D&B

Decide with Confidence

Industry & Financial Consulting Services

INDUSTRY NORMS
AND KEY BUSINESS RATIOS

One Year
Desk-Top Edition
SIC #0100-8999

CONTENTS

INDUSTRY NORMS AND KEY BUSINESS RATIOS

APPENDIX - SIC Numbers Appearing in This Directory

The Desk-Top Edition of The D&B Industry Norms and Key Business Ratios is made possible through over one million financial statements in the D&B Financial Information Base. This file consists of U.S. corporations, partnerships and proprietorships both public and privately owned, in all size ranges, and includes over 800 different lines of business as defined by the U.S. Standard Industrial Classification (SIC) code numbers. Our data is collected weekly, maintained daily, and constantly edited and updated. All of these factors combine to make this financial information unequaled anywhere for scope and timeliness*.

It should be noted that only general data is supplied in the Desk-Top Edition, however, for more detailed asset/geographical breakdowns of this data, an expanded set of Industry Norms and Key Business Ratios are also published by D&B for the Corporate Marketplace in the following five segments:

1. Agriculture, Mining, Construction/ Transportation/Communication/Utilities
2. Manufacturing
3. Wholesaling
4. Retailing
5. Finance/Real Estate/Services

All five segments are available in three different formats. The three formats are as follows:

1. Industry Norms and Key Business Ratios, Three Year Edition.
Directories and diskettes available.

2. Industry Norms and Key Business Ratios, One Year Edition.
Directories and diskettes available.

3. Key Business Ratios, One Year Edition.
Directories only.

Note that the Industry Norms contain "typical" balance sheets and income statements, and "common-size" financial figures, <u>as well as Key Business Ratios</u>. The Key Business Ratios books contain fourteen indicators of performance.

*To provide the most current information available, fiscal years January 1 - December 31 were utilized to calculate the Norms.

INDUSTRY NORM FORMAT

At the top of each industry norm will be identifying information: SIC code number and short title. Beside the year date, in parenthesis, is the number of companies in the sample. The "typical" balance-sheet figures are in the first column and the "common-size" balance-sheet figures are in the second. The respective income statements begin with the item "Net Sales", and the respective Key Business Ratios begin with the item "Ratios." The latter are further broken down, or refined, into the median, and the upper quartile and lower quartile.

THE COMMON - SIZE FINANCIAL STATEMENT

The common-size balance-sheet and income statement present each item of the financial statement as a percentage of its respective aggregate total. Common-size percentages are computed for all statement items of all the individual companies used in the industry sample. An average for each statement item is then determined and presented as the industry norm.

This enables the analyst to examine the current composition of assets, liabilities and sales of a particular industry.

THE TYPICAL FINANCIAL STATEMENT

The typical balance-sheet figures are the result of translating the common-size percentages into dollar figures. They permit, for example, a quick check of the relative size of assets and liabilities between one's own company and that company's own line of business.

After the common-size percentages have been computed for the particular sample, the actual financial statements are then sequenced by both *total assets* and *total sales*, with the median, or mid-point figure in both these groups serving as the "typical" amount. We then compute the typical balance-sheet and income statement dollar figures by multiplying the common-size percentages for each statement item by their respective total amounts.

(For example, if the median total assets for an SIC category are $669,599, and the common-size figure for cash is 9.2 percent, then by multiplying the two we derive a cash figure of $61,603 for the typical balance sheet.)

KEY BUSINESS RATIOS

The Fourteen Key Business Ratios are broken down into median figures, with upper and lower quartiles, giving the analyst an even more refined set of figures to work with. These ratios cover all those critical areas of business performance with indicators of solvency, efficiency and profitability.

They provide a profound and well-documented insight into all aspects for everyone interested in the financial workings of business—business executives and managers, credit executives, bankers, lenders, investors, academicians and students.

In the ratio tables appearing in this book, the figures are broken down into the median—which is the midpoint of all companies in the sample—and the upper quartile and lower quartile—which are mid-points of the upper and lower halves.

Upper quartile figures are not always the highest numerical value, nor are lower quartile figures always the lowest numerical value. The quartile listings reflect *judgmental ranking*, thus the upper quartile represents the best condition in any given ratio and is not necessarily the highest numerical value. (For example, see the items Total Liabilities-to-Net Worth or Collection Period, where a lower numerical value represents a better condition.)

Each of the fourteen ratios is calculated individually for every concern in the sample. These individual figures are then sequenced for each ratio according to condition (best to worst), and the figure that falls in the middle of this series becomes the median (or mid-point) for that ratio in that line of business. The figure halfway between the median and the best condition of the series becomes the upper quartile; and the number halfway between the median and the least favorable condition of the series is the lower quartile.

In a statistical sense, each median is considered the *typical* ratio figure for a concern in a given category.

SOLVENCY RATIOS

Quick Ratio

Cash + Accounts Receivable
Current Liabilities

The Quick Ratio is computed by dividing cash plus accounts receivable by total current liabilities. Current liabilities are all the liabilities that fall due within one year. This ratio reveals the protection afforded short-term creditors in cash or near-cash assets. It shows the number of dollars of liquid assets available to cover each dollar of current debt. Any time this ratio is as much as 1 to 1 (1.0) the business is said to be in a liquid condition. The larger the ratio the greater the liquidity.

Current Ratio

Current Assets
Current Liabilities

Total current assets are divided by total current liabilities. Current assets include cash, accounts and notes receivable (less reserves for bad debts), advances on inventories, merchandise inventories and marketable securities. This ratio measures the degree to which current assets cover current liabilities. The higher the ratio the more assurance exists that the retirement of current liabilities can be made. The current ratio measures the margin of safety available to cover any possible shrinkage in the value of current assets. Normally a ratio of 2 to 1 (2.0) or better is considered good.

Current Liabilities to Net Worth

Current Liabilities
Net Worth

Current Liabilities to Net Worth is derived by dividing current liabilities by net worth. This contrasts the funds that creditors temporarily are risking with the funds permanently invested by the owners. The smaller the net worth and the larger the liabilities, the less security for the creditors. Care should be exercised when selling any firm with current liabilities exceeding two-thirds (66.6 percent) of net worth.

Current Liabilities to Inventory

Current Liabilities
Inventory

Dividing current liabilities by inventory yields another indication of the extent to which the business relies on funds from disposal of unsold inventories to meet its debts. This ratio combines with Net Sales to Inventory to indicate how management controls inventory. It is possible to have decreasing liquidity while maintaining consistent sales-to-inventory ratios. Large increases in sales with corresponding increases in inventory levels can cause an inappropriate rise in current liabilities if growth isn't made wisely.

Total Liabilities to Net Worth

Total Liabilities
Net Worth

Obtained by dividing total current plus long-term and deferred liabilities by net worth. The effect of long-term (funded) debt on a business can be determined by comparing this ratio with Current Liabilities to Net Worth. The difference will pinpoint the relative size of long-term debt, which, if sizable, can burden a firm with substantial interest charges. In general, total liabilities shouldn't exceed net worth (100 percent) since in such cases creditors have more at stake than owners.

Fixed Assets to Net Worth

Fixed Assets
Net Worth

Fixed assets are divided by net worth. The proportion of net worth that consists of fixed assets will vary greatly from industry to industry but generally a smaller proportion is desirable. A high ratio is unfavorable because heavy investment in fixed assets indicates that either the concern has a low net working capital and is overtrading or has utilized large funded debt to supplement working capital. Also, the larger the fixed assets, the bigger the annual depreciation charge that must be deducted from the income statement. Normally, fixed assets above 75 percent of net worth indicate possible over-investment and should be examined with care.

EFFICIENCY RATIOS

Collection Period

$$\frac{\text{Accounts Receivable}}{\text{Sales}} \times 365$$

Accounts receivable are divided by sales and then multiplied by 365 days to obtain this figure. The quality of the receivables of a company can be determined by this relationship when compared with selling terms and industry norms. In some industries where credit sales are not the normal way of doing business, the percentage of cash sales should be taken into consideration. Generally, where most sales are for credit, any collection period more than one-third over normal selling terms (40.0 for 30-day terms) is indicative of some slow-turning receivables. When comparing the collection period of one concern with that of another, allowances should be made for possible variations in selling terms.

Sales to Inventory

$$\frac{\text{Annual Net Sales}}{\text{Inventory}}$$

Obtained by dividing annual net sales by inventory. Inventory control is a prime management objective since poor controls allow inventory to become costly to store, obsolete or insufficient to meet demands. The sales-to-inventory relationship is a guide to the rapidity at which merchandise is being moved and the effect on the flow of funds into the business. This ratio varies widely between lines of business and a company's figure is only meaningful when compared with industry norms. Individual figures that are outside either the upper or lower quartiles for a given industry should be examined with care. Although low figures are usually the biggest problem, as they indicate excessively high inventories, extremely high turnovers might reflect insufficient merchandise to meet customer demand and result in lost sales.

Asset to Sales

$$\frac{\text{Total Assets}}{\text{Net Sales}}$$

Assets to sales is calculated by dividing total assets by annual net sales. This ratio ties in sales and the total investment that is used to generate those sales. While figures vary greatly from industry to industry, by comparing a company's ratio with industry norms it can be determined whether a firm is overtrading (handling an excessive volume of sales in relation to investment) or undertrading (not generating sufficient sales to warrant the assets invested). Abnormally low percentages (above the upper quartile) can indicate overtrading which may lead to financial difficulties if not corrected. Extremely high percentages (below the lower quartile) can be the result of overly conservative or poor sales management, indicating a more aggressive sales policy may need to be followed.

Sales to Net Working Capital

$$\frac{\text{Sales}}{\text{Net Working Capital}}$$

Net sales are divided by net working capital (net working capital is current assets minus current liabilities.). This relationship indicates whether a company is overtrading or conversely carrying more liquid assets than needed for its volume. Each industry can vary substantially and it is necessary to compare a company with its peers to see if it is either overtrading on its available funds or being overly conservative. Companies with substantial sales gains often reach a level where their working capital becomes strained. Even if they maintain an adequate total investment for the volume being generated (Assets to Sales), that investment may be so centered in fixed assets or other noncurrent items that it will be difficult to continue meeting all current obligations without additional investment or reducing sales.

Accounts Payable to Sales

$$\frac{\text{Accounts Payable}}{\text{Annual Net Sales}}$$

Computed by dividing accounts payable by annual net sales. This ratio measures how the company is paying its suppliers in relation to the volume being transacted. An increasing percentage, or one larger than the industry norm, indicates the firm may be using suppliers to help finance operations. This ratio is especially important to short-term creditors since a high percentage could indicate potential problems in paying vendors.

PROFITABILITY RATIOS

Return on Sales (Profit Margin)

Net Profit After Taxes
Annual Net Sales

Obtained by dividing net profit after taxes by annual net sales. This reveals the profits earned per dollar of sales and therefore measures the efficiency of the operation. Return must be adequate for the firm to be able to achieve satisfactory profits for its owners. This ratio is an indicator of the firm's ability to withstand adverse conditions such as falling prices, rising costs and declining sales.

Return on Assets

Net Profit After Taxes
Total Assets

Net profit after taxes divided by total assets. This ratio is the key indicator of profitability for a firm. It matches operating profits with the assets available to earn a return. Companies efficiently using their assets will have a relatively high return while less well-run businesses will be relatively low.

Return on Net Worth (Return on Equity)

Net Profit After Taxes
Net Worth

Obtained by dividing net profit after tax by net worth. This ratio is used to analyze the ability of the firm's management to realize an adequate return on the capital invested by the owners of the firm. Tendency is to look increasingly to this ratio as a final criterion of profitability. Generally, a relationship of at least 10 percent is regarded as a desirable objective for providing dividends plus funds for future growth.

Using Industry Norms for Financial Analysis

The principal purpose of financial analysis is to identify irregularities that require explanations to completely understand an industry's or company's current status and future potential. These irregularities can be identified by comparing the industry norms with the figures of specific companies (*comparative analysis*). D&B's Industry Norms are specifically formatted to accommodate this analysis.

Relative Position

Common-size and typical balance sheets provide an excellent picture of the makeup of the industry's assets and liabilities. Are assets concentrated in inventories or accounts receivable? Are payables to the trade or bank loans more important as a method for financing operations? The answers to these and other important questions are clearly shown by the Industry Norms, its common-size balance sheet approach and is then further crystallized by the typical balance sheets.

Financial Ratio Trends

Key Business Ratio changes indicate trends in the important *relationships* between key financial items, such as the relationship between Net Profits and Net Sales (a common indicator of profitability). Ratios that reflect short and long-term liquidity, efficiency in managing assets and controlling debt, and different measures of profitability are all included in the Key Business Ratios sections of the Industry Norms.

Comparative Analysis

Comparing a company with its peers is a reliable method for evaluating financial status. The key to this technique is the composition of the peer group and the timeliness of the data. The D&B Industry Norms are unique in scope of sample size and in level of detail.

Sample Size

The number of firms in the sample must be representative or they will be unduly influenced by irregular figures from relatively few companies. The more than one million companies used as a basis for the Industry Norms allow for more than adequate sample sizes in most cases.

Key Business Ratios Analysis

Valuable insights into an industry's performance can be obtained by equating two related statement items in the form of a financial ratio. For really effective ratio analysis, the items compared must be meaningful and the comparison should reflect the combined effort of two potentially diverse trends. While dozens of different ratios can be computed from financial statements, the fourteen included in the Industry Norms and Key Business Ratio books are those most commonly used and were rated as the most significant as shown in a survey of financial analysts. Many of the other ratios in existence are variations on these fourteen.

The fourteen Key Business Ratios are categorized into three major groups:

Solvency, or liquidity, measurements are significant in evaluating a company's ability to meet short and long-term obligations. These figures are of prime interest to credit managers of commercial companies and financial institutions.

Efficiency ratios indicate how effectively a company uses and controls its assets. This is critical information for evaluating how a company is managed. Studying these ratios is useful for credit, marketing and investment purposes.

Profitability ratios show how successfully a business is earning a return to its owners. Those interested in mergers and acquisitions consider this key data for selecting candidates.

Recent research efforts have revealed that the use of financial analysis (via Industry Norms) is very useful in several functional areas. To follow are only a few of the more widely used applications of this unique data.

Credit

Industry Norm data has proven to be an invaluable tool in determining minimum acceptable standards for risk. The credit worthiness of an existing or potential account is immediately visible by ranking its solvency status and comparing its solvency trends to that of the industry. Short term solvency gauges, such as the quick and current ratios, are ideal indicators when evaluating an account. Balance sheet comparisons supplement this qualification by allowing a comparison of the make-up of current assets and liability items. Moreover, leverage ratios such as current liability to net worth and total liability to net worth provide valuable benchmarks to spot potential problem accounts while profitability and collection period figures provide cash flow comparisons for an overall evaluation of accounts.

In addition to evaluating individual accounts against industry standards, internal credit polices also benefit from Industry Norm data. Are receivables growing at an excessive rate as compared to the industry? If so, how does your firm's collections stack up to the industry?

Finance

Here exists a unique opportunity for financial executives to rank their firm, or their firm's subsidiaries and divisions, against its peers. Determine the efficiency of management via ratio quartile breakdowns which provides you the opportunity to pinpoint your firm's profitability position versus the industry. For example, are returns on sales and gross profit margins comparatively low thereby indicating that pricing per unit may be too low or that the cost of goods is unnecessarily high?

In much the same way, matching the firm's growth and efficiency trends to that of the industry reveals conditions which prove to be vital in projecting budgets. If asset expansion exceeds the industry standard while asset utilization (as indicated by the asset to sales ratio) is sub par, should growth be slowed?

Investment executives have also utilized this diverse information when identifying optimal investment opportunities. By uncovering which industries exhibit the strongest sales growth while maintaining adequate returns, risk is minimized.

Corporate Planning

Corporate plans, competitive strategies and merger/acquisition decisions dictate a comprehensive analysis of the industry in question. Industry Norm data provides invaluable information in scrutinizing the performance of today's highly competitive, and sometimes unstable, markets. Does the liquidity of an industry provide a sufficient cushion to endure the recent record-high interest levels or is it too volatile to risk an entry? Are the profitability and equity statuses of an acquisition candidate among the best in the industry thereby qualifying it as an ideal acquisition target?

Industry Norm data provides these all-important benchmarks for setting strategic goals and measuring overall corporate performance.

Marketing and Sales

Attaining an in-depth knowledge of a potential or existing customer base is a key factor when developing successful marketing strategies and sales projections. Industry Norm data provides a competitive edge when determining market potential and market candidates. Identify those industries that meet or exceed your qualifications and take it one step further by focusing in on the specific region or size category that exhibits the greatest potential. For example, isolate the industries which have experienced the strongest growth trends in sales and inventory turnover and then fine tune marketing and sales strategies by identifying the particular *segment* which is the most attractive (such as firms with assets of $1 million or more).

You can also utilize this information from a different perspective by examining the industries of existing accounts. If an account's industry shows signs of faltering profitability and stagnating sales, should precautionary measures be taken? Will the next sale be profitable for your company or will it be written-off? Industry Norm data assist in answering these and many other important questions.

FINAL NOTE

The SIC categories in this directory reflect those appearing in the 1987 edition of the Standard Industrial Classification Manual

The D&B Financial Information Base includes over one million U.S. companies and is the most extensive and complete source of financial information of its kind. This compilation of data should be regarded only as a source of financial information, to be used in conjunction with other sources of data, when performing financial analysis. When utilizing these figures, remember:

- Because of the size of this database, and in order to facilitate the many calculations and rankings, many of the very large group samples have been randomly reduced.

- On the other hand, some of the samples from our file are very small, and, therefore, may not present a true picture of an entire line of business. In these small groups there is a chance that a few extreme variations might have an undue influence on the overall figures in a particular category.

- The companies composing our database are organized by principal line of business without consideration for multiple-operation functions.

- Within the primary SIC numbers, no allowance has been made for differing accounting methods, terms of sale, or fiscal-year closing date, all of which might have had an effect on the composite data.

- Therefore, D&B advises users that the Industry Norms and Key Business Ratios be used as yardsticks and not as absolutes.

	SIC 01 AGRICULTURL CROPS (NO BREAKDOWN) 2002 (267 Establishments)		SIC 0115 CORN (NO BREAKDOWN) 2002 (12 Establishments)		SIC 0134 IRISH POTATOES (NO BREAKDOWN) 2002 (15 Establishments)		SIC 0161 VEGETABLES,MELONS (NO BREAKDOWN) 2002 (42 Establishments)	
	$	%	$	%	$	%	$	%
Cash	249,974	8.1	161,449	5.7	189,827	5.1	287,084	7.6
Accounts Receivable	416,624	13.5	133,124	4.7	383,376	10.3	770,593	20.4
Notes Receivable	21,603	0.7	0	0.0	18,610	0.5	26,442	0.7
Inventory	493,776	16.0	402,205	14.2	569,481	15.3	253,087	6.7
Other Current	225,285	7.3	79,309	2.8	104,219	2.8	373,963	9.9
Total Current	**1,407,262**	**45.6**	**776,087**	**27.4**	**1,265,513**	**34.0**	**1,711,169**	**45.3**
Fixed Assets	1,425,778	46.2	1,869,406	66.0	2,076,931	55.8	1,662,063	44.0
Other Non-current	253,060	8.2	186,940	6.6	379,654	10.2	404,183	10.7
Total Assets	**3,086,100**	**100.0**	**2,832,433**	**100.0**	**3,722,098**	**100.0**	**3,777,415**	**100.0**
Accounts Payable	271,577	8.8	220,930	7.8	286,602	7.7	321,080	8.5
Bank Loans	9,258	0.3	0	0.0	74,442	2.0	18,887	0.5
Notes Payable	160,477	5.2	84,973	3.0	208,437	5.6	166,206	4.4
Other Current	1,320,851	42.8	566,486	20.0	859,805	23.1	661,048	17.5
Total Current	**1,762,163**	**57.1**	**872,389**	**30.8**	**1,429,286**	**38.4**	**1,167,221**	**30.9**
Other Long Term	641,909	20.8	597,644	21.1	897,025	24.1	664,825	17.6
Deferred Credits	9,258	0.3	5,665	0.2	7,444	0.2	0	0.0
Net Worth	672,770	21.8	1,356,735	47.9	1,388,343	37.3	1,945,369	51.5
Total Liab & Net Worth	**3,086,100**	**100.0**	**2,832,433**	**100.0**	**3,722,098**	**100.0**	**3,777,415**	**100.0**
Net Sales	4,511,842	100.0	1,570,956	100.0	6,552,989	100.0	7,631,141	100.0
Gross Profit	1,746,083	38.7	529,412	33.7	2,516,348	38.4	2,686,162	35.2
Net Profit After Tax	157,914	3.5	204,224	13.0	327,649	5.0	328,139	4.3
Working Capital	(354,901)	—	(96,302)	—	(163,773)	—	543,948	—

RATIOS	UQ	MED	LQ	UQ	MED	LQ	UQ	MED	LQ	UQ	MED	LQ
SOLVENCY												
Quick Ratio (times)	1.7	0.7	0.2	0.7	0.1	0.0	0.8	0.4	0.2	3.1	0.8	0.4
Current Ratio (times)	3.5	1.7	0.9	1.4	0.6	0.4	1.2	1.0	0.9	3.7	1.5	1.0
Curr Liab To Nw (%)	13.8	37.6	113.5	13.8	56.2	116.6	32.3	84.2	137.8	12.8	51.7	97.4
Curr Liab To Inv (%)	69.2	137.7	385.3	167.3	215.6	371.8	127.4	179.1	419.2	140.8	269.1	670.6
Total Liab To Nw (%)	30.8	76.8	175.5	42.0	80.1	245.5	54.4	165.0	213.3	19.3	84.6	150.2
Fixed Assets To Nw (%)	46.0	84.9	136.4	101.7	135.9	228.9	70.2	125.1	240.4	41.4	69.3	126.9
EFFICIENCY												
Coll Period (days)	18.3	33.3	59.5	27.0	29.9	53.7	26.7	46.0	62.8	13.9	29.8	57.2
Sales To Inv (times)	18.3	7.9	3.8	5.8	3.3	1.3	26.1	12.0	4.6	44.6	18.3	8.4
Assets To Sales (%)	34.9	68.4	118.3	153.9	180.3	200.8	49.0	56.8	88.5	23.9	49.5	81.0
Sales To Nwc (times)	14.8	5.7	2.9	10.2	7.4	5.5	22.0	13.7	9.7	30.9	11.3	5.0
Acct Pay To Sales (%)	1.8	3.9	6.6	1.0	6.2	13.6	3.4	7.5	13.2	0.7	2.8	5.7
PROFITABILITY												
Return On Sales (%)	7.2	1.7	0.1	15.7	3.0	1.8	8.2	2.7	1.4	6.2	1.4	(0.3)
Return On Assets (%)	11.0	2.7	0.1	3.7	2.4	1.2	12.9	4.7	2.4	13.5	4.6	(0.7)
Return On Nw (%)	20.9	6.8	0.7	10.3	5.1	3.0	34.7	16.8	8.7	25.9	12.7	0.7

Balance Sheet / Income Data

	SIC 0172 GRAPES (NO BREAKDOWN) 2002 (11 Establishments)		SIC 0175 DECID TREE FRUITS (NO BREAKDOWN) 2002 (17 Establishments)		SIC 0181 ORNMNTL NURS PRDCTS (NO BREAKDOWN) 2002 (97 Establishments)		SIC 0191 GEN FARMS,PRIM CROP (NO BREAKDOWN) 2002 (19 Establishments)	
	$	%	$	%	$	%	$	%
Cash	1,278,335	6.1	114,464	9.6	221,392	9.0	172,729	7.2
Accounts Receivable	1,676,505	8.0	118,041	9.9	339,467	13.8	105,556	4.4
Notes Receivable	335,301	1.6	50,078	4.2	4,920	0.2	4,798	0.2
Inventory	5,888,724	28.1	50,078	4.2	582,998	23.7	263,891	11.0
Other Current	1,152,597	5.5	72,734	6.1	95,935	3.9	290,280	12.1
Total Current	**10,331,462**	**49.3**	**405,395**	**34.0**	**1,244,712**	**50.6**	**837,254**	**34.9**
Fixed Assets	9,283,646	44.3	690,364	57.9	1,065,139	43.3	1,223,494	51.0
Other Non-current	1,341,204	6.4	96,579	8.1	150,055	6.1	338,260	14.1
Total Assets	**20,956,312**	**100.0**	**1,192,338**	**100.0**	**2,459,906**	**100.0**	**2,399,008**	**100.0**
Accounts Payable	1,068,772	5.1	67,963	5.7	191,873	7.8	83,965	3.5
Bank Loans	230,519	1.1	0	0.0	7,380	0.3	0	0.0
Notes Payable	0	0.0	3,577	0.3	130,375	5.3	175,128	7.3
Other Current	4,610,389	22.0	296,892	24.9	435,403	17.7	395,836	16.5
Total Current	**5,909,680**	**28.2**	**368,432**	**30.9**	**765,031**	**31.1**	**654,929**	**27.3**
Other Long Term	4,589,433	21.9	394,664	33.1	516,580	21.0	575,762	24.0
Deferred Credits	419,126	2.0	(1,192)	(0.1)	4,920	0.2	0	0.0
Net Worth	10,038,073	47.9	430,434	36.1	1,173,375	47.7	1,168,317	48.7
Total Liab & Net Worth	**20,956,312**	**100.0**	**1,192,338**	**100.0**	**2,459,906**	**100.0**	**2,399,008**	**100.0**
Net Sales	15,674,130	100.0	1,215,431	100.0	4,440,264	100.0	2,674,479	100.0
Gross Profit	6,363,697	40.6	611,362	50.3	1,927,075	43.4	1,048,396	39.2
Net Profit After Tax	(109,719)	(0.7)	(71,710)	(5.9)	146,529	3.3	64,187	2.4
Working Capital	4,421,782	—	36,963	—	479,681	—	182,325	—

RATIOS

	UQ	MED	LQ	UQ	MED	LQ	UQ	MED	LQ	UQ	MED	LQ
SOLVENCY												
Quick Ratio (times)	0.8	0.7	0.2	2.7	0.4	0.1	1.8	0.7	0.4	1.0	0.5	0.2
Current Ratio (times)	2.6	1.7	1.4	4.2	0.8	0.6	3.9	2.1	1.1	3.1	1.8	0.6
Curr Liab To Nw (%)	14.1	29.5	134.0	5.1	63.4	242.5	16.4	34.7	97.7	4.9	33.8	104.4
Curr Liab To Inv (%)	60.7	92.8	147.7	315.2	415.2	999.9	40.0	84.5	221.3	56.4	116.8	468.8
Total Liab To Nw (%)	54.4	70.9	195.4	43.7	122.2	340.4	35.9	73.0	193.4	19.9	76.5	158.2
Fixed Assets To Nw (%)	57.3	86.3	122.2	66.3	109.3	322.5	43.9	74.5	130.7	56.9	94.0	172.1
EFFICIENCY												
Coll Period (days)	17.9	39.4	45.6	3.7	23.7	65.0	12.4	29.6	54.3	5.1	20.1	34.3
Sales To Inv (times)	9.1	4.6	1.2	68.7	25.4	7.9	14.6	7.0	2.4	8.9	4.8	3.5
Assets To Sales (%)	39.1	133.7	279.6	61.0	98.1	175.8	31.7	55.4	102.6	56.0	89.7	131.0
Sales To Nwc (times)	5.5	2.2	1.4	66.1	4.0	2.1	13.5	5.6	2.7	14.5	6.5	2.5
Acct Pay To Sales (%)	4.0	4.8	8.5	1.1	3.2	4.2	1.8	4.0	6.6	3.1	4.0	4.9
PROFITABILITY												
Return On Sales (%)	4.0	(0.5)	(17.5)	3.8	2.5	(20.1)	7.0	1.4	0.1	5.6	0.4	(2.4)
Return On Assets (%)	12.2	(1.4)	(8.0)	8.8	2.4	(7.9)	7.7	2.1	0.2	11.0	0.4	(2.8)
Return On Nw (%)	20.1	(7.2)	(15.8)	30.2	2.3	(12.2)	17.3	4.2	0.6	32.3	1.7	0.7

	SIC 02 AGRICULTURAL PRD LVSK (NO BREAKDOWN) 2002 (90 Establishments) $	%	SIC 0211 BEEF CATTLE,FEEDLOT (NO BREAKDOWN) 2002 (20 Establishments) $	%	SIC 0241 DAIRY FARMS (NO BREAKDOWN) 2002 (12 Establishments) $	%	SIC 0252 CHICKEN EGGS (NO BREAKDOWN) 2002 (12 Establishments) $	%
Cash	368,094	7.2	540,416	6.7	167,452	3.6	430,144	6.1
Accounts Receivable	516,354	10.1	895,316	11.1	507,007	10.9	451,299	6.4
Notes Receivable	97,136	1.9	209,714	2.6	4,651	0.1	21,155	0.3
Inventory	1,232,092	24.1	3,177,970	39.4	837,259	18.0	1,678,268	23.8
Other Current	408,993	8.0	854,987	10.6	130,240	2.8	571,175	8.1
Total Current	**2,622,669**	**51.3**	**5,678,403**	**70.4**	**1,646,609**	**35.4**	**3,152,041**	**44.7**
Fixed Assets	2,131,877	41.7	1,766,435	21.9	2,679,228	57.6	2,996,907	42.5
Other Non-current	357,869	7.0	621,076	7.7	325,601	7.0	902,597	12.8
Total Assets	**5,112,415**	**100.0**	**8,065,914**	**100.0**	**4,651,438**	**100.0**	**7,051,545**	**100.0**
Accounts Payable	342,532	6.7	362,966	4.5	534,915	11.5	366,680	5.2
Bank Loans	0	0.0	0	0.0	0	0.0	21,155	0.3
Notes Payable	582,815	11.4	1,653,512	20.5	344,206	7.4	542,969	7.7
Other Current	996,921	19.5	2,024,545	25.1	367,464	7.9	1,332,742	18.9
Total Current	**1,922,268**	**37.6**	**4,041,023**	**50.1**	**1,246,585**	**26.8**	**2,263,546**	**32.1**
Other Long Term	853,774	16.7	1,169,557	14.5	1,162,860	25.0	1,375,051	19.5
Deferred Credits	5,112	0.1	0	0.0	9,303	0.2	28,206	0.4
Net Worth	2,331,261	45.6	2,855,334	35.4	2,232,690	48.0	3,384,742	48.0
Total Liab & Net Worth	**5,112,415**	**100.0**	**8,065,914**	**100.0**	**4,651,438**	**100.0**	**7,051,545**	**100.0**
Net Sales	8,312,870	100.0	10,988,984	100.0	9,492,731	100.0	10,684,159	100.0
Gross Profit	2,211,223	26.6	2,780,213	25.3	5,230,495	55.1	1,335,520	12.5
Net Profit After Tax	(91,442)	(1.1)	(54,945)	(0.5)	104,420	1.1	(256,420)	(2.4)
Working Capital	700,401	—	1,637,380	—	400,024	—	888,495	—

RATIOS	UQ	MED	LQ	UQ	MED	LQ	UQ	MED	LQ	UQ	MED	LQ
SOLVENCY												
Quick Ratio (times)	1.1	0.5	0.2	1.0	0.3	0.1	1.2	0.4	0.1	0.6	0.5	0.3
Current Ratio (times)	2.9	1.4	1.1	1.4	1.3	1.1	3.2	1.8	0.9	2.0	1.3	1.0
Curr Liab To Nw (%)	25.4	44.5	133.2	91.3	154.5	316.6	17.5	29.1	50.0	34.7	57.9	85.7
Curr Liab To Inv (%)	71.6	141.0	249.4	96.8	132.5	192.8	44.1	63.2	290.5	95.2	144.1	183.2
Total Liab To Nw (%)	43.8	107.7	197.0	142.8	195.7	362.3	47.7	73.9	156.1	46.5	76.4	148.1
Fixed Assets To Nw (%)	45.9	93.5	135.9	24.0	77.7	117.8	79.2	125.3	150.8	54.4	85.7	129.3
EFFICIENCY												
Coll Period (days)	13.5	23.6	43.4	23.4	33.4	65.0	10.3	27.2	62.2	3.3	15.9	28.8
Sales To Inv (times)	12.8	7.1	3.9	5.9	3.7	2.1	999.9	8.7	2.0	14.7	9.0	5.1
Assets To Sales (%)	43.5	61.5	94.5	49.5	73.4	141.8	27.4	49.0	55.7	45.9	66.0	79.4
Sales To Nwc (times)	15.2	8.3	5.4	12.4	8.7	5.7	77.0	7.3	5.7	19.3	8.6	7.3
Acct Pay To Sales (%)	2.0	3.6	7.4	2.3	3.0	6.2	3.6	5.4	16.4	1.9	5.0	5.6
PROFITABILITY												
Return On Sales (%)	2.9	0.2	(3.1)	5.3	1.3	(1.8)	3.3	1.3	(1.0)	0.6	(2.7)	(6.1)
Return On Assets (%)	6.1	0.8	(4.7)	6.2	1.6	(3.7)	6.2	3.2	(1.6)	1.2	(4.6)	(6.8)
Return On Nw (%)	12.2	4.9	(10.3)	12.9	6.8	(10.6)	12.1	8.6	4.9	3.1	(11.4)	(12.3)

Page 4

	SIC 07 AGRICULTURAL SERVICES (NO BREAKDOWN) 2002 (699 Establishments)		SIC 0711 SOIL PREP SERVICES (NO BREAKDOWN) 2002 (20 Establishments)		SIC 0721 CROP PLNTNG,PRTCTNG (NO BREAKDOWN) 2002 (19 Establishments)		SIC 0723 CROP PREP SVCS,MRKT (NO BREAKDOWN) 2002 (99 Establishments)	
	$	%	$	%	$	%	$	%
Cash	123,343	11.1	155,768	11.0	106,289	10.2	296,746	8.8
Accounts Receivable	285,578	25.7	447,479	31.6	189,653	18.2	762,098	22.6
Notes Receivable	6,667	0.6	16,993	1.2	1,042	0.1	23,605	0.7
Inventory	92,230	8.3	66,555	4.7	95,869	9.2	492,328	14.6
Other Current	103,342	9.3	89,212	6.3	77,112	7.4	303,490	9.0
Total Current	**611,160**	**55.0**	**776,007**	**54.8**	**469,965**	**45.1**	**1,878,267**	**55.7**
Fixed Assets	428,923	38.6	553,684	39.1	437,662	42.0	1,278,031	37.9
Other Non-current	71,117	6.4	86,381	6.1	134,425	12.9	215,815	6.4
Total Assets	**1,111,200**	**100.0**	**1,416,072**	**100.0**	**1,042,052**	**100.0**	**3,372,113**	**100.0**
Accounts Payable	131,122	11.8	123,198	8.7	70,860	6.8	394,537	11.7
Bank Loans	4,445	0.4	0	0.0	10,421	1.0	3,372	0.1
Notes Payable	35,558	3.2	19,825	1.4	39,598	3.8	192,210	5.7
Other Current	225,573	20.3	263,390	18.6	150,055	14.4	613,725	18.2
Total Current	**396,698**	**35.7**	**406,413**	**28.7**	**270,934**	**26.0**	**1,203,844**	**35.7**
Other Long Term	250,021	22.5	303,039	21.4	218,830	21.0	718,261	21.3
Deferred Credits	2,222	0.2	9,913	0.7	11,463	1.1	3,372	0.1
Net Worth	462,259	41.6	696,707	49.2	540,825	51.9	1,446,636	42.9
Total Liab & Net Worth	**1,111,200**	**100.0**	**1,416,072**	**100.0**	**1,042,052**	**100.0**	**3,372,113**	**100.0**
Net Sales	2,849,231	100.0	2,251,307	100.0	2,189,185	100.0	5,794,009	100.0
Gross Profit	1,116,899	39.2	697,905	31.0	950,106	43.4	1,743,997	30.1
Net Profit After Tax	102,572	3.6	121,571	5.4	17,513	0.8	231,760	4.0
Working Capital	214,462	—	369,594	—	199,031	—	674,423	—

RATIOS	UQ	MED	LQ	UQ	MED	LQ	UQ	MED	LQ	UQ	MED	LQ
SOLVENCY												
Quick Ratio (times)	2.2	1.1	0.5	3.1	1.9	0.6	2.6	1.1	0.6	1.4	0.9	0.4
Current Ratio (times)	2.9	1.6	1.1	4.6	2.8	1.3	4.3	1.6	1.2	2.2	1.5	1.2
Curr Liab To Nw (%)	26.9	68.4	140.2	20.8	28.8	100.7	8.9	47.1	99.9	37.6	91.1	139.5
Curr Liab To Inv (%)	137.6	335.2	999.9	91.5	129.4	270.6	97.6	209.3	465.7	133.0	323.4	999.9
Total Liab To Nw (%)	52.0	116.2	237.5	27.4	62.2	177.3	54.2	110.0	136.8	71.5	135.4	255.8
Fixed Assets To Nw (%)	42.0	74.0	144.0	36.5	80.8	101.9	51.0	80.8	137.2	44.6	75.5	156.1
EFFICIENCY												
Coll Period (days)	19.7	35.8	61.0	27.9	52.0	75.8	8.4	29.8	78.3	17.5	35.8	59.1
Sales To Inv (times)	93.0	33.8	10.4	50.9	26.5	7.3	65.1	16.6	7.5	58.5	16.2	6.7
Assets To Sales (%)	26.4	39.0	58.0	44.2	62.9	116.0	36.5	47.6	55.9	36.0	58.2	94.0
Sales To Nwc (times)	21.5	10.0	5.7	6.9	6.4	5.2	16.5	8.6	7.0	20.0	9.3	4.8
Acct Pay To Sales (%)	1.7	3.7	6.8	1.3	5.9	14.5	0.9	2.7	5.8	2.2	4.4	9.9
PROFITABILITY												
Return On Sales (%)	6.6	2.2	0.2	7.7	2.7	(0.2)	1.9	0.2	(2.6)	6.2	1.9	0.3
Return On Assets (%)	15.7	5.9	0.6	13.7	1.9	(0.8)	6.7	0.3	(4.7)	10.3	3.9	0.9
Return On Nw (%)	36.8	14.1	2.8	21.6	7.2	(0.4)	12.9	0.6	(27.5)	26.6	9.6	3.2

	SIC 0724 COTTON GINNING (NO BREAKDOWN) 2002 (27 Establishments)		SIC 0742 VTRNRY SVCS,SPCLTES (NO BREAKDOWN) 2002 (19 Establishments)		SIC 0751 LVSTCK SVCS,EXC VET (NO BREAKDOWN) 2002 (11 Establishments)		SIC 0781 LNDSCPE CNSLNG,PLNG (NO BREAKDOWN) 2002 (106 Establishments)	
	$	%	$	%	$	%	$	%
Cash	268,164	14.0	63,252	21.3	501,282	20.9	94,562	11.2
Accounts Receivable	214,531	11.2	31,181	10.5	309,404	12.9	304,793	36.1
Notes Receivable	11,493	0.6	0	0.0	62,360	2.6	1,689	0.2
Inventory	195,377	10.2	44,544	15.0	275,825	11.5	70,921	8.4
Other Current	185,798	9.7	18,709	6.3	295,013	12.3	45,593	5.4
Total Current	**875,363**	**45.7**	**157,686**	**53.1**	**1,443,884**	**60.2**	**517,558**	**61.3**
Fixed Assets	716,381	37.4	76,022	25.6	702,754	29.3	295,506	35.0
Other Non-current	323,712	16.9	63,252	21.3	251,840	10.5	31,239	3.7
Total Assets	**1,915,456**	**100.0**	**296,960**	**100.0**	**2,398,478**	**100.0**	**844,303**	**100.0**
Accounts Payable	180,053	9.4	38,308	12.9	273,426	11.4	112,292	13.3
Bank Loans	0	0.0	6,236	2.1	0	0.0	2,533	0.3
Notes Payable	28,732	1.5	21,678	7.3	112,728	4.7	27,018	3.2
Other Current	189,630	9.9	40,090	13.5	278,224	11.6	183,214	21.7
Total Current	**398,415**	**20.8**	**106,312**	**35.8**	**664,378**	**27.7**	**325,057**	**38.5**
Other Long Term	371,599	19.4	83,148	28.0	201,473	8.4	166,327	19.7
Deferred Credits	1,915	0.1	0	0.0	4,797	0.2	0	0.0
Net Worth	1,143,527	59.7	107,500	36.2	1,527,830	63.7	352,919	41.8
Total Liab & Net Worth	**1,915,456**	**100.0**	**296,960**	**100.0**	**2,398,478**	**100.0**	**844,303**	**100.0**
Net Sales	2,455,713	100.0	1,027,543	100.0	4,777,845	100.0	2,351,819	100.0
Gross Profit	702,334	28.6	620,636	60.4	1,978,028	41.4	973,653	41.4
Net Profit After Tax	127,697	5.2	66,790	6.5	157,669	3.3	68,203	2.9
Working Capital	476,948	—	51,374	—	779,506	—	192,501	—

RATIOS	UQ	MED	LQ	UQ	MED	LQ	UQ	MED	LQ	UQ	MED	LQ
SOLVENCY												
Quick Ratio (times)	2.1	1.4	0.7	4.1	0.8	0.3	3.2	1.2	1.1	2.4	1.3	0.8
Current Ratio (times)	3.8	2.1	1.4	4.2	1.7	1.2	5.0	2.5	1.7	2.9	1.7	1.1
Curr Liab To Nw (%)	16.0	31.9	58.5	13.3	78.6	104.9	18.4	39.3	87.3	32.5	66.2	165.2
Curr Liab To Inv (%)	111.0	169.7	453.5	93.3	122.9	228.2	104.4	148.4	180.5	174.5	356.9	999.9
Total Liab To Nw (%)	22.1	64.1	88.8	13.3	109.0	195.0	21.1	50.7	106.7	48.7	115.4	251.9
Fixed Assets To Nw (%)	42.8	53.1	71.8	19.8	42.9	61.2	24.3	48.4	61.7	32.8	64.2	145.8
EFFICIENCY												
Coll Period (days)	17.5	27.9	39.1	2.6	9.9	16.8	16.6	34.7	53.7	23.2	40.5	83.8
Sales To Inv (times)	26.3	11.2	7.6	36.5	25.0	13.4	24.3	13.2	7.8	90.6	39.4	9.5
Assets To Sales (%)	58.3	78.0	95.3	12.7	28.9	46.8	21.9	50.2	56.4	27.3	35.9	49.4
Sales To Nwc (times)	11.4	6.2	3.0	27.2	15.8	12.5	9.1	7.5	4.4	18.8	10.3	4.8
Acct Pay To Sales (%)	3.1	5.7	6.8	2.0	2.5	4.0	2.1	3.4	5.9	1.5	3.8	7.1
PROFITABILITY												
Return On Sales (%)	10.1	0.5	(2.8)	11.4	2.5	1.2	5.6	4.3	1.3	5.9	3.0	0.8
Return On Assets (%)	13.7	0.7	(4.0)	87.6	15.5	4.1	16.7	9.4	0.9	17.4	7.9	1.2
Return On Nw (%)	26.5	5.3	(3.9)	120.1	34.7	15.7	23.3	16.2	1.4	38.6	19.0	4.0

	SIC 0782 LAWN GARDEN SVCS (NO BREAKDOWN) 2002 (339 Establishments) $	%	SIC 0783 ORMNTL TREE SVCS (NO BREAKDOWN) 2002 (34 Establishments) $	%	SIC 08 FORESTRY (NO BREAKDOWN) 2002 (40 Establishments) $	%	SIC 0811 TIMBER TRACTS (NO BREAKDOWN) 2002 (18 Establishments) $	%
Cash	90,724	10.9	89,110	9.0	264,990	13.7	297,703	6.8
Accounts Receivable	218,902	26.3	251,488	25.4	311,412	16.1	525,358	12.0
Notes Receivable	5,826	0.7	990	0.1	5,803	0.3	4,378	0.1
Inventory	53,269	6.4	39,604	4.0	145,068	7.5	520,980	11.9
Other Current	86,562	10.4	71,288	7.2	263,056	13.6	788,038	18.0
Total Current	**455,283**	**54.7**	**452,480**	**45.7**	**990,329**	**51.2**	**2,136,457**	**48.8**
Fixed Assets	337,092	40.5	500,996	50.6	632,495	32.7	1,243,348	28.4
Other Non-current	39,952	4.8	36,634	3.7	311,412	16.1	998,180	22.8
Total Assets	**832,327**	**100.0**	**990,110**	**100.0**	**1,934,236**	**100.0**	**4,377,985**	**100.0**
Accounts Payable	102,376	12.3	111,882	11.3	96,712	5.0	96,316	2.2
Bank Loans	4,994	0.6	2,970	0.3	0	0.0	0	0.0
Notes Payable	25,802	3.1	36,634	3.7	42,553	2.2	118,206	2.7
Other Current	183,945	22.1	228,716	23.1	321,083	16.6	442,176	10.1
Total Current	**317,117**	**38.1**	**380,202**	**38.4**	**460,348**	**23.8**	**656,698**	**15.0**
Other Long Term	202,255	24.3	259,409	26.2	344,294	17.8	963,156	22.0
Deferred Credits	2,497	0.3	7,921	0.8	1,934	0.1	8,756	0.2
Net Worth	310,458	37.3	342,578	34.6	1,127,660	58.3	2,749,375	62.8
Total Liab & Net Worth	**832,327**	**100.0**	**990,110**	**100.0**	**1,934,236**	**100.0**	**4,377,985**	**100.0**
Net Sales	2,378,077	100.0	2,765,670	100.0	3,663,326	100.0	3,888,086	100.0
Gross Profit	958,365	40.3	1,239,020	44.8	1,318,797	36.0	1,539,682	39.6
Net Profit After Tax	87,989	3.7	35,954	1.3	186,830	5.1	(15,552)	(0.4)
Working Capital	138,166	—	72,278	—	529,981	—	1,479,759	—

RATIOS	UQ	MED	LQ	UQ	MED	LQ	UQ	MED	LQ	UQ	MED	LQ
SOLVENCY												
Quick Ratio (times)	2.1	1.2	0.5	1.8	1.0	0.5	2.5	1.0	0.5	2.2	0.8	0.2
Current Ratio (times)	2.8	1.6	1.0	2.4	1.3	0.9	7.6	2.7	1.4	9.1	3.1	1.5
Curr Liab To Nw (%)	31.4	74.7	156.0	33.2	75.4	153.3	11.8	19.2	64.7	6.9	15.7	30.9
Curr Liab To Inv (%)	188.4	486.8	999.9	420.1	999.9	999.9	89.3	201.2	999.9	81.8	201.2	392.9
Total Liab To Nw (%)	62.6	130.7	265.5	97.1	157.0	270.2	14.5	38.2	148.9	14.0	24.9	109.0
Fixed Assets To Nw (%)	44.3	78.7	152.2	74.0	122.4	168.6	14.6	40.4	117.2	11.2	29.3	119.2
EFFICIENCY												
Coll Period (days)	21.5	37.5	59.5	23.0	37.6	48.9	7.9	19.0	39.7	7.7	16.5	29.9
Sales To Inv (times)	115.7	42.8	15.6	396.5	106.3	32.4	62.3	17.8	5.0	19.0	11.0	3.2
Assets To Sales (%)	24.8	35.0	47.9	29.9	35.8	51.4	32.9	52.8	113.1	54.2	112.6	181.0
Sales To Nwc (times)	23.7	11.1	6.0	20.7	11.0	7.7	15.4	6.6	2.3	9.2	3.4	2.0
Acct Pay To Sales (%)	1.6	3.5	6.1	1.1	3.4	6.5	0.8	1.6	2.9	1.3	2.6	4.0
PROFITABILITY												
Return On Sales (%)	6.9	2.2	0.3	4.8	1.3	(0.1)	12.8	4.0	0.1	15.0	1.8	(2.1)
Return On Assets (%)	16.2	6.5	0.7	10.9	3.2	(0.4)	20.1	8.0	0.5	16.3	3.4	(1.4)
Return On Nw (%)	43.4	14.4	3.6	29.7	11.0	3.9	46.1	21.3	1.1	24.0	6.7	(1.4)

SIC 0851 FORESTRY SERVICES (NO BREAKDOWN) 2002 (19 Establishments)

	$	%
Cash	309,708	20.1
Accounts Receivable	249,615	16.2
Notes Receivable	9,245	0.6
Inventory	41,603	2.7
Other Current	167,950	10.9
Total Current	**778,121**	**50.5**
Fixed Assets	574,731	37.3
Other Non-current	187,982	12.2
Total Assets	**1,540,834**	**100.0**
Accounts Payable	67,797	4.4
Bank Loans	0	0.0
Notes Payable	24,653	1.6
Other Current	374,423	24.3
Total Current	**466,873**	**30.3**
Other Long Term	234,206	15.2
Deferred Credits	0	0.0
Net Worth	839,755	54.5
Total Liab & Net Worth	**1,540,834**	**100.0**
Net Sales	3,695,046	100.0
Gross Profit	1,315,436	35.6
Net Profit After Tax	358,419	9.7
Working Capital	311,248	—

RATIOS	UQ	MED	LQ
SOLVENCY			
Quick Ratio (times)	2.9	0.8	0.6
Current Ratio (times)	6.7	1.9	1.0
Curr Liab To Nw (%)	12.8	21.8	104.7
Curr Liab To Inv (%)	180.2	999.9	999.9
Total Liab To Nw (%)	24.6	56.1	148.9
Fixed Assets To Nw (%)	22.2	60.7	130.3
EFFICIENCY			
Coll Period (days)	7.7	24.1	57.0
Sales To Inv (times)	66.9	57.7	19.2
Assets To Sales (%)	25.1	41.7	57.3
Sales To Nwc (times)	13.5	6.2	3.7
Acct Pay To Sales (%)	0.7	1.3	1.8
PROFITABILITY			
Return On Sales (%)	11.6	7.3	1.1
Return On Assets (%)	29.2	15.3	1.5
Return On Nw (%)	91.8	23.5	4.3

SIC 09 FISHERIES (NO BREAKDOWN) 2002 (12 Establishments)

	$	%
Cash	835,205	9.1
Accounts Receivable	495,616	5.4
Notes Receivable	9,178	0.1
Inventory	706,712	7.7
Other Current	569,042	6.2
Total Current	**2,615,753**	**28.5**
Fixed Assets	4,946,986	53.9
Other Non-current	1,615,343	17.6
Total Assets	**9,178,082**	**100.0**
Accounts Payable	660,822	7.2
Bank Loans	0	0.0
Notes Payable	633,288	6.9
Other Current	1,376,712	15.0
Total Current	**2,670,822**	**29.1**
Other Long Term	2,826,849	30.8
Deferred Credits	0	0.0
Net Worth	3,680,411	40.1
Total Liab & Net Worth	**9,178,082**	**100.0**
Net Sales	6,325,349	100.0
Gross Profit	2,302,427	36.4
Net Profit After Tax	(1,031,032)	(16.3)
Working Capital	(55,069)	—

RATIOS	UQ	MED	LQ
SOLVENCY			
Quick Ratio (times)	2.0	0.7	0.3
Current Ratio (times)	3.7	1.3	0.8
Curr Liab To Nw (%)	13.4	32.7	70.4
Curr Liab To Inv (%)	121.1	256.7	501.6
Total Liab To Nw (%)	50.2	64.9	105.2
Fixed Assets To Nw (%)	31.4	115.2	164.6
EFFICIENCY			
Coll Period (days)	12.8	24.5	36.4
Sales To Inv (times)	28.6	12.5	4.4
Assets To Sales (%)	86.5	145.1	272.6
Sales To Nwc (times)	12.3	8.1	3.5
Acct Pay To Sales (%)	4.0	6.1	8.5
PROFITABILITY			
Return On Sales (%)	5.1	(0.8)	(36.7)
Return On Assets (%)	2.1	(0.5)	(16.0)
Return On Nw (%)	8.8	(0.8)	(27.8)

SIC 10 METAL MINING (NO BREAKDOWN) 2002 (45 Establishments)

	$	%
Cash	789,247	13.4
Accounts Receivable	270,935	4.6
Notes Receivable	0	0.0
Inventory	241,486	4.1
Other Current	806,916	13.7
Total Current	**2,108,584**	**35.8**
Fixed Assets	2,308,841	39.2
Other Non-current	1,472,475	25.0
Total Assets	**5,889,900**	**100.0**
Accounts Payable	4,323,187	73.4
Bank Loans	0	0.0
Notes Payable	17,670	0.3
Other Current	24,808,258	421.2
Total Current	**29,149,115**	**494.9**
Other Long Term	6,573,129	111.6
Deferred Credits	35,339	0.6
Net Worth	(29,867,683)	(507.1)
Total Liab & Net Worth	**5,889,900**	**100.0**
Net Sales	2,868,924	100.0
Gross Profit	1,179,128	41.1
Net Profit After Tax	(34,427)	(1.2)
Working Capital	(27,040,531)	—

RATIOS	UQ	MED	LQ
SOLVENCY			
Quick Ratio (times)	1.2	0.5	0.0
Current Ratio (times)	1.8	1.4	0.1
Curr Liab To Nw (%)	8.5	25.0	61.8
Curr Liab To Inv (%)	129.2	206.8	999.9
Total Liab To Nw (%)	16.0	75.5	230.0
Fixed Assets To Nw (%)	21.9	68.5	173.6
EFFICIENCY			
Coll Period (days)	21.4	36.5	64.1
Sales To Inv (times)	6.8	5.7	3.7
Assets To Sales (%)	151.4	205.3	313.0
Sales To Nwc (times)	7.9	5.0	1.9
Acct Pay To Sales (%)	5.5	10.8	30.7
PROFITABILITY			
Return On Sales (%)	8.2	(4.6)	(85.9)
Return On Assets (%)	3.5	(5.9)	(39.6)
Return On Nw (%)	9.8	0.0	(42.8)

SIC 1041 GOLD ORES (NO BREAKDOWN) 2002 (18 Establishments)

	$	%
Cash	2,646,135	13.1
Accounts Receivable	181,796	0.9
Notes Receivable	0	0.0
Inventory	626,185	3.1
Other Current	2,706,732	13.4
Total Current	**6,160,848**	**30.5**
Fixed Assets	8,120,199	40.2
Other Non-current	5,918,453	29.3
Total Assets	**20,199,500**	**100.0**
Accounts Payable	15,755,610	78.0
Bank Loans	0	0.0
Notes Payable	121,197	0.6
Other Current	70,960,844	351.3
Total Current	**86,837,651**	**429.9**
Other Long Term	41,045,384	203.2
Deferred Credits	0	0.0
Net Worth	(107,683,535)	(533.1)
Total Liab & Net Worth	**20,199,500**	**100.0**
Net Sales	8,613,859	100.0
Gross Profit	4,427,524	51.4
Net Profit After Tax	361,782	4.2
Working Capital	(80,676,803)	—

RATIOS	UQ	MED	LQ
SOLVENCY			
Quick Ratio (times)	0.8	0.4	0.0
Current Ratio (times)	1.6	0.8	0.1
Curr Liab To Nw (%)	8.5	22.0	64.9
Curr Liab To Inv (%)	174.9	243.0	999.9
Total Liab To Nw (%)	34.1	87.4	213.5
Fixed Assets To Nw (%)	27.7	95.6	168.5
EFFICIENCY			
Coll Period (days)	10.0	16.3	46.0
Sales To Inv (times)	17.6	6.4	5.1
Assets To Sales (%)	167.4	234.5	684.9
Sales To Nwc (times)	7.1	5.0	1.4
Acct Pay To Sales (%)	6.3	14.0	24.9
PROFITABILITY			
Return On Sales (%)	7.9	1.5	(221.9)
Return On Assets (%)	6.0	0.7	(43.3)
Return On Nw (%)	10.1	2.9	(21.2)

SIC 1081 METAL MINING SVCS
(NO BREAKDOWN)
2002 (13 Establishments)

	$	%
Cash	955,173	23.9
Accounts Receivable	463,599	11.6
Notes Receivable	0	0.0
Inventory	87,924	2.2
Other Current	359,689	9.0
Total Current	**1,866,385**	**46.7**
Fixed Assets	1,011,125	25.3
Other Non-current	1,119,031	28.0
Total Assets	**3,996,541**	**100.0**
Accounts Payable	167,855	4.2
Bank Loans	0	0.0
Notes Payable	7,993	0.2
Other Current	24,135,111	603.9
Total Current	**24,310,959**	**608.3**
Other Long Term	2,613,737	65.4
Deferred Credits	19,983	0.5
Net Worth	(22,948,138)	(574.2)
Total Liab & Net Worth	**3,996,541**	**100.0**
Net Sales	3,011,711	100.0
Gross Profit	1,391,410	46.2
Net Profit After Tax	(337,312)	(11.2)
Working Capital	(22,444,574)	—

RATIOS	UQ	MED	LQ
SOLVENCY			
Quick Ratio (times)	3.3	1.3	0.1
Current Ratio (times)	6.7	1.5	1.2
Curr Liab To Nw (%)	6.5	9.5	35.8
Curr Liab To Inv (%)	101.3	999.9	999.9
Total Liab To Nw (%)	11.3	15.2	289.2
Fixed Assets To Nw (%)	6.9	44.6	49.9
EFFICIENCY			
Coll Period (days)	24.7	50.4	79.8
Sales To Inv (times)	2.3	2.3	2.3
Assets To Sales (%)	72.9	132.7	171.3
Sales To Nwc (times)	11.8	3.2	1.9
Acct Pay To Sales (%)	4.0	5.8	8.7
PROFITABILITY			
Return On Sales (%)	0.0	(13.8)	(30.0)
Return On Assets (%)	(8.8)	(27.0)	(513.7)
Return On Nw (%)	0.0	(44.2)	(121.5)

SIC 12 COAL MINING
(NO BREAKDOWN)
2002 (26 Establishments)

	$	%
Cash	22,192,635	10.6
Accounts Receivable	30,985,943	14.8
Notes Receivable	1,465,551	0.7
Inventory	8,793,308	4.2
Other Current	11,515,048	5.5
Total Current	**74,952,485**	**35.8**
Fixed Assets	108,660,166	51.9
Other Non-current	25,751,831	12.3
Total Assets	**209,364,482**	**100.0**
Accounts Payable	17,167,888	8.2
Bank Loans	0	0.0
Notes Payable	209,364	0.1
Other Current	29,939,121	14.3
Total Current	**47,316,373**	**22.6**
Other Long Term	78,930,409	37.7
Deferred Credits	2,093,645	1.0
Net Worth	81,024,055	38.7
Total Liab & Net Worth	**209,364,482**	**100.0**
Net Sales	155,893,136	100.0
Gross Profit	49,262,231	31.6
Net Profit After Tax	7,950,550	5.1
Working Capital	27,636,112	—

RATIOS	UQ	MED	LQ
SOLVENCY			
Quick Ratio (times)	1.4	0.8	0.4
Current Ratio (times)	1.9	1.5	0.9
Curr Liab To Nw (%)	33.1	58.4	216.0
Curr Liab To Inv (%)	275.0	380.1	584.0
Total Liab To Nw (%)	41.5	134.1	548.0
Fixed Assets To Nw (%)	72.4	130.5	491.6
EFFICIENCY			
Coll Period (days)	21.5	31.8	42.7
Sales To Inv (times)	25.8	16.7	9.5
Assets To Sales (%)	50.7	134.3	151.1
Sales To Nwc (times)	39.0	12.2	4.7
Acct Pay To Sales (%)	3.6	4.5	7.2
PROFITABILITY			
Return On Sales (%)	8.2	5.1	0.5
Return On Assets (%)	11.4	4.7	0.3
Return On Nw (%)	80.0	18.2	5.4

SIC 1221 BIT COAL LGNTE-SRFC
(NO BREAKDOWN)
2002 (15 Establishments)

	$	%
Cash	14,420,350	5.0
Accounts Receivable	38,934,945	13.5
Notes Receivable	1,730,442	0.6
Inventory	17,016,013	5.9
Other Current	14,997,164	5.2
Total Current	**87,098,914**	**30.2**
Fixed Assets	160,065,885	55.5
Other Non-current	41,242,201	14.3
Total Assets	**288,407,000**	**100.0**
Accounts Payable	19,900,083	6.9
Bank Loans	0	0.0
Notes Payable	0	0.0
Other Current	49,317,597	17.1
Total Current	**69,217,680**	**24.0**
Other Long Term	134,397,662	46.6
Deferred Credits	1,730,442	0.6
Net Worth	83,061,216	28.8
Total Liab & Net Worth	**288,407,000**	**100.0**
Net Sales	212,063,971	100.0
Gross Profit	53,228,057	25.1
Net Profit After Tax	14,420,350	6.8
Working Capital	17,881,234	—

RATIOS	UQ	MED	LQ
SOLVENCY			
Quick Ratio (times)	0.9	0.5	0.3
Current Ratio (times)	1.8	1.0	0.9
Curr Liab To Nw (%)	47.5	76.0	311.6
Curr Liab To Inv (%)	275.0	359.6	561.9
Total Liab To Nw (%)	99.7	242.7	857.5
Fixed Assets To Nw (%)	82.2	215.1	583.9
EFFICIENCY			
Coll Period (days)	20.4	28.0	42.3
Sales To Inv (times)	22.5	14.2	9.5
Assets To Sales (%)	55.7	136.0	151.1
Sales To Nwc (times)	26.0	5.8	5.2
Acct Pay To Sales (%)	4.0	5.7	8.2
PROFITABILITY			
Return On Sales (%)	10.9	5.7	3.2
Return On Assets (%)	11.4	7.3	2.2
Return On Nw (%)	80.0	25.7	9.8

SIC 13 OIL,GAS EXTRACTION
(NO BREAKDOWN)
2002 (330 Establishments)

	$	%
Cash	710,953	14.2
Accounts Receivable	746,000	14.9
Notes Receivable	20,027	0.4
Inventory	105,141	2.1
Other Current	395,531	7.9
Total Current	**1,977,652**	**39.5**
Fixed Assets	2,368,176	47.3
Other Non-current	660,886	13.2
Total Assets	**5,006,714**	**100.0**
Accounts Payable	630,846	12.6
Bank Loans	10,013	0.2
Notes Payable	125,168	2.5
Other Current	1,441,934	28.8
Total Current	**2,207,961**	**44.1**
Other Long Term	1,206,618	24.1
Deferred Credits	45,060	0.9
Net Worth	1,547,075	30.9
Total Liab & Net Worth	**5,006,714**	**100.0**
Net Sales	3,369,256	100.0
Gross Profit	1,499,319	44.5
Net Profit After Tax	47,170	1.4
Working Capital	(230,309)	—

RATIOS	UQ	MED	LQ
SOLVENCY			
Quick Ratio (times)	2.3	1.0	0.6
Current Ratio (times)	3.3	1.4	0.9
Curr Liab To Nw (%)	12.7	32.3	81.6
Curr Liab To Inv (%)	278.8	919.7	999.9
Total Liab To Nw (%)	32.1	91.4	193.0
Fixed Assets To Nw (%)	39.9	95.3	165.5
EFFICIENCY			
Coll Period (days)	34.0	55.5	83.2
Sales To Inv (times)	110.4	29.8	13.8
Assets To Sales (%)	51.1	148.6	330.8
Sales To Nwc (times)	13.2	6.0	2.9
Acct Pay To Sales (%)	3.8	7.6	18.6
PROFITABILITY			
Return On Sales (%)	12.8	3.3	(6.9)
Return On Assets (%)	8.9	2.8	(5.7)
Return On Nw (%)	19.1	6.2	(6.4)

SIC 1311 CRUDE PTRLM,NAT GAS
(NO BREAKDOWN)
2002 (131 Establishments)

	$	%
Cash	2,132,532	14.1
Accounts Receivable	1,482,185	9.8
Notes Receivable	75,622	0.5
Inventory	287,362	1.9
Other Current	1,119,201	7.4
Total Current	**5,096,902**	**33.7**
Fixed Assets	8,000,775	52.9
Other Non-current	2,026,662	13.4
Total Assets	**15,124,339**	**100.0**
Accounts Payable	1,346,066	8.9
Bank Loans	15,124	0.1
Notes Payable	257,114	1.7
Other Current	2,208,154	14.6
Total Current	**3,826,458**	**25.3**
Other Long Term	3,705,463	24.5
Deferred Credits	166,368	1.1
Net Worth	7,426,050	49.1
Total Liab & Net Worth	**15,124,339**	**100.0**
Net Sales	5,987,466	100.0
Gross Profit	3,179,344	53.1
Net Profit After Tax	(71,850)	(1.2)
Working Capital	1,270,444	—

RATIOS	UQ	MED	LQ
SOLVENCY			
Quick Ratio (times)	1.5	0.9	0.5
Current Ratio (times)	2.2	1.2	0.8
Curr Liab To Nw (%)	16.5	33.9	70.9
Curr Liab To Inv (%)	383.9	999.9	999.9
Total Liab To Nw (%)	32.9	104.6	213.3
Fixed Assets To Nw (%)	49.7	119.1	200.6
EFFICIENCY			
Coll Period (days)	36.0	59.1	93.7
Sales To Inv (times)	76.8	29.7	14.3
Assets To Sales (%)	124.8	252.6	376.9
Sales To Nwc (times)	17.9	5.7	1.8
Acct Pay To Sales (%)	6.3	12.9	29.7
PROFITABILITY			
Return On Sales (%)	16.2	4.6	(19.0)
Return On Assets (%)	6.6	1.8	(4.5)
Return On Nw (%)	13.5	4.4	(11.4)

SIC 1381 DRILL OIL,GAS WELLS
(NO BREAKDOWN)
2002 (37 Establishments)

	$	%
Cash	437,607	8.6
Accounts Receivable	422,342	8.3
Notes Receivable	0	0.0
Inventory	81,415	1.6
Other Current	162,830	3.2
Total Current	**1,104,194**	**21.7**
Fixed Assets	2,910,595	57.2
Other Non-current	1,073,664	21.1
Total Assets	**5,088,453**	**100.0**
Accounts Payable	473,226	9.3
Bank Loans	20,354	0.4
Notes Payable	351,103	6.9
Other Current	814,153	16.0
Total Current	**1,658,836**	**32.6**
Other Long Term	1,440,032	28.3
Deferred Credits	55,973	1.1
Net Worth	1,933,612	38.0
Total Liab & Net Worth	**5,088,453**	**100.0**
Net Sales	2,301,426	100.0
Gross Profit	886,049	38.5
Net Profit After Tax	128,880	5.6
Working Capital	(554,642)	—

RATIOS	UQ	MED	LQ
SOLVENCY			
Quick Ratio (times)	2.6	1.1	0.7
Current Ratio (times)	3.3	1.7	0.9
Curr Liab To Nw (%)	8.2	33.1	81.6
Curr Liab To Inv (%)	278.8	505.2	999.9
Total Liab To Nw (%)	37.2	102.6	156.7
Fixed Assets To Nw (%)	61.7	114.8	186.8
EFFICIENCY			
Coll Period (days)	32.7	57.1	69.0
Sales To Inv (times)	168.5	22.7	18.1
Assets To Sales (%)	53.8	221.1	340.6
Sales To Nwc (times)	10.9	4.5	1.7
Acct Pay To Sales (%)	4.9	7.5	16.1
PROFITABILITY			
Return On Sales (%)	9.7	4.4	(0.8)
Return On Assets (%)	6.8	3.2	(2.9)
Return On Nw (%)	15.9	4.4	(6.7)

SIC 1382 OIL GAS EXPLOR SVCS
(NO BREAKDOWN)
2002 (45 Establishments)

	$	%
Cash	1,504,373	13.4
Accounts Receivable	1,044,080	9.3
Notes Receivable	22,453	0.2
Inventory	112,267	1.0
Other Current	819,547	7.3
Total Current	**3,502,720**	**31.2**
Fixed Assets	6,017,494	53.6
Other Non-current	1,706,453	15.2
Total Assets	**11,226,667**	**100.0**
Accounts Payable	3,570,080	31.8
Bank Loans	11,227	0.1
Notes Payable	134,720	1.2
Other Current	12,001,307	106.9
Total Current	**15,717,334**	**140.0**
Other Long Term	3,019,973	26.9
Deferred Credits	11,227	0.1
Net Worth	(7,521,867)	(67.0)
Total Liab & Net Worth	**11,226,667**	**100.0**
Net Sales	4,515,956	100.0
Gross Profit	1,774,771	39.3
Net Profit After Tax	221,282	4.9
Working Capital	(12,214,614)	—

RATIOS	UQ	MED	LQ
SOLVENCY			
Quick Ratio (times)	1.5	0.6	0.3
Current Ratio (times)	2.0	1.3	0.5
Curr Liab To Nw (%)	11.3	26.6	77.4
Curr Liab To Inv (%)	634.2	999.9	999.9
Total Liab To Nw (%)	27.6	100.2	195.9
Fixed Assets To Nw (%)	48.0	106.8	200.0
EFFICIENCY			
Coll Period (days)	39.3	62.8	91.1
Sales To Inv (times)	81.5	20.7	11.5
Assets To Sales (%)	136.2	248.6	486.0
Sales To Nwc (times)	13.3	5.8	2.7
Acct Pay To Sales (%)	5.4	10.0	26.3
PROFITABILITY			
Return On Sales (%)	13.0	(0.6)	(95.1)
Return On Assets (%)	6.4	(0.2)	(11.9)
Return On Nw (%)	22.9	4.4	(19.7)

SIC 1389 OIL GAS FLD SVC,NEC
(NO BREAKDOWN)
2002 (108 Establishments)

	$	%
Cash	253,713	17.3
Accounts Receivable	381,302	26.0
Notes Receivable	7,333	0.5
Inventory	41,063	2.8
Other Current	149,588	10.2
Total Current	**832,999**	**56.8**
Fixed Assets	498,626	34.0
Other Non-current	134,922	9.2
Total Assets	**1,466,547**	**100.0**
Accounts Payable	143,722	9.8
Bank Loans	4,400	0.3
Notes Payable	33,731	2.3
Other Current	294,775	20.1
Total Current	**476,628**	**32.5**
Other Long Term	302,109	20.6
Deferred Credits	2,993	0.2
Net Worth	684,877	46.7
Total Liab & Net Worth	**1,466,547**	**100.0**
Net Sales	3,074,522	100.0
Gross Profit	1,214,436	39.5
Net Profit After Tax	55,341	1.8
Working Capital	356,371	—

RATIOS	UQ	MED	LQ
SOLVENCY			
Quick Ratio (times)	3.4	1.5	1.0
Current Ratio (times)	4.2	2.2	1.2
Curr Liab To Nw (%)	15.2	33.7	88.5
Curr Liab To Inv (%)	159.0	373.9	999.9
Total Liab To Nw (%)	25.0	77.5	157.4
Fixed Assets To Nw (%)	27.4	60.6	107.9
EFFICIENCY			
Coll Period (days)	32.5	50.7	80.5
Sales To Inv (times)	186.4	38.0	17.3
Assets To Sales (%)	34.0	47.7	71.6
Sales To Nwc (times)	12.2	6.5	3.6
Acct Pay To Sales (%)	2.1	4.1	7.5
PROFITABILITY			
Return On Sales (%)	8.0	3.3	(0.9)
Return On Assets (%)	14.0	5.5	(3.6)
Return On Nw (%)	26.1	10.9	1.5

	SIC 14 NONMETALLIC MINERALS (NO BREAKDOWN) 2002 (118 Establishments) $	%	SIC 1422 CRUSHED BRKN LMSTNE (NO BREAKDOWN) 2002 (29 Establishments) $	%	SIC 1442 CNSTR SAND,GRAVEL (NO BREAKDOWN) 2002 (45 Establishments) $	%	SIC 15 GEN'L BLDG CONTRS (NO BREAKDOWN) 2002 (5129 Establishments) $	%
Cash	379,933	10.7	1,035,328	14.9	210,237	9.6	392,816	20.3
Accounts Receivable	440,296	12.4	632,315	9.1	278,127	12.7	592,127	30.6
Notes Receivable	14,203	0.4	97,279	1.4	2,190	0.1	13,545	0.7
Inventory	351,527	9.9	861,616	12.4	179,578	8.2	92,883	4.8
Other Current	220,148	6.2	389,117	5.6	131,398	6.0	458,608	23.7
Total Current	**1,406,107**	**39.6**	**3,015,655**	**43.4**	**801,530**	**36.6**	**1,549,979**	**80.1**
Fixed Assets	1,746,981	49.2	3,078,191	44.3	1,151,926	52.6	284,453	14.7
Other Non-current	397,687	11.2	854,667	12.3	236,517	10.8	100,623	5.2
Total Assets	**3,550,775**	**100.0**	**6,948,513**	**100.0**	**2,189,973**	**100.0**	**1,935,055**	**100.0**
Accounts Payable	259,207	7.3	229,301	3.3	162,058	7.4	506,984	26.2
Bank Loans	24,855	0.7	0	0.0	17,520	0.8	5,805	0.3
Notes Payable	145,582	4.1	257,095	3.7	131,398	6.0	52,246	2.7
Other Current	2,918,737	82.2	375,220	5.4	227,757	10.4	493,440	25.5
Total Current	**3,348,381**	**94.3**	**861,616**	**12.4**	**538,733**	**24.6**	**1,058,475**	**54.7**
Other Long Term	788,272	22.2	965,843	13.9	604,433	27.6	143,194	7.4
Deferred Credits	14,203	0.4	0	0.0	10,950	0.5	3,870	0.2
Net Worth	(600,081)	(16.9)	5,121,054	73.7	1,035,857	47.3	729,516	37.7
Total Liab & Net Worth	**3,550,775**	**100.0**	**6,948,513**	**100.0**	**2,189,973**	**100.0**	**1,935,055**	**100.0**
Net Sales	4,262,635	100.0	6,231,850	100.0	2,707,012	100.0	6,450,183	100.0
Gross Profit	1,581,438	37.1	2,100,133	33.7	1,044,907	38.6	1,102,981	17.1
Net Profit After Tax	221,657	5.2	548,403	8.8	135,351	5.0	148,354	2.3
Working Capital	(1,942,274)	—	2,154,039	—	262,797	—	491,504	—

RATIOS	SIC 14 UQ	MED	LQ	SIC 1422 UQ	MED	LQ	SIC 1442 UQ	MED	LQ	SIC 15 UQ	MED	LQ
SOLVENCY												
Quick Ratio (times)	2.4	1.0	0.5	10.0	1.9	1.0	2.5	0.7	0.4	1.6	1.1	0.5
Current Ratio (times)	4.1	2.0	1.0	15.8	3.8	1.8	3.2	1.3	1.0	2.3	1.5	1.2
Curr Liab To Nw (%)	12.4	32.8	57.4	3.9	12.2	34.8	16.4	42.9	135.9	54.7	130.1	275.9
Curr Liab To Inv (%)	82.5	161.9	789.2	34.2	88.6	166.4	140.7	348.9	842.1	161.0	999.9	999.9
Total Liab To Nw (%)	21.4	68.3	135.0	8.5	27.8	67.1	37.4	118.7	426.2	67.9	154.1	311.6
Fixed Assets To Nw (%)	51.9	86.1	139.9	36.8	60.8	89.4	56.3	110.4	267.2	10.3	23.3	50.1
EFFICIENCY												
Coll Period (days)	24.0	38.7	55.1	25.6	37.6	46.9	26.7	41.1	53.7	25.6	44.5	65.7
Sales To Inv (times)	44.1	11.3	6.6	30.8	8.0	2.9	60.9	19.1	7.7	525.3	95.1	13.8
Assets To Sales (%)	62.7	83.3	142.6	78.1	111.5	185.3	56.5	80.9	133.5	22.2	30.0	43.2
Sales To Nwc (times)	11.7	5.2	2.7	11.7	3.3	1.8	14.4	7.4	3.9	22.2	11.5	6.3
Acct Pay To Sales (%)	2.6	4.3	8.0	2.0	3.6	5.3	2.6	4.5	8.1	3.7	7.4	12.5
PROFITABILITY												
Return On Sales (%)	10.3	4.3	(0.7)	15.2	6.7	2.0	10.4	4.1	(0.5)	4.0	1.4	0.2
Return On Assets (%)	10.5	3.8	(0.9)	12.2	4.6	1.3	10.8	4.6	(1.0)	12.5	4.5	0.8
Return On Nw (%)	23.7	6.6	0.1	17.8	6.1	1.9	22.3	11.9	(2.9)	35.8	12.9	2.5

	SIC 1521 SNGL-FAM HSNG CNSTR (NO BREAKDOWN) 2002 (1011 Establishments)		SIC 1522 RSDNTL CNSTR, NEC (NO BREAKDOWN) 2002 (237 Establishments)		SIC 1531 OPERATIVE BUILDERS (NO BREAKDOWN) 2002 (63 Establishments)		SIC 1541 INDL BLDNGS,WRHSES (NO BREAKDOWN) 2002 (728 Establishments)	
	$	%	$	%	$	%	$	%
Cash	179,300	17.3	428,242	18.4	764,835	12.8	452,123	20.2
Accounts Receivable	225,939	21.8	651,672	28.0	448,146	7.5	734,140	32.8
Notes Receivable	10,364	1.0	27,929	1.2	59,753	1.0	13,429	0.6
Inventory	153,390	14.8	114,043	4.9	2,067,445	34.6	35,812	1.6
Other Current	206,248	19.9	609,779	26.2	1,457,967	24.4	525,984	23.5
Total Current	**775,241**	**74.8**	**1,831,665**	**78.7**	**4,798,146**	**80.3**	**1,761,488**	**78.7**
Fixed Assets	195,883	18.9	339,801	14.6	525,824	8.8	358,117	16.0
Other Non-current	65,295	6.3	155,935	6.7	651,305	10.9	118,626	5.3
Total Assets	**1,036,419**	**100.0**	**2,327,401**	**100.0**	**5,975,275**	**100.0**	**2,238,231**	**100.0**
Accounts Payable	169,973	16.4	500,391	21.5	549,725	9.2	564,034	25.2
Bank Loans	8,291	0.8	13,964	0.6	65,728	1.1	4,476	0.2
Notes Payable	58,039	5.6	83,786	3.6	621,429	10.4	49,241	2.2
Other Current	370,002	35.7	600,471	25.8	1,655,151	27.7	474,506	21.2
Total Current	**606,305**	**58.5**	**1,198,612**	**51.5**	**2,892,033**	**48.4**	**1,092,257**	**48.8**
Other Long Term	128,516	12.4	179,210	7.7	746,909	12.5	174,582	7.8
Deferred Credits	2,073	0.2	6,982	0.3	11,951	0.2	4,476	0.2
Net Worth	299,525	28.9	942,597	40.5	2,324,382	38.9	966,916	43.2
Total Liab & Net Worth	**1,036,419**	**100.0**	**2,327,401**	**100.0**	**5,975,275**	**100.0**	**2,238,231**	**100.0**
Net Sales	3,354,107	100.0	7,706,626	100.0	9,975,417	100.0	7,105,495	100.0
Gross Profit	778,153	23.2	1,456,552	18.9	2,064,911	20.7	1,186,618	16.7
Net Profit After Tax	124,102	3.7	308,265	4.0	428,943	4.3	113,688	1.6
Working Capital	168,936	—	633,053	—	1,906,113	—	669,231	—

RATIOS	UQ	MED	LQ	UQ	MED	LQ	UQ	MED	LQ	UQ	MED	LQ
SOLVENCY												
Quick Ratio (times)	1.6	0.8	0.2	1.5	1.0	0.3	1.1	0.3	0.0	1.7	1.2	0.7
Current Ratio (times)	2.4	1.4	1.1	2.1	1.5	1.2	2.5	1.6	1.3	2.5	1.5	1.2
Curr Liab To Nw (%)	45.2	123.1	299.7	51.1	126.6	281.0	44.6	124.1	303.4	46.6	123.3	246.0
Curr Liab To Inv (%)	96.2	186.0	999.9	99.2	470.8	999.9	41.5	88.0	130.0	478.8	999.9	999.9
Total Liab To Nw (%)	65.4	161.6	379.2	71.0	153.0	327.4	59.8	177.5	331.5	58.3	147.9	286.0
Fixed Assets To Nw (%)	12.1	31.1	76.9	5.7	19.5	46.2	4.7	11.8	25.2	12.7	26.0	55.2
EFFICIENCY												
Coll Period (days)	7.7	28.1	52.1	26.3	42.7	69.6	0.7	4.4	24.1	31.8	48.6	71.9
Sales To Inv (times)	116.7	16.2	3.2	332.6	66.1	3.9	5.5	2.6	1.4	777.4	254.1	42.8
Assets To Sales (%)	20.2	30.9	51.4	21.3	30.2	51.8	42.2	59.9	100.7	22.9	31.5	46.2
Sales To Nwc (times)	22.8	11.0	6.1	23.2	12.3	6.2	11.4	5.0	2.7	21.3	10.8	5.6
Acct Pay To Sales (%)	2.3	4.3	7.8	3.8	7.5	12.6	1.8	3.5	6.0	3.9	7.5	12.0
PROFITABILITY												
Return On Sales (%)	5.6	2.4	0.5	5.5	2.6	0.7	7.3	3.4	1.8	3.2	1.0	0.0
Return On Assets (%)	17.9	6.8	1.5	17.8	7.4	1.5	13.3	5.8	2.7	9.0	3.4	0.0
Return On Nw (%)	55.8	22.1	6.0	51.0	24.5	6.2	47.4	22.7	8.9	25.5	9.0	0.3

SIC 1542 NONRESID CONSTR, NEC
(NO BREAKDOWN)
2002 (3090 Establishments)

	$	%
Cash	457,603	21.6
Accounts Receivable	711,826	33.6
Notes Receivable	12,711	0.6
Inventory	36,015	1.7
Other Current	525,396	24.8
Total Current	**1,743,551**	**82.3**
Fixed Assets	277,528	13.1
Other Non-current	97,452	4.6
Total Assets	**2,118,531**	**100.0**
Accounts Payable	644,033	30.4
Bank Loans	4,237	0.2
Notes Payable	33,896	1.6
Other Current	487,263	23.0
Total Current	**1,169,429**	**55.2**
Other Long Term	118,638	5.6
Deferred Credits	4,237	0.2
Net Worth	826,227	39.0
Total Liab & Net Worth	**2,118,531**	**100.0**
Net Sales	7,230,481	100.0
Gross Profit	1,084,572	15.0
Net Profit After Tax	137,379	1.9
Working Capital	574,122	—

RATIOS	UQ	MED	LQ
SOLVENCY			
Quick Ratio (times)	1.6	1.1	0.7
Current Ratio (times)	2.2	1.5	1.2
Curr Liab To Nw (%)	60.5	135.0	276.8
Curr Liab To Inv (%)	486.2	999.9	999.9
Total Liab To Nw (%)	70.8	153.7	303.7
Fixed Assets To Nw (%)	10.2	21.9	44.6
EFFICIENCY			
Coll Period (days)	30.7	48.4	67.9
Sales To Inv (times)	780.1	181.0	40.5
Assets To Sales (%)	22.4	29.3	39.6
Sales To Nwc (times)	22.3	11.9	6.8
Acct Pay To Sales (%)	4.6	8.6	13.5
PROFITABILITY			
Return On Sales (%)	3.5	1.2	0.2
Return On Assets (%)	11.4	4.0	0.7
Return On Nw (%)	31.2	11.4	2.1

SIC 16 HEAVY CONSTR CONTRS
(NO BREAKDOWN)
2002 (2218 Establishments)

	$	%
Cash	397,136	15.6
Accounts Receivable	636,437	25.0
Notes Receivable	15,274	0.6
Inventory	45,823	1.8
Other Current	442,961	17.4
Total Current	**1,537,631**	**60.4**
Fixed Assets	857,916	33.7
Other Non-current	150,199	5.9
Total Assets	**2,545,746**	**100.0**
Accounts Payable	361,496	14.2
Bank Loans	7,637	0.3
Notes Payable	71,281	2.8
Other Current	470,963	18.5
Total Current	**911,377**	**35.8**
Other Long Term	379,316	14.9
Deferred Credits	10,183	0.4
Net Worth	1,244,870	48.9
Total Liab & Net Worth	**2,545,746**	**100.0**
Net Sales	5,462,974	100.0
Gross Profit	1,207,317	22.1
Net Profit After Tax	152,963	2.8
Working Capital	626,254	—

RATIOS	UQ	MED	LQ
Quick Ratio (times)	1.9	1.2	0.7
Current Ratio (times)	2.8	1.7	1.2
Curr Liab To Nw (%)	29.5	66.6	131.7
Curr Liab To Inv (%)	480.9	999.9	999.9
Total Liab To Nw (%)	43.9	98.9	202.3
Fixed Assets To Nw (%)	34.1	63.9	110.7
Coll Period (days)	30.7	51.1	72.6
Sales To Inv (times)	262.8	103.4	34.5
Assets To Sales (%)	34.3	46.6	62.8
Sales To Nwc (times)	15.7	8.4	5.0
Acct Pay To Sales (%)	2.6	5.6	9.8
Return On Sales (%)	5.5	2.1	0.2
Return On Assets (%)	11.5	4.5	0.5
Return On Nw (%)	25.8	9.7	1.6

SIC 1611 HIGHWAY,ST CONSTR
(NO BREAKDOWN)
2002 (738 Establishments)

	$	%
Cash	461,300	16.0
Accounts Receivable	703,483	24.4
Notes Receivable	14,416	0.5
Inventory	54,779	1.9
Other Current	461,301	16.0
Total Current	**1,695,279**	**58.8**
Fixed Assets	1,029,276	35.7
Other Non-current	158,572	5.5
Total Assets	**2,883,127**	**100.0**
Accounts Payable	420,937	14.6
Bank Loans	8,649	0.3
Notes Payable	77,844	2.7
Other Current	521,846	18.1
Total Current	**1,029,276**	**35.7**
Other Long Term	469,950	16.3
Deferred Credits	20,182	0.7
Net Worth	1,363,719	47.3
Total Liab & Net Worth	**2,883,127**	**100.0**
Net Sales	6,364,519	100.0
Gross Profit	1,291,997	20.3
Net Profit After Tax	165,477	2.6
Working Capital	666,003	—

RATIOS	UQ	MED	LQ
Quick Ratio (times)	2.0	1.2	0.7
Current Ratio (times)	2.7	1.7	1.2
Curr Liab To Nw (%)	32.5	67.5	130.5
Curr Liab To Inv (%)	447.6	999.9	999.9
Total Liab To Nw (%)	47.5	107.9	209.5
Fixed Assets To Nw (%)	40.1	72.3	118.0
Coll Period (days)	26.7	48.6	69.9
Sales To Inv (times)	255.3	91.9	38.4
Assets To Sales (%)	34.2	45.3	61.0
Sales To Nwc (times)	17.2	8.9	5.2
Acct Pay To Sales (%)	2.7	5.4	9.7
Return On Sales (%)	4.8	1.9	0.2
Return On Assets (%)	10.5	4.4	0.5
Return On Nw (%)	23.2	9.6	1.7

SIC 1622 BRDGE,TNNEL,ELV HGY
(NO BREAKDOWN)
2002 (126 Establishments)

	$	%
Cash	587,233	19.3
Accounts Receivable	642,001	21.1
Notes Receivable	3,043	0.1
Inventory	45,640	1.5
Other Current	678,513	22.3
Total Current	**1,956,430**	**64.3**
Fixed Assets	897,584	29.5
Other Non-current	188,645	6.2
Total Assets	**3,042,659**	**100.0**
Accounts Payable	441,186	14.5
Bank Loans	6,085	0.2
Notes Payable	51,725	1.7
Other Current	608,532	20.0
Total Current	**1,107,528**	**36.4**
Other Long Term	398,588	13.1
Deferred Credits	9,128	0.3
Net Worth	1,527,415	50.2
Total Liab & Net Worth	**3,042,659**	**100.0**
Net Sales	6,501,408	100.0
Gross Profit	1,105,239	17.0
Net Profit After Tax	221,048	3.4
Working Capital	848,902	—

RATIOS	UQ	MED	LQ
Quick Ratio (times)	1.9	1.1	0.6
Current Ratio (times)	2.9	1.7	1.3
Curr Liab To Nw (%)	30.9	77.2	141.2
Curr Liab To Inv (%)	550.2	999.9	999.9
Total Liab To Nw (%)	43.1	110.8	196.7
Fixed Assets To Nw (%)	30.0	63.6	100.8
Coll Period (days)	33.6	48.2	74.5
Sales To Inv (times)	311.2	163.6	72.8
Assets To Sales (%)	34.8	46.8	63.3
Sales To Nwc (times)	18.4	8.6	4.3
Acct Pay To Sales (%)	3.2	5.3	9.0
Return On Sales (%)	5.9	1.7	0.3
Return On Assets (%)	11.7	4.0	1.1
Return On Nw (%)	22.8	8.3	1.8

SIC 1623 WTER,SWER,UTIL LNES (NO BREAKDOWN) — 2002 (835 Establishments)
SIC 1629 HEAVY CONSTR,NEC (NO BREAKDOWN) — 2002 (519 Establishments)
SIC 17 SPECIAL TRADE CONTRS (NO BREAKDOWN) — 2002 (9976 Establishments)
SIC 1711 PLBNG,HTNG,AIR-COND (NO BREAKDOWN) — 2002 (2620 Establishments)

	SIC 1623 $	%	SIC 1629 $	%	SIC 17 $	%	SIC 1711 $	%
Cash	325,773	14.8	408,204	15.5	173,092	15.9	178,533	17.0
Accounts Receivable	574,505	26.1	661,026	25.1	388,640	35.7	384,371	36.6
Notes Receivable	19,811	0.9	15,801	0.6	5,443	0.5	4,201	0.4
Inventory	33,018	1.5	63,206	2.4	64,229	5.9	76,664	7.3
Other Current	383,001	17.4	466,142	17.7	169,825	15.6	157,529	15.0
Total Current	**1,336,108**	**60.7**	**1,614,379**	**61.3**	**801,229**	**73.6**	**801,298**	**76.3**
Fixed Assets	732,989	33.3	850,643	32.3	236,232	21.7	199,537	19.0
Other Non-current	132,070	6.0	168,549	6.4	51,166	4.7	49,359	4.7
Total Assets	**2,201,167**	**100.0**	**2,633,571**	**100.0**	**1,088,627**	**100.0**	**1,050,194**	**100.0**
Accounts Payable	305,962	13.9	376,601	14.3	173,092	15.9	199,537	19.0
Bank Loans	6,604	0.3	5,267	0.2	4,355	0.4	2,100	0.2
Notes Payable	68,236	3.1	71,106	2.7	33,747	3.1	28,355	2.7
Other Current	398,411	18.1	505,646	19.2	235,143	21.6	228,943	21.8
Total Current	**779,213**	**35.4**	**958,620**	**36.4**	**446,337**	**41.0**	**458,935**	**43.7**
Other Long Term	314,766	14.3	376,601	14.3	133,901	12.3	119,722	11.4
Deferred Credits	6,604	0.3	5,267	0.2	2,177	0.2	2,100	0.2
Net Worth	1,100,584	50.0	1,293,083	49.1	506,212	46.5	469,437	44.7
Total Liab & Net Worth	**2,201,167**	**100.0**	**2,633,571**	**100.0**	**1,088,627**	**100.0**	**1,050,194**	**100.0**
Net Sales	4,673,391	100.0	5,627,288	100.0	3,249,633	100.0	3,312,915	100.0
Gross Profit	1,121,614	24.0	1,271,767	22.6	971,640	29.9	990,562	29.9
Net Profit After Tax	135,528	2.9	163,191	2.9	87,740	2.7	89,449	2.7
Working Capital	556,895	—	655,759	—	354,892	—	342,363	—

RATIOS	UQ	MED	LQ	UQ	MED	LQ	UQ	MED	LQ	UQ	MED	LQ
SOLVENCY												
Quick Ratio (times)	1.9	1.2	0.7	1.9	1.2	0.7	2.5	1.4	0.8	2.3	1.4	0.8
Current Ratio (times)	2.8	1.8	1.2	2.8	1.7	1.2	3.4	1.9	1.3	3.1	1.8	1.3
Curr Liab To Nw (%)	27.5	63.0	127.4	27.2	71.4	143.6	29.8	72.1	155.4	35.9	83.9	176.5
Curr Liab To Inv (%)	601.9	999.9	999.9	352.7	999.9	999.9	226.2	668.1	999.9	226.8	668.7	999.9
Total Liab To Nw (%)	41.8	89.7	187.6	43.5	103.8	198.2	39.7	94.3	202.4	45.4	105.0	218.3
Fixed Assets To Nw (%)	33.0	63.1	109.1	28.2	54.1	103.4	15.6	32.3	68.3	15.4	30.7	60.7
EFFICIENCY												
Coll Period (days)	35.8	52.9	73.9	28.1	52.2	70.8	32.5	51.1	73.4	31.0	48.9	69.4
Sales To Inv (times)	272.3	113.1	38.9	263.7	79.7	23.1	167.0	57.6	23.2	149.0	54.3	23.0
Assets To Sales (%)	35.0	47.1	61.9	33.1	46.8	72.2	25.3	33.5	45.0	24.7	31.7	41.3
Sales To Nwc (times)	15.3	7.8	5.0	14.5	8.9	4.8	14.5	8.1	4.9	15.4	8.9	5.3
Acct Pay To Sales (%)	2.5	5.6	10.0	2.4	5.6	10.0	2.5	4.5	7.8	2.9	5.1	8.4
PROFITABILITY												
Return On Sales (%)	6.1	2.4	0.2	5.7	2.1	0.3	5.1	1.8	0.2	4.6	1.6	0.2
Return On Assets (%)	11.9	5.1	0.6	12.1	4.4	0.6	14.7	5.3	0.6	14.0	4.7	0.6
Return On Nw (%)	25.9	9.6	1.4	28.4	10.1	1.7	32.5	11.8	1.8	30.9	11.2	1.7

SIC 1721 PNTNG, PAPER HANGING
(NO BREAKDOWN)
2002 (356 Establishments)

	$	%
Cash	131,505	15.2
Accounts Receivable	302,807	35.0
Notes Receivable	6,056	0.7
Inventory	16,438	1.9
Other Current	159,191	18.4
Total Current	**615,997**	**71.2**
Fixed Assets	194,662	22.5
Other Non-current	54,505	6.3
Total Assets	**865,164**	**100.0**
Accounts Payable	99,494	11.5
Bank Loans	5,191	0.6
Notes Payable	35,472	4.1
Other Current	170,437	19.7
Total Current	**310,594**	**35.9**
Other Long Term	102,955	11.9
Deferred Credits	1,730	0.2
Net Worth	449,885	52.0
Total Liab & Net Worth	**865,164**	**100.0**
Net Sales	2,383,372	100.0
Gross Profit	745,995	31.3
Net Profit After Tax	50,051	2.1
Working Capital	305,403	—

RATIOS	UQ	MED	LQ
SOLVENCY			
Quick Ratio (times)	2.8	1.5	0.9
Current Ratio (times)	3.6	2.1	1.4
Curr Liab To Nw (%)	25.6	56.2	119.7
Curr Liab To Inv (%)	508.0	999.9	999.9
Total Liab To Nw (%)	32.9	70.9	152.4
Fixed Assets To Nw (%)	16.5	30.9	61.1
EFFICIENCY			
Coll Period (days)	39.4	58.4	77.8
Sales To Inv (times)	306.4	125.9	45.6
Assets To Sales (%)	27.3	36.3	48.5
Sales To Nwc (times)	12.4	6.8	4.5
Acct Pay To Sales (%)	1.7	3.3	6.4
PROFITABILITY			
Return On Sales (%)	5.4	1.7	(0.6)
Return On Assets (%)	13.2	4.4	(1.4)
Return On Nw (%)	27.0	9.1	(1.7)

SIC 1731 ELECTRICAL WORK
(NO BREAKDOWN)
2002 (2323 Establishments)

	$	%
Cash	188,265	16.9
Accounts Receivable	425,545	38.2
Notes Receivable	5,570	0.5
Inventory	63,498	5.7
Other Current	182,694	16.4
Total Current	**865,572**	**77.7**
Fixed Assets	197,177	17.7
Other Non-current	51,243	4.6
Total Assets	**1,113,992**	**100.0**
Accounts Payable	169,327	15.2
Bank Loans	4,456	0.4
Notes Payable	36,762	3.3
Other Current	253,990	22.8
Total Current	**464,535**	**41.7**
Other Long Term	114,741	10.3
Deferred Credits	2,228	0.2
Net Worth	532,488	47.8
Total Liab & Net Worth	**1,113,992**	**100.0**
Net Sales	3,295,834	100.0
Gross Profit	988,750	30.0
Net Profit After Tax	85,692	2.6
Working Capital	401,037	—

RATIOS	UQ	MED	LQ
Quick Ratio	2.6	1.4	0.9
Current Ratio	3.5	2.0	1.4
Curr Liab To Nw	28.6	70.8	151.9
Curr Liab To Inv	257.0	794.9	999.9
Total Liab To Nw	36.1	88.8	183.5
Fixed Assets To Nw	12.8	25.9	52.3
Coll Period	36.9	54.8	76.7
Sales To Inv	198.4	64.0	25.2
Assets To Sales	26.3	33.8	44.9
Sales To Nwc	13.1	7.5	4.6
Acct Pay To Sales	2.6	4.5	7.5
Return On Sales	5.3	1.9	0.1
Return On Assets	15.0	5.3	0.3
Return On Nw	32.6	11.7	1.1

SIC 1741 MSNRY, OTHER STNWRK
(NO BREAKDOWN)
2002 (245 Establishments)

	$	%
Cash	237,939	15.4
Accounts Receivable	531,500	34.4
Notes Receivable	4,635	0.3
Inventory	43,262	2.8
Other Current	299,740	19.4
Total Current	**1,117,076**	**72.3**
Fixed Assets	353,818	22.9
Other Non-current	74,163	4.8
Total Assets	**1,545,057**	**100.0**
Accounts Payable	213,218	13.8
Bank Loans	1,545	0.1
Notes Payable	61,802	4.0
Other Current	373,904	24.2
Total Current	**650,469**	**42.1**
Other Long Term	185,407	12.0
Deferred Credits	12,360	0.8
Net Worth	696,821	45.1
Total Liab & Net Worth	**1,545,057**	**100.0**
Net Sales	4,465,483	100.0
Gross Profit	1,085,112	24.3
Net Profit After Tax	138,430	3.1
Working Capital	466,607	—

RATIOS	UQ	MED	LQ
Quick Ratio	2.3	1.3	0.7
Current Ratio	3.1	1.8	1.3
Curr Liab To Nw	35.3	75.3	167.3
Curr Liab To Inv	413.4	999.9	999.9
Total Liab To Nw	45.1	106.4	231.1
Fixed Assets To Nw	18.5	37.5	75.4
Coll Period	40.7	62.1	78.5
Sales To Inv	280.8	108.4	34.7
Assets To Sales	25.7	34.6	44.4
Sales To Nwc	15.5	8.1	5.6
Acct Pay To Sales	2.6	4.0	6.6
Return On Sales	5.2	2.2	0.3
Return On Assets	16.5	6.3	1.3
Return On Nw	37.9	13.6	3.0

SIC 1742 PLSTRNG, DWALL, INSUL
(NO BREAKDOWN)
2002 (447 Establishments)

	$	%
Cash	197,510	15.1
Accounts Receivable	520,590	39.8
Notes Receivable	7,848	0.6
Inventory	58,861	4.5
Other Current	273,375	20.9
Total Current	**1,058,184**	**80.9**
Fixed Assets	185,738	14.2
Other Non-current	64,093	4.9
Total Assets	**1,308,015**	**100.0**
Accounts Payable	179,198	13.7
Bank Loans	6,540	0.5
Notes Payable	34,008	2.6
Other Current	298,228	22.8
Total Current	**517,974**	**39.6**
Other Long Term	107,257	8.2
Deferred Credits	1,308	0.1
Net Worth	681,476	52.1
Total Liab & Net Worth	**1,308,015**	**100.0**
Net Sales	4,037,083	100.0
Gross Profit	1,033,493	25.6
Net Profit After Tax	113,038	2.8
Working Capital	540,210	—

RATIOS	UQ	MED	LQ
Quick Ratio	2.8	1.5	0.9
Current Ratio	4.3	2.1	1.5
Curr Liab To Nw	26.0	69.8	133.9
Curr Liab To Inv	300.8	773.1	999.9
Total Liab To Nw	34.2	86.0	166.8
Fixed Assets To Nw	9.0	20.9	38.5
Coll Period	38.0	56.9	79.6
Sales To Inv	219.2	72.7	29.4
Assets To Sales	24.6	32.4	41.5
Sales To Nwc	11.8	7.6	4.5
Acct Pay To Sales	1.9	3.5	6.2
Return On Sales	4.9	1.9	0.2
Return On Assets	15.5	5.8	0.7
Return On Nw	29.2	11.6	2.2

	SIC 1743 TRZ,TILE,MRBL,MSAIC (NO BREAKDOWN) 2002 (84 Establishments) $	%	SIC 1751 CARPENTRY WORK (NO BREAKDOWN) 2002 (214 Establishments) $	%	SIC 1752 FLR LAYING WORK,NEC (NO BREAKDOWN) 2002 (259 Establishments) $	%	SIC 1761 RRNF,SDNG,SHT MTLWK (NO BREAKDOWN) 2002 (821 Establishments) $	%
Cash	229,779	17.1	134,499	15.8	92,195	11.4	158,789	16.0
Accounts Receivable	505,244	37.6	302,197	35.5	358,267	44.3	341,396	34.4
Notes Receivable	8,062	0.6	4,256	0.5	5,661	0.7	3,970	0.4
Inventory	92,718	6.9	77,465	9.1	97,856	12.1	60,538	6.1
Other Current	209,622	15.6	119,177	14.0	100,284	12.4	165,735	16.7
Total Current	**1,045,425**	**77.8**	**637,594**	**74.9**	**654,263**	**80.9**	**730,428**	**73.6**
Fixed Assets	241,872	18.0	188,980	22.2	118,075	14.6	209,403	21.1
Other Non-current	56,437	4.2	24,686	2.9	36,392	4.5	52,598	5.3
Total Assets	**1,343,734**	**100.0**	**851,260**	**100.0**	**808,730**	**100.0**	**992,429**	**100.0**
Accounts Payable	210,966	15.7	137,904	16.2	131,014	16.2	164,743	16.6
Bank Loans	2,687	0.2	4,256	0.5	5,661	0.7	2,977	0.3
Notes Payable	28,218	2.1	30,645	3.6	29,923	3.7	26,796	2.7
Other Current	349,372	26.0	208,559	24.5	186,008	23.0	192,531	19.4
Total Current	**591,243**	**44.0**	**381,364**	**44.8**	**352,606**	**43.6**	**387,047**	**39.0**
Other Long Term	122,280	9.1	125,987	14.8	102,709	12.7	123,061	12.4
Deferred Credits	5,375	0.4	2,554	0.3	1,617	0.2	1,985	0.2
Net Worth	624,836	46.5	341,355	40.1	351,798	43.5	480,336	48.4
Total Liab & Net Worth	**1,343,734**	**100.0**	**851,260**	**100.0**	**808,730**	**100.0**	**992,429**	**100.0**
Net Sales	3,861,305	100.0	3,073,141	100.0	2,940,836	100.0	3,091,679	100.0
Gross Profit	1,023,246	26.5	952,674	31.0	879,310	29.9	918,229	29.7
Net Profit After Tax	100,394	2.6	89,121	2.9	76,462	2.6	77,292	2.5
Working Capital	454,182	—	256,230	—	301,657	—	343,381	—

RATIOS	UQ	MED	LQ	UQ	MED	LQ	UQ	MED	LQ	UQ	MED	LQ
SOLVENCY												
Quick Ratio (times)	2.3	1.3	0.7	2.6	1.2	0.7	2.4	1.3	0.9	2.7	1.4	0.9
Current Ratio (times)	3.1	1.8	1.3	3.6	1.9	1.2	3.4	2.0	1.4	3.8	2.0	1.3
Curr Liab To Nw (%)	34.2	77.2	166.8	30.8	76.6	185.9	33.7	73.6	182.5	24.6	62.2	171.3
Curr Liab To Inv (%)	377.6	999.9	999.9	124.2	307.0	858.1	143.8	377.2	903.3	231.4	583.5	999.9
Total Liab To Nw (%)	46.4	100.2	194.4	39.3	106.1	273.5	44.0	91.6	223.7	31.5	85.5	205.8
Fixed Assets To Nw (%)	10.1	20.6	53.9	14.4	29.9	83.9	10.0	23.1	45.3	18.2	34.1	66.3
EFFICIENCY												
Coll Period (days)	39.8	59.5	80.7	23.0	41.3	64.8	31.6	48.6	68.1	25.9	46.0	66.3
Sales To Inv (times)	318.9	100.8	23.3	115.6	34.4	16.6	83.5	31.9	17.5	137.2	57.5	26.6
Assets To Sales (%)	25.2	34.8	42.8	20.5	27.7	34.9	21.2	27.5	35.6	23.2	32.1	42.2
Sales To Nwc (times)	13.0	7.4	4.4	21.5	8.5	5.5	16.1	8.4	5.3	16.2	8.3	5.4
Acct Pay To Sales (%)	3.3	5.6	9.7	1.6	3.5	7.8	2.1	3.7	6.3	2.6	4.5	7.7
PROFITABILITY												
Return On Sales (%)	5.4	2.2	0.4	6.2	2.4	0.4	4.5	1.6	0.2	4.5	1.8	0.2
Return On Assets (%)	16.8	5.7	1.0	23.4	7.9	1.3	15.3	5.4	0.6	14.5	5.9	0.7
Return On Nw (%)	34.0	16.1	1.4	52.0	26.4	5.2	35.0	10.7	2.3	34.3	12.4	1.9

Page 16

SIC 1771 CONCRETE WORK (NO BREAKDOWN) — 2002 (501 Establishments)
SIC 1781 WATER WELL DRILLING (NO BREAKDOWN) — 2002 (91 Establishments)
SIC 1791 STRUCT STEEL ERCTN (NO BREAKDOWN) — 2002 (188 Establishments)
SIC 1793 GLASS, GLAZING WORK (NO BREAKDOWN) — 2002 (213 Establishments)

	SIC 1771 $	%	SIC 1781 $	%	SIC 1791 $	%	SIC 1793 $	%
Cash	174,461	14.0	145,979	14.0	245,067	17.0	130,264	16.8
Accounts Receivable	423,692	34.0	232,524	22.3	498,783	34.6	320,233	41.3
Notes Receivable	6,231	0.5	2,085	0.2	10,091	0.7	6,978	0.9
Inventory	19,938	1.6	77,160	7.4	43,247	3.0	73,661	9.5
Other Current	189,415	15.2	109,485	10.5	249,390	17.3	89,170	11.5
Total Current	**813,737**	**65.3**	**567,233**	**54.4**	**1,046,578**	**72.6**	**620,306**	**80.0**
Fixed Assets	381,323	30.6	408,741	39.2	340,210	23.6	125,612	16.2
Other Non-current	51,092	4.1	66,733	6.4	54,780	3.8	29,465	3.8
Total Assets	**1,246,152**	**100.0**	**1,042,707**	**100.0**	**1,441,568**	**100.0**	**775,383**	**100.0**
Accounts Payable	195,646	15.7	139,723	13.4	203,261	14.1	126,387	16.3
Bank Loans	8,723	0.7	0	0.0	4,325	0.3	3,102	0.4
Notes Payable	37,385	3.0	30,239	2.9	57,663	4.0	20,160	2.6
Other Current	235,522	18.9	152,234	14.6	304,170	21.1	156,627	20.2
Total Current	**477,276**	**38.3**	**322,196**	**30.9**	**569,419**	**39.5**	**306,276**	**39.5**
Other Long Term	185,677	14.9	192,902	18.5	207,586	14.4	76,764	9.9
Deferred Credits	2,492	0.2	2,085	0.2	2,883	0.2	775	0.1
Net Worth	580,707	46.6	525,524	50.4	661,680	45.9	391,568	50.5
Total Liab & Net Worth	**1,246,152**	**100.0**	**1,042,707**	**100.0**	**1,441,568**	**100.0**	**775,383**	**100.0**
Net Sales	3,570,636	100.0	2,386,057	100.0	4,015,510	100.0	2,550,602	100.0
Gross Profit	946,219	26.5	1,030,777	43.2	1,148,436	28.6	872,306	34.2
Net Profit After Tax	103,548	2.9	93,056	3.9	128,496	3.2	58,664	2.3
Working Capital	336,461	—	245,037	—	477,159	—	314,030	—

RATIOS

	1771 UQ	MED	LQ	1781 UQ	MED	LQ	1791 UQ	MED	LQ	1793 UQ	MED	LQ
SOLVENCY												
Quick Ratio (times)	2.3	1.4	0.8	2.3	1.2	0.6	2.5	1.5	0.8	3.1	1.8	1.1
Current Ratio (times)	3.0	1.7	1.2	3.6	1.8	1.2	3.4	1.9	1.2	4.0	2.3	1.6
Curr Liab To Nw (%)	31.8	71.8	141.4	19.9	53.6	108.4	28.7	69.1	171.4	27.2	55.5	124.1
Curr Liab To Inv (%)	498.4	999.9	999.9	143.4	301.4	668.6	393.1	848.1	999.9	145.6	447.1	999.9
Total Liab To Nw (%)	46.5	105.8	203.4	39.4	101.7	173.8	38.2	93.0	218.1	32.7	70.2	141.9
Fixed Assets To Nw (%)	26.7	53.2	97.2	40.6	82.1	129.8	16.3	36.8	77.3	11.4	20.5	43.3
EFFICIENCY												
Coll Period (days)	31.8	52.2	75.2	23.0	46.0	70.8	40.9	57.7	81.8	33.2	53.3	70.5
Sales To Inv (times)	333.6	155.5	43.3	43.9	17.7	11.9	321.4	60.5	26.6	139.4	42.0	18.8
Assets To Sales (%)	26.2	34.9	47.9	34.2	43.7	64.8	26.2	35.9	48.5	23.8	30.4	38.9
Sales To Nwc (times)	16.6	9.5	5.8	12.2	6.6	4.3	15.8	7.6	4.1	10.9	7.0	5.0
Acct Pay To Sales (%)	2.4	4.9	8.5	2.4	4.1	7.1	1.7	4.0	7.8	2.5	5.0	8.1
PROFITABILITY												
Return On Sales (%)	5.1	1.7	0.4	5.9	2.5	0.2	5.5	2.4	0.2	4.4	1.7	0.2
Return On Assets (%)	13.2	4.9	1.0	10.9	4.3	0.3	15.1	6.0	0.5	13.1	5.8	0.9
Return On Nw (%)	32.0	11.8	3.1	24.6	9.4	0.3	33.1	14.0	2.0	27.3	11.1	2.4

	SIC 1794 EXCAVATION WORK (NO BREAKDOWN) 2002 (529 Establishments) $	%	SIC 1795 WRCKNG, DMLTN WORK (NO BREAKDOWN) 2002 (69 Establishments) $	%	SIC 1796 INSTL BLDG EQPT, NEC (NO BREAKDOWN) 2002 (123 Establishments) $	%	SIC 1799 SPCL TRD CNTRS, NEC (NO BREAKDOWN) 2002 (893 Establishments) $	%
Cash	190,951	11.5	199,652	14.5	192,166	13.3	148,817	15.5
Accounts Receivable	411,791	24.8	374,520	27.2	549,046	38.0	309,155	32.2
Notes Receivable	11,623	0.7	2,754	0.2	8,669	0.6	5,761	0.6
Inventory	19,925	1.2	8,261	0.6	80,912	5.6	78,729	8.2
Other Current	194,273	11.7	203,784	14.8	182,052	12.6	135,374	14.1
Total Current	**828,563**	**49.9**	**788,971**	**57.3**	**1,012,845**	**70.1**	**677,836**	**70.6**
Fixed Assets	775,429	46.7	524,603	38.1	349,655	24.2	226,585	23.6
Other Non-current	56,455	3.4	63,338	4.6	82,357	5.7	55,687	5.8
Total Assets	**1,660,447**	**100.0**	**1,376,912**	**100.0**	**1,444,857**	**100.0**	**960,108**	**100.0**
Accounts Payable	210,877	12.7	152,837	11.1	203,725	14.1	135,375	14.1
Bank Loans	4,981	0.3	4,131	0.3	7,224	0.5	5,761	0.6
Notes Payable	58,116	3.5	52,323	3.8	59,239	4.1	30,723	3.2
Other Current	312,164	18.8	243,713	17.7	306,310	21.2	218,905	22.8
Total Current	**586,138**	**35.3**	**453,004**	**32.9**	**576,498**	**39.9**	**390,764**	**40.7**
Other Long Term	381,902	23.0	326,328	23.7	203,725	14.1	114,253	11.9
Deferred Credits	6,642	0.4	4,131	0.3	10,114	0.7	960	0.1
Net Worth	685,765	41.3	593,449	43.1	654,520	45.3	454,131	47.3
Total Liab & Net Worth	**1,660,447**	**100.0**	**1,376,912**	**100.0**	**1,444,857**	**100.0**	**960,108**	**100.0**
Net Sales	3,205,496	100.0	2,917,186	100.0	4,116,402	100.0	2,766,882	100.0
Gross Profit	836,634	26.1	971,423	33.3	1,325,481	32.2	949,041	34.3
Net Profit After Tax	102,576	3.2	96,267	3.3	49,397	1.2	88,540	3.2
Working Capital	242,425	—	335,967	—	436,347	—	287,072	—

RATIOS	UQ	MED	LQ	UQ	MED	LQ	UQ	MED	LQ	UQ	MED	LQ
SOLVENCY												
Quick Ratio (times)	1.8	1.1	0.7	3.2	1.3	0.5	2.1	1.3	0.9	2.7	1.3	0.8
Current Ratio (times)	2.5	1.5	1.1	4.0	1.7	1.1	2.7	1.8	1.3	3.7	1.9	1.3
Curr Liab To Nw (%)	31.1	64.5	135.5	23.7	54.9	169.5	33.8	74.8	156.8	26.1	64.4	145.6
Curr Liab To Inv (%)	552.6	999.9	999.9	543.6	999.9	999.9	134.5	615.3	999.9	145.9	392.8	999.9
Total Liab To Nw (%)	53.0	113.9	221.6	34.0	88.5	297.2	54.0	106.9	231.5	37.3	86.8	199.6
Fixed Assets To Nw (%)	56.5	95.7	156.7	27.5	67.0	148.3	21.0	42.0	84.1	17.2	36.3	71.8
EFFICIENCY												
Coll Period (days)	27.7	50.4	77.8	34.3	72.3	82.1	33.2	54.8	77.0	28.8	47.8	73.7
Sales To Inv (times)	262.3	86.3	40.8	935.0	138.6	54.0	188.2	41.1	11.3	111.6	40.0	15.2
Assets To Sales (%)	37.4	51.8	68.5	35.4	47.2	67.6	25.6	35.1	48.6	24.7	34.7	46.9
Sales To Nwc (times)	19.7	9.3	5.1	12.5	5.3	3.5	17.5	8.9	5.1	14.1	7.9	4.6
Acct Pay To Sales (%)	2.5	5.1	9.3	1.9	4.1	9.0	2.3	4.6	8.0	1.8	3.7	7.4
PROFITABILITY												
Return On Sales (%)	6.2	2.6	0.6	4.8	1.7	0.4	5.1	1.8	(0.2)	5.9	2.2	0.2
Return On Assets (%)	11.2	5.0	1.0	10.1	4.1	0.7	13.5	4.4	(0.6)	16.7	6.1	0.5
Return On Nw (%)	28.1	11.0	2.8	21.2	7.3	2.3	27.6	8.3	(0.1)	34.7	13.3	2.5

	SIC 20 FOOD,KINDRED PRODUCT (NO BREAKDOWN) 2002 (847 Establishments) $	%	SIC 2011 MEAT PACKING PLANTS (NO BREAKDOWN) 2002 (45 Establishments) $	%	SIC 2013 SAUSG,OTHR PREP MTS (NO BREAKDOWN) 2002 (61 Establishments) $	%	SIC 2015 PLTRY SLGHTRNG PROC (NO BREAKDOWN) 2002 (15 Establishments) $	%
Cash	440,134	8.6	650,502	7.8	293,398	14.3	1,667,256	3.9
Accounts Receivable	951,919	18.6	1,592,895	19.1	402,139	19.6	6,968,274	16.3
Notes Receivable	20,471	0.4	8,340	0.1	16,414	0.8	0	0.0
Inventory	1,064,511	20.8	1,634,594	19.6	369,312	18.0	7,866,027	18.4
Other Current	281,482	5.5	350,270	4.2	112,844	5.5	2,436,759	5.7
Total Current	**2,758,517**	**53.9**	**4,236,601**	**50.8**	**1,194,107**	**58.2**	**18,938,316**	**44.3**
Fixed Assets	1,816,834	35.5	3,069,034	36.8	693,485	33.8	20,947,573	49.0
Other Non-current	542,492	10.6	1,034,131	12.4	164,139	8.0	2,864,259	6.7
Total Assets	**5,117,843**	**100.0**	**8,339,766**	**100.0**	**2,051,731**	**100.0**	**42,750,148**	**100.0**
Accounts Payable	731,852	14.3	800,618	9.6	203,121	9.9	4,403,265	10.3
Bank Loans	25,589	0.5	58,378	0.7	16,414	0.8	0	0.0
Notes Payable	199,596	3.9	400,309	4.8	55,397	2.7	3,420,012	8.0
Other Current	1,069,629	20.9	1,017,451	12.2	262,622	12.8	7,524,026	17.6
Total Current	**2,026,666**	**39.6**	**2,276,756**	**27.3**	**537,554**	**26.2**	**15,347,303**	**35.9**
Other Long Term	1,207,810	23.6	1,659,613	19.9	309,811	15.1	9,661,534	22.6
Deferred Credits	15,354	0.3	8,340	0.1	2,052	0.1	555,752	1.3
Net Worth	1,868,013	36.5	4,395,057	52.7	1,202,314	58.6	17,185,559	40.2
Total Liab & Net Worth	**5,117,843**	**100.0**	**8,339,766**	**100.0**	**2,051,731**	**100.0**	**42,750,148**	**100.0**
Net Sales	11,684,573	100.0	29,891,634	100.0	7,353,875	100.0	100,825,821	100.0
Gross Profit	3,633,902	31.1	5,769,085	19.3	1,912,008	26.0	17,644,519	17.5
Net Profit After Tax	350,537	3.0	597,833	2.0	264,740	3.6	2,218,168	2.2
Working Capital	731,851	—	1,959,845	—	656,553	—	3,591,013	—

RATIOS	UQ	MED	LQ	UQ	MED	LQ	UQ	MED	LQ	UQ	MED	LQ
SOLVENCY												
Quick Ratio (times)	1.6	0.9	0.5	2.4	0.8	0.4	2.2	1.4	0.8	0.8	0.5	0.4
Current Ratio (times)	3.2	1.8	1.2	4.1	1.6	1.2	3.9	2.5	1.7	1.6	1.4	1.0
Curr Liab To Nw (%)	24.5	54.6	118.9	9.3	54.8	131.3	16.0	35.5	79.2	61.9	78.4	206.1
Curr Liab To Inv (%)	85.2	144.6	281.2	97.2	146.1	244.3	73.5	123.2	208.7	93.9	126.0	309.0
Total Liab To Nw (%)	39.9	105.8	205.3	15.8	145.8	255.5	25.0	74.1	133.3	109.3	191.8	312.8
Fixed Assets To Nw (%)	35.0	70.6	123.2	42.6	83.4	129.8	33.0	54.1	83.9	88.1	129.2	193.0
EFFICIENCY												
Coll Period (days)	19.0	27.0	38.0	11.3	18.1	23.7	15.0	18.3	24.1	12.1	19.7	29.2
Sales To Inv (times)	24.4	13.9	7.6	35.4	19.5	14.0	34.9	20.5	15.4	22.2	12.0	8.8
Assets To Sales (%)	29.6	43.8	69.4	17.8	27.9	47.2	20.5	27.9	39.1	24.0	42.4	49.2
Sales To Nwc (times)	16.9	8.9	5.1	30.1	13.6	7.6	18.9	10.5	8.0	20.1	14.0	12.0
Acct Pay To Sales (%)	2.3	4.2	6.9	1.3	2.4	3.6	1.4	2.5	3.6	3.0	4.5	6.1
PROFITABILITY												
Return On Sales (%)	5.9	2.5	0.5	3.3	1.9	0.7	6.9	2.7	0.9	3.4	1.1	0.6
Return On Assets (%)	12.4	5.3	1.2	11.4	6.5	2.2	16.1	8.7	2.5	11.4	3.9	1.2
Return On Nw (%)	27.0	12.0	3.2	22.9	14.4	6.4	43.1	14.6	4.2	27.0	12.0	3.6

Balance Sheet

	SIC 2022 CHEESE,NTRAL,PROCD (31 Est.) $	%	SIC 2023 CONDNS,EVPRTD PRDCT (16 Est.) $	%	SIC 2024 ICE CRM,FRZN DSSRTS (16 Est.) $	%	SIC 2026 FLUID MILK (23 Est.) $	%
Cash	563,525	9.8	849,257	5.8	681,391	11.9	1,612,669	10.8
Accounts Receivable	1,196,053	20.8	3,192,034	21.8	944,786	16.5	3,404,522	22.8
Notes Receivable	51,752	0.9	0	0.0	5,726	0.1	29,864	0.2
Inventory	1,276,557	22.2	2,430,631	16.6	1,110,839	19.4	1,597,736	10.7
Other Current	529,023	9.2	307,490	2.1	280,572	4.9	866,063	5.8
Total Current	3,616,910	62.9	6,779,412	46.3	3,023,314	52.8	7,510,854	50.3
Fixed Assets	1,592,821	27.7	5,212,679	35.6	1,568,917	27.4	5,644,340	37.8
Other Non-current	540,524	9.4	2,650,267	18.1	1,133,742	19.8	1,776,922	11.9
Total Assets	5,750,255	100.0	14,642,358	100.0	5,725,973	100.0	14,932,116	100.0
Accounts Payable	914,291	15.9	1,596,017	10.9	440,900	7.7	2,344,342	15.7
Bank Loans	80,504	1.4	0	0.0	217,587	3.8	0	0.0
Notes Payable	189,758	3.3	4,465,919	30.5	131,697	2.3	179,185	1.2
Other Current	684,280	11.9	15,652,681	106.9	561,146	9.8	1,538,009	10.3
Total Current	1,868,833	32.5	21,714,617	148.3	1,351,330	23.6	4,061,536	27.2
Other Long Term	816,536	14.2	3,470,239	23.7	1,053,579	18.4	2,971,491	19.9
Deferred Credits	17,251	0.3	14,642	0.1	11,452	0.2	0	0.0
Net Worth	3,047,635	53.0	(10,557,140)	(72.1)	3,309,612	57.8	7,899,089	52.9
Total Liab & Net Worth	5,750,255	100.0	14,642,358	100.0	5,725,973	100.0	14,932,116	100.0
Net Sales	16,476,375	100.0	25,643,359	100.0	14,496,134	100.0	38,584,279	100.0
Gross Profit	3,015,177	18.3	7,539,148	29.4	5,001,166	34.5	10,494,924	27.2
Net Profit After Tax	362,480	2.2	(179,504)	(0.7)	289,923	2.0	1,543,371	4.0
Working Capital	1,748,077	—	(14,935,205)	—	1,671,984	—	3,449,318	—

RATIOS

	2022 UQ	MED	LQ	2023 UQ	MED	LQ	2024 UQ	MED	LQ	2026 UQ	MED	LQ
SOLVENCY												
Quick Ratio (times)	1.8	0.9	0.4	1.1	0.8	0.4	5.3	1.3	0.7	2.0	1.2	0.9
Current Ratio (times)	4.1	1.7	1.2	2.6	1.2	1.0	8.9	2.8	1.6	2.4	1.9	1.4
Curr Liab To Nw (%)	22.6	67.0	118.7	36.5	88.5	122.1	12.1	30.7	70.5	30.3	44.3	75.9
Curr Liab To Inv (%)	91.7	199.5	256.9	103.9	207.6	533.2	33.7	74.5	198.6	184.1	251.7	374.7
Total Liab To Nw (%)	46.6	99.0	161.7	82.5	118.1	148.5	25.0	65.6	186.5	39.9	75.3	174.2
Fixed Assets To Nw (%)	15.4	58.0	105.7	75.6	93.8	117.8	27.1	58.5	100.3	45.0	76.4	138.8
EFFICIENCY												
Coll Period (days)	17.9	24.7	33.2	22.6	23.9	29.2	15.5	21.5	31.3	23.0	24.5	28.8
Sales To Inv (times)	33.5	18.2	7.8	31.3	12.4	7.8	19.6	11.6	8.9	44.5	34.2	23.7
Assets To Sales (%)	18.4	34.9	49.7	26.3	57.1	82.5	32.3	39.5	53.0	32.4	38.7	40.9
Sales To Nwc (times)	40.1	14.0	6.1	57.3	6.7	5.2	10.7	6.3	4.1	26.6	10.6	6.3
Acct Pay To Sales (%)	2.2	4.0	6.0	2.3	3.6	5.4	1.5	3.1	4.4	2.4	4.5	5.9
PROFITABILITY												
Return On Sales (%)	3.0	1.1	0.3	5.1	0.7	(13.4)	4.9	1.5	(0.8)	4.3	2.7	2.0
Return On Assets (%)	10.4	3.8	0.5	15.5	3.1	(14.1)	10.2	4.1	(1.5)	12.4	7.6	5.1
Return On Nw (%)	21.9	6.5	1.3	33.2	10.3	(4.3)	12.6	11.4	(0.5)	19.6	12.7	10.7

(NO BREAKDOWN) 2002

SIC 2032 CANNED SPECIALTIES (NO BREAKDOWN) 2002 (13 Establishments)

	$	%
Cash	242,172	7.0
Accounts Receivable	664,243	19.2
Notes Receivable	13,838	0.4
Inventory	913,334	26.4
Other Current	183,360	5.3
Total Current	**2,016,947**	**58.3**
Fixed Assets	996,365	28.8
Other Non-current	446,288	12.9
Total Assets	**3,459,600**	**100.0**
Accounts Payable	470,506	13.6
Bank Loans	96,869	2.8
Notes Payable	190,278	5.5
Other Current	691,919	20.0
Total Current	**1,449,572**	**41.9**
Other Long Term	885,658	25.6
Deferred Credits	0	0.0
Net Worth	1,124,370	32.5
Total Liab & Net Worth	**3,459,600**	**100.0**
Net Sales	8,500,246	100.0
Gross Profit	2,626,576	30.9
Net Profit After Tax	314,509	3.7
Working Capital	567,375	—

RATIOS	UQ	MED	LQ
SOLVENCY			
Quick Ratio (times)	1.8	0.5	0.3
Current Ratio (times)	2.5	1.3	0.8
Curr Liab To Nw (%)	17.4	92.8	129.8
Curr Liab To Inv (%)	102.2	125.2	306.1
Total Liab To Nw (%)	42.4	147.5	186.2
Fixed Assets To Nw (%)	12.6	91.0	118.3
EFFICIENCY			
Coll Period (days)	18.1	24.5	38.9
Sales To Inv (times)	9.6	7.8	5.2
Assets To Sales (%)	30.9	40.7	56.9
Sales To Nwc (times)	13.2	7.1	4.6
Acct Pay To Sales (%)	3.0	5.9	8.1
PROFITABILITY			
Return On Sales (%)	6.2	1.6	0.9
Return On Assets (%)	17.6	5.5	2.3
Return On Nw (%)	30.9	9.3	5.4

SIC 2033 CANNED FRTS,VGTBLS (NO BREAKDOWN) 2002 (39 Establishments)

	$	%
Cash	694,346	4.5
Accounts Receivable	2,268,198	14.7
Notes Receivable	0	0.0
Inventory	4,814,134	31.2
Other Current	432,038	2.8
Total Current	**8,208,716**	**53.2**
Fixed Assets	5,863,368	38.0
Other Non-current	1,357,833	8.8
Total Assets	**15,429,917**	**100.0**
Accounts Payable	1,913,310	12.4
Bank Loans	185,159	1.2
Notes Payable	663,486	4.3
Other Current	2,592,226	16.8
Total Current	**5,354,181**	**34.7**
Other Long Term	4,628,975	30.0
Deferred Credits	15,430	0.1
Net Worth	5,431,331	35.2
Total Liab & Net Worth	**15,429,917**	**100.0**
Net Sales	25,673,739	100.0
Gross Profit	8,472,334	33.0
Net Profit After Tax	1,052,623	4.1
Working Capital	2,854,535	—

RATIOS	UQ	MED	LQ
SOLVENCY			
Quick Ratio (times)	0.8	0.6	0.4
Current Ratio (times)	2.2	1.5	1.2
Curr Liab To Nw (%)	47.7	90.6	142.6
Curr Liab To Inv (%)	76.1	111.2	168.7
Total Liab To Nw (%)	110.7	185.5	234.8
Fixed Assets To Nw (%)	58.1	102.7	147.0
EFFICIENCY			
Coll Period (days)	19.6	28.3	39.8
Sales To Inv (times)	10.7	6.7	3.6
Assets To Sales (%)	43.8	60.1	74.1
Sales To Nwc (times)	18.9	7.8	4.8
Acct Pay To Sales (%)	4.1	6.1	8.5
PROFITABILITY			
Return On Sales (%)	5.7	2.7	0.9
Return On Assets (%)	9.7	5.3	1.9
Return On Nw (%)	30.1	13.6	5.0

SIC 2035 PCKLD,SAUCS,SLD DRS (NO BREAKDOWN) 2002 (14 Establishments)

	$	%
Cash	499,184	9.7
Accounts Receivable	674,155	13.1
Notes Receivable	0	0.0
Inventory	1,476,966	28.7
Other Current	308,774	6.0
Total Current	**2,959,079**	**57.5**
Fixed Assets	1,641,645	31.9
Other Non-current	545,500	10.6
Total Assets	**5,146,224**	**100.0**
Accounts Payable	458,014	8.9
Bank Loans	0	0.0
Notes Payable	30,877	0.6
Other Current	591,816	11.5
Total Current	**1,080,707**	**21.0**
Other Long Term	1,698,254	33.0
Deferred Credits	0	0.0
Net Worth	2,367,263	46.0
Total Liab & Net Worth	**5,146,224**	**100.0**
Net Sales	11,643,041	100.0
Gross Profit	3,551,128	30.5
Net Profit After Tax	384,220	3.3
Working Capital	1,878,372	—

RATIOS	UQ	MED	LQ
SOLVENCY			
Quick Ratio (times)	2.0	1.2	0.8
Current Ratio (times)	4.2	3.0	2.0
Curr Liab To Nw (%)	17.8	46.8	103.8
Curr Liab To Inv (%)	51.5	60.2	81.1
Total Liab To Nw (%)	33.8	140.1	451.6
Fixed Assets To Nw (%)	33.1	70.6	133.1
EFFICIENCY			
Coll Period (days)	19.7	25.4	31.2
Sales To Inv (times)	12.4	6.6	4.7
Assets To Sales (%)	33.1	44.2	61.2
Sales To Nwc (times)	6.4	5.1	4.3
Acct Pay To Sales (%)	2.2	3.6	5.1
PROFITABILITY			
Return On Sales (%)	4.4	3.0	1.4
Return On Assets (%)	8.0	4.9	3.2
Return On Nw (%)	21.5	16.6	8.2

SIC 2037 FRZN FRTS,VGTBLS (NO BREAKDOWN) 2002 (11 Establishments)

	$	%
Cash	467,011	1.9
Accounts Receivable	5,235,436	21.3
Notes Receivable	147,477	0.6
Inventory	7,595,069	30.9
Other Current	1,032,339	4.2
Total Current	**14,477,332**	**58.9**
Fixed Assets	9,389,373	38.2
Other Non-current	712,806	2.9
Total Assets	**24,579,511**	**100.0**
Accounts Payable	2,507,110	10.2
Bank Loans	0	0.0
Notes Payable	1,597,668	6.5
Other Current	5,137,118	20.9
Total Current	**9,241,896**	**37.6**
Other Long Term	4,473,471	18.2
Deferred Credits	147,477	0.6
Net Worth	10,716,667	43.6
Total Liab & Net Worth	**24,579,511**	**100.0**
Net Sales	28,026,808	100.0
Gross Profit	3,755,592	13.4
Net Profit After Tax	980,938	3.5
Working Capital	5,235,436	—

RATIOS	UQ	MED	LQ
SOLVENCY			
Quick Ratio (times)	1.2	0.5	0.3
Current Ratio (times)	4.0	1.8	1.1
Curr Liab To Nw (%)	21.6	45.7	166.3
Curr Liab To Inv (%)	57.0	98.7	134.3
Total Liab To Nw (%)	52.7	104.6	201.7
Fixed Assets To Nw (%)	26.2	72.4	105.3
EFFICIENCY			
Coll Period (days)	21.6	32.1	75.6
Sales To Inv (times)	12.4	3.7	2.5
Assets To Sales (%)	56.5	87.7	97.5
Sales To Nwc (times)	21.1	5.2	2.6
Acct Pay To Sales (%)	1.1	5.2	15.2
PROFITABILITY			
Return On Sales (%)	3.5	3.3	1.4
Return On Assets (%)	4.6	3.2	2.5
Return On Nw (%)	23.0	8.7	4.4

Balance Sheet

	SIC 2038 FRZN SPCLTS, NEC (NO BREAKDOWN) 2002 (18 Establishments) $	%	SIC 2041 FLR, GRN MILL PRDCTS (NO BREAKDOWN) 2002 (18 Establishments) $	%	SIC 2047 DOG AND CAT FOOD (NO BREAKDOWN) 2002 (13 Establishments) $	%	SIC 2048 PREPARED FEEDS, NEC (NO BREAKDOWN) 2002 (94 Establishments) $	%
Cash	627,021	6.7	235,066	3.8	777,421	11.4	276,765	8.7
Accounts Receivable	2,189,893	23.4	1,082,543	17.5	1,193,410	17.5	687,140	21.6
Notes Receivable	37,434	0.4	0	0.0	0	0.0	28,631	0.9
Inventory	1,497,363	16.0	1,453,700	23.5	1,097,937	16.1	655,328	20.6
Other Current	290,114	3.1	272,183	4.4	593,296	8.7	206,779	6.5
Total Current	**4,641,825**	**49.6**	**3,043,492**	**49.2**	**3,662,064**	**53.7**	**1,854,643**	**58.3**
Fixed Assets	2,957,292	31.6	2,591,917	41.9	2,229,972	32.7	1,046,617	32.9
Other Non-current	1,759,402	18.8	550,550	8.9	927,450	13.6	279,946	8.8
Total Assets	**9,358,519**	**100.0**	**6,185,959**	**100.0**	**6,819,486**	**100.0**	**3,181,206**	**100.0**
Accounts Payable	1,300,834	13.9	569,108	9.2	838,797	12.3	407,194	12.8
Bank Loans	74,868	0.8	0	0.0	0	0.0	9,544	0.3
Notes Payable	486,643	5.2	408,273	6.6	115,931	1.7	139,973	4.4
Other Current	1,029,437	11.0	903,151	14.6	1,002,464	14.7	505,812	15.9
Total Current	**2,891,782**	**30.9**	**1,880,532**	**30.4**	**1,957,192**	**28.7**	**1,062,523**	**33.4**
Other Long Term	3,911,861	41.8	1,478,444	23.9	1,213,869	17.8	524,899	16.5
Deferred Credits	28,076	0.3	0	0.0	0	0.0	3,181	0.1
Net Worth	2,526,800	27.0	2,826,983	45.7	3,648,425	53.5	1,590,603	50.0
Total Liab & Net Worth	**9,358,519**	**100.0**	**6,185,959**	**100.0**	**6,819,486**	**100.0**	**3,181,206**	**100.0**
Net Sales	18,792,207	100.0	11,649,640	100.0	17,898,913	100.0	7,398,153	100.0
Gross Profit	6,558,480	34.9	3,308,498	28.4	5,852,945	32.7	1,871,733	25.3
Net Profit After Tax	131,545	0.7	396,088	3.4	680,159	3.8	162,759	2.2
Working Capital	1,750,043	—	1,162,960	—	1,704,872	—	792,120	—

RATIOS

	SIC 2038 UQ	MED	LQ	SIC 2041 UQ	MED	LQ	SIC 2047 UQ	MED	LQ	SIC 2048 UQ	MED	LQ
SOLVENCY												
Quick Ratio (times)	1.6	0.9	0.6	1.0	0.7	0.5	3.9	0.9	0.7	1.6	0.9	0.4
Current Ratio (times)	2.6	1.4	1.1	2.1	2.0	1.5	4.0	2.3	1.2	2.9	1.8	1.2
Curr Liab To Nw (%)	34.9	129.5	195.3	41.6	62.6	102.0	12.7	36.4	103.7	27.6	67.1	135.2
Curr Liab To Inv (%)	120.7	174.9	318.2	89.7	117.4	195.8	89.9	209.1	288.3	102.4	150.6	331.9
Total Liab To Nw (%)	59.7	176.5	409.1	61.2	98.4	172.3	22.5	45.5	141.7	40.9	94.1	199.4
Fixed Assets To Nw (%)	41.8	112.0	164.3	52.9	74.5	158.0	24.0	53.6	85.0	29.1	58.6	115.3
EFFICIENCY												
Coll Period (days)	24.1	35.4	46.7	24.3	26.7	38.3	19.0	21.9	28.5	21.2	29.9	43.8
Sales To Inv (times)	33.4	14.1	8.2	23.4	10.2	7.9	32.1	19.9	13.9	22.1	12.9	7.8
Assets To Sales (%)	27.2	49.8	56.9	39.0	53.1	68.4	27.6	38.1	56.1	31.5	43.0	53.9
Sales To Nwc (times)	21.0	11.8	5.0	11.6	7.2	5.3	13.1	9.7	6.7	14.8	8.7	6.3
Acct Pay To Sales (%)	4.9	5.9	8.4	2.5	4.0	5.7	4.1	5.0	5.5	1.9	4.9	7.1
PROFITABILITY												
Return On Sales (%)	5.3	2.5	1.3	5.0	1.6	0.3	4.8	3.9	1.3	4.4	1.4	0.0
Return On Assets (%)	10.6	6.2	3.5	4.6	3.4	0.7	10.0	7.3	3.0	9.9	3.3	(0.3)
Return On Nw (%)	26.0	19.2	8.8	14.6	7.2	3.7	35.2	14.6	5.7	23.0	6.2	(0.1)

	SIC 2051 BRD,CKE,RLTD PRDCTS (NO BREAKDOWN) 2002 (39 Establishments)		SIC 2052 COOKIES,CRACKERS (NO BREAKDOWN) 2002 (12 Establishments)		SIC 2064 CNDY CNFCTNR PRDCTS (NO BREAKDOWN) 2002 (30 Establishments)		SIC 2082 MALT BEVERAGES (NO BREAKDOWN) 2002 (16 Establishments)	
	$	%	$	%	$	%	$	%
Cash	131,221	8.1	1,236,230	14.6	117,910	8.8	558,464	5.9
Accounts Receivable	322,383	19.9	1,634,194	19.3	222,422	16.6	1,287,306	13.6
Notes Receivable	6,480	0.4	0	0.0	1,340	0.1	0	0.0
Inventory	162,001	10.0	1,557,988	18.4	329,613	24.6	1,050,669	11.1
Other Current	92,341	5.7	355,628	4.2	65,654	4.9	378,618	4.0
Total Current	**714,426**	**44.1**	**4,784,040**	**56.5**	**736,939**	**55.0**	**3,275,057**	**34.6**
Fixed Assets	691,746	42.7	2,946,630	34.8	460,922	34.4	5,414,257	57.2
Other Non-current	213,841	13.2	736,658	8.7	142,028	10.6	776,170	8.2
Total Assets	**1,620,013**	**100.0**	**8,467,328**	**100.0**	**1,339,889**	**100.0**	**9,465,484**	**100.0**
Accounts Payable	208,982	12.9	1,041,481	12.3	101,832	7.6	889,755	9.4
Bank Loans	3,240	0.2	177,814	2.1	0	0.0	0	0.0
Notes Payable	35,640	2.2	84,673	1.0	4,020	0.3	0	0.0
Other Current	374,223	23.1	660,452	7.8	338,991	25.3	1,438,754	15.2
Total Current	**622,085**	**38.4**	**1,964,420**	**23.2**	**444,843**	**33.2**	**2,328,509**	**24.6**
Other Long Term	372,603	23.0	1,464,848	17.3	309,515	23.1	2,943,766	31.1
Deferred Credits	9,720	0.6	0	0.0	0	0.0	28,396	0.3
Net Worth	615,605	38.0	5,038,060	59.5	585,531	43.7	4,164,813	44.0
Total Liab & Net Worth	**1,620,013**	**100.0**	**8,467,328**	**100.0**	**1,339,889**	**100.0**	**9,465,484**	**100.0**
Net Sales	4,778,799	100.0	14,854,961	100.0	3,228,648	100.0	11,322,349	100.0
Gross Profit	1,682,137	35.2	6,120,244	41.2	1,601,409	49.6	4,506,295	39.8
Net Profit After Tax	52,567	1.1	609,053	4.1	238,920	7.4	498,183	4.4
Working Capital	92,341	—	2,819,620	—	292,096	—	946,548	—

RATIOS	UQ	MED	LQ	UQ	MED	LQ	UQ	MED	LQ	UQ	MED	LQ
SOLVENCY												
Quick Ratio (times)	1.5	0.7	0.5	3.1	1.2	1.0	2.0	1.1	0.7	1.3	0.8	0.6
Current Ratio (times)	2.2	1.3	0.8	4.4	2.1	1.6	4.9	2.9	1.8	2.1	1.5	1.0
Curr Liab To Nw (%)	35.2	54.1	134.3	17.0	25.0	88.9	12.0	25.7	85.2	30.0	38.6	87.8
Curr Liab To Inv (%)	222.1	417.1	815.9	63.6	95.8	178.6	49.0	96.5	157.5	150.1	244.6	307.7
Total Liab To Nw (%)	64.9	118.3	232.7	29.4	68.8	119.8	19.4	48.4	185.6	53.3	125.2	225.5
Fixed Assets To Nw (%)	44.7	82.4	185.1	19.2	63.8	83.6	29.2	61.5	107.9	91.9	140.6	202.7
EFFICIENCY												
Coll Period (days)	16.1	23.4	32.7	18.6	26.7	34.7	20.8	27.2	38.0	23.6	29.0	36.5
Sales To Inv (times)	66.4	37.4	21.4	20.8	18.8	11.1	15.1	10.7	7.9	19.2	14.2	10.8
Assets To Sales (%)	26.2	33.9	54.7	50.0	57.0	71.7	31.3	41.5	51.5	57.6	83.6	108.2
Sales To Nwc (times)	27.2	14.1	8.7	14.6	8.5	5.5	10.6	8.2	6.7	13.4	9.4	8.4
Acct Pay To Sales (%)	2.1	3.6	5.5	2.5	5.6	8.6	1.8	3.1	4.5	4.0	6.1	9.5
PROFITABILITY												
Return On Sales (%)	4.6	1.8	(0.4)	3.9	3.0	1.4	10.8	5.2	0.3	10.8	2.0	0.8
Return On Assets (%)	17.1	5.3	(0.6)	9.9	6.5	2.9	16.7	10.3	1.0	14.7	3.2	1.2
Return On Nw (%)	34.5	15.1	4.6	15.1	11.0	3.1	40.1	22.6	8.1	25.8	9.2	1.7

SIC 2084 WINES,BRANDY,SPRTS (NO BREAKDOWN) 2002 (29 Establishments)

	$	%
Cash	638,977	5.1
Accounts Receivable	964,730	7.7
Notes Receivable	0	0.0
Inventory	5,099,289	40.7
Other Current	613,920	4.9
Total Current	**7,316,916**	**58.4**
Fixed Assets	4,071,914	32.5
Other Non-current	1,140,135	9.1
Total Assets	**12,528,965**	**100.0**
Accounts Payable	476,101	3.8
Bank Loans	0	0.0
Notes Payable	563,803	4.5
Other Current	2,681,199	21.4
Total Current	**3,721,103**	**29.7**
Other Long Term	2,580,966	20.6
Deferred Credits	75,174	0.6
Net Worth	6,151,722	49.1
Total Liab & Net Worth	**12,528,965**	**100.0**
Net Sales	8,010,847	100.0
Gross Profit	3,644,935	45.5
Net Profit After Tax	528,716	6.6
Working Capital	3,595,813	—

RATIOS	UQ	MED	LQ
SOLVENCY			
Quick Ratio (times)	1.1	0.4	0.2
Current Ratio (times)	5.1	2.1	1.2
Curr Liab To Nw (%)	23.9	51.2	99.6
Curr Liab To Inv (%)	37.3	78.3	118.2
Total Liab To Nw (%)	52.3	119.8	220.7
Fixed Assets To Nw (%)	41.3	63.3	95.1
EFFICIENCY			
Coll Period (days)	31.6	44.9	59.1
Sales To Inv (times)	2.7	1.4	1.0
Assets To Sales (%)	108.8	156.4	243.3
Sales To Nwc (times)	6.6	2.4	1.2
Acct Pay To Sales (%)	3.8	5.6	7.0
PROFITABILITY			
Return On Sales (%)	17.4	7.0	2.7
Return On Assets (%)	10.6	4.5	1.5
Return On Nw (%)	20.5	11.0	4.1

SIC 2086 BOTL,CND SFT DRNKS (NO BREAKDOWN) 2002 (40 Establishments)

	$	%
Cash	466,186	7.4
Accounts Receivable	1,222,163	19.4
Notes Receivable	6,300	0.1
Inventory	1,096,167	17.4
Other Current	390,587	6.2
Total Current	**3,181,403**	**50.5**
Fixed Assets	2,091,536	33.2
Other Non-current	1,026,869	16.3
Total Assets	**6,299,808**	**100.0**
Accounts Payable	1,152,865	18.3
Bank Loans	0	0.0
Notes Payable	163,795	2.6
Other Current	1,026,869	16.3
Total Current	**2,343,529**	**37.2**
Other Long Term	1,763,946	28.0
Deferred Credits	6,300	0.1
Net Worth	2,186,033	34.7
Total Liab & Net Worth	**6,299,808**	**100.0**
Net Sales	13,606,497	100.0
Gross Profit	4,340,473	31.9
Net Profit After Tax	(231,310)	(1.7)
Working Capital	837,874	—

RATIOS	UQ	MED	LQ
Quick Ratio (times)	1.7	0.7	0.5
Current Ratio (times)	2.7	1.4	1.0
Curr Liab To Nw (%)	22.9	66.1	106.1
Curr Liab To Inv (%)	137.1	210.3	403.3
Total Liab To Nw (%)	63.7	127.9	240.8
Fixed Assets To Nw (%)	33.5	87.1	120.0
Coll Period (days)	21.9	32.7	44.8
Sales To Inv (times)	24.0	18.7	12.4
Assets To Sales (%)	30.4	46.3	114.2
Sales To Nwc (times)	21.7	12.1	4.8
Acct Pay To Sales (%)	3.6	6.1	9.2
Return On Sales (%)	7.1	2.3	0.5
Return On Assets (%)	8.4	3.0	0.5
Return On Nw (%)	22.3	10.3	3.2

SIC 2087 EXTRCTS,SYRPS,NEC (NO BREAKDOWN) 2002 (24 Establishments)

	$	%
Cash	296,894	9.2
Accounts Receivable	755,145	23.4
Notes Receivable	0	0.0
Inventory	810,006	25.1
Other Current	264,623	8.2
Total Current	**2,126,668**	**65.9**
Fixed Assets	748,690	23.2
Other Non-current	351,756	10.9
Total Assets	**3,227,114**	**100.0**
Accounts Payable	2,675,278	82.9
Bank Loans	0	0.0
Notes Payable	74,224	2.3
Other Current	1,871,725	58.0
Total Current	**4,621,227**	**143.2**
Other Long Term	2,714,004	84.1
Deferred Credits	12,908	0.4
Net Worth	(4,121,025)	(127.7)
Total Liab & Net Worth	**3,227,114**	**100.0**
Net Sales	6,327,675	100.0
Gross Profit	2,379,206	37.6
Net Profit After Tax	253,107	4.0
Working Capital	(2,494,559)	—

RATIOS	UQ	MED	LQ
Quick Ratio (times)	2.1	1.0	0.7
Current Ratio (times)	3.4	2.0	1.4
Curr Liab To Nw (%)	30.7	57.3	122.7
Curr Liab To Inv (%)	91.3	113.2	210.6
Total Liab To Nw (%)	56.2	109.2	188.7
Fixed Assets To Nw (%)	13.8	42.0	66.3
Coll Period (days)	27.0	41.3	62.1
Sales To Inv (times)	15.1	10.5	4.6
Assets To Sales (%)	40.8	51.0	65.7
Sales To Nwc (times)	14.9	7.2	3.5
Acct Pay To Sales (%)	3.8	6.3	10.5
Return On Sales (%)	8.3	4.1	1.0
Return On Assets (%)	12.4	6.7	2.1
Return On Nw (%)	35.0	15.5	3.4

SIC 2092 FRSH,FZN PCKGD FISH (NO BREAKDOWN) 2002 (11 Establishments)

	$	%
Cash	479,549	3.8
Accounts Receivable	2,675,379	21.2
Notes Receivable	0	0.0
Inventory	3,748,055	29.7
Other Current	479,549	3.8
Total Current	**7,382,532**	**58.5**
Fixed Assets	4,114,026	32.6
Other Non-current	1,123,155	8.9
Total Assets	**12,619,713**	**100.0**
Accounts Payable	1,299,830	10.3
Bank Loans	0	0.0
Notes Payable	959,098	7.6
Other Current	2,195,831	17.4
Total Current	**4,454,759**	**35.3**
Other Long Term	1,892,957	15.0
Deferred Credits	88,338	0.7
Net Worth	6,183,659	49.0
Total Liab & Net Worth	**12,619,713**	**100.0**
Net Sales	28,616,129	100.0
Gross Profit	5,150,903	18.0
Net Profit After Tax	1,001,565	3.5
Working Capital	2,927,773	—

RATIOS	UQ	MED	LQ
Quick Ratio (times)	1.0	0.6	0.6
Current Ratio (times)	1.9	1.6	1.4
Curr Liab To Nw (%)	45.3	74.6	88.8
Curr Liab To Inv (%)	104.1	136.1	195.3
Total Liab To Nw (%)	67.9	90.7	159.1
Fixed Assets To Nw (%)	37.4	72.3	83.2
Coll Period (days)	24.8	34.2	44.5
Sales To Inv (times)	25.5	13.9	8.1
Assets To Sales (%)	38.4	44.1	58.9
Sales To Nwc (times)	21.6	15.5	10.7
Acct Pay To Sales (%)	1.4	3.9	5.5
Return On Sales (%)	2.7	0.6	(1.0)
Return On Assets (%)	4.6	1.5	(2.7)
Return On Nw (%)	7.7	3.7	(4.4)

SIC 2095 ROASTED COFFEE
(NO BREAKDOWN)
2002 (15 Establishments)

	$	%
Cash	152,857	5.5
Accounts Receivable	508,596	18.3
Notes Receivable	13,896	0.5
Inventory	614,206	22.1
Other Current	344,622	12.4
Total Current	**1,634,177**	**58.8**
Fixed Assets	722,595	26.0
Other Non-current	422,441	15.2
Total Assets	**2,779,213**	**100.0**
Accounts Payable	247,350	8.9
Bank Loans	0	0.0
Notes Payable	25,013	0.9
Other Current	516,933	18.6
Total Current	**789,296**	**28.4**
Other Long Term	547,506	19.7
Deferred Credits	5,558	0.2
Net Worth	1,436,853	51.7
Total Liab & Net Worth	**2,779,213**	**100.0**
Net Sales	6,273,619	100.0
Gross Profit	2,716,477	43.3
Net Profit After Tax	338,775	5.4
Working Capital	844,881	—

RATIOS	UQ	MED	LQ
SOLVENCY			
Quick Ratio (times)	1.7	1.1	0.7
Current Ratio (times)	3.8	2.2	1.5
Curr Liab To Nw (%)	26.2	52.6	88.2
Curr Liab To Inv (%)	54.8	104.5	165.5
Total Liab To Nw (%)	34.4	102.1	205.3
Fixed Assets To Nw (%)	37.1	54.0	79.3
EFFICIENCY			
Coll Period (days)	23.2	25.8	40.0
Sales To Inv (times)	15.2	11.8	7.6
Assets To Sales (%)	37.2	44.3	62.6
Sales To Nwc (times)	12.5	10.1	6.7
Acct Pay To Sales (%)	2.3	3.5	6.0
PROFITABILITY			
Return On Sales (%)	8.6	3.3	2.1
Return On Assets (%)	12.1	7.5	4.5
Return On Nw (%)	49.0	13.6	8.8

SIC 2096 POTATO CHIPS,SNACKS
(NO BREAKDOWN)
2002 (17 Establishments)

	$	%
Cash	290,975	6.0
Accounts Receivable	775,932	16.0
Notes Receivable	9,699	0.2
Inventory	877,773	18.1
Other Current	305,523	6.3
Total Current	**2,259,902**	**46.6**
Fixed Assets	1,993,176	41.1
Other Non-current	596,498	12.3
Total Assets	**4,849,576**	**100.0**
Accounts Payable	834,127	17.2
Bank Loans	0	0.0
Notes Payable	242,479	5.0
Other Current	640,144	13.2
Total Current	**1,716,750**	**35.4**
Other Long Term	1,091,154	22.5
Deferred Credits	4,850	0.1
Net Worth	2,036,822	42.0
Total Liab & Net Worth	**4,849,576**	**100.0**
Net Sales	12,466,776	100.0
Gross Profit	4,026,769	32.3
Net Profit After Tax	336,603	2.7
Working Capital	543,152	—

RATIOS	UQ	MED	LQ
SOLVENCY			
Quick Ratio (times)	1.8	0.7	0.6
Current Ratio (times)	2.9	1.3	0.9
Curr Liab To Nw (%)	22.8	33.7	151.1
Curr Liab To Inv (%)	114.0	190.7	353.4
Total Liab To Nw (%)	27.6	152.5	264.0
Fixed Assets To Nw (%)	53.1	79.5	185.8
EFFICIENCY			
Coll Period (days)	20.1	30.3	31.4
Sales To Inv (times)	31.9	20.9	17.6
Assets To Sales (%)	33.4	38.9	51.0
Sales To Nwc (times)	30.3	14.3	6.6
Acct Pay To Sales (%)	2.6	4.4	6.5
PROFITABILITY			
Return On Sales (%)	4.6	1.5	(0.7)
Return On Assets (%)	11.9	4.0	(1.4)
Return On Nw (%)	36.0	23.6	(1.0)

SIC 2097 MANUFACTURED ICE
(NO BREAKDOWN)
2002 (10 Establishments)

	$	%
Cash	305,759	16.3
Accounts Receivable	116,301	6.2
Notes Receivable	1,876	0.1
Inventory	99,419	5.3
Other Current	116,301	6.2
Total Current	**639,656**	**34.1**
Fixed Assets	971,677	51.8
Other Non-current	264,492	14.1
Total Assets	**1,875,825**	**100.0**
Accounts Payable	43,144	2.3
Bank Loans	0	0.0
Notes Payable	73,157	3.9
Other Current	292,629	15.6
Total Current	**408,930**	**21.8**
Other Long Term	504,597	26.9
Deferred Credits	16,882	0.9
Net Worth	945,416	50.4
Total Liab & Net Worth	**1,875,825**	**100.0**
Net Sales	2,368,466	100.0
Gross Profit	1,468,449	62.0
Net Profit After Tax	78,159	3.3
Working Capital	230,726	—

RATIOS	UQ	MED	LQ
SOLVENCY			
Quick Ratio (times)	5.1	0.5	0.4
Current Ratio (times)	5.8	1.2	0.6
Curr Liab To Nw (%)	16.0	44.8	122.7
Curr Liab To Inv (%)	259.1	446.6	628.0
Total Liab To Nw (%)	21.0	195.7	322.3
Fixed Assets To Nw (%)	49.5	180.9	242.3
EFFICIENCY			
Coll Period (days)	15.0	21.6	63.5
Sales To Inv (times)	37.7	19.7	8.7
Assets To Sales (%)	47.8	79.2	119.4
Sales To Nwc (times)	5.4	4.6	1.5
Acct Pay To Sales (%)	0.8	1.6	7.7
PROFITABILITY			
Return On Sales (%)	10.9	7.8	3.6
Return On Assets (%)	14.3	9.5	6.9
Return On Nw (%)	29.1	19.7	14.4

SIC 2099 FOOD PRPRTNS,NEC
(NO BREAKDOWN)
2002 (83 Establishments)

	$	%
Cash	215,953	12.3
Accounts Receivable	393,281	22.4
Notes Receivable	10,534	0.6
Inventory	317,785	18.1
Other Current	98,321	5.6
Total Current	**1,035,874**	**59.0**
Fixed Assets	607,478	34.6
Other Non-current	112,366	6.4
Total Assets	**1,755,718**	**100.0**
Accounts Payable	351,144	20.0
Bank Loans	12,290	0.7
Notes Payable	40,382	2.3
Other Current	730,378	41.6
Total Current	**1,134,194**	**64.6**
Other Long Term	409,082	23.3
Deferred Credits	5,267	0.3
Net Worth	207,175	11.8
Total Liab & Net Worth	**1,755,718**	**100.0**
Net Sales	5,240,949	100.0
Gross Profit	1,750,477	33.4
Net Profit After Tax	83,855	1.6
Working Capital	(98,320)	—

RATIOS	UQ	MED	LQ
SOLVENCY			
Quick Ratio (times)	2.0	0.9	0.5
Current Ratio (times)	3.3	1.8	1.3
Curr Liab To Nw (%)	20.6	50.7	113.7
Curr Liab To Inv (%)	79.0	182.0	418.6
Total Liab To Nw (%)	43.6	86.9	162.9
Fixed Assets To Nw (%)	27.0	52.8	120.7
EFFICIENCY			
Coll Period (days)	23.2	31.0	39.5
Sales To Inv (times)	26.7	15.2	7.7
Assets To Sales (%)	26.2	33.5	68.3
Sales To Nwc (times)	17.1	8.6	3.7
Acct Pay To Sales (%)	3.7	5.6	8.7
PROFITABILITY			
Return On Sales (%)	6.9	2.5	(0.1)
Return On Assets (%)	15.3	6.4	(0.3)
Return On Nw (%)	30.3	13.9	2.2

	SIC 22 TEXTILE MILL PDTS (NO BREAKDOWN) 2002 (360 Establishments) $	%	SIC 2211 FABRIC MILLS, COTTON (NO BREAKDOWN) 2002 (48 Establishments) $	%	SIC 2221 FABRIC MILLS, MNMADE (NO BREAKDOWN) 2002 (29 Establishments) $	%	SIC 2231 FABRIC MILLS, WOOL (NO BREAKDOWN) 2002 (10 Establishments) $	%
Cash	298,168	12.0	238,278	17.0	704,703	10.2	763,192	4.0
Accounts Receivable	573,973	23.1	329,385	23.5	1,506,130	21.8	3,548,842	18.6
Notes Receivable	2,485	0.1	0	0.0	6,909	0.1	0	0.0
Inventory	618,699	24.9	308,360	22.0	1,851,573	26.8	4,502,832	23.6
Other Current	203,748	8.2	107,927	7.7	504,346	7.3	2,613,932	13.7
Total Current	**1,697,073**	**68.3**	**983,950**	**70.2**	**4,573,661**	**66.2**	**11,428,798**	**59.9**
Fixed Assets	613,729	24.7	315,369	22.5	1,789,393	25.9	5,571,300	29.2
Other Non-current	173,931	7.0	102,319	7.3	545,800	7.9	2,079,698	10.9
Total Assets	**2,484,733**	**100.0**	**1,401,638**	**100.0**	**6,908,854**	**100.0**	**19,079,796**	**100.0**
Accounts Payable	367,740	14.8	217,254	15.5	1,022,510	14.8	2,728,411	14.3
Bank Loans	2,485	0.1	0	0.0	0	0.0	0	0.0
Notes Payable	84,481	3.4	23,828	1.7	352,352	5.1	171,718	0.9
Other Current	521,794	21.0	236,877	16.9	1,450,859	21.0	5,075,226	26.6
Total Current	**976,500**	**39.3**	**477,959**	**34.1**	**2,825,721**	**40.9**	**7,975,355**	**41.8**
Other Long Term	452,222	18.2	183,614	13.1	1,678,852	24.3	5,475,901	28.7
Deferred Credits	7,454	0.3	1,402	0.1	13,818	0.2	0	0.0
Net Worth	1,048,557	42.2	738,663	52.7	2,390,463	34.6	5,628,540	29.5
Total Liab & Net Worth	**2,484,733**	**100.0**	**1,401,638**	**100.0**	**6,908,854**	**100.0**	**19,079,796**	**100.0**
Net Sales	5,297,938	100.0	2,825,883	100.0	17,715,010	100.0	35,073,154	100.0
Gross Profit	1,441,039	27.2	794,073	28.1	4,783,053	27.0	4,243,852	12.1
Net Profit After Tax	105,959	2.0	42,388	1.5	283,440	1.6	175,366	0.5
Working Capital	720,573	—	505,991	—	1,747,940	—	3,453,443	—

RATIOS	UQ	MED	LQ	UQ	MED	LQ	UQ	MED	LQ	UQ	MED	LQ
SOLVENCY												
Quick Ratio (times)	2.1	1.2	0.6	2.2	1.4	0.6	1.6	0.9	0.5	1.0	0.5	0.4
Current Ratio (times)	3.7	2.3	1.4	3.4	2.3	1.5	3.4	2.1	1.1	3.0	1.4	0.9
Curr Liab To Nw (%)	20.3	51.4	130.5	18.8	47.1	115.2	20.4	46.6	111.2	43.1	123.7	464.3
Curr Liab To Inv (%)	63.3	108.8	213.8	75.4	109.1	199.0	51.4	98.6	193.8	84.2	195.3	459.1
Total Liab To Nw (%)	31.7	78.5	204.6	27.5	70.6	160.0	35.0	111.5	231.7	58.9	159.1	762.6
Fixed Assets To Nw (%)	15.6	42.4	97.1	13.2	37.6	104.4	37.0	76.8	98.1	28.5	75.0	172.3
EFFICIENCY												
Coll Period (days)	26.7	38.3	54.0	26.7	42.3	56.2	24.8	42.0	52.6	31.8	43.1	50.0
Sales To Inv (times)	16.4	8.8	5.7	16.0	8.2	4.6	12.3	7.5	5.7	19.8	9.5	6.8
Assets To Sales (%)	32.1	46.9	66.0	27.9	49.6	75.3	31.9	39.0	70.4	25.1	54.4	92.0
Sales To Nwc (times)	10.9	5.7	3.6	14.1	5.7	3.5	7.2	5.8	4.0	34.9	7.2	2.4
Acct Pay To Sales (%)	2.9	5.4	8.5	4.4	6.0	8.0	4.2	6.5	12.4	3.6	5.3	21.8
PROFITABILITY												
Return On Sales (%)	4.0	1.4	0.0	3.8	1.1	0.0	4.4	0.8	(0.9)	4.1	(0.4)	(10.1)
Return On Assets (%)	8.7	3.3	0.0	11.8	3.6	0.1	8.6	3.1	(1.1)	7.6	0.1	(11.0)
Return On Nw (%)	20.5	7.2	0.2	21.0	9.3	0.2	22.5	9.3	(1.4)	59.9	20.4	(2.9)

SIC 2241 NARROW FABRIC MILLS (NO BREAKDOWN) 2002 (26 Establishments)

	$	%
Cash	109,348	4.1
Accounts Receivable	594,746	22.3
Notes Receivable	2,667	0.1
Inventory	888,118	33.3
Other Current	154,687	5.8
Total Current	**1,749,566**	**65.6**
Fixed Assets	704,094	26.4
Other Non-current	213,361	8.0
Total Assets	**2,667,021**	**100.0**
Accounts Payable	333,378	12.5
Bank Loans	0	0.0
Notes Payable	82,678	3.1
Other Current	381,383	14.3
Total Current	**797,439**	**29.9**
Other Long Term	304,041	11.4
Deferred Credits	2,667	0.1
Net Worth	1,562,874	58.6
Total Liab & Net Worth	**2,667,021**	**100.0**
Net Sales	4,957,288	100.0
Gross Profit	1,269,066	25.6
Net Profit After Tax	74,359	1.5
Working Capital	952,127	—

RATIOS	UQ	MED	LQ
SOLVENCY			
Quick Ratio (times)	1.7	0.9	0.5
Current Ratio (times)	4.3	1.9	1.4
Curr Liab To Nw (%)	16.4	54.5	120.3
Curr Liab To Inv (%)	42.8	90.3	117.8
Total Liab To Nw (%)	16.5	65.3	176.0
Fixed Assets To Nw (%)	27.9	48.5	72.1
EFFICIENCY			
Coll Period (days)	34.3	38.0	44.9
Sales To Inv (times)	9.8	7.0	5.4
Assets To Sales (%)	35.0	53.8	57.8
Sales To Nwc (times)	10.0	6.4	3.9
Acct Pay To Sales (%)	2.1	3.5	8.5
PROFITABILITY			
Return On Sales (%)	4.0	1.5	0.1
Return On Assets (%)	7.1	2.5	0.1
Return On Nw (%)	12.1	7.0	0.1

SIC 2252 HOSIERY, NEC (NO BREAKDOWN) 2002 (35 Establishments)

	$	%
Cash	298,237	12.2
Accounts Receivable	576,918	23.6
Notes Receivable	0	0.0
Inventory	601,364	24.6
Other Current	273,792	11.2
Total Current	**1,750,311**	**71.6**
Fixed Assets	616,031	25.2
Other Non-current	78,226	3.2
Total Assets	**2,444,568**	**100.0**
Accounts Payable	330,017	13.5
Bank Loans	0	0.0
Notes Payable	78,226	3.2
Other Current	268,902	11.0
Total Current	**677,145**	**27.7**
Other Long Term	308,015	12.6
Deferred Credits	2,445	0.1
Net Worth	1,456,963	59.6
Total Liab & Net Worth	**2,444,568**	**100.0**
Net Sales	5,593,977	100.0
Gross Profit	1,202,705	21.5
Net Profit After Tax	128,661	2.3
Working Capital	1,073,166	—

RATIOS	UQ	MED	LQ
SOLVENCY			
Quick Ratio (times)	3.7	1.4	0.7
Current Ratio (times)	5.3	2.8	1.8
Curr Liab To Nw (%)	16.1	44.3	136.5
Curr Liab To Inv (%)	56.8	96.7	206.7
Total Liab To Nw (%)	23.5	56.2	191.2
Fixed Assets To Nw (%)	23.1	35.2	64.6
EFFICIENCY			
Coll Period (days)	24.8	33.6	45.3
Sales To Inv (times)	22.2	10.7	6.0
Assets To Sales (%)	32.4	43.7	53.8
Sales To Nwc (times)	8.5	4.9	3.7
Acct Pay To Sales (%)	1.8	3.7	5.8
PROFITABILITY			
Return On Sales (%)	3.6	2.0	0.3
Return On Assets (%)	7.7	4.5	0.5
Return On Nw (%)	16.1	7.1	1.0

SIC 2253 KNIT OUTERWR MILLS (NO BREAKDOWN) 2002 (40 Establishments)

	$	%
Cash	428,683	13.2
Accounts Receivable	636,530	19.6
Notes Receivable	6,495	0.2
Inventory	954,795	29.4
Other Current	263,056	8.1
Total Current	**2,289,559**	**70.5**
Fixed Assets	694,987	21.4
Other Non-current	263,056	8.1
Total Assets	**3,247,602**	**100.0**
Accounts Payable	532,607	16.4
Bank Loans	0	0.0
Notes Payable	97,428	3.0
Other Current	2,296,054	70.7
Total Current	**2,926,089**	**90.1**
Other Long Term	620,292	19.1
Deferred Credits	3,248	0.1
Net Worth	(302,027)	(9.3)
Total Liab & Net Worth	**3,247,602**	**100.0**
Net Sales	6,794,146	100.0
Gross Profit	2,017,861	29.7
Net Profit After Tax	47,559	0.7
Working Capital	(636,530)	—

RATIOS	UQ	MED	LQ
SOLVENCY			
Quick Ratio (times)	2.6	1.2	0.5
Current Ratio (times)	5.8	2.2	1.3
Curr Liab To Nw (%)	13.4	51.0	108.2
Curr Liab To Inv (%)	57.5	106.7	215.2
Total Liab To Nw (%)	27.3	54.4	140.3
Fixed Assets To Nw (%)	9.0	17.7	57.7
EFFICIENCY			
Coll Period (days)	21.6	34.0	48.8
Sales To Inv (times)	15.1	6.3	4.8
Assets To Sales (%)	34.2	47.8	61.1
Sales To Nwc (times)	7.0	5.1	3.4
Acct Pay To Sales (%)	2.3	5.3	8.7
PROFITABILITY			
Return On Sales (%)	5.0	1.3	(0.4)
Return On Assets (%)	9.2	2.7	(0.9)
Return On Nw (%)	11.3	6.5	(0.5)

SIC 2258 LACE WRP KNIT MILLS (NO BREAKDOWN) 2002 (12 Establishments)

	$	%
Cash	1,487,180	13.5
Accounts Receivable	2,511,682	22.8
Notes Receivable	33,048	0.3
Inventory	2,621,843	23.8
Other Current	1,685,472	15.3
Total Current	**8,339,225**	**75.7**
Fixed Assets	2,269,327	20.6
Other Non-current	407,597	3.7
Total Assets	**11,016,149**	**100.0**
Accounts Payable	1,068,566	9.7
Bank Loans	0	0.0
Notes Payable	55,081	0.5
Other Current	1,784,616	16.2
Total Current	**2,908,263**	**26.4**
Other Long Term	1,905,794	17.3
Deferred Credits	22,032	0.2
Net Worth	6,180,060	56.1
Total Liab & Net Worth	**11,016,149**	**100.0**
Net Sales	12,294,809	100.0
Gross Profit	2,963,049	24.1
Net Profit After Tax	270,486	2.2
Working Capital	5,430,962	—

RATIOS	UQ	MED	LQ
SOLVENCY			
Quick Ratio (times)	1.9	1.6	1.2
Current Ratio (times)	7.8	3.1	2.0
Curr Liab To Nw (%)	14.7	44.5	154.2
Curr Liab To Inv (%)	77.0	96.6	126.3
Total Liab To Nw (%)	22.4	70.8	261.6
Fixed Assets To Nw (%)	8.9	34.5	124.0
EFFICIENCY			
Coll Period (days)	48.0	55.1	72.1
Sales To Inv (times)	7.5	5.5	4.3
Assets To Sales (%)	65.7	89.6	133.1
Sales To Nwc (times)	3.8	1.5	1.1
Acct Pay To Sales (%)	4.9	7.5	8.6
PROFITABILITY			
Return On Sales (%)	7.9	3.1	0.7
Return On Assets (%)	10.2	4.4	0.4
Return On Nw (%)	11.5	7.7	0.7

	SIC 2261 FNSHNG PLNTS,COTTON (NO BREAKDOWN) 2002 (30 Establishments) $	%	SIC 2269 FNSHNG PLNTS,NEC (NO BREAKDOWN) 2002 (12 Establishments) $	%	SIC 2273 CARPETS AND RUGS (NO BREAKDOWN) 2002 (20 Establishments) $	%	SIC 2281 YARN SPINNING MILLS (NO BREAKDOWN) 2002 (15 Establishments) $	%
Cash	174,617	18.9	280,958	13.1	269,329	7.7	273,097	3.0
Accounts Receivable	272,550	29.5	656,282	30.6	828,973	23.7	1,474,725	16.2
Notes Receivable	0	0.0	0	0.0	0	0.0	0	0.0
Inventory	193,095	20.9	287,392	13.4	1,056,329	30.2	2,239,398	24.6
Other Current	64,673	7.0	98,657	4.6	199,373	5.7	946,738	10.4
Total Current	**704,935**	**76.3**	**1,323,289**	**61.7**	**2,354,004**	**67.3**	**4,933,958**	**54.2**
Fixed Assets	181,084	19.6	632,691	29.5	940,902	26.9	3,723,226	40.9
Other Non-current	37,880	4.1	188,734	8.8	202,871	5.8	446,059	4.9
Total Assets	**923,899**	**100.0**	**2,144,714**	**100.0**	**3,497,777**	**100.0**	**9,103,243**	**100.0**
Accounts Payable	144,128	15.6	223,050	10.4	549,151	15.7	864,808	9.5
Bank Loans	0	0.0	0	0.0	0	0.0	36,413	0.4
Notes Payable	60,977	6.6	92,223	4.3	227,356	6.5	509,782	5.6
Other Current	92,390	10.0	379,614	17.7	654,084	18.7	1,156,112	12.7
Total Current	**297,495**	**32.2**	**694,887**	**32.4**	**1,430,591**	**40.9**	**2,567,115**	**28.2**
Other Long Term	135,814	14.7	519,021	24.2	591,124	16.9	3,340,890	36.7
Deferred Credits	0	0.0	0	0.0	45,471	1.3	36,413	0.4
Net Worth	490,590	53.1	930,806	43.4	1,430,591	40.9	3,158,825	34.7
Total Liab & Net Worth	**923,899**	**100.0**	**2,144,714**	**100.0**	**3,497,777**	**100.0**	**9,103,243**	**100.0**
Net Sales	2,970,736	100.0	5,308,698	100.0	7,123,782	100.0	17,990,599	100.0
Gross Profit	1,111,055	37.4	1,587,301	29.9	1,659,841	23.3	2,878,496	16.0
Net Profit After Tax	145,566	4.9	191,113	3.6	85,485	1.2	(143,925)	(0.8)
Working Capital	407,440	—	628,402	—	923,413	—	2,366,843	—

RATIOS	UQ	MED	LQ	UQ	MED	LQ	UQ	MED	LQ	UQ	MED	LQ
SOLVENCY												
Quick Ratio (times)	3.1	1.7	0.8	2.6	1.5	0.8	1.1	0.8	0.4	1.4	0.9	0.3
Current Ratio (times)	5.7	2.8	1.7	3.5	2.5	1.2	2.6	2.0	1.1	3.0	2.4	1.3
Curr Liab To Nw (%)	14.6	47.8	110.9	24.2	29.9	155.2	40.9	75.3	110.8	32.4	47.6	180.8
Curr Liab To Inv (%)	75.3	122.1	234.5	110.0	134.4	385.2	94.2	128.3	245.8	68.4	99.9	168.5
Total Liab To Nw (%)	15.2	69.3	142.4	42.4	89.5	220.0	74.5	108.5	259.6	58.5	103.0	291.6
Fixed Assets To Nw (%)	11.3	23.5	53.5	33.2	59.3	72.5	17.3	81.1	125.6	44.7	94.2	116.5
EFFICIENCY												
Coll Period (days)	24.1	30.7	52.9	34.0	54.9	72.3	22.9	31.8	50.2	27.0	34.0	56.9
Sales To Inv (times)	31.2	14.4	9.5	30.0	11.3	10.1	12.8	7.1	6.0	12.7	9.5	7.1
Assets To Sales (%)	20.8	31.1	49.7	38.6	40.4	57.0	34.1	49.1	80.8	46.1	50.6	78.2
Sales To Nwc (times)	7.7	5.3	4.6	7.1	4.6	3.4	11.2	7.4	5.9	9.2	5.3	4.4
Acct Pay To Sales (%)	2.6	4.9	6.6	1.5	3.5	7.9	3.9	5.7	8.6	2.8	4.4	7.4
PROFITABILITY												
Return On Sales (%)	6.2	2.1	0.5	3.7	0.8	0.0	3.7	1.7	0.2	3.0	1.4	0.1
Return On Assets (%)	17.0	4.9	1.8	6.2	1.9	(0.1)	9.2	3.7	0.1	7.1	2.5	0.2
Return On Nw (%)	41.2	7.3	3.1	11.9	4.5	(1.4)	17.9	10.7	(3.3)	11.8	4.3	4.1

Balance Sheet

	SIC 2295 CTD FBRCS, NOT RBRZD (NO BREAKDOWN) 2002 (15 Establishments) $	%	SIC 2298 CORDAGE AND TWINE (NO BREAKDOWN) 2002 (10 Establishments) $	%	SIC 2299 TEXTILE GOODS, NEC (NO BREAKDOWN) 2002 (15 Establishments) $	%	SIC 23 APPAREL, RELATED PDTS (NO BREAKDOWN) 2002 (714 Establishments) $	%
Cash	370,973	8.9	152,454	14.6	254,407	18.6	177,888	11.6
Accounts Receivable	1,025,387	24.6	164,985	15.8	428,115	31.3	364,977	23.8
Notes Receivable	4,168	0.1	11,486	1.1	0	0.0	6,134	0.4
Inventory	1,196,285	28.7	325,793	31.2	257,142	18.8	510,661	33.3
Other Current	158,394	3.8	29,238	2.8	93,008	6.8	147,217	9.6
Total Current	**2,755,207**	**66.1**	**683,956**	**65.5**	**1,032,672**	**75.5**	**1,206,877**	**78.7**
Fixed Assets	825,312	19.8	274,627	26.3	258,510	18.9	230,027	15.0
Other Non-current	587,721	14.1	85,625	8.2	76,596	5.6	96,612	6.3
Total Assets	**4,168,240**	**100.0**	**1,044,208**	**100.0**	**1,367,778**	**100.0**	**1,533,516**	**100.0**
Accounts Payable	775,293	18.6	79,360	7.6	310,486	22.7	253,030	16.5
Bank Loans	16,673	0.4	0	0.0	6,839	0.5	10,735	0.7
Notes Payable	95,870	2.3	68,918	6.6	0	0.0	47,539	3.1
Other Current	529,366	12.7	77,271	7.4	175,075	12.8	338,907	22.1
Total Current	**1,417,202**	**34.0**	**225,549**	**21.6**	**492,400**	**36.0**	**650,211**	**42.4**
Other Long Term	496,020	11.9	163,940	15.7	203,799	14.9	182,488	11.9
Deferred Credits	16,673	0.4	48,034	4.6	1,368	0.1	3,067	0.2
Net Worth	2,238,345	53.7	606,685	58.1	670,211	49.0	697,750	45.5
Total Liab & Net Worth	**4,168,240**	**100.0**	**1,044,208**	**100.0**	**1,367,778**	**100.0**	**1,533,516**	**100.0**
Net Sales	7,312,702	100.0	2,031,533	100.0	3,144,317	100.0	4,307,629	100.0
Gross Profit	2,647,198	36.2	686,658	33.8	748,347	23.8	1,486,132	34.5
Net Profit After Tax	760,521	10.4	77,198	3.8	44,020	1.4	133,536	3.1
Working Capital	1,338,005	—	458,407	—	540,272	—	556,666	—

RATIOS

	SIC 2295 UQ	MED	LQ	SIC 2298 UQ	MED	LQ	SIC 2299 UQ	MED	LQ	SIC 23 UQ	MED	LQ
SOLVENCY												
Quick Ratio (times)	2.0	1.2	0.6	5.3	1.3	0.4	1.7	1.3	1.1	2.0	1.0	0.5
Current Ratio (times)	3.6	1.9	1.5	9.2	2.8	1.8	3.3	2.0	1.5	4.2	2.1	1.4
Curr Liab To Nw (%)	27.9	78.3	113.9	10.0	24.6	54.4	41.5	65.6	145.3	23.5	68.5	171.1
Curr Liab To Inv (%)	58.8	86.7	238.7	29.0	62.8	90.7	110.2	208.3	547.4	59.6	101.4	200.7
Total Liab To Nw (%)	39.5	100.4	180.8	15.3	50.1	58.2	51.8	122.9	216.8	34.5	87.3	214.2
Fixed Assets To Nw (%)	6.7	31.7	110.6	10.7	25.1	65.1	12.6	26.3	77.9	7.4	19.9	45.9
EFFICIENCY												
Coll Period (days)	25.9	40.5	59.9	21.6	26.7	39.1	37.2	49.3	62.8	16.8	33.2	51.8
Sales To Inv (times)	11.5	5.7	4.4	9.2	7.8	6.4	38.7	17.2	7.9	17.2	8.3	4.9
Assets To Sales (%)	36.8	57.0	73.2	34.8	51.4	68.4	27.6	43.5	98.5	25.4	35.6	55.1
Sales To Nwc (times)	10.1	5.2	3.3	8.9	5.9	3.3	15.7	9.1	3.8	13.0	6.7	4.0
Acct Pay To Sales (%)	3.6	7.6	12.9	2.6	3.8	6.4	6.1	6.6	29.4	2.6	5.3	8.7
PROFITABILITY												
Return On Sales (%)	15.4	9.1	0.5	3.7	0.9	(0.4)	1.8	1.3	0.7	5.0	1.6	0.2
Return On Assets (%)	19.5	11.9	1.5	4.7	2.4	(0.5)	4.2	2.7	0.9	12.9	3.9	0.6
Return On Nw (%)	39.9	17.7	3.2	21.2	2.3	(2.8)	15.7	6.7	3.2	29.2	9.1	1.5

SIC 2311 MENS,BOYS SUITS CTS (NO BREAKDOWN) 2002 (28 Establishments)

	$	%
Cash	254,960	9.2
Accounts Receivable	626,314	22.6
Notes Receivable	0	0.0
Inventory	1,075,265	38.8
Other Current	163,506	5.9
Total Current	**2,120,045**	**76.5**
Fixed Assets	435,094	15.7
Other Non-current	216,162	7.8
Total Assets	**2,771,301**	**100.0**
Accounts Payable	426,780	15.4
Bank Loans	0	0.0
Notes Payable	116,395	4.2
Other Current	498,834	18.0
Total Current	**1,042,009**	**37.6**
Other Long Term	421,238	15.2
Deferred Credits	11,085	0.4
Net Worth	1,296,969	46.8
Total Liab & Net Worth	**2,771,301**	**100.0**
Net Sales	5,678,895	100.0
Gross Profit	1,732,063	30.5
Net Profit After Tax	170,367	3.0
Working Capital	1,078,036	—

RATIOS	UQ	MED	LQ
SOLVENCY			
Quick Ratio (times)	1.5	1.0	0.6
Current Ratio (times)	3.3	2.0	1.7
Curr Liab To Nw (%)	30.0	87.3	153.4
Curr Liab To Inv (%)	78.5	90.7	130.4
Total Liab To Nw (%)	44.9	106.6	188.2
Fixed Assets To Nw (%)	6.9	18.6	29.9
EFFICIENCY			
Coll Period (days)	25.1	41.1	55.3
Sales To Inv (times)	10.8	6.5	4.1
Assets To Sales (%)	33.9	48.8	71.7
Sales To Nwc (times)	8.1	5.6	4.6
Acct Pay To Sales (%)	3.0	6.4	9.7
PROFITABILITY			
Return On Sales (%)	2.4	1.4	0.5
Return On Assets (%)	6.8	3.0	0.9
Return On Nw (%)	10.6	5.9	2.0

SIC 2321 MENS,BOYS SHIRTS (NO BREAKDOWN) 2002 (14 Establishments)

	$	%
Cash	296,341	9.9
Accounts Receivable	634,590	21.2
Notes Receivable	32,927	1.1
Inventory	1,296,119	43.3
Other Current	164,634	5.5
Total Current	**2,424,611**	**81.0**
Fixed Assets	401,108	13.4
Other Non-current	167,628	5.6
Total Assets	**2,993,347**	**100.0**
Accounts Payable	416,075	13.9
Bank Loans	14,967	0.5
Notes Payable	125,721	4.2
Other Current	667,516	22.3
Total Current	**1,224,279**	**40.9**
Other Long Term	350,222	11.7
Deferred Credits	0	0.0
Net Worth	1,418,846	47.4
Total Liab & Net Worth	**2,993,347**	**100.0**
Net Sales	6,133,908	100.0
Gross Profit	1,729,762	28.2
Net Profit After Tax	177,883	2.9
Working Capital	1,200,332	—

RATIOS	UQ	MED	LQ
SOLVENCY			
Quick Ratio (times)	1.1	0.8	0.6
Current Ratio (times)	3.2	2.2	1.6
Curr Liab To Nw (%)	44.6	85.3	166.4
Curr Liab To Inv (%)	56.4	78.5	117.3
Total Liab To Nw (%)	62.7	115.6	166.8
Fixed Assets To Nw (%)	9.1	16.8	50.8
EFFICIENCY			
Coll Period (days)	20.4	46.2	71.5
Sales To Inv (times)	8.9	5.0	3.5
Assets To Sales (%)	30.1	48.8	58.3
Sales To Nwc (times)	9.8	3.7	2.8
Acct Pay To Sales (%)	2.4	3.8	5.1
PROFITABILITY			
Return On Sales (%)	5.0	1.1	0.5
Return On Assets (%)	13.2	3.6	1.0
Return On Nw (%)	23.6	7.5	2.6

SIC 2325 MNS,BYS TRSRS,SLCKS (NO BREAKDOWN) 2002 (16 Establishments)

	$	%
Cash	892,659	5.7
Accounts Receivable	4,635,564	29.6
Notes Receivable	0	0.0
Inventory	5,684,830	36.3
Other Current	1,237,196	7.9
Total Current	**12,450,249**	**79.5**
Fixed Assets	1,707,015	10.9
Other Non-current	1,503,426	9.6
Total Assets	**15,660,690**	**100.0**
Accounts Payable	2,114,193	13.5
Bank Loans	469,821	3.0
Notes Payable	532,463	3.4
Other Current	2,834,585	18.1
Total Current	**5,951,062**	**38.0**
Other Long Term	3,053,835	19.5
Deferred Credits	0	0.0
Net Worth	6,655,793	42.5
Total Liab & Net Worth	**15,660,690**	**100.0**
Net Sales	28,841,050	100.0
Gross Profit	8,738,838	30.3
Net Profit After Tax	490,298	1.7
Working Capital	6,499,187	—

RATIOS	UQ	MED	LQ
SOLVENCY			
Quick Ratio (times)	1.7	1.1	0.8
Current Ratio (times)	3.3	2.2	1.6
Curr Liab To Nw (%)	39.4	59.1	142.6
Curr Liab To Inv (%)	72.7	93.2	126.1
Total Liab To Nw (%)	69.5	115.0	205.0
Fixed Assets To Nw (%)	12.0	26.8	33.3
EFFICIENCY			
Coll Period (days)	43.5	50.9	64.8
Sales To Inv (times)	7.2	6.3	4.2
Assets To Sales (%)	40.2	54.3	71.9
Sales To Nwc (times)	7.7	4.6	3.1
Acct Pay To Sales (%)	3.5	6.5	8.3
PROFITABILITY			
Return On Sales (%)	5.6	1.2	(0.7)
Return On Assets (%)	11.0	2.1	(1.4)
Return On Nw (%)	21.5	8.3	(2.5)

SIC 2326 MNS,BYS WORK CLTHNG (NO BREAKDOWN) 2002 (20 Establishments)

	$	%
Cash	95,415	8.4
Accounts Receivable	301,011	26.5
Notes Receivable	11,359	1.0
Inventory	448,677	39.5
Other Current	52,251	4.6
Total Current	**908,713**	**80.0**
Fixed Assets	189,694	16.7
Other Non-current	37,484	3.3
Total Assets	**1,135,891**	**100.0**
Accounts Payable	173,791	15.3
Bank Loans	0	0.0
Notes Payable	82,920	7.3
Other Current	209,004	18.4
Total Current	**465,715**	**41.0**
Other Long Term	81,784	7.2
Deferred Credits	0	0.0
Net Worth	588,392	51.8
Total Liab & Net Worth	**1,135,891**	**100.0**
Net Sales	2,763,725	100.0
Gross Profit	859,518	31.1
Net Profit After Tax	74,621	2.7
Working Capital	442,998	—

RATIOS	UQ	MED	LQ
SOLVENCY			
Quick Ratio (times)	2.0	1.0	0.5
Current Ratio (times)	5.7	2.0	1.4
Curr Liab To Nw (%)	14.8	72.2	248.9
Curr Liab To Inv (%)	50.2	91.9	157.3
Total Liab To Nw (%)	35.8	93.2	255.5
Fixed Assets To Nw (%)	13.2	25.3	59.6
EFFICIENCY			
Coll Period (days)	25.9	35.4	50.7
Sales To Inv (times)	29.6	7.8	3.4
Assets To Sales (%)	24.1	41.1	68.8
Sales To Nwc (times)	17.7	7.0	2.5
Acct Pay To Sales (%)	1.5	5.1	7.9
PROFITABILITY			
Return On Sales (%)	1.8	0.9	0.1
Return On Assets (%)	11.6	1.9	0.4
Return On Nw (%)	17.9	7.0	0.6

	SIC 2329 MEN, BOYS CLTHNG, NEC (NO BREAKDOWN) 2002 (76 Establishments)		SIC 2331 WMNS, MISSES BLOUSES (NO BREAKDOWN) 2002 (22 Establishments)		SIC 2335 WMNS, MISSES DRESSES (NO BREAKDOWN) 2002 (36 Establishments)		SIC 2337 WMNS, MISSES STS, CTS (NO BREAKDOWN) 2002 (13 Establishments)	
	$	%	$	%	$	%	$	%
Cash	274,753	12.5	232,123	14.3	192,398	12.9	165,116	11.3
Accounts Receivable	562,693	25.6	321,401	19.8	372,864	25.0	175,345	12.0
Notes Receivable	10,990	0.5	0	0.0	28,338	1.9	0	0.0
Inventory	815,466	37.1	491,841	30.3	504,112	33.8	616,629	42.2
Other Current	127,485	5.8	295,429	18.2	195,380	13.1	252,789	17.3
Total Current	**1,791,387**	**81.5**	**1,340,794**	**82.6**	**1,293,092**	**86.7**	**1,209,879**	**82.8**
Fixed Assets	287,941	13.1	193,165	11.9	77,556	5.2	150,504	10.3
Other Non-current	118,693	5.4	89,278	5.5	120,808	8.1	100,823	6.9
Total Assets	**2,198,021**	**100.0**	**1,623,237**	**100.0**	**1,491,456**	**100.0**	**1,461,206**	**100.0**
Accounts Payable	351,683	16.0	394,447	24.3	335,578	22.5	286,396	19.6
Bank Loans	28,574	1.3	1,623	0.1	5,966	0.4	0	0.0
Notes Payable	59,347	2.7	51,944	3.2	35,795	2.4	56,987	3.9
Other Current	393,446	17.9	361,981	22.3	259,513	17.4	176,806	12.1
Total Current	**833,050**	**37.9**	**809,995**	**49.9**	**636,852**	**42.7**	**520,189**	**35.6**
Other Long Term	301,129	13.7	123,367	7.6	47,726	3.2	371,146	25.4
Deferred Credits	2,198	0.1	3,246	0.2	0	0.0	4,384	0.3
Net Worth	1,061,644	48.3	686,629	42.3	806,878	54.1	565,487	38.7
Total Liab & Net Worth	**2,198,021**	**100.0**	**1,623,237**	**100.0**	**1,491,456**	**100.0**	**1,461,206**	**100.0**
Net Sales	5,347,983	100.0	5,153,133	100.0	5,628,136	100.0	2,945,980	100.0
Gross Profit	1,829,010	34.2	1,726,300	33.5	1,862,913	33.1	1,054,661	35.8
Net Profit After Tax	224,615	4.2	252,504	4.9	0	0.0	20,622	0.7
Working Capital	958,337	—	530,799	—	656,240	—	689,690	—

RATIOS	UQ	MED	LQ	UQ	MED	LQ	UQ	MED	LQ	UQ	MED	LQ
SOLVENCY												
Quick Ratio (times)	1.9	1.1	0.5	1.7	0.8	0.2	2.2	0.9	0.2	2.2	0.7	0.5
Current Ratio (times)	4.4	2.3	1.4	2.5	1.5	1.3	3.7	2.0	1.4	7.6	2.1	1.7
Curr Liab To Nw (%)	21.2	61.3	147.3	66.6	158.7	200.5	33.1	86.2	152.7	13.9	68.0	236.6
Curr Liab To Inv (%)	51.7	93.8	160.4	90.3	149.3	308.7	69.8	135.6	218.1	38.9	84.8	138.1
Total Liab To Nw (%)	31.8	68.1	193.1	73.1	185.2	240.2	38.5	86.2	153.4	26.5	165.2	492.3
Fixed Assets To Nw (%)	7.8	13.8	41.1	11.0	25.8	39.7	3.7	6.5	11.3	5.0	7.0	48.9
EFFICIENCY												
Coll Period (days)	22.3	38.7	61.0	8.2	18.6	31.8	6.0	35.4	52.8	1.8	13.9	42.3
Sales To Inv (times)	11.3	6.4	4.2	17.5	10.9	8.1	17.3	11.0	6.9	8.0	7.5	3.3
Assets To Sales (%)	25.5	41.1	59.0	22.6	31.5	36.2	21.2	26.5	44.2	24.4	49.6	56.8
Sales To Nwc (times)	11.9	6.4	3.7	16.0	9.7	6.8	13.6	8.4	4.4	10.0	5.7	3.1
Acct Pay To Sales (%)	4.2	5.7	9.2	3.9	7.7	11.7	4.9	6.8	8.0	5.5	7.1	11.6
PROFITABILITY												
Return On Sales (%)	6.4	2.3	0.3	8.7	2.9	1.3	3.2	0.5	0.2	4.1	1.5	0.3
Return On Assets (%)	18.5	5.2	0.4	25.5	8.8	5.3	9.7	2.6	0.7	2.8	2.7	1.1
Return On Nw (%)	33.7	13.3	1.8	60.8	32.0	17.4	15.6	5.2	1.2	21.5	10.7	2.5

Balance Sheet / Ratios

	SIC 2339 WMNS,MS OUTRWR,NEC (NO BREAKDOWN) 2002 (118 Establishments) $	%	SIC 2341 WMNS,CHLDRNS UNDRWR (NO BREAKDOWN) 2002 (21 Establishments) $	%	SIC 2353 HATS,CAPS,MILLINERY (NO BREAKDOWN) 2002 (11 Establishments) $	%	SIC 2361 GRLS DRSSES,BLOUSES (NO BREAKDOWN) 2002 (12 Establishments) $	%
Cash	315,456	11.8	651,362	14.2	292,275	13.5	195,055	12.1
Accounts Receivable	494,570	18.5	830,257	18.1	655,995	30.3	372,377	23.1
Notes Receivable	10,693	0.4	0	0.0	0	0.0	1,612	0.1
Inventory	957,060	35.8	1,967,847	42.9	469,805	21.7	644,809	40.0
Other Current	502,591	18.8	467,881	10.2	203,510	9.4	148,306	9.2
Total Current	**2,280,370**	**85.3**	**3,917,347**	**85.4**	**1,621,585**	**74.9**	**1,362,159**	**84.5**
Fixed Assets	270,009	10.1	472,467	10.3	480,630	22.2	191,831	11.9
Other Non-current	122,974	4.6	197,243	4.3	62,785	2.9	58,033	3.6
Total Assets	**2,673,353**	**100.0**	**4,587,057**	**100.0**	**2,165,000**	**100.0**	**1,612,023**	**100.0**
Accounts Payable	521,304	19.5	435,770	9.5	160,210	7.4	319,181	19.8
Bank Loans	16,040	0.6	0	0.0	0	0.0	0	0.0
Notes Payable	61,487	2.3	243,114	5.3	30,310	1.4	101,557	6.3
Other Current	649,625	24.3	701,820	15.3	593,210	27.4	228,907	14.2
Total Current	**1,248,456**	**46.7**	**1,380,704**	**30.1**	**783,730**	**36.2**	**649,645**	**40.3**
Other Long Term	152,381	5.7	903,650	19.7	177,530	8.2	112,842	7.0
Deferred Credits	2,673	0.1	9,174	0.2	0	0.0	0	0.0
Net Worth	1,269,843	47.5	2,293,529	50.0	1,203,740	55.6	849,536	52.7
Total Liab & Net Worth	**2,673,353**	**100.0**	**4,587,057**	**100.0**	**2,165,000**	**100.0**	**1,612,023**	**100.0**
Net Sales	9,686,062	100.0	8,250,103	100.0	4,645,923	100.0	4,755,230	100.0
Gross Profit	2,944,563	30.4	2,607,033	31.6	1,556,384	33.5	1,526,429	32.1
Net Profit After Tax	368,070	3.8	206,253	2.5	102,210	2.2	218,741	4.6
Working Capital	1,031,914	—	2,536,643	—	837,855	—	712,514	—

RATIOS	UQ	MED	LQ	UQ	MED	LQ	UQ	MED	LQ	UQ	MED	LQ
SOLVENCY												
Quick Ratio (times)	1.4	0.6	0.1	2.7	1.3	0.9	1.5	0.9	0.8	2.3	1.5	0.8
Current Ratio (times)	3.1	1.9	1.3	8.1	3.3	1.8	4.1	2.0	1.3	3.4	2.8	1.7
Curr Liab To Nw (%)	40.8	97.9	214.0	21.0	60.2	137.2	19.3	51.8	181.9	30.1	42.0	102.6
Curr Liab To Inv (%)	73.8	121.2	222.9	29.3	58.7	129.7	56.4	85.6	233.3	66.0	87.5	127.6
Total Liab To Nw (%)	51.1	105.2	224.4	33.4	116.9	313.5	26.6	59.3	213.9	31.2	50.6	175.3
Fixed Assets To Nw (%)	5.3	11.6	32.0	4.1	8.8	40.1	4.4	61.3	91.9	5.0	18.6	40.0
EFFICIENCY												
Coll Period (days)	3.7	18.5	40.5	33.2	46.2	70.1	32.9	39.1	56.2	12.1	27.0	89.4
Sales To Inv (times)	18.2	11.0	7.4	5.9	4.2	1.7	16.0	8.8	3.9	10.5	8.4	7.3
Assets To Sales (%)	20.1	27.6	42.5	49.5	55.6	92.2	38.9	46.6	52.2	27.5	33.9	38.8
Sales To Nwc (times)	16.3	8.6	4.9	8.8	2.5	1.4	11.6	4.2	3.4	7.3	5.6	3.5
Acct Pay To Sales (%)	3.2	6.0	8.7	3.7	5.9	7.2	1.6	1.9	3.4	3.4	5.5	6.2
PROFITABILITY												
Return On Sales (%)	4.1	1.1	0.2	4.7	2.3	1.1	2.6	2.5	1.8	7.0	4.2	0.1
Return On Assets (%)	13.8	3.5	0.5	12.9	4.0	2.3	7.1	4.9	3.7	18.1	8.8	0.2
Return On Nw (%)	32.6	11.1	1.7	33.6	8.2	3.0	18.9	11.4	5.5	30.8	12.8	0.0

SIC 2369 GRLS OUTERWR, NEC (NO BREAKDOWN) 2002 (24 Establishments)

	$	%
Cash	203,353	13.9
Accounts Receivable	361,354	24.7
Notes Receivable	1,463	0.1
Inventory	531,059	36.3
Other Current	112,649	7.7
Total Current	**1,209,878**	**82.7**
Fixed Assets	93,630	6.4
Other Non-current	159,464	10.9
Total Assets	**1,462,972**	**100.0**
Accounts Payable	253,094	17.3
Bank Loans	24,871	1.7
Notes Payable	13,167	0.9
Other Current	421,335	28.8
Total Current	**712,467**	**48.7**
Other Long Term	143,372	9.8
Deferred Credits	1,463	0.1
Net Worth	605,670	41.4
Total Liab & Net Worth	**1,462,972**	**100.0**
Net Sales	4,191,897	100.0
Gross Profit	1,249,185	29.8
Net Profit After Tax	121,565	2.9
Working Capital	497,411	—

RATIOS	UQ	MED	LQ
SOLVENCY			
Quick Ratio (times)	1.6	0.9	0.3
Current Ratio (times)	3.5	1.7	1.2
Curr Liab To Nw (%)	26.9	73.1	288.8
Curr Liab To Inv (%)	73.5	111.1	220.4
Total Liab To Nw (%)	26.9	78.8	299.7
Fixed Assets To Nw (%)	6.5	13.6	36.1
EFFICIENCY			
Coll Period (days)	17.4	34.0	47.3
Sales To Inv (times)	16.8	7.0	5.9
Assets To Sales (%)	20.5	34.9	48.7
Sales To Nwc (times)	24.3	9.0	4.5
Acct Pay To Sales (%)	3.2	5.5	8.0
PROFITABILITY			
Return On Sales (%)	5.1	2.7	0.6
Return On Assets (%)	13.8	5.1	1.1
Return On Nw (%)	44.1	15.6	4.0

SIC 2389 APPAREL ACCS, NEC (NO BREAKDOWN) 2002 (21 Establishments)

	$	%
Cash	151,799	14.8
Accounts Receivable	194,877	19.0
Notes Receivable	0	0.0
Inventory	426,677	41.6
Other Current	59,489	5.8
Total Current	**832,842**	**81.2**
Fixed Assets	130,260	12.7
Other Non-current	62,565	6.1
Total Assets	**1,025,667**	**100.0**
Accounts Payable	111,798	10.9
Bank Loans	0	0.0
Notes Payable	20,513	2.0
Other Current	178,466	17.4
Total Current	**310,777**	**30.3**
Other Long Term	125,131	12.2
Deferred Credits	0	0.0
Net Worth	589,759	57.5
Total Liab & Net Worth	**1,025,667**	**100.0**
Net Sales	2,757,169	100.0
Gross Profit	1,160,768	42.1
Net Profit After Tax	151,644	5.5
Working Capital	522,065	—

RATIOS	UQ	MED	LQ
SOLVENCY			
Quick Ratio (times)	2.7	1.3	0.5
Current Ratio (times)	6.0	2.5	2.0
Curr Liab To Nw (%)	14.5	63.8	118.8
Curr Liab To Inv (%)	24.7	65.8	97.7
Total Liab To Nw (%)	14.5	81.6	205.5
Fixed Assets To Nw (%)	8.9	21.6	35.6
EFFICIENCY			
Coll Period (days)	6.6	26.0	52.2
Sales To Inv (times)	11.9	5.0	3.1
Assets To Sales (%)	29.0	37.2	52.4
Sales To Nwc (times)	9.0	4.7	4.0
Acct Pay To Sales (%)	2.2	3.8	6.0
PROFITABILITY			
Return On Sales (%)	8.4	4.5	1.2
Return On Assets (%)	26.2	8.3	4.6
Return On Nw (%)	35.7	32.2	8.3

SIC 2391 CURTAINS, DRAPERIES (NO BREAKDOWN) 2002 (27 Establishments)

	$	%
Cash	(7,905)	(1.0)
Accounts Receivable	306,732	38.8
Notes Receivable	791	0.1
Inventory	194,474	24.6
Other Current	98,027	12.4
Total Current	**592,119**	**74.9**
Fixed Assets	137,555	17.4
Other Non-current	60,872	7.7
Total Assets	**790,546**	**100.0**
Accounts Payable	173,920	22.0
Bank Loans	3,162	0.4
Notes Payable	30,831	3.9
Other Current	595,282	75.3
Total Current	**803,195**	**101.6**
Other Long Term	62,453	7.9
Deferred Credits	0	0.0
Net Worth	(75,102)	(9.5)
Total Liab & Net Worth	**790,546**	**100.0**
Net Sales	1,961,653	100.0
Gross Profit	819,971	41.8
Net Profit After Tax	11,770	0.6
Working Capital	(211,076)	—

RATIOS	UQ	MED	LQ
SOLVENCY			
Quick Ratio (times)	1.8	1.3	0.6
Current Ratio (times)	4.2	2.5	1.5
Curr Liab To Nw (%)	26.4	52.7	137.2
Curr Liab To Inv (%)	69.2	108.2	251.8
Total Liab To Nw (%)	33.0	68.5	155.2
Fixed Assets To Nw (%)	17.8	29.3	52.5
EFFICIENCY			
Coll Period (days)	29.4	46.6	61.3
Sales To Inv (times)	57.1	15.1	5.7
Assets To Sales (%)	27.7	40.3	49.9
Sales To Nwc (times)	13.8	6.8	3.4
Acct Pay To Sales (%)	2.6	5.6	7.7
PROFITABILITY			
Return On Sales (%)	3.9	0.5	(2.5)
Return On Assets (%)	7.8	1.2	(9.8)
Return On Nw (%)	10.4	2.1	(13.8)

SIC 2392 HSEHLD FRNSHNGS, NEC (NO BREAKDOWN) 2002 (43 Establishments)

	$	%
Cash	273,258	12.3
Accounts Receivable	630,938	28.4
Notes Receivable	2,222	0.1
Inventory	708,695	31.9
Other Current	102,194	4.6
Total Current	**1,717,307**	**77.3**
Fixed Assets	377,674	17.0
Other Non-current	126,632	5.7
Total Assets	**2,221,613**	**100.0**
Accounts Payable	410,998	18.5
Bank Loans	0	0.0
Notes Payable	75,535	3.4
Other Current	353,237	15.9
Total Current	**839,770**	**37.8**
Other Long Term	346,571	15.6
Deferred Credits	0	0.0
Net Worth	1,035,272	46.6
Total Liab & Net Worth	**2,221,613**	**100.0**
Net Sales	6,004,359	100.0
Gross Profit	1,861,351	31.0
Net Profit After Tax	252,183	4.2
Working Capital	877,537	—

RATIOS	UQ	MED	LQ
SOLVENCY			
Quick Ratio (times)	2.8	1.0	0.5
Current Ratio (times)	5.5	2.4	1.4
Curr Liab To Nw (%)	15.6	38.5	145.2
Curr Liab To Inv (%)	40.1	89.6	163.5
Total Liab To Nw (%)	19.0	87.0	239.4
Fixed Assets To Nw (%)	12.9	29.8	52.7
EFFICIENCY			
Coll Period (days)	29.1	44.5	54.6
Sales To Inv (times)	26.6	6.6	4.9
Assets To Sales (%)	28.1	37.0	54.3
Sales To Nwc (times)	16.8	5.1	3.8
Acct Pay To Sales (%)	3.0	4.3	8.7
PROFITABILITY			
Return On Sales (%)	7.4	1.9	0.2
Return On Assets (%)	19.5	4.8	0.6
Return On Nw (%)	26.0	7.4	0.7

SIC 2393 TEXTILE BAGS (NO BREAKDOWN) 2002 (14 Establishments)

	$	%
Cash	244,143	13.3
Accounts Receivable	567,220	30.9
Notes Receivable	0	0.0
Inventory	609,441	33.2
Other Current	45,892	2.5
Total Current	**1,466,696**	**79.9**
Fixed Assets	251,486	13.7
Other Non-current	117,483	6.4
Total Assets	**1,835,665**	**100.0**
Accounts Payable	301,049	16.4
Bank Loans	0	0.0
Notes Payable	18,357	1.0
Other Current	659,003	35.9
Total Current	**978,409**	**53.3**
Other Long Term	168,882	9.2
Deferred Credits	(1,836)	(0.1)
Net Worth	690,210	37.6
Total Liab & Net Worth	**1,835,665**	**100.0**
Net Sales	5,127,556	100.0
Gross Profit	1,276,761	24.9
Net Profit After Tax	117,934	2.3
Working Capital	488,287	—

RATIOS	UQ	MED	LQ
SOLVENCY			
Quick Ratio (times)	1.9	0.8	0.5
Current Ratio (times)	2.8	1.8	1.1
Curr Liab To Nw (%)	41.0	104.8	165.1
Curr Liab To Inv (%)	105.8	130.7	253.4
Total Liab To Nw (%)	41.0	134.2	224.5
Fixed Assets To Nw (%)	5.1	15.1	77.6
EFFICIENCY			
Coll Period (days)	36.1	39.8	53.7
Sales To Inv (times)	10.6	8.0	6.5
Assets To Sales (%)	31.6	35.8	51.1
Sales To Nwc (times)	15.3	6.1	5.1
Acct Pay To Sales (%)	4.3	9.9	10.1
PROFITABILITY			
Return On Sales (%)	1.9	1.1	0.9
Return On Assets (%)	3.8	3.3	2.6
Return On Nw (%)	20.7	9.1	5.3

SIC 2394 CANVAS RLTD PRDCTS (NO BREAKDOWN) 2002 (49 Establishments)

	$	%
Cash	92,845	15.1
Accounts Receivable	114,981	18.7
Notes Receivable	615	0.1
Inventory	153,103	24.9
Other Current	45,500	7.4
Total Current	**407,044**	**66.2**
Fixed Assets	143,265	23.3
Other Non-current	64,561	10.5
Total Assets	**614,870**	**100.0**
Accounts Payable	57,798	9.4
Bank Loans	4,919	0.8
Notes Payable	26,439	4.3
Other Current	83,008	13.5
Total Current	**172,164**	**28.0**
Other Long Term	68,250	11.1
Deferred Credits	1,230	0.2
Net Worth	373,226	60.7
Total Liab & Net Worth	**614,870**	**100.0**
Net Sales	1,782,232	100.0
Gross Profit	777,053	43.6
Net Profit After Tax	60,596	3.4
Working Capital	234,880	—

RATIOS	UQ	MED	LQ
SOLVENCY			
Quick Ratio (times)	4.7	1.8	0.7
Current Ratio (times)	7.7	3.1	1.8
Curr Liab To Nw (%)	12.8	20.8	70.9
Curr Liab To Inv (%)	56.8	104.9	158.4
Total Liab To Nw (%)	17.1	48.7	86.0
Fixed Assets To Nw (%)	11.4	25.9	52.1
EFFICIENCY			
Coll Period (days)	13.9	22.5	29.2
Sales To Inv (times)	27.9	12.4	5.6
Assets To Sales (%)	28.8	34.5	54.7
Sales To Nwc (times)	7.8	5.8	4.0
Acct Pay To Sales (%)	1.2	2.4	4.4
PROFITABILITY			
Return On Sales (%)	5.1	1.3	(0.4)
Return On Assets (%)	17.8	2.6	(1.2)
Return On Nw (%)	25.9	4.8	(2.0)

SIC 2395 PLEATING, STITCHING (NO BREAKDOWN) 2002 (38 Establishments)

	$	%
Cash	34,978	10.3
Accounts Receivable	97,125	28.6
Notes Receivable	4,415	1.3
Inventory	55,015	16.2
Other Current	28,865	8.5
Total Current	**220,398**	**64.9**
Fixed Assets	110,369	32.5
Other Non-current	8,830	2.6
Total Assets	**339,597**	**100.0**
Accounts Payable	55,694	16.4
Bank Loans	9,169	2.7
Notes Payable	8,150	2.4
Other Current	70,297	20.7
Total Current	**143,310**	**42.2**
Other Long Term	88,974	26.2
Deferred Credits	0	0.0
Net Worth	107,313	31.6
Total Liab & Net Worth	**339,597**	**100.0**
Net Sales	1,078,086	100.0
Gross Profit	478,670	44.4
Net Profit After Tax	34,499	3.2
Working Capital	77,088	—

RATIOS	UQ	MED	LQ
SOLVENCY			
Quick Ratio (times)	2.1	1.1	0.6
Current Ratio (times)	5.7	1.6	1.0
Curr Liab To Nw (%)	14.4	101.1	207.4
Curr Liab To Inv (%)	113.5	240.3	436.5
Total Liab To Nw (%)	54.8	121.5	376.3
Fixed Assets To Nw (%)	33.7	86.2	179.7
EFFICIENCY			
Coll Period (days)	20.3	28.7	42.4
Sales To Inv (times)	57.1	18.9	9.8
Assets To Sales (%)	22.8	31.5	45.6
Sales To Nwc (times)	18.8	7.0	3.3
Acct Pay To Sales (%)	2.3	3.3	7.1
PROFITABILITY			
Return On Sales (%)	5.7	1.9	0.4
Return On Assets (%)	11.2	3.7	0.9
Return On Nw (%)	46.3	10.7	2.3

SIC 2396 AUTO APPAREL, TRMNGS (NO BREAKDOWN) 2002 (44 Establishments)

	$	%
Cash	89,215	13.1
Accounts Receivable	164,810	24.2
Notes Receivable	10,215	1.5
Inventory	160,043	23.5
Other Current	27,923	4.1
Total Current	**452,206**	**66.4**
Fixed Assets	185,922	27.3
Other Non-current	42,905	6.3
Total Assets	**681,033**	**100.0**
Accounts Payable	106,922	15.7
Bank Loans	2,724	0.4
Notes Payable	6,129	0.9
Other Current	141,655	20.8
Total Current	**257,430**	**37.8**
Other Long Term	115,776	17.0
Deferred Credits	6,810	1.0
Net Worth	301,017	44.2
Total Liab & Net Worth	**681,033**	**100.0**
Net Sales	2,196,881	100.0
Gross Profit	929,281	42.3
Net Profit After Tax	32,953	1.5
Working Capital	194,776	—

RATIOS	UQ	MED	LQ
SOLVENCY			
Quick Ratio (times)	1.9	1.0	0.6
Current Ratio (times)	3.3	2.1	1.2
Curr Liab To Nw (%)	27.0	71.7	171.4
Curr Liab To Inv (%)	68.1	138.8	339.3
Total Liab To Nw (%)	38.0	96.3	250.2
Fixed Assets To Nw (%)	22.6	45.2	83.5
EFFICIENCY			
Coll Period (days)	24.5	33.4	42.7
Sales To Inv (times)	44.5	14.8	6.3
Assets To Sales (%)	20.5	31.0	58.4
Sales To Nwc (times)	17.7	8.9	5.2
Acct Pay To Sales (%)	1.3	4.0	8.4
PROFITABILITY			
Return On Sales (%)	3.0	0.9	0.1
Return On Assets (%)	9.3	3.6	0.3
Return On Nw (%)	16.9	6.9	1.6

	SIC 2399 FAB TXTLE PRDTS, NEC (NO BREAKDOWN) 2002 (29 Establishments)		SIC 24 LUMBER, WOOD PRODUCTS (NO BREAKDOWN) 2002 (965 Establishments)		SIC 2411 LOGGING (NO BREAKDOWN) 2002 (32 Establishments)		SIC 2421 SAWML PLNG, MILL, GNRL (NO BREAKDOWN) 2002 (162 Establishments)	
	$	%	$	%	$	%	$	%
Cash	120,418	11.4	218,192	11.6	122,019	10.0	292,385	8.8
Accounts Receivable	250,343	23.7	400,646	21.3	117,138	9.6	405,352	12.2
Notes Receivable	1,056	0.1	15,048	0.8	3,661	0.3	39,871	1.2
Inventory	369,705	35.0	430,742	22.9	80,533	6.6	963,541	29.0
Other Current	51,759	4.9	118,501	6.3	65,890	5.4	199,353	6.0
Total Current	**793,281**	**75.1**	**1,183,129**	**62.9**	**389,241**	**31.9**	**1,900,502**	**57.2**
Fixed Assets	164,783	15.6	586,862	31.2	696,730	57.1	1,219,378	36.7
Other Non-current	98,235	9.3	110,977	5.9	134,221	11.0	202,676	6.1
Total Assets	**1,056,299**	**100.0**	**1,880,968**	**100.0**	**1,220,192**	**100.0**	**3,322,556**	**100.0**
Accounts Payable	141,544	13.4	182,454	9.7	93,955	7.7	209,321	6.3
Bank Loans	3,169	0.3	7,524	0.4	0	0.0	9,968	0.3
Notes Payable	19,013	1.8	77,120	4.1	80,533	6.6	149,515	4.5
Other Current	180,627	17.1	323,526	17.2	317,249	26.0	491,738	14.8
Total Current	**344,353**	**32.6**	**590,624**	**31.4**	**491,737**	**40.3**	**860,542**	**25.9**
Other Long Term	82,392	7.8	336,693	17.9	462,453	37.9	661,188	19.9
Deferred Credits	3,169	0.3	3,762	0.2	3,661	0.3	9,968	0.3
Net Worth	626,385	59.3	949,889	50.5	262,341	21.5	1,790,858	53.9
Total Liab & Net Worth	**1,056,299**	**100.0**	**1,880,968**	**100.0**	**1,220,192**	**100.0**	**3,322,556**	**100.0**
Net Sales	2,917,953	100.0	4,667,414	100.0	2,096,550	100.0	6,527,615	100.0
Gross Profit	1,021,284	35.0	1,292,874	27.7	855,392	40.8	1,325,106	20.3
Net Profit After Tax	151,734	5.2	116,685	2.5	25,159	1.2	32,638	0.5
Working Capital	448,928	—	592,505	—	(102,496)	—	1,039,960	—

RATIOS	UQ	MED	LQ	UQ	MED	LQ	UQ	MED	LQ	UQ	MED	LQ
SOLVENCY												
Quick Ratio (times)	2.2	1.2	0.7	2.6	1.1	0.5	0.8	0.4	0.2	2.3	0.7	0.3
Current Ratio (times)	4.7	2.8	1.7	4.8	2.3	1.4	1.5	0.9	0.5	6.7	2.3	1.4
Curr Liab To Nw (%)	18.5	36.9	85.5	17.6	46.1	123.9	26.3	94.8	187.9	9.7	40.1	101.1
Curr Liab To Inv (%)	39.2	76.8	123.4	55.7	116.3	228.6	93.7	208.9	601.9	37.4	73.0	154.3
Total Liab To Nw (%)	23.5	47.7	97.8	26.3	76.5	213.2	71.5	258.4	838.2	19.0	76.8	221.8
Fixed Assets To Nw (%)	10.4	23.3	41.5	26.1	51.7	113.7	72.7	160.5	426.3	28.5	52.3	139.1
EFFICIENCY												
Coll Period (days)	16.3	32.1	42.9	16.6	27.6	41.1	7.0	16.4	33.3	12.1	18.8	27.4
Sales To Inv (times)	13.1	8.8	6.4	21.9	11.8	6.5	56.0	24.3	8.2	12.9	6.1	4.3
Assets To Sales (%)	27.9	36.2	51.6	28.6	40.3	56.1	32.6	58.2	76.2	35.6	50.9	79.8
Sales To Nwc (times)	8.3	5.4	4.2	13.0	7.2	4.3	203.5	22.6	19.6	11.6	6.1	4.0
Acct Pay To Sales (%)	1.5	4.0	9.0	1.6	3.0	5.3	1.7	3.1	5.8	1.1	2.4	4.1
PROFITABILITY												
Return On Sales (%)	9.6	3.9	1.3	5.0	1.9	0.1	3.7	0.5	(0.8)	3.4	0.9	(2.1)
Return On Assets (%)	19.8	9.0	3.5	12.6	4.6	0.2	4.7	1.1	(1.6)	6.2	2.0	(2.9)
Return On Nw (%)	34.3	20.5	10.3	27.0	9.7	1.2	10.7	6.5	(0.2)	13.3	3.7	(4.9)

	SIC 2426 HDWD DNSN,FLRG MLLS (NO BREAKDOWN) 2002 (41 Establishments) $	%	SIC 2431 MILLWORK (NO BREAKDOWN) 2002 (192 Establishments) $	%	SIC 2434 WOOD KTCHN CABINETS (NO BREAKDOWN) 2002 (113 Establishments) $	%	SIC 2435 HDWD VENEER PLYWOOD (NO BREAKDOWN) 2002 (17 Establishments) $	%
Cash	230,235	10.5	168,636	12.7	163,306	13.2	242,994	6.4
Accounts Receivable	267,511	12.2	398,352	30.0	326,612	26.4	801,122	21.1
Notes Receivable	6,578	0.3	5,311	0.4	8,660	0.7	64,545	1.7
Inventory	673,162	30.7	274,863	20.7	214,030	17.3	1,051,709	27.7
Other Current	94,286	4.3	88,965	6.7	72,992	5.9	148,075	3.9
Total Current	**1,271,772**	**58.0**	**936,127**	**70.5**	**785,600**	**63.5**	**2,308,445**	**60.8**
Fixed Assets	798,146	36.4	325,321	24.5	398,367	32.2	1,199,784	31.6
Other Non-current	122,792	5.6	66,392	5.0	53,199	4.3	288,556	7.6
Total Assets	**2,192,710**	**100.0**	**1,327,840**	**100.0**	**1,237,166**	**100.0**	**3,796,785**	**100.0**
Accounts Payable	166,646	7.6	146,062	11.0	150,934	12.2	478,395	12.6
Bank Loans	0	0.0	1,328	0.1	4,949	0.4	91,123	2.4
Notes Payable	72,359	3.3	42,491	3.2	48,249	3.9	68,342	1.8
Other Current	280,667	12.8	256,273	19.3	230,113	18.6	379,678	10.0
Total Current	**519,672**	**23.7**	**446,154**	**33.6**	**434,245**	**35.1**	**1,017,538**	**26.8**
Other Long Term	357,412	16.3	181,914	13.7	233,825	18.9	470,802	12.4
Deferred Credits	2,193	0.1	1,328	0.1	1,237	0.1	0	0.0
Net Worth	1,313,433	59.9	698,444	52.6	567,859	45.9	2,308,445	60.8
Total Liab & Net Worth	**2,192,710**	**100.0**	**1,327,840**	**100.0**	**1,237,166**	**100.0**	**3,796,785**	**100.0**
Net Sales	4,291,018	100.0	3,522,122	100.0	3,352,753	100.0	7,372,398	100.0
Gross Profit	798,129	18.6	1,039,026	29.5	1,186,875	35.4	1,238,563	16.8
Net Profit After Tax	(4,291)	(0.1)	98,619	2.8	174,343	5.2	73,724	1.0
Working Capital	752,100	—	489,973	—	351,355	—	1,290,907	—

RATIOS	UQ	MED	LQ	UQ	MED	LQ	UQ	MED	LQ	UQ	MED	LQ
SOLVENCY												
Quick Ratio (times)	3.0	1.6	0.5	3.0	1.2	0.7	2.2	1.2	0.7	1.9	0.9	0.5
Current Ratio (times)	9.7	4.1	1.4	4.4	2.4	1.4	4.0	2.2	1.3	3.8	2.5	1.5
Curr Liab To Nw (%)	5.2	19.2	96.1	21.8	57.9	136.4	23.9	55.3	163.3	19.1	45.0	78.1
Curr Liab To Inv (%)	24.5	51.9	105.0	66.9	134.2	333.6	105.1	176.7	423.4	53.4	75.6	112.8
Total Liab To Nw (%)	11.6	28.7	132.8	29.1	81.4	197.3	39.8	86.3	249.9	19.6	58.8	144.8
Fixed Assets To Nw (%)	29.9	56.3	88.5	20.5	43.3	81.4	29.2	57.4	137.7	39.5	57.0	78.2
EFFICIENCY												
Coll Period (days)	11.2	19.9	29.9	24.5	36.9	53.9	20.6	34.3	44.4	23.2	27.4	53.1
Sales To Inv (times)	15.8	7.2	4.6	33.1	14.1	7.6	54.0	18.9	11.4	10.7	6.5	5.3
Assets To Sales (%)	36.3	51.1	64.2	27.9	37.7	50.9	28.5	36.9	48.4	41.1	51.5	63.3
Sales To Nwc (times)	13.2	4.3	3.3	13.2	7.2	4.2	15.2	8.3	5.3	6.9	4.6	2.7
Acct Pay To Sales (%)	1.3	2.0	5.0	1.9	3.4	5.7	2.3	3.4	5.5	1.8	3.7	4.9
PROFITABILITY												
Return On Sales (%)	2.6	1.0	(3.1)	5.2	2.0	0.6	7.8	4.1	1.1	6.2	0.4	(2.7)
Return On Assets (%)	6.3	1.9	(5.8)	13.4	5.2	1.6	19.2	10.4	3.6	14.1	0.2	(4.4)
Return On Nw (%)	14.6	2.0	(13.0)	30.6	10.2	3.8	42.2	22.9	8.8	18.5	0.3	(11.1)

SIC 2439 — STRCTRL WD MBRS, NEC (NO BREAKDOWN) — 2002 (82 Establishments)

	$	%
Cash	182,327	12.1
Accounts Receivable	340,545	22.6
Notes Receivable	6,027	0.4
Inventory	326,984	21.7
Other Current	96,439	6.4
Total Current	**952,322**	**63.2**
Fixed Assets	486,709	32.3
Other Non-current	67,807	4.5
Total Assets	**1,506,838**	**100.0**
Accounts Payable	116,027	7.7
Bank Loans	0	0.0
Notes Payable	45,205	3.0
Other Current	206,436	13.7
Total Current	**367,668**	**24.4**
Other Long Term	212,464	14.1
Deferred Credits	1,507	0.1
Net Worth	925,199	61.4
Total Liab & Net Worth	**1,506,838**	**100.0**
Net Sales	4,220,835	100.0
Gross Profit	1,489,955	35.3
Net Profit After Tax	202,600	4.8
Working Capital	584,654	—

RATIOS	UQ	MED	LQ
SOLVENCY			
Quick Ratio (times)	4.1	1.6	0.7
Current Ratio (times)	7.3	3.2	1.6
Curr Liab To Nw (%)	12.0	33.7	93.0
Curr Liab To Inv (%)	47.8	103.3	185.6
Total Liab To Nw (%)	17.6	56.1	175.9
Fixed Assets To Nw (%)	29.9	52.7	97.8
EFFICIENCY			
Coll Period (days)	19.4	27.2	37.6
Sales To Inv (times)	22.5	13.6	8.0
Assets To Sales (%)	26.8	35.7	49.7
Sales To Nwc (times)	12.2	7.2	4.3
Acct Pay To Sales (%)	1.0	2.4	4.3
PROFITABILITY			
Return On Sales (%)	6.5	3.6	1.5
Return On Assets (%)	18.0	9.2	3.6
Return On Nw (%)	35.7	15.5	9.5

SIC 2441 — NLED WD BOXES SHOOK (NO BREAKDOWN) — 2002 (12 Establishments)

	$	%
Cash	63,902	7.0
Accounts Receivable	257,432	28.2
Notes Receivable	5,477	0.6
Inventory	192,618	21.1
Other Current	85,810	9.4
Total Current	**605,239**	**66.3**
Fixed Assets	301,250	33.0
Other Non-current	6,391	0.7
Total Assets	**912,880**	**100.0**
Accounts Payable	212,701	23.3
Bank Loans	0	0.0
Notes Payable	150,625	16.5
Other Current	259,258	28.4
Total Current	**622,584**	**68.2**
Other Long Term	258,345	28.3
Deferred Credits	0	0.0
Net Worth	31,951	3.5
Total Liab & Net Worth	**912,880**	**100.0**
Net Sales	2,638,382	100.0
Gross Profit	564,614	21.4
Net Profit After Tax	(84,428)	(3.2)
Working Capital	(17,345)	—

RATIOS	UQ	MED	LQ
SOLVENCY			
Quick Ratio (times)	1.3	0.9	0.3
Current Ratio (times)	2.4	1.4	0.9
Curr Liab To Nw (%)	50.4	135.9	389.1
Curr Liab To Inv (%)	105.6	253.4	331.2
Total Liab To Nw (%)	159.8	258.3	520.7
Fixed Assets To Nw (%)	67.5	141.6	433.1
EFFICIENCY			
Coll Period (days)	17.4	28.8	45.3
Sales To Inv (times)	15.7	13.0	11.9
Assets To Sales (%)	22.6	34.6	43.1
Sales To Nwc (times)	16.0	11.9	9.2
Acct Pay To Sales (%)	2.8	5.5	10.8
PROFITABILITY			
Return On Sales (%)	3.1	2.0	(0.7)
Return On Assets (%)	10.8	6.1	(1.1)
Return On Nw (%)	39.8	21.8	4.6

SIC 2448 — WOOD PALLETS, SKIDS (NO BREAKDOWN) — 2002 (73 Establishments)

	$	%
Cash	128,428	10.1
Accounts Receivable	278,473	21.9
Notes Receivable	12,716	1.0
Inventory	259,399	20.4
Other Current	63,578	5.0
Total Current	**742,594**	**58.4**
Fixed Assets	441,233	34.7
Other Non-current	87,738	6.9
Total Assets	**1,271,565**	**100.0**
Accounts Payable	114,441	9.0
Bank Loans	8,901	0.7
Notes Payable	58,492	4.6
Other Current	189,463	14.9
Total Current	**371,297**	**29.2**
Other Long Term	292,460	23.0
Deferred Credits	2,543	0.2
Net Worth	605,265	47.6
Total Liab & Net Worth	**1,271,565**	**100.0**
Net Sales	3,355,053	100.0
Gross Profit	828,698	24.7
Net Profit After Tax	114,072	3.4
Working Capital	371,297	—

RATIOS	UQ	MED	LQ
SOLVENCY			
Quick Ratio (times)	2.9	1.1	0.6
Current Ratio (times)	5.0	2.3	1.3
Curr Liab To Nw (%)	17.2	41.1	105.2
Curr Liab To Inv (%)	61.0	145.8	220.7
Total Liab To Nw (%)	27.4	70.8	211.2
Fixed Assets To Nw (%)	28.6	67.8	133.6
EFFICIENCY			
Coll Period (days)	23.7	30.9	38.0
Sales To Inv (times)	18.9	12.8	9.2
Assets To Sales (%)	28.9	37.9	48.5
Sales To Nwc (times)	15.2	8.7	4.8
Acct Pay To Sales (%)	1.4	2.4	4.7
PROFITABILITY			
Return On Sales (%)	4.6	1.9	0.2
Return On Assets (%)	13.0	5.0	0.3
Return On Nw (%)	23.3	6.9	0.3

SIC 2449 — WOOD CONTAINERS, NEC (NO BREAKDOWN) — 2002 (16 Establishments)

	$	%
Cash	153,027	13.8
Accounts Receivable	226,214	20.4
Notes Receivable	0	0.0
Inventory	251,718	22.7
Other Current	54,336	4.9
Total Current	**685,295**	**61.8**
Fixed Assets	352,628	31.8
Other Non-current	70,969	6.4
Total Assets	**1,108,892**	**100.0**
Accounts Payable	60,989	5.5
Bank Loans	0	0.0
Notes Payable	21,069	1.9
Other Current	136,394	12.3
Total Current	**218,452**	**19.7**
Other Long Term	270,569	24.4
Deferred Credits	0	0.0
Net Worth	619,871	55.9
Total Liab & Net Worth	**1,108,892**	**100.0**
Net Sales	2,469,693	100.0
Gross Profit	874,271	35.4
Net Profit After Tax	180,288	7.3
Working Capital	466,843	—

RATIOS	UQ	MED	LQ
SOLVENCY			
Quick Ratio (times)	6.1	1.7	0.7
Current Ratio (times)	8.5	3.3	1.8
Curr Liab To Nw (%)	11.9	31.5	50.5
Curr Liab To Inv (%)	47.4	76.7	126.9
Total Liab To Nw (%)	26.2	51.9	142.1
Fixed Assets To Nw (%)	16.1	40.9	81.3
EFFICIENCY			
Coll Period (days)	19.6	27.4	38.6
Sales To Inv (times)	20.2	11.5	7.3
Assets To Sales (%)	31.4	44.9	54.0
Sales To Nwc (times)	8.2	7.2	4.8
Acct Pay To Sales (%)	1.0	1.3	3.7
PROFITABILITY			
Return On Sales (%)	12.9	2.1	1.3
Return On Assets (%)	17.7	4.7	2.8
Return On Nw (%)	24.9	12.3	5.8

	SIC 2451 MOBILE HOMES (NO BREAKDOWN) 2002 (24 Establishments)		SIC 2452 PREFABRCTD WD BLDGS (NO BREAKDOWN) 2002 (71 Establishments)		SIC 2491 WOOD PRESERVING (NO BREAKDOWN) 2002 (35 Establishments)		SIC 2493 RECONSTTD WD PRDTS (NO BREAKDOWN) 2002 (15 Establishments)	
	$	%	$	%	$	%	$	%
Cash	1,540,189	19.1	418,277	14.0	409,957	8.8	746,460	14.3
Accounts Receivable	1,241,828	15.4	519,858	17.4	968,989	20.8	1,090,980	20.9
Notes Receivable	24,191	0.3	53,778	1.8	4,659	0.1	67,860	1.3
Inventory	1,701,466	21.1	770,824	25.8	1,509,386	32.4	903,060	17.3
Other Current	1,080,552	13.4	146,397	4.9	177,026	3.8	250,560	4.8
Total Current	**5,588,226**	**69.3**	**1,909,134**	**63.9**	**3,070,017**	**65.9**	**3,058,920**	**58.6**
Fixed Assets	1,846,614	22.9	833,566	27.9	1,309,066	28.1	1,727,820	33.1
Other Non-current	628,978	7.8	244,990	8.2	279,516	6.0	433,260	8.3
Total Assets	**8,063,818**	**100.0**	**2,987,690**	**100.0**	**4,658,599**	**100.0**	**5,220,000**	**100.0**
Accounts Payable	467,701	5.8	367,486	12.3	256,223	5.5	835,200	16.0
Bank Loans	0	0.0	2,988	0.1	9,317	0.2	0	0.0
Notes Payable	40,319	0.5	158,348	5.3	265,540	5.7	276,660	5.3
Other Current	2,072,402	25.7	591,562	19.8	968,989	20.8	746,460	14.3
Total Current	**2,580,422**	**32.0**	**1,120,384**	**37.5**	**1,500,069**	**32.2**	**1,858,320**	**35.6**
Other Long Term	1,056,360	13.1	415,288	13.9	1,029,550	22.1	2,067,120	39.6
Deferred Credits	8,064	0.1	11,951	0.4	4,659	0.1	52,200	1.0
Net Worth	4,418,972	54.8	1,440,067	48.2	2,124,321	45.6	1,242,360	23.8
Total Liab & Net Worth	**8,063,818**	**100.0**	**2,987,690**	**100.0**	**4,658,599**	**100.0**	**5,220,000**	**100.0**
Net Sales	22,275,740	100.0	7,544,672	100.0	12,624,930	100.0	6,666,667	100.0
Gross Profit	5,413,005	24.3	1,999,338	26.5	1,994,739	15.8	2,000,000	30.0
Net Profit After Tax	334,136	1.5	150,893	2.0	378,748	3.0	60,000	0.9
Working Capital	3,007,804	—	788,750	—	1,569,948	—	1,200,600	—

RATIOS	UQ	MED	LQ	UQ	MED	LQ	UQ	MED	LQ	UQ	MED	LQ
SOLVENCY												
Quick Ratio (times)	1.7	1.0	0.6	1.8	0.9	0.4	2.3	1.1	0.4	2.5	0.8	0.6
Current Ratio (times)	3.1	2.5	1.4	2.8	1.9	1.4	5.7	2.8	1.5	4.4	1.7	1.2
Curr Liab To Nw (%)	37.7	51.9	125.0	34.5	72.7	145.9	21.2	42.4	102.5	11.5	35.0	235.0
Curr Liab To Inv (%)	87.0	168.8	261.1	83.8	139.5	205.1	28.9	65.6	106.9	111.4	164.9	525.6
Total Liab To Nw (%)	44.4	54.7	179.8	45.7	105.6	198.6	40.4	99.2	183.4	24.1	176.8	305.8
Fixed Assets To Nw (%)	18.5	47.8	91.7	25.8	51.4	97.1	26.8	39.7	77.2	28.7	40.5	246.0
EFFICIENCY												
Coll Period (days)	10.2	19.4	24.8	8.4	21.9	40.4	13.9	21.2	34.7	22.3	27.4	39.8
Sales To Inv (times)	19.4	14.2	8.9	18.7	11.8	8.3	11.1	9.2	6.4	17.9	9.9	7.9
Assets To Sales (%)	28.9	36.2	53.1	25.5	39.6	53.2	28.6	36.9	47.8	30.4	78.3	390.6
Sales To Nwc (times)	17.5	8.7	3.9	13.9	8.2	5.4	10.5	6.6	4.9	18.7	9.2	3.7
Acct Pay To Sales (%)	1.5	1.9	3.6	2.3	3.7	5.8	0.6	1.8	3.2	2.6	6.1	11.3
PROFITABILITY												
Return On Sales (%)	4.0	2.3	0.6	4.1	1.5	(0.3)	3.6	2.3	1.0	9.8	3.6	0.9
Return On Assets (%)	10.6	5.5	1.3	13.9	3.8	(0.8)	15.9	5.9	1.8	9.9	4.0	2.4
Return On Nw (%)	28.7	9.7	6.2	28.4	7.6	(0.2)	32.4	7.3	3.1	32.2	17.4	6.6

SIC 2499 WOOD PRODUCTS, NEC (NO BREAKDOWN) 2002 (72 Establishments)
SIC 25 FURNITURE, FIXTURES (NO BREAKDOWN) 2002 (544 Establishments)
SIC 2511 WOOD HSHLD FURNTR (NO BREAKDOWN) 2002 (92 Establishments)
SIC 2512 UPHLSTRD HSHLD FURN (NO BREAKDOWN) 2002 (79 Establishments)

	SIC 2499 $	%	SIC 25 $	%	SIC 2511 $	%	SIC 2512 $	%
Cash	155,763	12.5	210,269	11.9	161,075	8.5	263,163	11.0
Accounts Receivable	307,788	24.7	436,441	24.7	392,265	20.7	547,858	22.9
Notes Receivable	16,199	1.3	7,068	0.4	1,895	0.1	7,177	0.3
Inventory	302,804	24.3	427,606	24.2	596,925	31.5	677,048	28.3
Other Current	102,182	8.2	141,359	8.0	153,495	8.1	188,999	7.9
Total Current	**884,736**	**71.0**	**1,222,743**	**69.2**	**1,305,655**	**68.9**	**1,684,245**	**70.4**
Fixed Assets	290,343	23.3	447,043	25.3	513,545	27.1	550,251	23.0
Other Non-current	71,028	5.7	97,183	5.5	75,800	4.0	157,898	6.6
Total Assets	**1,246,107**	**100.0**	**1,766,969**	**100.0**	**1,895,000**	**100.0**	**2,392,394**	**100.0**
Accounts Payable	153,271	12.3	226,172	12.8	227,400	12.0	311,011	13.0
Bank Loans	24,922	2.0	5,301	0.3	1,895	0.1	28,709	1.2
Notes Payable	41,122	3.3	56,543	3.2	121,280	6.4	40,671	1.7
Other Current	193,146	15.5	319,821	18.1	358,155	18.9	294,264	12.3
Total Current	**412,461**	**33.1**	**607,837**	**34.4**	**708,730**	**37.4**	**674,655**	**28.2**
Other Long Term	170,718	13.7	300,385	17.0	301,305	15.9	322,974	13.5
Deferred Credits	4,984	0.4	1,767	0.1	1,895	0.1	2,392	0.1
Net Worth	657,944	52.8	856,980	48.5	883,070	46.6	1,392,373	58.2
Total Liab & Net Worth	**1,246,107**	**100.0**	**1,766,969**	**100.0**	**1,895,000**	**100.0**	**2,392,394**	**100.0**
Net Sales	3,331,837	100.0	4,613,496	100.0	4,690,594	100.0	7,249,679	100.0
Gross Profit	1,066,188	32.0	1,513,227	32.8	1,491,609	31.8	1,921,165	26.5
Net Profit After Tax	83,296	2.5	101,497	2.2	150,099	3.2	28,999	0.4
Working Capital	472,275	—	614,906	—	596,925	—	1,009,590	—

RATIOS	UQ	MED	LQ	UQ	MED	LQ	UQ	MED	LQ	UQ	MED	LQ
SOLVENCY												
Quick Ratio (times)	3.1	1.5	0.6	2.0	1.2	0.6	1.7	0.9	0.5	2.4	1.2	0.8
Current Ratio (times)	5.5	2.7	1.4	3.9	2.2	1.4	4.3	2.3	1.3	5.0	2.7	1.8
Curr Liab To Nw (%)	16.6	42.6	120.2	24.8	52.4	136.5	19.1	50.0	142.3	19.8	36.3	88.8
Curr Liab To Inv (%)	51.9	111.6	216.3	70.0	123.8	217.6	42.9	84.8	167.9	58.7	94.5	136.7
Total Liab To Nw (%)	23.2	60.7	158.0	31.9	85.2	199.6	26.9	80.3	229.6	27.9	55.9	130.8
Fixed Assets To Nw (%)	12.8	40.9	93.0	19.8	42.2	83.3	23.6	48.0	104.0	14.3	28.7	59.1
EFFICIENCY												
Coll Period (days)	26.3	33.1	47.7	21.5	34.7	49.3	18.6	31.8	42.0	15.0	29.6	41.8
Sales To Inv (times)	20.0	10.2	5.7	21.1	12.0	6.6	11.5	6.2	4.8	15.6	11.4	8.3
Assets To Sales (%)	27.2	37.4	56.9	26.9	38.3	55.5	27.1	40.4	58.5	23.2	33.0	47.7
Sales To Nwc (times)	11.1	5.5	3.3	13.4	6.9	4.3	13.8	6.3	3.8	11.4	6.2	4.3
Acct Pay To Sales (%)	2.7	4.2	5.7	2.5	4.0	6.6	2.2	3.7	5.6	1.9	3.2	5.2
PROFITABILITY												
Return On Sales (%)	4.3	1.8	(0.2)	4.4	1.7	0.1	3.6	1.5	0.1	3.5	1.6	0.3
Return On Assets (%)	10.7	4.8	(0.3)	12.1	4.9	0.4	7.8	4.2	0.4	12.1	4.9	0.8
Return On Nw (%)	24.7	10.8	0.6	30.8	9.6	1.4	24.6	8.7	0.7	23.6	8.1	1.7

	SIC 2514 METAL HSEHLD FURNTR (NO BREAKDOWN) 2002 (17 Establishments)		SIC 2515 MATTRESSES, BDSPRNGS (NO BREAKDOWN) 2002 (51 Establishments)		SIC 2519 HSEHLD FURNTR, NEC (NO BREAKDOWN) 2002 (16 Establishments)		SIC 2521 WOOD OFFICE FURNTR (NO BREAKDOWN) 2002 (32 Establishments)	
	$	%	$	%	$	%	$	%
Cash	107,214	5.5	315,356	13.6	156,499	9.6	256,941	12.6
Accounts Receivable	487,338	25.0	521,728	22.5	312,998	19.2	558,744	27.4
Notes Receivable	11,696	0.6	0	0.0	47,276	2.9	0	0.0
Inventory	551,667	28.3	544,916	23.5	506,992	31.1	413,960	20.3
Other Current	253,417	13.0	190,142	8.2	91,292	5.6	132,549	6.5
Total Current	**1,411,332**	**72.4**	**1,572,142**	**67.8**	**1,115,057**	**68.4**	**1,362,194**	**66.8**
Fixed Assets	430,807	22.1	540,279	23.3	401,029	24.6	595,450	29.2
Other Non-current	107,214	5.5	206,372	8.9	114,114	7.0	81,568	4.0
Total Assets	**1,949,353**	**100.0**	**2,318,793**	**100.0**	**1,630,200**	**100.0**	**2,039,212**	**100.0**
Accounts Payable	237,821	12.2	331,587	14.3	329,300	20.2	214,117	10.5
Bank Loans	0	0.0	2,319	0.1	0	0.0	0	0.0
Notes Payable	48,734	2.5	41,738	1.8	30,974	1.9	67,294	3.3
Other Current	397,668	20.4	361,732	15.6	262,462	16.1	438,431	21.5
Total Current	**684,223**	**35.1**	**737,376**	**31.8**	**622,736**	**38.2**	**719,842**	**35.3**
Other Long Term	124,758	6.4	361,732	15.6	306,478	18.8	536,312	26.3
Deferred Credits	0	0.0	2,319	0.1	0	0.0	6,118	0.3
Net Worth	1,140,372	58.5	1,217,366	52.5	700,986	43.0	776,940	38.1
Total Liab & Net Worth	**1,949,353**	**100.0**	**2,318,793**	**100.0**	**1,630,200**	**100.0**	**2,039,212**	**100.0**
Net Sales	4,708,582	100.0	7,652,782	100.0	3,937,681	100.0	4,302,135	100.0
Gross Profit	1,389,032	29.5	2,609,599	34.1	1,535,696	39.0	1,479,934	34.4
Net Profit After Tax	70,629	1.5	198,972	2.6	137,819	3.5	163,481	3.8
Working Capital	727,109	—	834,766	—	492,321	—	642,352	—

RATIOS	UQ	MED	LQ	UQ	MED	LQ	UQ	MED	LQ	UQ	MED	LQ
SOLVENCY												
Quick Ratio (times)	2.0	0.6	0.4	1.9	1.2	0.7	1.6	0.6	0.4	1.7	1.2	0.6
Current Ratio (times)	3.2	2.2	1.3	3.2	1.9	1.5	3.5	1.9	1.3	2.8	1.8	1.4
Curr Liab To Nw (%)	19.7	48.7	144.7	28.4	60.9	115.6	31.4	113.2	166.4	33.4	88.7	173.2
Curr Liab To Inv (%)	62.0	109.7	174.7	84.1	131.9	202.3	58.8	117.1	298.3	86.0	161.3	389.5
Total Liab To Nw (%)	19.7	95.2	158.5	39.7	77.1	154.8	52.6	193.9	375.4	77.4	199.6	257.2
Fixed Assets To Nw (%)	16.7	36.1	86.6	20.5	44.9	73.6	14.2	28.7	119.1	28.2	58.3	119.9
EFFICIENCY												
Coll Period (days)	22.9	48.9	65.0	13.2	27.8	43.3	6.6	21.2	41.7	27.6	38.7	45.5
Sales To Inv (times)	8.8	6.5	5.7	20.4	16.1	11.3	8.7	5.0	5.0	24.8	14.5	7.9
Assets To Sales (%)	30.5	41.4	49.9	22.4	30.3	44.1	27.2	41.4	51.3	35.0	47.4	60.5
Sales To Nwc (times)	13.3	7.3	5.3	17.4	8.6	5.8	23.6	6.9	4.9	13.5	8.4	5.1
Acct Pay To Sales (%)	4.0	5.0	7.7	3.1	4.6	6.4	5.3	6.6	7.9	3.0	3.7	5.8
PROFITABILITY												
Return On Sales (%)	2.7	1.4	0.3	3.6	1.7	0.5	5.0	3.4	1.4	4.3	0.8	(1.5)
Return On Assets (%)	5.9	3.2	0.6	14.3	6.3	1.0	12.9	5.4	4.4	10.1	1.8	(3.2)
Return On Nw (%)	31.1	6.8	1.4	24.2	12.0	1.4	34.6	12.7	6.5	17.6	6.1	(21.3)

	SIC 2522 OFFC FURN, EXC WOOD (NO BREAKDOWN) 2002 (17 Establishments)		SIC 2531 PBLC BLG, RLTD FURN (NO BREAKDOWN) 2002 (50 Establishments)		SIC 2541 WD PARTNS, FXTRS (NO BREAKDOWN) 2002 (89 Establishments)		SIC 2542 PRTNS, FXTRS, EXC WD (NO BREAKDOWN) 2002 (45 Establishments)	
	$	%	$	%	$	%	$	%
Cash	368,310	15.4	460,662	16.9	143,924	11.7	193,042	9.8
Accounts Receivable	361,135	15.1	621,485	22.8	394,868	32.1	581,096	29.5
Notes Receivable	14,350	0.6	8,177	0.3	2,460	0.2	31,517	1.6
Inventory	533,332	22.3	575,147	21.1	215,271	17.5	435,330	22.1
Other Current	246,337	10.3	215,340	7.9	94,719	7.7	122,129	6.2
Total Current	**1,523,464**	**63.7**	**1,880,811**	**69.0**	**851,242**	**69.2**	**1,363,114**	**69.2**
Fixed Assets	784,452	32.8	659,647	24.2	343,203	27.9	504,273	25.6
Other Non-current	83,707	3.5	185,355	6.8	35,674	2.9	102,431	5.2
Total Assets	**2,391,623**	**100.0**	**2,725,813**	**100.0**	**1,230,119**	**100.0**	**1,969,818**	**100.0**
Accounts Payable	251,120	10.5	299,839	11.0	158,685	12.9	275,775	14.0
Bank Loans	7,175	0.3	2,726	0.1	4,920	0.4	9,849	0.5
Notes Payable	33,483	1.4	8,177	0.3	46,745	3.8	86,672	4.4
Other Current	365,918	15.3	447,034	16.4	274,317	22.3	427,450	21.7
Total Current	**657,696**	**27.5**	**757,776**	**27.8**	**484,667**	**39.4**	**799,746**	**40.6**
Other Long Term	492,674	20.6	452,485	16.6	263,246	21.4	285,624	14.5
Deferred Credits	2,392	0.1	5,452	0.2	2,460	0.2	0	0.0
Net Worth	1,238,861	51.8	1,510,100	55.4	479,746	39.0	884,448	44.9
Total Liab & Net Worth	**2,391,623**	**100.0**	**2,725,813**	**100.0**	**1,230,119**	**100.0**	**1,969,818**	**100.0**
Net Sales	4,364,276	100.0	5,836,859	100.0	3,650,205	100.0	3,641,068	100.0
Gross Profit	1,510,039	34.6	1,844,447	31.6	1,252,020	34.3	1,296,220	35.6
Net Profit After Tax	17,457	0.4	58,369	1.0	120,457	3.3	(65,539)	(1.8)
Working Capital	865,768	—	1,123,035	—	366,575	—	563,368	—

RATIOS	UQ	MED	LQ	UQ	MED	LQ	UQ	MED	LQ	UQ	MED	LQ
SOLVENCY												
Quick Ratio (times)	1.3	0.9	0.6	2.2	1.5	0.9	2.1	1.3	0.7	1.9	1.0	0.6
Current Ratio (times)	4.8	1.8	1.7	5.3	2.7	1.7	3.1	2.0	1.4	3.4	1.9	1.2
Curr Liab To Nw (%)	24.5	44.8	96.8	18.2	41.1	86.6	32.4	78.7	159.7	27.7	93.0	179.0
Curr Liab To Inv (%)	65.5	137.6	349.7	55.6	113.9	268.2	96.1	184.1	456.1	90.8	161.5	297.9
Total Liab To Nw (%)	40.5	88.3	167.3	24.6	73.3	152.9	45.0	93.9	231.9	42.7	113.8	250.2
Fixed Assets To Nw (%)	37.1	56.2	102.7	15.1	38.5	68.8	28.2	47.6	113.5	21.8	41.9	74.5
EFFICIENCY												
Coll Period (days)	16.5	30.5	42.9	27.7	36.1	49.3	25.8	36.2	57.1	38.0	56.6	70.8
Sales To Inv (times)	21.0	13.7	4.4	25.4	12.5	6.9	43.7	21.7	11.1	36.4	11.9	6.5
Assets To Sales (%)	41.2	54.8	85.0	35.4	46.7	60.6	25.0	33.7	46.7	34.2	54.1	62.8
Sales To Nwc (times)	10.5	8.7	2.8	9.7	5.6	3.3	14.8	7.9	4.6	15.0	7.5	5.0
Acct Pay To Sales (%)	3.4	4.6	6.8	1.4	3.9	6.4	2.3	3.6	5.7	2.9	6.0	8.5
PROFITABILITY												
Return On Sales (%)	5.7	0.7	0.0	6.2	2.1	(1.5)	6.2	2.0	0.4	3.9	0.3	(3.8)
Return On Assets (%)	12.9	2.2	0.0	13.2	5.1	(3.3)	16.8	5.4	1.6	6.6	0.6	(6.9)
Return On Nw (%)	19.4	5.2	(3.8)	28.8	8.0	(6.9)	48.0	21.3	4.0	12.8	2.8	(11.8)

Balance Sheet

	SIC 2591 DRPRY,HRDWR,BLINDS (NO BREAKDOWN) 2002 (21 Establishments) $	%	SIC 2599 FURN,FIXTURES, NEC (NO BREAKDOWN) 2002 (33 Establishments) $	%	SIC 26 PAPER,ALLIED PDTS (NO BREAKDOWN) 2002 (304 Establishments) $	%	SIC 2621 PAPER MILLS (NO BREAKDOWN) 2002 (29 Establishments) $	%
Cash	98,912	15.2	286,276	16.2	288,172	6.5	1,303,905	3.8
Accounts Receivable	175,698	27.0	432,948	24.5	1,148,255	25.9	7,480,300	21.8
Notes Receivable	0	0.0	0	0.0	13,300	0.3	137,253	0.4
Inventory	186,110	28.6	323,386	18.3	846,783	19.1	4,220,536	12.3
Other Current	59,216	9.1	155,508	8.8	106,403	2.4	892,146	2.6
Total Current	**519,936**	**79.9**	**1,198,118**	**67.8**	**2,402,913**	**54.2**	**14,034,140**	**40.9**
Fixed Assets	92,404	14.2	406,441	23.0	1,591,597	35.9	14,068,453	41.0
Other Non-current	38,394	5.9	162,576	9.2	438,908	9.9	6,210,708	18.1
Total Assets	**650,734**	**100.0**	**1,767,135**	**100.0**	**4,433,418**	**100.0**	**34,313,301**	**100.0**
Accounts Payable	115,831	17.8	187,316	10.6	704,913	15.9	9,230,278	26.9
Bank Loans	0	0.0	0	0.0	22,167	0.5	549,013	1.6
Notes Payable	40,346	6.2	28,274	1.6	133,003	3.0	1,372,532	4.0
Other Current	127,543	19.6	289,811	16.4	824,616	18.6	13,416,501	39.1
Total Current	**283,720**	**43.6**	**505,401**	**28.6**	**1,684,699**	**38.0**	**24,568,324**	**71.6**
Other Long Term	106,070	16.3	293,344	16.6	1,068,453	24.1	11,426,328	33.3
Deferred Credits	0	0.0	1,767	0.1	17,734	0.4	171,567	0.5
Net Worth	260,944	40.1	966,623	54.7	1,662,532	37.5	(1,852,918)	(5.4)
Total Liab & Net Worth	**650,734**	**100.0**	**1,767,135**	**100.0**	**4,433,418**	**100.0**	**34,313,301**	**100.0**
Net Sales	1,990,012	100.0	4,247,921	100.0	9,066,294	100.0	35,013,572	100.0
Gross Profit	776,105	39.0	1,503,764	35.4	2,529,496	27.9	9,208,569	26.3
Net Profit After Tax	(43,780)	(2.2)	352,577	8.3	208,525	2.3	245,095	0.7
Working Capital	236,216	—	692,717	—	718,214	—	(10,534,184)	—

RATIOS

	SIC 2591 UQ	MED	LQ	SIC 2599 UQ	MED	LQ	SIC 26 UQ	MED	LQ	SIC 2621 UQ	MED	LQ
SOLVENCY												
Quick Ratio (times)	2.2	1.1	0.6	2.5	1.4	1.0	1.6	0.9	0.6	1.0	0.7	0.5
Current Ratio (times)	3.2	2.0	1.3	4.3	2.3	1.6	2.9	1.7	1.2	1.8	1.4	1.1
Curr Liab To Nw (%)	31.2	79.7	141.5	20.1	38.7	98.2	26.6	65.7	148.9	36.7	59.7	121.0
Curr Liab To Inv (%)	95.5	122.5	178.6	95.7	155.1	274.3	97.5	159.2	253.7	128.5	159.0	252.4
Total Liab To Nw (%)	35.5	98.8	200.3	21.9	71.0	200.1	56.2	153.2	316.6	148.7	218.4	280.4
Fixed Assets To Nw (%)	15.9	24.5	36.7	18.8	35.8	67.0	42.7	91.8	173.4	85.3	145.6	192.0
EFFICIENCY												
Coll Period (days)	23.7	36.1	45.3	26.3	43.1	60.6	32.9	40.2	49.6	36.0	46.7	59.7
Sales To Inv (times)	16.9	11.6	6.5	19.4	12.9	9.1	18.8	11.5	7.9	11.4	9.1	7.9
Assets To Sales (%)	24.7	32.7	40.6	31.6	41.6	69.1	35.0	48.9	73.2	46.5	98.0	130.5
Sales To Nwc (times)	15.1	10.0	5.7	11.6	5.7	2.9	15.5	8.3	5.4	28.3	10.0	7.1
Acct Pay To Sales (%)	3.5	6.7	8.5	2.5	4.3	7.5	3.2	5.9	9.5	5.4	7.4	12.9
PROFITABILITY												
Return On Sales (%)	1.4	0.9	0.3	8.8	3.4	1.1	5.2	1.7	0.2	4.8	2.6	(1.0)
Return On Assets (%)	6.1	4.0	1.0	24.3	8.1	1.9	9.5	3.3	0.3	7.1	2.8	(1.8)
Return On Nw (%)	14.5	7.9	1.5	34.4	19.9	2.7	25.9	9.2	1.0	20.5	8.1	(6.6)

SIC 2631 PAPERBOARD MILLS
(NO BREAKDOWN)
2002 (19 Establishments)

	$	%
Cash	468,972	4.2
Accounts Receivable	2,266,697	20.3
Notes Receivable	78,162	0.7
Inventory	1,563,239	14.0
Other Current	569,465	5.1
Total Current	**4,946,535**	**44.3**
Fixed Assets	3,807,604	34.1
Other Non-current	2,411,855	21.6
Total Assets	**11,165,994**	**100.0**
Accounts Payable	1,261,757	11.3
Bank Loans	133,992	1.2
Notes Payable	301,482	2.7
Other Current	1,429,247	12.8
Total Current	**3,126,478**	**28.0**
Other Long Term	4,287,742	38.4
Deferred Credits	0	0.0
Net Worth	3,751,774	33.6
Total Liab & Net Worth	**11,165,994**	**100.0**
Net Sales	16,112,545	100.0
Gross Profit	3,802,561	23.6
Net Profit After Tax	32,225	0.2
Working Capital	1,820,057	—

RATIOS	UQ	MED	LQ
SOLVENCY			
Quick Ratio (times)	1.0	0.6	0.4
Current Ratio (times)	2.1	1.3	1.1
Curr Liab To Nw (%)	49.4	69.2	197.8
Curr Liab To Inv (%)	153.0	203.4	245.4
Total Liab To Nw (%)	57.1	307.7	489.1
Fixed Assets To Nw (%)	65.0	132.9	223.7
EFFICIENCY			
Coll Period (days)	28.1	31.0	40.5
Sales To Inv (times)	15.2	11.3	8.7
Assets To Sales (%)	37.3	69.3	124.3
Sales To Nwc (times)	24.9	12.7	6.6
Acct Pay To Sales (%)	6.3	6.7	9.0
PROFITABILITY			
Return On Sales (%)	2.7	0.6	(0.6)
Return On Assets (%)	3.8	1.1	(1.4)
Return On Nw (%)	7.0	1.4	(8.1)

SIC 2653 CRRGTD SLD FBR BXS
(NO BREAKDOWN)
2002 (63 Establishments)

	$	%
Cash	297,230	7.6
Accounts Receivable	934,709	23.9
Notes Receivable	7,822	0.2
Inventory	563,172	14.4
Other Current	234,655	6.0
Total Current	**2,037,588**	**52.1**
Fixed Assets	1,474,416	37.7
Other Non-current	398,913	10.2
Total Assets	**3,910,917**	**100.0**
Accounts Payable	453,666	11.6
Bank Loans	15,644	0.4
Notes Payable	19,555	0.5
Other Current	598,370	15.3
Total Current	**1,087,235**	**27.8**
Other Long Term	868,223	22.2
Deferred Credits	23,466	0.6
Net Worth	1,931,993	49.4
Total Liab & Net Worth	**3,910,917**	**100.0**
Net Sales	8,164,754	100.0
Gross Profit	2,163,660	26.5
Net Profit After Tax	220,448	2.7
Working Capital	950,353	—

RATIOS	UQ	MED	LQ
Quick Ratio (times)	1.9	1.1	0.7
Current Ratio (times)	3.4	2.1	1.2
Curr Liab To Nw (%)	23.9	64.3	139.3
Curr Liab To Inv (%)	128.2	202.3	342.3
Total Liab To Nw (%)	55.2	141.0	322.1
Fixed Assets To Nw (%)	54.1	97.0	197.3
Coll Period (days)	32.1	38.7	46.4
Sales To Inv (times)	27.0	17.5	11.2
Assets To Sales (%)	34.5	47.9	65.9
Sales To Nwc (times)	19.3	8.7	6.3
Acct Pay To Sales (%)	3.0	4.3	9.5
Return On Sales (%)	4.8	1.2	0.1
Return On Assets (%)	9.5	2.0	0.2
Return On Nw (%)	19.8	7.7	0.6

SIC 2657 FLDNG PAPERBRD BXS
(NO BREAKDOWN)
2002 (24 Establishments)

	$	%
Cash	390,333	4.8
Accounts Receivable	1,780,895	21.9
Notes Receivable	0	0.0
Inventory	1,601,992	19.7
Other Current	268,355	3.3
Total Current	**4,041,575**	**49.7**
Fixed Assets	3,431,679	42.2
Other Non-current	658,687	8.1
Total Assets	**8,131,941**	**100.0**
Accounts Payable	674,951	8.3
Bank Loans	0	0.0
Notes Payable	504,180	6.2
Other Current	1,089,681	13.4
Total Current	**2,268,812**	**27.9**
Other Long Term	1,967,929	24.2
Deferred Credits	65,056	0.8
Net Worth	3,830,144	47.1
Total Liab & Net Worth	**8,131,941**	**100.0**
Net Sales	13,690,136	100.0
Gross Profit	3,614,196	26.4
Net Profit After Tax	205,352	1.5
Working Capital	1,772,763	—

RATIOS	UQ	MED	LQ
Quick Ratio (times)	1.3	0.9	0.6
Current Ratio (times)	2.6	2.1	1.1
Curr Liab To Nw (%)	22.5	49.7	154.0
Curr Liab To Inv (%)	77.1	100.8	215.5
Total Liab To Nw (%)	56.8	126.8	253.3
Fixed Assets To Nw (%)	55.7	106.1	152.1
Coll Period (days)	33.6	39.8	51.5
Sales To Inv (times)	15.4	11.2	7.0
Assets To Sales (%)	35.6	59.4	93.5
Sales To Nwc (times)	9.3	7.3	4.2
Acct Pay To Sales (%)	2.7	4.0	7.9
Return On Sales (%)	5.2	1.3	0.6
Return On Assets (%)	6.8	1.8	1.3
Return On Nw (%)	11.0	4.1	3.2

SIC 2671 PAPER CTD LMND,PCKG
(NO BREAKDOWN)
2002 (17 Establishments)

	$	%
Cash	560,956	5.9
Accounts Receivable	2,072,685	21.8
Notes Receivable	19,015	0.2
Inventory	1,920,561	20.2
Other Current	275,725	2.9
Total Current	**4,848,942**	**51.0**
Fixed Assets	3,622,445	38.1
Other Non-current	1,036,343	10.9
Total Assets	**9,507,730**	**100.0**
Accounts Payable	1,445,175	15.2
Bank Loans	85,570	0.9
Notes Payable	142,616	1.5
Other Current	1,806,468	19.0
Total Current	**3,479,829**	**36.6**
Other Long Term	2,643,149	27.8
Deferred Credits	0	0.0
Net Worth	3,384,752	35.6
Total Liab & Net Worth	**9,507,730**	**100.0**
Net Sales	16,449,360	100.0
Gross Profit	4,276,834	26.0
Net Profit After Tax	674,424	4.1
Working Capital	1,369,113	—

RATIOS	UQ	MED	LQ
Quick Ratio (times)	1.3	0.8	0.6
Current Ratio (times)	2.2	1.6	1.0
Curr Liab To Nw (%)	40.7	83.8	139.4
Curr Liab To Inv (%)	108.9	192.8	221.4
Total Liab To Nw (%)	91.6	164.4	301.9
Fixed Assets To Nw (%)	62.4	95.4	180.4
Coll Period (days)	36.5	44.9	49.3
Sales To Inv (times)	18.1	14.0	9.1
Assets To Sales (%)	37.8	57.8	73.2
Sales To Nwc (times)	12.4	8.7	6.7
Acct Pay To Sales (%)	3.9	9.0	10.0
Return On Sales (%)	6.2	4.3	0.7
Return On Assets (%)	11.0	7.3	2.0
Return On Nw (%)	22.3	13.2	6.0

Page 43

Balance Sheet Items

	SIC 2672 PAPER CTD LMND,NEC (NO BREAKDOWN) 2002 (25 Establishments) $	%	SIC 2673 BAGS:PLSTC,LMND,CTD (NO BREAKDOWN) 2002 (27 Establishments) $	%	SIC 2675 DIE-CUT PAPER BOARD (NO BREAKDOWN) 2002 (10 Establishments) $	%	SIC 2677 ENVELOPES (NO BREAKDOWN) 2002 (10 Establishments) $	%
Cash	290,829	6.7	302,721	7.6	64,649	8.2	514,780	9.3
Accounts Receivable	1,085,182	25.0	2,230,577	56.0	195,523	24.8	1,688,258	30.5
Notes Receivable	13,022	0.3	19,916	0.5	1,577	0.2	0	0.0
Inventory	863,804	19.9	1,179,020	29.6	209,714	26.6	597,809	10.8
Other Current	329,895	7.6	(1,370,212)	(34.4)	57,553	7.3	188,200	3.4
Total Current	**2,582,732**	**59.5**	**2,362,022**	**59.3**	**529,016**	**67.1**	**2,989,047**	**54.0**
Fixed Assets	1,341,284	30.9	1,366,229	34.3	214,445	27.2	1,965,022	35.5
Other Non-current	416,710	9.6	254,923	6.4	44,939	5.7	581,204	10.5
Total Assets	**4,340,726**	**100.0**	**3,983,174**	**100.0**	**788,400**	**100.0**	**5,535,273**	**100.0**
Accounts Payable	568,635	13.1	1,593,270	40.0	86,724	11.0	669,768	12.1
Bank Loans	0	0.0	0	0.0	11,826	1.5	22,141	0.4
Notes Payable	56,429	1.3	219,075	5.5	6,307	0.8	215,876	3.9
Other Current	798,694	18.4	541,711	13.6	197,100	25.0	1,223,295	22.1
Total Current	**1,423,758**	**32.8**	**2,354,056**	**59.1**	**301,957**	**38.3**	**2,131,080**	**38.5**
Other Long Term	811,716	18.7	645,274	16.2	253,077	32.1	1,400,424	25.3
Deferred Credits	0	0.0	0	0.0	0	0.0	33,212	0.6
Net Worth	2,105,252	48.5	983,844	24.7	233,366	29.6	1,970,557	35.6
Total Liab & Net Worth	**4,340,726**	**100.0**	**3,983,174**	**100.0**	**788,400**	**100.0**	**5,535,273**	**100.0**
Net Sales	7,964,635	100.0	9,177,820	100.0	2,418,405	100.0	11,319,577	100.0
Gross Profit	2,747,799	34.5	2,285,277	24.9	899,647	37.2	3,746,780	33.1
Net Profit After Tax	390,267	4.9	284,512	3.1	74,971	3.1	203,752	1.8
Working Capital	1,158,974	—	7,966	—	227,059	—	857,967	—

RATIOS

	SIC 2672 UQ	MED	LQ	SIC 2673 UQ	MED	LQ	SIC 2675 UQ	MED	LQ	SIC 2677 UQ	MED	LQ
SOLVENCY												
Quick Ratio (times)	2.2	1.1	0.6	1.3	0.8	0.5	2.5	1.0	0.3	2.6	1.4	0.8
Current Ratio (times)	5.0	1.7	1.2	2.4	1.5	1.2	3.4	1.7	1.2	3.7	1.9	1.2
Curr Liab To Nw (%)	14.4	73.3	122.8	44.8	143.0	212.2	20.3	94.9	237.3	23.0	54.1	111.7
Curr Liab To Inv (%)	119.2	147.4	245.7	138.1	188.7	288.5	77.4	107.8	129.8	77.0	202.1	682.4
Total Liab To Nw (%)	38.1	149.1	228.9	57.5	155.1	367.9	23.3	106.2	388.1	88.6	120.9	292.9
Fixed Assets To Nw (%)	36.1	77.7	114.7	24.5	68.0	163.3	17.4	48.5	141.5	60.4	91.5	175.9
EFFICIENCY												
Coll Period (days)	38.7	41.3	51.8	30.5	36.5	49.5	29.2	33.8	34.7	41.6	50.7	53.7
Sales To Inv (times)	17.0	12.8	8.2	17.6	12.6	7.7	15.0	12.3	6.2	52.0	18.2	11.1
Assets To Sales (%)	36.2	54.5	69.3	28.9	43.4	49.1	26.2	32.6	34.2	41.0	48.9	56.6
Sales To Nwc (times)	10.2	7.8	3.8	13.6	8.9	4.4	13.2	8.4	4.0	20.2	6.7	5.6
Acct Pay To Sales (%)	1.7	4.8	8.9	4.0	7.2	13.1	1.4	2.6	8.6	1.7	3.8	6.9
PROFITABILITY												
Return On Sales (%)	7.6	1.7	0.7	3.9	2.1	0.3	7.3	4.1	0.6	5.7	2.5	0.0
Return On Assets (%)	8.9	3.7	1.6	12.1	5.5	1.3	29.6	11.5	1.0	12.1	4.5	0.0
Return On Nw (%)	26.8	10.0	3.8	38.9	15.6	4.2	44.5	36.6	7.6	30.4	7.5	0.8

Balance Sheet

	SIC 2679 CNVTD PPR PRDTS, NEC (NO BREAKDOWN) 2002 (46 Establishments) $	%	SIC 27 PRINTING, PUBLISHING (NO BREAKDOWN) 2002 (1289 Establishments) $	%	SIC 2711 NEWSPAPERS (NO BREAKDOWN) 2002 (65 Establishments) $	%	SIC 2721 PERIODICALS (NO BREAKDOWN) 2002 (82 Establishments) $	%
Cash	142,014	7.3	178,378	12.4	234,121	13.5	560,457	21.6
Accounts Receivable	496,076	25.5	368,264	25.6	362,453	20.9	601,972	23.2
Notes Receivable	5,836	0.3	10,070	0.7	5,203	0.3	10,379	0.4
Inventory	396,861	20.4	151,046	10.5	46,824	2.7	88,220	3.4
Other Current	171,196	8.8	94,942	6.6	140,472	8.1	293,201	11.3
Total Current	**1,211,983**	**62.3**	**802,700**	**55.8**	**789,073**	**45.5**	**1,554,229**	**59.9**
Fixed Assets	622,527	32.0	490,539	34.1	534,142	30.8	438,505	16.9
Other Non-current	110,888	5.7	145,292	10.1	411,011	23.7	601,973	23.2
Total Assets	**1,945,398**	**100.0**	**1,438,531**	**100.0**	**1,734,226**	**100.0**	**2,594,707**	**100.0**
Accounts Payable	305,427	15.7	204,271	14.2	142,207	8.2	978,205	37.7
Bank Loans	7,782	0.4	7,193	0.5	0	0.0	0	0.0
Notes Payable	99,215	5.1	71,927	5.0	15,608	0.9	848,469	32.7
Other Current	252,902	13.0	304,968	21.2	277,476	16.0	1,816,295	70.0
Total Current	**665,326**	**34.2**	**588,359**	**40.9**	**435,291**	**25.1**	**3,642,969**	**140.4**
Other Long Term	453,278	23.3	385,526	26.8	452,633	26.1	508,562	19.6
Deferred Credits	3,891	0.2	10,070	0.7	1,734	0.1	140,114	5.4
Net Worth	822,903	42.3	454,576	31.6	844,568	48.7	(1,696,938)	(65.4)
Total Liab & Net Worth	**1,945,398**	**100.0**	**1,438,531**	**100.0**	**1,734,226**	**100.0**	**2,594,707**	**100.0**
Net Sales	4,744,873	100.0	3,067,230	100.0	3,322,272	100.0	4,980,244	100.0
Gross Profit	1,447,186	30.5	1,331,178	43.4	1,853,828	55.8	2,275,972	45.7
Net Profit After Tax	156,581	3.3	55,210	1.8	172,758	5.2	(49,802)	(1.0)
Working Capital	546,657	—	214,341	—	353,782	—	(2,088,740)	—

RATIOS

	UQ	MED	LQ	UQ	MED	LQ	UQ	MED	LQ	UQ	MED	LQ
SOLVENCY												
Quick Ratio (times)	1.7	1.1	0.6	2.3	1.2	0.7	2.6	1.3	0.8	2.3	1.1	0.5
Current Ratio (times)	3.8	2.0	1.3	3.4	1.8	1.1	4.0	1.8	1.2	3.4	1.6	0.8
Curr Liab To Nw (%)	28.2	65.9	148.8	22.6	57.4	133.4	11.1	27.2	71.5	27.5	50.7	164.8
Curr Liab To Inv (%)	78.9	145.6	252.0	141.9	328.2	762.7	305.7	800.8	999.9	178.8	789.1	999.9
Total Liab To Nw (%)	53.4	146.4	297.7	39.5	113.2	288.6	17.3	87.3	163.4	34.6	123.7	357.0
Fixed Assets To Nw (%)	35.3	64.8	142.4	28.4	67.1	163.1	19.0	44.0	94.3	12.6	27.7	62.5
EFFICIENCY												
Coll Period (days)	30.5	39.8	44.5	30.7	40.9	54.8	31.0	35.4	42.3	27.0	45.8	56.8
Sales To Inv (times)	24.3	10.8	6.6	62.0	29.7	13.7	107.4	64.3	45.1	72.7	26.8	14.1
Assets To Sales (%)	32.6	41.0	59.8	32.1	46.9	68.9	32.1	52.2	96.0	31.2	52.1	112.1
Sales To Nwc (times)	15.1	9.7	4.9	15.2	8.1	4.4	18.8	10.4	5.3	12.5	5.5	2.4
Acct Pay To Sales (%)	3.4	6.3	9.5	2.6	4.4	7.4	1.8	3.2	4.4	1.9	4.1	6.9
PROFITABILITY												
Return On Sales (%)	5.9	1.7	0.5	4.9	1.4	(0.8)	9.2	3.8	1.0	5.0	1.8	(7.8)
Return On Assets (%)	14.4	3.9	0.9	10.3	3.1	(1.7)	11.3	6.5	2.7	10.7	3.4	(7.3)
Return On Nw (%)	34.4	14.2	4.0	28.0	9.2	(1.8)	26.9	15.3	5.0	32.4	14.2	(13.1)

…

SIC 2731 BOOK PUBLISHING (NO BREAKDOWN) 2002 (113 Establishments)

	$	%
Cash	278,720	11.0
Accounts Receivable	559,973	22.1
Notes Receivable	25,338	1.0
Inventory	724,671	28.6
Other Current	263,517	10.4
Total Current	**1,852,219**	**73.1**
Fixed Assets	352,200	13.9
Other Non-current	329,396	13.0
Total Assets	**2,533,815**	**100.0**
Accounts Payable	329,396	13.0
Bank Loans	5,068	0.2
Notes Payable	40,541	1.6
Other Current	757,610	29.9
Total Current	**1,132,615**	**44.7**
Other Long Term	478,891	18.9
Deferred Credits	15,203	0.6
Net Worth	907,106	35.8
Total Liab & Net Worth	**2,533,815**	**100.0**
Net Sales	3,666,881	100.0
Gross Profit	2,046,120	55.8
Net Profit After Tax	62,337	1.7
Working Capital	719,604	—

RATIOS	UQ	MED	LQ
SOLVENCY			
Quick Ratio (times)	1.8	1.0	0.5
Current Ratio (times)	3.8	2.4	1.5
Curr Liab To Nw (%)	20.3	47.2	98.7
Curr Liab To Inv (%)	56.7	92.6	165.4
Total Liab To Nw (%)	27.6	68.1	179.7
Fixed Assets To Nw (%)	6.1	18.0	54.6
EFFICIENCY			
Coll Period (days)	30.3	51.1	79.1
Sales To Inv (times)	8.6	4.5	2.6
Assets To Sales (%)	43.1	69.1	99.6
Sales To Nwc (times)	6.6	3.5	2.1
Acct Pay To Sales (%)	4.1	6.2	11.2
PROFITABILITY			
Return On Sales (%)	6.6	2.1	(2.6)
Return On Assets (%)	9.2	3.1	(3.4)
Return On Nw (%)	24.3	7.3	(3.9)

SIC 2732 BOOK PRINTING (NO BREAKDOWN) 2002 (16 Establishments)

	$	%
Cash	518,506	14.9
Accounts Receivable	800,379	23.0
Notes Receivable	3,480	0.1
Inventory	647,263	18.6
Other Current	69,599	2.0
Total Current	**2,039,227**	**58.6**
Fixed Assets	1,224,928	35.2
Other Non-current	215,754	6.2
Total Assets	**3,479,909**	**100.0**
Accounts Payable	452,388	13.0
Bank Loans	10,440	0.3
Notes Payable	27,839	0.8
Other Current	361,911	10.4
Total Current	**852,578**	**24.5**
Other Long Term	838,658	24.1
Deferred Credits	0	0.0
Net Worth	1,788,673	51.4
Total Liab & Net Worth	**3,479,909**	**100.0**
Net Sales	5,838,773	100.0
Gross Profit	1,950,150	33.4
Net Profit After Tax	87,582	1.5
Working Capital	1,186,649	—

RATIOS	UQ	MED	LQ
SOLVENCY			
Quick Ratio (times)	3.4	1.6	1.3
Current Ratio (times)	4.2	2.4	2.0
Curr Liab To Nw (%)	16.9	30.9	68.5
Curr Liab To Inv (%)	130.8	176.8	273.0
Total Liab To Nw (%)	17.8	47.6	133.0
Fixed Assets To Nw (%)	20.1	48.5	74.9
EFFICIENCY			
Coll Period (days)	40.9	49.1	56.6
Sales To Inv (times)	19.7	14.8	9.4
Assets To Sales (%)	43.8	59.6	86.6
Sales To Nwc (times)	9.3	6.3	3.8
Acct Pay To Sales (%)	2.8	4.6	7.5
PROFITABILITY			
Return On Sales (%)	3.5	1.8	(0.7)
Return On Assets (%)	4.9	2.3	(0.8)
Return On Nw (%)	10.0	4.0	(0.5)

SIC 2741 MISC PUBLISHING (NO BREAKDOWN) 2002 (58 Establishments)

	$	%
Cash	251,844	16.5
Accounts Receivable	453,320	29.7
Notes Receivable	18,316	1.2
Inventory	120,580	7.9
Other Current	170,949	11.2
Total Current	**1,015,009**	**66.5**
Fixed Assets	280,845	18.4
Other Non-current	230,476	15.1
Total Assets	**1,526,330**	**100.0**
Accounts Payable	149,580	9.8
Bank Loans	15,263	1.0
Notes Payable	38,158	2.5
Other Current	438,058	28.7
Total Current	**641,059**	**42.0**
Other Long Term	415,162	27.2
Deferred Credits	6,105	0.4
Net Worth	464,004	30.4
Total Liab & Net Worth	**1,526,330**	**100.0**
Net Sales	3,445,440	100.0
Gross Profit	1,812,301	52.6
Net Profit After Tax	75,800	2.2
Working Capital	373,950	—

RATIOS	UQ	MED	LQ
SOLVENCY			
Quick Ratio (times)	1.9	1.2	0.7
Current Ratio (times)	2.8	2.0	1.2
Curr Liab To Nw (%)	33.0	61.6	109.7
Curr Liab To Inv (%)	94.2	222.3	547.7
Total Liab To Nw (%)	40.2	94.6	166.3
Fixed Assets To Nw (%)	9.4	32.5	73.4
EFFICIENCY			
Coll Period (days)	24.5	42.7	74.8
Sales To Inv (times)	76.6	14.7	9.3
Assets To Sales (%)	30.9	44.3	72.9
Sales To Nwc (times)	10.5	6.4	4.2
Acct Pay To Sales (%)	1.6	3.2	7.8
PROFITABILITY			
Return On Sales (%)	8.1	2.7	(0.1)
Return On Assets (%)	12.0	4.3	(0.1)
Return On Nw (%)	33.1	12.2	1.7

SIC 2752 COMMRCL PRTNG, LITH (NO BREAKDOWN) 2002 (635 Establishments)

	$	%
Cash	134,348	10.7
Accounts Receivable	323,942	25.8
Notes Receivable	7,534	0.6
Inventory	97,936	7.8
Other Current	66,545	5.3
Total Current	**630,305**	**50.2**
Fixed Assets	537,392	42.8
Other Non-current	87,891	7.0
Total Assets	**1,255,588**	**100.0**
Accounts Payable	160,715	12.8
Bank Loans	7,534	0.6
Notes Payable	42,690	3.4
Other Current	195,872	15.6
Total Current	**406,811**	**32.4**
Other Long Term	404,299	32.2
Deferred Credits	5,022	0.4
Net Worth	439,456	35.0
Total Liab & Net Worth	**1,255,588**	**100.0**
Net Sales	2,784,009	100.0
Gross Profit	1,116,388	40.1
Net Profit After Tax	33,408	1.2
Working Capital	223,494	—

RATIOS	UQ	MED	LQ
SOLVENCY			
Quick Ratio (times)	2.2	1.2	0.8
Current Ratio (times)	3.0	1.6	1.1
Curr Liab To Nw (%)	26.5	66.3	146.7
Curr Liab To Inv (%)	219.5	438.4	870.2
Total Liab To Nw (%)	57.5	162.7	355.9
Fixed Assets To Nw (%)	50.5	109.6	215.6
EFFICIENCY			
Coll Period (days)	30.7	39.8	52.9
Sales To Inv (times)	75.2	38.1	21.0
Assets To Sales (%)	32.1	45.1	61.6
Sales To Nwc (times)	17.8	9.7	5.9
Acct Pay To Sales (%)	2.7	4.4	6.9
PROFITABILITY			
Return On Sales (%)	3.5	1.0	(1.1)
Return On Assets (%)	8.2	2.1	(2.2)
Return On Nw (%)	22.5	7.0	(2.8)

SIC 2754 COMMRCL PRTNG,GRVRE (NO BREAKDOWN) 2002 (18 Establishments)
SIC 2759 COMMRCL PRTNG, NEC (NO BREAKDOWN) 2002 (216 Establishments)
SIC 2761 MANIFOLD BUS FORMS (NO BREAKDOWN) 2002 (21 Establishments)
SIC 2782 BLNKBKS,LSLF BNDRS (NO BREAKDOWN) 2002 (16 Establishments)

	SIC 2754 $	%	SIC 2759 $	%	SIC 2761 $	%	SIC 2782 $	%
Cash	470,685	11.5	135,508	13.2	412,682	13.6	202,949	10.4
Accounts Receivable	1,375,219	33.6	280,256	27.3	907,293	29.9	491,761	25.2
Notes Receivable	4,093	0.1	7,186	0.7	3,034	0.1	78,057	4.0
Inventory	597,565	14.6	126,269	12.3	379,303	12.5	446,878	22.9
Other Current	306,968	7.5	58,515	5.7	136,550	4.5	167,822	8.6
Total Current	**2,754,530**	**67.3**	**607,734**	**59.2**	**1,838,862**	**60.6**	**1,387,467**	**71.1**
Fixed Assets	1,289,268	31.5	346,983	33.8	837,502	27.6	251,735	12.9
Other Non-current	49,115	1.2	71,861	7.0	358,062	11.8	312,229	16.0
Total Assets	**4,092,913**	**100.0**	**1,026,578**	**100.0**	**3,034,426**	**100.0**	**1,951,431**	**100.0**
Accounts Payable	683,516	16.7	134,482	13.1	518,887	17.1	341,500	17.5
Bank Loans	12,279	0.3	5,133	0.5	87,998	2.9	0	0.0
Notes Payable	171,902	4.2	37,983	3.7	12,138	0.4	78,057	4.0
Other Current	798,119	19.5	173,492	16.9	324,683	10.7	321,987	16.5
Total Current	**1,665,816**	**40.7**	**351,090**	**34.2**	**943,706**	**31.1**	**741,544**	**38.0**
Other Long Term	794,024	19.4	230,980	22.5	713,091	23.5	175,629	9.0
Deferred Credits	12,279	0.3	0	0.0	9,103	0.3	81,960	4.2
Net Worth	1,620,794	39.6	444,508	43.3	1,368,526	45.1	952,298	48.8
Total Liab & Net Worth	**4,092,913**	**100.0**	**1,026,578**	**100.0**	**3,034,426**	**100.0**	**1,951,431**	**100.0**
Net Sales	8,801,963	100.0	2,612,158	100.0	5,996,889	100.0	4,496,385	100.0
Gross Profit	2,816,628	32.0	1,162,410	44.5	1,631,154	27.2	1,654,670	36.8
Net Profit After Tax	360,880	4.1	70,528	2.7	173,910	2.9	179,855	4.0
Working Capital	1,088,714	—	256,644	—	895,156	—	645,923	—

RATIOS	UQ	MED	LQ	UQ	MED	LQ	UQ	MED	LQ	UQ	MED	LQ
SOLVENCY												
Quick Ratio (times)	1.8	1.2	0.7	2.7	1.4	0.7	2.7	1.6	1.0	1.3	1.0	0.6
Current Ratio (times)	2.2	1.5	1.2	4.0	1.9	1.1	4.8	2.0	1.6	2.3	1.7	1.4
Curr Liab To Nw (%)	42.3	72.1	104.4	19.3	48.7	121.7	15.8	49.1	88.1	61.1	87.9	150.3
Curr Liab To Inv (%)	128.2	201.9	461.4	110.4	218.9	592.9	127.7	239.5	394.8	91.4	159.1	372.5
Total Liab To Nw (%)	75.6	156.8	253.5	30.0	84.0	197.1	32.5	95.6	137.9	68.7	137.7	172.4
Fixed Assets To Nw (%)	40.4	61.2	118.2	28.9	59.8	131.8	14.3	52.5	79.4	11.2	27.1	44.8
EFFICIENCY												
Coll Period (days)	40.4	51.7	61.5	30.3	40.4	50.0	33.2	39.8	46.7	28.1	40.9	49.6
Sales To Inv (times)	24.1	14.4	11.2	48.3	22.3	11.3	29.2	18.4	12.8	23.7	15.5	7.1
Assets To Sales (%)	31.4	46.5	66.0	27.7	39.3	57.8	37.8	50.6	73.8	30.6	43.4	52.1
Sales To Nwc (times)	17.9	8.3	6.6	15.4	7.3	4.7	10.3	3.6	2.7	15.1	8.2	4.9
Acct Pay To Sales (%)	4.5	5.6	7.0	2.6	4.4	6.9	3.1	4.5	13.8	2.9	4.7	6.3
PROFITABILITY												
Return On Sales (%)	4.0	1.0	0.6	7.1	2.4	(0.1)	3.5	2.1	0.1	6.8	1.8	0.5
Return On Assets (%)	9.2	2.7	0.9	17.4	6.9	(0.1)	15.5	2.5	0.5	16.7	5.3	1.1
Return On Nw (%)	15.6	7.7	3.4	36.8	18.4	0.4	20.9	7.5	1.9	29.8	15.3	2.1

Page 47

	SIC 2789 BKBNDNG,RLTD WORK (NO BREAKDOWN) 2002 (17 Establishments) $	%	SIC 2791 TYPESETTING (NO BREAKDOWN) 2002 (10 Establishments) $	%	SIC 2796 PLATEMAKING SRVCS (NO BREAKDOWN) 2002 (17 Establishments) $	%	SIC 28 CHEMICALS,ALLIED PDT (NO BREAKDOWN) 2002 (1022 Establishments) $	%
Cash	199,087	13.6	73,026	8.6	249,952	13.8	791,345	12.8
Accounts Receivable	332,300	22.7	230,966	27.2	565,109	31.2	1,180,835	19.1
Notes Receivable	7,319	0.5	0	0.0	1,811	0.1	49,459	0.8
Inventory	124,429	8.5	45,004	5.3	159,390	8.8	1,131,376	18.3
Other Current	141,996	9.7	5,945	0.7	115,920	6.4	605,873	9.8
Total Current	**805,131**	**55.0**	**354,941**	**41.8**	**1,092,182**	**60.3**	**3,758,888**	**60.8**
Fixed Assets	442,090	30.2	494,199	58.2	393,041	21.7	1,607,419	26.0
Other Non-current	216,654	14.8	0	0.0	326,024	18.0	816,074	13.2
Total Assets	**1,463,875**	**100.0**	**849,140**	**100.0**	**1,811,247**	**100.0**	**6,182,381**	**100.0**
Accounts Payable	60,019	4.1	136,712	16.1	284,366	15.7	902,628	14.6
Bank Loans	0	0.0	0	0.0	9,056	0.5	18,547	0.3
Notes Payable	52,700	3.6	78,121	9.2	119,542	6.6	185,471	3.0
Other Current	175,664	12.0	305,690	36.0	287,989	15.9	1,885,626	30.5
Total Current	**288,383**	**19.7**	**520,523**	**61.3**	**700,953**	**38.7**	**2,992,272**	**48.4**
Other Long Term	238,612	16.3	270,027	31.8	302,478	16.7	1,323,030	21.4
Deferred Credits	2,928	0.2	1,698	0.2	1,811	0.1	37,094	0.6
Net Worth	933,952	63.8	56,892	6.7	806,005	44.5	1,829,985	29.6
Total Liab & Net Worth	**1,463,875**	**100.0**	**849,140**	**100.0**	**1,811,247**	**100.0**	**6,182,381**	**100.0**
Net Sales	2,368,730	100.0	1,521,756	100.0	3,972,033	100.0	8,610,558	100.0
Gross Profit	1,324,120	55.9	558,484	36.7	1,235,302	31.1	3,633,655	42.2
Net Profit After Tax	75,799	3.2	4,565	0.3	(83,413)	(2.1)	43,053	0.5
Working Capital	516,748	—	(165,582)	—	391,229	—	766,616	—

RATIOS	UQ	MED	LQ	UQ	MED	LQ	UQ	MED	LQ	UQ	MED	LQ
SOLVENCY												
Quick Ratio (times)	4.9	2.1	1.1	1.4	0.7	0.5	2.2	1.4	0.6	2.0	1.1	0.6
Current Ratio (times)	6.8	4.6	1.4	2.0	1.0	0.6	3.7	1.9	1.0	4.1	2.1	1.3
Curr Liab To Nw (%)	10.7	20.7	43.3	73.5	133.8	595.8	18.8	53.3	247.8	20.1	43.7	92.6
Curr Liab To Inv (%)	40.7	421.2	955.0	109.6	109.6	999.9	290.8	424.2	741.7	89.2	155.1	286.4
Total Liab To Nw (%)	19.0	38.6	76.9	194.5	577.7	898.0	49.1	75.6	269.9	30.6	72.0	177.1
Fixed Assets To Nw (%)	22.0	35.6	89.5	145.8	388.0	558.2	30.8	60.5	85.0	16.7	41.8	87.4
EFFICIENCY												
Coll Period (days)	33.2	51.8	56.2	46.7	49.3	66.8	47.9	61.7	65.3	30.3	44.9	60.8
Sales To Inv (times)	146.4	65.6	21.2	108.6	11.8	4.4	45.7	32.1	24.1	14.8	8.8	5.6
Assets To Sales (%)	53.7	61.8	63.1	35.4	55.8	110.7	43.4	45.6	65.7	42.2	71.8	127.2
Sales To Nwc (times)	9.6	3.8	2.9	8.3	6.8	5.6	11.1	7.1	3.4	9.4	4.8	2.4
Acct Pay To Sales (%)	1.5	1.8	5.4	2.6	5.0	16.8	2.3	2.7	9.5	3.8	6.7	11.0
PROFITABILITY												
Return On Sales (%)	6.8	3.3	(2.8)	6.8	1.6	(6.6)	2.4	(0.2)	(4.4)	6.6	1.9	(5.1)
Return On Assets (%)	10.4	5.3	(4.9)	8.7	4.6	(3.9)	5.3	(0.7)	(9.7)	9.8	3.3	(7.2)
Return On Nw (%)	11.9	6.5	(9.7)	48.5	37.0	2.5	9.5	(2.4)	(25.9)	21.3	8.1	(10.4)

SIC 2819 IND INORG CHEM,NEC (NO BREAKDOWN) 2002 (63 Establishments)
SIC 2821 PLASTICS MTRLS,RSNS (NO BREAKDOWN) 2002 (63 Establishments)
SIC 2833 MEDCNLS,BOTANICALS (NO BREAKDOWN) 2002 (31 Establishments)
SIC 2834 PHRMCTCL PREPRTNS (NO BREAKDOWN) 2002 (201 Establishments)

	SIC 2819 $	%	SIC 2821 $	%	SIC 2833 $	%	SIC 2834 $	%
Cash	398,811	7.3	592,231	12.1	546,515	8.1	7,937,352	21.6
Accounts Receivable	1,109,022	20.3	1,101,256	22.5	1,214,479	18.0	4,299,399	11.7
Notes Receivable	60,095	1.1	39,156	0.8	6,747	0.1	36,747	0.1
Inventory	863,180	15.8	748,854	15.3	1,504,604	22.3	4,630,122	12.6
Other Current	366,031	6.7	254,511	5.2	479,045	7.1	6,504,219	17.7
Total Current	**2,797,139**	**51.2**	**2,736,008**	**55.9**	**3,751,390**	**55.6**	**23,407,839**	**63.7**
Fixed Assets	1,917,570	35.1	1,556,441	31.8	2,435,705	36.1	7,239,159	19.7
Other Non-current	748,453	13.7	602,020	12.3	560,009	8.3	6,100,002	16.6
Total Assets	**5,463,162**	**100.0**	**4,894,469**	**100.0**	**6,747,104**	**100.0**	**36,747,000**	**100.0**
Accounts Payable	732,064	13.4	973,999	19.9	3,717,654	55.1	4,924,098	13.4
Bank Loans	0	0.0	14,683	0.3	67,471	1.0	220,482	0.6
Notes Payable	229,453	4.2	97,889	2.0	310,367	4.6	955,422	2.6
Other Current	1,038,000	19.0	1,184,463	24.2	8,103,272	120.1	22,783,140	62.0
Total Current	**1,999,517**	**36.6**	**2,271,034**	**46.4**	**12,198,764**	**180.8**	**28,883,142**	**78.6**
Other Long Term	1,507,833	27.6	1,076,783	22.0	1,464,122	21.7	10,031,931	27.3
Deferred Credits	16,389	0.3	14,683	0.3	141,689	2.1	330,723	0.9
Net Worth	1,939,423	35.5	1,531,969	31.3	(7,057,471)	(104.6)	(2,498,796)	(6.8)
Total Liab & Net Worth	**5,463,162**	**100.0**	**4,894,469**	**100.0**	**6,747,104**	**100.0**	**36,747,000**	**100.0**
Net Sales	9,501,151	100.0	9,200,130	100.0	10,176,627	100.0	23,939,414	100.0
Gross Profit	3,277,897	34.5	2,566,836	27.9	4,192,770	41.2	13,358,193	55.8
Net Profit After Tax	351,543	3.7	147,202	1.6	223,886	2.2	(790,001)	(3.3)
Working Capital	797,622	—	464,974	—	(8,447,374)	—	(5,475,303)	—

RATIOS	SIC 2819 UQ	MED	LQ	SIC 2821 UQ	MED	LQ	SIC 2833 UQ	MED	LQ	SIC 2834 UQ	MED	LQ
SOLVENCY												
Quick Ratio (times)	1.6	1.0	0.6	1.6	1.0	0.6	1.7	0.8	0.4	2.6	1.4	0.7
Current Ratio (times)	3.5	2.0	1.3	2.5	1.6	1.2	2.4	1.6	1.2	5.1	2.7	1.5
Curr Liab To Nw (%)	20.5	51.5	89.7	27.7	65.4	136.6	26.0	57.5	101.1	15.0	29.9	63.2
Curr Liab To Inv (%)	101.9	163.6	323.0	116.1	193.0	324.8	76.1	149.9	243.5	118.6	196.5	345.2
Total Liab To Nw (%)	27.5	86.7	184.6	43.8	110.0	242.7	40.3	111.6	155.0	25.2	50.2	129.6
Fixed Assets To Nw (%)	30.3	69.7	104.1	21.9	66.9	118.6	32.0	50.4	101.7	8.0	28.6	61.4
EFFICIENCY												
Coll Period (days)	34.3	46.0	61.0	36.7	48.6	69.2	32.5	40.7	53.7	31.1	50.7	65.7
Sales To Inv (times)	15.8	9.9	6.1	15.5	8.8	7.2	12.0	8.1	4.8	12.9	7.2	4.2
Assets To Sales (%)	48.4	57.5	100.5	36.3	53.2	112.0	43.1	66.3	87.1	77.4	153.5	375.5
Sales To Nwc (times)	8.8	5.4	3.3	14.9	8.1	4.1	12.7	6.7	2.6	4.2	2.0	0.5
Acct Pay To Sales (%)	3.6	6.0	9.6	4.3	7.9	12.8	3.9	7.3	11.0	4.9	9.1	18.8
PROFITABILITY												
Return On Sales (%)	8.7	2.2	0.0	3.8	1.2	(1.1)	6.9	3.9	(9.8)	10.6	(5.1)	(88.8)
Return On Assets (%)	11.9	2.7	0.1	6.3	2.8	(1.0)	14.4	7.6	(8.2)	8.6	(6.7)	(37.8)
Return On Nw (%)	29.3	10.4	0.7	14.2	8.2	(2.5)	30.0	15.1	(11.6)	19.0	(0.8)	(45.0)

	SIC 2835 DGNOSTIC SUBSTANCES (NO BREAKDOWN) 2002 (51 Establishments) $	%	SIC 2836 BIOL PRD,EXC DGNSTC (NO BREAKDOWN) 2002 (40 Establishments) $	%	SIC 2841 SOAP,OTHER DTRGENTS (NO BREAKDOWN) 2002 (19 Establishments) $	%	SIC 2842 POLISHES,SANT GOODS (NO BREAKDOWN) 2002 (64 Establishments) $	%
Cash	3,750,397	18.9	4,005,134	26.7	116,375	9.9	225,341	11.5
Accounts Receivable	2,797,915	14.1	1,950,065	13.0	263,313	22.4	450,681	23.0
Notes Receivable	59,530	0.3	0	0.0	4,702	0.4	13,716	0.7
Inventory	2,897,132	14.6	1,845,062	12.3	243,329	20.7	407,572	20.8
Other Current	3,770,240	19.0	1,500,049	10.0	118,726	10.1	178,313	9.1
Total Current	**13,275,214**	**66.9**	**9,300,310**	**62.0**	**746,445**	**63.5**	**1,275,623**	**65.1**
Fixed Assets	3,551,963	17.9	2,835,095	18.9	209,240	17.8	433,046	22.1
Other Non-current	3,016,192	15.2	2,865,095	19.1	219,819	18.7	250,814	12.8
Total Assets	**19,843,369**	**100.0**	**15,000,500**	**100.0**	**1,175,504**	**100.0**	**1,959,483**	**100.0**
Accounts Payable	2,996,349	15.1	1,005,034	6.7	159,869	13.6	235,138	12.0
Bank Loans	0	0.0	105,004	0.7	0	0.0	11,757	0.6
Notes Payable	1,012,012	5.1	225,008	1.5	5,878	0.5	39,190	2.0
Other Current	5,992,697	30.2	3,060,101	20.4	211,590	18.0	354,666	18.1
Total Current	**10,001,058**	**50.4**	**4,395,147**	**29.3**	**377,337**	**32.1**	**640,751**	**32.7**
Other Long Term	2,718,541	13.7	2,520,083	16.8	136,358	11.6	350,748	17.9
Deferred Credits	257,964	1.3	285,010	1.9	1,176	0.1	1,959	0.1
Net Worth	6,865,806	34.6	7,800,260	52.0	660,633	56.2	966,025	49.3
Total Liab & Net Worth	**19,843,369**	**100.0**	**15,000,500**	**100.0**	**1,175,504**	**100.0**	**1,959,483**	**100.0**
Net Sales	16,345,444	100.0	12,953,800	100.0	2,544,381	100.0	4,241,305	100.0
Gross Profit	8,319,831	50.9	7,241,174	55.9	1,106,806	43.5	1,934,035	45.6
Net Profit After Tax	(800,927)	(4.9)	(1,010,396)	(7.8)	111,953	4.4	(63,620)	(1.5)
Working Capital	3,274,156	—	4,905,163	—	369,108	—	634,872	—

RATIOS	UQ	MED	LQ	UQ	MED	LQ	UQ	MED	LQ	UQ	MED	LQ
SOLVENCY												
Quick Ratio (times)	2.5	1.6	1.1	3.0	1.7	0.8	3.0	1.4	0.6	2.2	1.1	0.7
Current Ratio (times)	5.4	3.4	1.7	4.1	2.7	1.4	6.2	2.7	1.3	4.7	2.2	1.3
Curr Liab To Nw (%)	13.4	24.3	49.5	13.8	40.2	127.8	9.5	31.0	79.2	20.7	43.1	95.6
Curr Liab To Inv (%)	56.0	182.4	312.8	122.2	189.1	387.4	63.7	106.8	200.9	65.4	130.2	239.8
Total Liab To Nw (%)	19.8	40.0	119.1	26.1	62.7	208.1	15.2	39.8	161.7	28.2	74.1	195.3
Fixed Assets To Nw (%)	15.8	24.8	45.0	11.3	43.4	58.8	14.2	29.3	63.2	15.3	34.2	61.5
EFFICIENCY												
Coll Period (days)	36.9	54.1	70.8	37.6	52.6	67.5	24.5	33.2	48.9	26.3	40.9	50.7
Sales To Inv (times)	10.8	7.2	3.7	14.3	7.7	4.3	12.6	10.6	6.6	15.7	10.1	7.8
Assets To Sales (%)	79.0	121.4	182.0	69.2	115.8	680.0	31.6	46.2	77.8	35.7	46.2	75.0
Sales To Nwc (times)	2.8	1.9	1.1	3.8	2.4	0.6	22.8	5.2	4.2	10.5	6.1	4.1
Acct Pay To Sales (%)	3.3	5.8	12.8	4.3	8.5	15.5	2.7	4.6	6.7	3.6	6.3	8.4
PROFITABILITY												
Return On Sales (%)	6.8	(4.9)	(81.1)	6.8	(27.1)	(429.4)	8.3	3.2	1.2	3.6	2.2	(1.1)
Return On Assets (%)	7.7	(3.0)	(29.6)	7.9	(21.6)	(62.9)	13.5	5.6	1.8	9.5	4.1	(1.8)
Return On Nw (%)	9.8	(1.2)	(34.8)	19.3	(24.4)	(94.1)	22.3	14.7	3.2	20.2	7.8	(4.9)

	SIC 2844 TOILET PREPARATIONS (NO BREAKDOWN) 2002 (65 Establishments)		SIC 2851 PAINTS,ALLIED PRDTS (NO BREAKDOWN) 2002 (77 Establishments)		SIC 2865 CYCL CRDS,INTRMDTES (NO BREAKDOWN) 2002 (12 Establishments)		SIC 2869 IND ORG CHEM, NEC (NO BREAKDOWN) 2002 (63 Establishments)	
	$	%	$	%	$	%	$	%
Cash	516,509	14.8	(121,983)	(4.9)	373,284	7.3	2,035,033	8.8
Accounts Receivable	715,434	20.5	702,022	28.2	802,817	15.7	3,630,684	15.7
Notes Receivable	13,960	0.4	169,282	6.8	189,199	3.7	23,125	0.1
Inventory	977,179	28.0	704,512	28.3	1,416,435	27.7	3,168,176	13.7
Other Current	247,784	7.1	134,430	5.4	245,447	4.8	1,410,649	6.1
Total Current	**2,470,866**	**70.8**	**1,588,263**	**63.8**	**3,027,182**	**59.2**	**10,267,667**	**44.4**
Fixed Assets	596,777	17.1	629,828	25.3	1,421,548	27.8	9,412,028	40.7
Other Non-current	422,281	12.1	271,349	10.9	664,753	13.0	3,445,680	14.9
Total Assets	**3,489,924**	**100.0**	**2,489,440**	**100.0**	**5,113,483**	**100.0**	**23,125,375**	**100.0**
Accounts Payable	453,690	13.0	365,948	14.7	490,894	9.6	1,711,278	7.4
Bank Loans	10,470	0.3	2,489	0.1	0	0.0	0	0.0
Notes Payable	52,349	1.5	59,747	2.4	5,113	0.1	578,134	2.5
Other Current	792,213	22.7	360,968	14.5	490,895	9.6	3,538,183	15.3
Total Current	**1,308,722**	**37.5**	**789,152**	**31.7**	**986,902**	**19.3**	**5,827,595**	**25.2**
Other Long Term	966,708	27.7	355,990	14.3	1,661,882	32.5	6,544,481	28.3
Deferred Credits	6,980	0.2	4,979	0.2	10,227	0.2	69,376	0.3
Net Worth	1,207,514	34.6	1,339,319	53.8	2,454,472	48.0	10,683,923	46.2
Total Liab & Net Worth	**3,489,924**	**100.0**	**2,489,440**	**100.0**	**5,113,483**	**100.0**	**23,125,375**	**100.0**
Net Sales	6,427,116	100.0	5,411,826	100.0	8,181,573	100.0	28,339,920	100.0
Gross Profit	3,207,131	49.9	1,910,375	35.3	2,896,277	35.4	9,210,474	32.5
Net Profit After Tax	147,824	2.3	156,943	2.9	605,436	7.4	935,217	3.3
Working Capital	1,162,144	—	799,111	—	2,040,280	—	4,440,072	—

RATIOS	**UQ**	**MED**	**LQ**	**UQ**	**MED**	**LQ**	**UQ**	**MED**	**LQ**	**UQ**	**MED**	**LQ**
SOLVENCY												
Quick Ratio (times)	2.2	1.1	0.6	2.0	1.1	0.7	2.7	1.3	0.7	1.5	1.0	0.7
Current Ratio (times)	3.8	2.4	1.4	4.3	2.2	1.5	7.9	3.0	2.1	2.7	1.8	1.1
Curr Liab To Nw (%)	28.6	60.7	146.0	24.1	47.5	95.9	8.1	21.8	23.5	24.6	43.9	76.1
Curr Liab To Inv (%)	72.7	115.4	240.7	57.6	109.5	180.2	30.6	97.5	147.5	100.4	210.9	393.7
Total Liab To Nw (%)	32.9	77.8	287.7	35.9	69.6	132.3	21.3	31.1	76.5	50.1	90.3	284.1
Fixed Assets To Nw (%)	9.2	28.7	70.1	21.5	32.7	52.5	17.1	45.6	88.1	28.4	87.2	162.5
EFFICIENCY												
Coll Period (days)	26.3	35.0	50.0	32.5	42.3	59.1	27.6	44.4	53.1	23.7	38.0	56.9
Sales To Inv (times)	11.1	7.7	4.0	10.5	7.9	6.0	11.3	6.9	4.9	22.7	12.0	7.3
Assets To Sales (%)	41.1	54.3	75.6	37.7	46.0	63.8	47.9	62.5	110.0	50.9	81.6	143.9
Sales To Nwc (times)	7.0	4.8	2.8	10.2	6.0	3.8	9.3	5.8	3.9	13.5	6.2	4.5
Acct Pay To Sales (%)	2.9	5.6	8.9	4.1	5.7	8.5	3.4	8.6	10.7	3.2	5.9	8.6
PROFITABILITY												
Return On Sales (%)	7.8	3.8	(0.3)	5.5	1.8	(0.1)	8.7	4.2	1.7	10.7	2.2	(2.0)
Return On Assets (%)	16.8	5.6	(1.2)	8.6	4.5	(0.3)	10.1	6.2	2.7	10.0	3.7	(2.1)
Return On Nw (%)	44.2	18.7	6.4	16.5	8.2	(1.7)	134.9	20.2	10.1	30.6	9.0	(3.6)

	SIC 2873 NITROGENOUS FRTLZRS (NO BREAKDOWN) 2002 (18 Establishments)		SIC 2875 FRTLZRS, MIXING ONLY (NO BREAKDOWN) 2002 (24 Establishments)		SIC 2879 AGRCLTRL CHEM, NEC (NO BREAKDOWN) 2002 (26 Establishments)		SIC 2891 ADHESIVES, SEALANTS (NO BREAKDOWN) 2002 (50 Establishments)	
	$	%	$	%	$	%	$	%
Cash	391,168	7.1	402,456	15.4	521,747	15.7	296,754	9.8
Accounts Receivable	953,128	17.3	488,696	18.7	850,747	25.6	763,080	25.2
Notes Receivable	0	0.0	2,613	0.1	0	0.0	3,028	0.1
Inventory	1,294,712	23.5	642,884	24.6	794,252	23.9	669,209	22.1
Other Current	424,225	7.7	182,935	7.0	255,890	7.7	187,742	6.2
Total Current	**3,063,233**	**55.6**	**1,719,584**	**65.8**	**2,422,636**	**72.9**	**1,919,813**	**63.4**
Fixed Assets	1,994,407	36.2	702,991	26.9	744,404	22.4	775,193	25.6
Other Non-current	451,771	8.2	190,775	7.3	156,192	4.7	333,091	11.0
Total Assets	**5,509,411**	**100.0**	**2,613,350**	**100.0**	**3,323,232**	**100.0**	**3,028,097**	**100.0**
Accounts Payable	1,410,409	25.6	363,256	13.9	538,364	16.2	351,259	11.6
Bank Loans	22,038	0.4	0	0.0	0	0.0	15,140	0.5
Notes Payable	325,055	5.9	177,708	6.8	219,333	6.6	54,506	1.8
Other Current	1,101,882	20.0	402,455	15.4	545,010	16.4	390,625	12.9
Total Current	**2,859,384**	**51.9**	**943,419**	**36.1**	**1,302,707**	**39.2**	**811,530**	**26.8**
Other Long Term	826,412	15.0	196,002	7.5	362,232	10.9	375,484	12.4
Deferred Credits	16,528	0.3	2,613	0.1	3,323	0.1	9,084	0.3
Net Worth	1,807,087	32.8	1,471,316	56.3	1,654,970	49.8	1,831,999	60.5
Total Liab & Net Worth	**5,509,411**	**100.0**	**2,613,350**	**100.0**	**3,323,232**	**100.0**	**3,028,097**	**100.0**
Net Sales	8,689,923	100.0	5,478,721	100.0	5,104,811	100.0	6,512,037	100.0
Gross Profit	2,120,341	24.4	2,038,084	37.2	2,011,296	39.4	2,031,756	31.2
Net Profit After Tax	17,380	0.2	136,968	2.5	51,048	1.0	78,144	1.2
Working Capital	203,849	—	776,165	—	1,119,929	—	1,108,283	—

RATIOS	UQ	MED	LQ	UQ	MED	LQ	UQ	MED	LQ	UQ	MED	LQ
SOLVENCY												
Quick Ratio (times)	1.4	0.8	0.4	2.1	1.0	0.5	2.0	1.2	0.6	2.9	1.1	0.9
Current Ratio (times)	2.1	1.6	1.3	3.7	1.9	1.2	3.1	2.2	1.3	4.9	2.3	1.7
Curr Liab To Nw (%)	31.5	56.6	87.6	22.8	55.5	136.6	30.6	57.1	189.2	19.7	40.2	64.1
Curr Liab To Inv (%)	103.3	161.7	174.2	101.0	145.2	231.0	93.4	151.4	376.1	78.0	130.7	175.4
Total Liab To Nw (%)	61.4	95.3	176.4	22.8	62.9	174.9	42.3	71.6	282.0	23.5	69.7	108.7
Fixed Assets To Nw (%)	50.6	67.6	100.8	28.5	45.7	71.1	10.7	32.7	48.8	14.7	44.6	74.2
EFFICIENCY												
Coll Period (days)	24.5	30.3	51.5	24.5	31.1	46.7	24.1	59.5	80.9	30.7	40.5	55.9
Sales To Inv (times)	13.7	6.8	5.5	23.0	11.3	5.9	15.9	5.6	4.1	12.0	9.2	7.3
Assets To Sales (%)	34.7	63.4	108.0	31.3	47.7	61.6	47.1	65.1	85.8	33.6	46.5	68.3
Sales To Nwc (times)	10.6	7.0	6.3	11.9	9.1	5.6	9.2	4.4	3.4	9.0	6.9	5.0
Acct Pay To Sales (%)	4.2	7.6	12.0	3.5	5.9	11.9	4.9	7.2	14.4	3.3	4.6	8.6
PROFITABILITY												
Return On Sales (%)	4.7	1.9	(3.9)	4.0	2.8	1.5	5.1	2.6	(5.5)	4.2	2.2	0.0
Return On Assets (%)	10.4	4.2	(5.5)	6.8	5.7	3.6	11.5	4.4	(6.4)	10.9	3.2	0.1
Return On Nw (%)	25.5	11.6	(7.0)	14.5	8.6	6.4	28.7	15.6	(12.2)	14.8	7.6	0.8

SIC 2893 PRINTING INK
(NO BREAKDOWN)
2002 (16 Establishments)

	$	%
Cash	559,981	17.9
Accounts Receivable	785,225	25.1
Notes Receivable	0	0.0
Inventory	678,860	21.7
Other Current	250,270	8.0
Total Current	**2,274,336**	**72.7**
Fixed Assets	591,265	18.9
Other Non-current	262,784	8.4
Total Assets	**3,128,385**	**100.0**
Accounts Payable	416,075	13.3
Bank Loans	0	0.0
Notes Payable	394,177	12.6
Other Current	416,075	13.3
Total Current	**1,226,327**	**39.2**
Other Long Term	340,994	10.9
Deferred Credits	0	0.0
Net Worth	1,561,064	49.9
Total Liab & Net Worth	**3,128,385**	**100.0**
Net Sales	5,708,732	100.0
Gross Profit	2,426,211	42.5
Net Profit After Tax	399,611	7.0
Working Capital	1,048,009	—

RATIOS	UQ	MED	LQ
SOLVENCY			
Quick Ratio (times)	2.0	0.8	0.6
Current Ratio (times)	4.2	1.5	1.3
Curr Liab To Nw (%)	28.4	76.0	226.3
Curr Liab To Inv (%)	111.9	156.9	249.5
Total Liab To Nw (%)	28.4	107.8	298.4
Fixed Assets To Nw (%)	14.1	39.2	117.8
EFFICIENCY			
Coll Period (days)	47.8	52.9	56.9
Sales To Inv (times)	16.8	7.1	6.7
Assets To Sales (%)	41.3	54.8	65.7
Sales To Nwc (times)	14.2	6.5	4.2
Acct Pay To Sales (%)	3.3	7.3	12.6
PROFITABILITY			
Return On Sales (%)	7.5	2.2	0.3
Return On Assets (%)	17.2	4.6	0.4
Return On Nw (%)	44.6	9.0	1.4

SIC 2899 CHEM PRPRTNS, NEC
(NO BREAKDOWN)
2002 (76 Establishments)

	$	%
Cash	189,534	10.4
Accounts Receivable	464,722	25.5
Notes Receivable	3,645	0.2
Inventory	311,637	17.1
Other Current	178,599	9.8
Total Current	**1,148,137**	**63.0**
Fixed Assets	493,881	27.1
Other Non-current	180,422	9.9
Total Assets	**1,822,440**	**100.0**
Accounts Payable	267,899	14.7
Bank Loans	5,467	0.3
Notes Payable	52,851	2.9
Other Current	411,871	22.6
Total Current	**738,088**	**40.5**
Other Long Term	331,684	18.2
Deferred Credits	10,935	0.6
Net Worth	741,733	40.7
Total Liab & Net Worth	**1,822,440**	**100.0**
Net Sales	3,153,010	100.0
Gross Profit	1,491,374	47.3
Net Profit After Tax	69,366	2.2
Working Capital	410,049	—

RATIOS	UQ	MED	LQ
SOLVENCY			
Quick Ratio (times)	2.1	1.1	0.7
Current Ratio (times)	4.6	1.9	1.3
Curr Liab To Nw (%)	18.0	46.9	97.9
Curr Liab To Inv (%)	76.2	168.2	394.6
Total Liab To Nw (%)	32.7	71.8	198.4
Fixed Assets To Nw (%)	25.2	52.9	84.9
EFFICIENCY			
Coll Period (days)	30.5	43.8	58.1
Sales To Inv (times)	25.4	13.7	9.3
Assets To Sales (%)	30.0	57.8	93.8
Sales To Nwc (times)	12.7	6.2	3.1
Acct Pay To Sales (%)	3.5	5.7	8.8
PROFITABILITY			
Return On Sales (%)	5.4	2.0	(0.8)
Return On Assets (%)	9.8	4.5	(1.2)
Return On Nw (%)	27.0	12.2	0.4

SIC 29 PETRO RFNG RLTD IND
(NO BREAKDOWN)
2002 (117 Establishments)

	$	%
Cash	602,083	9.5
Accounts Receivable	1,362,609	21.5
Notes Receivable	25,351	0.4
Inventory	918,969	14.5
Other Current	304,210	4.8
Total Current	**3,213,222**	**50.7**
Fixed Assets	2,363,968	37.3
Other Non-current	760,525	12.0
Total Assets	**6,337,715**	**100.0**
Accounts Payable	1,007,697	15.9
Bank Loans	6,338	0.1
Notes Payable	158,443	2.5
Other Current	887,279	14.0
Total Current	**2,059,757**	**32.5**
Other Long Term	1,723,859	27.2
Deferred Credits	38,026	0.6
Net Worth	2,516,073	39.7
Total Liab & Net Worth	**6,337,715**	**100.0**
Net Sales	13,898,498	100.0
Gross Profit	3,849,884	27.7
Net Profit After Tax	236,274	1.7
Working Capital	1,153,465	—

RATIOS	UQ	MED	LQ
SOLVENCY			
Quick Ratio (times)	1.9	1.0	0.6
Current Ratio (times)	3.0	1.6	1.1
Curr Liab To Nw (%)	27.8	60.5	113.4
Curr Liab To Inv (%)	111.0	185.5	496.6
Total Liab To Nw (%)	38.8	108.8	232.9
Fixed Assets To Nw (%)	30.6	70.5	176.8
EFFICIENCY			
Coll Period (days)	20.4	37.1	55.5
Sales To Inv (times)	32.3	15.2	9.5
Assets To Sales (%)	33.1	45.6	75.1
Sales To Nwc (times)	21.1	8.8	4.8
Acct Pay To Sales (%)	2.7	6.9	10.4
PROFITABILITY			
Return On Sales (%)	3.7	1.0	(0.7)
Return On Assets (%)	8.1	2.4	(1.6)
Return On Nw (%)	17.1	6.9	(1.1)

SIC 2911 PETROLEUM REFINING
(NO BREAKDOWN)
2002 (47 Establishments)

	$	%
Cash	9,784,412	6.7
Accounts Receivable	24,534,048	16.8
Notes Receivable	1,168,288	0.8
Inventory	18,838,644	12.9
Other Current	5,987,476	4.1
Total Current	**60,312,868**	**41.3**
Fixed Assets	62,795,480	43.0
Other Non-current	22,927,652	15.7
Total Assets	**146,036,000**	**100.0**
Accounts Payable	30,959,632	21.2
Bank Loans	0	0.0
Notes Payable	2,336,576	1.6
Other Current	22,343,508	15.3
Total Current	**55,639,716**	**38.1**
Other Long Term	54,471,428	37.3
Deferred Credits	1,460,360	1.0
Net Worth	34,464,496	23.6
Total Liab & Net Worth	**146,036,000**	**100.0**
Net Sales	325,973,214	100.0
Gross Profit	63,238,804	19.4
Net Profit After Tax	(977,920)	(0.3)
Working Capital	4,673,152	—

RATIOS	UQ	MED	LQ
SOLVENCY			
Quick Ratio (times)	1.1	0.7	0.4
Current Ratio (times)	1.6	1.3	0.9
Curr Liab To Nw (%)	42.4	77.4	127.4
Curr Liab To Inv (%)	154.5	229.1	493.8
Total Liab To Nw (%)	77.7	171.9	338.0
Fixed Assets To Nw (%)	68.3	131.2	235.6
EFFICIENCY			
Coll Period (days)	16.4	20.6	51.5
Sales To Inv (times)	27.0	18.2	12.4
Assets To Sales (%)	32.7	44.8	73.1
Sales To Nwc (times)	34.0	22.0	10.1
Acct Pay To Sales (%)	6.9	8.6	14.0
PROFITABILITY			
Return On Sales (%)	1.0	0.1	(2.4)
Return On Assets (%)	2.8	0.3	(5.1)
Return On Nw (%)	9.4	3.0	(7.3)

SIC 2951 ASPH PVNG MXT,BLCKS (NO BREAKDOWN) 2002 (26 Establishments)

	$	%
Cash	259,410	11.7
Accounts Receivable	518,819	23.4
Notes Receivable	2,217	0.1
Inventory	250,541	11.3
Other Current	152,986	6.9
Total Current	1,183,973	53.4
Fixed Assets	928,997	41.9
Other Non-current	104,207	4.7
Total Assets	2,217,177	100.0
Accounts Payable	317,056	14.3
Bank Loans	0	0.0
Notes Payable	113,076	5.1
Other Current	325,925	14.7
Total Current	756,057	34.1
Other Long Term	521,037	23.5
Deferred Credits	11,086	0.5
Net Worth	928,997	41.9
Total Liab & Net Worth	2,217,177	100.0
Net Sales	5,834,676	100.0
Gross Profit	1,493,677	25.6
Net Profit After Tax	52,512	0.9
Working Capital	427,916	—

RATIOS	UQ	MED	LQ
SOLVENCY			
Quick Ratio (times)	3.4	0.9	0.6
Current Ratio (times)	4.4	1.6	0.9
Curr Liab To Nw (%)	16.0	72.8	128.3
Curr Liab To Inv (%)	131.3	415.7	999.9
Total Liab To Nw (%)	31.1	104.8	207.4
Fixed Assets To Nw (%)	34.5	59.6	150.9
EFFICIENCY			
Coll Period (days)	24.1	38.0	55.1
Sales To Inv (times)	68.6	28.7	13.0
Assets To Sales (%)	27.6	38.0	68.5
Sales To Nwc (times)	14.9	8.8	4.7
Acct Pay To Sales (%)	1.2	6.5	10.7
PROFITABILITY			
Return On Sales (%)	3.5	1.1	(0.5)
Return On Assets (%)	9.9	2.6	(1.3)
Return On Nw (%)	23.2	11.9	0.5

SIC 2952 ASPH FELTS,COATINGS (NO BREAKDOWN) 2002 (11 Establishments)

	$	%
Cash	1,527,793	15.9
Accounts Receivable	2,555,930	26.6
Notes Receivable	48,044	0.5
Inventory	1,191,486	12.4
Other Current	586,133	6.1
Total Current	5,909,386	61.5
Fixed Assets	2,873,019	29.9
Other Non-current	826,353	8.6
Total Assets	9,608,758	100.0
Accounts Payable	749,483	7.8
Bank Loans	0	0.0
Notes Payable	9,609	0.1
Other Current	1,306,791	13.6
Total Current	2,065,883	21.5
Other Long Term	1,960,187	20.4
Deferred Credits	105,696	1.1
Net Worth	5,476,992	57.0
Total Liab & Net Worth	9,608,758	100.0
Net Sales	19,852,806	100.0
Gross Profit	7,325,685	36.9
Net Profit After Tax	1,766,900	8.9
Working Capital	3,843,503	—

RATIOS	UQ	MED	LQ
Quick Ratio (times)	6.7	2.1	1.1
Current Ratio (times)	7.7	2.6	2.1
Curr Liab To Nw (%)	5.2	31.0	52.4
Curr Liab To Inv (%)	111.0	135.1	230.2
Total Liab To Nw (%)	5.2	63.9	116.6
Fixed Assets To Nw (%)	5.8	31.3	117.3
Coll Period (days)	35.4	57.3	71.9
Sales To Inv (times)	43.9	13.0	10.9
Assets To Sales (%)	43.9	48.4	85.0
Sales To Nwc (times)	9.1	5.3	2.6
Acct Pay To Sales (%)	2.2	2.8	5.9
Return On Sales (%)	13.8	7.6	2.5
Return On Assets (%)	30.4	5.2	3.5
Return On Nw (%)	45.4	16.3	6.8

SIC 2992 LBRCTNG OILS,GRSES (NO BREAKDOWN) 2002 (29 Establishments)

	$	%
Cash	199,165	10.6
Accounts Receivable	481,002	25.6
Notes Receivable	3,758	0.2
Inventory	390,815	20.8
Other Current	73,278	3.9
Total Current	1,148,018	61.1
Fixed Assets	509,186	27.1
Other Non-current	221,712	11.8
Total Assets	1,878,916	100.0
Accounts Payable	240,501	12.8
Bank Loans	7,516	0.4
Notes Payable	46,973	2.5
Other Current	227,349	12.1
Total Current	522,339	27.8
Other Long Term	261,169	13.9
Deferred Credits	0	0.0
Net Worth	1,095,408	58.3
Total Liab & Net Worth	1,878,916	100.0
Net Sales	4,194,009	100.0
Gross Profit	1,564,365	37.3
Net Profit After Tax	50,328	1.2
Working Capital	625,679	—

RATIOS	UQ	MED	LQ
Quick Ratio (times)	2.3	1.4	0.9
Current Ratio (times)	4.1	2.5	1.6
Curr Liab To Nw (%)	21.9	40.9	63.4
Curr Liab To Inv (%)	74.5	127.5	186.3
Total Liab To Nw (%)	34.3	64.9	148.7
Fixed Assets To Nw (%)	24.1	50.0	69.5
Coll Period (days)	34.3	41.3	51.7
Sales To Inv (times)	15.8	10.7	7.4
Assets To Sales (%)	33.5	44.8	76.4
Sales To Nwc (times)	9.6	6.0	4.4
Acct Pay To Sales (%)	2.5	5.2	9.5
Return On Sales (%)	4.9	2.2	(0.1)
Return On Assets (%)	9.5	5.4	(0.6)
Return On Nw (%)	16.2	8.2	(1.4)

SIC 30 RUBBER & PLASTICS (NO BREAKDOWN) 2002 (829 Establishments)

	$	%
Cash	287,461	10.7
Accounts Receivable	644,771	24.0
Notes Receivable	16,119	0.6
Inventory	521,190	19.4
Other Current	145,074	5.4
Total Current	1,614,615	60.1
Fixed Assets	851,635	31.7
Other Non-current	220,297	8.2
Total Assets	2,686,547	100.0
Accounts Payable	325,072	12.1
Bank Loans	8,060	0.3
Notes Payable	94,029	3.5
Other Current	488,952	18.2
Total Current	916,113	34.1
Other Long Term	580,294	21.6
Deferred Credits	5,373	0.2
Net Worth	1,184,767	44.1
Total Liab & Net Worth	2,686,547	100.0
Net Sales	5,373,094	100.0
Gross Profit	1,579,690	29.4
Net Profit After Tax	112,835	2.1
Working Capital	698,502	—

RATIOS	UQ	MED	LQ
Quick Ratio (times)	2.3	1.1	0.7
Current Ratio (times)	3.9	2.0	1.3
Curr Liab To Nw (%)	21.5	51.9	134.5
Curr Liab To Inv (%)	86.5	152.2	248.7
Total Liab To Nw (%)	38.2	94.7	220.9
Fixed Assets To Nw (%)	28.2	62.3	121.8
Coll Period (days)	33.1	44.9	57.9
Sales To Inv (times)	17.2	10.4	7.2
Assets To Sales (%)	37.5	50.0	71.2
Sales To Nwc (times)	12.6	6.7	4.2
Acct Pay To Sales (%)	3.0	5.3	8.1
Return On Sales (%)	4.8	1.9	(0.6)
Return On Assets (%)	9.8	3.7	(1.0)
Return On Nw (%)	23.4	8.9	(0.8)

Page 54

SIC 3011 — TIRES, INNER TUBES (NO BREAKDOWN) 2002 (10 Establishments)
SIC 3052 — RBBR, PLSTC HSE BTNG (NO BREAKDOWN) 2002 (14 Establishments)
SIC 3053 — GSKTS, PKNG SLNG DVC (NO BREAKDOWN) 2002 (43 Establishments)
SIC 3061 — MECH RUBBER GOODS (NO BREAKDOWN) 2002 (22 Establishments)

Item	3011 $	3011 %	3052 $	3052 %	3053 $	3053 %	3061 $	3061 %
Cash	2,005,404	9.2	404,417	13.3	292,882	12.2	861,074	15.0
Accounts Receivable	3,487,660	16.0	602,064	19.8	628,976	26.2	1,446,604	25.2
Notes Receivable	0	0.0	48,652	1.6	2,401	0.1	28,702	0.5
Inventory	7,236,894	33.2	906,137	29.8	609,770	25.4	878,295	15.3
Other Current	959,106	4.4	328,397	10.8	122,433	5.1	177,955	3.1
Total Current	**13,689,064**	**62.8**	**2,289,667**	**75.3**	**1,656,462**	**69.0**	**3,392,630**	**59.1**
Fixed Assets	6,038,011	27.7	602,064	19.8	530,548	22.1	1,831,217	31.9
Other Non-current	2,070,798	9.5	148,996	4.9	213,660	8.9	516,644	9.0
Total Assets	**21,797,873**	**100.0**	**3,040,727**	**100.0**	**2,400,670**	**100.0**	**5,740,491**	**100.0**
Accounts Payable	3,291,479	15.1	304,073	10.0	240,067	10.0	556,828	9.7
Bank Loans	0	0.0	0	0.0	0	0.0	0	0.0
Notes Payable	414,160	1.9	127,711	4.2	55,215	2.3	918,479	16.0
Other Current	3,989,010	18.3	559,493	18.4	276,077	11.5	1,102,173	19.2
Total Current	**7,694,649**	**35.3**	**991,277**	**32.6**	**571,359**	**23.8**	**2,577,480**	**44.9**
Other Long Term	5,536,660	25.4	413,539	13.6	446,525	18.6	1,280,130	22.3
Deferred Credits	21,798	0.1	6,081	0.2	2,401	0.1	17,221	0.3
Net Worth	8,544,766	39.2	1,629,830	53.6	1,380,385	57.5	1,865,660	32.5
Total Liab & Net Worth	**21,797,873**	**100.0**	**3,040,727**	**100.0**	**2,400,670**	**100.0**	**5,740,491**	**100.0**
Net Sales	29,141,541	100.0	5,059,446	100.0	5,956,998	100.0	10,178,176	100.0
Gross Profit	6,148,865	21.1	1,477,358	29.2	2,210,046	37.1	2,412,228	23.7
Net Profit After Tax	524,548	1.8	50,594	1.0	125,097	2.1	305,345	3.0
Working Capital	5,994,415	—	1,298,390	—	1,085,103	—	815,150	—

RATIOS

Ratio	3011 UQ	3011 MED	3011 LQ	3052 UQ	3052 MED	3052 LQ	3053 UQ	3053 MED	3053 LQ	3061 UQ	3061 MED	3061 LQ
SOLVENCY												
Quick Ratio (times)	1.2	0.7	0.5	1.7	1.3	0.7	3.8	1.5	0.9	2.7	1.5	0.8
Current Ratio (times)	2.7	1.8	1.3	5.3	2.9	2.1	5.2	2.9	1.9	3.3	2.5	1.3
Curr Liab To Nw (%)	34.8	107.9	445.0	14.5	41.2	81.4	18.5	34.3	72.3	22.2	34.2	73.5
Curr Liab To Inv (%)	70.7	133.1	171.7	37.8	88.4	176.2	56.1	83.5	154.9	90.1	177.9	364.4
Total Liab To Nw (%)	45.5	213.2	469.4	24.3	58.4	123.6	19.4	68.5	136.0	32.9	62.7	98.3
Fixed Assets To Nw (%)	31.7	77.4	272.2	18.8	36.2	55.6	13.6	33.8	65.8	26.8	46.9	99.7
EFFICIENCY												
Coll Period (days)	36.5	42.7	53.3	28.1	41.1	56.4	34.7	42.5	47.9	36.5	45.5	63.0
Sales To Inv (times)	8.7	5.8	3.1	10.1	6.7	5.9	13.7	10.4	6.7	20.4	14.1	7.4
Assets To Sales (%)	66.6	74.8	93.6	34.1	60.1	71.5	31.3	40.3	69.7	45.8	56.4	102.8
Sales To Nwc (times)	14.0	6.9	3.9	6.5	4.3	2.3	8.1	6.0	4.2	8.1	5.8	3.9
Acct Pay To Sales (%)	6.2	10.2	12.8	2.7	5.9	8.5	2.2	3.8	5.4	2.8	4.8	7.7
PROFITABILITY												
Return On Sales (%)	3.6	1.1	0.3	3.3	1.1	(4.7)	2.6	0.7	(0.7)	6.0	2.1	(0.9)
Return On Assets (%)	8.5	1.5	0.5	10.4	1.9	(10.4)	6.9	1.8	(1.0)	10.9	2.9	(1.7)
Return On Nw (%)	18.3	8.4	0.7	15.0	2.3	(42.5)	18.7	5.9	(0.8)	16.6	8.3	4.8

Balance Sheet

	SIC 3069 FBRTD RBBR PRDS,NEC (NO BREAKDOWN) 2002 (89 Establishments) $	%	SIC 3081 UNSPTD PLSTC FLM,ST (NO BREAKDOWN) 2002 (42 Establishments) $	%	SIC 3083 LMNTD PLSTC PLT,SHT (NO BREAKDOWN) 2002 (11 Establishments) $	%	SIC 3084 PLASTICS PIPE (NO BREAKDOWN) 2002 (13 Establishments) $	%
Cash	378,004	12.1	1,171,782	11.3	213,591	8.7	389,299	5.7
Accounts Receivable	727,892	23.3	2,810,203	27.1	667,779	27.2	1,311,323	19.2
Notes Receivable	28,116	0.9	103,698	1.0	2,455	0.1	6,830	0.1
Inventory	627,924	20.1	2,229,497	21.5	613,768	25.0	1,953,325	28.6
Other Current	221,805	7.1	373,310	3.6	83,473	3.4	259,532	3.8
Total Current	**1,983,741**	**63.5**	**6,688,490**	**64.5**	**1,581,066**	**64.4**	**3,920,309**	**57.4**
Fixed Assets	890,341	28.5	3,027,968	29.2	729,156	29.7	2,472,390	36.2
Other Non-current	249,920	8.0	653,294	6.3	144,849	5.9	437,107	6.4
Total Assets	**3,124,002**	**100.0**	**10,369,752**	**100.0**	**2,455,071**	**100.0**	**6,829,806**	**100.0**
Accounts Payable	337,392	10.8	1,513,984	14.6	525,385	21.4	710,300	10.4
Bank Loans	3,124	0.1	124,437	1.2	0	0.0	0	0.0
Notes Payable	121,836	3.9	300,723	2.9	108,023	4.4	177,575	2.6
Other Current	759,133	24.3	1,814,706	17.5	655,504	26.7	963,002	14.1
Total Current	**1,221,485**	**39.1**	**3,753,850**	**36.2**	**1,288,912**	**52.5**	**1,850,877**	**27.1**
Other Long Term	496,716	15.9	2,353,934	22.7	989,394	40.3	894,705	13.1
Deferred Credits	3,124	0.1	0	0.0	0	0.0	34,149	0.5
Net Worth	1,402,677	44.9	4,261,968	41.1	176,765	7.2	4,050,075	59.3
Total Liab & Net Worth	**3,124,002**	**100.0**	**10,369,752**	**100.0**	**2,455,071**	**100.0**	**6,829,806**	**100.0**
Net Sales	6,042,557	100.0	16,834,013	100.0	7,350,512	100.0	12,862,158	100.0
Gross Profit	1,691,916	28.0	4,393,677	26.1	2,322,762	31.6	3,099,780	24.1
Net Profit After Tax	102,723	1.7	168,340	1.0	242,567	3.3	578,797	4.5
Working Capital	762,256	—	2,934,640	—	292,154	—	2,069,432	—

RATIOS

	SIC 3069 UQ	MED	LQ	SIC 3081 UQ	MED	LQ	SIC 3083 UQ	MED	LQ	SIC 3084 UQ	MED	LQ
SOLVENCY												
Quick Ratio (times)	2.9	1.1	0.6	1.8	1.1	0.7	1.1	0.9	0.4	1.9	0.8	0.5
Current Ratio (times)	4.0	2.0	1.4	2.9	1.8	1.3	1.9	1.3	1.2	4.9	1.5	1.2
Curr Liab To Nw (%)	18.2	38.6	123.9	37.6	61.2	166.8	78.2	150.6	283.1	13.3	72.3	133.8
Curr Liab To Inv (%)	78.1	144.3	231.4	116.4	158.2	191.4	174.9	234.2	318.9	39.7	123.8	179.4
Total Liab To Nw (%)	29.8	66.6	166.4	64.0	145.2	283.0	99.2	173.1	392.8	14.6	91.4	169.8
Fixed Assets To Nw (%)	24.9	47.3	92.9	27.7	70.2	127.5	52.3	67.9	88.7	51.7	77.1	90.7
EFFICIENCY												
Coll Period (days)	29.6	44.5	57.9	41.6	55.9	63.5	32.0	42.7	54.0	28.1	38.0	57.5
Sales To Inv (times)	16.7	10.6	7.2	10.1	8.1	5.8	26.2	12.2	10.3	8.8	7.6	6.6
Assets To Sales (%)	36.6	51.7	71.5	44.1	61.6	77.3	29.6	33.4	64.5	47.3	53.1	63.1
Sales To Nwc (times)	9.9	5.9	3.9	15.6	7.2	4.4	24.2	11.8	6.9	13.6	8.1	4.5
Acct Pay To Sales (%)	2.8	4.3	6.4	3.1	6.2	11.8	5.5	7.5	9.0	3.7	4.6	8.9
PROFITABILITY												
Return On Sales (%)	5.5	2.0	(1.5)	5.4	1.5	(0.7)	3.6	1.2	(0.4)	7.3	3.9	1.4
Return On Assets (%)	9.1	3.1	(2.0)	7.4	3.2	(1.3)	14.3	6.6	(0.7)	13.8	6.9	3.1
Return On Nw (%)	22.8	6.1	(3.6)	27.9	8.6	(0.1)	43.1	16.3	2.1	22.7	14.2	6.9

	SIC 3086 PLSTCS FOAM PRDCTS (NO BREAKDOWN) 2002 (46 Establishments)		SIC 3087 CSTM CPND PCHSD RSN (NO BREAKDOWN) 2002 (13 Establishments)		SIC 3088 PLSTCS PLMBNG FXTRS (NO BREAKDOWN) 2002 (11 Establishments)		SIC 3089 PLSTCS PRODUCTS, NEC (NO BREAKDOWN) 2002 (495 Establishments)	
	$	%	$	%	$	%	$	%
Cash	424,481	9.2	357,411	6.9	184,354	8.8	245,247	10.4
Accounts Receivable	1,199,619	26.0	1,403,744	27.1	488,119	23.3	556,521	23.6
Notes Receivable	4,614	0.1	0	0.0	0	0.0	14,149	0.6
Inventory	747,455	16.2	1,263,887	24.4	641,049	30.6	417,391	17.7
Other Current	198,399	4.3	274,533	5.3	232,539	11.1	127,339	5.4
Total Current	**2,574,568**	**55.8**	**3,299,575**	**63.7**	**1,546,061**	**73.8**	**1,360,647**	**57.7**
Fixed Assets	1,531,822	33.2	1,367,485	26.4	442,031	21.1	804,126	34.1
Other Non-current	507,531	11.0	512,806	9.9	106,841	5.1	193,367	8.2
Total Assets	**4,613,921**	**100.0**	**5,179,866**	**100.0**	**2,094,933**	**100.0**	**2,358,140**	**100.0**
Accounts Payable	788,980	17.1	1,041,153	20.1	247,202	11.8	275,902	11.7
Bank Loans	0	0.0	0	0.0	56,563	2.7	7,074	0.3
Notes Payable	110,734	2.4	62,158	1.2	8,380	0.4	82,535	3.5
Other Current	793,595	17.2	476,548	9.2	534,208	25.5	422,108	17.9
Total Current	**1,693,309**	**36.7**	**1,579,859**	**30.5**	**846,353**	**40.4**	**787,619**	**33.4**
Other Long Term	1,088,885	23.6	1,160,290	22.4	263,961	12.6	544,731	23.1
Deferred Credits	27,684	0.6	0	0.0	2,095	0.1	7,074	0.3
Net Worth	1,804,043	39.1	2,439,717	47.1	982,524	46.9	1,018,716	43.2
Total Liab & Net Worth	**4,613,921**	**100.0**	**5,179,866**	**100.0**	**2,094,933**	**100.0**	**2,358,140**	**100.0**
Net Sales	10,907,615	100.0	7,595,111	100.0	6,386,991	100.0	4,902,578	100.0
Gross Profit	3,119,578	28.6	2,384,865	31.4	1,948,032	30.5	1,451,163	29.6
Net Profit After Tax	250,875	2.3	151,902	2.0	191,610	3.0	102,954	2.1
Working Capital	881,259	—	1,719,716	—	699,708	—	573,028	—

RATIOS	UQ	MED	LQ	UQ	MED	LQ	UQ	MED	LQ	UQ	MED	LQ
SOLVENCY												
Quick Ratio (times)	1.8	1.0	0.6	1.8	1.1	0.6	1.0	0.7	0.6	2.2	1.1	0.7
Current Ratio (times)	2.7	1.6	1.2	3.3	1.9	1.1	2.2	1.7	1.5	3.9	2.0	1.2
Curr Liab To Nw (%)	44.3	61.9	143.6	47.9	85.2	141.8	52.9	80.5	143.4	21.2	53.3	138.6
Curr Liab To Inv (%)	119.0	197.9	322.6	85.7	138.3	184.7	96.2	157.1	187.5	94.2	159.5	282.4
Total Liab To Nw (%)	64.2	136.8	187.1	49.0	126.8	404.7	65.6	100.6	192.4	41.1	99.2	233.2
Fixed Assets To Nw (%)	47.1	76.8	135.4	29.9	56.4	124.6	15.9	27.0	93.6	34.7	70.5	128.3
EFFICIENCY												
Coll Period (days)	37.4	45.5	53.7	25.6	49.3	60.2	32.5	37.6	54.0	32.9	44.5	58.8
Sales To Inv (times)	22.9	13.3	9.3	12.8	9.8	9.7	15.1	10.8	6.0	19.4	10.9	7.5
Assets To Sales (%)	34.5	42.3	58.2	37.5	68.2	85.4	26.4	32.8	68.7	38.6	48.1	69.7
Sales To Nwc (times)	19.2	11.0	5.3	36.0	14.1	5.9	12.2	8.9	4.5	12.7	6.9	4.2
Acct Pay To Sales (%)	4.9	6.6	9.1	2.6	8.6	9.7	1.7	3.5	6.0	3.0	5.4	7.8
PROFITABILITY												
Return On Sales (%)	3.2	1.8	0.4	6.3	3.1	(1.8)	8.1	3.3	1.8	5.0	1.9	(0.7)
Return On Assets (%)	7.2	4.0	0.8	18.8	6.2	(2.2)	14.1	8.7	5.4	10.0	3.9	(1.2)
Return On Nw (%)	22.1	11.3	2.5	24.9	15.1	(9.8)	32.5	24.4	11.1	24.4	9.2	(1.3)

SIC 31 LEATHER,LEATHER PDTS (NO BREAKDOWN) 2002 (54 Establishments)

	$	%
Cash	182,272	10.4
Accounts Receivable	481,970	27.5
Notes Receivable	0	0.0
Inventory	566,096	32.3
Other Current	98,147	5.6
Total Current	**1,328,485**	**75.8**
Fixed Assets	266,398	15.2
Other Non-current	157,736	9.0
Total Assets	**1,752,619**	**100.0**
Accounts Payable	240,109	13.7
Bank Loans	19,279	1.1
Notes Payable	45,568	2.6
Other Current	259,387	14.8
Total Current	**564,343**	**32.2**
Other Long Term	247,119	14.1
Deferred Credits	1,753	0.1
Net Worth	939,404	53.6
Total Liab & Net Worth	**1,752,619**	**100.0**
Net Sales	3,591,432	100.0
Gross Profit	1,300,098	36.2
Net Profit After Tax	86,194	2.4
Working Capital	764,142	—

RATIOS	UQ	MED	LQ
SOLVENCY			
Quick Ratio (times)	1.9	1.0	0.8
Current Ratio (times)	3.8	2.6	1.9
Curr Liab To Nw (%)	26.5	42.7	107.6
Curr Liab To Inv (%)	53.8	97.9	154.4
Total Liab To Nw (%)	32.0	66.9	117.9
Fixed Assets To Nw (%)	10.4	19.2	36.4
EFFICIENCY			
Coll Period (days)	24.9	43.3	60.6
Sales To Inv (times)	10.9	6.6	4.9
Assets To Sales (%)	36.6	48.8	64.6
Sales To Nwc (times)	8.6	4.9	3.1
Acct Pay To Sales (%)	3.6	5.3	8.3
PROFITABILITY			
Return On Sales (%)	5.1	2.8	(0.2)
Return On Assets (%)	10.4	4.8	(0.4)
Return On Nw (%)	17.9	8.9	2.0

SIC 3161 LUGGAGE (NO BREAKDOWN) 2002 (11 Establishments)

	$	%
Cash	156,997	9.3
Accounts Receivable	411,907	24.4
Notes Receivable	1,688	0.1
Inventory	498,002	29.5
Other Current	156,997	9.3
Total Current	**1,225,591**	**72.6**
Fixed Assets	313,994	18.6
Other Non-current	148,557	8.8
Total Assets	**1,688,142**	**100.0**
Accounts Payable	251,533	14.9
Bank Loans	0	0.0
Notes Payable	0	0.0
Other Current	319,059	18.9
Total Current	**570,592**	**33.8**
Other Long Term	584,097	34.6
Deferred Credits	0	0.0
Net Worth	533,453	31.6
Total Liab & Net Worth	**1,688,142**	**100.0**
Net Sales	4,317,499	100.0
Gross Profit	1,873,795	43.4
Net Profit After Tax	34,540	0.8
Working Capital	654,999	—

RATIOS	UQ	MED	LQ
Quick Ratio	1.5	0.9	0.7
Current Ratio	3.1	2.3	2.0
Curr Liab To Nw	32.4	43.9	117.2
Curr Liab To Inv	89.3	121.4	154.4
Total Liab To Nw	45.5	117.2	312.8
Fixed Assets To Nw	12.0	27.1	92.7
Coll Period	24.8	39.8	60.6
Sales To Inv	11.9	8.0	6.2
Assets To Sales	30.5	39.1	48.2
Sales To Nwc	10.8	7.4	5.0
Acct Pay To Sales	3.9	5.8	9.5
Return On Sales	5.2	0.7	(4.6)
Return On Assets	13.2	1.8	(6.3)
Return On Nw	42.0	14.0	(25.5)

SIC 32 STONE CLAY,GLASS PDT (NO BREAKDOWN) 2002 (517 Establishments)

	$	%
Cash	275,949	11.9
Accounts Receivable	542,622	23.4
Notes Receivable	11,594	0.5
Inventory	366,386	15.8
Other Current	157,685	6.8
Total Current	**1,354,236**	**58.4**
Fixed Assets	809,295	34.9
Other Non-current	155,366	6.7
Total Assets	**2,318,897**	**100.0**
Accounts Payable	255,079	11.0
Bank Loans	6,957	0.3
Notes Payable	71,886	3.1
Other Current	347,834	15.0
Total Current	**681,756**	**29.4**
Other Long Term	447,546	19.3
Deferred Credits	9,276	0.4
Net Worth	1,180,319	50.9
Total Liab & Net Worth	**2,318,897**	**100.0**
Net Sales	4,628,537	100.0
Gross Profit	1,592,217	34.4
Net Profit After Tax	138,856	3.0
Working Capital	672,480	—

RATIOS	UQ	MED	LQ
Quick Ratio	2.6	1.2	0.7
Current Ratio	4.1	2.2	1.4
Curr Liab To Nw	18.1	46.0	107.0
Curr Liab To Inv	87.3	163.8	397.7
Total Liab To Nw	29.5	85.9	188.9
Fixed Assets To Nw	31.3	60.4	121.2
Coll Period	28.5	39.1	55.0
Sales To Inv	31.7	13.2	7.7
Assets To Sales	35.8	50.1	73.4
Sales To Nwc	11.4	6.3	3.6
Acct Pay To Sales	2.7	4.5	7.4
Return On Sales	6.2	2.5	0.3
Return On Assets	10.7	4.7	0.7
Return On Nw	21.9	10.3	1.9

SIC 3211 FLAT GLASS (NO BREAKDOWN) 2002 (16 Establishments)

	$	%
Cash	171,231	9.9
Accounts Receivable	460,075	26.6
Notes Receivable	1,730	0.1
Inventory	330,355	19.1
Other Current	174,689	10.1
Total Current	**1,138,080**	**65.8**
Fixed Assets	404,728	23.4
Other Non-current	186,797	10.8
Total Assets	**1,729,605**	**100.0**
Accounts Payable	257,711	14.9
Bank Loans	0	0.0
Notes Payable	44,970	2.6
Other Current	506,774	29.3
Total Current	**809,455**	**46.8**
Other Long Term	250,793	14.5
Deferred Credits	0	0.0
Net Worth	669,357	38.7
Total Liab & Net Worth	**1,729,605**	**100.0**
Net Sales	3,197,052	100.0
Gross Profit	1,256,441	39.3
Net Profit After Tax	303,720	9.5
Working Capital	328,625	—

RATIOS	UQ	MED	LQ
Quick Ratio	2.3	0.6	0.4
Current Ratio	3.0	1.4	1.0
Curr Liab To Nw	45.3	103.5	286.1
Curr Liab To Inv	109.5	235.1	325.1
Total Liab To Nw	45.3	184.6	460.8
Fixed Assets To Nw	12.4	70.2	181.5
Coll Period	19.2	29.2	77.6
Sales To Inv	24.8	11.8	3.8
Assets To Sales	47.9	54.1	95.8
Sales To Nwc	26.3	15.4	6.6
Acct Pay To Sales	4.2	7.1	12.5
Return On Sales	11.3	0.9	(0.1)
Return On Assets	13.0	5.3	(0.1)
Return On Nw	31.9	7.4	(7.3)

SIC 3229 PRSSD BLWN GLSS,NEC (NO BREAKDOWN) 2002 (23 Establishments)

Item	$	%
Cash	608,710	18.3
Accounts Receivable	575,447	17.3
Notes Receivable	6,653	0.2
Inventory	618,689	18.6
Other Current	269,429	8.1
Total Current	**2,078,928**	**62.5**
Fixed Assets	841,550	25.3
Other Non-current	405,806	12.2
Total Assets	**3,326,284**	**100.0**
Accounts Payable	272,755	8.2
Bank Loans	16,631	0.5
Notes Payable	76,505	2.3
Other Current	449,049	13.5
Total Current	**814,940**	**24.5**
Other Long Term	582,099	17.5
Deferred Credits	46,568	1.4
Net Worth	1,882,677	56.6
Total Liab & Net Worth	**3,326,284**	**100.0**
Net Sales	5,866,462	100.0
Gross Profit	1,953,532	33.3
Net Profit After Tax	70,398	1.2
Working Capital	1,263,988	—

RATIOS	UQ	MED	LQ
SOLVENCY			
Quick Ratio (times)	2.6	1.4	0.9
Current Ratio (times)	4.8	2.4	1.9
Curr Liab To Nw (%)	18.5	41.9	69.9
Curr Liab To Inv (%)	57.0	137.1	254.2
Total Liab To Nw (%)	27.4	60.9	121.6
Fixed Assets To Nw (%)	23.7	38.7	83.9
EFFICIENCY			
Coll Period (days)	31.8	37.1	51.1
Sales To Inv (times)	11.0	7.3	5.8
Assets To Sales (%)	46.2	56.7	114.2
Sales To Nwc (times)	9.1	5.4	3.1
Acct Pay To Sales (%)	1.7	5.2	8.2
PROFITABILITY			
Return On Sales (%)	6.4	1.5	(6.3)
Return On Assets (%)	9.4	3.2	(9.0)
Return On Nw (%)	20.0	4.1	(16.7)

SIC 3231 PRDS OF PRCHSD GLSS (NO BREAKDOWN) 2002 (34 Establishments)

Item	$	%
Cash	291,656	12.7
Accounts Receivable	592,498	25.8
Notes Receivable	2,297	0.1
Inventory	521,306	22.7
Other Current	137,790	6.0
Total Current	**1,545,547**	**67.3**
Fixed Assets	514,417	22.4
Other Non-current	236,539	10.3
Total Assets	**2,296,503**	**100.0**
Accounts Payable	261,801	11.4
Bank Loans	13,779	0.6
Notes Payable	140,087	6.1
Other Current	296,249	12.9
Total Current	**711,916**	**31.0**
Other Long Term	541,974	23.6
Deferred Credits	2,297	0.1
Net Worth	1,040,316	45.3
Total Liab & Net Worth	**2,296,503**	**100.0**
Net Sales	5,092,024	100.0
Gross Profit	1,940,061	38.1
Net Profit After Tax	203,681	4.0
Working Capital	833,631	—

RATIOS	UQ	MED	LQ
SOLVENCY			
Quick Ratio (times)	2.7	1.3	0.7
Current Ratio (times)	5.3	2.4	1.3
Curr Liab To Nw (%)	21.3	62.7	144.8
Curr Liab To Inv (%)	65.5	125.7	241.9
Total Liab To Nw (%)	42.5	119.0	213.1
Fixed Assets To Nw (%)	23.6	42.7	103.4
EFFICIENCY			
Coll Period (days)	19.4	35.1	51.8
Sales To Inv (times)	22.3	13.9	5.9
Assets To Sales (%)	35.4	45.1	58.4
Sales To Nwc (times)	11.8	6.0	4.3
Acct Pay To Sales (%)	3.0	3.7	6.8
PROFITABILITY			
Return On Sales (%)	5.8	2.6	0.5
Return On Assets (%)	10.2	4.5	1.0
Return On Nw (%)	27.8	15.0	1.9

SIC 3251 BRCK,STRL CLAY TILE (NO BREAKDOWN) 2002 (13 Establishments)

Item	$	%
Cash	1,494,755	12.0
Accounts Receivable	1,370,192	11.0
Notes Receivable	62,281	0.5
Inventory	2,553,540	20.5
Other Current	1,282,998	10.3
Total Current	**6,763,766**	**54.3**
Fixed Assets	5,069,710	40.7
Other Non-current	622,815	5.0
Total Assets	**12,456,291**	**100.0**
Accounts Payable	1,008,960	8.1
Bank Loans	124,563	1.0
Notes Payable	0	0.0
Other Current	1,183,347	9.5
Total Current	**2,316,870**	**18.6**
Other Long Term	1,806,162	14.5
Deferred Credits	0	0.0
Net Worth	8,333,259	66.9
Total Liab & Net Worth	**12,456,291**	**100.0**
Net Sales	14,517,822	100.0
Gross Profit	5,371,594	37.0
Net Profit After Tax	1,422,747	9.8
Working Capital	4,446,896	—

RATIOS	UQ	MED	LQ
SOLVENCY			
Quick Ratio (times)	3.7	1.7	0.7
Current Ratio (times)	7.1	3.4	3.2
Curr Liab To Nw (%)	5.8	18.9	47.0
Curr Liab To Inv (%)	41.8	62.6	119.7
Total Liab To Nw (%)	20.9	37.3	81.3
Fixed Assets To Nw (%)	42.7	57.0	82.5
EFFICIENCY			
Coll Period (days)	28.5	32.9	39.4
Sales To Inv (times)	11.3	6.9	6.0
Assets To Sales (%)	62.4	85.8	109.3
Sales To Nwc (times)	5.1	3.1	2.6
Acct Pay To Sales (%)	2.7	3.4	4.4
PROFITABILITY			
Return On Sales (%)	14.1	11.1	2.7
Return On Assets (%)	15.3	10.2	4.0
Return On Nw (%)	17.6	13.6	5.9

SIC 3271 CONCRETE BLCK,BRCK (NO BREAKDOWN) 2002 (36 Establishments)

Item	$	%
Cash	230,344	13.6
Accounts Receivable	299,785	17.7
Notes Receivable	6,775	0.4
Inventory	362,452	21.4
Other Current	81,298	4.8
Total Current	**980,654**	**57.9**
Fixed Assets	662,238	39.1
Other Non-current	50,811	3.0
Total Assets	**1,693,703**	**100.0**
Accounts Payable	182,920	10.8
Bank Loans	0	0.0
Notes Payable	50,811	3.0
Other Current	264,218	15.6
Total Current	**497,949**	**29.4**
Other Long Term	318,416	18.8
Deferred Credits	6,775	0.4
Net Worth	870,563	51.4
Total Liab & Net Worth	**1,693,703**	**100.0**
Net Sales	3,513,907	100.0
Gross Profit	1,134,992	32.3
Net Profit After Tax	80,820	2.3
Working Capital	482,705	—

RATIOS	UQ	MED	LQ
SOLVENCY			
Quick Ratio (times)	2.7	1.3	0.5
Current Ratio (times)	4.6	2.5	1.4
Curr Liab To Nw (%)	17.7	33.8	119.4
Curr Liab To Inv (%)	66.8	133.8	302.4
Total Liab To Nw (%)	29.8	80.2	156.4
Fixed Assets To Nw (%)	31.2	75.9	139.7
EFFICIENCY			
Coll Period (days)	23.7	30.3	45.1
Sales To Inv (times)	19.3	9.8	7.7
Assets To Sales (%)	35.6	48.2	66.0
Sales To Nwc (times)	10.2	5.8	3.2
Acct Pay To Sales (%)	3.2	4.7	6.7
PROFITABILITY			
Return On Sales (%)	5.4	1.9	(1.7)
Return On Assets (%)	11.8	3.7	(1.9)
Return On Nw (%)	24.0	10.6	(1.1)

SIC 3272 CONCRETE PRDCTS,NEC (NO BREAKDOWN) 2002 (128 Establishments)

	$	%
Cash	237,376	10.8
Accounts Receivable	558,273	25.4
Notes Receivable	28,573	1.3
Inventory	305,512	13.9
Other Current	171,438	7.8
Total Current	**1,301,172**	**59.2**
Fixed Assets	771,472	35.1
Other Non-current	125,281	5.7
Total Assets	**2,197,925**	**100.0**
Accounts Payable	206,605	9.4
Bank Loans	4,396	0.2
Notes Payable	43,959	2.0
Other Current	353,865	16.1
Total Current	**608,825**	**27.7**
Other Long Term	452,773	20.6
Deferred Credits	4,396	0.2
Net Worth	1,131,931	51.5
Total Liab & Net Worth	**2,197,925**	**100.0**
Net Sales	4,378,337	100.0
Gross Profit	1,598,093	36.5
Net Profit After Tax	197,025	4.5
Working Capital	692,347	—

RATIOS	UQ	MED	LQ
SOLVENCY			
Quick Ratio (times)	2.7	1.5	0.8
Current Ratio (times)	4.4	2.6	1.5
Curr Liab To Nw (%)	17.8	45.4	100.1
Curr Liab To Inv (%)	90.5	170.1	372.8
Total Liab To Nw (%)	27.3	82.3	180.5
Fixed Assets To Nw (%)	34.9	59.6	130.6
EFFICIENCY			
Coll Period (days)	29.6	42.0	63.9
Sales To Inv (times)	27.0	14.4	9.0
Assets To Sales (%)	36.1	50.2	70.2
Sales To Nwc (times)	10.9	5.7	3.8
Acct Pay To Sales (%)	2.4	3.8	6.7
PROFITABILITY			
Return On Sales (%)	7.0	3.2	1.2
Return On Assets (%)	14.0	5.7	2.2
Return On Nw (%)	28.8	11.5	5.4

SIC 3273 READY-MIX CONCRETE (NO BREAKDOWN) 2002 (107 Establishments)

	$	%
Cash	314,274	13.2
Accounts Receivable	528,551	22.2
Notes Receivable	7,143	0.3
Inventory	164,279	6.9
Other Current	133,328	5.6
Total Current	**1,147,575**	**48.2**
Fixed Assets	1,138,052	47.8
Other Non-current	95,234	4.0
Total Assets	**2,380,861**	**100.0**
Accounts Payable	297,608	12.5
Bank Loans	0	0.0
Notes Payable	80,949	3.4
Other Current	257,133	10.8
Total Current	**635,690**	**26.7**
Other Long Term	488,077	20.5
Deferred Credits	9,523	0.4
Net Worth	1,247,571	52.4
Total Liab & Net Worth	**2,380,861**	**100.0**
Net Sales	4,970,482	100.0
Gross Profit	1,749,610	35.2
Net Profit After Tax	154,085	3.1
Working Capital	511,885	—

RATIOS	UQ	MED	LQ
SOLVENCY			
Quick Ratio (times)	2.4	1.2	0.8
Current Ratio (times)	3.5	1.9	1.2
Curr Liab To Nw (%)	18.7	43.1	110.4
Curr Liab To Inv (%)	177.1	408.4	999.9
Total Liab To Nw (%)	31.2	89.4	196.5
Fixed Assets To Nw (%)	50.8	74.0	170.7
EFFICIENCY			
Coll Period (days)	26.3	37.2	47.8
Sales To Inv (times)	95.2	35.8	20.3
Assets To Sales (%)	36.6	47.9	64.5
Sales To Nwc (times)	13.5	8.3	4.9
Acct Pay To Sales (%)	2.9	4.6	8.1
PROFITABILITY			
Return On Sales (%)	5.0	2.5	0.3
Return On Assets (%)	10.0	4.7	1.0
Return On Nw (%)	19.2	9.5	2.0

SIC 3281 CUT STNE,STNE PRDS (NO BREAKDOWN) 2002 (37 Establishments)

	$	%
Cash	163,705	13.7
Accounts Receivable	308,291	25.8
Notes Receivable	4,780	0.4
Inventory	209,112	17.5
Other Current	72,891	6.1
Total Current	**758,779**	**63.5**
Fixed Assets	350,114	29.3
Other Non-current	86,034	7.2
Total Assets	**1,194,927**	**100.0**
Accounts Payable	132,637	11.1
Bank Loans	0	0.0
Notes Payable	37,043	3.1
Other Current	161,315	13.5
Total Current	**330,995**	**27.7**
Other Long Term	197,163	16.5
Deferred Credits	1,195	0.1
Net Worth	665,574	55.7
Total Liab & Net Worth	**1,194,927**	**100.0**
Net Sales	3,433,698	100.0
Gross Profit	1,146,855	33.4
Net Profit After Tax	178,552	5.2
Working Capital	427,784	—

RATIOS	UQ	MED	LQ
SOLVENCY			
Quick Ratio (times)	4.4	1.4	0.7
Current Ratio (times)	4.6	2.5	1.4
Curr Liab To Nw (%)	17.1	52.8	99.3
Curr Liab To Inv (%)	69.9	153.4	271.3
Total Liab To Nw (%)	23.8	81.1	144.0
Fixed Assets To Nw (%)	29.1	46.2	74.2
EFFICIENCY			
Coll Period (days)	26.3	34.7	45.3
Sales To Inv (times)	47.2	22.9	8.7
Assets To Sales (%)	25.8	34.8	49.0
Sales To Nwc (times)	15.0	6.3	4.4
Acct Pay To Sales (%)	2.1	4.1	5.8
PROFITABILITY			
Return On Sales (%)	7.4	3.9	0.3
Return On Assets (%)	18.9	5.7	0.6
Return On Nw (%)	50.9	13.4	1.9

SIC 3291 ABRASIVE PRODUCTS (NO BREAKDOWN) 2002 (17 Establishments)

	$	%
Cash	458,086	11.9
Accounts Receivable	900,774	23.4
Notes Receivable	0	0.0
Inventory	1,008,559	26.2
Other Current	161,676	4.2
Total Current	**2,529,095**	**65.7**
Fixed Assets	1,027,806	26.7
Other Non-current	292,559	7.6
Total Assets	**3,849,460**	**100.0**
Accounts Payable	384,946	10.0
Bank Loans	0	0.0
Notes Payable	26,946	0.7
Other Current	581,269	15.1
Total Current	**993,161**	**25.8**
Other Long Term	735,247	19.1
Deferred Credits	0	0.0
Net Worth	2,121,052	55.1
Total Liab & Net Worth	**3,849,460**	**100.0**
Net Sales	6,405,092	100.0
Gross Profit	1,953,553	30.5
Net Profit After Tax	262,609	4.1
Working Capital	1,535,934	—

RATIOS	UQ	MED	LQ
SOLVENCY			
Quick Ratio (times)	2.1	1.3	0.9
Current Ratio (times)	3.9	2.6	1.8
Curr Liab To Nw (%)	18.7	39.1	94.9
Curr Liab To Inv (%)	68.4	103.7	203.9
Total Liab To Nw (%)	36.6	65.9	177.0
Fixed Assets To Nw (%)	15.7	47.9	61.9
EFFICIENCY			
Coll Period (days)	37.6	45.3	54.8
Sales To Inv (times)	10.7	8.5	5.8
Assets To Sales (%)	41.3	60.1	72.5
Sales To Nwc (times)	9.6	6.4	2.7
Acct Pay To Sales (%)	4.4	6.5	8.3
PROFITABILITY			
Return On Sales (%)	6.0	2.7	0.6
Return On Assets (%)	9.9	5.2	1.2
Return On Nw (%)	19.1	9.8	3.4

Balance Sheet

	SIC 3295 MNRLS, GRND TREATED (NO BREAKDOWN) 2002 (12 Establishments) $	%	SIC 3296 MINERAL WOOL (NO BREAKDOWN) 2002 (16 Establishments) $	%	SIC 3297 NONCLAY RFRCTRS (NO BREAKDOWN) 2002 (12 Establishments) $	%	SIC 3299 NMTL MNRL PRDTS,NEC (NO BREAKDOWN) 2002 (16 Establishments) $	%
Cash	416,292	10.0	336,828	10.6	145,837	11.4	312,066	9.0
Accounts Receivable	691,044	16.6	1,067,682	33.6	512,988	40.1	932,731	26.9
Notes Receivable	8,326	0.2	0	0.0	0	0.0	6,935	0.2
Inventory	595,297	14.3	654,591	20.6	173,981	13.6	852,981	24.6
Other Current	274,752	6.6	212,902	6.7	253,297	19.8	235,783	6.8
Total Current	**1,985,711**	**47.7**	**2,272,003**	**71.5**	**1,086,103**	**84.9**	**2,340,496**	**67.5**
Fixed Assets	1,748,425	42.0	645,058	20.3	176,540	13.8	936,199	27.0
Other Non-current	428,780	10.3	260,565	8.2	16,630	1.3	190,707	5.5
Total Assets	**4,162,916**	**100.0**	**3,177,626**	**100.0**	**1,279,273**	**100.0**	**3,467,402**	**100.0**
Accounts Payable	312,219	7.5	374,960	11.8	356,917	27.9	416,088	12.0
Bank Loans	29,140	0.7	0	0.0	0	0.0	86,685	2.5
Notes Payable	287,241	6.9	114,395	3.6	10,234	0.8	263,523	7.6
Other Current	441,269	10.6	670,478	21.1	309,584	24.2	520,110	15.0
Total Current	**1,069,869**	**25.7**	**1,159,833**	**36.5**	**676,735**	**52.9**	**1,286,406**	**37.1**
Other Long Term	874,213	21.0	651,414	20.5	140,720	11.0	502,773	14.5
Deferred Credits	79,095	1.9	9,533	0.3	0	0.0	17,337	0.5
Net Worth	2,139,739	51.4	1,356,846	42.7	461,818	36.1	1,660,886	47.9
Total Liab & Net Worth	**4,162,916**	**100.0**	**3,177,626**	**100.0**	**1,279,273**	**100.0**	**3,467,402**	**100.0**
Net Sales	4,457,084	100.0	6,689,739	100.0	4,167,013	100.0	7,164,054	100.0
Gross Profit	1,060,786	23.8	1,926,645	28.8	1,075,089	25.8	2,665,028	37.2
Net Profit After Tax	(124,798)	(2.8)	(60,208)	(0.9)	(50,004)	(1.2)	(286,562)	(4.0)
Working Capital	915,842	—	1,112,170	—	409,368	—	1,054,090	—

RATIOS

	SIC 3295 UQ	MED	LQ	SIC 3296 UQ	MED	LQ	SIC 3297 UQ	MED	LQ	SIC 3299 UQ	MED	LQ
SOLVENCY												
Quick Ratio (times)	3.6	0.9	0.5	2.3	1.3	0.8	2.8	1.3	0.9	1.3	1.0	0.7
Current Ratio (times)	4.6	2.1	1.3	4.2	2.0	1.5	3.9	1.9	1.5	3.5	2.0	1.4
Curr Liab To Nw (%)	14.5	54.5	113.8	48.3	71.3	120.2	22.3	88.8	252.4	25.0	50.3	213.7
Curr Liab To Inv (%)	100.0	131.4	641.5	94.5	172.3	232.5	123.2	175.9	999.9	92.1	159.0	250.4
Total Liab To Nw (%)	32.2	109.0	267.9	66.2	127.5	175.0	22.3	99.3	252.4	40.9	89.7	276.6
Fixed Assets To Nw (%)	55.3	66.0	162.0	18.1	24.0	73.8	9.8	18.6	32.1	20.3	56.0	73.5
EFFICIENCY												
Coll Period (days)	32.5	38.9	66.1	31.8	58.0	95.6	47.1	63.2	75.8	33.4	48.6	62.8
Sales To Inv (times)	42.7	6.2	4.8	19.2	10.2	6.4	31.5	14.1	7.4	11.5	8.9	6.3
Assets To Sales (%)	59.6	93.4	158.0	34.8	47.5	60.9	25.2	30.7	63.4	34.5	48.4	85.6
Sales To Nwc (times)	9.8	2.9	1.8	7.6	6.3	3.1	12.0	6.1	3.9	21.4	8.0	2.5
Acct Pay To Sales (%)	2.7	6.2	8.0	2.5	4.7	9.9	4.6	7.9	13.2	3.0	5.2	7.4
PROFITABILITY												
Return On Sales (%)	7.7	0.7	(5.7)	5.5	1.6	1.0	4.7	1.0	0.0	5.5	4.2	0.7
Return On Assets (%)	5.1	0.0	(6.5)	8.9	4.5	1.6	9.2	3.7	0.0	7.6	6.0	3.0
Return On Nw (%)	13.3	(0.4)	(21.5)	14.4	11.0	4.9	57.2	8.9	(0.1)	23.4	11.3	6.2

Balance Sheet Data ($ and %)

Item	SIC 33 PRIMARY METAL INDS (454 Est.) $	%	SIC 3312 BLST FRNCS, STL MLLS (91 Est.) $	%	SIC 3315 STL WIRE RLTD PRDS (30 Est.) $	%	SIC 3316 COLD FNSH STL SHPES (16 Est.) $	%
Cash	336,015	9.3	264,565	9.0	372,631	8.5	785,781	15.1
Accounts Receivable	816,553	22.6	605,560	20.6	1,100,359	25.1	1,280,147	24.6
Notes Receivable	25,291	0.7	20,577	0.7	61,375	1.4	0	0.0
Inventory	632,287	17.5	505,613	17.2	1,231,876	28.1	1,202,089	23.1
Other Current	231,236	6.4	252,806	8.6	197,275	4.5	145,709	2.8
Total Current	**2,041,382**	**56.5**	**1,649,121**	**56.1**	**2,963,516**	**67.6**	**3,413,726**	**65.6**
Fixed Assets	1,242,895	34.4	1,011,226	34.4	1,201,188	27.4	1,758,901	33.8
Other Non-current	328,789	9.1	279,263	9.5	219,195	5.0	31,223	0.6
Total Assets	**3,613,066**	**100.0**	**2,939,610**	**100.0**	**4,383,899**	**100.0**	**5,203,850**	**100.0**
Accounts Payable	390,211	10.8	308,659	10.5	490,997	11.2	645,277	12.4
Bank Loans	10,839	0.3	14,698	0.5	0	0.0	0	0.0
Notes Payable	79,487	2.2	102,886	3.5	131,517	3.0	223,766	4.3
Other Current	588,931	16.3	473,278	16.1	547,987	12.5	447,531	8.6
Total Current	**1,069,468**	**29.6**	**899,521**	**30.6**	**1,170,501**	**26.7**	**1,316,574**	**25.3**
Other Long Term	910,492	25.2	964,191	32.8	622,514	14.2	525,589	10.1
Deferred Credits	10,839	0.3	17,638	0.6	21,919	0.5	31,223	0.6
Net Worth	1,622,267	44.9	1,058,260	36.0	2,568,965	58.6	3,330,464	64.0
Total Liab & Net Worth	**3,613,066**	**100.0**	**2,939,610**	**100.0**	**4,383,899**	**100.0**	**5,203,850**	**100.0**
Net Sales	6,229,424	100.0	5,077,047	100.0	7,898,917	100.0	10,555,477	100.0
Gross Profit	1,588,503	25.5	1,264,185	24.9	2,488,159	31.5	2,554,425	24.2
Net Profit After Tax	(24,918)	(0.4)	35,539	0.7	379,148	4.8	158,332	1.5
Working Capital	971,914	—	749,600	—	1,793,015	—	2,097,152	—

RATIOS

	SIC 33 UQ	MED	LQ	SIC 3312 UQ	MED	LQ	SIC 3315 UQ	MED	LQ	SIC 3316 UQ	MED	LQ
SOLVENCY												
Quick Ratio (times)	2.1	1.1	0.7	1.7	0.9	0.5	2.8	1.6	0.9	6.5	1.1	0.8
Current Ratio (times)	4.0	2.2	1.3	3.2	1.9	1.3	6.0	2.7	1.7	7.9	2.1	1.5
Curr Liab To Nw (%)	18.0	46.7	103.5	23.9	60.7	150.5	16.0	28.8	126.4	11.2	45.1	66.0
Curr Liab To Inv (%)	72.1	140.5	284.4	74.1	148.5	332.4	37.5	96.4	129.5	45.9	98.1	154.3
Total Liab To Nw (%)	31.2	81.3	200.7	47.4	114.3	290.2	17.6	51.3	172.1	11.2	50.7	115.9
Fixed Assets To Nw (%)	29.8	63.1	122.9	30.8	75.4	151.1	24.9	49.5	90.5	26.6	48.8	89.9
EFFICIENCY												
Coll Period (days)	35.4	46.4	59.1	31.8	41.3	50.4	40.7	50.0	64.4	27.7	49.5	69.4
Sales To Inv (times)	17.7	9.2	5.7	24.5	7.8	5.0	8.1	6.1	4.4	11.0	6.6	5.1
Assets To Sales (%)	41.3	58.0	89.1	36.8	57.9	84.6	43.1	55.5	87.4	43.5	49.3	64.6
Sales To Nwc (times)	11.3	5.9	3.3	13.6	6.6	4.2	6.0	3.9	2.9	9.1	4.2	3.1
Acct Pay To Sales (%)	3.0	5.5	8.4	3.0	5.8	7.8	3.6	7.0	10.1	3.1	5.4	13.1
PROFITABILITY												
Return On Sales (%)	3.4	0.9	(2.4)	4.7	1.7	(2.2)	8.9	2.6	0.5	4.0	1.9	0.4
Return On Assets (%)	6.6	1.7	(3.8)	8.5	2.7	(3.2)	11.6	5.0	0.6	6.2	3.8	0.4
Return On Nw (%)	13.6	3.6	(5.7)	18.4	6.5	(6.6)	37.1	10.4	1.5	10.7	6.1	1.1

SIC 33 PRIMARY METAL INDS (NO BREAKDOWN) 2002 (454 Establishments)
SIC 3312 BLST FRNCS, STL MLLS (NO BREAKDOWN) 2002 (91 Establishments)
SIC 3315 STL WIRE RLTD PRDS (NO BREAKDOWN) 2002 (30 Establishments)
SIC 3316 COLD FNSH STL SHPES (NO BREAKDOWN) 2002 (16 Establishments)

SIC 3317 — STEEL PIPE TUBES (NO BREAKDOWN) — 2002 (18 Establishments)

	$	%
Cash	1,385,112	8.9
Accounts Receivable	3,579,503	23.0
Notes Receivable	124,504	0.8
Inventory	3,875,201	24.9
Other Current	653,650	4.2
Total Current	**9,617,970**	**61.8**
Fixed Assets	5,291,440	34.0
Other Non-current	653,648	4.2
Total Assets	**15,563,058**	**100.0**
Accounts Payable	2,038,761	13.1
Bank Loans	124,504	0.8
Notes Payable	140,068	0.9
Other Current	2,350,021	15.1
Total Current	**4,653,354**	**29.9**
Other Long Term	3,470,562	22.3
Deferred Credits	0	0.0
Net Worth	7,439,142	47.8
Total Liab & Net Worth	**15,563,058**	**100.0**
Net Sales	21,261,008	100.0
Gross Profit	3,274,195	15.4
Net Profit After Tax	(807,918)	(3.8)
Working Capital	4,964,616	—

RATIOS — SIC 3317

	UQ	MED	LQ
SOLVENCY			
Quick Ratio (times)	1.8	0.9	0.7
Current Ratio (times)	3.6	2.4	1.6
Curr Liab To Nw (%)	31.8	43.5	104.4
Curr Liab To Inv (%)	70.7	118.4	153.3
Total Liab To Nw (%)	76.1	100.3	205.5
Fixed Assets To Nw (%)	53.0	64.0	79.1
EFFICIENCY			
Coll Period (days)	41.1	48.8	60.1
Sales To Inv (times)	8.5	6.8	4.0
Assets To Sales (%)	45.0	73.2	88.5
Sales To Nwc (times)	5.6	4.2	3.3
Acct Pay To Sales (%)	7.2	8.1	10.4
PROFITABILITY			
Return On Sales (%)	1.0	(0.3)	(6.5)
Return On Assets (%)	1.2	(0.5)	(10.6)
Return On Nw (%)	7.3	(0.9)	(22.1)

SIC 3321 — GRY, DCTLE IRN FNDRS (NO BREAKDOWN) — 2002 (40 Establishments)

	$	%
Cash	239,698	7.6
Accounts Receivable	618,169	19.6
Notes Receivable	25,231	0.8
Inventory	492,012	15.6
Other Current	242,853	7.7
Total Current	**1,617,963**	**51.3**
Fixed Assets	1,308,878	41.5
Other Non-current	227,083	7.2
Total Assets	**3,153,924**	**100.0**
Accounts Payable	186,082	5.9
Bank Loans	3,154	0.1
Notes Payable	47,309	1.5
Other Current	596,091	18.9
Total Current	**832,636**	**26.4**
Other Long Term	703,325	22.3
Deferred Credits	12,616	0.4
Net Worth	1,605,347	50.9
Total Liab & Net Worth	**3,153,924**	**100.0**
Net Sales	5,562,476	100.0
Gross Profit	1,062,433	19.1
Net Profit After Tax	(155,749)	(2.8)
Working Capital	785,327	—

RATIOS — SIC 3321

	UQ	MED	LQ
SOLVENCY			
Quick Ratio (times)	1.8	1.1	0.7
Current Ratio (times)	3.0	1.8	1.3
Curr Liab To Nw (%)	29.3	53.2	80.4
Curr Liab To Inv (%)	97.6	174.2	267.5
Total Liab To Nw (%)	56.9	86.0	197.9
Fixed Assets To Nw (%)	44.9	105.5	130.0
EFFICIENCY			
Coll Period (days)	40.4	47.1	62.4
Sales To Inv (times)	17.2	12.2	7.8
Assets To Sales (%)	49.5	56.7	92.2
Sales To Nwc (times)	13.9	6.7	3.6
Acct Pay To Sales (%)	2.5	5.1	7.7
PROFITABILITY			
Return On Sales (%)	1.7	0.3	(7.3)
Return On Assets (%)	3.6	0.3	(8.6)
Return On Nw (%)	7.4	0.5	(21.2)

SIC 3324 — STL INVSTMNT FNDRS (NO BREAKDOWN) — 2002 (12 Establishments)

	$	%
Cash	266,580	11.0
Accounts Receivable	811,856	33.5
Notes Receivable	0	0.0
Inventory	310,202	12.8
Other Current	169,640	7.0
Total Current	**1,558,278**	**64.3**
Fixed Assets	593,745	24.5
Other Non-current	271,427	11.2
Total Assets	**2,423,450**	**100.0**
Accounts Payable	198,723	8.2
Bank Loans	0	0.0
Notes Payable	31,505	1.3
Other Current	375,635	15.5
Total Current	**605,863**	**25.0**
Other Long Term	310,201	12.8
Deferred Credits	0	0.0
Net Worth	1,507,386	62.2
Total Liab & Net Worth	**2,423,450**	**100.0**
Net Sales	3,858,997	100.0
Gross Profit	1,045,788	27.1
Net Profit After Tax	(119,629)	(3.1)
Working Capital	952,415	—

RATIOS — SIC 3324

	UQ	MED	LQ
SOLVENCY			
Quick Ratio (times)	3.3	2.0	0.8
Current Ratio (times)	4.8	2.8	1.8
Curr Liab To Nw (%)	16.2	30.4	82.9
Curr Liab To Inv (%)	102.1	123.6	176.2
Total Liab To Nw (%)	18.5	44.9	147.7
Fixed Assets To Nw (%)	23.7	36.6	59.7
EFFICIENCY			
Coll Period (days)	47.7	50.0	57.9
Sales To Inv (times)	14.5	12.0	8.4
Assets To Sales (%)	42.3	62.8	79.0
Sales To Nwc (times)	9.5	4.8	3.6
Acct Pay To Sales (%)	3.1	4.7	8.8
PROFITABILITY			
Return On Sales (%)	3.4	0.7	(7.9)
Return On Assets (%)	7.7	1.0	(7.0)
Return On Nw (%)	9.9	1.2	(17.6)

SIC 3325 — STL FOUNDRIES, NEC (NO BREAKDOWN) — 2002 (21 Establishments)

	$	%
Cash	153,322	9.9
Accounts Receivable	405,760	26.2
Notes Receivable	1,549	0.1
Inventory	257,085	16.6
Other Current	46,460	3.0
Total Current	**864,176**	**55.8**
Fixed Assets	481,647	31.1
Other Non-current	202,880	13.1
Total Assets	**1,548,703**	**100.0**
Accounts Payable	153,322	9.9
Bank Loans	0	0.0
Notes Payable	43,364	2.8
Other Current	286,509	18.5
Total Current	**483,195**	**31.2**
Other Long Term	278,767	18.0
Deferred Credits	3,097	0.2
Net Worth	783,644	50.6
Total Liab & Net Worth	**1,548,703**	**100.0**
Net Sales	2,564,078	100.0
Gross Profit	725,634	28.3
Net Profit After Tax	(5,128)	(0.2)
Working Capital	380,981	—

RATIOS — SIC 3325

	UQ	MED	LQ
SOLVENCY			
Quick Ratio (times)	3.4	1.5	0.8
Current Ratio (times)	4.7	2.5	1.2
Curr Liab To Nw (%)	12.8	53.3	125.3
Curr Liab To Inv (%)	62.9	203.5	325.2
Total Liab To Nw (%)	25.8	111.5	243.4
Fixed Assets To Nw (%)	27.4	48.0	132.3
EFFICIENCY			
Coll Period (days)	51.5	61.3	63.9
Sales To Inv (times)	12.3	9.0	7.7
Assets To Sales (%)	44.8	60.4	73.1
Sales To Nwc (times)	11.0	5.8	4.2
Acct Pay To Sales (%)	2.4	4.8	8.4
PROFITABILITY			
Return On Sales (%)	2.2	0.1	(2.1)
Return On Assets (%)	6.0	0.0	(3.5)
Return On Nw (%)	6.6	(0.1)	(15.5)

	SIC 3341 SCDRY NFER MTLS (NO BREAKDOWN) 2002 (13 Establishments) $	%	SIC 3354 ALM EXTRDED PRDCTS (NO BREAKDOWN) 2002 (15 Establishments) $	%	SIC 3357 NFER WRDRWNG, INSUL (NO BREAKDOWN) 2002 (34 Establishments) $	%	SIC 3363 ALUM DIE-CASTINGS (NO BREAKDOWN) 2002 (19 Establishments) $	%
Cash	257,213	5.1	976,562	6.8	2,474,138	7.9	236,634	9.1
Accounts Receivable	1,644,149	32.6	3,331,801	23.2	6,420,232	20.5	608,487	23.4
Notes Receivable	237,040	4.7	43,084	0.3	0	0.0	0	0.0
Inventory	978,420	19.4	2,340,878	16.3	6,921,323	22.1	306,844	11.8
Other Current	196,692	3.9	775,506	5.4	1,816,456	5.8	130,017	5.0
Total Current	**3,313,514**	**65.7**	**7,467,831**	**52.0**	**17,632,149**	**56.3**	**1,281,982**	**49.3**
Fixed Assets	1,316,328	26.1	5,055,147	35.2	10,021,825	32.0	1,071,352	41.2
Other Non-current	413,559	8.2	1,838,235	12.8	3,664,230	11.7	247,036	9.5
Total Assets	**5,043,401**	**100.0**	**14,361,213**	**100.0**	**31,318,204**	**100.0**	**2,600,370**	**100.0**
Accounts Payable	1,013,724	20.1	1,507,927	10.5	2,818,638	9.0	291,241	11.2
Bank Loans	141,215	2.8	0	0.0	125,273	0.4	2,600	0.1
Notes Payable	221,910	4.4	186,696	1.3	532,409	1.7	65,009	2.5
Other Current	791,813	15.7	2,154,182	15.0	5,418,050	17.3	483,670	18.6
Total Current	**2,168,662**	**43.0**	**3,848,805**	**26.8**	**8,894,370**	**28.4**	**842,520**	**32.4**
Other Long Term	559,818	11.1	1,910,041	13.3	7,234,505	23.1	522,674	20.1
Deferred Credits	0	0.0	0	0.0	0	0.0	28,604	1.1
Net Worth	2,314,921	45.9	8,602,367	59.9	15,189,329	48.5	1,206,572	46.4
Total Liab & Net Worth	**5,043,401**	**100.0**	**14,361,213**	**100.0**	**31,318,204**	**100.0**	**2,600,370**	**100.0**
Net Sales	12,094,487	100.0	23,542,972	100.0	40,151,544	100.0	4,788,895	100.0
Gross Profit	1,838,362	15.2	5,391,341	22.9	10,840,917	27.0	1,249,902	26.1
Net Profit After Tax	36,283	0.3	282,516	1.2	(2,529,547)	(6.3)	(52,678)	(1.1)
Working Capital	1,144,852	—	3,619,026	—	8,737,779	—	439,462	—

RATIOS	3341 UQ	MED	LQ	3354 UQ	MED	LQ	3357 UQ	MED	LQ	3363 UQ	MED	LQ
SOLVENCY												
Quick Ratio (times)	0.9	0.7	0.5	1.8	1.2	0.8	2.5	1.2	0.7	1.7	1.2	0.8
Current Ratio (times)	2.0	1.6	1.0	3.0	1.9	1.4	7.1	2.6	1.3	3.5	2.2	1.2
Curr Liab To Nw (%)	53.2	100.0	183.3	20.3	44.1	116.4	11.3	18.9	51.7	21.2	39.6	150.8
Curr Liab To Inv (%)	143.8	224.6	415.7	135.6	155.1	294.4	55.9	79.3	183.7	114.8	210.1	527.8
Total Liab To Nw (%)	61.8	104.0	256.6	22.9	57.5	184.4	13.0	47.6	148.3	42.5	89.9	234.4
Fixed Assets To Nw (%)	12.9	41.8	160.4	42.2	68.3	91.1	21.9	57.3	93.0	40.3	78.5	144.5
EFFICIENCY												
Coll Period (days)	36.1	43.5	46.4	38.0	47.5	66.3	32.5	41.4	63.5	38.0	45.3	51.5
Sales To Inv (times)	20.0	16.1	9.9	19.0	11.7	5.9	8.7	5.8	4.1	27.5	13.7	9.0
Assets To Sales (%)	24.0	41.7	62.0	49.6	61.0	87.2	42.8	78.0	134.4	42.3	54.3	68.0
Sales To Nwc (times)	24.2	9.0	6.4	17.0	8.7	3.6	8.8	3.8	2.2	15.6	7.4	4.5
Acct Pay To Sales (%)	5.1	7.4	11.3	4.2	5.8	7.8	4.5	7.8	16.1	2.7	4.5	6.9
PROFITABILITY												
Return On Sales (%)	1.9	0.8	0.0	5.0	0.1	(0.5)	4.1	0.0	(10.9)	3.2	0.5	(1.4)
Return On Assets (%)	5.6	2.9	0.2	6.6	0.2	(0.8)	5.6	0.3	(5.8)	5.9	1.1	(1.9)
Return On Nw (%)	11.8	6.9	0.2	7.3	0.5	(2.0)	13.6	1.0	(16.2)	16.4	3.1	(2.9)

SIC 3364 NFER DCSTNG, EXC ALM (NO BREAKDOWN) 2002 (10 Establishments)

	$	%
Cash	278,222	10.7
Accounts Receivable	595,447	22.9
Notes Receivable	0	0.0
Inventory	429,034	16.5
Other Current	239,220	9.2
Total Current	**1,541,923**	**59.3**
Fixed Assets	785,263	30.2
Other Non-current	273,021	10.5
Total Assets	**2,600,207**	**100.0**
Accounts Payable	234,019	9.0
Bank Loans	0	0.0
Notes Payable	5,200	0.2
Other Current	413,433	15.9
Total Current	**652,652**	**25.1**
Other Long Term	416,033	16.0
Deferred Credits	0	0.0
Net Worth	1,531,522	58.9
Total Liab & Net Worth	**2,600,207**	**100.0**
Net Sales	4,933,979	100.0
Gross Profit	838,776	17.0
Net Profit After Tax	93,746	1.9
Working Capital	889,271	—

RATIOS	UQ	MED	LQ
SOLVENCY			
Quick Ratio (times)	3.4	1.6	0.9
Current Ratio (times)	5.4	2.7	1.3
Curr Liab To Nw (%)	18.7	23.3	184.5
Curr Liab To Inv (%)	61.4	106.6	323.0
Total Liab To Nw (%)	18.8	48.5	381.0
Fixed Assets To Nw (%)	16.3	40.4	259.4
EFFICIENCY			
Coll Period (days)	32.5	35.0	48.2
Sales To Inv (times)	19.9	15.9	9.4
Assets To Sales (%)	41.0	52.7	61.6
Sales To Nwc (times)	9.4	5.3	4.6
Acct Pay To Sales (%)	1.7	1.8	5.9
PROFITABILITY			
Return On Sales (%)	5.9	1.9	(1.2)
Return On Assets (%)	11.8	5.7	(1.8)
Return On Nw (%)	15.9	9.3	(0.9)

SIC 3365 ALUMINUM FOUNDRIES (NO BREAKDOWN) 2002 (19 Establishments)

	$	%
Cash	199,079	11.6
Accounts Receivable	398,157	23.2
Notes Receivable	34,324	2.0
Inventory	334,658	19.5
Other Current	63,499	3.7
Total Current	**1,029,717**	**60.0**
Fixed Assets	578,358	33.7
Other Non-current	108,120	6.3
Total Assets	**1,716,195**	**100.0**
Accounts Payable	204,227	11.9
Bank Loans	8,581	0.5
Notes Payable	20,594	1.2
Other Current	219,673	12.8
Total Current	**453,075**	**26.4**
Other Long Term	408,455	23.8
Deferred Credits	1,716	0.1
Net Worth	852,949	49.7
Total Liab & Net Worth	**1,716,195**	**100.0**
Net Sales	2,933,667	100.0
Gross Profit	692,345	23.6
Net Profit After Tax	8,801	0.3
Working Capital	576,642	—

RATIOS	UQ	MED	LQ
SOLVENCY			
Quick Ratio (times)	2.0	1.2	0.9
Current Ratio (times)	2.8	2.4	1.7
Curr Liab To Nw (%)	21.8	56.8	76.8
Curr Liab To Inv (%)	94.4	147.1	227.0
Total Liab To Nw (%)	47.6	97.9	147.6
Fixed Assets To Nw (%)	29.9	67.2	108.6
EFFICIENCY			
Coll Period (days)	35.0	44.4	54.4
Sales To Inv (times)	14.7	10.7	7.5
Assets To Sales (%)	49.0	58.5	72.3
Sales To Nwc (times)	10.0	5.8	3.3
Acct Pay To Sales (%)	3.3	5.0	8.9
PROFITABILITY			
Return On Sales (%)	3.6	1.5	(1.6)
Return On Assets (%)	7.0	2.2	(4.1)
Return On Nw (%)	12.3	5.3	(15.0)

SIC 3366 COPPER FOUNDRIES (NO BREAKDOWN) 2002 (15 Establishments)

	$	%
Cash	225,082	14.7
Accounts Receivable	385,855	25.2
Notes Receivable	(10,718)	(0.7)
Inventory	195,990	12.8
Other Current	81,151	5.3
Total Current	**877,360**	**57.3**
Fixed Assets	552,752	36.1
Other Non-current	101,057	6.6
Total Assets	**1,531,169**	**100.0**
Accounts Payable	124,025	8.1
Bank Loans	0	0.0
Notes Payable	16,843	1.1
Other Current	367,480	24.0
Total Current	**508,348**	**33.2**
Other Long Term	195,990	12.8
Deferred Credits	0	0.0
Net Worth	826,831	54.0
Total Liab & Net Worth	**1,531,169**	**100.0**
Net Sales	2,477,620	100.0
Gross Profit	837,436	33.8
Net Profit After Tax	22,299	0.9
Working Capital	369,012	—

RATIOS	UQ	MED	LQ
SOLVENCY			
Quick Ratio (times)	3.8	1.6	1.0
Current Ratio (times)	4.9	2.1	1.7
Curr Liab To Nw (%)	14.2	22.9	48.1
Curr Liab To Inv (%)	87.1	119.3	357.3
Total Liab To Nw (%)	18.8	50.5	66.0
Fixed Assets To Nw (%)	34.6	43.6	65.9
EFFICIENCY			
Coll Period (days)	34.7	44.9	67.9
Sales To Inv (times)	19.4	16.6	11.8
Assets To Sales (%)	37.5	61.8	73.5
Sales To Nwc (times)	6.2	3.5	2.8
Acct Pay To Sales (%)	2.5	4.1	5.3
PROFITABILITY			
Return On Sales (%)	5.9	1.4	(0.9)
Return On Assets (%)	8.3	3.8	(1.5)
Return On Nw (%)	24.0	4.6	1.7

SIC 3369 NFER FOUNDRIES, NEC (NO BREAKDOWN) 2002 (15 Establishments)

	$	%
Cash	407,101	13.9
Accounts Receivable	694,122	23.7
Notes Receivable	2,929	0.1
Inventory	521,323	17.8
Other Current	216,730	7.4
Total Current	**1,842,205**	**62.9**
Fixed Assets	928,424	31.7
Other Non-current	158,154	5.4
Total Assets	**2,928,783**	**100.0**
Accounts Payable	322,166	11.0
Bank Loans	0	0.0
Notes Payable	20,501	0.7
Other Current	609,187	20.8
Total Current	**951,854**	**32.5**
Other Long Term	547,683	18.7
Deferred Credits	2,929	0.1
Net Worth	1,426,317	48.7
Total Liab & Net Worth	**2,928,783**	**100.0**
Net Sales	5,822,630	100.0
Gross Profit	1,775,902	30.5
Net Profit After Tax	87,339	1.5
Working Capital	890,351	—

RATIOS	UQ	MED	LQ
SOLVENCY			
Quick Ratio (times)	2.4	1.1	0.8
Current Ratio (times)	4.2	1.7	1.3
Curr Liab To Nw (%)	15.7	67.0	99.4
Curr Liab To Inv (%)	120.3	178.3	212.5
Total Liab To Nw (%)	17.0	83.9	117.3
Fixed Assets To Nw (%)	22.5	44.1	80.8
EFFICIENCY			
Coll Period (days)	35.8	48.2	53.7
Sales To Inv (times)	17.6	13.9	8.2
Assets To Sales (%)	41.9	50.3	72.6
Sales To Nwc (times)	12.6	8.4	3.1
Acct Pay To Sales (%)	2.9	3.0	5.1
PROFITABILITY			
Return On Sales (%)	2.8	1.7	0.1
Return On Assets (%)	5.2	2.6	0.7
Return On Nw (%)	7.2	3.6	1.7

	SIC 3398 METAL HEAT TREATING (NO BREAKDOWN) 2002 (29 Establishments) $	%	SIC 3399 PRIM METAL PRODUCTS (NO BREAKDOWN) 2002 (18 Establishments) $	%	SIC 34 FABRICATED METAL PDT (NO BREAKDOWN) 2002 (2301 Establishments) $	%	SIC 3423 HAND EDGE TOOLS,NEC (NO BREAKDOWN) 2002 (41 Establishments) $	%
Cash	129,007	7.8	221,789	6.4	230,057	12.6	463,220	12.2
Accounts Receivable	454,833	27.5	589,128	17.0	478,372	26.2	793,549	20.9
Notes Receivable	1,654	0.1	6,931	0.2	9,129	0.5	34,172	0.9
Inventory	49,618	3.0	398,528	11.5	314,046	17.2	1,044,144	27.5
Other Current	117,430	7.1	339,614	9.8	140,590	7.7	193,642	5.1
Total Current	**752,542**	**45.5**	**1,555,990**	**44.9**	**1,172,194**	**64.2**	**2,528,727**	**66.6**
Fixed Assets	749,234	45.3	1,396,579	40.3	531,321	29.1	846,706	22.3
Other Non-current	152,162	9.2	512,888	14.8	122,332	6.7	421,454	11.1
Total Assets	**1,653,938**	**100.0**	**3,465,457**	**100.0**	**1,825,847**	**100.0**	**3,796,887**	**100.0**
Accounts Payable	125,699	7.6	291,098	8.4	220,927	12.1	326,532	8.6
Bank Loans	0	0.0	0	0.0	7,303	0.4	0	0.0
Notes Payable	49,618	3.0	6,931	0.2	58,427	3.2	53,156	1.4
Other Current	276,208	16.7	471,302	13.6	319,524	17.5	717,612	18.9
Total Current	**451,525**	**27.3**	**769,331**	**22.2**	**606,181**	**33.2**	**1,097,300**	**28.9**
Other Long Term	350,635	21.2	1,105,481	31.9	328,652	18.0	710,018	18.7
Deferred Credits	3,308	0.2	0	0.0	5,478	0.3	3,797	0.1
Net Worth	848,470	51.3	1,590,645	45.9	885,536	48.5	1,985,772	52.3
Total Liab & Net Worth	**1,653,938**	**100.0**	**3,465,457**	**100.0**	**1,825,847**	**100.0**	**3,796,887**	**100.0**
Net Sales	3,091,473	100.0	5,681,077	100.0	3,726,218	100.0	5,960,576	100.0
Gross Profit	1,180,943	38.2	1,761,134	31.0	1,207,295	32.4	2,026,596	34.0
Net Profit After Tax	(3,091)	(0.1)	215,881	3.8	59,619	1.6	184,778	3.1
Working Capital	301,017	—	786,659	—	566,013	—	1,431,427	—

RATIOS	UQ	MED	LQ	UQ	MED	LQ	UQ	MED	LQ	UQ	MED	LQ
SOLVENCY												
Quick Ratio (times)	2.3	1.2	0.7	3.4	1.2	0.8	2.7	1.3	0.7	4.5	1.4	0.9
Current Ratio (times)	3.4	1.7	1.0	3.2	2.0	1.3	4.5	2.2	1.4	9.8	3.1	1.8
Curr Liab To Nw (%)	18.8	47.4	105.8	22.8	51.7	99.8	18.4	48.4	113.2	9.7	30.3	70.4
Curr Liab To Inv (%)	314.4	797.6	999.9	64.2	168.8	307.6	79.3	161.4	383.9	45.1	81.9	135.4
Total Liab To Nw (%)	40.1	82.9	217.3	36.1	109.3	222.2	28.1	81.6	182.5	12.6	63.3	149.8
Fixed Assets To Nw (%)	47.7	86.2	170.2	27.0	87.9	197.3	22.9	47.4	96.6	11.2	31.7	76.8
EFFICIENCY												
Coll Period (days)	42.7	49.7	58.0	43.1	50.2	65.2	34.0	46.7	62.1	35.1	42.9	53.7
Sales To Inv (times)	131.1	41.3	25.8	15.6	9.6	6.7	28.7	12.3	6.8	8.1	6.0	4.4
Assets To Sales (%)	33.7	53.5	92.5	49.0	61.0	79.0	35.2	49.0	70.3	56.9	63.7	91.6
Sales To Nwc (times)	16.3	8.1	4.1	11.2	5.7	3.6	10.8	6.0	3.5	6.5	3.9	1.9
Acct Pay To Sales (%)	2.4	2.9	5.3	3.6	5.5	6.8	2.7	4.8	7.8	1.5	3.9	6.5
PROFITABILITY												
Return On Sales (%)	2.0	0.3	(2.2)	3.8	1.2	(0.3)	4.9	1.7	(0.6)	6.9	2.8	0.7
Return On Assets (%)	2.7	1.0	(5.6)	8.5	2.3	(0.3)	9.6	3.3	(1.2)	10.7	5.0	0.4
Return On Nw (%)	5.1	1.8	(8.1)	20.4	7.5	0.9	21.3	6.9	(1.2)	19.4	10.3	1.3

	SIC 3429 HAEDWARE, NEC (NO BREAKDOWN) 2002 (67 Establishments) $	%	SIC 3433 HTNG EQPT, EXC ELEC (NO BREAKDOWN) 2002 (28 Establishments) $	%	SIC 3441 FBRCTED STRCTRL MTL (NO BREAKDOWN) 2002 (418 Establishments) $	%	SIC 3442 MTL DOORS, SASH, TRIM (NO BREAKDOWN) 2002 (91 Establishments) $	%
Cash	269,817	10.0	236,212	9.8	203,026	12.7	295,287	11.2
Accounts Receivable	509,955	18.9	597,761	24.8	500,372	31.3	656,487	24.9
Notes Receivable	18,887	0.7	0	0.0	7,993	0.5	7,909	0.3
Inventory	831,037	30.8	785,767	32.6	174,251	10.9	696,034	26.4
Other Current	159,193	5.9	96,414	4.0	164,659	10.3	150,280	5.7
Total Current	**1,788,889**	**66.3**	**1,716,154**	**71.2**	**1,050,301**	**65.7**	**1,805,997**	**68.5**
Fixed Assets	623,278	23.1	513,400	21.3	463,603	29.0	606,393	23.0
Other Non-current	286,006	10.6	180,774	7.5	84,727	5.3	224,102	8.5
Total Assets	**2,698,173**	**100.0**	**2,410,328**	**100.0**	**1,598,631**	**100.0**	**2,636,492**	**100.0**
Accounts Payable	237,439	8.8	679,712	28.2	220,611	13.8	358,563	13.6
Bank Loans	5,396	0.2	9,641	0.4	7,993	0.5	2,636	0.1
Notes Payable	91,738	3.4	60,258	2.5	46,360	2.9	118,642	4.5
Other Current	445,199	16.5	2,330,788	96.7	266,972	16.7	406,020	15.4
Total Current	**779,772**	**28.9**	**3,080,399**	**127.8**	**541,936**	**33.9**	**885,861**	**33.6**
Other Long Term	515,351	19.1	416,987	17.3	250,985	15.7	424,475	16.1
Deferred Credits	5,396	0.2	40,976	1.7	3,197	0.2	10,546	0.4
Net Worth	1,397,654	51.8	(1,128,034)	(46.8)	802,513	50.2	1,315,610	49.9
Total Liab & Net Worth	**2,698,173**	**100.0**	**2,410,328**	**100.0**	**1,598,631**	**100.0**	**2,636,492**	**100.0**
Net Sales	4,452,431	100.0	3,657,554	100.0	3,584,374	100.0	5,978,440	100.0
Gross Profit	1,442,588	32.4	1,126,527	30.8	1,071,728	29.9	1,966,907	32.9
Net Profit After Tax	129,120	2.9	25,603	0.7	53,766	1.5	197,289	3.3
Working Capital	1,009,117	—	(1,364,245)	—	508,365	—	920,136	—

RATIOS	UQ	MED	LQ	UQ	MED	LQ	UQ	MED	LQ	UQ	MED	LQ
SOLVENCY												
Quick Ratio (times)	2.6	1.1	0.5	1.5	0.9	0.4	2.6	1.3	0.8	2.3	1.2	0.6
Current Ratio (times)	5.9	2.6	1.5	2.9	1.8	1.3	3.8	1.9	1.3	4.1	2.4	1.5
Curr Liab To Nw (%)	13.8	36.8	114.5	37.7	63.5	112.7	21.7	59.5	126.2	24.8	50.5	99.5
Curr Liab To Inv (%)	41.4	87.9	150.7	71.4	92.9	210.2	131.2	367.2	881.0	64.2	107.4	191.5
Total Liab To Nw (%)	21.2	63.5	175.3	57.9	115.0	178.3	33.7	93.0	178.8	27.2	89.1	179.4
Fixed Assets To Nw (%)	19.1	39.8	74.3	18.8	34.8	59.5	22.5	47.2	94.8	18.8	37.4	78.2
EFFICIENCY												
Coll Period (days)	29.9	38.7	47.5	23.6	49.7	63.3	37.8	54.0	73.6	25.9	38.4	52.9
Sales To Inv (times)	8.4	6.1	4.7	9.6	6.6	2.9	70.2	26.2	10.9	14.9	10.9	6.3
Assets To Sales (%)	41.9	60.6	82.0	38.5	65.9	82.8	32.8	44.6	61.6	33.4	44.1	66.7
Sales To Nwc (times)	10.6	4.7	3.1	8.9	5.3	3.3	12.5	7.2	3.9	9.0	6.0	3.7
Acct Pay To Sales (%)	2.3	4.4	6.8	3.6	5.5	10.8	2.9	5.4	8.2	2.9	5.2	8.9
PROFITABILITY												
Return On Sales (%)	5.3	2.5	(0.9)	4.2	2.3	0.5	4.3	1.4	(0.2)	6.1	2.6	0.8
Return On Assets (%)	9.9	3.4	(1.1)	10.2	5.1	1.2	9.3	3.0	(0.6)	13.5	5.7	1.1
Return On Nw (%)	20.3	6.9	(2.0)	36.1	8.8	3.7	18.2	5.8	(0.9)	26.1	12.9	3.4

	SIC 3443 FBRCT PLT WK BLR SH (180 Establishments) $	%	SIC 3444 SHEET METALWORK (307 Establishments) $	%	SIC 3446 ARCHTCTRL METALWORK (82 Establishments) $	%	SIC 3448 PREFBRCTD MTL BLDGS (61 Establishments) $	%
Cash	292,225	12.7	188,448	14.2	133,711	12.2	272,334	10.2
Accounts Receivable	602,859	26.2	384,858	29.0	335,374	30.6	568,698	21.3
Notes Receivable	2,301	0.1	5,308	0.4	9,864	0.9	16,020	0.6
Inventory	414,178	18.0	200,391	15.1	144,671	13.2	517,969	19.4
Other Current	209,390	9.1	88,916	6.7	146,864	13.4	280,344	10.5
Total Current	**1,520,953**	**66.1**	**867,921**	**65.4**	**770,484**	**70.3**	**1,655,365**	**62.0**
Fixed Assets	618,966	26.9	391,493	29.5	258,655	23.6	830,352	31.1
Other Non-current	161,069	7.0	67,682	5.1	66,856	6.1	184,226	6.9
Total Assets	**2,300,988**	**100.0**	**1,327,096**	**100.0**	**1,095,995**	**100.0**	**2,669,943**	**100.0**
Accounts Payable	260,012	11.3	149,962	11.3	135,903	12.4	424,521	15.9
Bank Loans	4,602	0.2	6,635	0.5	8,768	0.8	10,680	0.4
Notes Payable	73,632	3.2	35,832	2.7	18,632	1.7	48,059	1.8
Other Current	467,100	20.3	222,952	16.8	191,799	17.5	528,648	19.8
Total Current	**805,346**	**35.0**	**415,381**	**31.3**	**355,102**	**32.4**	**1,011,908**	**37.9**
Other Long Term	393,469	17.1	230,915	17.4	135,904	12.4	648,796	24.3
Deferred Credits	4,602	0.2	3,981	0.3	3,288	0.3	8,010	0.3
Net Worth	1,097,571	47.7	676,819	51.0	601,701	54.9	1,001,229	37.5
Total Liab & Net Worth	**2,300,988**	**100.0**	**1,327,096**	**100.0**	**1,095,995**	**100.0**	**2,669,943**	**100.0**
Net Sales	4,592,790	100.0	3,009,288	100.0	2,548,826	100.0	5,741,813	100.0
Gross Profit	1,327,316	28.9	1,014,130	33.7	953,261	37.4	1,693,835	29.5
Net Profit After Tax	45,928	1.0	72,223	2.4	73,916	2.9	11,484	0.2
Working Capital	715,607	—	452,540	—	415,382	—	643,457	—

RATIOS	UQ	MED	LQ	UQ	MED	LQ	UQ	MED	LQ	UQ	MED	LQ
SOLVENCY												
Quick Ratio (times)	2.2	1.1	0.7	3.2	1.5	0.9	2.5	1.5	0.7	1.6	0.9	0.5
Current Ratio (times)	3.9	1.9	1.3	4.3	2.3	1.5	4.5	2.3	1.5	2.8	1.8	1.2
Curr Liab To Nw (%)	25.6	64.7	121.3	21.0	41.0	91.6	18.1	55.6	97.2	25.2	60.0	146.2
Curr Liab To Inv (%)	79.4	162.0	387.8	83.5	181.8	408.8	95.5	245.6	966.8	82.9	172.7	344.0
Total Liab To Nw (%)	38.0	92.9	198.8	31.2	72.1	159.2	21.9	59.3	131.5	36.1	123.3	232.4
Fixed Assets To Nw (%)	22.8	46.9	101.4	24.6	46.3	95.4	21.4	37.9	65.9	30.3	53.9	112.6
EFFICIENCY												
Coll Period (days)	33.2	48.6	65.0	34.0	44.7	64.5	29.2	46.0	64.4	21.9	38.9	64.6
Sales To Inv (times)	26.1	12.1	7.0	35.3	14.6	8.8	84.7	18.5	9.4	24.1	13.2	6.7
Assets To Sales (%)	35.6	50.1	65.3	32.6	44.1	63.0	29.0	43.0	56.0	28.7	46.5	66.9
Sales To Nwc (times)	12.1	6.6	3.7	10.2	6.1	3.8	10.3	5.7	3.8	11.7	7.1	4.2
Acct Pay To Sales (%)	3.2	4.8	7.8	2.2	4.1	6.9	2.2	4.0	7.7	3.3	5.5	10.0
PROFITABILITY												
Return On Sales (%)	3.2	1.1	(1.0)	5.0	2.0	(0.5)	5.5	2.0	0.1	6.0	1.9	(0.5)
Return On Assets (%)	7.4	2.4	(1.7)	12.5	3.8	(1.3)	16.6	5.5	0.3	11.4	4.3	(1.0)
Return On Nw (%)	21.9	4.5	(2.0)	28.5	7.2	(1.6)	27.5	12.2	2.7	35.0	11.4	0.9

(NO BREAKDOWN)
2002

SIC 3449 MISC METALWORK (NO BREAKDOWN) 2002 (29 Establishments)

	$	%
Cash	167,914	11.1
Accounts Receivable	402,388	26.6
Notes Receivable	25,716	1.7
Inventory	222,372	14.7
Other Current	86,226	5.7
Total Current	**904,616**	**59.8**
Fixed Assets	476,512	31.5
Other Non-current	131,607	8.7
Total Assets	**1,512,735**	**100.0**
Accounts Payable	187,579	12.4
Bank Loans	15,127	1.0
Notes Payable	125,557	8.3
Other Current	299,522	19.8
Total Current	**627,785**	**41.5**
Other Long Term	269,267	17.8
Deferred Credits	0	0.0
Net Worth	615,683	40.7
Total Liab & Net Worth	**1,512,735**	**100.0**
Net Sales	2,870,465	100.0
Gross Profit	961,606	33.5
Net Profit After Tax	97,596	3.4
Working Capital	276,831	—

RATIOS	UQ	MED	LQ
SOLVENCY			
Quick Ratio (times)	2.8	1.0	0.6
Current Ratio (times)	4.5	1.6	1.1
Curr Liab To Nw (%)	11.3	35.7	130.7
Curr Liab To Inv (%)	58.5	172.1	247.7
Total Liab To Nw (%)	18.5	46.5	195.4
Fixed Assets To Nw (%)	16.7	51.4	94.1
EFFICIENCY			
Coll Period (days)	38.0	44.9	53.1
Sales To Inv (times)	21.8	10.7	6.6
Assets To Sales (%)	35.1	52.7	71.6
Sales To Nwc (times)	14.7	5.7	3.0
Acct Pay To Sales (%)	2.3	4.0	8.6
PROFITABILITY			
Return On Sales (%)	6.7	3.6	0.7
Return On Assets (%)	12.7	4.6	0.8
Return On Nw (%)	18.9	12.1	2.6

SIC 3451 SCREW MACHINE PRDTS (NO BREAKDOWN) 2002 (86 Establishments)

	$	%
Cash	201,703	14.1
Accounts Receivable	301,839	21.1
Notes Receivable	10,014	0.7
Inventory	256,062	17.9
Other Current	85,830	6.0
Total Current	**855,448**	**59.8**
Fixed Assets	499,250	34.9
Other Non-current	75,817	5.3
Total Assets	**1,430,515**	**100.0**
Accounts Payable	123,024	8.6
Bank Loans	7,153	0.5
Notes Payable	37,193	2.6
Other Current	251,771	17.6
Total Current	**419,141**	**29.3**
Other Long Term	264,645	18.5
Deferred Credits	1,431	0.1
Net Worth	745,298	52.1
Total Liab & Net Worth	**1,430,515**	**100.0**
Net Sales	2,545,400	100.0
Gross Profit	814,528	32.0
Net Profit After Tax	(27,999)	(1.1)
Working Capital	436,307	—

RATIOS	UQ	MED	LQ
SOLVENCY			
Quick Ratio (times)	3.2	1.2	0.6
Current Ratio (times)	5.3	2.3	1.4
Curr Liab To Nw (%)	11.9	46.8	92.0
Curr Liab To Inv (%)	76.8	130.0	238.0
Total Liab To Nw (%)	22.8	71.4	180.1
Fixed Assets To Nw (%)	24.9	57.8	125.8
EFFICIENCY			
Coll Period (days)	31.2	44.2	55.2
Sales To Inv (times)	17.8	10.0	5.9
Assets To Sales (%)	42.5	56.2	79.0
Sales To Nwc (times)	9.3	5.3	2.5
Acct Pay To Sales (%)	2.6	3.6	7.0
PROFITABILITY			
Return On Sales (%)	2.6	0.5	(3.6)
Return On Assets (%)	3.5	0.6	(6.7)
Return On Nw (%)	7.4	1.3	(9.5)

SIC 3452 BLTS,NUTS,RVTS,WSHR (NO BREAKDOWN) 2002 (38 Establishments)

	$	%
Cash	317,399	9.0
Accounts Receivable	853,451	24.2
Notes Receivable	10,580	0.3
Inventory	973,357	27.6
Other Current	144,593	4.1
Total Current	**2,299,380**	**65.2**
Fixed Assets	1,015,677	28.8
Other Non-current	211,600	6.0
Total Assets	**3,526,657**	**100.0**
Accounts Payable	292,713	8.3
Bank Loans	0	0.0
Notes Payable	102,273	2.9
Other Current	433,778	12.3
Total Current	**828,764**	**23.5**
Other Long Term	892,244	25.3
Deferred Credits	3,527	0.1
Net Worth	1,802,122	51.1
Total Liab & Net Worth	**3,526,657**	**100.0**
Net Sales	6,388,871	100.0
Gross Profit	1,673,884	26.2
Net Profit After Tax	76,666	1.2
Working Capital	1,470,616	—

RATIOS	UQ	MED	LQ
SOLVENCY			
Quick Ratio (times)	3.2	1.4	0.9
Current Ratio (times)	5.7	2.7	1.9
Curr Liab To Nw (%)	18.0	31.3	73.9
Curr Liab To Inv (%)	36.4	77.2	136.1
Total Liab To Nw (%)	25.9	58.7	153.8
Fixed Assets To Nw (%)	20.4	50.9	72.5
EFFICIENCY			
Coll Period (days)	40.2	48.9	55.5
Sales To Inv (times)	13.7	5.2	4.8
Assets To Sales (%)	44.1	55.2	99.4
Sales To Nwc (times)	8.1	4.1	2.9
Acct Pay To Sales (%)	2.4	4.1	5.8
PROFITABILITY			
Return On Sales (%)	5.6	1.0	(1.0)
Return On Assets (%)	7.4	2.7	(1.9)
Return On Nw (%)	13.0	4.5	0.6

SIC 3462 IRON,STEEL FORGINGS (NO BREAKDOWN) 2002 (32 Establishments)

	$	%
Cash	417,324	11.8
Accounts Receivable	689,646	19.5
Notes Receivable	74,270	2.1
Inventory	725,013	20.5
Other Current	321,835	9.1
Total Current	**2,228,088**	**63.0**
Fixed Assets	1,156,484	32.7
Other Non-current	152,075	4.3
Total Assets	**3,536,647**	**100.0**
Accounts Payable	360,738	10.2
Bank Loans	0	0.0
Notes Payable	42,440	1.2
Other Current	364,274	10.3
Total Current	**767,452**	**21.7**
Other Long Term	848,796	24.0
Deferred Credits	7,073	0.2
Net Worth	1,913,326	54.1
Total Liab & Net Worth	**3,536,647**	**100.0**
Net Sales	5,732,005	100.0
Gross Profit	1,496,053	26.1
Net Profit After Tax	(206,352)	(3.6)
Working Capital	1,460,636	—

RATIOS	UQ	MED	LQ
SOLVENCY			
Quick Ratio (times)	3.2	1.4	0.8
Current Ratio (times)	5.8	3.4	2.0
Curr Liab To Nw (%)	16.0	25.9	92.7
Curr Liab To Inv (%)	64.2	108.8	134.1
Total Liab To Nw (%)	18.9	49.9	129.2
Fixed Assets To Nw (%)	26.9	64.7	83.2
EFFICIENCY			
Coll Period (days)	36.1	50.7	66.1
Sales To Inv (times)	10.1	7.3	4.8
Assets To Sales (%)	50.8	61.7	84.5
Sales To Nwc (times)	4.7	3.6	2.7
Acct Pay To Sales (%)	4.1	5.2	9.8
PROFITABILITY			
Return On Sales (%)	2.3	1.8	(1.0)
Return On Assets (%)	4.3	3.0	(1.7)
Return On Nw (%)	13.0	4.9	(1.2)

	SIC 3465 AUTOMOTIVE STAMPINGS (NO BREAKDOWN) 2002 (41 Establishments)		SIC 3469 METAL STAMPINGS, NEC (NO BREAKDOWN) 2002 (221 Establishments)		SIC 3471 PLATING, POLISHING (NO BREAKDOWN) 2002 (97 Establishments)		SIC 3479 MTL CTNG, ALLD SVCS (NO BREAKDOWN) 2002 (94 Establishments)	
	$	%	$	%	$	%	$	%
Cash	640,090	6.4	285,652	13.5	181,722	14.4	184,596	14.8
Accounts Receivable	3,090,436	30.9	490,898	23.2	326,846	25.9	329,280	26.4
Notes Receivable	90,013	0.9	8,464	0.4	3,786	0.3	2,495	0.2
Inventory	1,710,241	17.1	368,174	17.4	69,408	5.5	101,029	8.1
Other Current	330,047	3.3	143,884	6.8	113,575	9.0	91,050	7.3
Total Current	**5,860,827**	**58.6**	**1,297,072**	**61.3**	**695,337**	**55.1**	**708,450**	**56.8**
Fixed Assets	3,580,505	35.8	679,217	32.1	469,447	37.2	457,749	36.7
Other Non-current	560,080	5.6	139,652	6.6	97,171	7.7	81,073	6.5
Total Assets	**10,001,412**	**100.0**	**2,115,941**	**100.0**	**1,261,955**	**100.0**	**1,247,272**	**100.0**
Accounts Payable	1,670,236	16.7	234,869	11.1	106,004	8.4	127,222	10.2
Bank Loans	0	0.0	14,812	0.7	10,096	0.8	2,495	0.2
Notes Payable	510,072	5.1	61,362	2.9	36,597	2.9	37,418	3.0
Other Current	2,110,298	21.1	275,073	13.0	227,151	18.0	203,305	16.3
Total Current	**4,290,606**	**42.9**	**586,116**	**27.7**	**379,848**	**30.1**	**370,440**	**29.7**
Other Long Term	2,220,313	22.2	404,144	19.1	283,940	22.5	261,927	21.0
Deferred Credits	40,006	0.4	12,696	0.6	7,572	0.6	1,247	0.1
Net Worth	3,450,487	34.5	1,112,985	52.6	590,595	46.8	613,658	49.2
Total Liab & Net Worth	**10,001,412**	**100.0**	**2,115,941**	**100.0**	**1,261,955**	**100.0**	**1,247,272**	**100.0**
Net Sales	17,333,470	100.0	4,069,117	100.0	2,528,968	100.0	2,636,939	100.0
Gross Profit	3,397,360	19.6	1,281,772	31.5	1,046,993	41.4	1,054,776	40.0
Net Profit After Tax	156,001	0.9	65,106	1.6	(20,232)	(0.8)	47,465	1.8
Working Capital	1,570,221	—	710,956	—	315,489	—	338,010	—

RATIOS	UQ	MED	LQ	UQ	MED	LQ	UQ	MED	LQ	UQ	MED	LQ
SOLVENCY												
Quick Ratio (times)	1.2	0.8	0.6	3.1	1.4	0.8	3.2	1.4	0.8	4.2	1.6	0.9
Current Ratio (times)	2.2	1.2	0.9	5.3	2.6	1.4	4.2	2.1	1.1	5.5	2.1	1.3
Curr Liab To Nw (%)	56.5	138.9	309.8	16.7	40.0	91.5	11.7	38.4	93.5	12.5	50.8	115.8
Curr Liab To Inv (%)	179.8	302.9	455.6	83.9	157.8	253.5	218.1	468.4	999.9	123.1	282.3	548.2
Total Liab To Nw (%)	105.9	275.0	467.6	27.8	72.1	193.6	28.9	64.1	141.6	15.8	72.9	208.4
Fixed Assets To Nw (%)	66.1	151.1	215.2	25.6	56.2	113.1	35.3	70.4	111.8	30.7	57.6	134.7
EFFICIENCY												
Coll Period (days)	44.6	51.8	61.7	32.5	45.3	56.6	42.3	51.1	62.4	37.6	43.8	56.9
Sales To Inv (times)	17.9	12.1	9.0	18.6	11.3	7.4	128.7	44.5	19.5	52.3	20.9	13.4
Assets To Sales (%)	38.5	57.7	66.5	38.8	52.0	66.8	37.4	49.9	72.1	34.1	47.3	78.2
Sales To Nwc (times)	27.2	16.4	6.6	10.6	5.6	3.6	12.3	5.6	3.6	14.6	6.7	3.5
Acct Pay To Sales (%)	5.5	8.8	12.1	2.8	4.9	7.0	1.8	3.4	6.6	2.1	3.9	6.6
PROFITABILITY												
Return On Sales (%)	2.7	0.9	(0.6)	4.8	1.5	(0.7)	2.9	0.4	(3.9)	6.5	2.7	0.1
Return On Assets (%)	6.6	2.1	(0.9)	10.1	3.0	(1.3)	7.0	0.9	(6.8)	15.6	5.1	0.2
Return On Nw (%)	23.3	6.9	(1.0)	18.2	8.0	(0.7)	10.4	2.4	(10.4)	36.1	10.8	1.1

Balance Sheet Data

	SIC 3484 SMALL ARMS (NO BREAKDOWN) 2002 (12 Establishments) $	%	SIC 3491 INDUSTRIAL VALVES (NO BREAKDOWN) 2002 (24 Establishments) $	%	SIC 3492 FLD PWR VLVS,FTTNGS (NO BREAKDOWN) 2002 (17 Establishments) $	%	SIC 3493 STL SPRNGS,EXC WIRE (NO BREAKDOWN) 2002 (14 Establishments) $	%
Cash	598,292	12.0	473,751	9.1	331,945	10.1	444,355	18.2
Accounts Receivable	707,979	14.2	1,202,598	23.1	785,493	23.9	527,366	21.6
Notes Receivable	19,943	0.4	5,206	0.1	3,287	0.1	0	0.0
Inventory	1,465,815	29.4	1,431,664	27.5	1,015,554	30.9	485,860	19.9
Other Current	403,846	8.1	301,950	5.8	147,896	4.5	187,996	7.7
Total Current	**3,195,875**	**64.1**	**3,415,169**	**65.6**	**2,284,175**	**69.5**	**1,645,577**	**67.4**
Fixed Assets	1,151,712	23.1	1,051,622	20.2	765,774	23.3	739,777	30.3
Other Non-current	638,178	12.8	739,260	14.2	236,634	7.2	56,155	2.3
Total Assets	**4,985,765**	**100.0**	**5,206,051**	**100.0**	**3,286,583**	**100.0**	**2,441,509**	**100.0**
Accounts Payable	324,075	6.5	515,399	9.9	335,231	10.2	275,891	11.3
Bank Loans	9,972	0.2	0	0.0	0	0.0	0	0.0
Notes Payable	962,253	19.3	614,314	11.8	55,872	1.7	51,272	2.1
Other Current	498,575	10.0	853,792	16.4	637,597	19.4	456,561	18.7
Total Current	**1,794,875**	**36.0**	**1,983,505**	**38.1**	**1,028,700**	**31.3**	**783,724**	**32.1**
Other Long Term	1,216,527	24.4	1,353,574	26.0	272,786	8.3	344,253	14.1
Deferred Credits	9,972	0.2	0	0.0	3,287	0.1	0	0.0
Net Worth	1,964,391	39.4	1,868,972	35.9	1,981,810	60.3	1,313,532	53.8
Total Liab & Net Worth	**4,985,765**	**100.0**	**5,206,051**	**100.0**	**3,286,583**	**100.0**	**2,441,509**	**100.0**
Net Sales	6,508,832	100.0	6,379,964	100.0	4,218,977	100.0	3,518,024	100.0
Gross Profit	2,779,271	42.7	2,354,207	36.9	1,632,744	38.7	1,020,227	29.0
Net Profit After Tax	175,738	2.7	(82,940)	(1.3)	160,321	3.8	(28,144)	(0.8)
Working Capital	1,401,000	—	1,431,664	—	1,255,475	—	861,853	—

Ratios

RATIOS	SIC 3484 UQ	MED	LQ	SIC 3491 UQ	MED	LQ	SIC 3492 UQ	MED	LQ	SIC 3493 UQ	MED	LQ
SOLVENCY												
Quick Ratio (times)	3.8	0.9	0.6	2.0	1.2	0.8	2.2	1.0	0.8	3.5	1.1	0.8
Current Ratio (times)	7.3	3.3	2.2	3.7	2.3	1.8	3.9	2.5	1.8	4.4	2.9	1.6
Curr Liab To Nw (%)	11.1	35.1	54.0	23.3	35.2	66.6	16.8	44.8	62.6	10.2	34.5	64.8
Curr Liab To Inv (%)	29.3	69.5	127.5	49.6	111.9	183.6	51.6	89.3	157.1	93.4	157.2	246.8
Total Liab To Nw (%)	33.5	75.1	162.8	25.4	77.0	108.9	32.4	57.0	92.9	20.7	42.3	134.6
Fixed Assets To Nw (%)	37.4	44.7	60.7	11.8	24.5	49.4	10.6	19.0	59.4	19.8	45.9	115.0
EFFICIENCY												
Coll Period (days)	30.9	36.1	51.5	39.7	50.6	71.6	36.7	51.0	67.7	33.3	38.4	57.5
Sales To Inv (times)	7.5	4.3	3.4	7.9	6.4	3.0	11.8	7.1	3.6	20.2	8.0	5.6
Assets To Sales (%)	63.2	76.6	97.2	43.4	81.6	110.7	57.1	77.9	95.5	46.5	69.4	92.4
Sales To Nwc (times)	4.0	2.9	2.5	8.2	4.3	2.6	5.5	3.6	1.9	7.7	3.8	3.1
Acct Pay To Sales (%)	2.9	5.4	9.7	2.9	5.8	10.5	1.6	2.6	4.2	1.9	4.3	7.5
PROFITABILITY												
Return On Sales (%)	5.1	3.9	0.2	4.7	1.9	0.2	6.6	2.1	(1.2)	3.3	(0.5)	(5.1)
Return On Assets (%)	6.3	4.2	0.5	6.6	4.4	0.2	7.0	2.9	(1.0)	5.5	(0.5)	(6.3)
Return On Nw (%)	13.2	4.1	0.9	11.6	6.8	1.9	8.1	4.1	(1.9)	15.7	3.8	(9.3)

	SIC 3494 VLVS,PPE FTTNGS,NEC (NO BREAKDOWN) 2002 (29 Establishments) $	%	SIC 3495 WIRE SPRINGS (NO BREAKDOWN) 2002 (29 Establishments) $	%	SIC 3496 MISC FBRCTD WRE PRD (NO BREAKDOWN) 2002 (71 Establishments) $	%	SIC 3498 FBRCTD PIPE,FITTNGS (NO BREAKDOWN) 2002 (45 Establishments) $	%
Cash	436,218	10.7	199,982	9.1	258,270	13.1	174,674	9.9
Accounts Receivable	888,743	21.8	443,916	20.2	459,366	23.3	483,442	27.4
Notes Receivable	89,690	2.2	35,162	1.6	3,943	0.2	1,764	0.1
Inventory	1,092,583	26.8	382,383	17.4	471,195	23.9	344,055	19.5
Other Current	264,991	6.5	101,088	4.6	120,264	6.1	146,445	8.3
Total Current	**2,772,225**	**68.0**	**1,162,531**	**52.9**	**1,313,038**	**66.6**	**1,150,380**	**65.2**
Fixed Assets	925,434	22.7	824,101	37.5	512,597	26.0	449,918	25.5
Other Non-current	379,142	9.3	210,970	9.6	145,893	7.4	164,088	9.3
Total Assets	**4,076,801**	**100.0**	**2,197,602**	**100.0**	**1,971,528**	**100.0**	**1,764,386**	**100.0**
Accounts Payable	529,984	13.0	199,982	9.1	277,985	14.1	271,715	15.4
Bank Loans	16,307	0.4	87,904	4.0	0	0.0	0	0.0
Notes Payable	362,835	8.9	6,593	0.3	47,317	2.4	81,162	4.6
Other Current	599,290	14.7	307,664	14.0	254,327	12.9	238,192	13.5
Total Current	**1,508,416**	**37.0**	**602,143**	**27.4**	**579,629**	**29.4**	**591,069**	**33.5**
Other Long Term	456,602	11.2	837,286	38.1	283,900	14.4	250,543	14.2
Deferred Credits	0	0.0	2,198	0.1	1,972	0.1	0	0.0
Net Worth	2,111,783	51.8	755,975	34.4	1,106,027	56.1	922,774	52.3
Total Liab & Net Worth	**4,076,801**	**100.0**	**2,197,602**	**100.0**	**1,971,528**	**100.0**	**1,764,386**	**100.0**
Net Sales	6,291,360	100.0	3,782,448	100.0	4,230,747	100.0	4,093,703	100.0
Gross Profit	2,422,174	38.5	1,338,987	35.4	1,243,840	29.4	1,326,360	32.4
Net Profit After Tax	232,780	3.7	26,477	0.7	101,538	2.4	77,780	1.9
Working Capital	1,263,809	—	560,388	—	733,409	—	559,311	—

RATIOS	UQ	MED	LQ	UQ	MED	LQ	UQ	MED	LQ	UQ	MED	LQ
SOLVENCY												
Quick Ratio (times)	3.9	0.9	0.6	2.2	1.0	0.7	3.4	1.7	0.8	2.2	1.2	0.8
Current Ratio (times)	6.1	3.3	1.5	4.1	2.0	1.4	5.9	2.7	1.4	3.3	1.9	1.4
Curr Liab To Nw (%)	11.9	27.9	85.0	15.0	49.6	84.4	13.2	35.8	142.9	28.3	72.4	131.7
Curr Liab To Inv (%)	40.9	65.4	161.1	62.0	143.4	235.9	61.5	95.3	199.2	83.0	146.5	324.2
Total Liab To Nw (%)	16.4	52.6	150.6	32.9	81.4	211.4	18.2	62.2	192.8	43.3	94.6	166.2
Fixed Assets To Nw (%)	18.8	35.9	65.9	33.5	76.6	156.9	15.1	45.7	87.9	25.8	44.2	67.2
EFFICIENCY												
Coll Period (days)	34.2	53.3	63.0	38.3	44.2	48.9	31.4	41.6	60.2	32.4	48.6	65.9
Sales To Inv (times)	9.2	5.9	3.9	13.5	9.9	7.9	16.2	8.7	5.9	28.8	9.1	5.0
Assets To Sales (%)	41.9	64.8	86.1	46.0	58.1	79.4	35.5	46.6	66.7	34.4	43.1	72.7
Sales To Nwc (times)	7.7	3.8	2.2	9.1	6.1	3.7	7.9	4.5	3.3	16.0	6.7	5.1
Acct Pay To Sales (%)	3.2	5.7	9.9	1.6	3.7	7.6	2.1	4.8	7.6	4.6	5.8	9.8
PROFITABILITY												
Return On Sales (%)	5.4	2.8	0.4	5.3	2.1	(3.0)	3.6	1.9	0.2	4.1	1.0	(0.3)
Return On Assets (%)	7.9	4.1	0.2	9.2	3.5	(4.5)	8.0	3.2	0.3	7.8	3.6	(0.9)
Return On Nw (%)	17.9	5.9	0.7	21.1	5.5	(17.1)	22.8	6.5	0.7	13.9	8.7	(0.7)

SIC 3499 FBRCTD MTL PRDS,NEC (NO BREAKDOWN) 2002 (92 Establishments)

	$	%
Cash	261,121	13.6
Accounts Receivable	495,362	25.8
Notes Receivable	5,760	0.3
Inventory	424,322	22.1
Other Current	90,240	4.7
Total Current	**1,276,805**	**66.5**
Fixed Assets	481,922	25.1
Other Non-current	161,281	8.4
Total Assets	**1,920,008**	**100.0**
Accounts Payable	236,161	12.3
Bank Loans	5,760	0.3
Notes Payable	48,000	2.5
Other Current	360,962	18.8
Total Current	**650,883**	**33.9**
Other Long Term	282,241	14.7
Deferred Credits	7,680	0.4
Net Worth	979,204	51.0
Total Liab & Net Worth	**1,920,008**	**100.0**
Net Sales	4,582,358	100.0
Gross Profit	1,553,419	33.9
Net Profit After Tax	114,559	2.5
Working Capital	625,922	—

RATIOS	UQ	MED	LQ
SOLVENCY			
Quick Ratio (times)	3.9	1.3	0.7
Current Ratio (times)	6.0	2.1	1.3
Curr Liab To Nw (%)	14.6	53.0	124.8
Curr Liab To Inv (%)	64.2	138.3	266.8
Total Liab To Nw (%)	27.1	85.0	159.3
Fixed Assets To Nw (%)	17.0	46.3	87.2
EFFICIENCY			
Coll Period (days)	30.3	43.8	56.2
Sales To Inv (times)	18.8	10.6	6.3
Assets To Sales (%)	31.4	41.9	63.8
Sales To Nwc (times)	12.2	6.5	3.9
Acct Pay To Sales (%)	2.5	4.2	7.5
PROFITABILITY			
Return On Sales (%)	5.3	1.8	(0.7)
Return On Assets (%)	14.6	4.2	(1.3)
Return On Nw (%)	29.6	8.1	(2.2)

SIC 35 MACHINERY EX ELECTRL (NO BREAKDOWN) 2002 (3372 Establishments)

	$	%
Cash	196,409	12.7
Accounts Receivable	364,981	23.6
Notes Receivable	7,733	0.5
Inventory	304,666	19.7
Other Current	106,711	6.9
Total Current	**980,500**	**63.4**
Fixed Assets	453,133	29.3
Other Non-current	112,897	7.3
Total Assets	**1,546,530**	**100.0**
Accounts Payable	224,247	14.5
Bank Loans	7,733	0.5
Notes Payable	98,978	6.4
Other Current	295,387	19.1
Total Current	**626,345**	**40.5**
Other Long Term	323,224	20.9
Deferred Credits	3,093	0.2
Net Worth	593,868	38.4
Total Liab & Net Worth	**1,546,530**	**100.0**
Net Sales	2,832,473	100.0
Gross Profit	1,002,695	35.4
Net Profit After Tax	0	0.0
Working Capital	354,155	—

RATIOS	UQ	MED	LQ
SOLVENCY			
Quick Ratio (times)	2.5	1.2	0.7
Current Ratio (times)	4.4	2.1	1.3
Curr Liab To Nw (%)	18.1	47.7	125.0
Curr Liab To Inv (%)	76.1	153.6	344.4
Total Liab To Nw (%)	29.0	86.4	215.2
Fixed Assets To Nw (%)	21.1	48.6	102.2
EFFICIENCY			
Coll Period (days)	31.8	45.6	61.7
Sales To Inv (times)	24.0	9.6	5.3
Assets To Sales (%)	38.3	54.6	80.5
Sales To Nwc (times)	10.2	5.4	3.0
Acct Pay To Sales (%)	2.2	4.4	8.0
PROFITABILITY			
Return On Sales (%)	4.6	1.3	(2.9)
Return On Assets (%)	9.0	2.3	(5.0)
Return On Nw (%)	19.9	5.2	(6.5)

SIC 3519 INTRNL CMB ENGS,NEC (NO BREAKDOWN) 2002 (19 Establishments)

	$	%
Cash	472,223	10.4
Accounts Receivable	1,071,583	23.6
Notes Receivable	0	0.0
Inventory	1,412,129	31.1
Other Current	168,003	3.7
Total Current	**3,123,938**	**68.8**
Fixed Assets	844,553	18.6
Other Non-current	572,117	12.6
Total Assets	**4,540,608**	**100.0**
Accounts Payable	735,578	16.2
Bank Loans	0	0.0
Notes Payable	245,193	5.4
Other Current	635,685	14.0
Total Current	**1,616,456**	**35.6**
Other Long Term	1,680,025	37.0
Deferred Credits	4,541	0.1
Net Worth	1,239,586	27.3
Total Liab & Net Worth	**4,540,608**	**100.0**
Net Sales	8,331,391	100.0
Gross Profit	2,849,336	34.2
Net Profit After Tax	474,889	5.7
Working Capital	1,507,482	—

RATIOS	UQ	MED	LQ
SOLVENCY			
Quick Ratio (times)	1.6	1.0	0.8
Current Ratio (times)	3.3	1.8	1.5
Curr Liab To Nw (%)	44.4	72.6	161.2
Curr Liab To Inv (%)	45.8	139.3	169.7
Total Liab To Nw (%)	55.4	181.1	276.4
Fixed Assets To Nw (%)	12.6	30.7	72.6
EFFICIENCY			
Coll Period (days)	27.7	42.0	48.9
Sales To Inv (times)	9.6	6.8	5.1
Assets To Sales (%)	40.7	54.5	79.3
Sales To Nwc (times)	8.0	4.0	3.1
Acct Pay To Sales (%)	5.2	6.7	8.5
PROFITABILITY			
Return On Sales (%)	7.3	2.6	0.9
Return On Assets (%)	9.1	5.3	2.2
Return On Nw (%)	25.0	15.9	8.6

SIC 3523 FARM MCHNRY,EQPMT (NO BREAKDOWN) 2002 (122 Establishments)

	$	%
Cash	169,459	8.3
Accounts Receivable	373,625	18.3
Notes Receivable	16,333	0.8
Inventory	810,543	39.7
Other Current	98,000	4.8
Total Current	**1,467,960**	**71.9**
Fixed Assets	463,459	22.7
Other Non-current	110,250	5.4
Total Assets	**2,041,669**	**100.0**
Accounts Payable	206,209	10.1
Bank Loans	26,542	1.3
Notes Payable	187,834	9.2
Other Current	336,874	16.5
Total Current	**757,459**	**37.1**
Other Long Term	275,625	13.5
Deferred Credits	2,042	0.1
Net Worth	1,006,543	49.3
Total Liab & Net Worth	**2,041,669**	**100.0**
Net Sales	3,979,862	100.0
Gross Profit	1,333,254	33.5
Net Profit After Tax	87,557	2.2
Working Capital	710,501	—

RATIOS	UQ	MED	LQ
SOLVENCY			
Quick Ratio (times)	1.9	0.7	0.4
Current Ratio (times)	4.8	2.5	1.4
Curr Liab To Nw (%)	20.8	50.0	109.6
Curr Liab To Inv (%)	41.8	82.9	117.0
Total Liab To Nw (%)	27.9	69.6	202.5
Fixed Assets To Nw (%)	13.5	40.2	78.7
EFFICIENCY			
Coll Period (days)	17.9	30.5	49.6
Sales To Inv (times)	7.8	4.7	3.1
Assets To Sales (%)	41.0	51.3	75.4
Sales To Nwc (times)	9.0	4.4	2.6
Acct Pay To Sales (%)	1.9	3.8	8.0
PROFITABILITY			
Return On Sales (%)	4.5	2.0	(0.1)
Return On Assets (%)	8.7	3.3	0.0
Return On Nw (%)	20.8	8.2	0.1

SIC 3524 LAWN,GARDEN EQPMT (NO BREAKDOWN) 2002 (22 Establishments)

	$	%
Cash	341,889	8.6
Accounts Receivable	771,238	19.4
Notes Receivable	0	0.0
Inventory	1,526,574	38.4
Other Current	206,723	5.2
Total Current	**2,846,424**	**71.6**
Fixed Assets	779,189	19.6
Other Non-current	349,839	8.8
Total Assets	**3,975,452**	**100.0**
Accounts Payable	544,637	13.7
Bank Loans	43,730	1.1
Notes Payable	258,404	6.5
Other Current	548,613	13.8
Total Current	**1,395,384**	**35.1**
Other Long Term	799,065	20.1
Deferred Credits	7,951	0.2
Net Worth	1,773,052	44.6
Total Liab & Net Worth	**3,975,452**	**100.0**
Net Sales	8,031,216	100.0
Gross Profit	2,152,366	26.8
Net Profit After Tax	0	0.0
Working Capital	1,451,040	—

RATIOS	UQ	MED	LQ
SOLVENCY			
Quick Ratio (times)	1.6	0.6	0.5
Current Ratio (times)	2.7	1.8	1.4
Curr Liab To Nw (%)	38.4	105.7	133.4
Curr Liab To Inv (%)	60.1	94.0	130.9
Total Liab To Nw (%)	50.0	128.8	206.6
Fixed Assets To Nw (%)	18.9	31.5	49.4
EFFICIENCY			
Coll Period (days)	27.4	34.0	44.2
Sales To Inv (times)	7.6	5.5	3.3
Assets To Sales (%)	34.6	49.5	59.3
Sales To Nwc (times)	8.1	6.9	4.7
Acct Pay To Sales (%)	3.5	7.0	9.0
PROFITABILITY			
Return On Sales (%)	3.3	1.8	0.2
Return On Assets (%)	7.8	3.9	0.6
Return On Nw (%)	19.4	11.6	2.1

SIC 3531 CONSTR MACHINERY (NO BREAKDOWN) 2002 (80 Establishments)

	$	%
Cash	286,379	11.1
Accounts Receivable	562,439	21.8
Notes Receivable	5,160	0.2
Inventory	681,119	26.4
Other Current	203,820	7.9
Total Current	**1,738,917**	**67.4**
Fixed Assets	614,039	23.8
Other Non-current	227,039	8.8
Total Assets	**2,579,995**	**100.0**
Accounts Payable	273,479	10.6
Bank Loans	28,380	1.1
Notes Payable	87,720	3.4
Other Current	479,879	18.6
Total Current	**869,458**	**33.7**
Other Long Term	407,639	15.8
Deferred Credits	12,900	0.5
Net Worth	1,289,998	50.0
Total Liab & Net Worth	**2,579,995**	**100.0**
Net Sales	4,425,377	100.0
Gross Profit	1,526,755	34.5
Net Profit After Tax	119,485	2.7
Working Capital	869,459	—

RATIOS	UQ	MED	LQ
SOLVENCY			
Quick Ratio (times)	2.5	0.9	0.5
Current Ratio (times)	4.2	2.1	1.4
Curr Liab To Nw (%)	16.6	45.1	192.2
Curr Liab To Inv (%)	62.5	100.7	193.3
Total Liab To Nw (%)	25.2	81.2	291.9
Fixed Assets To Nw (%)	15.7	43.7	117.7
EFFICIENCY			
Coll Period (days)	32.4	48.9	65.7
Sales To Inv (times)	10.5	4.7	3.5
Assets To Sales (%)	40.2	58.3	85.6
Sales To Nwc (times)	7.0	5.1	2.7
Acct Pay To Sales (%)	2.5	5.3	8.9
PROFITABILITY			
Return On Sales (%)	4.0	1.9	0.3
Return On Assets (%)	9.7	2.9	0.4
Return On Nw (%)	17.1	6.0	0.8

SIC 3532 MINING MACHINERY (NO BREAKDOWN) 2002 (23 Establishments)

	$	%
Cash	221,815	11.1
Accounts Receivable	435,637	21.8
Notes Receivable	3,997	0.2
Inventory	571,524	28.6
Other Current	97,919	4.9
Total Current	**1,330,892**	**66.6**
Fixed Assets	515,571	25.8
Other Non-current	151,873	7.6
Total Assets	**1,998,336**	**100.0**
Accounts Payable	205,829	10.3
Bank Loans	0	0.0
Notes Payable	55,953	2.8
Other Current	459,617	23.0
Total Current	**721,399**	**36.1**
Other Long Term	211,824	10.6
Deferred Credits	0	0.0
Net Worth	1,065,113	53.3
Total Liab & Net Worth	**1,998,336**	**100.0**
Net Sales	4,053,420	100.0
Gross Profit	1,588,941	39.2
Net Profit After Tax	263,472	6.5
Working Capital	609,493	—

RATIOS	UQ	MED	LQ
SOLVENCY			
Quick Ratio (times)	2.4	1.0	0.5
Current Ratio (times)	4.4	2.2	1.5
Curr Liab To Nw (%)	13.7	62.0	187.7
Curr Liab To Inv (%)	61.6	104.0	174.6
Total Liab To Nw (%)	13.8	85.0	235.6
Fixed Assets To Nw (%)	23.6	54.4	72.7
EFFICIENCY			
Coll Period (days)	35.0	43.8	54.8
Sales To Inv (times)	14.9	7.1	3.2
Assets To Sales (%)	37.7	49.3	70.9
Sales To Nwc (times)	8.1	5.2	3.0
Acct Pay To Sales (%)	2.4	4.0	7.0
PROFITABILITY			
Return On Sales (%)	6.4	1.4	0.4
Return On Assets (%)	14.2	2.4	0.6
Return On Nw (%)	41.2	5.4	1.8

SIC 3533 OIL,GAS FLD MCHNRY (NO BREAKDOWN) 2002 (51 Establishments)

	$	%
Cash	237,603	11.2
Accounts Receivable	521,877	24.6
Notes Receivable	2,121	0.1
Inventory	517,635	24.4
Other Current	112,437	5.3
Total Current	**1,391,673**	**65.6**
Fixed Assets	572,792	27.0
Other Non-current	156,988	7.4
Total Assets	**2,121,453**	**100.0**
Accounts Payable	246,089	11.6
Bank Loans	0	0.0
Notes Payable	86,980	4.1
Other Current	379,739	17.9
Total Current	**712,808**	**33.6**
Other Long Term	415,805	19.6
Deferred Credits	0	0.0
Net Worth	992,840	46.8
Total Liab & Net Worth	**2,121,453**	**100.0**
Net Sales	3,741,540	100.0
Gross Profit	1,530,290	40.9
Net Profit After Tax	101,022	2.7
Working Capital	678,865	—

RATIOS	UQ	MED	LQ
SOLVENCY			
Quick Ratio (times)	2.4	1.4	0.7
Current Ratio (times)	4.0	2.2	1.5
Curr Liab To Nw (%)	21.3	55.7	103.8
Curr Liab To Inv (%)	58.1	101.4	178.7
Total Liab To Nw (%)	39.5	88.4	197.6
Fixed Assets To Nw (%)	26.2	52.3	80.3
EFFICIENCY			
Coll Period (days)	34.5	47.7	67.6
Sales To Inv (times)	9.8	5.9	4.8
Assets To Sales (%)	40.9	56.7	83.1
Sales To Nwc (times)	7.7	4.3	3.0
Acct Pay To Sales (%)	2.5	5.0	8.3
PROFITABILITY			
Return On Sales (%)	5.4	3.2	0.9
Return On Assets (%)	10.0	4.1	1.8
Return On Nw (%)	19.5	8.9	3.5

Balance Sheet

	SIC 3535 CNVYRS,CNVYNG EQPMT (NO BREAKDOWN) 2002 (74 Establishments)		SIC 3536 HSTS,CRNES,MONORLS (NO BREAKDOWN) 2002 (17 Establishments)		SIC 3537 INDL TRUCKS,TRCTORS (NO BREAKDOWN) 2002 (25 Establishments)		SIC 3541 MACH TLS,MTL CTTNG (NO BREAKDOWN) 2002 (62 Establishments)	
	$	%	$	%	$	%	$	%
Cash	358,068	16.7	120,499	4.5	337,556	9.5	137,485	9.8
Accounts Receivable	621,795	29.0	776,548	29.0	643,134	18.1	345,115	24.6
Notes Receivable	6,432	0.3	0	0.0	3,553	0.1	5,612	0.4
Inventory	343,059	16.0	827,426	30.9	1,097,947	30.9	308,639	22.0
Other Current	220,844	10.3	299,908	11.2	280,705	7.9	44,893	3.2
Total Current	**1,550,198**	**72.3**	**2,024,381**	**75.6**	**2,362,895**	**66.5**	**841,744**	**60.0**
Fixed Assets	441,689	20.6	490,029	18.3	685,773	19.3	468,571	33.4
Other Non-current	152,232	7.1	163,343	6.1	504,558	14.2	92,591	6.6
Total Assets	**2,144,119**	**100.0**	**2,677,753**	**100.0**	**3,553,226**	**100.0**	**1,402,906**	**100.0**
Accounts Payable	261,583	12.2	441,829	16.5	397,961	11.2	158,528	11.3
Bank Loans	8,576	0.4	0	0.0	0	0.0	11,223	0.8
Notes Payable	62,179	2.9	74,977	2.8	149,235	4.2	39,281	2.8
Other Current	497,436	23.2	364,175	13.6	1,154,799	32.5	343,713	24.5
Total Current	**829,774**	**38.7**	**880,981**	**32.9**	**1,701,995**	**47.9**	**552,745**	**39.4**
Other Long Term	349,492	16.3	613,205	22.9	564,963	15.9	270,761	19.3
Deferred Credits	4,288	0.2	8,033	0.3	0	0.0	1,403	0.1
Net Worth	960,565	44.8	1,175,534	43.9	1,286,268	36.2	577,997	41.2
Total Liab & Net Worth	**2,144,119**	**100.0**	**2,677,753**	**100.0**	**3,553,226**	**100.0**	**1,402,906**	**100.0**
Net Sales	4,411,767	100.0	5,746,251	100.0	5,595,631	100.0	2,444,087	100.0
Gross Profit	1,380,883	31.3	1,798,577	31.3	1,348,547	24.1	928,753	38.0
Net Profit After Tax	39,706	0.9	5,746	0.1	(106,317)	(1.9)	(2,444)	(0.1)
Working Capital	720,424	—	1,143,400	—	660,900	—	288,999	—

Ratios

RATIOS	SIC 3535			SIC 3536			SIC 3537			SIC 3541		
	UQ	MED	LQ	UQ	MED	LQ	UQ	MED	LQ	UQ	MED	LQ
SOLVENCY												
Quick Ratio (times)	2.3	1.2	0.8	1.5	1.1	0.6	1.8	0.6	0.4	3.0	1.1	0.8
Current Ratio (times)	4.4	2.0	1.3	5.8	2.4	1.4	4.0	2.0	1.2	4.3	2.2	1.3
Curr Liab To Nw (%)	24.7	58.8	205.7	38.4	60.4	309.0	29.1	76.4	178.8	18.7	43.5	120.2
Curr Liab To Inv (%)	111.2	231.4	391.4	36.5	135.9	246.8	61.5	88.6	204.4	68.6	146.0	317.7
Total Liab To Nw (%)	32.1	80.5	279.8	50.8	74.6	529.5	37.4	108.6	230.3	29.8	91.6	218.3
Fixed Assets To Nw (%)	16.9	35.7	63.6	23.3	36.7	89.6	19.2	41.3	111.5	29.5	53.4	109.9
EFFICIENCY												
Coll Period (days)	33.6	52.8	76.3	47.6	58.8	80.0	24.8	40.0	54.4	38.3	49.3	60.6
Sales To Inv (times)	29.4	13.1	7.9	11.2	5.8	5.1	10.1	6.3	4.3	25.3	8.2	4.5
Assets To Sales (%)	35.8	48.6	63.4	38.0	46.6	79.6	43.7	63.5	94.6	41.3	57.4	87.4
Sales To Nwc (times)	12.1	7.3	4.1	10.2	5.1	2.9	8.9	3.9	2.2	9.7	5.6	3.5
Acct Pay To Sales (%)	2.7	5.6	8.3	4.0	9.4	12.3	3.8	5.4	7.4	2.1	4.0	8.1
PROFITABILITY												
Return On Sales (%)	3.8	0.5	(2.7)	6.8	2.0	(1.3)	1.8	(0.6)	(4.0)	4.0	0.6	(3.3)
Return On Assets (%)	9.6	1.6	(5.3)	9.8	3.5	(5.4)	2.4	(1.0)	(6.0)	9.2	0.9	(3.8)
Return On Nw (%)	20.3	2.7	(11.0)	18.2	6.8	(8.6)	7.6	0.2	(28.4)	16.4	1.6	(5.5)

	SIC 3542 MACH TLS, MTL FRMNG (38 Est.) $	%	SIC 3543 INDUSTRIAL PATTERNS (16 Est.) $	%	SIC 3544 SPCL DIES, TLS, FXTRS (326 Est.) $	%	SIC 3545 MACHINE TOOL, ACCS (137 Est.) $	%
Cash	285,830	10.8	140,156	16.4	144,239	10.8	138,780	12.8
Accounts Receivable	558,426	21.1	240,146	28.1	351,248	26.3	228,769	21.1
Notes Receivable	5,293	0.2	3,418	0.4	4,007	0.3	6,505	0.6
Inventory	643,117	24.3	101,699	11.9	165,607	12.4	223,348	20.6
Other Current	259,363	9.8	35,894	4.2	70,783	5.3	81,317	7.5
Total Current	**1,752,029**	**66.2**	**521,313**	**61.0**	**735,884**	**55.1**	**678,719**	**62.6**
Fixed Assets	719,867	27.2	275,185	32.2	514,184	38.5	315,507	29.1
Other Non-current	174,674	6.6	58,114	6.8	85,475	6.4	89,989	8.3
Total Assets	**2,646,570**	**100.0**	**854,612**	**100.0**	**1,335,543**	**100.0**	**1,084,215**	**100.0**
Accounts Payable	280,536	10.6	48,713	5.7	112,186	8.4	118,179	10.9
Bank Loans	0	0.0	10,255	1.2	5,342	0.4	6,505	0.6
Notes Payable	63,518	2.4	2,564	0.3	68,113	5.1	32,526	3.0
Other Current	648,410	24.5	117,937	13.8	277,792	20.8	199,497	18.4
Total Current	**992,464**	**37.5**	**179,469**	**21.0**	**463,433**	**34.7**	**356,707**	**32.9**
Other Long Term	481,676	18.2	204,252	23.9	283,135	21.2	282,980	26.1
Deferred Credits	42,345	1.6	1,709	0.2	4,007	0.3	4,337	0.4
Net Worth	1,130,085	42.7	469,182	54.9	584,968	43.8	440,191	40.6
Total Liab & Net Worth	**2,646,570**	**100.0**	**854,612**	**100.0**	**1,335,543**	**100.0**	**1,084,215**	**100.0**
Net Sales	4,200,905	100.0	1,520,662	100.0	2,367,984	100.0	1,783,248	100.0
Gross Profit	1,365,294	32.5	621,951	40.9	786,171	33.2	663,368	37.2
Net Profit After Tax	4,201	0.1	27,372	1.8	(16,576)	(0.7)	(41,015)	(2.3)
Working Capital	759,565	—	341,844	—	272,451	—	322,012	—

RATIOS	3542 UQ	MED	LQ	3543 UQ	MED	LQ	3544 UQ	MED	LQ	3545 UQ	MED	LQ
SOLVENCY												
Quick Ratio (times)	3.6	1.1	0.6	5.6	2.8	1.1	2.5	1.2	0.7	2.6	1.1	0.6
Current Ratio (times)	6.2	2.5	1.2	6.2	4.8	1.8	3.7	1.9	1.2	5.8	2.5	1.3
Curr Liab To Nw (%)	13.3	54.8	152.6	12.4	18.8	68.6	18.5	49.9	131.7	13.1	35.5	94.8
Curr Liab To Inv (%)	46.3	105.7	319.2	85.1	227.2	364.5	130.7	231.2	533.8	48.9	119.9	288.7
Total Liab To Nw (%)	21.3	94.0	240.9	20.5	49.8	98.5	33.2	97.7	227.7	20.8	88.6	222.7
Fixed Assets To Nw (%)	23.0	55.4	82.0	25.4	49.8	110.3	40.2	81.0	138.1	21.1	53.8	106.3
EFFICIENCY												
Coll Period (days)	38.9	46.7	64.8	28.1	57.0	78.5	40.2	50.7	66.4	33.6	44.5	60.2
Sales To Inv (times)	17.0	5.9	4.3	65.8	24.3	6.4	35.6	16.2	8.7	20.6	9.7	5.0
Assets To Sales (%)	42.6	63.0	74.7	34.2	56.2	78.5	44.1	56.4	76.8	41.3	60.8	82.9
Sales To Nwc (times)	12.0	5.0	2.6	11.6	4.7	2.5	10.9	6.4	4.1	11.6	4.6	2.5
Acct Pay To Sales (%)	2.3	5.6	10.2	1.5	2.5	3.4	1.8	3.5	6.7	1.9	3.9	7.3
PROFITABILITY												
Return On Sales (%)	5.1	1.2	(2.8)	5.9	2.5	(0.5)	4.3	1.0	(4.5)	3.4	0.5	(5.7)
Return On Assets (%)	6.5	2.0	(4.0)	9.7	5.3	(0.8)	7.5	1.7	(7.0)	6.3	0.5	(10.6)
Return On Nw (%)	15.7	7.4	(6.9)	15.2	8.2	(1.7)	16.9	4.2	(11.9)	13.8	2.8	(20.4)

SIC 3542 MACH TLS, MTL FRMNG (NO BREAKDOWN) 2002 (38 Establishments)
SIC 3543 INDUSTRIAL PATTERNS (NO BREAKDOWN) 2002 (16 Establishments)
SIC 3544 SPCL DIES, TLS, FXTRS (NO BREAKDOWN) 2002 (326 Establishments)
SIC 3545 MACHINE TOOL, ACCS (NO BREAKDOWN) 2002 (137 Establishments)

SIC 3546 POWER-DRIVEN HNDTLS (NO BREAKDOWN) 2002 (10 Establishments)

	$	%
Cash	188,919	8.7
Accounts Receivable	473,384	21.8
Notes Receivable	4,343	0.2
Inventory	957,626	44.1
Other Current	52,116	2.4
Total Current	**1,676,388**	**77.2**
Fixed Assets	286,636	13.2
Other Non-current	208,463	9.6
Total Assets	**2,171,487**	**100.0**
Accounts Payable	204,120	9.4
Bank Loans	0	0.0
Notes Payable	241,035	11.1
Other Current	371,324	17.1
Total Current	**816,479**	**37.6**
Other Long Term	236,692	10.9
Deferred Credits	0	0.0
Net Worth	1,118,316	51.5
Total Liab & Net Worth	**2,171,487**	**100.0**
Net Sales	2,922,594	100.0
Gross Profit	1,052,134	36.0
Net Profit After Tax	58,452	2.0
Working Capital	859,909	—

RATIOS	UQ	MED	LQ
SOLVENCY			
Quick Ratio (times)	1.2	0.9	0.4
Current Ratio (times)	2.8	2.1	1.5
Curr Liab To Nw (%)	38.9	65.5	242.4
Curr Liab To Inv (%)	60.1	71.1	131.6
Total Liab To Nw (%)	39.6	90.5	398.6
Fixed Assets To Nw (%)	13.0	29.0	39.9
EFFICIENCY			
Coll Period (days)	43.6	62.4	80.5
Sales To Inv (times)	5.7	3.8	2.3
Assets To Sales (%)	47.2	74.3	92.8
Sales To Nwc (times)	7.7	6.5	4.7
Acct Pay To Sales (%)	3.7	6.1	14.5
PROFITABILITY			
Return On Sales (%)	6.3	1.0	(1.5)
Return On Assets (%)	6.8	1.9	(1.8)
Return On Nw (%)	39.0	12.5	(2.7)

SIC 3548 WELDING APPARATUS (NO BREAKDOWN) 2002 (25 Establishments)

	$	%
Cash	184,762	9.9
Accounts Receivable	436,710	23.4
Notes Receivable	0	0.0
Inventory	582,281	31.2
Other Current	123,175	6.6
Total Current	**1,326,928**	**71.1**
Fixed Assets	373,257	20.0
Other Non-current	166,099	8.9
Total Assets	**1,866,284**	**100.0**
Accounts Payable	195,960	10.5
Bank Loans	(1,866)	(0.1)
Notes Payable	54,122	2.9
Other Current	244,483	13.1
Total Current	**492,699**	**26.4**
Other Long Term	610,275	32.7
Deferred Credits	0	0.0
Net Worth	763,310	40.9
Total Liab & Net Worth	**1,866,284**	**100.0**
Net Sales	2,768,967	100.0
Gross Profit	999,597	36.1
Net Profit After Tax	27,690	1.0
Working Capital	834,229	—

RATIOS	UQ	MED	LQ
SOLVENCY			
Quick Ratio (times)	2.3	1.2	0.8
Current Ratio (times)	5.3	2.9	1.7
Curr Liab To Nw (%)	16.4	43.5	126.0
Curr Liab To Inv (%)	34.9	81.4	128.0
Total Liab To Nw (%)	21.9	90.8	213.0
Fixed Assets To Nw (%)	16.8	28.7	96.5
EFFICIENCY			
Coll Period (days)	38.2	50.7	74.8
Sales To Inv (times)	8.3	4.8	2.6
Assets To Sales (%)	55.0	67.4	92.2
Sales To Nwc (times)	5.0	3.0	2.4
Acct Pay To Sales (%)	4.1	6.4	10.4
PROFITABILITY			
Return On Sales (%)	4.8	2.7	(1.1)
Return On Assets (%)	6.8	3.2	(1.7)
Return On Nw (%)	16.9	5.9	(0.9)

SIC 3549 MTLWRKNG MCHNRY, NEC (NO BREAKDOWN) 2002 (31 Establishments)

	$	%
Cash	377,766	12.1
Accounts Receivable	999,052	32.0
Notes Receivable	0	0.0
Inventory	493,282	15.8
Other Current	184,200	5.9
Total Current	**2,054,300**	**65.8**
Fixed Assets	836,706	26.8
Other Non-current	231,030	7.4
Total Assets	**3,122,036**	**100.0**
Accounts Payable	499,526	16.0
Bank Loans	59,319	1.9
Notes Payable	34,342	1.1
Other Current	536,990	17.2
Total Current	**1,130,177**	**36.2**
Other Long Term	590,065	18.9
Deferred Credits	0	0.0
Net Worth	1,401,794	44.9
Total Liab & Net Worth	**3,122,036**	**100.0**
Net Sales	5,019,350	100.0
Gross Profit	1,566,037	31.2
Net Profit After Tax	(95,368)	(1.9)
Working Capital	924,123	—

RATIOS	UQ	MED	LQ
SOLVENCY			
Quick Ratio (times)	2.7	1.3	0.9
Current Ratio (times)	4.0	2.1	1.4
Curr Liab To Nw (%)	26.4	51.0	170.8
Curr Liab To Inv (%)	80.4	188.5	331.1
Total Liab To Nw (%)	30.9	90.0	265.5
Fixed Assets To Nw (%)	11.7	36.0	112.3
EFFICIENCY			
Coll Period (days)	38.7	48.6	85.1
Sales To Inv (times)	17.0	7.4	3.9
Assets To Sales (%)	44.1	62.2	137.4
Sales To Nwc (times)	10.5	3.6	1.9
Acct Pay To Sales (%)	2.3	5.2	7.9
PROFITABILITY			
Return On Sales (%)	7.2	(0.2)	(8.9)
Return On Assets (%)	13.0	(0.1)	(12.2)
Return On Nw (%)	22.7	0.7	(21.5)

SIC 3552 TEXTILE MACHINERY (NO BREAKDOWN) 2002 (30 Establishments)

	$	%
Cash	138,814	11.3
Accounts Receivable	309,568	25.2
Notes Receivable	7,371	0.6
Inventory	367,305	29.9
Other Current	98,275	8.0
Total Current	**921,333**	**75.0**
Fixed Assets	240,775	19.6
Other Non-current	66,336	5.4
Total Assets	**1,228,444**	**100.0**
Accounts Payable	149,870	12.2
Bank Loans	22,112	1.8
Notes Payable	95,819	7.8
Other Current	189,180	15.4
Total Current	**456,981**	**37.2**
Other Long Term	152,327	12.4
Deferred Credits	2,457	0.2
Net Worth	616,679	50.2
Total Liab & Net Worth	**1,228,444**	**100.0**
Net Sales	1,968,660	100.0
Gross Profit	706,749	35.9
Net Profit After Tax	(100,402)	(5.1)
Working Capital	464,352	—

RATIOS	UQ	MED	LQ
SOLVENCY			
Quick Ratio (times)	2.1	1.0	0.6
Current Ratio (times)	5.4	2.0	1.2
Curr Liab To Nw (%)	16.8	82.2	161.4
Curr Liab To Inv (%)	45.1	109.7	238.3
Total Liab To Nw (%)	26.2	93.8	228.8
Fixed Assets To Nw (%)	13.8	26.7	52.6
EFFICIENCY			
Coll Period (days)	38.3	44.2	72.3
Sales To Inv (times)	9.7	5.6	3.4
Assets To Sales (%)	36.7	62.4	89.3
Sales To Nwc (times)	10.6	5.3	2.9
Acct Pay To Sales (%)	3.2	5.2	8.6
PROFITABILITY			
Return On Sales (%)	3.3	0.3	(5.6)
Return On Assets (%)	7.7	0.7	(10.2)
Return On Nw (%)	17.3	1.7	(14.9)

	SIC 3553 WOODWRKNG MACHINERY (NO BREAKDOWN) 2002 (19 Establishments) $	%	SIC 3554 PAPER IND MACHINERY (NO BREAKDOWN) 2002 (17 Establishments) $	%	SIC 3555 PRNTNG TRDES MCHNRY (NO BREAKDOWN) 2002 (20 Establishments) $	%	SIC 3556 FOOD PRDCTS MCHNRY (NO BREAKDOWN) 2002 (51 Establishments) $	%
Cash	137,248	8.2	155,730	10.4	588,130	11.2	245,848	11.8
Accounts Receivable	374,923	22.4	303,973	20.3	981,968	18.7	437,526	21.0
Notes Receivable	1,674	0.1	85,352	5.7	36,758	0.7	10,417	0.5
Inventory	533,930	31.9	317,450	21.2	1,276,033	24.3	572,951	27.5
Other Current	145,617	8.7	169,208	11.3	509,364	9.7	118,758	5.7
Total Current	**1,193,392**	**71.3**	**1,031,713**	**68.9**	**3,392,253**	**64.6**	**1,385,500**	**66.5**
Fixed Assets	379,944	22.7	342,906	22.9	1,239,275	23.6	500,030	24.0
Other Non-current	100,426	6.0	122,787	8.2	619,637	11.8	197,929	9.5
Total Assets	**1,673,762**	**100.0**	**1,497,406**	**100.0**	**5,251,165**	**100.0**	**2,083,459**	**100.0**
Accounts Payable	254,412	15.2	175,197	11.7	467,354	8.9	247,932	11.9
Bank Loans	0	0.0	0	0.0	0	0.0	0	0.0
Notes Payable	40,170	2.4	14,974	1.0	68,265	1.3	137,508	6.6
Other Current	388,313	23.2	314,455	21.0	1,144,754	21.8	670,874	32.2
Total Current	**682,895**	**40.8**	**504,626**	**33.7**	**1,680,373**	**32.0**	**1,056,314**	**50.7**
Other Long Term	167,376	10.0	184,181	12.3	1,050,233	20.0	420,858	20.2
Deferred Credits	0	0.0	0	0.0	31,507	0.6	16,668	0.8
Net Worth	823,491	49.2	808,599	54.0	2,489,052	47.4	589,619	28.3
Total Liab & Net Worth	**1,673,762**	**100.0**	**1,497,406**	**100.0**	**5,251,165**	**100.0**	**2,083,459**	**100.0**
Net Sales	3,327,559	100.0	3,859,294	100.0	6,973,659	100.0	3,694,076	100.0
Gross Profit	1,291,093	38.8	1,431,798	37.1	2,461,702	35.3	1,189,492	32.2
Net Profit After Tax	26,620	0.8	77,186	2.0	6,974	0.1	14,776	0.4
Working Capital	510,497	—	527,087	—	1,711,880	—	329,186	—

RATIOS	UQ	MED	LQ	UQ	MED	LQ	UQ	MED	LQ	UQ	MED	LQ
SOLVENCY												
Quick Ratio (times)	1.6	0.8	0.6	1.6	0.9	0.7	2.4	1.0	0.5	2.2	1.0	0.5
Current Ratio (times)	5.4	1.7	1.2	4.0	2.0	1.5	4.2	2.5	1.5	4.1	2.2	1.3
Curr Liab To Nw (%)	18.3	71.6	162.2	31.0	47.4	142.8	21.1	62.5	132.8	21.9	37.4	143.2
Curr Liab To Inv (%)	34.7	108.4	343.1	67.9	167.5	249.1	88.1	139.7	216.0	53.8	116.4	234.9
Total Liab To Nw (%)	43.2	92.6	175.1	31.0	105.6	241.4	31.7	136.8	206.2	28.6	83.5	254.8
Fixed Assets To Nw (%)	23.4	34.8	106.0	15.7	32.3	86.2	19.3	32.3	56.5	24.8	42.9	83.2
EFFICIENCY												
Coll Period (days)	28.8	40.7	59.1	32.5	44.8	58.4	28.8	42.6	66.1	25.2	40.9	52.2
Sales To Inv (times)	16.4	6.7	3.5	12.1	6.5	5.1	11.6	7.1	5.0	14.5	7.6	4.7
Assets To Sales (%)	42.2	50.3	83.2	29.6	38.8	77.9	39.8	75.3	108.9	36.1	56.4	89.9
Sales To Nwc (times)	7.9	3.9	2.9	11.5	7.3	2.7	6.5	3.7	2.3	15.6	5.6	3.1
Acct Pay To Sales (%)	2.3	4.2	9.3	3.3	5.2	8.1	2.0	4.7	6.5	2.9	4.6	6.8
PROFITABILITY												
Return On Sales (%)	1.7	1.0	(0.4)	5.5	2.8	(2.0)	3.3	1.3	(2.7)	4.5	1.5	(1.6)
Return On Assets (%)	4.5	1.3	(1.1)	24.5	5.5	(2.6)	7.1	2.0	(4.0)	11.0	3.1	(2.9)
Return On Nw (%)	8.3	0.9	(2.6)	42.3	8.1	(14.8)	12.3	2.9	(7.2)	19.0	8.9	(0.4)

SIC 3559 SPEC IND MCHNRY, NEC
(NO BREAKDOWN)
2002 (119 Establishments)

	$	%
Cash	343,577	14.1
Accounts Receivable	577,501	23.7
Notes Receivable	14,620	0.6
Inventory	596,995	24.5
Other Current	216,868	8.9
Total Current	**1,749,561**	**71.8**
Fixed Assets	453,229	18.6
Other Non-current	233,924	9.6
Total Assets	**2,436,714**	**100.0**
Accounts Payable	1,917,694	78.7
Bank Loans	14,620	0.6
Notes Payable	85,285	3.5
Other Current	(506,836)	(20.8)
Total Current	**1,510,763**	**62.0**
Other Long Term	460,539	18.9
Deferred Credits	7,310	0.3
Net Worth	458,102	18.8
Total Liab & Net Worth	**2,436,714**	**100.0**
Net Sales	3,819,301	100.0
Gross Profit	1,260,369	33.0
Net Profit After Tax	(99,302)	(2.6)
Working Capital	238,798	—

RATIOS	UQ	MED	LQ
SOLVENCY			
Quick Ratio (times)	1.8	1.0	0.6
Current Ratio (times)	3.4	2.1	1.4
Curr Liab To Nw (%)	27.8	60.9	140.3
Curr Liab To Inv (%)	84.1	134.5	236.4
Total Liab To Nw (%)	43.6	94.5	188.9
Fixed Assets To Nw (%)	12.3	25.7	61.5
EFFICIENCY			
Coll Period (days)	31.4	51.1	76.3
Sales To Inv (times)	13.5	6.2	4.1
Assets To Sales (%)	39.8	63.8	112.3
Sales To Nwc (times)	7.7	4.4	2.0
Acct Pay To Sales (%)	2.3	5.5	9.8
PROFITABILITY			
Return On Sales (%)	5.3	0.4	(9.5)
Return On Assets (%)	8.4	0.5	(16.4)
Return On Nw (%)	21.1	0.8	(28.8)

SIC 3561 PUMPS, PUMPING EQPMT
(NO BREAKDOWN)
2002 (44 Establishments)

	$	%
Cash	279,889	9.8
Accounts Receivable	736,851	25.8
Notes Receivable	0	0.0
Inventory	868,228	30.4
Other Current	185,641	6.5
Total Current	**2,070,609**	**72.5**
Fixed Assets	434,114	15.2
Other Non-current	351,289	12.3
Total Assets	**2,856,012**	**100.0**
Accounts Payable	342,721	12.0
Bank Loans	14,280	0.5
Notes Payable	119,953	4.2
Other Current	422,690	14.8
Total Current	**899,644**	**31.5**
Other Long Term	591,194	20.7
Deferred Credits	0	0.0
Net Worth	1,365,174	47.8
Total Liab & Net Worth	**2,856,012**	**100.0**
Net Sales	5,524,201	100.0
Gross Profit	1,950,043	35.3
Net Profit After Tax	182,299	3.3
Working Capital	1,170,965	—

RATIOS	UQ	MED	LQ
SOLVENCY			
Quick Ratio (times)	2.0	1.3	0.9
Current Ratio (times)	4.2	2.8	1.9
Curr Liab To Nw (%)	23.9	41.5	92.0
Curr Liab To Inv (%)	51.3	105.0	159.0
Total Liab To Nw (%)	29.0	96.9	167.2
Fixed Assets To Nw (%)	14.1	24.1	42.7
EFFICIENCY			
Coll Period (days)	37.6	52.2	64.4
Sales To Inv (times)	9.6	5.7	4.4
Assets To Sales (%)	40.4	51.7	102.4
Sales To Nwc (times)	7.3	4.2	3.1
Acct Pay To Sales (%)	3.0	5.5	7.7
PROFITABILITY			
Return On Sales (%)	5.4	2.4	0.1
Return On Assets (%)	7.0	2.9	0.3
Return On Nw (%)	12.6	7.4	3.8

SIC 3562 BALL, ROLLER BEARNGS
(NO BREAKDOWN)
2002 (14 Establishments)

	$	%
Cash	3,557,828	8.4
Accounts Receivable	8,216,888	19.4
Notes Receivable	381,196	0.9
Inventory	10,292,287	24.3
Other Current	2,795,436	6.6
Total Current	**25,243,635**	**59.6**
Fixed Assets	11,520,585	27.2
Other Non-current	5,590,872	13.2
Total Assets	**42,355,092**	**100.0**
Accounts Payable	4,320,219	10.2
Bank Loans	0	0.0
Notes Payable	804,747	1.9
Other Current	4,659,060	11.0
Total Current	**9,784,026**	**23.1**
Other Long Term	11,308,810	26.7
Deferred Credits	0	0.0
Net Worth	21,262,256	50.2
Total Liab & Net Worth	**42,355,092**	**100.0**
Net Sales	39,290,438	100.0
Gross Profit	13,201,587	33.6
Net Profit After Tax	589,357	1.5
Working Capital	15,459,609	—

RATIOS	UQ	MED	LQ
SOLVENCY			
Quick Ratio (times)	2.9	1.0	0.8
Current Ratio (times)	6.0	2.1	1.5
Curr Liab To Nw (%)	13.5	51.9	113.2
Curr Liab To Inv (%)	70.4	122.8	129.7
Total Liab To Nw (%)	43.8	131.0	303.0
Fixed Assets To Nw (%)	28.2	77.8	127.6
EFFICIENCY			
Coll Period (days)	35.4	50.0	56.6
Sales To Inv (times)	8.0	5.9	3.6
Assets To Sales (%)	46.7	107.8	164.0
Sales To Nwc (times)	8.0	4.5	2.4
Acct Pay To Sales (%)	4.2	8.2	11.6
PROFITABILITY			
Return On Sales (%)	4.3	1.2	(1.5)
Return On Assets (%)	3.1	1.8	(1.6)
Return On Nw (%)	13.8	5.3	(5.2)

SIC 3563 AIR, GAS COMPRESSORS
(NO BREAKDOWN)
2002 (13 Establishments)

	$	%
Cash	575,135	17.8
Accounts Receivable	697,917	21.6
Notes Receivable	0	0.0
Inventory	743,152	23.0
Other Current	397,425	12.3
Total Current	**2,413,629**	**74.7**
Fixed Assets	445,891	13.8
Other Non-current	371,577	11.5
Total Assets	**3,231,097**	**100.0**
Accounts Payable	323,110	10.0
Bank Loans	0	0.0
Notes Payable	42,004	1.3
Other Current	526,669	16.3
Total Current	**891,783**	**27.6**
Other Long Term	420,042	13.0
Deferred Credits	0	0.0
Net Worth	1,919,272	59.4
Total Liab & Net Worth	**3,231,097**	**100.0**
Net Sales	3,504,444	100.0
Gross Profit	1,240,573	35.4
Net Profit After Tax	(10,513)	(0.3)
Working Capital	1,521,846	—

RATIOS	UQ	MED	LQ
SOLVENCY			
Quick Ratio (times)	1.7	1.3	0.8
Current Ratio (times)	4.7	2.7	1.7
Curr Liab To Nw (%)	14.6	31.9	89.6
Curr Liab To Inv (%)	73.8	124.8	205.2
Total Liab To Nw (%)	16.0	35.9	103.9
Fixed Assets To Nw (%)	7.5	14.8	43.4
EFFICIENCY			
Coll Period (days)	41.1	54.4	83.4
Sales To Inv (times)	9.3	5.7	3.5
Assets To Sales (%)	49.3	92.2	124.7
Sales To Nwc (times)	5.4	3.4	1.8
Acct Pay To Sales (%)	2.0	7.8	9.1
PROFITABILITY			
Return On Sales (%)	2.3	0.1	(2.5)
Return On Assets (%)	2.7	0.1	(6.5)
Return On Nw (%)	8.2	0.8	(5.3)

	SIC 3564 BLOWERS AND FANS (NO BREAKDOWN) 2002 (52 Establishments) $	%	SIC 3565 PACKAGING MACHINERY (NO BREAKDOWN) 2002 (36 Establishments) $	%	SIC 3566 SPD CHNGRS,DRVS,GRS (NO BREAKDOWN) 2002 (14 Establishments) $	%	SIC 3567 INDL FURNACES,OVENS (NO BREAKDOWN) 2002 (29 Establishments) $	%
Cash	315,131	19.4	165,259	11.5	143,432	6.4	268,512	18.0
Accounts Receivable	646,506	39.8	419,613	29.2	472,877	21.1	438,570	29.4
Notes Receivable	6,498	0.4	24,430	1.7	0	0.0	0	0.0
Inventory	334,624	20.6	436,858	30.4	578,209	25.8	289,396	19.4
Other Current	(216,044)	(13.3)	107,777	7.5	33,616	1.5	138,732	9.3
Total Current	**1,086,715**	**66.9**	**1,153,937**	**80.3**	**1,228,134**	**54.8**	**1,135,210**	**76.1**
Fixed Assets	383,355	23.6	202,622	14.1	853,867	38.1	261,053	17.5
Other Non-current	154,317	9.5	80,473	5.6	159,120	7.1	95,471	6.4
Total Assets	**1,624,387**	**100.0**	**1,437,032**	**100.0**	**2,241,121**	**100.0**	**1,491,734**	**100.0**
Accounts Payable	294,014	18.1	254,355	17.7	192,736	8.6	184,975	12.4
Bank Loans	0	0.0	11,496	0.8	0	0.0	10,442	0.7
Notes Payable	58,478	3.6	25,867	1.8	24,652	1.1	29,835	2.0
Other Current	253,404	15.6	428,235	29.8	510,976	22.8	265,528	17.8
Total Current	**605,896**	**37.3**	**719,953**	**50.1**	**728,364**	**32.5**	**490,780**	**32.9**
Other Long Term	289,141	17.8	175,318	12.2	396,679	17.7	159,616	10.7
Deferred Credits	0	0.0	5,748	0.4	0	0.0	0	0.0
Net Worth	729,350	44.9	536,013	37.3	1,116,078	49.8	841,338	56.4
Total Liab & Net Worth	**1,624,387**	**100.0**	**1,437,032**	**100.0**	**2,241,121**	**100.0**	**1,491,734**	**100.0**
Net Sales	3,328,662	100.0	3,583,621	100.0	3,229,281	100.0	2,742,158	100.0
Gross Profit	981,955	29.5	1,386,861	38.7	907,428	28.1	976,208	35.6
Net Profit After Tax	36,615	1.1	121,843	3.4	(193,757)	(6.0)	2,742	0.1
Working Capital	480,819	—	433,984	—	499,770	—	644,430	—

RATIOS	UQ	MED	LQ	UQ	MED	LQ	UQ	MED	LQ	UQ	MED	LQ
SOLVENCY												
Quick Ratio (times)	3.2	1.2	0.7	1.4	0.8	0.6	2.2	1.1	0.6	2.9	1.4	0.9
Current Ratio (times)	5.1	2.1	1.2	2.2	1.7	1.3	3.0	2.5	1.6	4.4	2.4	1.7
Curr Liab To Nw (%)	16.0	39.0	133.9	49.7	138.0	348.1	18.8	28.3	47.5	20.7	52.4	114.1
Curr Liab To Inv (%)	81.8	140.2	396.3	89.0	144.8	333.2	53.8	122.5	307.1	89.4	157.9	466.0
Total Liab To Nw (%)	20.0	62.1	190.5	65.6	143.8	430.8	34.7	71.1	83.8	21.4	66.8	183.7
Fixed Assets To Nw (%)	11.9	28.0	62.6	16.8	38.9	58.3	37.4	63.7	98.9	10.6	26.7	55.0
EFFICIENCY												
Coll Period (days)	41.3	56.4	67.9	21.9	52.8	69.0	43.8	54.8	61.9	28.1	54.4	78.8
Sales To Inv (times)	27.9	8.8	6.4	13.0	7.9	5.0	18.6	4.8	4.3	22.6	8.4	4.1
Assets To Sales (%)	33.3	48.8	72.2	31.7	40.1	52.9	52.6	69.4	89.9	31.0	54.4	81.9
Sales To Nwc (times)	8.5	5.7	3.3	18.6	7.5	4.3	7.7	6.1	3.8	8.3	6.5	2.3
Acct Pay To Sales (%)	2.6	5.5	10.2	2.8	5.4	7.8	1.7	4.1	7.9	2.3	4.8	7.8
PROFITABILITY												
Return On Sales (%)	4.4	1.6	(0.1)	6.8	2.5	0.7	1.4	(1.5)	(7.6)	4.7	1.1	(5.2)
Return On Assets (%)	8.6	4.2	(0.3)	19.0	6.7	1.4	1.6	(2.4)	(16.3)	8.4	2.9	(5.4)
Return On Nw (%)	20.5	9.1	5.4	44.6	15.4	4.7	5.5	1.3	(18.4)	14.3	3.3	(11.6)

	SIC 3568 PWR TRANS EQPT,NEC (NO BREAKDOWN) 2002 (24 Establishments)		SIC 3569 GNRL IND MCHNRY,NEC (NO BREAKDOWN) 2002 (93 Establishments)		SIC 3571 ELECTRNC COMPUTERS (NO BREAKDOWN) 2002 (76 Establishments)		SIC 3572 COMPTR STRGE DVCES (NO BREAKDOWN) 2002 (34 Establishments)	
	$	%	$	%	$	%	$	%
Cash	533,082	9.9	225,498	9.7	1,059,957	18.8	2,743,827	26.6
Accounts Receivable	823,854	15.3	588,155	25.3	1,437,708	25.5	2,166,179	21.0
Notes Receivable	43,077	0.8	6,974	0.3	0	0.0	20,630	0.2
Inventory	1,394,629	25.9	527,712	22.7	1,088,147	19.3	1,763,889	17.1
Other Current	376,927	7.0	330,110	14.2	597,635	10.6	845,842	8.2
Total Current	**3,171,569**	**58.9**	**1,678,449**	**72.2**	**4,183,447**	**74.2**	**7,540,367**	**73.1**
Fixed Assets	1,507,707	28.0	497,491	21.4	851,348	15.1	1,371,914	13.3
Other Non-current	705,392	13.1	148,782	6.4	603,274	10.7	1,402,859	13.6
Total Assets	**5,384,668**	**100.0**	**2,324,722**	**100.0**	**5,638,069**	**100.0**	**10,315,140**	**100.0**
Accounts Payable	452,312	8.4	253,395	10.9	1,105,062	19.6	1,990,822	19.3
Bank Loans	10,769	0.2	11,624	0.5	33,828	0.6	0	0.0
Notes Payable	140,001	2.6	111,587	4.8	124,038	2.2	165,042	1.6
Other Current	640,776	11.9	550,958	23.7	1,302,393	23.1	2,816,033	27.3
Total Current	**1,243,858**	**23.1**	**927,564**	**39.9**	**2,565,321**	**45.5**	**4,971,897**	**48.2**
Other Long Term	1,383,860	25.7	383,579	16.5	732,950	13.0	1,175,927	11.4
Deferred Credits	5,385	0.1	9,299	0.4	11,276	0.2	30,945	0.3
Net Worth	2,751,565	51.1	1,004,280	43.2	2,328,522	41.3	4,136,371	40.1
Total Liab & Net Worth	**5,384,668**	**100.0**	**2,324,722**	**100.0**	**5,638,069**	**100.0**	**10,315,140**	**100.0**
Net Sales	7,132,011	100.0	4,883,870	100.0	9,572,273	100.0	16,504,224	100.0
Gross Profit	2,004,095	28.1	1,704,471	34.9	3,110,989	32.5	5,248,343	31.8
Net Profit After Tax	71,320	1.0	151,400	3.1	(775,354)	(8.1)	(907,732)	(5.5)
Working Capital	1,927,711	—	750,885	—	1,618,126	—	2,568,470	—

RATIOS	UQ	MED	LQ	UQ	MED	LQ	UQ	MED	LQ	UQ	MED	LQ
SOLVENCY												
Quick Ratio (times)	2.0	0.9	0.6	1.8	0.9	0.6	1.5	0.9	0.7	2.0	1.4	0.7
Current Ratio (times)	4.8	2.4	1.6	3.6	2.0	1.4	2.3	1.6	1.2	3.9	1.9	1.2
Curr Liab To Nw (%)	12.6	47.1	84.8	19.7	55.5	116.2	45.1	91.8	181.2	28.0	68.1	218.4
Curr Liab To Inv (%)	56.4	78.2	151.5	68.6	148.7	300.4	148.0	224.7	441.9	159.2	204.8	401.3
Total Liab To Nw (%)	24.9	137.7	189.1	30.5	75.8	161.5	54.3	114.3	238.3	33.2	98.0	298.6
Fixed Assets To Nw (%)	20.0	61.4	89.1	15.1	35.3	61.2	11.2	21.5	53.9	8.3	19.1	63.9
EFFICIENCY												
Coll Period (days)	39.8	48.7	58.8	36.5	48.9	66.1	27.4	40.9	68.5	36.1	46.0	59.1
Sales To Inv (times)	7.3	4.5	3.5	23.0	8.0	5.3	31.6	11.3	6.8	16.6	12.5	7.2
Assets To Sales (%)	64.5	75.5	93.2	36.8	47.6	72.3	24.6	58.9	104.1	41.1	62.5	118.2
Sales To Nwc (times)	5.8	3.7	2.4	8.7	5.6	3.7	17.5	6.3	3.1	12.9	3.3	2.5
Acct Pay To Sales (%)	2.7	4.7	6.0	3.3	5.0	7.7	5.0	8.2	12.4	7.9	9.7	14.1
PROFITABILITY												
Return On Sales (%)	2.9	1.3	(1.0)	5.6	2.1	(0.1)	3.4	0.5	(9.7)	4.6	0.6	(10.3)
Return On Assets (%)	7.6	1.8	(1.4)	11.7	3.2	(0.3)	7.3	1.3	(10.4)	5.5	2.4	(19.0)
Return On Nw (%)	11.7	2.4	(4.0)	22.9	9.2	0.6	20.6	4.6	(20.6)	18.5	4.9	(41.8)

SIC 3575 — COMPUTER TERMINALS (NO BREAKDOWN) — 2002 (26 Establishments)

	$	%
Cash	510,145	21.1
Accounts Receivable	534,322	22.1
Notes Receivable	2,418	0.1
Inventory	582,677	24.1
Other Current	74,950	3.1
Total Current	**1,704,512**	**70.5**
Fixed Assets	299,801	12.4
Other Non-current	413,435	17.1
Total Assets	**2,417,748**	**100.0**
Accounts Payable	534,322	22.1
Bank Loans	0	0.0
Notes Payable	5,070,018	209.7
Other Current	1,436,142	59.4
Total Current	**7,040,482**	**291.2**
Other Long Term	597,184	24.7
Deferred Credits	0	0.0
Net Worth	(5,219,918)	(215.9)
Total Liab & Net Worth	**2,417,748**	**100.0**
Net Sales	4,797,119	100.0
Gross Profit	1,290,425	26.9
Net Profit After Tax	(143,914)	(3.0)
Working Capital	(5,335,970)	—

RATIOS	UQ	MED	LQ
SOLVENCY			
Quick Ratio (times)	2.6	1.2	0.6
Current Ratio (times)	4.0	2.7	1.1
Curr Liab To Nw (%)	16.2	48.2	103.2
Curr Liab To Inv (%)	65.5	143.0	367.9
Total Liab To Nw (%)	16.8	66.0	181.0
Fixed Assets To Nw (%)	4.2	19.8	46.9
EFFICIENCY			
Coll Period (days)	34.3	48.4	69.0
Sales To Inv (times)	16.4	5.8	3.9
Assets To Sales (%)	43.1	50.4	111.8
Sales To Nwc (times)	5.5	3.3	2.5
Acct Pay To Sales (%)	3.0	5.4	8.9
PROFITABILITY			
Return On Sales (%)	9.4	1.9	(14.3)
Return On Assets (%)	14.8	4.7	(16.0)
Return On Nw (%)	30.0	13.1	(2.9)

SIC 3577 — CMPTR PRPRL EQP,NEC (NO BREAKDOWN) — 2002 (144 Establishments)

	$	%
Cash	1,476,982	18.3
Accounts Receivable	1,904,742	23.6
Notes Receivable	8,071	0.1
Inventory	1,904,742	23.6
Other Current	807,095	10.0
Total Current	**6,101,632**	**75.6**
Fixed Assets	1,065,364	13.2
Other Non-current	903,946	11.2
Total Assets	**8,070,942**	**100.0**
Accounts Payable	2,736,049	33.9
Bank Loans	72,638	0.9
Notes Payable	1,121,861	13.9
Other Current	2,276,006	28.2
Total Current	**6,206,554**	**76.9**
Other Long Term	1,533,479	19.0
Deferred Credits	32,284	0.4
Net Worth	298,625	3.7
Total Liab & Net Worth	**8,070,942**	**100.0**
Net Sales	13,915,417	100.0
Gross Profit	4,717,326	33.9
Net Profit After Tax	(1,308,049)	(9.4)
Working Capital	(104,922)	—

RATIOS	UQ	MED	LQ
SOLVENCY			
Quick Ratio (times)	2.2	1.3	0.6
Current Ratio (times)	4.2	2.3	1.3
Curr Liab To Nw (%)	21.4	44.1	116.3
Curr Liab To Inv (%)	79.8	166.9	332.5
Total Liab To Nw (%)	33.1	67.2	169.2
Fixed Assets To Nw (%)	7.4	15.8	44.1
EFFICIENCY			
Coll Period (days)	32.1	47.8	66.1
Sales To Inv (times)	13.8	8.7	5.2
Assets To Sales (%)	37.0	58.0	130.7
Sales To Nwc (times)	8.4	3.4	1.6
Acct Pay To Sales (%)	4.7	8.6	12.2
PROFITABILITY			
Return On Sales (%)	3.4	(0.5)	(40.0)
Return On Assets (%)	5.0	(1.0)	(33.0)
Return On Nw (%)	13.3	(0.7)	(40.1)

SIC 3578 — CLCTNG,ACCTNG EQPMT (NO BREAKDOWN) — 2002 (13 Establishments)

	$	%
Cash	350,801	15.9
Accounts Receivable	450,085	20.4
Notes Receivable	0	0.0
Inventory	439,053	19.9
Other Current	183,123	8.3
Total Current	**1,423,062**	**64.5**
Fixed Assets	542,749	24.6
Other Non-current	240,487	10.9
Total Assets	**2,206,298**	**100.0**
Accounts Payable	383,896	17.4
Bank Loans	13,238	0.6
Notes Payable	103,696	4.7
Other Current	324,325	14.7
Total Current	**825,155**	**37.4**
Other Long Term	284,613	12.9
Deferred Credits	6,619	0.3
Net Worth	1,089,911	49.4
Total Liab & Net Worth	**2,206,298**	**100.0**
Net Sales	3,605,062	100.0
Gross Profit	1,434,815	39.8
Net Profit After Tax	223,514	6.2
Working Capital	597,907	—

RATIOS	UQ	MED	LQ
SOLVENCY			
Quick Ratio (times)	1.0	0.8	0.8
Current Ratio (times)	1.9	1.5	1.3
Curr Liab To Nw (%)	57.6	106.2	137.7
Curr Liab To Inv (%)	127.2	197.5	251.5
Total Liab To Nw (%)	70.7	122.9	212.0
Fixed Assets To Nw (%)	25.2	51.8	96.0
EFFICIENCY			
Coll Period (days)	28.7	46.4	80.7
Sales To Inv (times)	16.1	8.0	6.0
Assets To Sales (%)	35.3	61.2	91.7
Sales To Nwc (times)	13.8	8.4	4.4
Acct Pay To Sales (%)	5.3	8.9	13.3
PROFITABILITY			
Return On Sales (%)	6.1	4.9	0.3
Return On Assets (%)	11.6	6.1	1.9
Return On Nw (%)	44.5	15.2	2.1

SIC 3585 — RRFGRTN,HTNG EQPMT (NO BREAKDOWN) — 2002 (79 Establishments)

	$	%
Cash	317,277	11.0
Accounts Receivable	683,588	23.7
Notes Receivable	2,884	0.1
Inventory	738,390	25.6
Other Current	181,714	6.3
Total Current	**1,923,853**	**66.7**
Fixed Assets	608,595	21.1
Other Non-current	351,889	12.2
Total Assets	**2,884,337**	**100.0**
Accounts Payable	594,173	20.6
Bank Loans	20,190	0.7
Notes Payable	550,908	19.1
Other Current	1,289,300	44.7
Total Current	**2,454,571**	**85.1**
Other Long Term	810,498	28.1
Deferred Credits	5,769	0.2
Net Worth	(386,501)	(13.4)
Total Liab & Net Worth	**2,884,337**	**100.0**
Net Sales	5,159,816	100.0
Gross Profit	1,563,424	30.3
Net Profit After Tax	227,032	4.4
Working Capital	(530,718)	—

RATIOS	UQ	MED	LQ
SOLVENCY			
Quick Ratio (times)	1.7	1.0	0.6
Current Ratio (times)	3.5	1.9	1.4
Curr Liab To Nw (%)	40.1	76.8	126.1
Curr Liab To Inv (%)	87.0	142.4	244.7
Total Liab To Nw (%)	62.6	108.3	232.9
Fixed Assets To Nw (%)	16.9	39.5	68.1
EFFICIENCY			
Coll Period (days)	31.0	42.3	57.9
Sales To Inv (times)	13.8	8.3	4.9
Assets To Sales (%)	41.0	55.9	75.5
Sales To Nwc (times)	9.3	6.6	3.8
Acct Pay To Sales (%)	3.5	5.7	8.9
PROFITABILITY			
Return On Sales (%)	5.6	2.1	(1.2)
Return On Assets (%)	14.7	4.0	(1.9)
Return On Nw (%)	25.7	10.3	(0.9)

	SIC 3589 SVC IND MCHNRY,NEC (NO BREAKDOWN) 2002 (92 Establishments)		SIC 3593 FLD PWR CYLS,ACTRS (NO BREAKDOWN) 2002 (21 Establishments)		SIC 3594 FLUID PWR PMPS,MTRS (NO BREAKDOWN) 2002 (14 Establishments)		SIC 3599 IND MACHINERY,NEC (NO BREAKDOWN) 2002 (1156 Establishments)	
	$	%	$	%	$	%	$	%
Cash	353,536	14.0	216,541	8.1	2,695,011	8.2	117,289	12.9
Accounts Receivable	606,062	24.0	598,829	22.4	5,981,610	18.2	208,210	22.9
Notes Receivable	32,828	1.3	0	0.0	0	0.0	5,455	0.6
Inventory	613,638	24.3	588,136	22.0	8,840,952	26.9	120,017	13.2
Other Current	209,598	8.3	197,827	7.4	2,399,218	7.3	59,099	6.5
Total Current	**1,815,662**	**71.9**	**1,601,333**	**59.9**	**19,916,791**	**60.6**	**510,070**	**56.1**
Fixed Assets	482,325	19.1	927,650	34.7	10,549,983	32.1	355,503	39.1
Other Non-current	227,273	9.0	144,361	5.4	2,399,217	7.3	43,643	4.8
Total Assets	**2,525,260**	**100.0**	**2,673,344**	**100.0**	**32,865,991**	**100.0**	**909,216**	**100.0**
Accounts Payable	376,264	14.9	211,194	7.9	3,680,991	11.2	84,557	9.3
Bank Loans	5,051	0.2	0	0.0	1,051,712	3.2	4,546	0.5
Notes Payable	123,738	4.9	34,753	1.3	1,413,238	4.3	32,732	3.6
Other Current	500,000	19.8	489,223	18.3	4,864,166	14.8	160,022	17.6
Total Current	**1,005,053**	**39.8**	**735,170**	**27.5**	**11,010,107**	**33.5**	**281,857**	**31.0**
Other Long Term	371,214	14.7	1,088,051	40.7	7,657,776	23.3	219,121	24.1
Deferred Credits	2,525	0.1	2,673	0.1	197,196	0.6	1,818	0.2
Net Worth	1,146,468	45.4	847,450	31.7	14,000,912	42.6	406,420	44.7
Total Liab & Net Worth	**2,525,260**	**100.0**	**2,673,344**	**100.0**	**32,865,991**	**100.0**	**909,216**	**100.0**
Net Sales	4,773,648	100.0	5,581,094	100.0	43,131,222	100.0	1,755,243	100.0
Gross Profit	1,761,476	36.9	1,568,287	28.1	11,343,511	26.3	670,503	38.2
Net Profit After Tax	205,267	4.3	150,690	2.7	(948,887)	(2.2)	17,552	1.0
Working Capital	810,609	—	866,163	—	8,906,684	—	228,213	—

RATIOS	UQ	MED	LQ	UQ	MED	LQ	UQ	MED	LQ	UQ	MED	LQ
SOLVENCY												
Quick Ratio (times)	2.2	1.1	0.6	2.3	1.3	0.6	1.1	0.8	0.6	3.3	1.3	0.6
Current Ratio (times)	4.9	2.3	1.3	3.8	2.6	2.0	2.6	1.6	1.5	4.8	2.2	1.2
Curr Liab To Nw (%)	19.6	44.0	125.4	20.1	38.1	58.9	39.3	60.2	200.5	13.7	39.8	108.1
Curr Liab To Inv (%)	57.5	122.8	328.1	64.4	99.0	180.5	80.9	130.5	159.4	94.7	188.9	510.3
Total Liab To Nw (%)	27.1	77.5	183.2	32.9	42.5	166.4	45.0	152.2	307.3	23.8	81.2	208.1
Fixed Assets To Nw (%)	11.6	32.3	66.9	27.2	55.9	110.3	38.7	61.8	131.3	35.8	66.0	140.3
EFFICIENCY												
Coll Period (days)	29.9	47.5	66.8	34.3	38.0	59.5	40.2	47.5	70.1	29.9	42.7	57.7
Sales To Inv (times)	10.3	7.3	4.8	13.1	9.1	5.8	9.8	5.8	4.7	43.7	16.8	7.6
Assets To Sales (%)	37.0	52.9	89.2	43.1	47.9	63.1	69.2	76.2	102.0	36.5	51.8	71.2
Sales To Nwc (times)	8.5	5.2	3.6	9.1	6.7	3.5	9.3	5.7	3.0	11.5	6.2	3.6
Acct Pay To Sales (%)	3.0	6.5	12.0	2.2	3.9	5.6	4.3	7.2	7.6	1.7	3.3	6.3
PROFITABILITY												
Return On Sales (%)	5.0	1.8	(1.5)	6.1	0.9	(0.6)	2.1	(0.3)	(7.3)	4.9	1.3	(2.3)
Return On Assets (%)	10.7	4.2	(3.3)	14.5	2.0	(0.9)	2.3	(0.7)	(5.3)	9.9	2.6	(4.1)
Return On Nw (%)	23.9	8.1	(3.1)	27.5	2.6	(2.3)	5.0	(3.0)	(11.2)	21.6	5.7	(5.7)

	SIC 36 ELECTRICAL EQUIPMENT (NO BREAKDOWN) 2002 (1682 Establishments)		SIC 3612 TRNSFRMRS, EXC ELEC (NO BREAKDOWN) 2002 (36 Establishments)		SIC 3613 SWTCHGR, BRD APPRTUS (NO BREAKDOWN) 2002 (79 Establishments)		SIC 3621 MOTORS, GENERATORS (NO BREAKDOWN) 2002 (46 Establishments)	
	$	%	$	%	$	%	$	%
Cash	572,544	16.0	366,373	12.1	211,310	15.4	538,303	16.1
Accounts Receivable	783,670	21.9	856,889	28.3	478,879	34.9	722,195	21.6
Notes Receivable	10,735	0.3	3,028	0.1	5,489	0.4	3,343	0.1
Inventory	823,032	23.0	699,439	23.1	238,753	17.4	835,874	25.0
Other Current	339,949	9.5	99,919	3.3	112,516	8.2	247,420	7.4
Total Current	**2,529,930**	**70.7**	**2,025,648**	**66.9**	**1,046,947**	**76.3**	**2,347,135**	**70.2**
Fixed Assets	712,102	19.9	575,296	19.0	246,986	18.0	655,325	19.6
Other Non-current	336,370	9.4	426,931	14.1	78,212	5.7	341,037	10.2
Total Assets	**3,578,402**	**100.0**	**3,027,875**	**100.0**	**1,372,145**	**100.0**	**3,343,497**	**100.0**
Accounts Payable	715,680	20.0	529,878	17.5	175,635	12.8	454,716	13.6
Bank Loans	10,735	0.3	24,223	0.8	4,116	0.3	10,030	0.3
Notes Payable	325,635	9.1	66,613	2.2	63,119	4.6	76,900	2.3
Other Current	783,670	21.9	705,495	23.3	268,940	19.6	795,753	23.8
Total Current	**1,835,720**	**51.3**	**1,326,209**	**43.8**	**511,810**	**37.3**	**1,337,399**	**40.0**
Other Long Term	883,866	24.7	1,804,614	59.6	166,030	12.1	896,057	26.8
Deferred Credits	10,735	0.3	0	0.0	0	0.0	6,687	0.2
Net Worth	848,081	23.7	(102,948)	(3.4)	694,305	50.6	1,103,354	33.0
Total Liab & Net Worth	**3,578,402**	**100.0**	**3,027,875**	**100.0**	**1,372,145**	**100.0**	**3,343,497**	**100.0**
Net Sales	5,818,540	100.0	6,456,023	100.0	3,620,435	100.0	5,563,223	100.0
Gross Profit	1,966,667	33.8	1,678,566	26.0	1,147,678	31.7	1,763,542	31.7
Net Profit After Tax	(104,734)	(1.8)	(96,840)	(1.5)	83,270	2.3	100,138	1.8
Working Capital	694,210	—	699,439	—	535,137	—	1,009,736	—

RATIOS	UQ	MED	LQ	UQ	MED	LQ	UQ	MED	LQ	UQ	MED	LQ
SOLVENCY												
Quick Ratio (times)	2.5	1.3	0.7	1.9	1.1	0.7	2.8	1.7	0.9	1.6	1.0	0.6
Current Ratio (times)	4.7	2.4	1.4	3.4	1.9	1.2	4.4	2.7	1.4	2.9	2.1	1.2
Curr Liab To Nw (%)	17.3	41.1	102.2	25.3	58.5	166.3	21.8	38.3	115.9	30.3	62.2	149.1
Curr Liab To Inv (%)	72.1	135.0	269.6	71.1	125.4	321.2	84.5	226.3	470.6	75.0	121.3	200.7
Total Liab To Nw (%)	24.7	63.5	158.1	25.4	82.6	240.7	25.7	58.1	149.5	47.0	116.5	172.4
Fixed Assets To Nw (%)	12.1	26.6	57.2	17.5	35.8	83.2	12.1	26.1	49.5	16.4	45.7	69.5
EFFICIENCY												
Coll Period (days)	34.7	48.2	64.1	36.9	46.7	56.6	35.1	49.6	69.6	38.2	47.7	62.1
Sales To Inv (times)	12.6	7.1	4.5	13.1	8.7	4.6	33.9	14.2	8.6	10.9	7.1	4.0
Assets To Sales (%)	38.5	61.5	106.3	33.2	46.9	68.3	29.5	37.9	60.3	41.2	60.1	84.7
Sales To Nwc (times)	7.9	4.1	2.1	14.6	6.2	3.6	8.9	5.2	3.6	11.6	6.2	3.4
Acct Pay To Sales (%)	3.2	6.2	10.5	3.8	7.0	8.5	2.4	5.2	7.3	4.8	7.9	12.1
PROFITABILITY												
Return On Sales (%)	5.7	1.3	(8.3)	6.5	1.6	(1.8)	4.8	2.5	0.3	4.3	1.4	0.3
Return On Assets (%)	9.7	2.2	(10.1)	10.1	1.8	(6.0)	13.0	4.9	0.7	6.1	3.9	0.5
Return On Nw (%)	19.4	5.4	(12.0)	19.8	7.8	(9.3)	19.5	9.3	1.2	19.9	10.0	2.4

	SIC 3625 RELAYS,IND CONTROLS (NO BREAKDOWN) 2002 (98 Establishments)		SIC 3629 ELE IND APPRTUS,NEC (NO BREAKDOWN) 2002 (21 Establishments)		SIC 3634 ELEC HSEWRS,FANS (NO BREAKDOWN) 2002 (22 Establishments)		SIC 3643 CUR-CRRYNG WRNG DVC (NO BREAKDOWN) 2002 (51 Establishments)	
	$	%	$	%	$	%	$	%
Cash	232,167	12.2	1,458,201	17.4	1,552,171	14.5	407,953	13.2
Accounts Receivable	397,729	20.9	1,516,864	18.1	2,483,474	23.2	803,544	26.0
Notes Receivable	1,903	0.1	0	0.0	0	0.0	3,091	0.1
Inventory	622,284	32.7	1,650,951	19.7	2,590,520	24.2	781,910	25.3
Other Current	175,078	9.2	1,508,484	18.0	834,961	7.8	234,883	7.6
Total Current	**1,429,161**	**75.1**	**6,134,500**	**73.2**	**7,461,126**	**69.7**	**2,231,381**	**72.2**
Fixed Assets	378,699	19.9	1,826,941	21.8	1,776,968	16.6	602,658	19.5
Other Non-current	95,150	5.0	419,023	5.0	1,466,534	13.7	256,516	8.3
Total Assets	**1,903,010**	**100.0**	**8,380,464**	**100.0**	**10,704,628**	**100.0**	**3,090,555**	**100.0**
Accounts Payable	255,003	13.4	1,642,571	19.6	1,027,644	9.6	485,217	15.7
Bank Loans	1,903	0.1	83,805	1.0	85,637	0.8	30,906	1.0
Notes Payable	43,769	2.3	662,057	7.9	117,751	1.1	24,724	0.8
Other Current	430,081	22.6	1,508,483	18.0	1,862,605	17.4	587,206	19.0
Total Current	**730,756**	**38.4**	**3,896,916**	**46.5**	**3,093,637**	**28.9**	**1,128,053**	**36.5**
Other Long Term	420,565	22.1	1,081,080	12.9	2,301,496	21.5	355,414	11.5
Deferred Credits	5,709	0.3	368,740	4.4	0	0.0	6,181	0.2
Net Worth	745,980	39.2	3,033,728	36.2	5,309,495	49.6	1,600,907	51.8
Total Liab & Net Worth	**1,903,010**	**100.0**	**8,380,464**	**100.0**	**10,704,628**	**100.0**	**3,090,555**	**100.0**
Net Sales	3,813,647	100.0	12,470,929	100.0	16,243,745	100.0	6,718,598	100.0
Gross Profit	1,472,068	38.6	2,219,825	17.8	6,107,648	37.6	2,102,921	31.3
Net Profit After Tax	49,577	1.3	261,890	2.1	81,219	0.5	154,528	2.3
Working Capital	698,405	—	2,237,584	—	4,367,489	—	1,103,328	—

RATIOS	UQ	MED	LQ	UQ	MED	LQ	UQ	MED	LQ	UQ	MED	LQ
SOLVENCY												
Quick Ratio (times)	2.5	1.2	0.7	3.1	1.5	0.6	2.6	1.4	1.0	2.4	1.1	0.7
Current Ratio (times)	4.8	2.1	1.4	7.0	2.6	1.5	4.7	2.8	2.0	4.3	2.4	1.6
Curr Liab To Nw (%)	23.7	55.4	164.1	11.1	26.4	115.3	21.3	47.1	78.7	13.5	47.6	110.1
Curr Liab To Inv (%)	55.5	128.8	211.9	83.3	121.2	277.0	51.7	81.1	155.1	72.0	118.1	166.0
Total Liab To Nw (%)	31.4	99.0	218.9	14.8	31.4	117.1	32.3	93.4	157.0	17.3	83.8	157.7
Fixed Assets To Nw (%)	13.2	29.0	69.7	10.7	20.5	50.3	24.6	34.2	52.7	17.5	30.3	46.3
EFFICIENCY												
Coll Period (days)	36.5	49.8	65.0	45.3	62.1	83.1	28.8	42.4	75.9	37.6	42.9	52.4
Sales To Inv (times)	12.6	7.0	4.8	8.5	6.1	4.7	7.7	5.6	4.0	12.8	8.0	6.4
Assets To Sales (%)	36.6	49.9	73.5	44.2	67.2	116.0	39.8	65.9	82.5	32.5	46.0	59.9
Sales To Nwc (times)	10.4	5.3	2.6	4.9	3.0	0.8	4.9	3.6	2.7	9.4	6.4	3.6
Acct Pay To Sales (%)	2.4	3.7	8.1	5.9	8.0	16.9	1.8	4.7	10.9	3.7	4.8	8.4
PROFITABILITY												
Return On Sales (%)	6.9	1.8	(1.7)	6.5	(0.3)	(118.5)	6.5	3.5	0.2	4.8	0.8	(0.8)
Return On Assets (%)	11.1	3.7	(3.5)	9.4	(0.7)	(21.8)	8.9	3.6	0.5	10.8	2.1	(2.6)
Return On Nw (%)	26.5	7.5	(5.3)	20.5	6.3	(14.4)	19.4	6.7	1.5	18.1	4.8	(6.9)

SIC 3644 NCUR-CRYNG WRNG DVC (NO BREAKDOWN) 2002 (20 Establishments)

	$	%
Cash	274,202	12.3
Accounts Receivable	526,112	23.6
Notes Receivable	0	0.0
Inventory	336,622	15.1
Other Current	135,987	6.1
Total Current	**1,272,923**	**57.1**
Fixed Assets	715,601	32.1
Other Non-current	240,763	10.8
Total Assets	**2,229,287**	**100.0**
Accounts Payable	169,426	7.6
Bank Loans	24,522	1.1
Notes Payable	20,064	0.9
Other Current	329,934	14.8
Total Current	**543,946**	**24.4**
Other Long Term	258,597	11.6
Deferred Credits	0	0.0
Net Worth	1,426,744	64.0
Total Liab & Net Worth	**2,229,287**	**100.0**
Net Sales	4,397,016	100.0
Gross Profit	1,723,630	39.2
Net Profit After Tax	320,982	7.3
Working Capital	728,977	—

RATIOS	UQ	MED	LQ
SOLVENCY			
Quick Ratio (times)	3.2	1.5	0.8
Current Ratio (times)	4.9	2.7	1.4
Curr Liab To Nw (%)	11.5	33.4	73.4
Curr Liab To Inv (%)	85.0	181.9	312.7
Total Liab To Nw (%)	13.6	33.4	95.0
Fixed Assets To Nw (%)	34.5	45.5	72.3
EFFICIENCY			
Coll Period (days)	31.1	43.6	58.6
Sales To Inv (times)	23.2	12.8	8.2
Assets To Sales (%)	35.8	50.7	82.3
Sales To Nwc (times)	15.2	6.7	4.3
Acct Pay To Sales (%)	2.3	3.6	5.0
PROFITABILITY			
Return On Sales (%)	9.0	4.9	1.1
Return On Assets (%)	27.2	7.9	2.2
Return On Nw (%)	31.7	13.7	2.6

SIC 3645 RSDNTL LGHTNG FXTRS (NO BREAKDOWN) 2002 (17 Establishments)

	$	%
Cash	158,651	11.0
Accounts Receivable	376,436	26.1
Notes Receivable	0	0.0
Inventory	462,973	32.1
Other Current	77,882	5.4
Total Current	**1,075,942**	**74.6**
Fixed Assets	186,054	12.9
Other Non-current	180,286	12.5
Total Assets	**1,442,282**	**100.0**
Accounts Payable	227,881	15.8
Bank Loans	1,442	0.1
Notes Payable	18,750	1.3
Other Current	245,187	17.0
Total Current	**493,260**	**34.2**
Other Long Term	373,551	25.9
Deferred Credits	0	0.0
Net Worth	575,471	39.9
Total Liab & Net Worth	**1,442,282**	**100.0**
Net Sales	2,850,360	100.0
Gross Profit	1,140,144	40.0
Net Profit After Tax	91,212	3.2
Working Capital	582,682	—

RATIOS	UQ	MED	LQ
SOLVENCY			
Quick Ratio (times)	2.2	1.2	0.6
Current Ratio (times)	4.7	2.2	1.7
Curr Liab To Nw (%)	16.4	41.9	153.0
Curr Liab To Inv (%)	51.6	109.5	190.5
Total Liab To Nw (%)	43.9	71.7	180.1
Fixed Assets To Nw (%)	11.7	20.6	52.0
EFFICIENCY			
Coll Period (days)	26.7	53.9	66.8
Sales To Inv (times)	12.1	5.6	3.6
Assets To Sales (%)	38.2	50.6	58.3
Sales To Nwc (times)	6.3	4.8	3.1
Acct Pay To Sales (%)	5.0	8.5	10.2
PROFITABILITY			
Return On Sales (%)	8.4	2.2	0.1
Return On Assets (%)	19.8	4.3	0.1
Return On Nw (%)	17.0	3.5	0.2

SIC 3646 COMRCL LGHTNG FXTRS (NO BREAKDOWN) 2002 (23 Establishments)

	$	%
Cash	122,521	9.0
Accounts Receivable	378,454	27.8
Notes Receivable	1,361	0.1
Inventory	378,454	27.8
Other Current	74,875	5.5
Total Current	**955,665**	**70.2**
Fixed Assets	225,983	16.6
Other Non-current	179,698	13.2
Total Assets	**1,361,346**	**100.0**
Accounts Payable	185,143	13.6
Bank Loans	1,361	0.1
Notes Payable	49,008	3.6
Other Current	274,993	20.2
Total Current	**510,505**	**37.5**
Other Long Term	245,042	18.0
Deferred Credits	0	0.0
Net Worth	605,799	44.5
Total Liab & Net Worth	**1,361,346**	**100.0**
Net Sales	3,911,914	100.0
Gross Profit	1,603,885	41.0
Net Profit After Tax	156,477	4.0
Working Capital	445,160	—

RATIOS	UQ	MED	LQ
SOLVENCY			
Quick Ratio (times)	1.4	1.2	0.7
Current Ratio (times)	2.4	1.9	1.4
Curr Liab To Nw (%)	47.9	69.0	107.2
Curr Liab To Inv (%)	94.1	140.4	170.4
Total Liab To Nw (%)	61.8	86.1	200.4
Fixed Assets To Nw (%)	12.7	29.2	46.3
EFFICIENCY			
Coll Period (days)	34.9	43.8	56.2
Sales To Inv (times)	14.1	9.1	7.1
Assets To Sales (%)	28.1	34.8	68.1
Sales To Nwc (times)	13.4	7.9	4.5
Acct Pay To Sales (%)	4.3	5.2	8.2
PROFITABILITY			
Return On Sales (%)	7.3	3.4	1.0
Return On Assets (%)	14.6	6.4	3.8
Return On Nw (%)	32.7	14.0	6.3

SIC 3648 LGHTNG EQPMNT, NEC (NO BREAKDOWN) 2002 (21 Establishments)

	$	%
Cash	490,420	16.0
Accounts Receivable	655,937	21.4
Notes Receivable	42,912	1.4
Inventory	726,435	23.7
Other Current	196,168	6.4
Total Current	**2,111,872**	**68.9**
Fixed Assets	646,742	21.1
Other Non-current	306,512	10.0
Total Assets	**3,065,126**	**100.0**
Accounts Payable	334,099	10.9
Bank Loans	0	0.0
Notes Payable	542,527	17.7
Other Current	1,388,502	45.3
Total Current	**2,265,128**	**73.9**
Other Long Term	168,582	5.5
Deferred Credits	3,065	0.1
Net Worth	628,351	20.5
Total Liab & Net Worth	**3,065,126**	**100.0**
Net Sales	5,583,107	100.0
Gross Profit	2,054,583	36.8
Net Profit After Tax	100,496	1.8
Working Capital	(153,256)	—

RATIOS	UQ	MED	LQ
SOLVENCY			
Quick Ratio (times)	1.7	1.3	0.5
Current Ratio (times)	3.4	2.5	1.2
Curr Liab To Nw (%)	28.9	42.3	106.3
Curr Liab To Inv (%)	78.2	105.4	186.2
Total Liab To Nw (%)	35.2	51.6	139.6
Fixed Assets To Nw (%)	10.4	25.9	38.7
EFFICIENCY			
Coll Period (days)	28.1	46.2	55.1
Sales To Inv (times)	14.1	6.7	4.7
Assets To Sales (%)	35.7	54.9	85.7
Sales To Nwc (times)	9.4	5.8	3.0
Acct Pay To Sales (%)	1.9	4.0	7.8
PROFITABILITY			
Return On Sales (%)	6.2	3.0	0.8
Return On Assets (%)	10.9	4.4	1.6
Return On Nw (%)	23.2	9.4	2.2

	SIC 3651 HSHLD AUDIO,VDEO EQ (NO BREAKDOWN) 2002 (45 Establishments) $	%	SIC 3652 PRERECRD RCDS,TAPES (NO BREAKDOWN) 2002 (13 Establishments) $	%	SIC 3661 TLPHNE,TLGPH APPTUS (NO BREAKDOWN) 2002 (112 Establishments) $	%	SIC 3663 RDIO,TV CMMNCTNS EQ (NO BREAKDOWN) 2002 (154 Establishments) $	%
Cash	238,737	10.6	299,059	14.3	5,506,795	21.4	1,174,834	21.4
Accounts Receivable	565,311	25.1	315,789	15.1	3,962,834	15.4	955,239	17.4
Notes Receivable	0	0.0	23,005	1.1	25,733	0.1	16,470	0.3
Inventory	743,238	33.0	518,647	24.8	4,503,221	17.5	1,339,531	24.4
Other Current	213,963	9.5	207,041	9.9	4,117,230	16.0	527,028	9.6
Total Current	**1,761,249**	**78.2**	**1,363,541**	**65.2**	**18,115,813**	**70.4**	**4,013,102**	**73.1**
Fixed Assets	335,583	14.9	495,643	23.7	4,091,498	15.9	839,952	15.3
Other Non-current	155,405	6.9	232,136	11.1	3,525,378	13.7	636,826	11.6
Total Assets	**2,252,237**	**100.0**	**2,091,320**	**100.0**	**25,732,689**	**100.0**	**5,489,880**	**100.0**
Accounts Payable	445,943	19.8	140,118	6.7	2,496,071	9.7	3,996,633	72.8
Bank Loans	0	0.0	0	0.0	0	0.0	21,960	0.4
Notes Payable	58,558	2.6	41,826	2.0	1,029,308	4.0	3,744,098	68.2
Other Current	736,482	32.7	353,434	16.9	7,436,747	28.9	(2,668,082)	(48.6)
Total Current	**1,240,983**	**55.1**	**535,378**	**25.6**	**10,962,126**	**42.6**	**5,094,609**	**92.8**
Other Long Term	416,663	18.5	75,288	3.6	3,731,239	14.5	4,990,300	90.9
Deferred Credits	(4,504)	(0.2)	60,648	2.9	102,931	0.4	16,470	0.3
Net Worth	599,095	26.6	1,420,006	67.9	10,936,393	42.5	(4,611,499)	(84.0)
Total Liab & Net Worth	**2,252,237**	**100.0**	**2,091,320**	**100.0**	**25,732,689**	**100.0**	**5,489,880**	**100.0**
Net Sales	4,960,874	100.0	5,975,200	100.0	22,792,461	100.0	6,727,794	100.0
Gross Profit	1,766,071	35.6	2,413,981	40.4	7,316,380	32.1	2,435,461	36.2
Net Profit After Tax	(24,804)	(0.5)	394,363	6.6	(2,803,473)	(12.3)	(208,562)	(3.1)
Working Capital	520,266	—	828,163	—	7,153,687	—	(1,081,507)	—

RATIOS	UQ	MED	LQ	UQ	MED	LQ	UQ	MED	LQ	UQ	MED	LQ
SOLVENCY												
Quick Ratio (times)	1.9	0.7	0.5	3.0	1.4	0.3	3.0	1.2	0.7	2.4	1.4	0.6
Current Ratio (times)	4.6	2.0	1.1	6.4	2.9	1.4	5.0	2.6	1.4	5.0	2.9	1.4
Curr Liab To Nw (%)	23.8	53.0	242.8	17.3	41.7	62.9	15.1	33.0	90.6	17.0	30.1	76.7
Curr Liab To Inv (%)	68.2	139.8	254.2	34.4	89.8	293.6	101.1	189.6	385.8	58.0	126.8	252.8
Total Liab To Nw (%)	25.7	103.3	270.9	28.1	49.3	69.0	23.5	55.0	158.3	19.8	41.3	138.0
Fixed Assets To Nw (%)	9.9	21.6	81.6	24.3	27.6	36.3	7.9	14.3	46.7	9.6	20.4	32.5
EFFICIENCY												
Coll Period (days)	31.0	51.1	68.3	20.8	37.6	42.0	36.9	49.9	65.0	27.7	48.6	66.4
Sales To Inv (times)	11.6	6.1	4.2	25.9	17.8	9.0	10.6	6.7	3.3	8.2	5.5	3.4
Assets To Sales (%)	32.1	45.4	65.9	31.7	35.0	75.9	64.6	112.9	222.8	50.0	81.6	123.8
Sales To Nwc (times)	12.0	5.1	2.9	10.6	5.2	2.8	4.7	2.4	1.0	4.9	2.9	1.7
Acct Pay To Sales (%)	3.6	7.2	11.8	2.1	6.0	6.9	4.0	7.0	13.5	3.5	7.0	12.6
PROFITABILITY												
Return On Sales (%)	4.4	1.0	(3.1)	9.4	4.3	2.8	5.1	(14.8)	(95.4)	4.3	0.3	(20.6)
Return On Assets (%)	6.5	1.0	(7.2)	31.6	10.2	6.1	4.4	(15.5)	(48.4)	5.5	0.5	(18.6)
Return On Nw (%)	27.3	7.1	(0.8)	35.1	15.5	12.8	10.0	(15.0)	(113.4)	9.4	2.0	(25.8)

SIC 3669 CMMNCTNS EQPMNT,NEC
(NO BREAKDOWN) 2002 (39 Establishments)

	$	%
Cash	726,521	18.5
Accounts Receivable	993,567	25.3
Notes Receivable	15,709	0.4
Inventory	915,024	23.3
Other Current	443,766	11.3
Total Current	**3,094,587**	**78.8**
Fixed Assets	600,853	15.3
Other Non-current	231,701	5.9
Total Assets	**3,927,141**	**100.0**
Accounts Payable	502,674	12.8
Bank Loans	0	0.0
Notes Payable	74,616	1.9
Other Current	863,971	22.0
Total Current	**1,441,261**	**36.7**
Other Long Term	259,191	6.6
Deferred Credits	47,126	1.2
Net Worth	2,179,563	55.5
Total Liab & Net Worth	**3,927,141**	**100.0**
Net Sales	5,357,628	100.0
Gross Profit	2,469,867	46.1
Net Profit After Tax	16,073	0.3
Working Capital	1,653,326	—

RATIOS	UQ	MED	LQ
SOLVENCY			
Quick Ratio (times)	3.0	1.5	0.9
Current Ratio (times)	5.0	2.7	1.6
Curr Liab To Nw (%)	12.9	39.1	89.8
Curr Liab To Inv (%)	52.1	128.3	311.7
Total Liab To Nw (%)	33.2	52.1	139.4
Fixed Assets To Nw (%)	11.2	17.0	40.8
EFFICIENCY			
Coll Period (days)	33.6	49.3	63.9
Sales To Inv (times)	10.3	6.0	3.8
Assets To Sales (%)	46.7	73.3	99.0
Sales To Nwc (times)	6.0	3.4	2.0
Acct Pay To Sales (%)	2.6	4.6	9.3
PROFITABILITY			
Return On Sales (%)	6.0	0.9	(11.7)
Return On Assets (%)	12.0	2.8	(10.1)
Return On Nw (%)	25.4	10.2	(16.5)

SIC 3672 PRINTED CIRCT BRDS
(NO BREAKDOWN) 2002 (137 Establishments)

	$	%
Cash	289,652	11.2
Accounts Receivable	677,580	26.2
Notes Receivable	18,103	0.7
Inventory	491,375	19.0
Other Current	235,342	9.1
Total Current	**1,712,052**	**66.2**
Fixed Assets	765,510	29.6
Other Non-current	108,620	4.2
Total Assets	**2,586,182**	**100.0**
Accounts Payable	488,788	18.9
Bank Loans	7,759	0.3
Notes Payable	64,655	2.5
Other Current	1,606,019	62.1
Total Current	**2,167,221**	**83.8**
Other Long Term	628,442	24.3
Deferred Credits	2,586	0.1
Net Worth	(212,067)	(8.2)
Total Liab & Net Worth	**2,586,182**	**100.0**
Net Sales	5,561,682	100.0
Gross Profit	1,557,271	28.0
Net Profit After Tax	(61,179)	(1.1)
Working Capital	(455,169)	—

RATIOS	UQ	MED	LQ
SOLVENCY			
Quick Ratio (times)	2.0	1.2	0.6
Current Ratio (times)	3.7	2.2	1.4
Curr Liab To Nw (%)	21.0	52.2	102.9
Curr Liab To Inv (%)	97.3	165.2	344.8
Total Liab To Nw (%)	35.6	89.4	182.2
Fixed Assets To Nw (%)	20.7	44.3	102.9
EFFICIENCY			
Coll Period (days)	32.5	45.3	59.9
Sales To Inv (times)	23.5	9.8	6.2
Assets To Sales (%)	33.9	46.5	72.0
Sales To Nwc (times)	11.1	6.1	3.6
Acct Pay To Sales (%)	2.9	6.1	10.1
PROFITABILITY			
Return On Sales (%)	5.0	1.8	(4.9)
Return On Assets (%)	12.5	3.5	(5.4)
Return On Nw (%)	24.8	8.9	(1.7)

SIC 3674 SMCNDCTRS,RLTD DVCS
(NO BREAKDOWN) 2002 (204 Establishments)

	$	%
Cash	8,471,460	21.6
Accounts Receivable	4,863,246	12.4
Notes Receivable	78,439	0.2
Inventory	5,765,299	14.7
Other Current	5,765,300	14.7
Total Current	**24,943,744**	**63.6**
Fixed Assets	9,020,537	23.0
Other Non-current	5,255,443	13.4
Total Assets	**39,219,724**	**100.0**
Accounts Payable	3,412,116	8.7
Bank Loans	78,439	0.2
Notes Payable	705,955	1.8
Other Current	6,549,694	16.7
Total Current	**10,746,204**	**27.4**
Other Long Term	6,432,035	16.4
Deferred Credits	117,659	0.3
Net Worth	21,923,826	55.9
Total Liab & Net Worth	**39,219,724**	**100.0**
Net Sales	26,807,740	100.0
Gross Profit	8,792,939	32.8
Net Profit After Tax	(2,600,351)	(9.7)
Working Capital	14,197,540	—

RATIOS	UQ	MED	LQ
SOLVENCY			
Quick Ratio (times)	3.1	1.6	0.8
Current Ratio (times)	5.8	3.3	1.7
Curr Liab To Nw (%)	12.6	24.1	53.8
Curr Liab To Inv (%)	99.6	194.2	380.6
Total Liab To Nw (%)	19.5	40.2	106.1
Fixed Assets To Nw (%)	10.2	26.7	57.2
EFFICIENCY			
Coll Period (days)	35.0	47.0	63.2
Sales To Inv (times)	11.4	7.4	4.1
Assets To Sales (%)	73.8	146.3	236.3
Sales To Nwc (times)	4.1	1.7	0.9
Acct Pay To Sales (%)	4.5	8.0	12.5
PROFITABILITY			
Return On Sales (%)	4.1	(5.6)	(50.4)
Return On Assets (%)	5.4	(3.5)	(31.4)
Return On Nw (%)	8.1	(4.0)	(51.5)

SIC 3675 ELEC CAPACITORS
(NO BREAKDOWN) 2002 (12 Establishments)

	$	%
Cash	832,276	12.8
Accounts Receivable	949,314	14.6
Notes Receivable	0	0.0
Inventory	1,729,573	26.6
Other Current	851,782	13.1
Total Current	**4,362,945**	**67.1**
Fixed Assets	1,586,525	24.4
Other Non-current	552,683	8.5
Total Assets	**6,502,153**	**100.0**
Accounts Payable	643,713	9.9
Bank Loans	65,022	1.0
Notes Payable	26,009	0.4
Other Current	1,254,915	19.3
Total Current	**1,989,659**	**30.6**
Other Long Term	572,189	8.8
Deferred Credits	45,515	0.7
Net Worth	3,894,790	59.9
Total Liab & Net Worth	**6,502,153**	**100.0**
Net Sales	7,890,962	100.0
Gross Profit	2,319,943	29.4
Net Profit After Tax	(118,364)	(1.5)
Working Capital	2,373,286	—

RATIOS	UQ	MED	LQ
SOLVENCY			
Quick Ratio (times)	2.2	1.6	0.9
Current Ratio (times)	5.4	3.6	2.1
Curr Liab To Nw (%)	13.4	17.8	45.9
Curr Liab To Inv (%)	43.8	54.3	103.3
Total Liab To Nw (%)	32.3	41.9	62.5
Fixed Assets To Nw (%)	31.3	34.5	57.0
EFFICIENCY			
Coll Period (days)	27.7	41.7	46.4
Sales To Inv (times)	5.3	4.5	2.2
Assets To Sales (%)	54.3	82.4	186.6
Sales To Nwc (times)	4.0	2.2	1.7
Acct Pay To Sales (%)	2.3	4.0	9.7
PROFITABILITY			
Return On Sales (%)	2.7	(0.1)	(8.0)
Return On Assets (%)	4.6	(0.1)	(3.6)
Return On Nw (%)	6.9	0.1	(3.2)

SIC 3677 ELE COILS, TRNSFRMRS (NO BREAKDOWN) 2002 (32 Establishments)
SIC 3678 ELEC CONNECTORS (NO BREAKDOWN) 2002 (32 Establishments)
SIC 3679 ELEC COMPONENTS, NEC (NO BREAKDOWN) 2002 (242 Establishments)
SIC 3691 STORAGE BATTERIES (NO BREAKDOWN) 2002 (16 Establishments)

	SIC 3677 $	SIC 3677 %	SIC 3678 $	SIC 3678 %	SIC 3679 $	SIC 3679 %	SIC 3691 $	SIC 3691 %
Cash	401,797	16.2	511,550	10.6	323,278	15.1	2,604,590	13.2
Accounts Receivable	505,967	20.4	1,095,488	22.7	550,215	25.7	3,827,959	19.4
Notes Receivable	4,960	0.2	4,826	0.1	6,423	0.3	19,732	0.1
Inventory	649,820	26.2	1,322,308	27.4	554,496	25.9	3,847,690	19.5
Other Current	156,255	6.3	255,774	5.3	145,582	6.8	2,150,760	10.9
Total Current	**1,718,799**	**69.3**	**3,189,946**	**66.1**	**1,579,994**	**73.8**	**12,450,731**	**63.1**
Fixed Assets	501,006	20.2	1,230,615	25.5	402,492	18.8	4,498,838	22.8
Other Non-current	260,425	10.5	405,379	8.4	158,427	7.4	2,782,176	14.1
Total Assets	**2,480,230**	**100.0**	**4,825,940**	**100.0**	**2,140,913**	**100.0**	**19,731,745**	**100.0**
Accounts Payable	310,029	12.5	704,587	14.6	265,473	12.4	2,328,346	11.8
Bank Loans	0	0.0	0	0.0	4,282	0.2	276,244	1.4
Notes Payable	29,763	1.2	130,300	2.7	51,382	2.4	710,343	3.6
Other Current	352,192	14.2	1,288,527	26.7	466,719	21.8	2,900,567	14.7
Total Current	**691,984**	**27.9**	**2,123,414**	**44.0**	**787,856**	**36.8**	**6,215,500**	**31.5**
Other Long Term	414,198	16.7	723,891	15.0	368,237	17.2	5,564,352	28.2
Deferred Credits	7,441	0.3	0	0.0	4,282	0.2	0	0.0
Net Worth	1,366,607	55.1	1,978,635	41.0	980,538	45.8	7,951,893	40.3
Total Liab & Net Worth	**2,480,230**	**100.0**	**4,825,940**	**100.0**	**2,140,913**	**100.0**	**19,731,745**	**100.0**
Net Sales	4,013,317	100.0	6,002,413	100.0	4,181,471	100.0	21,948,548	100.0
Gross Profit	1,452,821	36.2	1,878,755	31.3	1,409,156	33.7	4,433,607	20.2
Net Profit After Tax	20,067	0.5	132,053	2.2	(33,452)	(0.8)	(548,714)	(2.5)
Working Capital	1,026,815	—	1,066,532	—	792,138	—	6,235,231	—

RATIOS	SIC 3677 UQ	MED	LQ	SIC 3678 UQ	MED	LQ	SIC 3679 UQ	MED	LQ	SIC 3691 UQ	MED	LQ
SOLVENCY												
Quick Ratio (times)	3.3	1.8	0.9	2.4	1.1	0.5	2.6	1.3	0.7	1.8	1.0	0.6
Current Ratio (times)	6.1	3.3	1.7	3.9	2.3	1.6	4.7	2.3	1.5	3.9	2.0	1.4
Curr Liab To Nw (%)	9.0	28.1	48.5	19.7	35.7	96.9	18.2	53.7	119.7	21.2	36.9	104.9
Curr Liab To Inv (%)	48.2	90.3	132.0	69.0	134.1	175.5	58.1	118.7	204.3	93.8	144.7	256.0
Total Liab To Nw (%)	15.8	31.3	93.7	25.9	82.8	142.6	26.3	78.2	165.4	41.1	59.3	136.4
Fixed Assets To Nw (%)	13.8	25.0	53.4	23.2	42.3	72.6	12.7	28.3	56.7	11.6	19.7	68.9
EFFICIENCY												
Coll Period (days)	39.3	47.8	57.5	45.5	55.9	68.8	35.0	47.8	62.4	32.5	46.9	67.6
Sales To Inv (times)	7.7	5.4	4.6	8.0	5.2	4.4	12.6	7.1	4.7	7.5	6.1	3.1
Assets To Sales (%)	47.2	61.8	103.8	47.9	80.4	96.4	34.5	51.2	85.1	51.6	89.9	207.9
Sales To Nwc (times)	4.9	4.0	2.3	6.4	4.4	2.6	8.1	4.9	3.0	6.6	4.0	2.2
Acct Pay To Sales (%)	2.0	3.5	7.6	3.3	6.2	10.7	3.0	5.4	9.1	6.4	8.8	23.7
PROFITABILITY												
Return On Sales (%)	5.3	1.5	(5.4)	5.8	1.7	0.4	6.4	1.6	(3.9)	8.3	1.6	(50.1)
Return On Assets (%)	8.0	1.7	(7.7)	7.9	3.3	0.7	12.2	3.5	(5.5)	11.4	2.9	(15.7)
Return On Nw (%)	15.8	4.1	(6.1)	26.4	5.2	1.4	25.6	10.2	(7.8)	24.3	11.2	(14.0)

	SIC 3694 ENGINE ELEC EQPMNT (NO BREAKDOWN) 2002 (26 Establishments) $	%	SIC 3695 MAG,OPTCL RCDNG MED (NO BREAKDOWN) 2002 (16 Establishments) $	%	SIC 3699 ELEC EQPT,SPPLS,NEC (NO BREAKDOWN) 2002 (118 Establishments) $	%	SIC 37 TRANSPORTATION EQPT (NO BREAKDOWN) 2002 (725 Establishments) $	%
Cash	261,802	12.0	253,218	24.9	341,881	16.3	414,211	10.6
Accounts Receivable	506,151	23.2	285,760	28.1	520,163	24.8	715,101	18.3
Notes Receivable	6,545	0.3	0	0.0	18,877	0.9	19,538	0.5
Inventory	748,318	34.3	82,372	8.1	509,676	24.3	1,101,958	28.2
Other Current	93,813	4.3	94,576	9.3	167,794	8.0	281,352	7.2
Total Current	**1,616,629**	**74.1**	**715,926**	**70.4**	**1,558,391**	**74.3**	**2,532,160**	**64.8**
Fixed Assets	436,337	20.0	176,948	17.4	339,784	16.2	1,055,067	27.0
Other Non-current	128,719	5.9	124,066	12.2	199,256	9.5	320,427	8.2
Total Assets	**2,181,685**	**100.0**	**1,016,940**	**100.0**	**2,097,431**	**100.0**	**3,907,654**	**100.0**
Accounts Payable	447,245	20.5	738,298	72.6	536,942	25.6	539,256	13.8
Bank Loans	6,545	0.3	0	0.0	6,292	0.3	7,815	0.2
Notes Payable	80,722	3.7	375,251	36.9	58,728	2.8	136,768	3.5
Other Current	726,502	33.3	766,773	75.4	1,174,562	56.0	828,423	21.2
Total Current	**1,261,014**	**57.8**	**1,880,322**	**184.9**	**1,776,524**	**84.7**	**1,512,262**	**38.7**
Other Long Term	316,344	14.5	411,861	40.5	264,277	12.6	777,624	19.9
Deferred Credits	13,090	0.6	1,017	0.1	2,097	0.1	7,815	0.2
Net Worth	591,237	27.1	(1,276,260)	(125.5)	54,533	2.6	1,609,953	41.2
Total Liab & Net Worth	**2,181,685**	**100.0**	**1,016,940**	**100.0**	**2,097,431**	**100.0**	**3,907,654**	**100.0**
Net Sales	5,282,530	100.0	1,918,755	100.0	3,404,920	100.0	7,991,112	100.0
Gross Profit	1,864,733	35.3	711,858	37.1	1,263,225	37.1	2,253,494	28.2
Net Profit After Tax	(174,323)	(3.3)	69,075	3.6	27,239	0.8	167,813	2.1
Working Capital	355,615	—	(1,164,396)	—	(218,133)	—	1,019,898	—

RATIOS	UQ	MED	LQ	UQ	MED	LQ	UQ	MED	LQ	UQ	MED	LQ
SOLVENCY												
Quick Ratio (times)	1.1	0.8	0.5	2.4	1.6	0.9	2.2	1.2	0.6	1.7	0.8	0.4
Current Ratio (times)	2.7	1.8	1.1	3.4	1.9	1.1	4.2	2.2	1.2	3.6	1.9	1.3
Curr Liab To Nw (%)	40.1	70.1	159.7	18.1	63.0	223.2	19.7	49.9	100.3	25.3	59.2	125.4
Curr Liab To Inv (%)	72.8	100.7	251.0	150.8	223.0	726.7	70.0	136.7	321.5	58.8	114.6	219.4
Total Liab To Nw (%)	50.8	70.8	165.8	19.5	101.9	268.5	33.6	68.5	139.4	40.3	94.4	228.9
Fixed Assets To Nw (%)	12.4	29.3	54.4	9.2	20.8	27.3	11.4	20.1	44.1	21.0	49.6	97.9
EFFICIENCY												
Coll Period (days)	27.0	44.7	63.2	32.1	50.0	73.8	34.0	51.7	74.5	17.5	32.1	52.2
Sales To Inv (times)	8.8	5.8	3.9	45.3	6.9	5.1	12.8	6.7	4.1	13.5	7.9	4.8
Assets To Sales (%)	32.3	41.3	74.4	27.8	53.0	89.5	37.1	61.6	103.2	32.7	48.9	77.6
Sales To Nwc (times)	11.8	5.6	4.0	23.7	8.4	2.3	6.2	3.7	2.2	11.6	6.2	3.6
Acct Pay To Sales (%)	2.1	7.8	10.5	3.5	7.5	28.6	3.3	6.1	11.9	2.8	5.0	8.9
PROFITABILITY												
Return On Sales (%)	8.2	4.4	(1.3)	9.9	1.3	(18.3)	7.3	1.5	(7.4)	5.4	1.8	(0.1)
Return On Assets (%)	14.8	7.9	(3.4)	14.1	6.7	(34.4)	11.9	2.3	(8.5)	11.7	4.1	(0.1)
Return On Nw (%)	47.2	15.8	10.1	52.1	10.2	(46.0)	37.4	5.7	(4.9)	26.2	10.6	1.2

	SIC 3711 MTR VHCL,CAR BODIES (NO BREAKDOWN) 2002 (42 Establishments) $	%	SIC 3713 TRUCK,BUS BODIES (NO BREAKDOWN) 2002 (53 Establishments) $	%	SIC 3714 MTR VHCLE PRTS,ACCS (NO BREAKDOWN) 2002 (197 Establishments) $	%	SIC 3715 TRUCK TRAILERS (NO BREAKDOWN) 2002 (35 Establishments) $	%
Cash	391,722	9.9	190,874	9.5	671,286	7.7	365,084	14.3
Accounts Receivable	739,919	18.7	433,988	21.6	1,900,524	21.8	416,144	16.3
Notes Receivable	47,481	1.2	2,009	0.1	61,026	0.7	5,106	0.2
Inventory	1,380,918	34.9	693,175	34.5	2,214,372	25.4	916,539	35.9
Other Current	257,191	6.5	128,589	6.4	479,490	5.5	97,015	3.8
Total Current	**2,817,231**	**71.2**	**1,448,635**	**72.1**	**5,326,698**	**61.1**	**1,799,888**	**70.5**
Fixed Assets	751,789	19.0	387,776	19.3	2,650,272	30.4	615,281	24.1
Other Non-current	387,765	9.8	172,792	8.6	741,030	8.5	137,864	5.4
Total Assets	**3,956,785**	**100.0**	**2,009,203**	**100.0**	**8,718,000**	**100.0**	**2,553,033**	**100.0**
Accounts Payable	569,777	14.4	301,380	15.0	1,386,162	15.9	354,872	13.9
Bank Loans	0	0.0	0	0.0	34,872	0.4	0	0.0
Notes Payable	245,321	6.2	144,663	7.2	252,822	2.9	51,061	2.0
Other Current	799,270	20.2	407,868	20.3	2,040,012	23.4	390,613	15.3
Total Current	**1,614,368**	**40.8**	**853,911**	**42.5**	**3,713,868**	**42.6**	**796,546**	**31.2**
Other Long Term	783,443	19.8	357,638	17.8	2,057,448	23.6	382,955	15.0
Deferred Credits	3,957	0.1	0	0.0	26,154	0.3	10,212	0.4
Net Worth	1,555,017	39.3	797,654	39.7	2,920,530	33.5	1,363,320	53.4
Total Liab & Net Worth	**3,956,785**	**100.0**	**2,009,203**	**100.0**	**8,718,000**	**100.0**	**2,553,033**	**100.0**
Net Sales	10,579,639	100.0	5,151,803	100.0	16,669,216	100.0	7,191,642	100.0
Gross Profit	2,359,259	22.3	1,313,710	25.5	4,667,380	28.0	1,769,144	24.6
Net Profit After Tax	31,739	0.3	41,214	0.8	200,031	1.2	165,408	2.3
Working Capital	1,202,863	—	594,724	—	1,612,830	—	1,003,342	—

RATIOS	UQ	MED	LQ	UQ	MED	LQ	UQ	MED	LQ	UQ	MED	LQ
SOLVENCY												
Quick Ratio (times)	1.1	0.7	0.5	1.3	0.6	0.5	1.5	0.8	0.5	2.3	1.1	0.4
Current Ratio (times)	2.9	1.7	1.2	3.2	1.7	1.3	3.2	1.8	1.2	4.4	3.0	1.6
Curr Liab To Nw (%)	46.8	94.9	276.6	32.3	83.3	238.2	35.1	69.0	172.9	20.2	49.4	85.2
Curr Liab To Inv (%)	56.4	110.7	189.9	55.8	93.0	181.8	76.8	140.8	288.6	47.2	91.0	126.2
Total Liab To Nw (%)	56.4	150.8	357.2	48.0	115.8	314.4	57.1	119.9	269.4	21.5	76.5	139.0
Fixed Assets To Nw (%)	24.9	34.3	130.4	15.7	37.4	61.0	26.5	72.5	129.6	17.9	36.2	76.7
EFFICIENCY												
Coll Period (days)	16.1	24.1	40.5	20.8	30.5	47.8	27.8	42.6	61.7	10.6	18.9	35.2
Sales To Inv (times)	11.4	8.3	5.5	14.3	8.5	4.3	14.0	8.2	5.0	13.7	8.6	6.0
Assets To Sales (%)	27.8	37.4	47.3	27.0	39.0	50.6	39.3	52.3	82.3	24.4	35.5	59.4
Sales To Nwc (times)	12.4	8.6	5.4	12.5	7.3	4.8	11.4	6.2	3.9	14.9	5.2	3.6
Acct Pay To Sales (%)	3.4	5.6	7.2	2.0	3.7	7.2	4.1	8.0	11.4	2.9	3.9	6.6
PROFITABILITY												
Return On Sales (%)	4.2	1.5	0.2	2.6	0.5	(0.7)	5.0	1.6	(1.2)	5.5	2.0	0.3
Return On Assets (%)	10.3	4.1	0.8	7.3	2.7	(1.2)	10.2	3.6	(2.0)	20.9	4.0	0.9
Return On Nw (%)	26.9	9.6	1.2	23.1	3.5	(0.7)	23.9	11.2	0.9	42.3	9.8	1.5

SIC 3716 MOTOR HOMES (NO BREAKDOWN) 2002 (15 Establishments)

	$	%
Cash	2,357,528	6.4
Accounts Receivable	5,672,803	15.4
Notes Receivable	36,836	0.1
Inventory	16,318,517	44.3
Other Current	2,026,001	5.5
Total Current	**26,411,685**	**71.7**
Fixed Assets	7,993,495	21.7
Other Non-current	2,431,201	6.6
Total Assets	**36,836,381**	**100.0**
Accounts Payable	5,120,257	13.9
Bank Loans	0	0.0
Notes Payable	1,878,655	5.1
Other Current	7,698,804	20.9
Total Current	**14,697,716**	**39.9**
Other Long Term	3,388,947	9.2
Deferred Credits	0	0.0
Net Worth	18,749,718	50.9
Total Liab & Net Worth	**36,836,381**	**100.0**
Net Sales	86,066,311	100.0
Gross Profit	10,414,024	12.1
Net Profit After Tax	(4,475,448)	(5.2)
Working Capital	11,713,969	—

RATIOS	UQ	MED	LQ
SOLVENCY			
Quick Ratio (times)	0.9	0.6	0.3
Current Ratio (times)	2.7	2.2	1.8
Curr Liab To Nw (%)	39.0	50.8	92.8
Curr Liab To Inv (%)	61.9	71.5	103.4
Total Liab To Nw (%)	40.1	69.6	110.0
Fixed Assets To Nw (%)	22.9	34.4	51.9
EFFICIENCY			
Coll Period (days)	11.0	14.3	25.6
Sales To Inv (times)	7.5	5.2	4.5
Assets To Sales (%)	33.4	42.8	49.3
Sales To Nwc (times)	8.9	6.1	5.7
Acct Pay To Sales (%)	3.8	5.9	6.9
PROFITABILITY			
Return On Sales (%)	4.3	1.5	(4.2)
Return On Assets (%)	9.1	3.4	(10.0)
Return On Nw (%)	30.4	6.7	(13.5)

SIC 3721 AIRCRAFT (NO BREAKDOWN) 2002 (15 Establishments)

	$	%
Cash	388,439	10.5
Accounts Receivable	443,931	12.0
Notes Receivable	55,491	1.5
Inventory	1,198,613	32.4
Other Current	314,451	8.5
Total Current	**2,400,925**	**64.9**
Fixed Assets	939,653	25.4
Other Non-current	358,844	9.7
Total Assets	**3,699,422**	**100.0**
Accounts Payable	325,549	8.8
Bank Loans	0	0.0
Notes Payable	81,387	2.2
Other Current	1,368,787	37.0
Total Current	**1,775,723**	**48.0**
Other Long Term	603,005	16.3
Deferred Credits	18,497	0.5
Net Worth	1,302,197	35.2
Total Liab & Net Worth	**3,699,422**	**100.0**
Net Sales	4,979,034	100.0
Gross Profit	1,573,375	31.6
Net Profit After Tax	209,119	4.2
Working Capital	625,202	—

RATIOS	UQ	MED	LQ
SOLVENCY			
Quick Ratio (times)	0.8	0.7	0.4
Current Ratio (times)	2.5	1.9	0.9
Curr Liab To Nw (%)	54.7	105.4	189.2
Curr Liab To Inv (%)	50.4	80.2	320.3
Total Liab To Nw (%)	86.8	153.4	346.6
Fixed Assets To Nw (%)	35.6	59.4	78.1
EFFICIENCY			
Coll Period (days)	20.8	33.6	44.5
Sales To Inv (times)	8.7	4.6	2.5
Assets To Sales (%)	45.0	74.3	109.6
Sales To Nwc (times)	6.0	3.4	2.9
Acct Pay To Sales (%)	1.7	4.1	7.3
PROFITABILITY			
Return On Sales (%)	4.9	1.7	1.2
Return On Assets (%)	6.7	3.8	1.3
Return On Nw (%)	22.7	11.9	7.5

SIC 3724 AIRCRAFT ENG,ENG PRT (NO BREAKDOWN) 2002 (38 Establishments)

	$	%
Cash	1,230,819	11.0
Accounts Receivable	1,678,389	15.0
Notes Receivable	11,189	0.1
Inventory	2,976,344	26.6
Other Current	704,924	6.3
Total Current	**6,601,665**	**59.0**
Fixed Assets	2,953,965	26.4
Other Non-current	1,633,633	14.6
Total Assets	**11,189,263**	**100.0**
Accounts Payable	995,844	8.9
Bank Loans	67,136	0.6
Notes Payable	179,028	1.6
Other Current	2,103,582	18.8
Total Current	**3,345,590**	**29.9**
Other Long Term	2,898,019	25.9
Deferred Credits	11,189	0.1
Net Worth	4,934,465	44.1
Total Liab & Net Worth	**11,189,263**	**100.0**
Net Sales	16,169,455	100.0
Gross Profit	4,575,956	28.3
Net Profit After Tax	210,203	1.3
Working Capital	3,256,075	—

RATIOS	UQ	MED	LQ
SOLVENCY			
Quick Ratio (times)	1.5	0.9	0.4
Current Ratio (times)	3.4	1.9	1.5
Curr Liab To Nw (%)	27.2	54.6	96.5
Curr Liab To Inv (%)	65.2	103.2	168.6
Total Liab To Nw (%)	55.6	87.4	208.8
Fixed Assets To Nw (%)	19.3	42.0	91.8
EFFICIENCY			
Coll Period (days)	24.1	39.8	49.7
Sales To Inv (times)	8.0	5.1	3.8
Assets To Sales (%)	50.9	69.2	102.4
Sales To Nwc (times)	9.5	6.0	3.5
Acct Pay To Sales (%)	3.2	4.4	8.7
PROFITABILITY			
Return On Sales (%)	6.3	1.7	(0.5)
Return On Assets (%)	7.3	2.9	(0.5)
Return On Nw (%)	14.5	7.9	0.4

SIC 3728 AIRCRFT PRT,EQP,NEC (NO BREAKDOWN) 2002 (129 Establishments)

	$	%
Cash	380,754	12.8
Accounts Receivable	624,675	21.0
Notes Receivable	5,949	0.2
Inventory	755,559	25.4
Other Current	246,896	8.3
Total Current	**2,013,833**	**67.7**
Fixed Assets	776,382	26.1
Other Non-current	184,428	6.2
Total Assets	**2,974,643**	**100.0**
Accounts Payable	306,388	10.3
Bank Loans	8,924	0.3
Notes Payable	92,214	3.1
Other Current	437,273	14.7
Total Current	**844,799**	**28.4**
Other Long Term	520,562	17.5
Deferred Credits	5,949	0.2
Net Worth	1,603,333	53.9
Total Liab & Net Worth	**2,974,643**	**100.0**
Net Sales	5,128,695	100.0
Gross Profit	1,743,756	34.0
Net Profit After Tax	210,276	4.1
Working Capital	1,169,034	—

RATIOS	UQ	MED	LQ
SOLVENCY			
Quick Ratio (times)	3.6	1.3	0.6
Current Ratio (times)	6.5	3.0	1.5
Curr Liab To Nw (%)	13.2	33.6	90.1
Curr Liab To Inv (%)	41.4	98.0	214.3
Total Liab To Nw (%)	23.1	61.2	159.5
Fixed Assets To Nw (%)	15.4	37.2	84.0
EFFICIENCY			
Coll Period (days)	28.1	38.9	59.2
Sales To Inv (times)	16.5	6.8	4.0
Assets To Sales (%)	39.3	58.0	89.5
Sales To Nwc (times)	8.5	4.3	2.5
Acct Pay To Sales (%)	2.3	3.9	6.5
PROFITABILITY			
Return On Sales (%)	8.3	3.3	0.5
Return On Assets (%)	14.9	4.5	1.0
Return On Nw (%)	23.3	9.5	2.9

	SIC 3731 SHIPBLDING,REPAIRNG (NO BREAKDOWN) 2002 (44 Establishments) $	%	SIC 3732 BOATBLDING,REPAIRNG (NO BREAKDOWN) 2002 (66 Establishments) $	%	SIC 3751 MTRCYCLS, BCYL,PRTS (NO BREAKDOWN) 2002 (13 Establishments) $	%	SIC 3792 TRVL TRLRS,CAMPERS (NO BREAKDOWN) 2002 (24 Establishments) $	%
Cash	725,011	12.9	350,613	13.4	116,980	5.5	374,657	13.5
Accounts Receivable	1,045,364	18.6	240,719	9.2	227,579	10.7	388,534	14.0
Notes Receivable	16,861	0.3	18,316	0.7	0	0.0	55,505	2.0
Inventory	500,201	8.9	881,765	33.7	778,449	36.6	1,032,389	37.2
Other Current	820,554	14.6	225,019	8.6	212,691	10.0	202,593	7.3
Total Current	**3,107,991**	**55.3**	**1,716,432**	**65.6**	**1,335,699**	**62.8**	**2,053,678**	**74.0**
Fixed Assets	2,073,867	36.9	748,322	28.6	542,362	25.5	560,598	20.2
Other Non-current	438,379	7.8	151,758	5.8	248,848	11.7	160,964	5.8
Total Assets	**5,620,237**	**100.0**	**2,616,512**	**100.0**	**2,126,909**	**100.0**	**2,775,240**	**100.0**
Accounts Payable	831,795	14.8	410,792	15.7	531,727	25.0	266,423	9.6
Bank Loans	16,861	0.3	0	0.0	0	0.0	0	0.0
Notes Payable	140,506	2.5	125,593	4.8	59,553	2.8	74,931	2.7
Other Current	865,516	15.4	709,075	27.1	1,197,450	56.3	563,374	20.3
Total Current	**1,854,678**	**33.0**	**1,245,460**	**47.6**	**1,788,730**	**84.1**	**904,728**	**32.6**
Other Long Term	831,796	14.8	622,729	23.8	489,189	23.0	277,524	10.0
Deferred Credits	11,240	0.2	2,617	0.1	6,381	0.3	0	0.0
Net Worth	2,922,523	52.0	745,706	28.5	(157,391)	(7.4)	1,592,988	57.4
Total Liab & Net Worth	**5,620,237**	**100.0**	**2,616,512**	**100.0**	**2,126,909**	**100.0**	**2,775,240**	**100.0**
Net Sales	9,021,247	100.0	7,475,749	100.0	3,064,710	100.0	9,129,079	100.0
Gross Profit	2,814,629	31.2	1,996,025	26.7	1,238,143	40.4	2,145,334	23.5
Net Profit After Tax	451,062	5.0	179,418	2.4	(162,430)	(5.3)	392,550	4.3
Working Capital	1,253,313	—	470,972	—	(453,031)	—	1,148,950	—

RATIOS	UQ	MED	LQ	UQ	MED	LQ	UQ	MED	LQ	UQ	MED	LQ
SOLVENCY												
Quick Ratio (times)	1.9	1.2	0.6	1.1	0.6	0.3	1.4	0.8	0.3	1.7	0.7	0.3
Current Ratio (times)	2.8	1.7	1.2	2.4	1.7	1.0	3.3	2.6	1.5	5.0	2.3	1.7
Curr Liab To Nw (%)	27.0	59.2	87.8	32.5	67.1	143.2	13.5	39.7	97.7	15.2	45.4	76.7
Curr Liab To Inv (%)	152.2	381.4	999.9	77.2	112.9	219.6	30.9	66.4	254.8	45.9	112.8	159.1
Total Liab To Nw (%)	47.9	73.3	153.4	43.4	97.4	229.4	39.4	53.2	261.1	22.0	66.7	111.8
Fixed Assets To Nw (%)	35.9	66.2	101.2	18.0	55.9	100.6	20.2	46.2	78.4	15.4	22.7	83.0
EFFICIENCY												
Coll Period (days)	23.7	47.1	66.1	6.9	13.0	23.0	5.5	14.3	24.5	4.4	14.1	27.7
Sales To Inv (times)	81.9	21.4	9.3	14.0	8.7	6.2	10.2	7.4	5.0	14.8	9.6	7.3
Assets To Sales (%)	35.9	62.3	103.5	25.4	35.0	52.1	34.6	69.4	81.2	24.5	30.4	40.3
Sales To Nwc (times)	10.0	6.4	3.8	17.3	7.6	4.9	11.5	4.2	3.2	19.1	6.9	3.6
Acct Pay To Sales (%)	3.9	7.0	8.8	2.0	4.1	8.9	4.0	8.1	14.5	1.6	2.7	4.7
PROFITABILITY												
Return On Sales (%)	5.9	2.3	(1.1)	4.9	1.9	0.7	8.1	0.1	(6.5)	5.1	2.8	1.1
Return On Assets (%)	9.4	5.2	(1.0)	15.1	7.5	1.0	17.3	0.5	(8.2)	18.6	12.2	1.9
Return On Nw (%)	28.3	10.6	(1.7)	34.2	18.5	4.5	26.0	0.8	(1.9)	40.7	20.3	3.1

SIC 3799 TRNSPRTN EQPMNT, NEC
(NO BREAKDOWN)
2002 (35 Establishments)

	$	%
Cash	136,944	12.6
Accounts Receivable	127,162	11.7
Notes Receivable	8,695	0.8
Inventory	373,879	34.4
Other Current	66,299	6.1
Total Current	**712,979**	**65.6**
Fixed Assets	286,931	26.4
Other Non-current	86,948	8.0
Total Assets	**1,086,858**	**100.0**
Accounts Payable	160,855	14.8
Bank Loans	2,174	0.2
Notes Payable	23,911	2.2
Other Current	240,195	22.1
Total Current	**427,135**	**39.3**
Other Long Term	226,067	20.8
Deferred Credits	0	0.0
Net Worth	433,656	39.9
Total Liab & Net Worth	**1,086,858**	**100.0**
Net Sales	2,985,874	100.0
Gross Profit	856,946	28.7
Net Profit After Tax	65,689	2.2
Working Capital	285,844	—

RATIOS	UQ	MED	LQ
SOLVENCY			
Quick Ratio (times)	1.6	0.6	0.3
Current Ratio (times)	4.1	2.1	1.5
Curr Liab To Nw (%)	19.4	43.5	93.6
Curr Liab To Inv (%)	53.9	80.6	126.1
Total Liab To Nw (%)	46.5	88.3	201.0
Fixed Assets To Nw (%)	22.8	40.8	81.1
EFFICIENCY			
Coll Period (days)	10.1	17.5	21.0
Sales To Inv (times)	12.8	7.5	5.8
Assets To Sales (%)	25.6	36.4	48.1
Sales To Nwc (times)	13.5	6.8	4.8
Acct Pay To Sales (%)	2.6	4.0	5.6
PROFITABILITY			
Return On Sales (%)	4.7	2.1	0.4
Return On Assets (%)	12.0	6.2	0.2
Return On Nw (%)	33.1	11.0	0.7

SIC 38 INSTRUMENTS RLTD PDTS
(NO BREAKDOWN)
2002 (1058 Establishments)

	$	%
Cash	645,714	17.0
Accounts Receivable	820,436	21.6
Notes Receivable	11,395	0.3
Inventory	847,024	22.3
Other Current	368,436	9.7
Total Current	**2,693,005**	**70.9**
Fixed Assets	660,907	17.4
Other Non-current	444,403	11.7
Total Assets	**3,798,315**	**100.0**
Accounts Payable	512,773	13.5
Bank Loans	7,597	0.2
Notes Payable	524,167	13.8
Other Current	736,873	19.4
Total Current	**1,781,410**	**46.9**
Other Long Term	676,099	17.8
Deferred Credits	18,992	0.5
Net Worth	1,321,814	34.8
Total Liab & Net Worth	**3,798,315**	**100.0**
Net Sales	5,496,838	100.0
Gross Profit	2,319,666	42.2
Net Profit After Tax	(82,453)	(1.5)
Working Capital	911,595	—

RATIOS	UQ	MED	LQ
SOLVENCY			
Quick Ratio (times)	2.6	1.4	0.7
Current Ratio (times)	4.8	2.7	1.5
Curr Liab To Nw (%)	17.7	36.8	90.4
Curr Liab To Inv (%)	67.0	120.7	241.2
Total Liab To Nw (%)	22.6	53.7	144.2
Fixed Assets To Nw (%)	10.3	24.1	48.0
EFFICIENCY			
Coll Period (days)	38.0	52.2	73.4
Sales To Inv (times)	11.0	6.3	3.9
Assets To Sales (%)	44.6	69.1	124.8
Sales To Nwc (times)	6.1	3.3	1.9
Acct Pay To Sales (%)	3.2	5.4	9.0
PROFITABILITY			
Return On Sales (%)	6.4	1.5	(8.0)
Return On Assets (%)	9.5	2.4	(8.6)
Return On Nw (%)	18.1	5.6	(8.5)

SIC 3812 SEARCH, NVGTN EQPMNT
(NO BREAKDOWN)
2002 (59 Establishments)

	$	%
Cash	1,023,203	13.4
Accounts Receivable	1,756,245	23.0
Notes Receivable	22,908	0.3
Inventory	1,824,967	23.9
Other Current	717,769	9.4
Total Current	**5,345,092**	**70.0**
Fixed Assets	1,481,354	19.4
Other Non-current	809,400	10.6
Total Assets	**7,635,846**	**100.0**
Accounts Payable	1,000,296	13.1
Bank Loans	7,636	0.1
Notes Payable	91,630	1.2
Other Current	2,214,395	29.0
Total Current	**3,313,957**	**43.4**
Other Long Term	763,585	10.0
Deferred Credits	0	0.0
Net Worth	3,558,304	46.6
Total Liab & Net Worth	**7,635,846**	**100.0**
Net Sales	11,196,255	100.0
Gross Profit	3,929,886	35.1
Net Profit After Tax	302,299	2.7
Working Capital	2,031,135	—

RATIOS	UQ	MED	LQ
SOLVENCY			
Quick Ratio (times)	1.8	1.2	0.6
Current Ratio (times)	3.9	2.1	1.4
Curr Liab To Nw (%)	24.7	55.8	95.1
Curr Liab To Inv (%)	51.1	118.3	278.6
Total Liab To Nw (%)	28.7	82.6	182.2
Fixed Assets To Nw (%)	11.3	29.0	55.1
EFFICIENCY			
Coll Period (days)	32.7	49.8	70.8
Sales To Inv (times)	7.7	5.4	3.8
Assets To Sales (%)	43.7	68.2	117.1
Sales To Nwc (times)	6.9	3.9	2.1
Acct Pay To Sales (%)	2.9	5.7	10.5
PROFITABILITY			
Return On Sales (%)	7.1	2.0	(4.1)
Return On Assets (%)	10.8	2.7	(3.1)
Return On Nw (%)	20.9	5.9	(3.3)

SIC 3821 LBRTRY APPTUS, FURN
(NO BREAKDOWN)
2002 (37 Establishments)

	$	%
Cash	334,062	11.0
Accounts Receivable	686,345	22.6
Notes Receivable	0	0.0
Inventory	543,609	17.9
Other Current	498,055	16.4
Total Current	**2,062,071**	**67.9**
Fixed Assets	622,569	20.5
Other Non-current	352,283	11.6
Total Assets	**3,036,923**	**100.0**
Accounts Payable	273,323	9.0
Bank Loans	3,037	0.1
Notes Payable	157,920	5.2
Other Current	610,422	20.1
Total Current	**1,044,702**	**34.4**
Other Long Term	1,008,257	33.2
Deferred Credits	18,222	0.6
Net Worth	965,742	31.8
Total Liab & Net Worth	**3,036,923**	**100.0**
Net Sales	4,760,067	100.0
Gross Profit	1,485,141	31.2
Net Profit After Tax	(152,322)	(3.2)
Working Capital	1,017,369	—

RATIOS	UQ	MED	LQ
SOLVENCY			
Quick Ratio (times)	3.0	1.6	0.7
Current Ratio (times)	5.9	3.5	1.7
Curr Liab To Nw (%)	12.5	22.4	61.9
Curr Liab To Inv (%)	69.7	118.3	289.1
Total Liab To Nw (%)	20.4	50.5	94.3
Fixed Assets To Nw (%)	9.4	24.2	46.7
EFFICIENCY			
Coll Period (days)	41.6	57.7	84.0
Sales To Inv (times)	10.1	6.8	3.7
Assets To Sales (%)	39.6	63.8	177.4
Sales To Nwc (times)	4.7	3.0	2.0
Acct Pay To Sales (%)	3.7	7.6	9.5
PROFITABILITY			
Return On Sales (%)	6.6	1.3	(32.1)
Return On Assets (%)	6.0	3.0	(17.2)
Return On Nw (%)	17.3	6.4	(12.1)

	SIC 3822 ENVIRNMNTL CNTRLS $	%	UQ	MED	LQ	SIC 3823 PROC CNTL INSTRMNTS $	%	UQ	MED	LQ	SIC 3824 FLD MTRS,CNTNG DVCS $	%	UQ	MED	LQ	SIC 3825 INSTRMNTS MEAS ELEC $	%	UQ	MED	LQ
	(NO BREAKDOWN) 2002 (24 Establishments)					(NO BREAKDOWN) 2002 (114 Establishments)					(NO BREAKDOWN) 2002 (11 Establishments)					(NO BREAKDOWN) 2002 (97 Establishments)				
Cash	306,506	13.5				310,029	13.6				440,717	15.6				688,364	18.9			
Accounts Receivable	610,741	26.9				615,499	27.0				579,147	20.5				764,849	21.0			
Notes Receivable	13,622	0.6				11,398	0.5				36,726	1.3				10,926	0.3			
Inventory	395,052	17.4				556,229	24.4				782,555	27.7				844,976	23.2			
Other Current	395,052	17.4				150,455	6.6				220,358	7.8				393,351	10.8			
Total Current	**1,720,973**	**75.8**				**1,643,610**	**72.1**				**2,059,503**	**72.9**				**2,702,466**	**74.2**			
Fixed Assets	356,455	15.7				387,536	17.0				468,968	16.6				542,678	14.9			
Other Non-current	192,985	8.5				248,480	10.9				296,636	10.5				396,993	10.9			
Total Assets	**2,270,413**	**100.0**				**2,279,626**	**100.0**				**2,825,107**	**100.0**				**3,642,137**	**100.0**			
Accounts Payable	290,613	12.8				243,920	10.7				313,587	11.1				349,645	9.6			
Bank Loans	0	0.0				9,119	0.4				0	0.0				10,926	0.3			
Notes Payable	56,760	2.5				88,905	3.9				11,300	0.4				76,485	2.1			
Other Current	429,108	18.9				403,494	17.7				641,300	22.7				622,806	17.1			
Total Current	**776,481**	**34.2**				**745,438**	**32.7**				**966,187**	**34.2**				**1,059,862**	**29.1**			
Other Long Term	308,776	13.6				259,877	11.4				274,035	9.7				684,721	18.8			
Deferred Credits	0	0.0				11,398	0.5				2,825	0.1				21,853	0.6			
Net Worth	1,185,156	52.2				1,262,913	55.4				1,582,060	56.0				1,875,701	51.5			
Total Liab & Net Worth	**2,270,413**	**100.0**				**2,279,626**	**100.0**				**2,825,107**	**100.0**				**3,642,137**	**100.0**			
Net Sales	4,434,400	100.0				3,964,567	100.0				5,340,467	100.0				5,195,631	100.0			
Gross Profit	1,458,918	32.9				1,554,110	39.2				2,146,868	40.2				2,052,274	39.5			
Net Profit After Tax	150,770	3.4				(39,646)	(1.0)				181,576	3.4				(358,499)	(6.9)			
Working Capital	944,492	—				898,172	—				1,093,316	—				1,642,604	—			
RATIOS			**UQ**	**MED**	**LQ**			**UQ**	**MED**	**LQ**			**UQ**	**MED**	**LQ**			**UQ**	**MED**	**LQ**
SOLVENCY																				
Quick Ratio (times)			2.1	1.2	0.7			3.3	1.7	0.8			1.8	1.3	0.9			2.7	1.5	0.8
Current Ratio (times)			3.5	2.4	1.6			5.5	3.2	1.8			3.2	2.6	1.8			4.9	2.9	1.8
Curr Liab To Nw (%)			31.0	47.2	136.6			13.4	30.4	76.6			28.1	45.8	101.0			18.4	40.2	90.6
Curr Liab To Inv (%)			82.0	183.6	980.9			44.9	81.3	177.6			83.8	109.2	156.1			60.3	112.9	196.2
Total Liab To Nw (%)			31.0	63.0	196.6			18.1	35.1	121.2			34.2	46.5	121.9			24.1	58.8	137.5
Fixed Assets To Nw (%)			17.6	25.3	34.1			11.5	22.3	40.6			15.2	21.8	32.2			10.8	26.2	45.6
EFFICIENCY																				
Coll Period (days)			37.6	49.0	65.3			40.9	53.2	74.1			30.3	34.0	41.6			36.7	51.5	74.1
Sales To Inv (times)			28.8	16.0	8.7			10.7	6.1	4.3			18.7	7.0	5.6			11.0	5.1	3.3
Assets To Sales (%)			43.0	51.2	74.1			43.7	57.5	81.1			40.1	52.9	75.6			47.8	70.1	136.5
Sales To Nwc (times)			16.2	5.4	3.2			5.2	3.3	2.1			15.7	5.2	3.2			5.5	3.0	1.6
Acct Pay To Sales (%)			3.8	5.6	8.1			2.2	4.5	7.3			3.1	3.8	7.0			3.2	5.9	8.7
PROFITABILITY																				
Return On Sales (%)			6.4	2.3	1.5			6.7	2.5	(1.7)			5.5	3.3	1.6			3.7	0.0	(18.1)
Return On Assets (%)			10.9	5.3	2.6			12.0	4.1	(2.7)			6.5	5.3	4.3			6.0	(0.2)	(15.6)
Return On Nw (%)			27.4	15.8	4.6			18.2	6.7	(2.0)			16.6	7.9	6.0			15.7	0.0	(17.6)

	SIC 3826 ANALYTCL INSTRMNTS (NO BREAKDOWN) 2002 (64 Establishments)		SIC 3827 OPTCL INSTRMNTS, LNS (NO BREAKDOWN) 2002 (57 Establishments)		SIC 3829 MEAS,CTLNG DVCS, NEC (NO BREAKDOWN) 2002 (119 Establishments)		SIC 3841 SRGL,MDCL INSTRMNTS (NO BREAKDOWN) 2002 (182 Establishments)	
	$	%	$	%	$	%	$	%
Cash	1,576,554	18.3	792,199	25.0	291,488	15.8	1,428,231	21.0
Accounts Receivable	1,791,930	20.8	570,383	18.0	479,664	26.0	1,183,391	17.4
Notes Receivable	25,845	0.3	0	0.0	(1,845)	(0.1)	20,403	0.3
Inventory	1,507,633	17.5	687,629	21.7	501,802	27.2	1,346,618	19.8
Other Current	1,094,111	12.7	282,024	8.9	158,658	8.6	768,524	11.3
Total Current	**5,996,073**	**69.6**	**2,332,235**	**73.6**	**1,429,767**	**77.5**	**4,747,167**	**69.8**
Fixed Assets	1,223,337	14.2	595,734	18.8	287,798	15.6	1,122,181	16.5
Other Non-current	1,395,638	16.2	240,828	7.6	127,296	6.9	931,751	13.7
Total Assets	**8,615,048**	**100.0**	**3,168,797**	**100.0**	**1,844,861**	**100.0**	**6,801,099**	**100.0**
Accounts Payable	1,275,027	14.8	405,606	12.8	232,452	12.6	1,251,402	18.4
Bank Loans	17,230	0.2	0	0.0	1,845	0.1	13,602	0.2
Notes Payable	1,464,558	17.0	5,051,062	159.4	53,501	2.9	761,723	11.2
Other Current	3,411,559	39.6	(3,260,692)	(102.9)	837,567	45.4	2,189,954	32.2
Total Current	**6,168,374**	**71.6**	**2,195,976**	**69.3**	**1,125,365**	**61.0**	**4,216,681**	**62.0**
Other Long Term	844,275	9.8	465,814	14.7	263,815	14.3	1,435,033	21.1
Deferred Credits	25,845	0.3	12,675	0.4	1,845	0.1	20,403	0.3
Net Worth	1,576,554	18.3	494,332	15.6	453,836	24.6	1,128,982	16.6
Total Liab & Net Worth	**8,615,048**	**100.0**	**3,168,797**	**100.0**	**1,844,861**	**100.0**	**6,801,099**	**100.0**
Net Sales	8,890,658	100.0	4,073,004	100.0	3,100,607	100.0	7,473,735	100.0
Gross Profit	4,534,236	51.0	1,340,018	32.9	1,330,160	42.9	3,363,181	45.0
Net Profit After Tax	(266,720)	(3.0)	(191,431)	(4.7)	(31,006)	(1.0)	(97,159)	(1.3)
Working Capital	(172,301)	—	136,259	—	304,402	—	530,486	—

RATIOS	UQ	MED	LQ	UQ	MED	LQ	UQ	MED	LQ	UQ	MED	LQ
SOLVENCY												
Quick Ratio (times)	2.9	1.4	0.8	2.6	1.3	0.6	2.5	1.4	0.7	2.9	1.5	0.7
Current Ratio (times)	5.5	2.7	1.5	6.5	2.3	1.4	4.8	2.7	1.4	5.1	3.1	1.6
Curr Liab To Nw (%)	14.5	37.8	71.2	9.2	35.4	101.2	22.5	43.9	117.6	15.4	29.7	62.5
Curr Liab To Inv (%)	94.7	138.6	302.5	52.8	120.1	273.0	55.2	116.6	210.9	82.1	133.4	284.9
Total Liab To Nw (%)	18.3	54.5	109.1	13.1	60.9	173.9	29.6	60.7	158.9	19.8	40.5	87.9
Fixed Assets To Nw (%)	10.2	20.7	37.0	8.0	21.2	58.3	11.7	22.5	47.2	8.9	18.1	46.8
EFFICIENCY												
Coll Period (days)	43.5	59.1	82.7	35.0	47.3	68.3	41.6	55.5	72.3	41.3	53.7	75.2
Sales To Inv (times)	11.9	6.3	4.6	9.7	5.7	3.5	10.1	5.8	3.8	10.4	6.6	4.0
Assets To Sales (%)	57.5	96.9	178.1	43.4	77.8	159.5	46.2	59.5	89.9	49.6	91.0	152.9
Sales To Nwc (times)	4.6	2.9	1.3	6.0	2.9	1.0	6.2	3.4	2.3	5.1	2.7	1.4
Acct Pay To Sales (%)	3.2	5.2	8.5	3.4	5.0	9.0	3.3	5.1	10.1	3.8	6.0	10.4
PROFITABILITY												
Return On Sales (%)	7.6	2.4	(10.1)	3.5	0.9	(24.3)	5.1	1.1	(5.1)	8.0	1.2	(31.9)
Return On Assets (%)	10.6	3.2	(6.8)	6.1	1.0	(15.8)	8.3	1.6	(8.4)	10.4	1.2	(29.6)
Return On Nw (%)	21.9	6.0	(8.0)	15.1	1.5	(25.6)	14.0	5.3	(7.2)	17.5	2.9	(26.6)

	SIC 3842 SRGCL APPL,SUPPLS (NO BREAKDOWN) 2002 (123 Establishments) $	%	SIC 3843 DENTAL EQPT,SUPPLS (NO BREAKDOWN) 2002 (25 Establishments) $	%	SIC 3844 X-RAY APPRTUS,TUBES (NO BREAKDOWN) 2002 (11 Establishments) $	%	SIC 3845 ELECTROMDCL EQPT (NO BREAKDOWN) 2002 (63 Establishments) $	%
Cash	496,403	13.0	480,527	13.4	290,693	24.2	3,951,797	22.3
Accounts Receivable	870,615	22.8	742,307	20.7	297,900	24.8	2,516,391	14.2
Notes Receivable	30,548	0.8	0	0.0	0	0.0	124,047	0.7
Inventory	889,707	23.3	968,226	27.0	294,296	24.5	3,154,350	17.8
Other Current	267,295	7.0	215,161	6.0	51,652	4.3	2,197,413	12.4
Total Current	**2,554,568**	**66.9**	**2,406,221**	**67.1**	**934,541**	**77.8**	**11,943,998**	**67.4**
Fixed Assets	820,975	21.5	649,070	18.1	223,425	18.6	2,534,112	14.3
Other Non-current	442,944	11.6	530,731	14.8	43,243	3.6	3,242,955	18.3
Total Assets	**3,818,487**	**100.0**	**3,586,022**	**100.0**	**1,201,209**	**100.0**	**17,721,065**	**100.0**
Accounts Payable	672,054	17.6	380,118	10.6	147,749	12.3	1,435,406	8.1
Bank Loans	0	0.0	0	0.0	0	0.0	0	0.0
Notes Payable	217,654	5.7	154,199	4.3	96,097	8.0	194,932	1.1
Other Current	672,053	17.6	968,226	27.0	212,613	17.7	4,004,961	22.6
Total Current	**1,561,761**	**40.9**	**1,502,543**	**41.9**	**456,459**	**38.0**	**5,635,299**	**31.8**
Other Long Term	778,972	20.4	365,774	10.2	56,457	4.7	4,323,940	24.4
Deferred Credits	7,637	0.2	0	0.0	0	0.0	124,047	0.7
Net Worth	1,470,117	38.5	1,717,705	47.9	688,293	57.3	7,637,779	43.1
Total Liab & Net Worth	**3,818,487**	**100.0**	**3,586,022**	**100.0**	**1,201,209**	**100.0**	**17,721,065**	**100.0**
Net Sales	5,768,107	100.0	7,288,663	100.0	2,053,349	100.0	15,159,166	100.0
Gross Profit	2,670,634	46.3	3,462,115	47.5	821,340	40.0	7,155,126	47.2
Net Profit After Tax	213,420	3.7	(349,856)	(4.8)	12,320	0.6	(1,500,757)	(9.9)
Working Capital	992,807	—	903,678	—	478,082	—	6,308,699	—

RATIOS	UQ	MED	LQ	UQ	MED	LQ	UQ	MED	LQ	UQ	MED	LQ
SOLVENCY												
Quick Ratio (times)	2.2	1.3	0.8	1.8	1.3	0.6	2.1	1.1	1.1	2.9	1.5	0.7
Current Ratio (times)	4.0	2.5	1.7	3.0	2.6	1.4	3.3	2.3	1.8	5.5	3.1	1.5
Curr Liab To Nw (%)	22.2	42.3	121.6	21.0	42.4	75.8	27.8	40.7	89.7	13.6	23.8	62.0
Curr Liab To Inv (%)	62.0	122.0	225.1	83.8	104.1	188.4	104.6	114.4	212.6	82.2	141.9	260.4
Total Liab To Nw (%)	29.3	83.7	169.1	25.6	50.8	149.7	29.4	61.5	89.7	17.5	40.0	91.8
Fixed Assets To Nw (%)	15.2	33.5	61.3	8.2	23.1	43.5	5.7	16.5	43.3	7.8	13.8	28.4
EFFICIENCY												
Coll Period (days)	36.5	49.7	69.9	41.3	55.9	62.1	42.9	48.6	55.0	46.7	58.4	87.2
Sales To Inv (times)	13.2	7.3	3.6	12.2	7.8	5.1	9.7	7.6	5.0	7.8	5.7	3.6
Assets To Sales (%)	36.9	66.2	117.4	36.0	49.2	107.4	40.2	58.5	86.9	80.4	116.9	168.1
Sales To Nwc (times)	7.3	3.9	2.0	8.1	5.6	3.6	7.5	4.9	1.9	2.8	1.8	1.2
Acct Pay To Sales (%)	2.7	5.5	8.8	3.3	4.7	6.6	3.0	4.6	8.3	4.2	6.5	13.5
PROFITABILITY												
Return On Sales (%)	8.9	3.6	0.2	8.2	3.9	(1.3)	8.9	0.4	(0.4)	6.0	(3.5)	(70.5)
Return On Assets (%)	12.5	5.5	0.4	15.4	7.9	(4.4)	17.3	1.2	(0.3)	3.9	(3.5)	(53.6)
Return On Nw (%)	29.4	10.7	1.9	24.0	17.1	(6.2)	37.0	3.1	0.1	7.8	(0.6)	(47.2)

	SIC 3851 OPHTHALMIC GOODS (NO BREAKDOWN) 2002 (26 Establishments)		SIC 3861 PHTGRPH EQPT,SUPPLS (NO BREAKDOWN) 2002 (40 Establishments)		SIC 39 MISC MANUFACTURING (NO BREAKDOWN) 2002 (616 Establishments)		SIC 3911 JEWELRY,PREC MTL (NO BREAKDOWN) 2002 (48 Establishments)	
	$	%	$	%	$	%	$	%
Cash	209,688	7.7	934,310	16.8	188,484	12.5	211,430	7.3
Accounts Receivable	708,039	26.0	1,056,661	19.0	382,998	25.4	793,586	27.4
Notes Receivable	5,446	0.2	5,561	0.1	7,539	0.5	0	0.0
Inventory	590,940	21.7	1,140,081	20.5	396,569	26.3	1,242,512	42.9
Other Current	223,305	8.2	506,086	9.1	101,028	6.7	115,852	4.0
Total Current	**1,737,418**	**63.8**	**3,642,699**	**65.5**	**1,076,618**	**71.4**	**2,363,380**	**81.6**
Fixed Assets	702,592	25.8	1,128,959	20.3	303,081	20.1	402,586	13.9
Other Non-current	283,215	10.4	789,714	14.2	128,169	8.5	130,333	4.5
Total Assets	**2,723,225**	**100.0**	**5,561,372**	**100.0**	**1,507,868**	**100.0**	**2,896,299**	**100.0**
Accounts Payable	471,118	17.3	628,435	11.3	232,212	15.4	518,438	17.9
Bank Loans	2,723	0.1	11,123	0.2	7,539	0.5	28,963	1.0
Notes Payable	51,741	1.9	66,736	1.2	155,310	10.3	153,504	5.3
Other Current	403,038	14.8	1,217,941	21.9	505,136	33.5	524,229	18.1
Total Current	**928,620**	**34.1**	**1,924,235**	**34.6**	**900,197**	**59.7**	**1,225,134**	**42.3**
Other Long Term	479,288	17.6	2,346,899	42.2	284,987	18.9	408,379	14.1
Deferred Credits	174,286	6.4	0	0.0	4,524	0.3	2,896	0.1
Net Worth	1,141,031	41.9	1,290,238	23.2	318,160	21.1	1,259,890	43.5
Total Liab & Net Worth	**2,723,225**	**100.0**	**5,561,372**	**100.0**	**1,507,868**	**100.0**	**2,896,299**	**100.0**
Net Sales	6,842,274	100.0	7,628,768	100.0	3,306,728	100.0	5,237,430	100.0
Gross Profit	2,887,440	42.2	3,143,052	41.2	1,365,679	41.3	1,618,366	30.9
Net Profit After Tax	225,795	3.3	(236,492)	(3.1)	99,202	3.0	89,036	1.7
Working Capital	808,798	—	1,718,464	—	176,421	—	1,138,246	—

RATIOS	UQ	MED	LQ	UQ	MED	LQ	UQ	MED	LQ	UQ	MED	LQ
SOLVENCY												
Quick Ratio (times)	2.0	1.2	0.7	3.0	1.2	0.7	2.1	1.1	0.6	1.9	0.9	0.6
Current Ratio (times)	3.4	2.0	1.5	4.9	1.8	1.4	4.0	2.1	1.3	3.8	2.3	1.4
Curr Liab To Nw (%)	25.2	54.7	89.2	20.2	71.7	105.2	23.6	57.9	149.8	30.2	61.6	166.2
Curr Liab To Inv (%)	94.9	138.7	197.8	75.8	139.2	296.0	67.0	139.6	284.3	45.1	96.4	172.8
Total Liab To Nw (%)	30.5	67.1	180.6	23.1	91.3	216.1	34.5	89.6	224.4	34.7	87.8	256.7
Fixed Assets To Nw (%)	30.9	48.8	74.9	15.4	35.8	86.1	14.1	31.8	64.6	5.9	22.4	38.0
EFFICIENCY												
Coll Period (days)	36.1	40.5	77.0	34.7	47.5	65.7	25.9	40.5	60.2	25.0	55.5	88.4
Sales To Inv (times)	17.4	10.1	4.8	11.5	6.8	4.7	18.4	9.1	5.1	9.7	5.3	2.9
Assets To Sales (%)	30.2	39.8	99.0	54.4	72.9	103.6	30.3	45.6	66.6	39.8	55.3	73.7
Sales To Nwc (times)	14.5	5.7	3.8	8.1	4.5	2.4	12.0	6.2	3.6	10.0	5.1	2.7
Acct Pay To Sales (%)	2.2	4.3	9.7	2.7	5.1	6.8	2.5	4.5	8.1	3.1	7.0	14.0
PROFITABILITY												
Return On Sales (%)	4.8	2.5	1.2	2.3	0.0	(8.6)	6.2	2.1	0.0	2.3	1.1	0.1
Return On Assets (%)	10.1	4.4	1.8	3.3	0.1	(8.9)	14.2	5.2	0.0	5.5	1.9	0.1
Return On Nw (%)	26.5	12.9	3.9	5.0	0.5	(10.0)	32.3	11.1	1.3	15.0	4.2	(0.4)

	SIC 3931 MUSICAL INSTRUMENTS (NO BREAKDOWN) 2002 (21 Establishments)		SIC 3944 GMES,TYS,CHLRN VHCL (NO BREAKDOWN) 2002 (39 Establishments)		SIC 3949 SPRTG,AHLTC GDS NEC (NO BREAKDOWN) 2002 (87 Establishments)		SIC 3953 MARKING DEVICES (NO BREAKDOWN) 2002 (14 Establishments)	
	$	%	$	%	$	%	$	%
Cash	339,655	17.0	372,215	16.1	183,422	9.9	147,219	19.8
Accounts Receivable	229,767	11.5	538,671	23.3	415,016	22.4	190,343	25.6
Notes Receivable	0	0.0	2,312	0.1	9,264	0.5	744	0.1
Inventory	709,280	35.5	610,340	26.4	679,959	36.7	93,685	12.6
Other Current	185,811	9.3	205,758	8.9	87,078	4.7	27,510	3.7
Total Current	**1,464,513**	**73.3**	**1,729,296**	**74.8**	**1,374,739**	**74.2**	**459,501**	**61.8**
Fixed Assets	337,657	16.9	256,620	11.1	305,703	16.5	221,572	29.8
Other Non-current	195,801	9.8	325,977	14.1	172,306	9.3	62,456	8.4
Total Assets	**1,997,971**	**100.0**	**2,311,893**	**100.0**	**1,852,748**	**100.0**	**743,529**	**100.0**
Accounts Payable	175,821	8.8	221,942	9.6	239,004	12.9	118,965	16.0
Bank Loans	0	0.0	4,624	0.2	11,116	0.6	0	0.0
Notes Payable	87,911	4.4	2,193,986	94.9	114,870	6.2	54,278	7.3
Other Current	547,444	27.4	834,593	36.1	457,630	24.7	101,119	13.6
Total Current	**811,176**	**40.6**	**3,255,145**	**140.8**	**822,620**	**44.4**	**274,362**	**36.9**
Other Long Term	349,645	17.5	316,730	13.7	459,482	24.8	58,739	7.9
Deferred Credits	0	0.0	0	0.0	3,705	0.2	0	0.0
Net Worth	837,150	41.9	(1,259,982)	(54.5)	566,941	30.6	410,428	55.2
Total Liab & Net Worth	**1,997,971**	**100.0**	**2,311,893**	**100.0**	**1,852,748**	**100.0**	**743,529**	**100.0**
Net Sales	3,380,662	100.0	3,350,570	100.0	3,750,502	100.0	2,059,637	100.0
Gross Profit	1,375,929	40.7	1,390,487	41.5	1,590,213	42.4	1,066,892	51.8
Net Profit After Tax	94,659	2.8	(16,753)	(0.5)	93,763	2.5	72,087	3.5
Working Capital	653,337	—	(1,525,849)	—	552,119	—	185,139	—

RATIOS	UQ	MED	LQ	UQ	MED	LQ	UQ	MED	LQ	UQ	MED	LQ
SOLVENCY												
Quick Ratio (times)	1.5	1.0	0.2	2.6	1.1	0.5	1.7	0.9	0.4	3.7	1.3	0.7
Current Ratio (times)	4.8	1.7	1.2	4.3	2.1	1.4	4.5	2.1	1.1	6.0	2.0	1.3
Curr Liab To Nw (%)	19.9	48.5	220.8	19.0	54.8	143.6	26.2	56.5	182.2	12.3	76.4	212.5
Curr Liab To Inv (%)	54.2	95.2	203.3	58.8	145.5	240.8	53.6	101.0	176.5	53.2	115.4	175.4
Total Liab To Nw (%)	23.0	66.3	221.5	28.9	78.7	163.8	33.6	106.1	329.9	12.3	92.2	212.5
Fixed Assets To Nw (%)	20.6	34.5	60.4	5.8	12.6	30.5	13.0	27.4	63.2	14.2	32.8	63.4
EFFICIENCY												
Coll Period (days)	8.8	25.2	39.8	32.0	50.0	77.0	22.5	37.6	64.3	20.5	34.7	52.1
Sales To Inv (times)	10.3	4.6	3.3	9.7	7.2	4.9	9.7	5.2	3.6	22.3	12.2	7.7
Assets To Sales (%)	44.3	59.1	82.3	48.5	69.0	101.2	37.3	49.4	72.9	26.7	36.1	54.0
Sales To Nwc (times)	9.9	4.2	2.2	6.5	4.0	2.2	12.0	4.9	2.8	9.7	6.7	4.1
Acct Pay To Sales (%)	1.1	3.4	6.9	3.6	5.9	8.2	3.1	4.9	7.8	1.9	3.2	8.0
PROFITABILITY												
Return On Sales (%)	6.8	3.8	(0.6)	8.3	2.5	(10.7)	8.3	2.4	(0.7)	3.6	1.4	0.2
Return On Assets (%)	9.4	4.6	(1.3)	12.0	3.8	(11.1)	13.8	5.5	(1.5)	18.9	3.3	0.0
Return On Nw (%)	26.4	10.5	5.7	35.2	10.2	(3.6)	42.2	12.8	(1.6)	62.2	4.8	(1.2)

SIC 3955 CRBN PAPR,INKD RBBN (NO BREAKDOWN) 2002 (16 Establishments)

	$	%
Cash	56,524	9.2
Accounts Receivable	173,872	28.3
Notes Receivable	1,843	0.3
Inventory	183,088	29.8
Other Current	52,837	8.6
Total Current	**468,164**	**76.2**
Fixed Assets	100,145	16.3
Other Non-current	46,079	7.5
Total Assets	**614,388**	**100.0**
Accounts Payable	200,905	32.7
Bank Loans	0	0.0
Notes Payable	19,046	3.1
Other Current	266,030	43.3
Total Current	**485,981**	**79.1**
Other Long Term	224,251	36.5
Deferred Credits	12,288	2.0
Net Worth	(108,132)	(17.6)
Total Liab & Net Worth	**614,388**	**100.0**
Net Sales	2,133,292	100.0
Gross Profit	648,521	30.4
Net Profit After Tax	57,599	2.7
Working Capital	(17,817)	—

RATIOS	UQ	MED	LQ
SOLVENCY			
Quick Ratio (times)	1.4	0.6	0.2
Current Ratio (times)	2.2	1.6	1.1
Curr Liab To Nw (%)	60.8	132.1	304.9
Curr Liab To Inv (%)	127.4	177.1	300.1
Total Liab To Nw (%)	76.2	158.6	359.6
Fixed Assets To Nw (%)	25.1	35.3	63.9
EFFICIENCY			
Coll Period (days)	15.4	30.7	37.8
Sales To Inv (times)	17.7	12.6	6.4
Assets To Sales (%)	21.1	28.8	46.7
Sales To Nwc (times)	13.2	12.6	10.2
Acct Pay To Sales (%)	3.7	7.2	12.8
PROFITABILITY			
Return On Sales (%)	2.2	1.5	(0.4)
Return On Assets (%)	9.8	5.5	(1.1)
Return On Nw (%)	42.2	13.9	0.0

SIC 3961 COSTUME JEWELRY (NO BREAKDOWN) 2002 (12 Establishments)

	$	%
Cash	312,169	16.0
Accounts Receivable	563,855	28.9
Notes Receivable	0	0.0
Inventory	556,051	28.5
Other Current	187,301	9.6
Total Current	**1,619,376**	**83.0**
Fixed Assets	265,343	13.6
Other Non-current	66,336	3.4
Total Assets	**1,951,055**	**100.0**
Accounts Payable	206,812	10.6
Bank Loans	1,951	0.1
Notes Payable	87,797	4.5
Other Current	485,813	24.9
Total Current	**782,373**	**40.1**
Other Long Term	56,581	2.9
Deferred Credits	0	0.0
Net Worth	1,112,101	57.0
Total Liab & Net Worth	**1,951,055**	**100.0**
Net Sales	4,232,223	100.0
Gross Profit	1,756,373	41.5
Net Profit After Tax	296,256	7.0
Working Capital	837,003	—

RATIOS	UQ	MED	LQ
SOLVENCY			
Quick Ratio (times)	1.6	1.1	0.8
Current Ratio (times)	3.2	2.3	1.6
Curr Liab To Nw (%)	34.0	68.2	134.3
Curr Liab To Inv (%)	93.3	144.5	249.1
Total Liab To Nw (%)	36.1	70.2	161.7
Fixed Assets To Nw (%)	6.6	18.7	48.8
EFFICIENCY			
Coll Period (days)	44.2	55.2	60.6
Sales To Inv (times)	10.2	7.3	4.9
Assets To Sales (%)	36.8	46.1	59.3
Sales To Nwc (times)	10.0	5.7	4.0
Acct Pay To Sales (%)	2.4	5.5	7.1
PROFITABILITY			
Return On Sales (%)	11.6	8.1	0.5
Return On Assets (%)	23.0	15.5	1.7
Return On Nw (%)	32.4	25.2	3.8

SIC 3965 FSTNR,BTNS,NDLS,PNS (NO BREAKDOWN) 2002 (12 Establishments)

	$	%
Cash	176,982	13.2
Accounts Receivable	407,594	30.4
Notes Receivable	0	0.0
Inventory	337,874	25.2
Other Current	135,417	10.1
Total Current	**1,057,867**	**78.9**
Fixed Assets	198,434	14.8
Other Non-current	84,468	6.3
Total Assets	**1,340,769**	**100.0**
Accounts Payable	214,523	16.0
Bank Loans	12,067	0.9
Notes Payable	8,045	0.6
Other Current	226,590	16.9
Total Current	**461,225**	**34.4**
Other Long Term	202,456	15.1
Deferred Credits	0	0.0
Net Worth	677,088	50.5
Total Liab & Net Worth	**1,340,769**	**100.0**
Net Sales	2,979,487	100.0
Gross Profit	1,239,467	41.6
Net Profit After Tax	291,990	9.8
Working Capital	596,642	—

RATIOS	UQ	MED	LQ
SOLVENCY			
Quick Ratio (times)	2.3	1.6	0.9
Current Ratio (times)	4.9	2.1	1.5
Curr Liab To Nw (%)	30.2	51.2	131.1
Curr Liab To Inv (%)	66.0	104.1	183.0
Total Liab To Nw (%)	35.8	119.7	227.4
Fixed Assets To Nw (%)	5.1	34.5	48.2
EFFICIENCY			
Coll Period (days)	35.8	38.2	65.0
Sales To Inv (times)	18.2	7.6	6.3
Assets To Sales (%)	31.1	45.0	59.8
Sales To Nwc (times)	15.2	5.2	3.3
Acct Pay To Sales (%)	4.3	6.4	8.6
PROFITABILITY			
Return On Sales (%)	6.1	2.9	1.2
Return On Assets (%)	17.3	8.2	1.8
Return On Nw (%)	37.9	14.5	4.3

SIC 3991 BROOMS AND BRUSHES (NO BREAKDOWN) 2002 (14 Establishments)

	$	%
Cash	132,646	8.3
Accounts Receivable	410,724	25.7
Notes Receivable	0	0.0
Inventory	586,520	36.7
Other Current	87,898	5.5
Total Current	**1,217,788**	**76.2**
Fixed Assets	278,078	17.4
Other Non-current	102,281	6.4
Total Assets	**1,598,147**	**100.0**
Accounts Payable	134,244	8.4
Bank Loans	0	0.0
Notes Payable	3,196	0.2
Other Current	244,517	15.3
Total Current	**381,957**	**23.9**
Other Long Term	107,076	6.7
Deferred Credits	0	0.0
Net Worth	1,109,114	69.4
Total Liab & Net Worth	**1,598,147**	**100.0**
Net Sales	4,527,329	100.0
Gross Profit	1,543,819	34.1
Net Profit After Tax	176,566	3.9
Working Capital	835,831	—

RATIOS	UQ	MED	LQ
SOLVENCY			
Quick Ratio (times)	5.3	2.3	1.0
Current Ratio (times)	6.7	4.8	2.3
Curr Liab To Nw (%)	7.4	20.7	94.9
Curr Liab To Inv (%)	33.6	56.2	97.4
Total Liab To Nw (%)	14.6	30.1	128.9
Fixed Assets To Nw (%)	11.3	23.2	53.8
EFFICIENCY			
Coll Period (days)	38.0	42.3	51.1
Sales To Inv (times)	9.4	7.0	6.9
Assets To Sales (%)	30.0	35.3	38.8
Sales To Nwc (times)	8.2	5.0	4.0
Acct Pay To Sales (%)	1.9	4.4	4.9
PROFITABILITY			
Return On Sales (%)	7.3	2.7	1.1
Return On Assets (%)	8.9	8.1	6.9
Return On Nw (%)	24.1	11.4	8.0

SIC 3993 SIGNS, ADVT SPCLTIES
(NO BREAKDOWN)
2002 (198 Establishments)

	$	%
Cash	149,498	13.5
Accounts Receivable	327,787	29.6
Notes Receivable	8,859	0.8
Inventory	177,182	16.0
Other Current	89,699	8.1
Total Current	**753,025**	**68.0**
Fixed Assets	282,384	25.5
Other Non-current	71,981	6.5
Total Assets	**1,107,390**	**100.0**
Accounts Payable	143,961	13.0
Bank Loans	1,107	0.1
Notes Payable	50,940	4.6
Other Current	256,915	23.2
Total Current	**452,923**	**40.9**
Other Long Term	214,833	19.4
Deferred Credits	4,430	0.4
Net Worth	435,204	39.3
Total Liab & Net Worth	**1,107,390**	**100.0**
Net Sales	2,906,535	100.0
Gross Profit	1,255,623	43.2
Net Profit After Tax	90,103	3.1
Working Capital	300,102	—

RATIOS	UQ	MED	LQ
SOLVENCY			
Quick Ratio (times)	2.1	1.2	0.7
Current Ratio (times)	3.4	1.9	1.2
Curr Liab To Nw (%)	25.1	63.5	142.7
Curr Liab To Inv (%)	117.7	206.6	494.7
Total Liab To Nw (%)	38.8	101.3	231.5
Fixed Assets To Nw (%)	22.2	41.1	87.0
EFFICIENCY			
Coll Period (days)	29.9	44.5	59.1
Sales To Inv (times)	33.5	16.8	8.9
Assets To Sales (%)	27.1	38.1	51.6
Sales To Nwc (times)	13.4	7.4	4.6
Acct Pay To Sales (%)	2.1	3.8	7.1
PROFITABILITY			
Return On Sales (%)	5.2	2.0	0.1
Return On Assets (%)	14.9	5.7	0.2
Return On Nw (%)	32.1	11.2	2.0

SIC 3999 MFG INDUSTRIES, NEC
(NO BREAKDOWN)
2002 (115 Establishments)

	$	%
Cash	185,660	12.2
Accounts Receivable	348,493	22.9
Notes Receivable	7,609	0.5
Inventory	380,451	25.0
Other Current	91,308	6.0
Total Current	**1,013,521**	**66.6**
Fixed Assets	336,318	22.1
Other Non-current	171,964	11.3
Total Assets	**1,521,803**	**100.0**
Accounts Payable	336,318	22.1
Bank Loans	22,827	1.5
Notes Payable	74,568	4.9
Other Current	1,185,485	77.9
Total Current	**1,619,198**	**106.4**
Other Long Term	310,448	20.4
Deferred Credits	3,044	0.2
Net Worth	(410,887)	(27.0)
Total Liab & Net Worth	**1,521,803**	**100.0**
Net Sales	3,344,622	100.0
Gross Profit	1,444,877	43.2
Net Profit After Tax	143,819	4.3
Working Capital	(605,677)	—

RATIOS	UQ	MED	LQ
SOLVENCY			
Quick Ratio (times)	2.3	1.0	0.5
Current Ratio (times)	4.0	1.9	1.2
Curr Liab To Nw (%)	22.0	51.0	144.9
Curr Liab To Inv (%)	80.6	150.5	268.3
Total Liab To Nw (%)	40.6	90.5	240.0
Fixed Assets To Nw (%)	14.0	36.4	67.0
EFFICIENCY			
Coll Period (days)	22.1	34.3	59.3
Sales To Inv (times)	17.8	9.4	6.1
Assets To Sales (%)	29.5	45.5	76.6
Sales To Nwc (times)	11.7	6.9	3.6
Acct Pay To Sales (%)	1.9	4.5	7.3
PROFITABILITY			
Return On Sales (%)	8.4	3.6	0.2
Return On Assets (%)	18.5	6.2	0.6
Return On Nw (%)	38.4	17.2	2.8

SIC 41 LOCAL PASSENGER TRAN
(NO BREAKDOWN)
2002 (170 Establishments)

	$	%
Cash	198,068	11.1
Accounts Receivable	303,348	17.0
Notes Receivable	8,922	0.5
Inventory	46,394	2.6
Other Current	119,555	6.7
Total Current	**676,287**	**37.9**
Fixed Assets	915,397	51.3
Other Non-current	192,715	10.8
Total Assets	**1,784,399**	**100.0**
Accounts Payable	128,477	7.2
Bank Loans	12,491	0.7
Notes Payable	64,238	3.6
Other Current	390,783	21.9
Total Current	**595,989**	**33.4**
Other Long Term	638,815	35.8
Deferred Credits	7,138	0.4
Net Worth	542,457	30.4
Total Liab & Net Worth	**1,784,399**	**100.0**
Net Sales	4,289,421	100.0
Gross Profit	1,587,086	37.0
Net Profit After Tax	132,972	3.1
Working Capital	80,298	—

RATIOS	UQ	MED	LQ
SOLVENCY			
Quick Ratio (times)	2.1	1.0	0.4
Current Ratio (times)	2.6	1.4	0.7
Curr Liab To Nw (%)	17.8	57.5	157.8
Curr Liab To Inv (%)	376.4	737.7	999.9
Total Liab To Nw (%)	45.1	128.6	315.1
Fixed Assets To Nw (%)	65.9	106.0	243.5
EFFICIENCY			
Coll Period (days)	12.8	30.9	50.4
Sales To Inv (times)	206.7	75.9	18.8
Assets To Sales (%)	27.0	41.6	75.1
Sales To Nwc (times)	24.4	13.3	5.3
Acct Pay To Sales (%)	1.2	2.1	4.8
PROFITABILITY			
Return On Sales (%)	6.1	1.4	(1.4)
Return On Assets (%)	12.6	3.6	(2.6)
Return On Nw (%)	42.6	11.4	0.1

SIC 4111 LCL SUBURBAN TRANS
(NO BREAKDOWN)
2002 (23 Establishments)

	$	%
Cash	1,489,012	15.0
Accounts Receivable	1,359,964	13.7
Notes Receivable	0	0.0
Inventory	277,949	2.8
Other Current	933,114	9.4
Total Current	**4,060,039**	**40.9**
Fixed Assets	4,139,453	41.7
Other Non-current	1,727,254	17.4
Total Assets	**9,926,746**	**100.0**
Accounts Payable	387,143	3.9
Bank Loans	0	0.0
Notes Payable	268,022	2.7
Other Current	1,022,455	10.3
Total Current	**1,677,620**	**16.9**
Other Long Term	4,526,596	45.6
Deferred Credits	49,634	0.5
Net Worth	3,672,896	37.0
Total Liab & Net Worth	**9,926,746**	**100.0**
Net Sales	8,231,133	100.0
Gross Profit	3,399,458	41.3
Net Profit After Tax	460,943	5.6
Working Capital	2,382,419	—

RATIOS	UQ	MED	LQ
SOLVENCY			
Quick Ratio (times)	3.5	1.4	1.0
Current Ratio (times)	5.2	2.4	1.7
Curr Liab To Nw (%)	5.4	13.0	47.0
Curr Liab To Inv (%)	265.1	452.6	651.2
Total Liab To Nw (%)	7.3	19.8	117.0
Fixed Assets To Nw (%)	52.6	84.3	100.3
EFFICIENCY			
Coll Period (days)	17.2	48.6	98.8
Sales To Inv (times)	27.6	10.8	5.1
Assets To Sales (%)	36.4	120.6	478.4
Sales To Nwc (times)	15.4	3.2	1.8
Acct Pay To Sales (%)	3.0	5.6	8.1
PROFITABILITY			
Return On Sales (%)	12.1	2.5	(10.5)
Return On Assets (%)	16.7	6.6	(3.3)
Return On Nw (%)	39.5	3.9	(5.7)

	SIC 4119 LCL PASS TRANS NEC (NO BREAKDOWN) 2002 (64 Establishments) $	%	SIC 4141 LCL BUS CHRTR SVCE (NO BREAKDOWN) 2002 (14 Establishments) $	%	SIC 4142 BS CHTR SVC,EXC LCL (NO BREAKDOWN) 2002 (16 Establishments) $	%	SIC 4151 SCHOOL BUSES (NO BREAKDOWN) 2002 (35 Establishments) $	%
Cash	211,874	13.1	78,598	5.5	91,111	5.5	163,316	12.0
Accounts Receivable	438,305	27.1	175,774	12.3	79,515	4.8	168,760	12.4
Notes Receivable	6,469	0.4	5,716	0.4	3,313	0.2	17,693	1.3
Inventory	29,113	1.8	37,155	2.6	57,979	3.5	58,521	4.3
Other Current	106,746	6.6	181,490	12.7	51,353	3.1	74,852	5.5
Total Current	**792,507**	**49.0**	**478,733**	**33.5**	**283,271**	**17.1**	**483,142**	**35.5**
Fixed Assets	695,466	43.0	798,842	55.9	1,262,295	76.2	717,228	52.7
Other Non-current	129,389	8.0	151,480	10.6	110,989	6.7	160,594	11.8
Total Assets	**1,617,362**	**100.0**	**1,429,055**	**100.0**	**1,656,555**	**100.0**	**1,360,964**	**100.0**
Accounts Payable	135,858	8.4	211,500	14.8	59,636	3.6	89,824	6.6
Bank Loans	29,113	1.8	1,429	0.1	4,970	0.3	0	0.0
Notes Payable	54,990	3.4	62,878	4.4	53,010	3.2	74,853	5.5
Other Current	430,219	26.6	394,420	27.6	248,483	15.0	254,500	18.7
Total Current	**650,180**	**40.2**	**670,227**	**46.9**	**366,099**	**22.1**	**419,177**	**30.8**
Other Long Term	394,636	24.4	790,267	55.3	1,268,921	76.6	431,425	31.7
Deferred Credits	3,235	0.2	0	0.0	9,939	0.6	6,805	0.5
Net Worth	569,311	35.2	(31,439)	(2.2)	11,596	0.7	503,557	37.0
Total Liab & Net Worth	**1,617,362**	**100.0**	**1,429,055**	**100.0**	**1,656,555**	**100.0**	**1,360,964**	**100.0**
Net Sales	4,701,634	100.0	3,862,311	100.0	1,942,034	100.0	3,271,548	100.0
Gross Profit	1,824,234	38.8	1,954,329	50.6	551,538	28.4	1,004,365	30.7
Net Profit After Tax	216,275	4.6	23,174	0.6	(66,029)	(3.4)	71,974	2.2
Working Capital	142,327	—	(191,494)	—	(82,828)	—	63,965	—

RATIOS	UQ	MED	LQ	UQ	MED	LQ	UQ	MED	LQ	UQ	MED	LQ
SOLVENCY												
Quick Ratio (times)	2.3	1.4	0.8	0.6	0.4	0.2	0.8	0.6	0.2	1.9	0.8	0.4
Current Ratio (times)	2.8	1.7	1.0	1.4	0.9	0.5	1.2	0.9	0.5	2.3	1.1	0.7
Curr Liab To Nw (%)	23.7	59.6	130.7	73.7	137.0	190.3	39.8	156.1	209.5	20.7	106.4	208.2
Curr Liab To Inv (%)	895.1	999.9	999.9	339.6	690.3	704.2	439.5	771.4	999.9	390.1	989.0	999.9
Total Liab To Nw (%)	54.2	109.5	241.3	232.7	315.4	431.4	125.8	394.0	743.5	50.2	233.0	406.5
Fixed Assets To Nw (%)	56.2	96.2	161.0	214.4	292.1	411.8	168.0	241.2	683.4	76.0	169.7	355.4
EFFICIENCY												
Coll Period (days)	31.1	43.6	61.2	22.8	32.1	39.8	6.2	13.1	17.5	8.4	16.6	31.4
Sales To Inv (times)	387.8	114.7	76.9	40.8	22.4	17.1	74.3	43.0	20.5	215.9	106.0	39.0
Assets To Sales (%)	23.7	34.4	56.8	30.9	37.0	82.3	44.4	85.3	101.5	28.4	41.6	73.9
Sales To Nwc (times)	27.3	15.6	6.5	17.7	17.0	14.5	35.6	29.8	24.0	17.4	12.2	8.5
Acct Pay To Sales (%)	1.2	2.0	3.5	2.1	2.4	4.5	1.3	1.8	3.8	0.9	1.6	3.9
PROFITABILITY												
Return On Sales (%)	6.7	2.3	0.5	1.0	(1.3)	(2.8)	0.5	(1.2)	(8.5)	7.5	1.1	(0.5)
Return On Assets (%)	24.0	6.6	2.3	1.2	(2.7)	(6.4)	1.4	(1.4)	(9.3)	13.4	3.4	(1.2)
Return On Nw (%)	48.2	19.0	4.5	6.4	(5.6)	(17.3)	5.4	4.1	1.9	82.4	11.5	0.1

	SIC 42 TRUCKING & WAREHSNG (NO BREAKDOWN) 2002 (1342 Establishments)		SIC 4212 LCL TRCKG W/O STRGE (NO BREAKDOWN) 2002 (321 Establishments)		SIC 4213 TRCKG, EXCEPT LOCAL (NO BREAKDOWN) 2002 (698 Establishments)		SIC 4214 LCL TRCKG WTH STRGE (NO BREAKDOWN) 2002 (125 Establishments)	
	$	%	$	%	$	%	$	%
Cash	136,288	9.9	93,165	9.5	149,699	9.2	126,350	13.1
Accounts Receivable	381,331	27.7	251,055	25.6	476,760	29.3	295,137	30.6
Notes Receivable	11,013	0.8	9,807	1.0	11,390	0.7	5,787	0.6
Inventory	26,156	1.9	16,672	1.7	21,153	1.3	7,716	0.8
Other Current	112,886	8.2	76,493	7.8	131,802	8.1	86,805	9.0
Total Current	**667,674**	**48.5**	**447,192**	**45.6**	**790,804**	**48.6**	**521,795**	**54.1**
Fixed Assets	608,478	44.2	466,806	47.6	728,971	44.8	365,546	37.9
Other Non-current	100,495	7.3	66,687	6.8	107,393	6.6	77,159	8.0
Total Assets	**1,376,647**	**100.0**	**980,685**	**100.0**	**1,627,168**	**100.0**	**964,500**	**100.0**
Accounts Payable	145,925	10.6	111,798	11.4	159,462	9.8	131,172	13.6
Bank Loans	2,753	0.2	1,961	0.2	1,627	0.1	5,787	0.6
Notes Payable	53,689	3.9	44,131	4.5	60,205	3.7	33,758	3.5
Other Current	329,019	23.9	329,510	33.6	353,096	21.7	208,332	21.6
Total Current	**531,386**	**38.6**	**487,400**	**49.7**	**574,390**	**35.3**	**379,049**	**39.3**
Other Long Term	368,941	26.8	270,670	27.6	423,064	26.0	366,509	38.0
Deferred Credits	8,260	0.6	8,826	0.9	8,136	0.5	1,929	0.2
Net Worth	468,060	34.0	213,789	21.8	621,578	38.2	217,013	22.5
Total Liab & Net Worth	**1,376,647**	**100.0**	**980,685**	**100.0**	**1,627,168**	**100.0**	**964,500**	**100.0**
Net Sales	4,159,054	100.0	3,133,179	100.0	4,945,799	100.0	3,183,168	100.0
Gross Profit	1,409,919	33.9	1,134,211	36.2	1,483,740	30.0	1,279,634	40.2
Net Profit After Tax	108,135	2.6	43,865	1.4	108,808	2.2	79,579	2.5
Working Capital	136,288	—	(40,208)	—	216,414	—	142,746	—

RATIOS	UQ	MED	LQ	UQ	MED	LQ	UQ	MED	LQ	UQ	MED	LQ
SOLVENCY												
Quick Ratio (times)	2.3	1.1	0.6	2.3	1.1	0.5	2.1	1.1	0.6	2.8	1.3	0.7
Current Ratio (times)	2.9	1.5	0.9	2.8	1.3	0.8	2.8	1.4	0.8	3.3	1.6	1.0
Curr Liab To Nw (%)	23.3	61.3	162.7	24.4	60.1	164.1	25.3	65.1	181.3	22.7	63.5	132.8
Curr Liab To Inv (%)	360.9	999.9	999.9	396.2	989.9	999.9	505.8	999.9	999.9	819.7	999.9	999.9
Total Liab To Nw (%)	49.4	123.4	298.4	52.5	128.1	300.2	52.5	129.2	324.6	37.1	111.3	229.9
Fixed Assets To Nw (%)	42.2	94.8	187.8	45.7	100.0	194.7	47.2	103.2	206.6	32.9	69.4	136.8
EFFICIENCY												
Coll Period (days)	23.7	34.3	45.6	21.9	33.8	46.7	25.8	34.7	44.4	22.6	38.3	52.6
Sales To Inv (times)	321.8	126.0	46.3	282.6	86.2	46.3	334.9	173.5	69.5	730.5	275.0	110.6
Assets To Sales (%)	21.2	33.1	52.1	20.9	31.3	48.3	20.7	32.9	51.5	22.4	30.3	43.5
Sales To Nwc (times)	28.0	12.7	7.1	27.3	12.6	7.2	29.9	14.3	7.6	26.0	11.3	6.6
Acct Pay To Sales (%)	1.2	2.6	4.7	1.2	2.9	5.2	1.2	2.4	4.3	1.4	3.0	5.0
PROFITABILITY												
Return On Sales (%)	4.1	1.4	0.0	4.0	1.3	(0.7)	3.4	1.4	0.0	4.8	1.8	0.2
Return On Assets (%)	11.5	4.0	(0.1)	12.2	3.9	(1.7)	10.0	3.8	0.1	14.7	5.3	0.5
Return On Nw (%)	35.0	10.7	1.6	36.2	10.0	(0.1)	34.5	10.5	1.8	33.1	13.0	2.6

SIC 4215 COURIER SVC,EXC AIR
(NO BREAKDOWN)
2002 (26 Establishments)

	$	%
Cash	109,314	8.2
Accounts Receivable	518,573	38.9
Notes Receivable	0	0.0
Inventory	0	0.0
Other Current	119,978	9.0
Total Current	**747,865**	**56.1**
Fixed Assets	386,597	29.0
Other Non-current	198,630	14.9
Total Assets	**1,333,092**	**100.0**
Accounts Payable	183,967	13.8
Bank Loans	0	0.0
Notes Payable	29,328	2.2
Other Current	365,267	27.4
Total Current	**578,562**	**43.4**
Other Long Term	403,927	30.3
Deferred Credits	1,333	0.1
Net Worth	349,270	26.2
Total Liab & Net Worth	**1,333,092**	**100.0**
Net Sales	6,288,170	100.0
Gross Profit	2,056,232	32.7
Net Profit After Tax	62,882	1.0
Working Capital	169,303	—

RATIOS	UQ	MED	LQ
SOLVENCY			
Quick Ratio (times)	1.9	1.1	0.7
Current Ratio (times)	2.1	1.4	0.9
Curr Liab To Nw (%)	49.6	110.0	275.3
Curr Liab To Inv (%)	999.9	999.9	999.9
Total Liab To Nw (%)	96.7	185.5	335.0
Fixed Assets To Nw (%)	32.3	66.8	142.2
EFFICIENCY			
Coll Period (days)	27.0	34.5	38.5
Sales To Inv (times)	999.9	999.9	999.9
Assets To Sales (%)	17.4	21.2	32.0
Sales To Nwc (times)	35.7	25.3	12.5
Acct Pay To Sales (%)	1.3	2.1	4.6
PROFITABILITY			
Return On Sales (%)	2.5	1.1	(1.0)
Return On Assets (%)	13.0	6.7	(2.6)
Return On Nw (%)	43.6	22.0	(5.7)

SIC 4221 FRM PRDT WRHSG,STRG
(NO BREAKDOWN)
2002 (29 Establishments)

	$	%
Cash	286,162	10.5
Accounts Receivable	367,923	13.5
Notes Receivable	35,430	1.3
Inventory	482,388	17.7
Other Current	179,874	6.6
Total Current	**1,351,777**	**49.6**
Fixed Assets	1,193,706	43.8
Other Non-current	179,874	6.6
Total Assets	**2,725,357**	**100.0**
Accounts Payable	223,479	8.2
Bank Loans	24,528	0.9
Notes Payable	258,909	9.5
Other Current	403,353	14.8
Total Current	**910,269**	**33.4**
Other Long Term	460,586	16.9
Deferred Credits	10,901	0.4
Net Worth	1,343,601	49.3
Total Liab & Net Worth	**2,725,357**	**100.0**
Net Sales	6,222,276	100.0
Gross Profit	1,636,459	26.3
Net Profit After Tax	367,114	5.9
Working Capital	441,508	—

RATIOS	UQ	MED	LQ
SOLVENCY			
Quick Ratio (times)	1.7	1.0	0.4
Current Ratio (times)	2.7	1.9	1.2
Curr Liab To Nw (%)	16.2	40.7	87.5
Curr Liab To Inv (%)	123.3	156.7	276.4
Total Liab To Nw (%)	35.0	80.6	137.4
Fixed Assets To Nw (%)	60.6	81.5	111.5
EFFICIENCY			
Coll Period (days)	10.2	24.3	43.8
Sales To Inv (times)	23.3	13.2	9.8
Assets To Sales (%)	33.2	43.8	91.7
Sales To Nwc (times)	15.5	10.4	4.2
Acct Pay To Sales (%)	1.3	2.8	4.4
PROFITABILITY			
Return On Sales (%)	4.4	2.4	0.1
Return On Assets (%)	7.4	4.2	0.1
Return On Nw (%)	12.8	8.2	1.0

SIC 4222 RFRGT WRHSG,STORAGE
(NO BREAKDOWN)
2002 (23 Establishments)

	$	%
Cash	336,233	8.5
Accounts Receivable	842,560	21.3
Notes Receivable	0	0.0
Inventory	35,601	0.9
Other Current	304,587	7.7
Total Current	**1,518,981**	**38.4**
Fixed Assets	2,175,624	55.0
Other Non-current	261,075	6.6
Total Assets	**3,955,680**	**100.0**
Accounts Payable	344,144	8.7
Bank Loans	0	0.0
Notes Payable	126,582	3.2
Other Current	399,524	10.1
Total Current	**870,250**	**22.0**
Other Long Term	1,024,520	25.9
Deferred Credits	15,823	0.4
Net Worth	2,045,087	51.7
Total Liab & Net Worth	**3,955,680**	**100.0**
Net Sales	8,362,960	100.0
Gross Profit	3,278,280	39.2
Net Profit After Tax	568,681	6.8
Working Capital	648,731	—

RATIOS	UQ	MED	LQ
SOLVENCY			
Quick Ratio (times)	2.9	1.2	0.9
Current Ratio (times)	3.1	1.5	1.1
Curr Liab To Nw (%)	19.8	44.1	89.3
Curr Liab To Inv (%)	487.5	898.1	999.9
Total Liab To Nw (%)	40.6	110.2	321.1
Fixed Assets To Nw (%)	52.5	146.9	213.9
EFFICIENCY			
Coll Period (days)	28.5	37.8	50.7
Sales To Inv (times)	259.7	56.8	28.7
Assets To Sales (%)	31.2	47.3	89.0
Sales To Nwc (times)	19.4	8.5	3.4
Acct Pay To Sales (%)	2.2	3.3	6.1
PROFITABILITY			
Return On Sales (%)	5.3	2.3	1.1
Return On Assets (%)	13.1	6.7	1.8
Return On Nw (%)	28.6	9.5	3.9

SIC 4225 GNRL WRHSG,STRGE
(NO BREAKDOWN)
2002 (86 Establishments)

	$	%
Cash	269,377	12.2
Accounts Receivable	494,593	22.4
Notes Receivable	33,120	1.5
Inventory	77,280	3.5
Other Current	242,881	11.0
Total Current	**1,117,251**	**50.6**
Fixed Assets	856,706	38.8
Other Non-current	234,049	10.6
Total Assets	**2,208,006**	**100.0**
Accounts Payable	211,969	9.6
Bank Loans	0	0.0
Notes Payable	72,864	3.3
Other Current	434,977	19.7
Total Current	**719,810**	**32.6**
Other Long Term	410,689	18.6
Deferred Credits	4,416	0.2
Net Worth	1,073,091	48.6
Total Liab & Net Worth	**2,208,006**	**100.0**
Net Sales	5,307,707	100.0
Gross Profit	2,128,391	40.1
Net Profit After Tax	291,924	5.5
Working Capital	397,441	—

RATIOS	UQ	MED	LQ
SOLVENCY			
Quick Ratio (times)	2.4	1.3	0.7
Current Ratio (times)	3.1	1.6	1.1
Curr Liab To Nw (%)	17.2	49.2	139.2
Curr Liab To Inv (%)	200.1	692.8	999.9
Total Liab To Nw (%)	26.6	89.6	209.4
Fixed Assets To Nw (%)	35.8	73.7	157.6
EFFICIENCY			
Coll Period (days)	23.0	32.5	46.0
Sales To Inv (times)	90.4	66.2	12.3
Assets To Sales (%)	23.3	41.6	94.8
Sales To Nwc (times)	26.6	12.3	6.6
Acct Pay To Sales (%)	1.3	2.7	5.0
PROFITABILITY			
Return On Sales (%)	5.7	2.0	(0.2)
Return On Assets (%)	10.8	3.8	(0.4)
Return On Nw (%)	27.5	10.4	0.2

SIC 4226 SPCL WRHSG,STRG,NEC
(NO BREAKDOWN)
2002 (33 Establishments)

	$	%
Cash	192,798	10.0
Accounts Receivable	485,850	25.2
Notes Receivable	23,136	1.2
Inventory	80,975	4.2
Other Current	158,093	8.2
Total Current	**940,852**	**48.8**
Fixed Assets	782,758	40.6
Other Non-current	204,365	10.6
Total Assets	**1,927,975**	**100.0**
Accounts Payable	204,365	10.6
Bank Loans	11,568	0.6
Notes Payable	13,496	0.7
Other Current	321,972	16.7
Total Current	**551,401**	**28.6**
Other Long Term	416,442	21.6
Deferred Credits	23,136	1.2
Net Worth	936,996	48.6
Total Liab & Net Worth	**1,927,975**	**100.0**
Net Sales	3,700,528	100.0
Gross Profit	2,020,488	54.6
Net Profit After Tax	407,058	11.0
Working Capital	389,451	—

RATIOS	UQ	MED	LQ
SOLVENCY			
Quick Ratio (times)	2.7	1.4	0.6
Current Ratio (times)	3.0	1.8	1.3
Curr Liab To Nw (%)	26.8	45.3	95.0
Curr Liab To Inv (%)	283.9	952.7	999.9
Total Liab To Nw (%)	41.7	67.1	269.7
Fixed Assets To Nw (%)	25.7	71.1	129.3
EFFICIENCY			
Coll Period (days)	24.5	37.1	53.7
Sales To Inv (times)	712.2	97.0	38.1
Assets To Sales (%)	31.0	52.1	93.3
Sales To Nwc (times)	14.2	6.8	4.6
Acct Pay To Sales (%)	2.0	3.9	5.8
PROFITABILITY			
Return On Sales (%)	16.7	5.2	1.4
Return On Assets (%)	26.5	11.8	2.2
Return On Nw (%)	56.1	37.9	4.9

SIC 44 WATER TRANSPORTATION
(NO BREAKDOWN)
2002 (90 Establishments)

	$	%
Cash	579,479	10.0
Accounts Receivable	979,319	16.9
Notes Receivable	17,384	0.3
Inventory	388,251	6.7
Other Current	318,714	5.5
Total Current	**2,283,147**	**39.4**
Fixed Assets	2,694,577	46.5
Other Non-current	817,065	14.1
Total Assets	**5,794,789**	**100.0**
Accounts Payable	533,121	9.2
Bank Loans	75,332	1.3
Notes Payable	260,766	4.5
Other Current	869,218	15.0
Total Current	**1,738,437**	**30.0**
Other Long Term	1,622,541	28.0
Deferred Credits	28,974	0.5
Net Worth	2,404,837	41.5
Total Liab & Net Worth	**5,794,789**	**100.0**
Net Sales	5,877,068	100.0
Gross Profit	2,339,073	39.8
Net Profit After Tax	352,624	6.0
Working Capital	544,710	—

RATIOS	UQ	MED	LQ
SOLVENCY			
Quick Ratio (times)	1.8	0.9	0.5
Current Ratio (times)	2.8	1.5	1.0
Curr Liab To Nw (%)	15.5	42.2	138.7
Curr Liab To Inv (%)	134.9	262.7	717.5
Total Liab To Nw (%)	51.6	125.8	341.8
Fixed Assets To Nw (%)	37.7	104.5	185.0
EFFICIENCY			
Coll Period (days)	23.8	46.7	74.0
Sales To Inv (times)	47.8	22.3	8.8
Assets To Sales (%)	51.6	98.6	179.8
Sales To Nwc (times)	16.2	7.2	4.7
Acct Pay To Sales (%)	2.3	5.0	9.7
PROFITABILITY			
Return On Sales (%)	10.3	4.6	0.6
Return On Assets (%)	11.3	4.4	0.7
Return On Nw (%)	25.9	9.2	3.0

SIC 4412 DPSEA FRGN TRNS FRT
(NO BREAKDOWN)
2002 (11 Establishments)

	$	%
Cash	132,542	12.2
Accounts Receivable	382,417	35.2
Notes Receivable	0	0.0
Inventory	1,086	0.1
Other Current	116,246	10.7
Total Current	**632,291**	**58.2**
Fixed Assets	330,269	30.4
Other Non-current	123,851	11.4
Total Assets	**1,086,411**	**100.0**
Accounts Payable	286,813	26.4
Bank Loans	0	0.0
Notes Payable	27,160	2.5
Other Current	283,553	26.1
Total Current	**597,526**	**55.0**
Other Long Term	281,381	25.9
Deferred Credits	10,864	1.0
Net Worth	196,640	18.1
Total Liab & Net Worth	**1,086,411**	**100.0**
Net Sales	2,061,501	100.0
Gross Profit	717,402	34.8
Net Profit After Tax	14,431	0.7
Working Capital	34,765	—

RATIOS	UQ	MED	LQ
SOLVENCY			
Quick Ratio (times)	1.4	0.8	0.7
Current Ratio (times)	1.7	1.1	0.9
Curr Liab To Nw (%)	55.3	160.2	456.6
Curr Liab To Inv (%)	999.9	999.9	999.9
Total Liab To Nw (%)	159.5	397.7	626.8
Fixed Assets To Nw (%)	25.4	46.7	209.2
EFFICIENCY			
Coll Period (days)	50.8	73.4	128.7
Sales To Inv (times)	230.9	148.0	65.1
Assets To Sales (%)	38.1	52.7	99.5
Sales To Nwc (times)	17.0	12.4	4.3
Acct Pay To Sales (%)	5.9	17.6	27.9
PROFITABILITY			
Return On Sales (%)	4.4	0.3	(6.6)
Return On Assets (%)	10.9	0.5	(10.9)
Return On Nw (%)	87.4	2.3	(22.5)

SIC 4449 WTR TRANS FRHT, NEC
(NO BREAKDOWN)
2002 (11 Establishments)

	$	%
Cash	1,469,808	10.0
Accounts Receivable	3,380,557	23.0
Notes Receivable	0	0.0
Inventory	308,660	2.1
Other Current	778,998	5.3
Total Current	**5,938,023**	**40.4**
Fixed Assets	7,878,169	53.6
Other Non-current	881,884	6.0
Total Assets	**14,698,076**	**100.0**
Accounts Payable	1,778,467	12.1
Bank Loans	0	0.0
Notes Payable	249,867	1.7
Other Current	2,072,429	14.1
Total Current	**4,100,763**	**27.9**
Other Long Term	4,350,631	29.6
Deferred Credits	44,094	0.3
Net Worth	6,202,588	42.2
Total Liab & Net Worth	**14,698,076**	**100.0**
Net Sales	17,051,132	100.0
Gross Profit	5,439,311	31.9
Net Profit After Tax	1,040,119	6.1
Working Capital	1,837,260	—

RATIOS	UQ	MED	LQ
SOLVENCY			
Quick Ratio (times)	1.8	1.1	0.8
Current Ratio (times)	2.2	1.8	1.0
Curr Liab To Nw (%)	20.5	42.2	74.9
Curr Liab To Inv (%)	373.9	793.4	999.9
Total Liab To Nw (%)	80.6	141.4	549.5
Fixed Assets To Nw (%)	74.6	104.5	281.9
EFFICIENCY			
Coll Period (days)	40.2	46.7	63.9
Sales To Inv (times)	107.2	48.4	14.1
Assets To Sales (%)	49.0	86.2	169.0
Sales To Nwc (times)	15.1	6.6	4.7
Acct Pay To Sales (%)	3.9	7.0	7.8
PROFITABILITY			
Return On Sales (%)	9.0	4.6	1.7
Return On Assets (%)	8.2	4.5	3.5
Return On Nw (%)	35.3	9.6	8.5

Balance Sheet / Income ($ and %)

	SIC 4492 TOWING TUGBOAT SVCE (14 Est.) $	%	SIC 4493 MARINAS (20 Est.) $	%	SIC 4499 WTR TRANS SRVC,NEC (16 Est.) $	%	SIC 45 TRANS BY AIR (155 Est.) $	%
Cash	1,026,447	14.1	163,055	8.4	3,889,421	6.1	488,939	12.5
Accounts Receivable	1,026,447	14.1	116,468	6.0	16,322,814	25.6	801,860	20.5
Notes Receivable	131,036	1.8	3,882	0.2	0	0.0	31,292	0.8
Inventory	262,072	3.6	452,283	23.3	1,020,176	1.6	391,151	10.0
Other Current	298,469	4.1	34,941	1.8	4,845,835	7.6	309,010	7.9
Total Current	**2,744,471**	**37.7**	**770,629**	**39.7**	**26,078,246**	**40.9**	**2,022,252**	**51.7**
Fixed Assets	3,829,156	52.6	978,330	50.4	15,302,638	24.0	1,505,932	38.5
Other Non-current	706,138	9.7	192,171	9.9	22,380,109	35.1	383,328	9.8
Total Assets	**7,279,765**	**100.0**	**1,941,130**	**100.0**	**63,760,993**	**100.0**	**3,911,512**	**100.0**
Accounts Payable	516,863	7.1	85,410	4.4	4,527,031	7.1	477,204	12.2
Bank Loans	444,066	6.1	0	0.0	318,805	0.5	7,823	0.2
Notes Payable	451,345	6.2	234,877	12.1	191,283	0.3	148,637	3.8
Other Current	647,899	8.9	380,461	19.6	7,268,753	11.4	848,799	21.7
Total Current	**2,060,173**	**28.3**	**700,748**	**36.1**	**12,305,872**	**19.3**	**1,482,463**	**37.9**
Other Long Term	2,620,716	36.0	498,870	25.7	6,121,055	9.6	1,263,419	32.3
Deferred Credits	0	0.0	13,588	0.7	0	0.0	31,292	0.8
Net Worth	2,598,876	35.7	727,924	37.5	45,334,066	71.1	1,134,338	29.0
Total Liab & Net Worth	**7,279,765**	**100.0**	**1,941,130**	**100.0**	**63,760,993**	**100.0**	**3,911,512**	**100.0**
Net Sales	6,893,717	100.0	2,387,614	100.0	70,845,548	100.0	6,959,986	100.0
Gross Profit	1,916,453	27.8	1,169,931	49.0	26,425,389	37.3	2,742,234	39.4
Net Profit After Tax	110,299	1.6	114,605	4.8	9,068,230	12.8	0	0.0
Working Capital	684,298	—	69,881	—	13,772,374	—	539,789	—

RATIOS

	SIC 4492 UQ	MED	LQ	SIC 4493 UQ	MED	LQ	SIC 4499 UQ	MED	LQ	SIC 45 UQ	MED	LQ
SOLVENCY												
Quick Ratio (times)	1.9	1.3	0.9	1.3	0.4	0.2	3.9	1.5	0.9	1.7	0.9	0.4
Current Ratio (times)	2.8	1.9	1.4	2.4	1.4	1.1	6.5	3.9	1.4	2.9	1.6	0.9
Curr Liab To Nw (%)	15.9	23.6	113.2	25.5	73.5	239.2	3.0	14.2	53.2	17.1	67.1	182.7
Curr Liab To Inv (%)	258.6	494.0	650.1	102.8	182.6	243.1	4.5	64.4	194.2	136.6	347.7	999.9
Total Liab To Nw (%)	38.8	128.4	256.1	98.2	142.5	309.9	4.7	15.1	139.8	65.5	137.5	327.9
Fixed Assets To Nw (%)	63.9	163.2	188.9	86.0	128.0	252.8	16.4	23.3	34.6	28.2	93.1	199.1
EFFICIENCY												
Coll Period (days)	37.4	56.2	77.2	5.1	10.2	25.4	64.2	77.8	90.9	19.4	32.1	56.6
Sales To Inv (times)	37.5	29.8	16.9	19.4	9.2	3.3	30.5	21.8	12.3	51.6	21.0	8.3
Assets To Sales (%)	59.1	105.6	180.7	69.9	81.3	124.3	35.3	90.0	327.4	30.7	56.2	99.2
Sales To Nwc (times)	11.6	6.1	4.7	15.4	9.0	5.0	22.9	7.0	4.7	18.9	7.8	3.6
Acct Pay To Sales (%)	3.2	7.1	10.3	0.9	2.4	4.2	1.9	5.1	9.6	2.3	5.0	8.5
PROFITABILITY												
Return On Sales (%)	9.5	1.6	(6.5)	6.7	4.0	0.9	17.2	6.2	(1.0)	4.3	1.2	(1.4)
Return On Assets (%)	8.2	3.6	(5.1)	11.1	3.8	0.9	17.4	9.5	(1.2)	11.0	2.6	(1.4)
Return On Nw (%)	26.3	12.1	2.2	23.3	15.7	5.2	24.1	9.5	(2.0)	35.1	9.1	0.0

Column headings:
- SIC 4492 TOWING TUGBOAT SVCE (NO BREAKDOWN) 2002 (14 Establishments)
- SIC 4493 MARINAS (NO BREAKDOWN) 2002 (20 Establishments)
- SIC 4499 WTR TRANS SRVC,NEC (NO BREAKDOWN) 2002 (16 Establishments)
- SIC 45 TRANS BY AIR (NO BREAKDOWN) 2002 (155 Establishments)

	SIC 4512 AIR TRANS, SCHEDULED (NO BREAKDOWN) 2002 (26 Establishments)		SIC 4513 AIR COURIER SVCS (NO BREAKDOWN) 2002 (11 Establishments)		SIC 4522 AIR TRANS, NONSCHED (NO BREAKDOWN) 2002 (45 Establishments)		SIC 4581 ARPTS, FLY FLDS, SVCS (NO BREAKDOWN) 2002 (73 Establishments)	
	$	%	$	%	$	%	$	%
Cash	3,454,771	14.7	269,173	11.0	583,602	14.3	279,293	10.8
Accounts Receivable	2,420,690	10.3	876,037	35.8	836,632	20.5	566,343	21.9
Notes Receivable	117,509	0.5	61,176	2.5	36,730	0.9	15,516	0.6
Inventory	752,059	3.2	19,576	0.8	281,598	6.9	403,423	15.6
Other Current	2,373,685	10.1	252,044	10.3	293,842	7.2	183,609	7.1
Total Current	**9,118,714**	**38.8**	**1,478,006**	**60.4**	**2,032,404**	**49.8**	**1,448,184**	**56.0**
Fixed Assets	11,069,367	47.1	623,993	25.5	1,754,887	43.0	894,771	34.6
Other Non-current	3,313,760	14.1	345,031	14.1	293,841	7.2	243,087	9.4
Total Assets	**23,501,841**	**100.0**	**2,447,030**	**100.0**	**4,081,132**	**100.0**	**2,586,042**	**100.0**
Accounts Payable	2,796,719	11.9	482,065	19.7	546,872	13.4	271,534	10.5
Bank Loans	0	0.0	0	0.0	8,162	0.2	10,344	0.4
Notes Payable	329,026	1.4	166,398	6.8	151,002	3.7	111,200	4.3
Other Current	5,522,932	23.5	371,949	15.2	938,660	23.0	540,483	20.9
Total Current	**8,648,677**	**36.8**	**1,020,412**	**41.7**	**1,644,696**	**40.3**	**933,561**	**36.1**
Other Long Term	10,740,342	45.7	871,142	35.6	1,465,126	35.9	643,925	24.9
Deferred Credits	282,022	1.2	17,129	0.7	16,325	0.4	23,274	0.9
Net Worth	3,830,800	16.3	538,347	22.0	954,985	23.4	985,282	38.1
Total Liab & Net Worth	**23,501,841**	**100.0**	**2,447,030**	**100.0**	**4,081,132**	**100.0**	**2,586,042**	**100.0**
Net Sales	25,968,885	100.0	8,184,047	100.0	5,507,601	100.0	4,954,103	100.0
Gross Profit	8,128,261	31.3	3,494,588	42.7	2,505,958	45.5	1,847,880	37.3
Net Profit After Tax	(986,818)	(3.8)	229,153	2.8	33,046	0.6	39,633	0.8
Working Capital	470,037	—	457,594	—	387,708	—	514,623	—

RATIOS	SIC 4512			SIC 4513			SIC 4522			SIC 4581		
	UQ	MED	LQ	UQ	MED	LQ	UQ	MED	LQ	UQ	MED	LQ
SOLVENCY												
Quick Ratio (times)	1.4	0.8	0.4	1.5	1.3	1.0	1.4	0.9	0.4	2.1	0.9	0.3
Current Ratio (times)	3.1	1.1	0.7	2.0	1.6	1.3	2.7	1.5	0.9	3.2	1.7	1.0
Curr Liab To Nw (%)	12.1	94.3	756.5	72.4	110.5	185.1	21.2	45.0	321.1	13.7	63.1	123.1
Curr Liab To Inv (%)	241.9	999.9	999.9	999.9	999.9	999.9	197.7	354.4	542.2	110.8	229.7	491.3
Total Liab To Nw (%)	27.7	159.1	999.9	123.7	162.1	305.4	60.0	147.1	343.8	65.5	120.0	239.9
Fixed Assets To Nw (%)	19.2	94.9	343.4	15.5	32.1	52.1	36.7	137.8	212.8	38.3	84.9	182.3
EFFICIENCY												
Coll Period (days)	17.0	25.2	50.8	10.8	28.5	54.2	26.5	35.2	75.6	20.4	32.1	49.6
Sales To Inv (times)	35.5	20.7	5.8	640.2	186.4	88.5	45.4	28.0	10.3	51.6	13.9	5.9
Assets To Sales (%)	37.2	90.5	217.1	22.3	29.9	59.7	35.5	74.1	124.9	25.3	52.2	81.7
Sales To Nwc (times)	29.6	7.2	3.8	25.8	13.7	8.0	20.2	5.9	3.3	10.4	7.8	3.6
Acct Pay To Sales (%)	2.0	6.9	15.2	2.9	4.8	7.8	3.6	5.9	9.6	1.9	4.4	6.6
PROFITABILITY												
Return On Sales (%)	3.0	0.2	(12.8)	3.4	1.8	0.5	4.7	0.8	(2.3)	4.4	1.7	(0.5)
Return On Assets (%)	8.1	0.7	(1.4)	8.0	4.7	1.3	9.0	2.0	(1.9)	13.0	3.7	(0.7)
Return On Nw (%)	43.2	12.5	0.2	24.0	8.1	1.8	46.8	7.8	(0.5)	29.2	9.4	0.2

	SIC 46 PIPE LINES EX NAT GAS (NO BREAKDOWN) 2002 (14 Establishments) $	%	SIC 47 TRANSPORTATION SVS (NO BREAKDOWN) 2002 (606 Establishments) $	%	SIC 4724 TRAVEL AGENCIES (NO BREAKDOWN) 2002 (62 Establishments) $	%	SIC 4725 TOUR OPERATORS (NO BREAKDOWN) 2002 (28 Establishments) $	%
Cash	21,745,263	2.5	158,808	17.1	217,147	37.6	1,195,090	32.0
Accounts Receivable	114,814,986	13.2	404,915	43.6	112,038	19.4	448,159	12.0
Notes Receivable	0	0.0	5,572	0.6	2,310	0.4	0	0.0
Inventory	22,615,073	2.6	10,216	1.1	12,705	2.2	41,081	1.1
Other Current	101,767,828	11.7	110,515	11.9	80,853	14.0	571,402	15.3
Total Current	**260,943,150**	**30.0**	**690,026**	**74.3**	**425,053**	**73.6**	**2,255,732**	**60.4**
Fixed Assets	483,614,638	55.6	165,309	17.8	92,403	16.0	1,083,050	29.0
Other Non-current	125,252,712	14.4	73,368	7.9	60,062	10.4	395,873	10.6
Total Assets	**869,810,500**	**100.0**	**928,703**	**100.0**	**577,518**	**100.0**	**3,734,655**	**100.0**
Accounts Payable	133,081,007	15.3	257,251	27.7	94,135	16.3	608,749	16.3
Bank Loans	0	0.0	4,644	0.5	1,733	0.3	0	0.0
Notes Payable	0	0.0	27,861	3.0	17,326	3.0	190,467	5.1
Other Current	72,194,271	8.3	259,107	27.9	303,196	52.5	1,243,640	33.3
Total Current	**205,275,278**	**23.6**	**548,863**	**59.1**	**416,390**	**72.1**	**2,042,856**	**54.7**
Other Long Term	346,184,578	39.8	128,162	13.8	56,020	9.7	825,359	22.1
Deferred Credits	869,811	0.1	1,857	0.2	2,310	0.4	18,673	0.5
Net Worth	317,480,833	36.5	249,821	26.9	102,798	17.8	847,767	22.7
Total Liab & Net Worth	**869,810,500**	**100.0**	**928,703**	**100.0**	**577,518**	**100.0**	**3,734,655**	**100.0**
Net Sales	356,333,675	100.0	5,074,880	100.0	5,397,364	100.0	14,879,104	100.0
Gross Profit	120,797,116	33.9	1,238,271	24.4	901,360	16.7	3,556,106	23.9
Net Profit After Tax	61,289,392	17.2	111,647	2.2	10,795	0.2	476,131	3.2
Working Capital	55,667,872	—	141,163	—	8,663	—	212,876	—

RATIOS	UQ	MED	LQ	UQ	MED	LQ	UQ	MED	LQ	UQ	MED	LQ
SOLVENCY												
Quick Ratio (times)	0.8	0.8	0.6	2.1	1.3	0.9	2.2	1.1	0.5	1.5	1.0	0.7
Current Ratio (times)	1.6	1.1	0.9	2.4	1.5	1.1	2.5	1.3	0.9	2.1	1.1	0.7
Curr Liab To Nw (%)	23.8	69.6	167.3	43.0	108.3	254.1	38.5	99.0	236.8	93.4	174.4	455.5
Curr Liab To Inv (%)	426.1	999.9	999.9	291.2	937.3	999.9	924.5	999.9	999.9	327.5	999.9	999.9
Total Liab To Nw (%)	144.5	195.0	264.7	62.7	137.0	320.7	38.5	130.2	253.4	101.0	203.4	475.6
Fixed Assets To Nw (%)	123.5	193.2	288.1	8.2	27.6	69.8	8.8	24.0	64.0	23.2	55.3	96.2
EFFICIENCY												
Coll Period (days)	31.6	41.3	48.4	22.3	36.9	51.1	1.8	5.0	21.9	4.8	11.0	31.3
Sales To Inv (times)	123.5	63.9	29.4	444.5	98.2	28.0	891.6	329.2	83.4	230.6	190.8	87.0
Assets To Sales (%)	178.0	244.1	348.5	11.7	18.3	31.8	4.6	10.7	23.5	17.1	25.1	47.1
Sales To Nwc (times)	37.1	5.0	3.8	40.4	16.8	8.7	112.4	29.8	13.6	48.7	14.2	8.3
Acct Pay To Sales (%)	5.7	8.8	19.5	2.5	6.0	9.1	0.3	1.1	3.0	0.6	3.6	7.4
PROFITABILITY												
Return On Sales (%)	25.9	16.6	6.6	3.8	1.1	0.1	2.2	0.4	(0.1)	3.6	0.9	0.4
Return On Assets (%)	8.0	6.2	3.8	18.4	5.5	3.8	18.0	4.9	(1.0)	18.7	8.5	1.3
Return On Nw (%)	22.8	18.7	13.3	47.1	17.0	4.0	49.4	13.6	2.0	40.0	25.1	4.7

SIC 4731 — FRGT TRANS ARNGMNT (NO BREAKDOWN) — 2002 (460 Establishments)

	$	%
Cash	128,594	14.0
Accounts Receivable	466,611	50.8
Notes Receivable	5,511	0.6
Inventory	3,674	0.4
Other Current	111,141	12.1
Total Current	**715,531**	**77.9**
Fixed Assets	135,942	14.8
Other Non-current	67,052	7.3
Total Assets	**918,525**	**100.0**
Accounts Payable	283,824	30.9
Bank Loans	5,511	0.6
Notes Payable	18,371	2.0
Other Current	176,357	19.2
Total Current	**484,063**	**52.7**
Other Long Term	116,652	12.7
Deferred Credits	919	0.1
Net Worth	316,891	34.5
Total Liab & Net Worth	**918,525**	**100.0**
Net Sales	5,189,407	100.0
Gross Profit	1,235,079	23.8
Net Profit After Tax	114,167	2.2
Working Capital	231,468	—

RATIOS	UQ	MED	LQ
SOLVENCY			
Quick Ratio (times)	2.0	1.3	1.0
Current Ratio (times)	2.3	1.5	1.1
Curr Liab To Nw (%)	50.2	109.7	250.8
Curr Liab To Inv (%)	422.1	989.1	999.9
Total Liab To Nw (%)	68.1	136.8	318.7
Fixed Assets To Nw (%)	7.5	24.2	62.6
EFFICIENCY			
Coll Period (days)	27.0	39.1	54.4
Sales To Inv (times)	679.5	108.6	55.8
Assets To Sales (%)	12.2	17.7	27.1
Sales To Nwc (times)	37.4	17.5	9.0
Acct Pay To Sales (%)	3.8	6.6	9.3
PROFITABILITY			
Return On Sales (%)	3.7	1.2	0.2
Return On Assets (%)	19.9	6.1	1.1
Return On Nw (%)	50.7	18.6	4.7

SIC 4783 — PACKING AND CRATING (NO BREAKDOWN) — 2002 (24 Establishments)

	$	%
Cash	98,639	11.2
Accounts Receivable	314,413	35.7
Notes Receivable	15,853	1.8
Inventory	81,906	9.3
Other Current	62,531	7.1
Total Current	**573,342**	**65.1**
Fixed Assets	241,314	27.4
Other Non-current	66,053	7.5
Total Assets	**880,709**	**100.0**
Accounts Payable	192,875	21.9
Bank Loans	0	0.0
Notes Payable	37,870	4.3
Other Current	95,998	10.9
Total Current	**326,743**	**37.1**
Other Long Term	131,226	14.9
Deferred Credits	0	0.0
Net Worth	422,740	48.0
Total Liab & Net Worth	**880,709**	**100.0**
Net Sales	2,380,295	100.0
Gross Profit	980,682	41.2
Net Profit After Tax	78,550	3.3
Working Capital	246,599	—

RATIOS	UQ	MED	LQ
SOLVENCY			
Quick Ratio (times)	3.0	1.4	0.7
Current Ratio (times)	4.7	1.8	1.1
Curr Liab To Nw (%)	11.4	62.9	237.5
Curr Liab To Inv (%)	124.1	350.5	496.6
Total Liab To Nw (%)	11.4	62.9	277.9
Fixed Assets To Nw (%)	24.4	47.6	60.8
EFFICIENCY			
Coll Period (days)	32.1	39.3	52.9
Sales To Inv (times)	69.3	39.7	14.9
Assets To Sales (%)	27.2	37.0	51.1
Sales To Nwc (times)	14.0	9.6	4.3
Acct Pay To Sales (%)	2.6	7.5	12.9
PROFITABILITY			
Return On Sales (%)	4.4	0.3	(0.5)
Return On Assets (%)	8.7	0.3	(1.1)
Return On Nw (%)	28.3	5.4	(1.1)

SIC 4789 — TRANS SRVCS, NEC (NO BREAKDOWN) — 2002 (20 Establishments)

	$	%
Cash	276,862	10.8
Accounts Receivable	574,233	22.4
Notes Receivable	0	0.0
Inventory	156,376	6.1
Other Current	176,884	6.9
Total Current	**1,184,355**	**46.2**
Fixed Assets	1,089,505	42.5
Other Non-current	289,680	11.3
Total Assets	**2,563,540**	**100.0**
Accounts Payable	538,343	21.0
Bank Loans	0	0.0
Notes Payable	548,598	21.4
Other Current	4,478,504	174.7
Total Current	**5,565,445**	**217.1**
Other Long Term	466,565	18.2
Deferred Credits	10,254	0.4
Net Worth	(3,478,724)	(135.7)
Total Liab & Net Worth	**2,563,540**	**100.0**
Net Sales	3,427,193	100.0
Gross Profit	928,769	27.1
Net Profit After Tax	44,554	1.3
Working Capital	(4,381,090)	—

RATIOS	UQ	MED	LQ
SOLVENCY			
Quick Ratio (times)	2.8	1.2	0.7
Current Ratio (times)	3.8	1.9	1.0
Curr Liab To Nw (%)	15.4	54.7	93.4
Curr Liab To Inv (%)	206.0	573.4	999.9
Total Liab To Nw (%)	29.4	64.8	280.8
Fixed Assets To Nw (%)	35.1	54.9	93.0
EFFICIENCY			
Coll Period (days)	18.1	44.6	68.6
Sales To Inv (times)	766.0	11.0	7.7
Assets To Sales (%)	39.5	74.8	105.5
Sales To Nwc (times)	42.6	8.6	3.0
Acct Pay To Sales (%)	1.2	4.6	6.8
PROFITABILITY			
Return On Sales (%)	4.8	1.4	(1.6)
Return On Assets (%)	8.0	3.0	(2.1)
Return On Nw (%)	15.7	9.7	0.3

SIC 48 — COMMUNICATION (NO BREAKDOWN) — 2002 (749 Establishments)

	$	%
Cash	1,064,083	17.4
Accounts Receivable	996,813	16.3
Notes Receivable	24,462	0.4
Inventory	232,386	3.8
Other Current	593,195	9.7
Total Current	**2,910,939**	**47.6**
Fixed Assets	2,054,780	33.6
Other Non-current	1,149,699	18.8
Total Assets	**6,115,418**	**100.0**
Accounts Payable	2,758,054	45.1
Bank Loans	18,346	0.3
Notes Payable	813,351	13.3
Other Current	3,626,442	59.3
Total Current	**7,216,193**	**118.0**
Other Long Term	1,638,932	26.8
Deferred Credits	55,039	0.9
Net Worth	(2,794,746)	(45.7)
Total Liab & Net Worth	**6,115,418**	**100.0**
Net Sales	6,554,574	100.0
Gross Profit	3,060,986	46.7
Net Profit After Tax	(85,209)	(1.3)
Working Capital	(4,305,254)	—

RATIOS	UQ	MED	LQ
SOLVENCY			
Quick Ratio (times)	1.9	0.9	0.4
Current Ratio (times)	2.9	1.4	0.7
Curr Liab To Nw (%)	15.2	39.1	120.0
Curr Liab To Inv (%)	297.6	831.4	999.9
Total Liab To Nw (%)	31.5	104.4	240.2
Fixed Assets To Nw (%)	23.4	63.2	155.1
EFFICIENCY			
Coll Period (days)	21.9	42.0	65.0
Sales To Inv (times)	118.2	39.2	16.6
Assets To Sales (%)	34.0	93.3	250.2
Sales To Nwc (times)	12.3	5.3	2.2
Acct Pay To Sales (%)	3.3	6.5	13.2
PROFITABILITY			
Return On Sales (%)	9.1	1.0	(28.8)
Return On Assets (%)	13.3	1.3	(21.0)
Return On Nw (%)	37.2	7.5	(10.9)

SIC 4812 RDIO TELPHON COMM (NO BREAKDOWN) 2002 (98 Establishments)

	$	%
Cash	815,687	16.5
Accounts Receivable	954,107	19.3
Notes Receivable	4,944	0.1
Inventory	439,977	8.9
Other Current	336,161	6.8
Total Current	**2,550,876**	**51.6**
Fixed Assets	1,542,390	31.2
Other Non-current	850,293	17.2
Total Assets	**4,943,559**	**100.0**
Accounts Payable	919,502	18.6
Bank Loans	14,831	0.3
Notes Payable	74,153	1.5
Other Current	1,161,736	23.5
Total Current	**2,170,222**	**43.9**
Other Long Term	1,310,043	26.5
Deferred Credits	24,718	0.5
Net Worth	1,438,576	29.1
Total Liab & Net Worth	**4,943,559**	**100.0**
Net Sales	7,185,406	100.0
Gross Profit	3,578,332	49.8
Net Profit After Tax	301,787	4.2
Working Capital	380,654	—

RATIOS	UQ	MED	LQ
SOLVENCY			
Quick Ratio (times)	2.1	1.0	0.6
Current Ratio (times)	3.1	1.6	0.9
Curr Liab To Nw (%)	22.0	61.4	162.8
Curr Liab To Inv (%)	158.1	592.7	999.9
Total Liab To Nw (%)	38.4	123.0	319.3
Fixed Assets To Nw (%)	21.2	46.1	164.4
EFFICIENCY			
Coll Period (days)	22.3	40.6	70.8
Sales To Inv (times)	66.3	26.9	14.0
Assets To Sales (%)	29.7	68.8	217.8
Sales To Nwc (times)	16.0	6.9	3.6
Acct Pay To Sales (%)	2.6	5.2	10.7
PROFITABILITY			
Return On Sales (%)	15.0	2.2	(10.9)
Return On Assets (%)	22.1	6.5	(8.1)
Return On Nw (%)	81.1	19.5	(0.2)

SIC 4813 TEL COMM,EXC RDIO (NO BREAKDOWN) 2002 (464 Establishments)

	$	%
Cash	1,007,946	19.3
Accounts Receivable	872,161	16.7
Notes Receivable	20,890	0.4
Inventory	167,121	3.2
Other Current	511,807	9.8
Total Current	**2,579,925**	**49.4**
Fixed Assets	1,859,217	35.6
Other Non-current	783,378	15.0
Total Assets	**5,222,520**	**100.0**
Accounts Payable	3,248,407	62.2
Bank Loans	0	0.0
Notes Payable	1,013,169	19.4
Other Current	4,052,676	77.6
Total Current	**8,314,252**	**159.2**
Other Long Term	1,279,517	24.5
Deferred Credits	52,225	1.0
Net Worth	(4,423,474)	(84.7)
Total Liab & Net Worth	**5,222,520**	**100.0**
Net Sales	6,447,556	100.0
Gross Profit	2,920,743	45.3
Net Profit After Tax	(58,028)	(0.9)
Working Capital	(5,734,327)	—

RATIOS	UQ	MED	LQ
SOLVENCY			
Quick Ratio (times)	1.9	0.9	0.4
Current Ratio (times)	2.8	1.3	0.6
Curr Liab To Nw (%)	16.4	44.2	135.2
Curr Liab To Inv (%)	402.2	899.2	999.9
Total Liab To Nw (%)	35.0	117.4	251.8
Fixed Assets To Nw (%)	26.5	80.2	182.5
EFFICIENCY			
Coll Period (days)	21.9	40.9	61.0
Sales To Inv (times)	137.5	50.5	19.2
Assets To Sales (%)	30.7	81.0	228.5
Sales To Nwc (times)	12.0	4.9	1.8
Acct Pay To Sales (%)	3.6	7.4	14.5
PROFITABILITY			
Return On Sales (%)	9.0	1.1	(30.6)
Return On Assets (%)	12.9	1.5	(38.9)
Return On Nw (%)	33.1	8.3	(14.1)

SIC 4832 RAD BRDCSTG STNS (NO BREAKDOWN) 2002 (37 Establishments)

	$	%
Cash	604,411	8.7
Accounts Receivable	687,778	9.9
Notes Receivable	104,209	1.5
Inventory	27,789	0.4
Other Current	583,569	8.4
Total Current	**2,007,756**	**28.9**
Fixed Assets	2,077,229	29.9
Other Non-current	2,862,268	41.2
Total Assets	**6,947,253**	**100.0**
Accounts Payable	97,262	1.4
Bank Loans	0	0.0
Notes Payable	48,631	0.7
Other Current	1,285,241	18.5
Total Current	**1,431,134**	**20.6**
Other Long Term	1,313,031	18.9
Deferred Credits	55,578	0.8
Net Worth	4,147,510	59.7
Total Liab & Net Worth	**6,947,253**	**100.0**
Net Sales	3,707,179	100.0
Gross Profit	3,099,202	83.6
Net Profit After Tax	(92,679)	(2.5)
Working Capital	576,622	—

RATIOS	UQ	MED	LQ
SOLVENCY			
Quick Ratio (times)	4.2	1.7	0.6
Current Ratio (times)	6.9	2.6	0.9
Curr Liab To Nw (%)	3.8	15.3	32.3
Curr Liab To Inv (%)	548.1	831.4	926.0
Total Liab To Nw (%)	10.5	67.8	125.8
Fixed Assets To Nw (%)	21.7	42.6	60.7
EFFICIENCY			
Coll Period (days)	35.5	64.8	74.0
Sales To Inv (times)	417.5	155.0	41.7
Assets To Sales (%)	80.0	187.4	468.2
Sales To Nwc (times)	9.9	4.1	2.5
Acct Pay To Sales (%)	1.2	2.6	4.6
PROFITABILITY			
Return On Sales (%)	10.3	1.9	(21.2)
Return On Assets (%)	8.9	1.7	(3.0)
Return On Nw (%)	15.0	2.3	(8.7)

SIC 4833 TEL BRDCSTG STNS (NO BREAKDOWN) 2002 (31 Establishments)

	$	%
Cash	1,631,290	9.9
Accounts Receivable	1,367,647	8.3
Notes Receivable	32,955	0.2
Inventory	32,955	0.2
Other Current	1,977,322	12.0
Total Current	**5,042,169**	**30.6**
Fixed Assets	4,366,584	26.5
Other Non-current	7,068,923	42.9
Total Assets	**16,477,676**	**100.0**
Accounts Payable	790,928	4.8
Bank Loans	148,299	0.9
Notes Payable	247,165	1.5
Other Current	2,356,308	14.3
Total Current	**3,542,700**	**21.5**
Other Long Term	5,371,723	32.6
Deferred Credits	82,388	0.5
Net Worth	7,480,865	45.4
Total Liab & Net Worth	**16,477,676**	**100.0**
Net Sales	8,338,905	100.0
Gross Profit	3,969,319	47.6
Net Profit After Tax	(241,828)	(2.9)
Working Capital	1,499,469	—

RATIOS	UQ	MED	LQ
SOLVENCY			
Quick Ratio (times)	1.6	1.2	0.6
Current Ratio (times)	3.1	1.7	1.2
Curr Liab To Nw (%)	9.4	16.5	32.1
Curr Liab To Inv (%)	999.9	999.9	999.9
Total Liab To Nw (%)	20.0	39.6	170.3
Fixed Assets To Nw (%)	30.8	57.6	106.5
EFFICIENCY			
Coll Period (days)	32.5	55.1	74.5
Sales To Inv (times)	144.3	143.0	91.2
Assets To Sales (%)	137.7	197.6	352.7
Sales To Nwc (times)	11.5	5.5	2.1
Acct Pay To Sales (%)	3.0	4.7	14.3
PROFITABILITY			
Return On Sales (%)	4.9	(1.4)	(13.5)
Return On Assets (%)	2.5	(1.2)	(5.5)
Return On Nw (%)	5.0	(0.8)	(6.8)

	SIC 4841 CABLE, PAY TV SVCS (NO BREAKDOWN) 2002 (58 Establishments) $	%	SIC 4899 COMMNCTN SVCS, NEC (NO BREAKDOWN) 2002 (52 Establishments) $	%	SIC 49 ELEC, GAS, SANITARY SV (NO BREAKDOWN) 2002 (869 Establishments) $	%	SIC 4911 ELECTRIC SERVICES (NO BREAKDOWN) 2002 (409 Establishments) $	%
Cash	2,274,241	6.6	356,503	22.6	2,892,923	6.7	3,525,175	4.1
Accounts Receivable	3,376,903	9.8	339,151	21.5	5,094,999	11.8	4,470,954	5.2
Notes Receivable	68,916	0.2	1,577	0.1	215,890	0.5	343,920	0.4
Inventory	1,033,746	3.0	67,830	4.3	949,915	2.2	1,633,618	1.9
Other Current	3,721,484	10.8	211,379	13.4	2,806,566	6.5	4,298,993	5.0
Total Current	**10,475,290**	**30.4**	**976,440**	**61.9**	**11,960,293**	**27.7**	**14,272,660**	**16.6**
Fixed Assets	13,438,694	39.0	384,897	24.4	25,129,569	58.2	56,402,801	65.6
Other Non-current	10,544,207	30.6	216,111	13.7	6,088,092	14.1	15,304,419	17.8
Total Assets	**34,458,191**	**100.0**	**1,577,448**	**100.0**	**43,177,954**	**100.0**	**85,979,880**	**100.0**
Accounts Payable	2,963,404	8.6	671,993	42.6	4,015,550	9.3	3,611,155	4.2
Bank Loans	0	0.0	37,859	2.4	0	0.0	0	0.0
Notes Payable	1,102,662	3.2	134,083	8.5	690,847	1.6	859,799	1.0
Other Current	8,097,675	23.5	1,030,073	65.3	10,103,641	23.4	8,597,988	10.0
Total Current	**12,163,741**	**35.3**	**1,874,008**	**118.8**	**14,810,038**	**34.3**	**13,068,942**	**15.2**
Other Long Term	14,954,855	43.4	550,529	34.9	15,544,064	36.0	36,455,469	42.4
Deferred Credits	516,873	1.5	3,155	0.2	949,915	2.2	2,923,316	3.4
Net Worth	6,822,722	19.8	(850,244)	(53.9)	11,873,937	27.5	33,532,153	39.0
Total Liab & Net Worth	**34,458,191**	**100.0**	**1,577,448**	**100.0**	**43,177,954**	**100.0**	**85,979,880**	**100.0**
Net Sales	16,566,438	100.0	2,878,555	100.0	20,054,786	100.0	35,310,012	100.0
Gross Profit	7,835,925	47.3	1,160,058	40.3	8,122,188	40.5	14,618,345	41.4
Net Profit After Tax	(2,103,938)	(12.7)	(11,514)	(0.4)	1,363,725	6.8	2,118,601	6.0
Working Capital	(1,688,451)	—	(897,568)	—	(2,849,745)	—	1,203,718	—

RATIOS	UQ	MED	LQ	UQ	MED	LQ	UQ	MED	LQ	UQ	MED	LQ
SOLVENCY												
Quick Ratio (times)	0.9	0.5	0.3	1.9	1.2	0.5	1.3	0.7	0.4	1.0	0.6	0.3
Current Ratio (times)	1.9	1.0	0.5	3.2	1.7	0.9	2.1	1.2	0.8	1.8	1.1	0.8
Curr Liab To Nw (%)	7.8	19.4	79.4	21.7	40.6	122.1	13.2	30.4	89.7	14.1	24.1	57.8
Curr Liab To Inv (%)	247.5	871.4	999.9	284.0	618.3	999.9	377.0	808.3	999.9	373.8	682.8	999.9
Total Liab To Nw (%)	16.4	92.2	207.1	34.0	71.2	225.4	72.3	147.6	256.5	95.7	157.1	256.2
Fixed Assets To Nw (%)	22.6	55.0	107.8	12.5	29.4	192.5	91.6	159.1	230.6	134.2	186.2	246.9
EFFICIENCY												
Coll Period (days)	21.7	38.3	52.2	35.0	50.0	69.0	27.0	37.6	55.5	26.3	34.7	47.8
Sales To Inv (times)	56.9	31.3	13.8	110.4	24.5	9.8	66.0	32.6	16.7	54.8	32.2	17.8
Assets To Sales (%)	80.4	208.0	447.2	28.6	54.8	158.6	91.8	215.3	305.6	183.3	243.5	299.8
Sales To Nwc (times)	11.5	4.7	2.9	8.1	4.7	2.5	19.3	8.2	3.3	20.7	9.9	5.1
Acct Pay To Sales (%)	4.4	8.5	18.6	1.4	7.4	12.5	4.7	7.0	10.4	5.5	7.1	9.8
PROFITABILITY												
Return On Sales (%)	2.0	(12.5)	(67.4)	11.3	0.9	(43.8)	10.2	5.8	1.9	10.0	6.7	3.6
Return On Assets (%)	1.0	(2.5)	(18.2)	32.5	1.3	(29.9)	5.1	3.1	1.3	4.2	2.8	1.6
Return On Nw (%)	7.9	(1.1)	(12.1)	55.9	16.2	(10.9)	13.9	8.0	3.7	11.3	7.4	4.6

	SIC 4922 NAT GAS TRNSMSSN (NO BREAKDOWN) 2002 (19 Establishments)		SIC 4923 GAS TRNSMSN DIST (NO BREAKDOWN) 2002 (23 Establishments)		SIC 4924 NTRL GAS DIST (NO BREAKDOWN) 2002 (75 Establishments)		SIC 4931 ELEC,OTHR SVCS COMB (NO BREAKDOWN) 2002 (16 Establishments)	
	$	%	$	%	$	%	$	%
Cash	23,130,464	12.4	7,449,045	7.4	5,057,325	6.2	9,483,701	10.8
Accounts Receivable	24,622,752	13.2	17,515,322	17.4	13,214,301	16.2	3,249,046	3.7
Notes Receivable	1,492,288	0.8	805,302	0.8	815,698	1.0	0	0.0
Inventory	3,544,184	1.9	3,422,534	3.4	2,691,802	3.3	1,844,053	2.1
Other Current	16,042,096	8.6	6,744,405	6.7	8,238,546	10.1	7,990,896	9.1
Total Current	**68,831,784**	**36.9**	**35,936,608**	**35.7**	**30,017,672**	**36.8**	**22,567,696**	**25.7**
Fixed Assets	85,246,952	45.7	55,465,185	55.1	44,455,520	54.5	54,443,469	62.0
Other Non-current	32,457,264	17.4	9,260,975	9.2	7,096,569	8.7	10,800,881	12.3
Total Assets	**186,536,000**	**100.0**	**100,662,768**	**100.0**	**81,569,761**	**100.0**	**87,812,046**	**100.0**
Accounts Payable	38,239,880	20.5	12,985,497	12.9	11,827,615	14.5	3,863,730	4.4
Bank Loans	1,305,752	0.7	100,663	0.1	0	0.0	0	0.0
Notes Payable	1,492,288	0.8	1,711,267	1.7	1,305,116	1.6	702,496	0.8
Other Current	29,472,688	15.8	13,992,125	13.9	10,848,779	13.3	14,313,364	16.3
Total Current	**70,510,608**	**37.8**	**28,789,552**	**28.6**	**23,981,510**	**29.4**	**18,879,590**	**21.5**
Other Long Term	41,784,064	22.4	23,655,750	23.5	18,516,335	22.7	17,650,221	20.1
Deferred Credits	2,424,968	1.3	2,315,244	2.3	2,120,814	2.6	1,668,429	1.9
Net Worth	71,816,360	38.5	45,902,222	45.6	36,951,102	45.3	49,613,806	56.5
Total Liab & Net Worth	**186,536,000**	**100.0**	**100,662,768**	**100.0**	**81,569,761**	**100.0**	**87,812,046**	**100.0**
Net Sales	44,980,950	100.0	65,965,117	100.0	45,041,282	100.0	44,171,049	100.0
Gross Profit	15,428,466	34.3	18,536,198	28.1	16,349,985	36.3	13,295,486	30.1
Net Profit After Tax	6,072,428	13.5	4,749,488	7.2	1,531,404	3.4	1,634,329	3.7
Working Capital	(1,678,824)	—	7,147,056	—	6,036,162	—	3,688,106	—

RATIOS	UQ	MED	LQ	UQ	MED	LQ	UQ	MED	LQ	UQ	MED	LQ
SOLVENCY												
Quick Ratio (times)	1.0	0.7	0.1	1.3	0.6	0.3	1.2	0.6	0.3	1.7	0.9	0.4
Current Ratio (times)	1.2	1.1	1.0	2.0	1.2	0.9	1.9	1.1	0.8	4.0	2.0	1.0
Curr Liab To Nw (%)	23.8	123.6	212.1	12.4	60.1	252.6	17.3	55.6	101.1	7.7	9.3	43.7
Curr Liab To Inv (%)	999.9	999.9	999.9	242.8	503.7	999.9	299.3	735.3	999.9	229.3	371.2	767.7
Total Liab To Nw (%)	86.9	227.3	390.4	38.5	209.5	324.2	48.1	169.4	260.1	24.8	67.6	108.9
Fixed Assets To Nw (%)	84.3	131.5	262.3	69.8	121.5	232.1	85.9	129.7	212.5	71.8	99.0	137.2
EFFICIENCY												
Coll Period (days)	34.0	53.0	157.7	25.9	36.9	58.8	27.4	38.7	58.4	29.9	33.8	44.9
Sales To Inv (times)	354.1	17.1	12.3	30.3	17.7	12.7	42.1	19.6	10.0	37.5	20.9	11.9
Assets To Sales (%)	50.8	414.7	760.4	86.4	152.6	283.1	126.5	181.1	227.3	125.7	198.8	395.0
Sales To Nwc (times)	54.5	20.5	3.6	39.3	13.5	1.7	23.1	6.6	3.3	10.1	3.6	1.9
Acct Pay To Sales (%)	7.6	14.7	26.5	2.0	6.4	11.3	6.7	8.7	14.3	6.0	8.3	10.4
PROFITABILITY												
Return On Sales (%)	27.2	2.9	(0.2)	9.0	5.5	2.0	8.2	5.5	1.8	6.2	4.0	1.8
Return On Assets (%)	4.7	2.9	0.4	11.3	3.9	2.3	5.1	3.3	1.9	5.2	2.5	0.2
Return On Nw (%)	16.8	11.3	1.2	22.3	10.6	6.6	14.4	8.5	3.7	10.7	4.2	2.2

Page 112

	SIC 4941 WATER SUPPLY (90 Establishments) $	%	SIC 4953 REFUSE SYSTEMS (122 Establishments) $	%	SIC 4959 SANITARY SVCS,NEC (70 Establishments) $	%	SIC 50 WHOLESALE TRADE (1525 Establishments) $	%
Cash	2,825,987	7.5	293,843	10.4	129,790	9.9	185,514	11.5
Accounts Receivable	1,431,833	3.8	692,225	24.5	445,743	34.0	498,467	30.9
Notes Receivable	0	0.0	8,476	0.3	23,598	1.8	8,066	0.5
Inventory	150,719	0.4	98,889	3.5	31,464	2.4	533,957	33.1
Other Current	2,110,070	5.6	163,874	5.8	149,455	11.4	96,790	6.0
Total Current	**6,518,609**	**17.3**	**1,257,307**	**44.5**	**780,050**	**59.5**	**1,322,794**	**82.0**
Fixed Assets	26,526,594	70.4	1,251,657	44.3	462,786	35.3	208,098	12.9
Other Non-current	4,634,618	12.3	316,446	11.2	68,173	5.2	82,271	5.1
Total Assets	**37,679,821**	**100.0**	**2,825,410**	**100.0**	**1,311,009**	**100.0**	**1,613,163**	**100.0**
Accounts Payable	1,168,074	3.1	647,019	22.9	211,072	16.1	337,151	20.9
Bank Loans	0	0.0	0	0.0	2,622	0.2	9,679	0.6
Notes Payable	150,719	0.4	73,461	2.6	73,417	5.6	75,819	4.7
Other Current	2,072,391	5.5	2,695,441	95.4	308,087	23.5	330,698	20.5
Total Current	**3,391,184**	**9.0**	**3,415,921**	**120.9**	**595,198**	**45.4**	**753,347**	**46.7**
Other Long Term	10,851,788	28.8	1,254,482	44.4	310,709	23.7	174,222	10.8
Deferred Credits	263,759	0.7	16,952	0.6	1,311	0.1	1,613	0.1
Net Worth	23,173,090	61.5	(1,861,945)	(65.9)	403,791	30.8	683,981	42.4
Total Liab & Net Worth	**37,679,821**	**100.0**	**2,825,410**	**100.0**	**1,311,009**	**100.0**	**1,613,163**	**100.0**
Net Sales	5,244,234	100.0	4,764,604	100.0	3,205,401	100.0	4,716,851	100.0
Gross Profit	2,685,048	51.2	1,882,019	39.5	1,371,912	42.8	1,363,170	28.9
Net Profit After Tax	949,206	18.1	247,759	5.2	118,600	3.7	84,903	1.8
Working Capital	3,127,425	—	(2,158,614)	—	184,852	—	569,447	—

RATIOS	UQ	MED	LQ	UQ	MED	LQ	UQ	MED	LQ	UQ	MED	LQ
SOLVENCY												
Quick Ratio (times)	2.9	1.3	0.5	1.6	1.0	0.5	1.6	1.1	0.6	1.8	1.0	0.6
Current Ratio (times)	4.7	2.3	1.2	1.9	1.2	0.8	2.1	1.4	1.0	3.4	1.9	1.3
Curr Liab To Nw (%)	4.4	8.2	15.0	34.9	88.9	177.6	49.3	106.2	250.4	34.8	86.7	200.4
Curr Liab To Inv (%)	698.8	999.9	999.9	398.7	999.9	999.9	830.5	999.9	999.9	65.6	115.3	216.2
Total Liab To Nw (%)	33.8	58.5	128.6	102.1	177.8	316.3	93.6	198.3	355.9	44.8	111.9	257.7
Fixed Assets To Nw (%)	88.9	119.7	159.5	64.4	128.0	225.7	39.9	81.4	191.9	7.9	20.0	45.3
EFFICIENCY												
Coll Period (days)	27.0	35.8	54.8	32.1	48.9	66.4	35.0	53.0	82.9	24.8	37.2	51.8
Sales To Inv (times)	76.1	49.6	24.6	197.1	92.4	25.4	138.4	55.0	23.1	16.5	8.5	5.0
Assets To Sales (%)	461.5	718.5	931.2	35.0	59.3	88.1	26.0	40.9	59.3	24.9	34.2	48.6
Sales To Nwc (times)	6.8	2.0	1.2	23.4	10.5	4.8	22.2	10.8	5.9	14.1	7.6	4.4
Acct Pay To Sales (%)	3.2	6.2	11.0	3.3	5.7	9.4	3.4	6.1	9.5	3.3	5.9	9.9
PROFITABILITY												
Return On Sales (%)	29.9	11.0	1.1	8.9	3.6	1.2	6.4	3.0	(0.3)	3.3	1.2	0.1
Return On Assets (%)	4.5	2.3	0.1	14.0	5.2	1.6	15.4	6.8	(0.9)	9.5	3.4	0.4
Return On Nw (%)	8.1	3.7	0.2	47.8	19.7	5.8	50.9	17.4	(1.8)	23.9	8.4	1.4

Page 113

Balance Sheet

	SIC 5012 AUTO,OTHR MTR VHCLS (NO BREAKDOWN) 2002 (167 Establishments) $	%	SIC 5013 MTR VHCL SPLS, PRTS (NO BREAKDOWN) 2002 (524 Establishments) $	%	SIC 5014 TIRES AND TUBES (NO BREAKDOWN) 2002 (115 Establishments) $	%	SIC 5015 MTR VHCL PRTS, USED (NO BREAKDOWN) 2002 (23 Establishments) $	%
Cash	422,746	11.3	137,399	9.3	233,211	7.0	79,725	5.7
Accounts Receivable	613,542	16.4	347,190	23.5	972,823	29.2	208,404	14.9
Notes Receivable	14,964	0.4	10,342	0.7	6,663	0.2	8,392	0.6
Inventory	1,690,982	45.2	664,832	45.0	1,246,013	37.4	661,578	47.3
Other Current	216,985	5.8	65,005	4.4	173,243	5.2	39,164	2.8
Total Current	**2,959,219**	**79.1**	**1,224,768**	**82.9**	**2,631,953**	**79.0**	**997,263**	**71.3**
Fixed Assets	591,096	15.8	186,153	12.6	526,391	15.8	296,521	21.2
Other Non-current	190,796	5.1	66,483	4.5	173,242	5.2	104,902	7.5
Total Assets	**3,741,111**	**100.0**	**1,477,404**	**100.0**	**3,331,586**	**100.0**	**1,398,686**	**100.0**
Accounts Payable	482,603	12.9	310,255	21.0	1,092,760	32.8	177,633	12.7
Bank Loans	14,964	0.4	8,864	0.6	0	0.0	0	0.0
Notes Payable	284,324	7.6	56,141	3.8	146,590	4.4	93,712	6.7
Other Current	1,118,593	29.9	228,998	15.5	459,759	13.8	251,764	18.0
Total Current	**1,900,484**	**50.8**	**604,258**	**40.9**	**1,699,109**	**51.0**	**523,109**	**37.4**
Other Long Term	501,309	13.4	189,108	12.8	359,811	10.8	269,946	19.3
Deferred Credits	3,741	0.1	1,477	0.1	3,332	0.1	0	0.0
Net Worth	1,335,577	35.7	682,561	46.2	1,269,334	38.1	605,631	43.3
Total Liab & Net Worth	**3,741,111**	**100.0**	**1,477,404**	**100.0**	**3,331,586**	**100.0**	**1,398,686**	**100.0**
Net Sales	11,167,496	100.0	3,857,452	100.0	9,827,687	100.0	3,642,411	100.0
Gross Profit	2,132,992	19.1	1,207,382	31.3	2,466,749	25.1	1,365,904	37.5
Net Profit After Tax	145,177	1.3	73,292	1.9	216,209	2.2	21,854	0.6
Working Capital	1,058,735	—	620,510	—	932,844	—	474,154	—

RATIOS

	5012 UQ	MED	LQ	5013 UQ	MED	LQ	5014 UQ	MED	LQ	5015 UQ	MED	LQ
SOLVENCY												
Quick Ratio (times)	0.9	0.5	0.2	1.6	0.9	0.5	1.0	0.7	0.5	1.0	0.6	0.2
Current Ratio (times)	2.2	1.5	1.2	4.1	2.2	1.4	2.5	1.5	1.2	3.1	2.0	1.3
Curr Liab To Nw (%)	62.0	147.8	362.3	30.3	75.5	198.3	65.7	152.6	332.6	26.3	72.2	134.5
Curr Liab To Inv (%)	76.0	113.8	161.6	43.5	78.3	132.3	87.5	123.4	175.4	42.6	76.7	117.4
Total Liab To Nw (%)	79.7	200.6	464.8	37.3	96.9	271.1	75.5	170.1	414.4	28.9	86.9	211.5
Fixed Assets To Nw (%)	12.9	37.7	76.9	7.6	18.4	41.8	18.9	42.2	85.7	19.2	27.9	65.4
EFFICIENCY												
Coll Period (days)	9.5	18.3	33.1	24.1	32.5	43.8	27.7	36.1	49.6	9.5	19.7	28.1
Sales To Inv (times)	10.4	6.7	5.1	9.4	5.7	3.6	10.8	6.9	5.5	8.7	7.4	4.7
Assets To Sales (%)	23.3	33.5	46.7	27.8	38.3	53.8	26.1	33.9	44.9	26.6	38.4	50.7
Sales To Nwc (times)	29.3	11.1	6.5	11.4	6.2	3.6	22.1	10.6	6.6	14.7	8.1	5.0
Acct Pay To Sales (%)	1.7	3.0	6.2	4.3	6.5	11.2	6.4	11.7	16.3	1.9	4.0	5.9
PROFITABILITY												
Return On Sales (%)	2.3	0.9	0.1	3.0	1.3	0.2	2.6	1.0	0.3	4.3	2.0	0.4
Return On Assets (%)	5.8	2.2	0.7	7.8	3.0	0.5	6.7	3.1	0.7	9.5	4.9	1.2
Return On Nw (%)	22.6	8.2	2.4	19.0	7.2	1.5	24.5	9.3	2.3	21.6	13.8	4.6

	SIC 5021 FURNITURE (NO BREAKDOWN) 2002 (302 Establishments) $	%	SIC 5023 HOMEFURNISHINGS (NO BREAKDOWN) 2002 (358 Establishments) $	%	SIC 5031 LBR,PLYWD,MILLWRK (NO BREAKDOWN) 2002 (860 Establishments) $	%	SIC 5032 BRCK,STN,RLTD MTRLS (NO BREAKDOWN) 2002 (192 Establishments) $	%
Cash	182,555	13.3	149,700	10.5	220,484	9.5	173,397	10.6
Accounts Receivable	542,173	39.5	503,279	35.3	798,382	34.4	507,105	31.0
Notes Receivable	2,745	0.2	4,277	0.3	11,604	0.5	13,087	0.8
Inventory	326,677	23.8	444,824	31.2	724,114	31.2	448,215	27.4
Other Current	76,865	5.6	89,821	6.3	116,044	5.0	98,149	6.0
Total Current	**1,131,015**	**82.4**	**1,191,901**	**83.6**	**1,870,628**	**80.6**	**1,239,953**	**75.8**
Fixed Assets	177,064	12.9	171,086	12.0	336,527	14.5	341,887	20.9
Other Non-current	64,512	4.7	62,732	4.4	113,724	4.9	53,982	3.3
Total Assets	**1,372,591**	**100.0**	**1,425,719**	**100.0**	**2,320,879**	**100.0**	**1,635,822**	**100.0**
Accounts Payable	300,597	21.9	307,955	21.6	338,848	14.6	359,881	22.0
Bank Loans	13,726	1.0	7,129	0.5	16,246	0.7	6,543	0.4
Notes Payable	49,413	3.6	49,900	3.5	116,044	5.0	50,710	3.1
Other Current	323,932	23.6	312,233	21.9	438,647	18.9	242,102	14.8
Total Current	**687,668**	**50.1**	**677,217**	**47.5**	**909,785**	**39.2**	**659,236**	**40.3**
Other Long Term	113,925	8.3	148,274	10.4	232,087	10.0	194,663	11.9
Deferred Credits	2,745	0.2	1,426	0.1	2,321	0.1	1,636	0.1
Net Worth	568,253	41.4	598,802	42.0	1,176,686	50.7	780,287	47.7
Total Liab & Net Worth	**1,372,591**	**100.0**	**1,425,719**	**100.0**	**2,320,879**	**100.0**	**1,635,822**	**100.0**
Net Sales	5,238,897	100.0	5,020,137	100.0	8,114,962	100.0	4,339,050	100.0
Gross Profit	1,487,847	28.4	1,470,900	29.3	1,760,947	21.7	1,310,393	30.2
Net Profit After Tax	83,822	1.6	110,443	2.2	162,299	2.0	125,832	2.9
Working Capital	443,347	—	514,684	—	960,843	—	580,717	—

RATIOS	UQ	MED	LQ	UQ	MED	LQ	UQ	MED	LQ	UQ	MED	LQ
SOLVENCY												
Quick Ratio (times)	1.7	1.0	0.7	1.6	1.0	0.6	2.2	1.1	0.7	1.8	1.0	0.7
Current Ratio (times)	2.7	1.6	1.2	3.1	1.9	1.2	4.1	2.1	1.4	3.2	2.0	1.4
Curr Liab To Nw (%)	44.3	120.1	239.5	43.2	107.9	240.6	25.9	73.4	181.8	32.8	73.1	154.8
Curr Liab To Inv (%)	89.9	212.3	523.5	80.1	128.9	265.1	58.5	108.6	199.0	69.5	123.4	222.6
Total Liab To Nw (%)	54.9	133.8	262.7	54.0	144.4	293.1	37.1	95.9	225.0	40.3	98.9	224.2
Fixed Assets To Nw (%)	9.4	20.5	53.0	7.9	21.1	45.8	9.4	23.1	49.0	16.0	31.7	73.3
EFFICIENCY												
Coll Period (days)	21.9	36.5	54.8	23.4	36.1	56.2	23.4	33.6	44.5	25.6	39.1	56.2
Sales To Inv (times)	43.8	18.0	7.7	25.9	11.0	6.0	17.1	10.7	6.8	19.8	9.6	5.7
Assets To Sales (%)	18.9	26.2	36.2	21.0	28.4	38.8	20.7	28.6	41.7	27.2	37.7	56.1
Sales To Nwc (times)	23.8	11.8	6.8	17.2	8.7	5.3	17.1	9.0	5.4	11.5	7.2	4.6
Acct Pay To Sales (%)	2.9	5.0	8.8	2.7	5.5	9.0	2.2	3.6	6.0	4.0	6.2	11.0
PROFITABILITY												
Return On Sales (%)	3.6	1.1	0.0	3.3	1.3	0.3	2.9	1.0	0.2	4.5	1.9	0.5
Return On Assets (%)	12.3	4.0	0.2	10.6	4.2	0.9	9.9	3.6	0.8	13.0	5.1	1.5
Return On Nw (%)	30.9	10.1	0.7	30.0	10.6	3.1	21.2	8.4	2.2	29.8	12.8	3.8

	SIC 5033 RFNG,SIDNG,INSULTN (NO BREAKDOWN) 2002 (103 Establishments)		SIC 5039 CONSTR MTRLS, NEC (NO BREAKDOWN) 2002 (84 Establishments)		SIC 5043 PHOTO EQUIP,SPPLS (NO BREAKDOWN) 2002 (47 Establishments)		SIC 5044 OFFICE EQUIPMENT (NO BREAKDOWN) 2002 (228 Establishments)	
	$	%	$	%	$	%	$	%
Cash	185,568	9.9	205,062	15.9	181,610	13.6	140,206	12.4
Accounts Receivable	671,044	35.8	397,227	30.8	393,933	29.5	317,724	28.1
Notes Receivable	5,623	0.3	20,635	1.6	1,335	0.1	7,915	0.7
Inventory	577,323	30.8	254,070	19.7	446,012	33.4	382,173	33.8
Other Current	93,722	5.0	100,596	7.8	89,469	6.7	53,142	4.7
Total Current	**1,533,280**	**81.8**	**977,590**	**75.8**	**1,112,359**	**83.3**	**901,160**	**79.7**
Fixed Assets	283,038	15.1	246,332	19.1	137,543	10.3	151,512	13.4
Other Non-current	58,107	3.1	65,775	5.1	85,463	6.4	78,018	6.9
Total Assets	**1,874,425**	**100.0**	**1,289,697**	**100.0**	**1,335,365**	**100.0**	**1,130,690**	**100.0**
Accounts Payable	447,988	23.9	215,379	16.7	263,067	19.7	205,786	18.2
Bank Loans	0	0.0	5,159	0.4	18,695	1.4	1,131	0.1
Notes Payable	73,103	3.9	49,008	3.8	97,482	7.3	52,012	4.6
Other Current	311,154	16.6	187,007	14.5	243,036	18.2	272,495	24.1
Total Current	**832,245**	**44.4**	**456,553**	**35.4**	**622,280**	**46.6**	**531,424**	**47.0**
Other Long Term	181,819	9.7	184,426	14.3	94,811	7.1	123,245	10.9
Deferred Credits	0	0.0	0	0.0	10,683	0.8	7,915	0.7
Net Worth	860,361	45.9	648,718	50.3	607,591	45.5	468,106	41.4
Total Liab & Net Worth	**1,874,425**	**100.0**	**1,289,697**	**100.0**	**1,335,365**	**100.0**	**1,130,690**	**100.0**
Net Sales	5,697,340	100.0	3,980,546	100.0	4,496,178	100.0	3,385,299	100.0
Gross Profit	1,378,756	24.2	1,241,930	31.2	1,366,838	30.4	1,347,349	39.8
Net Profit After Tax	62,671	1.1	91,553	2.3	13,489	0.3	84,632	2.5
Working Capital	701,035	—	521,037	—	490,079	—	369,736	—

RATIOS	UQ	MED	LQ	UQ	MED	LQ	UQ	MED	LQ	UQ	MED	LQ
SOLVENCY												
Quick Ratio (times)	1.6	1.0	0.7	2.4	1.2	0.6	1.8	0.8	0.6	1.5	0.8	0.5
Current Ratio (times)	2.9	1.8	1.4	3.9	2.1	1.5	2.9	1.7	1.3	2.7	1.8	1.3
Curr Liab To Nw (%)	43.2	86.5	184.9	27.6	60.6	148.0	44.5	121.8	271.2	46.8	92.6	197.1
Curr Liab To Inv (%)	90.7	137.1	193.5	95.4	170.1	342.4	92.5	141.8	179.6	74.2	129.7	212.1
Total Liab To Nw (%)	48.5	109.6	220.2	32.6	92.8	229.7	58.7	129.2	354.1	63.4	112.9	265.0
Fixed Assets To Nw (%)	12.3	28.4	55.4	13.7	24.4	67.1	6.8	24.8	48.6	11.9	26.0	47.7
EFFICIENCY												
Coll Period (days)	28.5	38.5	54.4	25.2	42.2	56.6	20.4	34.3	54.4	23.7	31.8	42.3
Sales To Inv (times)	12.7	9.5	7.0	32.0	15.0	9.6	16.1	11.3	6.3	15.6	9.0	6.2
Assets To Sales (%)	26.2	32.9	40.6	27.9	32.4	42.9	23.7	29.7	43.4	23.9	33.4	42.0
Sales To Nwc (times)	14.9	8.5	5.3	11.3	7.8	5.3	17.6	10.0	6.2	14.5	8.1	5.5
Acct Pay To Sales (%)	5.2	7.9	10.7	2.2	5.7	9.6	3.5	6.1	10.2	2.7	4.9	8.1
PROFITABILITY												
Return On Sales (%)	3.4	1.2	0.4	4.0	1.8	0.6	1.9	0.6	(1.2)	4.2	1.3	0.3
Return On Assets (%)	9.3	4.4	0.9	11.7	5.7	1.5	5.9	1.6	(4.2)	11.3	4.0	0.8
Return On Nw (%)	23.6	9.6	2.3	28.1	10.4	4.0	15.2	4.1	(7.1)	32.9	9.8	2.1

SIC 5045 CMPTRS, PERIPH SFTWR (NO BREAKDOWN) 2002 (646 Establishments)

	$	%
Cash	243,996	19.4
Accounts Receivable	510,631	40.6
Notes Receivable	3,773	0.3
Inventory	213,811	17.0
Other Current	94,328	7.5
Total Current	**1,066,539**	**84.8**
Fixed Assets	127,029	10.1
Other Non-current	64,143	5.1
Total Assets	**1,257,711**	**100.0**
Accounts Payable	353,417	28.1
Bank Loans	8,804	0.7
Notes Payable	60,370	4.8
Other Current	294,304	23.4
Total Current	**716,895**	**57.0**
Other Long Term	93,071	7.4
Deferred Credits	5,031	0.4
Net Worth	442,714	35.2
Total Liab & Net Worth	**1,257,711**	**100.0**
Net Sales	5,218,718	100.0
Gross Profit	1,482,116	28.4
Net Profit After Tax	93,937	1.8
Working Capital	349,644	—

RATIOS	UQ	MED	LQ
SOLVENCY			
Quick Ratio (times)	1.9	1.2	0.7
Current Ratio (times)	2.6	1.6	1.2
Curr Liab To Nw (%)	49.0	123.6	279.2
Curr Liab To Inv (%)	146.1	291.6	809.8
Total Liab To Nw (%)	54.2	148.1	342.8
Fixed Assets To Nw (%)	5.8	15.4	40.2
EFFICIENCY			
Coll Period (days)	20.8	34.3	55.5
Sales To Inv (times)	70.7	28.2	13.4
Assets To Sales (%)	16.2	24.1	37.8
Sales To Nwc (times)	29.0	12.9	6.7
Acct Pay To Sales (%)	2.9	5.6	9.7
PROFITABILITY			
Return On Sales (%)	4.4	1.2	0.1
Return On Assets (%)	17.3	5.5	0.6
Return On Nw (%)	47.4	18.0	3.0

SIC 5046 CMMRCL EQUIP, NEC (NO BREAKDOWN) 2002 (251 Establishments)

	$	%
Cash	120,180	11.8
Accounts Receivable	351,373	34.5
Notes Receivable	6,111	0.6
Inventory	299,431	29.4
Other Current	69,256	6.8
Total Current	**846,351**	**83.1**
Fixed Assets	129,346	12.7
Other Non-current	42,776	4.2
Total Assets	**1,018,473**	**100.0**
Accounts Payable	234,249	23.0
Bank Loans	2,037	0.2
Notes Payable	87,589	8.6
Other Current	214,897	21.1
Total Current	**538,772**	**52.9**
Other Long Term	126,291	12.4
Deferred Credits	0	0.0
Net Worth	353,410	34.7
Total Liab & Net Worth	**1,018,473**	**100.0**
Net Sales	3,372,427	100.0
Gross Profit	1,075,804	31.9
Net Profit After Tax	57,331	1.7
Working Capital	307,579	—

RATIOS	UQ	MED	LQ
SOLVENCY			
Quick Ratio (times)	1.8	1.2	0.7
Current Ratio (times)	3.8	2.1	1.3
Curr Liab To Nw (%)	32.3	74.4	204.6
Curr Liab To Inv (%)	58.7	135.3	252.4
Total Liab To Nw (%)	43.1	110.4	258.7
Fixed Assets To Nw (%)	6.6	17.1	39.1
EFFICIENCY			
Coll Period (days)	23.4	38.7	57.7
Sales To Inv (times)	19.2	10.2	6.5
Assets To Sales (%)	22.6	30.2	40.0
Sales To Nwc (times)	15.9	7.4	4.8
Acct Pay To Sales (%)	3.1	5.6	9.9
PROFITABILITY			
Return On Sales (%)	3.8	1.2	0.0
Return On Assets (%)	12.2	3.7	0.1
Return On Nw (%)	29.6	8.8	0.9

SIC 5047 MEDICAL HOSP EQUIP (NO BREAKDOWN) 2002 (308 Establishments)

	$	%
Cash	150,689	11.4
Accounts Receivable	437,526	33.1
Notes Receivable	5,287	0.4
Inventory	355,573	26.9
Other Current	93,850	7.1
Total Current	**1,042,925**	**78.9**
Fixed Assets	196,953	14.9
Other Non-current	81,953	6.2
Total Assets	**1,321,831**	**100.0**
Accounts Payable	284,194	21.5
Bank Loans	6,609	0.5
Notes Payable	54,195	4.1
Other Current	338,389	25.6
Total Current	**683,387**	**51.7**
Other Long Term	163,907	12.4
Deferred Credits	1,322	0.1
Net Worth	473,215	35.8
Total Liab & Net Worth	**1,321,831**	**100.0**
Net Sales	3,945,764	100.0
Gross Profit	1,436,258	36.4
Net Profit After Tax	138,102	3.5
Working Capital	359,538	—

RATIOS	UQ	MED	LQ
SOLVENCY			
Quick Ratio (times)	1.8	1.1	0.7
Current Ratio (times)	3.1	1.9	1.3
Curr Liab To Nw (%)	36.2	80.2	194.8
Curr Liab To Inv (%)	90.0	147.7	260.4
Total Liab To Nw (%)	51.1	107.4	262.2
Fixed Assets To Nw (%)	10.2	26.1	57.8
EFFICIENCY			
Coll Period (days)	31.0	43.1	64.2
Sales To Inv (times)	16.6	10.7	6.8
Assets To Sales (%)	24.5	33.5	54.9
Sales To Nwc (times)	11.8	7.5	4.6
Acct Pay To Sales (%)	3.5	6.0	11.0
PROFITABILITY			
Return On Sales (%)	6.2	1.9	0.4
Return On Assets (%)	14.6	5.8	1.2
Return On Nw (%)	38.9	15.1	4.1

SIC 5049 PRFSSNL EQUIP, NEC (NO BREAKDOWN) 2002 (134 Establishments)

	$	%
Cash	213,295	16.1
Accounts Receivable	377,572	28.5
Notes Receivable	11,923	0.9
Inventory	397,444	30.0
Other Current	94,062	7.1
Total Current	**1,094,296**	**82.6**
Fixed Assets	160,302	12.1
Other Non-current	70,215	5.3
Total Assets	**1,324,813**	**100.0**
Accounts Payable	270,262	20.4
Bank Loans	15,898	1.2
Notes Payable	45,044	3.4
Other Current	230,517	17.4
Total Current	**561,721**	**42.4**
Other Long Term	149,703	11.3
Deferred Credits	1,325	0.1
Net Worth	612,064	46.2
Total Liab & Net Worth	**1,324,813**	**100.0**
Net Sales	3,561,325	100.0
Gross Profit	1,335,497	37.5
Net Profit After Tax	64,104	1.8
Working Capital	532,575	—

RATIOS	UQ	MED	LQ
SOLVENCY			
Quick Ratio (times)	2.1	1.2	0.6
Current Ratio (times)	3.5	2.0	1.4
Curr Liab To Nw (%)	28.9	72.4	184.0
Curr Liab To Inv (%)	64.5	113.4	236.9
Total Liab To Nw (%)	41.6	86.8	226.7
Fixed Assets To Nw (%)	6.4	20.3	40.1
EFFICIENCY			
Coll Period (days)	20.6	38.0	56.6
Sales To Inv (times)	17.9	8.6	5.3
Assets To Sales (%)	25.7	37.2	57.8
Sales To Nwc (times)	13.2	6.5	4.0
Acct Pay To Sales (%)	3.7	6.0	10.7
PROFITABILITY			
Return On Sales (%)	4.2	1.3	0.0
Return On Assets (%)	10.4	3.9	0.0
Return On Nw (%)	24.9	9.4	0.9

SIC 5051 METLS SVC CNTRS, OFF
(NO BREAKDOWN)
2002 (436 Establishments)

	$	%
Cash	294,894	9.1
Accounts Receivable	1,011,066	31.2
Notes Receivable	29,165	0.9
Inventory	1,098,562	33.9
Other Current	158,789	4.9
Total Current	**2,592,476**	**80.0**
Fixed Assets	492,570	15.2
Other Non-current	155,549	4.8
Total Assets	**3,240,595**	**100.0**
Accounts Payable	615,713	19.0
Bank Loans	22,684	0.7
Notes Payable	204,157	6.3
Other Current	580,067	17.9
Total Current	**1,422,621**	**43.9**
Other Long Term	453,683	14.0
Deferred Credits	9,722	0.3
Net Worth	1,354,569	41.8
Total Liab & Net Worth	**3,240,595**	**100.0**
Net Sales	8,266,824	100.0
Gross Profit	1,967,504	23.8
Net Profit After Tax	140,536	1.7
Working Capital	1,169,855	—

RATIOS	UQ	MED	LQ
SOLVENCY			
Quick Ratio (times)	1.8	0.9	0.5
Current Ratio (times)	3.9	1.9	1.3
Curr Liab To Nw (%)	29.9	91.7	250.1
Curr Liab To Inv (%)	63.0	112.6	183.0
Total Liab To Nw (%)	41.7	132.5	320.6
Fixed Assets To Nw (%)	9.9	24.0	57.1
EFFICIENCY			
Coll Period (days)	31.8	43.1	56.8
Sales To Inv (times)	12.0	7.0	4.6
Assets To Sales (%)	28.8	39.2	55.6
Sales To Nwc (times)	14.4	7.2	3.9
Acct Pay To Sales (%)	3.9	6.4	10.7
PROFITABILITY			
Return On Sales (%)	2.9	1.2	0.2
Return On Assets (%)	6.7	3.0	0.5
Return On Nw (%)	22.0	8.2	1.8

SIC 5063 ELEC APPRATUS, EQUIP
(NO BREAKDOWN)
2002 (755 Establishments)

	$	%
Cash	147,064	10.4
Accounts Receivable	485,029	34.3
Notes Receivable	2,828	0.2
Inventory	455,333	32.2
Other Current	89,087	6.3
Total Current	**1,179,341**	**83.4**
Fixed Assets	164,033	11.6
Other Non-current	70,704	5.0
Total Assets	**1,414,078**	**100.0**
Accounts Payable	304,027	21.5
Bank Loans	7,070	0.5
Notes Payable	53,735	3.8
Other Current	222,010	15.7
Total Current	**586,842**	**41.5**
Other Long Term	144,236	10.2
Deferred Credits	1,414	0.1
Net Worth	681,586	48.2
Total Liab & Net Worth	**1,414,078**	**100.0**
Net Sales	4,098,777	100.0
Gross Profit	1,209,139	29.5
Net Profit After Tax	94,272	2.3
Working Capital	592,499	—

RATIOS	UQ	MED	LQ
SOLVENCY			
Quick Ratio (times)	1.8	1.1	0.7
Current Ratio (times)	3.4	2.1	1.5
Curr Liab To Nw (%)	35.4	76.8	157.6
Curr Liab To Inv (%)	63.1	109.1	186.6
Total Liab To Nw (%)	42.6	94.4	200.5
Fixed Assets To Nw (%)	6.9	16.7	35.9
EFFICIENCY			
Coll Period (days)	32.1	43.4	55.5
Sales To Inv (times)	13.5	8.1	5.4
Assets To Sales (%)	27.0	34.5	44.7
Sales To Nwc (times)	11.4	6.6	4.2
Acct Pay To Sales (%)	4.8	7.0	10.0
PROFITABILITY			
Return On Sales (%)	3.4	1.4	0.2
Return On Assets (%)	9.7	3.9	0.5
Return On Nw (%)	22.3	8.6	1.3

SIC 5064 ELEC APPL, TEL, RADIO
(NO BREAKDOWN)
2002 (166 Establishments)

	$	%
Cash	276,244	11.3
Accounts Receivable	721,167	29.5
Notes Receivable	2,445	0.1
Inventory	909,404	37.2
Other Current	176,013	7.2
Total Current	**2,085,273**	**85.3**
Fixed Assets	227,351	9.3
Other Non-current	132,010	5.4
Total Assets	**2,444,634**	**100.0**
Accounts Payable	574,489	23.5
Bank Loans	17,112	0.7
Notes Payable	124,676	5.1
Other Current	457,147	18.7
Total Current	**1,173,424**	**48.0**
Other Long Term	173,569	7.1
Deferred Credits	7,334	0.3
Net Worth	1,090,307	44.6
Total Liab & Net Worth	**2,444,634**	**100.0**
Net Sales	8,068,099	100.0
Gross Profit	1,952,480	24.2
Net Profit After Tax	193,634	2.4
Working Capital	911,849	—

RATIOS	UQ	MED	LQ
SOLVENCY			
Quick Ratio (times)	1.5	0.9	0.5
Current Ratio (times)	2.8	1.8	1.3
Curr Liab To Nw (%)	47.5	113.6	241.4
Curr Liab To Inv (%)	69.2	125.4	196.4
Total Liab To Nw (%)	51.7	135.5	269.8
Fixed Assets To Nw (%)	5.2	13.7	34.1
EFFICIENCY			
Coll Period (days)	19.4	30.2	44.2
Sales To Inv (times)	15.8	8.5	5.7
Assets To Sales (%)	21.6	30.3	43.5
Sales To Nwc (times)	18.7	9.0	4.9
Acct Pay To Sales (%)	3.8	6.4	10.5
PROFITABILITY			
Return On Sales (%)	3.7	1.5	0.3
Return On Assets (%)	11.0	5.2	0.9
Return On Nw (%)	27.3	10.4	2.6

SIC 5065 ELEC PARTS, EQUIP
(NO BREAKDOWN)
2002 (708 Establishments)

	$	%
Cash	216,825	15.4
Accounts Receivable	466,033	33.1
Notes Receivable	9,856	0.7
Inventory	354,805	25.2
Other Current	111,229	7.9
Total Current	**1,158,748**	**82.3**
Fixed Assets	167,547	11.9
Other Non-current	81,661	5.8
Total Assets	**1,407,956**	**100.0**
Accounts Payable	318,198	22.6
Bank Loans	8,448	0.6
Notes Payable	49,278	3.5
Other Current	343,542	24.4
Total Current	**719,466**	**51.1**
Other Long Term	157,690	11.2
Deferred Credits	2,816	0.2
Net Worth	527,984	37.5
Total Liab & Net Worth	**1,407,956**	**100.0**
Net Sales	4,266,533	100.0
Gross Profit	1,331,158	31.2
Net Profit After Tax	46,932	1.1
Working Capital	439,282	—

RATIOS	UQ	MED	LQ
SOLVENCY			
Quick Ratio (times)	1.9	1.1	0.7
Current Ratio (times)	3.3	1.9	1.2
Curr Liab To Nw (%)	32.4	79.8	200.1
Curr Liab To Inv (%)	78.8	163.8	360.0
Total Liab To Nw (%)	40.8	104.9	257.6
Fixed Assets To Nw (%)	5.3	16.5	42.2
EFFICIENCY			
Coll Period (days)	26.7	39.8	54.4
Sales To Inv (times)	25.6	11.6	6.2
Assets To Sales (%)	24.1	33.0	47.9
Sales To Nwc (times)	15.8	7.6	4.5
Acct Pay To Sales (%)	3.5	6.5	10.5
PROFITABILITY			
Return On Sales (%)	3.8	1.4	0.0
Return On Assets (%)	11.9	4.2	(0.1)
Return On Nw (%)	32.4	10.9	0.8

SIC 5072 HARDWARE
(NO BREAKDOWN)
2002 (296 Establishments)

	$	%
Cash	167,820	10.4
Accounts Receivable	479,255	29.7
Notes Receivable	3,227	0.2
Inventory	640,621	39.7
Other Current	67,774	4.2
Total Current	**1,358,697**	**84.2**
Fixed Assets	175,888	10.9
Other Non-current	79,069	4.9
Total Assets	**1,613,654**	**100.0**
Accounts Payable	285,617	17.7
Bank Loans	4,841	0.3
Notes Payable	51,637	3.2
Other Current	229,139	14.2
Total Current	**571,234**	**35.4**
Other Long Term	153,296	9.5
Deferred Credits	1,614	0.1
Net Worth	887,510	55.0
Total Liab & Net Worth	**1,613,654**	**100.0**
Net Sales	4,337,780	100.0
Gross Profit	1,396,765	32.2
Net Profit After Tax	82,418	1.9
Working Capital	787,463	—

RATIOS	UQ	MED	LQ
SOLVENCY			
Quick Ratio (times)	2.1	1.2	0.7
Current Ratio (times)	4.5	2.6	1.7
Curr Liab To Nw (%)	23.2	60.7	134.5
Curr Liab To Inv (%)	46.7	85.1	130.0
Total Liab To Nw (%)	28.6	79.1	165.5
Fixed Assets To Nw (%)	6.8	15.9	35.3
EFFICIENCY			
Coll Period (days)	28.7	38.7	51.3
Sales To Inv (times)	10.7	6.4	4.3
Assets To Sales (%)	28.8	37.2	51.1
Sales To Nwc (times)	8.3	5.6	3.6
Acct Pay To Sales (%)	3.7	6.4	9.3
PROFITABILITY			
Return On Sales (%)	3.7	1.4	0.3
Return On Assets (%)	7.7	3.4	0.6
Return On Nw (%)	21.7	6.2	1.5

SIC 5074 PLMBG HDRNC,HTG SUP
(NO BREAKDOWN)
2002 (448 Establishments)

	$	%
Cash	144,817	9.0
Accounts Receivable	469,851	29.2
Notes Receivable	4,827	0.3
Inventory	654,895	40.7
Other Current	77,236	4.8
Total Current	**1,351,626**	**84.0**
Fixed Assets	189,871	11.8
Other Non-current	67,581	4.2
Total Assets	**1,609,078**	**100.0**
Accounts Payable	321,816	20.0
Bank Loans	4,827	0.3
Notes Payable	57,927	3.6
Other Current	270,325	16.8
Total Current	**654,895**	**40.7**
Other Long Term	160,908	10.0
Deferred Credits	0	0.0
Net Worth	793,275	49.3
Total Liab & Net Worth	**1,609,078**	**100.0**
Net Sales	4,432,722	100.0
Gross Profit	1,250,028	28.2
Net Profit After Tax	62,058	1.4
Working Capital	696,731	—

RATIOS	UQ	MED	LQ
SOLVENCY			
Quick Ratio (times)	1.7	1.0	0.6
Current Ratio (times)	3.5	2.2	1.5
Curr Liab To Nw (%)	33.4	73.1	171.1
Curr Liab To Inv (%)	56.1	91.4	147.3
Total Liab To Nw (%)	40.3	97.9	221.3
Fixed Assets To Nw (%)	9.0	19.8	38.7
EFFICIENCY			
Coll Period (days)	30.7	38.3	48.2
Sales To Inv (times)	9.4	6.7	4.8
Assets To Sales (%)	29.2	36.3	46.9
Sales To Nwc (times)	11.6	6.3	4.2
Acct Pay To Sales (%)	4.6	6.7	10.0
PROFITABILITY			
Return On Sales (%)	3.0	1.2	0.2
Return On Assets (%)	8.5	3.6	0.7
Return On Nw (%)	20.5	7.7	1.9

SIC 5075 WRM AIR HTG,AC
(NO BREAKDOWN)
2002 (256 Establishments)

	$	%
Cash	187,104	11.2
Accounts Receivable	608,088	36.4
Notes Receivable	18,376	1.1
Inventory	527,900	31.6
Other Current	53,459	3.2
Total Current	**1,394,927**	**83.5**
Fixed Assets	180,422	10.8
Other Non-current	95,222	5.7
Total Assets	**1,670,571**	**100.0**
Accounts Payable	395,925	23.7
Bank Loans	5,012	0.3
Notes Payable	71,835	4.3
Other Current	285,667	17.1
Total Current	**758,439**	**45.4**
Other Long Term	187,104	11.2
Deferred Credits	6,682	0.4
Net Worth	718,346	43.0
Total Liab & Net Worth	**1,670,571**	**100.0**
Net Sales	4,759,462	100.0
Gross Profit	1,361,206	28.6
Net Profit After Tax	95,189	2.0
Working Capital	636,488	—

RATIOS	UQ	MED	LQ
SOLVENCY			
Quick Ratio (times)	1.6	1.0	0.7
Current Ratio (times)	2.9	1.8	1.4
Curr Liab To Nw (%)	43.7	108.4	205.6
Curr Liab To Inv (%)	65.3	120.6	322.8
Total Liab To Nw (%)	66.6	134.0	229.6
Fixed Assets To Nw (%)	8.3	17.3	39.5
EFFICIENCY			
Coll Period (days)	31.4	42.7	58.8
Sales To Inv (times)	29.2	7.6	4.8
Assets To Sales (%)	27.2	35.1	46.0
Sales To Nwc (times)	12.1	7.3	5.0
Acct Pay To Sales (%)	4.4	7.2	11.5
PROFITABILITY			
Return On Sales (%)	2.9	1.2	0.2
Return On Assets (%)	7.7	3.2	0.7
Return On Nw (%)	22.5	7.3	2.0

SIC 5078 RFGTN EQUIP,SPPLS
(NO BREAKDOWN)
2002 (66 Establishments)

	$	%
Cash	125,347	11.8
Accounts Receivable	298,496	28.1
Notes Receivable	3,187	0.3
Inventory	342,049	32.2
Other Current	74,359	7.0
Total Current	**843,438**	**79.4**
Fixed Assets	162,526	15.3
Other Non-current	56,300	5.3
Total Assets	**1,062,264**	**100.0**
Accounts Payable	213,515	20.1
Bank Loans	4,249	0.4
Notes Payable	52,051	4.9
Other Current	247,508	23.3
Total Current	**517,323**	**48.7**
Other Long Term	168,899	15.9
Deferred Credits	2,125	0.2
Net Worth	373,917	35.2
Total Liab & Net Worth	**1,062,264**	**100.0**
Net Sales	2,737,794	100.0
Gross Profit	824,076	30.1
Net Profit After Tax	13,689	0.5
Working Capital	326,115	—

RATIOS	UQ	MED	LQ
SOLVENCY			
Quick Ratio (times)	1.8	0.8	0.4
Current Ratio (times)	3.2	1.9	1.2
Curr Liab To Nw (%)	39.7	89.7	239.7
Curr Liab To Inv (%)	64.7	124.4	193.1
Total Liab To Nw (%)	53.9	122.1	285.9
Fixed Assets To Nw (%)	12.1	22.7	53.4
EFFICIENCY			
Coll Period (days)	25.6	36.9	57.3
Sales To Inv (times)	12.7	7.1	4.3
Assets To Sales (%)	26.0	38.8	51.2
Sales To Nwc (times)	11.0	6.6	4.4
Acct Pay To Sales (%)	3.2	5.8	11.0
PROFITABILITY			
Return On Sales (%)	2.7	1.0	0.2
Return On Assets (%)	7.4	2.4	0.4
Return On Nw (%)	16.5	5.5	1.8

SIC 5082 CONSTR, MINNG MACH (NO BREAKDOWN) 2002 (277 Establishments)

	$	%
Cash	218,954	8.4
Accounts Receivable	552,598	21.2
Notes Receivable	10,426	0.4
Inventory	1,079,130	41.4
Other Current	179,856	6.9
Total Current	**2,040,964**	**78.3**
Fixed Assets	440,515	16.9
Other Non-current	125,116	4.8
Total Assets	**2,606,595**	**100.0**
Accounts Payable	388,383	14.9
Bank Loans	15,640	0.6
Notes Payable	247,627	9.5
Other Current	518,711	19.9
Total Current	**1,170,361**	**44.9**
Other Long Term	375,350	14.4
Deferred Credits	5,213	0.2
Net Worth	1,055,671	40.5
Total Liab & Net Worth	**2,606,595**	**100.0**
Net Sales	5,202,784	100.0
Gross Profit	1,420,360	27.3
Net Profit After Tax	83,245	1.6
Working Capital	870,603	—

RATIOS	UQ	MED	LQ
SOLVENCY			
Quick Ratio (times)	1.3	0.6	0.3
Current Ratio (times)	3.0	1.7	1.2
Curr Liab To Nw (%)	45.8	114.6	205.5
Curr Liab To Inv (%)	63.3	98.0	153.7
Total Liab To Nw (%)	62.3	155.2	281.0
Fixed Assets To Nw (%)	11.0	26.5	61.9
EFFICIENCY			
Coll Period (days)	21.0	34.0	50.8
Sales To Inv (times)	8.5	4.3	2.6
Assets To Sales (%)	36.1	50.1	71.4
Sales To Nwc (times)	10.1	6.0	3.6
Acct Pay To Sales (%)	2.4	5.1	9.2
PROFITABILITY			
Return On Sales (%)	3.1	1.1	(0.2)
Return On Assets (%)	6.2	2.1	(0.3)
Return On Nw (%)	15.6	5.6	0.0

SIC 5083 FARM,GRDN MACH (NO BREAKDOWN) 2002 (527 Establishments)

	$	%
Cash	170,504	6.9
Accounts Receivable	271,817	11.0
Notes Receivable	19,769	0.8
Inventory	1,541,946	62.4
Other Current	135,908	5.5
Total Current	**2,139,944**	**86.6**
Fixed Assets	247,107	10.0
Other Non-current	84,016	3.4
Total Assets	**2,471,067**	**100.0**
Accounts Payable	390,429	15.8
Bank Loans	7,413	0.3
Notes Payable	195,214	7.9
Other Current	669,659	27.1
Total Current	**1,262,715**	**51.1**
Other Long Term	210,041	8.5
Deferred Credits	2,471	0.1
Net Worth	995,840	40.3
Total Liab & Net Worth	**2,471,067**	**100.0**
Net Sales	5,720,063	100.0
Gross Profit	1,161,173	20.3
Net Profit After Tax	62,921	1.1
Working Capital	877,229	—

RATIOS	UQ	MED	LQ
Quick Ratio (times)	0.7	0.3	0.1
Current Ratio (times)	2.3	1.6	1.3
Curr Liab To Nw (%)	65.3	140.8	256.6
Curr Liab To Inv (%)	61.7	79.6	98.7
Total Liab To Nw (%)	73.6	163.4	304.1
Fixed Assets To Nw (%)	8.7	19.2	38.4
Coll Period (days)	6.6	13.0	27.0
Sales To Inv (times)	5.3	3.3	2.4
Assets To Sales (%)	35.1	43.2	57.8
Sales To Nwc (times)	10.7	6.8	4.4
Acct Pay To Sales (%)	1.8	4.1	12.1
Return On Sales (%)	2.0	0.9	0.2
Return On Assets (%)	4.7	2.1	0.5
Return On Nw (%)	13.1	5.6	1.5

SIC 5084 INDL MCHNRY, EQPT (NO BREAKDOWN) 2002 (1316 Establishments)

	$	%
Cash	181,499	12.4
Accounts Receivable	480,095	32.8
Notes Receivable	8,782	0.6
Inventory	411,301	28.1
Other Current	96,605	6.6
Total Current	**1,178,282**	**80.5**
Fixed Assets	204,919	14.0
Other Non-current	80,503	5.5
Total Assets	**1,463,704**	**100.0**
Accounts Payable	307,378	21.0
Bank Loans	4,391	0.3
Notes Payable	60,012	4.1
Other Current	294,204	20.1
Total Current	**665,985**	**45.5**
Other Long Term	156,617	10.7
Deferred Credits	2,927	0.2
Net Worth	638,175	43.6
Total Liab & Net Worth	**1,463,704**	**100.0**
Net Sales	4,170,097	100.0
Gross Profit	1,242,689	29.8
Net Profit After Tax	58,381	1.4
Working Capital	512,297	—

RATIOS	UQ	MED	LQ
Quick Ratio (times)	1.8	1.0	0.6
Current Ratio (times)	3.2	1.9	1.3
Curr Liab To Nw (%)	37.0	87.1	205.9
Curr Liab To Inv (%)	79.0	135.8	248.4
Total Liab To Nw (%)	47.5	113.5	265.9
Fixed Assets To Nw (%)	9.0	22.1	54.0
Coll Period (days)	31.4	42.7	54.8
Sales To Inv (times)	17.6	9.0	5.4
Assets To Sales (%)	26.2	35.1	49.7
Sales To Nwc (times)	14.3	7.7	4.6
Acct Pay To Sales (%)	3.8	6.4	10.6
Return On Sales (%)	2.7	0.9	(0.1)
Return On Assets (%)	7.8	2.6	(0.2)
Return On Nw (%)	19.3	6.5	0.2

SIC 5085 INDUSTRIAL SUPPLIES (NO BREAKDOWN) 2002 (718 Establishments)

	$	%
Cash	133,723	9.7
Accounts Receivable	449,421	32.6
Notes Receivable	6,893	0.5
Inventory	474,235	34.4
Other Current	81,337	5.9
Total Current	**1,145,609**	**83.1**
Fixed Assets	162,674	11.8
Other Non-current	70,308	5.1
Total Assets	**1,378,591**	**100.0**
Accounts Payable	275,718	20.0
Bank Loans	12,407	0.9
Notes Payable	57,901	4.2
Other Current	210,925	15.3
Total Current	**556,951**	**40.4**
Other Long Term	143,373	10.4
Deferred Credits	1,379	0.1
Net Worth	676,888	49.1
Total Liab & Net Worth	**1,378,591**	**100.0**
Net Sales	4,042,789	100.0
Gross Profit	1,253,265	31.0
Net Profit After Tax	68,727	1.7
Working Capital	588,658	—

RATIOS	UQ	MED	LQ
Quick Ratio (times)	2.0	1.1	0.7
Current Ratio (times)	4.1	2.4	1.5
Curr Liab To Nw (%)	26.4	64.0	150.0
Curr Liab To Inv (%)	53.0	102.1	178.4
Total Liab To Nw (%)	33.2	78.9	201.4
Fixed Assets To Nw (%)	7.6	17.5	36.7
Coll Period (days)	31.8	40.0	50.7
Sales To Inv (times)	13.7	8.4	5.2
Assets To Sales (%)	25.9	34.1	47.4
Sales To Nwc (times)	11.6	6.2	3.9
Acct Pay To Sales (%)	3.6	5.7	8.4
Return On Sales (%)	3.2	1.1	0.0
Return On Assets (%)	8.8	3.0	0.0
Return On Nw (%)	19.7	6.5	0.2

	SIC 5087 SVC ESTBLSHMNT EQPT (NO BREAKDOWN) 2002 (243 Establishments)		SIC 5088 TRNSPRTN EQPT,SUPPL (NO BREAKDOWN) 2002 (205 Establishments)		SIC 5091 SPTG,RECRTNL GOODS (NO BREAKDOWN) 2002 (216 Establishments)		SIC 5092 TOYS,HBBY GDS,SUPPL (NO BREAKDOWN) 2002 (77 Establishments)	
	$	%	$	%	$	%	$	%
Cash	114,623	12.1	255,516	17.3	152,858	12.6	228,983	11.2
Accounts Receivable	298,400	31.5	415,029	28.1	326,341	26.9	519,300	25.4
Notes Receivable	6,631	0.7	5,908	0.4	10,918	0.9	26,578	1.3
Inventory	304,083	32.1	463,769	31.4	473,133	39.0	809,618	39.6
Other Current	57,786	6.1	109,295	7.4	67,938	5.6	124,715	6.1
Total Current	**781,523**	**82.5**	**1,249,517**	**84.6**	**1,031,188**	**85.0**	**1,709,194**	**83.6**
Fixed Assets	121,254	12.8	150,651	10.2	120,103	9.9	224,894	11.0
Other Non-current	44,523	4.7	76,803	5.2	61,871	5.1	110,402	5.4
Total Assets	**947,300**	**100.0**	**1,476,971**	**100.0**	**1,213,162**	**100.0**	**2,044,490**	**100.0**
Accounts Payable	191,355	20.2	264,378	17.9	322,701	26.6	378,231	18.5
Bank Loans	4,737	0.5	10,339	0.7	4,853	0.4	55,201	2.7
Notes Payable	38,839	4.1	51,694	3.5	88,561	7.3	55,201	2.7
Other Current	145,884	15.4	293,917	19.9	384,572	31.7	893,442	43.7
Total Current	**380,815**	**40.2**	**620,328**	**42.0**	**800,687**	**66.0**	**1,382,075**	**67.6**
Other Long Term	125,991	13.3	138,835	9.4	138,300	11.4	265,784	13.0
Deferred Credits	947	0.1	0	0.0	0	0.0	0	0.0
Net Worth	439,547	46.4	717,808	48.6	274,175	22.6	396,631	19.4
Total Liab & Net Worth	**947,300**	**100.0**	**1,476,971**	**100.0**	**1,213,162**	**100.0**	**2,044,490**	**100.0**
Net Sales	3,095,752	100.0	3,282,158	100.0	3,476,109	100.0	5,215,536	100.0
Gross Profit	1,040,173	33.6	1,053,573	32.1	1,021,976	29.4	1,731,558	33.2
Net Profit After Tax	74,298	2.4	72,207	2.2	97,331	2.8	125,173	2.4
Working Capital	400,708	—	629,189	—	230,501	—	327,119	—

RATIOS	5087 UQ	MED	LQ	5088 UQ	MED	LQ	5091 UQ	MED	LQ	5092 UQ	MED	LQ
SOLVENCY												
Quick Ratio (times)	2.2	1.2	0.7	2.1	1.0	0.6	1.9	1.1	0.5	1.5	0.9	0.4
Current Ratio (times)	4.2	2.3	1.4	3.8	2.1	1.4	3.7	2.2	1.5	3.6	2.1	1.3
Curr Liab To Nw (%)	26.4	69.1	166.0	32.8	76.6	191.5	30.9	74.4	161.8	28.1	80.1	219.8
Curr Liab To Inv (%)	62.0	111.1	174.3	57.6	119.3	213.5	53.1	101.8	158.9	48.6	90.0	200.7
Total Liab To Nw (%)	38.2	98.9	221.8	41.5	106.4	231.9	37.9	90.4	211.9	45.8	106.1	236.5
Fixed Assets To Nw (%)	9.8	17.8	43.6	4.3	14.0	33.1	5.5	15.3	32.8	4.2	14.7	34.3
EFFICIENCY												
Coll Period (days)	26.1	35.4	50.7	28.7	46.0	60.2	23.0	30.7	48.6	20.1	30.9	59.5
Sales To Inv (times)	15.2	9.8	6.7	16.6	5.9	3.4	11.8	7.1	4.5	12.2	6.8	4.8
Assets To Sales (%)	23.2	30.6	41.4	29.4	45.0	64.0	26.8	34.9	46.6	27.8	39.2	55.2
Sales To Nwc (times)	12.0	6.9	4.8	11.0	5.4	2.9	10.4	6.1	4.1	12.9	7.8	3.4
Acct Pay To Sales (%)	2.9	5.1	8.6	3.5	6.5	12.0	3.7	6.0	9.6	3.3	5.7	9.4
PROFITABILITY												
Return On Sales (%)	3.0	1.3	0.2	4.6	1.4	0.1	3.7	1.3	0.1	4.7	2.2	0.2
Return On Assets (%)	9.5	3.9	0.6	11.2	3.2	0.2	9.4	4.5	0.4	10.6	5.5	0.7
Return On Nw (%)	23.6	8.8	1.4	22.6	7.1	0.6	22.3	8.1	1.3	23.5	12.9	1.3

SIC 5093 — SCRAP, WASTE MTRLS (NO BREAKDOWN) — 2002 (144 Establishments)

	$	%
Cash	187,907	10.3
Accounts Receivable	530,884	29.1
Notes Receivable	25,541	1.4
Inventory	330,206	18.1
Other Current	122,232	6.7
Total Current	**1,196,770**	**65.6**
Fixed Assets	499,870	27.4
Other Non-current	127,704	7.0
Total Assets	**1,824,344**	**100.0**
Accounts Payable	279,125	15.3
Bank Loans	5,473	0.3
Notes Payable	118,582	6.5
Other Current	306,490	16.8
Total Current	**709,670**	**38.9**
Other Long Term	326,557	17.9
Deferred Credits	5,473	0.3
Net Worth	782,644	42.9
Total Liab & Net Worth	**1,824,344**	**100.0**
Net Sales	5,613,366	100.0
Gross Profit	1,526,836	27.2
Net Profit After Tax	117,881	2.1
Working Capital	487,100	—

RATIOS	UQ	MED	LQ
SOLVENCY			
Quick Ratio (times)	2.3	1.1	0.7
Current Ratio (times)	3.7	1.9	1.4
Curr Liab To Nw (%)	24.0	64.0	127.6
Curr Liab To Inv (%)	95.0	173.3	300.9
Total Liab To Nw (%)	40.9	107.6	215.5
Fixed Assets To Nw (%)	18.2	44.2	88.4
EFFICIENCY			
Coll Period (days)	19.7	34.0	49.3
Sales To Inv (times)	39.6	19.3	9.9
Assets To Sales (%)	21.1	32.5	47.1
Sales To Nwc (times)	19.7	10.5	6.1
Acct Pay To Sales (%)	1.9	3.8	6.7
PROFITABILITY			
Return On Sales (%)	3.4	1.2	0.3
Return On Assets (%)	9.8	3.3	1.1
Return On Nw (%)	23.8	8.8	3.3

SIC 5094 — JWLRY, PRCIOUS STNS (NO BREAKDOWN) — 2002 (105 Establishments)

	$	%
Cash	164,222	10.1
Accounts Receivable	465,024	28.6
Notes Receivable	0	0.0
Inventory	695,910	42.8
Other Current	121,948	7.5
Total Current	**1,447,104**	**89.0**
Fixed Assets	100,809	6.2
Other Non-current	78,046	4.8
Total Assets	**1,625,959**	**100.0**
Accounts Payable	1,152,805	70.9
Bank Loans	19,512	1.2
Notes Payable	47,153	2.9
Other Current	972,323	59.8
Total Current	**2,191,793**	**134.8**
Other Long Term	128,450	7.9
Deferred Credits	0	0.0
Net Worth	(694,284)	(42.7)
Total Liab & Net Worth	**1,625,959**	**100.0**
Net Sales	4,105,957	100.0
Gross Profit	1,125,032	27.4
Net Profit After Tax	49,271	1.2
Working Capital	(744,689)	—

RATIOS	UQ	MED	LQ
SOLVENCY			
Quick Ratio (times)	1.8	0.9	0.4
Current Ratio (times)	4.3	2.0	1.5
Curr Liab To Nw (%)	32.8	79.1	195.3
Curr Liab To Inv (%)	46.1	93.6	173.9
Total Liab To Nw (%)	39.5	99.8	272.7
Fixed Assets To Nw (%)	1.5	5.4	11.5
EFFICIENCY			
Coll Period (days)	23.0	38.9	66.1
Sales To Inv (times)	12.5	5.7	3.0
Assets To Sales (%)	28.2	39.6	71.9
Sales To Nwc (times)	9.7	5.0	2.8
Acct Pay To Sales (%)	3.3	8.6	17.5
PROFITABILITY			
Return On Sales (%)	3.2	0.8	0.1
Return On Assets (%)	9.6	1.9	0.1
Return On Nw (%)	20.4	7.2	0.6

SIC 5099 — DURABLE GOODS, NEC (NO BREAKDOWN) — 2002 (207 Establishments)

	$	%
Cash	187,447	11.9
Accounts Receivable	456,804	29.0
Notes Receivable	4,726	0.3
Inventory	527,688	33.5
Other Current	107,112	6.8
Total Current	**1,283,777**	**81.5**
Fixed Assets	193,748	12.3
Other Non-current	97,662	6.2
Total Assets	**1,575,187**	**100.0**
Accounts Payable	340,240	21.6
Bank Loans	11,026	0.7
Notes Payable	48,831	3.1
Other Current	398,523	25.3
Total Current	**798,620**	**50.7**
Other Long Term	184,297	11.7
Deferred Credits	0	0.0
Net Worth	592,270	37.6
Total Liab & Net Worth	**1,575,187**	**100.0**
Net Sales	4,375,519	100.0
Gross Profit	1,356,411	31.0
Net Profit After Tax	87,510	2.0
Working Capital	485,157	—

RATIOS	UQ	MED	LQ
SOLVENCY			
Quick Ratio (times)	1.5	0.9	0.6
Current Ratio (times)	3.1	1.8	1.3
Curr Liab To Nw (%)	41.1	99.9	219.4
Curr Liab To Inv (%)	64.4	132.4	213.2
Total Liab To Nw (%)	49.7	126.9	318.2
Fixed Assets To Nw (%)	6.5	19.2	48.6
EFFICIENCY			
Coll Period (days)	23.0	37.1	53.3
Sales To Inv (times)	15.1	8.1	4.8
Assets To Sales (%)	23.9	36.0	52.4
Sales To Nwc (times)	14.5	8.0	4.3
Acct Pay To Sales (%)	2.5	5.4	12.1
PROFITABILITY			
Return On Sales (%)	4.3	1.2	0.1
Return On Assets (%)	10.2	3.5	0.4
Return On Nw (%)	27.4	10.3	2.4

SIC 51 — WHLE TRD NONDURBL GDS (NO BREAKDOWN) — 2002 (6232 Establishments)

	$	%
Cash	249,553	10.8
Accounts Receivable	681,649	29.5
Notes Receivable	13,864	0.6
Inventory	584,601	25.3
Other Current	161,747	7.0
Total Current	**1,691,414**	**73.2**
Fixed Assets	441,339	19.1
Other Non-current	177,922	7.7
Total Assets	**2,310,675**	**100.0**
Accounts Payable	487,552	21.1
Bank Loans	16,175	0.7
Notes Payable	117,844	5.1
Other Current	441,340	19.1
Total Current	**1,062,911**	**46.0**
Other Long Term	268,037	11.6
Deferred Credits	2,311	0.1
Net Worth	977,416	42.3
Total Liab & Net Worth	**2,310,675**	**100.0**
Net Sales	8,079,283	100.0
Gross Profit	1,793,601	22.2
Net Profit After Tax	129,269	1.6
Working Capital	628,503	—

RATIOS	UQ	MED	LQ
SOLVENCY			
Quick Ratio (times)	1.6	0.9	0.5
Current Ratio (times)	2.7	1.6	1.2
Curr Liab To Nw (%)	37.5	88.2	199.5
Curr Liab To Inv (%)	92.3	156.2	306.4
Total Liab To Nw (%)	49.6	118.2	262.5
Fixed Assets To Nw (%)	11.8	32.8	73.3
EFFICIENCY			
Coll Period (days)	16.1	27.7	43.1
Sales To Inv (times)	33.5	14.2	7.5
Assets To Sales (%)	18.4	28.6	45.1
Sales To Nwc (times)	25.2	12.5	6.5
Acct Pay To Sales (%)	2.6	4.6	8.0
PROFITABILITY			
Return On Sales (%)	2.6	0.9	0.2
Return On Assets (%)	8.6	3.4	0.6
Return On Nw (%)	22.1	8.4	1.9

SIC 5111 PRNTNG,WRTNG PAPER (NO BREAKDOWN) — 2002 (37 Establishments); SIC 5112 STNRY,OFFC SUPPL (NO BREAKDOWN) — 2002 (267 Establishments); SIC 5113 INDL,PRSNL SVC PPR (NO BREAKDOWN) — 2002 (164 Establishments); SIC 5122 DRGS,PRPRTRS,SNDRS (NO BREAKDOWN) — 2002 (217 Establishments)

	SIC 5111 $	SIC 5111 %	SIC 5112 $	SIC 5112 %	SIC 5113 $	SIC 5113 %	SIC 5122 $	SIC 5122 %
Cash	649,230	13.6	89,628	12.6	174,386	10.3	331,910	10.4
Accounts Receivable	2,296,174	48.1	274,575	38.6	609,503	36.0	989,347	31.0
Notes Receivable	76,380	1.6	3,557	0.5	6,772	0.4	19,149	0.6
Inventory	1,040,678	21.8	156,493	22.0	496,068	29.3	1,059,559	33.2
Other Current	219,593	4.6	45,526	6.4	116,821	6.9	204,252	6.4
Total Current	**4,282,055**	**89.7**	**569,779**	**80.1**	**1,403,550**	**82.9**	**2,604,217**	**81.6**
Fixed Assets	324,615	6.8	96,030	13.5	194,702	11.5	351,059	11.0
Other Non-current	167,081	3.5	45,525	6.4	94,812	5.6	236,167	7.4
Total Assets	**4,773,751**	**100.0**	**711,334**	**100.0**	**1,693,064**	**100.0**	**3,191,443**	**100.0**
Accounts Payable	1,255,497	26.3	186,370	26.2	347,078	20.5	931,901	29.2
Bank Loans	4,774	0.1	3,557	0.5	10,158	0.6	41,489	1.3
Notes Payable	243,461	5.1	26,319	3.7	79,574	4.7	162,764	5.1
Other Current	782,895	16.4	118,792	16.7	240,416	14.2	887,221	27.8
Total Current	**2,286,627**	**47.9**	**335,038**	**47.1**	**677,226**	**40.0**	**2,023,375**	**63.4**
Other Long Term	295,972	6.2	34,856	4.9	179,464	10.6	322,336	10.1
Deferred Credits	4,774	0.1	0	0.0	1,693	0.1	3,191	0.1
Net Worth	2,186,378	45.8	341,440	48.0	834,681	49.3	842,541	26.4
Total Liab & Net Worth	**4,773,751**	**100.0**	**711,334**	**100.0**	**1,693,064**	**100.0**	**3,191,443**	**100.0**
Net Sales	19,890,629	100.0	2,903,404	100.0	6,639,467	100.0	11,004,976	100.0
Gross Profit	3,361,516	16.9	920,379	31.7	1,746,180	26.3	3,015,363	27.4
Net Profit After Tax	397,813	2.0	60,971	2.1	86,313	1.3	264,119	2.4
Working Capital	1,995,428	—	234,741	—	726,324	—	580,842	—

RATIOS	5111 UQ	5111 MED	5111 LQ	5112 UQ	5112 MED	5112 LQ	5113 UQ	5113 MED	5113 LQ	5122 UQ	5122 MED	5122 LQ
SOLVENCY												
Quick Ratio (times)	2.1	1.2	0.8	2.1	1.2	0.8	2.2	1.1	0.8	1.4	0.8	0.5
Current Ratio (times)	3.0	1.7	1.3	3.1	2.1	1.4	3.7	2.2	1.5	2.6	1.6	1.3
Curr Liab To Nw (%)	52.6	133.3	287.5	37.3	73.7	181.3	28.7	80.3	141.3	49.4	122.1	263.7
Curr Liab To Inv (%)	104.0	189.2	263.7	100.8	161.5	362.6	70.8	128.1	196.4	95.9	144.4	251.8
Total Liab To Nw (%)	52.6	162.5	304.9	41.1	99.3	241.8	41.6	101.3	188.9	61.2	164.9	337.7
Fixed Assets To Nw (%)	2.5	12.1	28.2	8.6	21.3	41.0	8.7	17.3	39.7	5.7	17.2	42.7
EFFICIENCY												
Coll Period (days)	37.6	42.7	51.5	25.2	33.4	43.4	26.7	34.9	45.6	20.1	34.9	52.2
Sales To Inv (times)	20.2	11.5	9.1	43.6	18.6	10.5	16.9	12.2	8.7	19.6	10.4	7.1
Assets To Sales (%)	19.6	24.0	33.9	17.9	24.5	33.0	21.5	25.5	36.5	19.6	29.0	46.8
Sales To Nwc (times)	24.6	12.7	6.9	18.6	10.8	6.4	15.3	8.8	5.8	21.7	10.9	5.9
Acct Pay To Sales (%)	3.8	5.5	9.0	3.5	5.1	6.9	2.9	4.9	7.6	4.0	6.9	10.6
PROFITABILITY												
Return On Sales (%)	3.6	1.0	0.4	2.7	1.0	(0.1)	1.9	0.8	0.1	3.9	1.2	0.2
Return On Assets (%)	6.9	3.6	1.6	11.4	4.2	(0.2)	7.1	3.0	0.4	13.4	4.5	0.6
Return On Nw (%)	27.2	10.6	3.0	29.2	8.5	0.0	16.7	6.3	0.5	32.8	13.7	3.3

	SIC 5131 PCE GDS,NOTIONS (NO BREAKDOWN) 2002 (227 Establishments)		SIC 5136 MENS, BOYS CLOTHING (NO BREAKDOWN) 2002 (244 Establishments)		SIC 5137 WMNS,CLDRNS CLTHNG (NO BREAKDOWN) 2002 (206 Establishments)		SIC 5139 FOOTWEAR (NO BREAKDOWN) 2002 (78 Establishments)	
	$	%	$	%	$	%	$	%
Cash	172,484	11.2	205,163	13.7	169,140	13.5	375,363	10.3
Accounts Receivable	420,430	27.3	392,355	26.2	328,257	26.2	1,078,714	29.6
Notes Receivable	3,080	0.2	7,488	0.5	8,770	0.7	3,644	0.1
Inventory	583,674	37.9	548,100	36.6	451,040	36.0	1,483,232	40.7
Other Current	169,404	11.0	149,754	10.0	141,577	11.3	258,747	7.1
Total Current	**1,349,072**	**87.6**	**1,302,860**	**87.0**	**1,098,784**	**87.7**	**3,199,700**	**87.8**
Fixed Assets	112,423	7.3	148,256	9.9	101,484	8.1	262,390	7.2
Other Non-current	78,541	5.1	46,424	3.1	52,621	4.2	182,215	5.0
Total Assets	**1,540,036**	**100.0**	**1,497,540**	**100.0**	**1,252,889**	**100.0**	**3,644,305**	**100.0**
Accounts Payable	304,927	19.8	304,001	20.3	309,464	24.7	692,418	19.0
Bank Loans	20,020	1.3	25,458	1.7	11,276	0.9	54,665	1.5
Notes Payable	56,981	3.7	73,379	4.9	56,380	4.5	182,215	5.0
Other Current	291,068	18.9	263,567	17.6	251,830	20.1	761,660	20.9
Total Current	**672,996**	**43.7**	**666,405**	**44.5**	**628,950**	**50.2**	**1,690,958**	**46.4**
Other Long Term	110,882	7.2	131,784	8.8	96,473	7.7	357,141	9.8
Deferred Credits	1,540	0.1	0	0.0	0	0.0	0	0.0
Net Worth	754,618	49.0	699,351	46.7	527,466	42.1	1,596,206	43.8
Total Liab & Net Worth	**1,540,036**	**100.0**	**1,497,540**	**100.0**	**1,252,889**	**100.0**	**3,644,305**	**100.0**
Net Sales	4,052,726	100.0	4,114,121	100.0	3,964,839	100.0	8,802,669	100.0
Gross Profit	1,171,238	28.9	1,139,612	27.7	1,129,979	28.5	2,746,433	31.2
Net Profit After Tax	64,844	1.6	143,994	3.5	103,086	2.6	123,237	1.4
Working Capital	676,076	—	636,455	—	469,834	—	1,508,742	—

RATIOS	UQ	MED	LQ	UQ	MED	LQ	UQ	MED	LQ	UQ	MED	LQ
SOLVENCY												
Quick Ratio (times)	1.8	1.0	0.4	1.8	0.8	0.4	1.6	0.8	0.3	1.7	0.9	0.5
Current Ratio (times)	3.6	2.2	1.5	3.7	2.0	1.4	3.0	1.8	1.2	3.5	1.9	1.3
Curr Liab To Nw (%)	30.4	82.9	174.9	36.5	88.3	211.6	41.8	96.9	250.3	34.4	87.9	247.8
Curr Liab To Inv (%)	57.4	107.1	188.6	71.6	117.9	206.0	64.3	120.5	271.3	63.3	98.7	214.3
Total Liab To Nw (%)	37.8	99.3	209.8	41.5	110.6	262.8	47.9	118.5	330.8	47.6	94.8	257.1
Fixed Assets To Nw (%)	2.3	7.5	20.2	3.9	12.6	29.4	3.0	9.9	34.0	5.1	10.3	21.9
EFFICIENCY												
Coll Period (days)	17.9	32.9	57.3	17.5	33.1	54.8	12.1	30.9	55.9	27.7	43.1	64.6
Sales To Inv (times)	13.2	7.1	4.1	14.8	8.0	4.5	17.9	8.9	5.2	12.8	6.2	4.2
Assets To Sales (%)	26.5	38.0	52.9	26.1	36.4	51.7	19.7	31.6	48.0	27.8	41.4	60.7
Sales To Nwc (times)	11.4	6.5	3.7	12.2	7.2	4.1	17.4	8.4	4.7	13.9	6.3	3.7
Acct Pay To Sales (%)	4.5	7.6	10.6	2.9	5.8	10.5	3.4	5.9	10.7	2.8	6.1	12.2
PROFITABILITY												
Return On Sales (%)	3.4	1.0	0.2	4.6	1.8	0.6	4.3	1.8	0.4	5.5	1.5	0.4
Return On Assets (%)	9.6	3.0	0.6	12.0	4.3	1.6	16.2	6.3	1.1	13.2	4.7	0.9
Return On Nw (%)	22.6	6.6	1.8	30.6	11.9	3.6	40.8	15.4	4.1	34.0	13.4	5.2

SIC 5141 GROCERIES, GNRL LNE
(NO BREAKDOWN)
2002 (290 Establishments)

	$	%
Cash	290,014	7.7
Accounts Receivable	1,239,149	32.9
Notes Receivable	18,832	0.5
Inventory	1,092,259	29.0
Other Current	293,780	7.8
Total Current	**2,934,034**	**77.9**
Fixed Assets	587,560	15.6
Other Non-current	244,817	6.5
Total Assets	**3,766,411**	**100.0**
Accounts Payable	892,639	23.7
Bank Loans	26,365	0.7
Notes Payable	195,853	5.2
Other Current	757,049	20.1
Total Current	**1,871,906**	**49.7**
Other Long Term	406,772	10.8
Deferred Credits	7,533	0.2
Net Worth	1,480,200	39.3
Total Liab & Net Worth	**3,766,411**	**100.0**
Net Sales	19,022,278	100.0
Gross Profit	2,834,319	14.9
Net Profit After Tax	76,089	0.4
Working Capital	1,062,128	—

RATIOS	UQ	MED	LQ
SOLVENCY			
Quick Ratio (times)	1.3	0.8	0.5
Current Ratio (times)	2.6	1.6	1.2
Curr Liab To Nw (%)	50.2	130.0	291.2
Curr Liab To Inv (%)	85.5	145.0	244.4
Total Liab To Nw (%)	64.0	169.1	364.9
Fixed Assets To Nw (%)	13.6	30.4	81.4
EFFICIENCY			
Coll Period (days)	12.1	22.6	35.4
Sales To Inv (times)	26.2	17.7	11.5
Assets To Sales (%)	13.6	19.8	27.3
Sales To Nwc (times)	31.6	17.8	11.1
Acct Pay To Sales (%)	2.1	4.2	6.7
PROFITABILITY			
Return On Sales (%)	1.5	0.7	0.2
Return On Assets (%)	8.8	3.2	1.2
Return On Nw (%)	25.4	9.7	3.6

SIC 5142 PCKGD FROZEN GOODS
(NO BREAKDOWN)
2002 (75 Establishments)

	$	%
Cash	332,661	7.2
Accounts Receivable	1,607,862	34.8
Notes Receivable	60,064	1.3
Inventory	1,242,859	26.9
Other Current	254,115	5.5
Total Current	**3,497,561**	**75.7**
Fixed Assets	827,032	17.9
Other Non-current	295,699	6.4
Total Assets	**4,620,292**	**100.0**
Accounts Payable	1,182,795	25.6
Bank Loans	64,684	1.4
Notes Payable	170,951	3.7
Other Current	725,385	15.7
Total Current	**2,143,815**	**46.4**
Other Long Term	559,056	12.1
Deferred Credits	27,722	0.6
Net Worth	1,889,699	40.9
Total Liab & Net Worth	**4,620,292**	**100.0**
Net Sales	23,815,938	100.0
Gross Profit	3,977,262	16.7
Net Profit After Tax	309,607	1.3
Working Capital	1,353,746	—

RATIOS	UQ	MED	LQ
SOLVENCY			
Quick Ratio (times)	1.5	0.8	0.5
Current Ratio (times)	2.5	1.6	1.2
Curr Liab To Nw (%)	48.3	122.6	226.4
Curr Liab To Inv (%)	103.1	160.0	265.6
Total Liab To Nw (%)	63.5	149.3	323.9
Fixed Assets To Nw (%)	8.8	28.0	74.6
EFFICIENCY			
Coll Period (days)	17.5	22.6	29.9
Sales To Inv (times)	35.4	16.5	11.7
Assets To Sales (%)	12.0	19.4	26.7
Sales To Nwc (times)	44.6	17.8	9.5
Acct Pay To Sales (%)	2.8	4.5	7.2
PROFITABILITY			
Return On Sales (%)	2.2	0.7	0.4
Return On Assets (%)	9.0	4.8	1.8
Return On Nw (%)	22.1	12.1	5.7

SIC 5143 DRY EXC DRIED,CNND
(NO BREAKDOWN)
2002 (57 Establishments)

	$	%
Cash	274,978	8.7
Accounts Receivable	1,017,735	32.2
Notes Receivable	44,249	1.4
Inventory	625,812	19.8
Other Current	208,604	6.6
Total Current	**2,171,378**	**68.7**
Fixed Assets	657,419	20.8
Other Non-current	331,870	10.5
Total Assets	**3,160,667**	**100.0**
Accounts Payable	900,790	28.5
Bank Loans	9,482	0.3
Notes Payable	88,499	2.8
Other Current	641,615	20.3
Total Current	**1,640,386**	**51.9**
Other Long Term	451,976	14.3
Deferred Credits	6,321	0.2
Net Worth	1,061,984	33.6
Total Liab & Net Worth	**3,160,667**	**100.0**
Net Sales	15,569,788	100.0
Gross Profit	3,067,248	19.7
Net Profit After Tax	140,128	0.9
Working Capital	530,992	—

RATIOS	UQ	MED	LQ
SOLVENCY			
Quick Ratio (times)	1.2	0.8	0.5
Current Ratio (times)	2.1	1.4	1.1
Curr Liab To Nw (%)	53.8	108.5	197.6
Curr Liab To Inv (%)	149.3	237.4	375.7
Total Liab To Nw (%)	74.8	151.3	349.5
Fixed Assets To Nw (%)	20.8	44.7	91.0
EFFICIENCY			
Coll Period (days)	17.5	24.5	28.1
Sales To Inv (times)	45.8	21.8	16.3
Assets To Sales (%)	13.5	20.3	27.2
Sales To Nwc (times)	32.2	17.5	11.6
Acct Pay To Sales (%)	4.1	5.1	6.3
PROFITABILITY			
Return On Sales (%)	1.7	0.8	0.1
Return On Assets (%)	8.5	3.9	0.5
Return On Nw (%)	20.8	11.4	3.2

SIC 5144 PLTRY,PLTRY PRDTS
(NO BREAKDOWN)
2002 (53 Establishments)

	$	%
Cash	229,558	11.9
Accounts Receivable	688,675	35.7
Notes Receivable	9,645	0.5
Inventory	362,664	18.8
Other Current	108,029	5.6
Total Current	**1,398,571**	**72.5**
Fixed Assets	441,755	22.9
Other Non-current	88,737	4.6
Total Assets	**1,929,063**	**100.0**
Accounts Payable	449,472	23.3
Bank Loans	0	0.0
Notes Payable	77,163	4.0
Other Current	270,068	14.0
Total Current	**796,703**	**41.3**
Other Long Term	248,849	12.9
Deferred Credits	(1,929)	(0.1)
Net Worth	885,440	45.9
Total Liab & Net Worth	**1,929,063**	**100.0**
Net Sales	13,489,951	100.0
Gross Profit	2,010,003	14.9
Net Profit After Tax	121,410	0.9
Working Capital	601,868	—

RATIOS	UQ	MED	LQ
SOLVENCY			
Quick Ratio (times)	1.7	1.0	0.7
Current Ratio (times)	3.0	1.7	1.3
Curr Liab To Nw (%)	37.8	93.6	214.5
Curr Liab To Inv (%)	104.0	159.8	285.1
Total Liab To Nw (%)	39.8	120.7	280.3
Fixed Assets To Nw (%)	16.3	36.4	130.7
EFFICIENCY			
Coll Period (days)	13.1	20.4	27.0
Sales To Inv (times)	46.0	28.7	17.1
Assets To Sales (%)	10.4	14.3	26.4
Sales To Nwc (times)	34.6	20.9	10.2
Acct Pay To Sales (%)	1.8	3.8	5.0
PROFITABILITY			
Return On Sales (%)	0.9	0.3	0.0
Return On Assets (%)	5.3	2.5	0.0
Return On Nw (%)	14.4	4.9	(0.2)

SIC 5145 CONFECTIONERY
(NO BREAKDOWN)
2002 (71 Establishments)

	$	%
Cash	150,539	10.6
Accounts Receivable	380,608	26.8
Notes Receivable	1,420	0.1
Inventory	512,684	36.1
Other Current	63,908	4.5
Total Current	**1,109,159**	**78.1**
Fixed Assets	241,430	17.0
Other Non-current	69,589	4.9
Total Assets	**1,420,178**	**100.0**
Accounts Payable	247,111	17.4
Bank Loans	12,782	0.9
Notes Payable	102,253	7.2
Other Current	251,371	17.7
Total Current	**613,517**	**43.2**
Other Long Term	203,085	14.3
Deferred Credits	0	0.0
Net Worth	603,576	42.5
Total Liab & Net Worth	**1,420,178**	**100.0**
Net Sales	5,504,566	100.0
Gross Profit	1,166,968	21.2
Net Profit After Tax	71,559	1.3
Working Capital	495,642	—

RATIOS	UQ	MED	LQ
SOLVENCY			
Quick Ratio (times)	2.0	1.0	0.4
Current Ratio (times)	4.6	2.0	1.1
Curr Liab To Nw (%)	19.6	82.3	253.3
Curr Liab To Inv (%)	42.7	109.5	171.1
Total Liab To Nw (%)	51.4	133.9	296.2
Fixed Assets To Nw (%)	9.2	25.8	71.3
EFFICIENCY			
Coll Period (days)	13.5	23.6	32.5
Sales To Inv (times)	22.5	11.6	7.1
Assets To Sales (%)	17.1	25.8	37.6
Sales To Nwc (times)	25.3	10.8	6.0
Acct Pay To Sales (%)	1.4	3.4	6.1
PROFITABILITY			
Return On Sales (%)	2.4	0.8	0.2
Return On Assets (%)	9.6	3.3	0.9
Return On Nw (%)	21.8	8.8	3.4

SIC 5146 FISH AND SEAFOODS
(NO BREAKDOWN)
2002 (83 Establishments)

	$	%
Cash	186,355	8.3
Accounts Receivable	911,565	40.6
Notes Receivable	8,981	0.4
Inventory	594,987	26.5
Other Current	123,488	5.5
Total Current	**1,825,376**	**81.3**
Fixed Assets	314,333	14.0
Other Non-current	105,526	4.7
Total Assets	**2,245,235**	**100.0**
Accounts Payable	565,799	25.2
Bank Loans	33,679	1.5
Notes Payable	110,017	4.9
Other Current	449,046	20.0
Total Current	**1,158,541**	**51.6**
Other Long Term	190,845	8.5
Deferred Credits	6,736	0.3
Net Worth	889,113	39.6
Total Liab & Net Worth	**2,245,235**	**100.0**
Net Sales	10,952,366	100.0
Gross Profit	1,620,950	14.8
Net Profit After Tax	186,190	1.7
Working Capital	666,835	—

RATIOS	UQ	MED	LQ
SOLVENCY			
Quick Ratio (times)	1.9	1.0	0.6
Current Ratio (times)	2.9	1.5	1.2
Curr Liab To Nw (%)	50.8	157.3	299.8
Curr Liab To Inv (%)	126.8	181.7	331.0
Total Liab To Nw (%)	71.5	184.6	376.2
Fixed Assets To Nw (%)	7.7	22.6	57.2
EFFICIENCY			
Coll Period (days)	22.6	32.3	41.3
Sales To Inv (times)	58.8	20.8	10.2
Assets To Sales (%)	15.5	20.5	30.9
Sales To Nwc (times)	27.0	15.7	9.0
Acct Pay To Sales (%)	2.9	5.0	7.6
PROFITABILITY			
Return On Sales (%)	2.4	0.9	0.2
Return On Assets (%)	11.2	4.1	1.2
Return On Nw (%)	36.3	11.6	5.1

SIC 5147 MEATS, MEAT PRDTS
(NO BREAKDOWN)
2002 (159 Establishments)

	$	%
Cash	201,004	11.4
Accounts Receivable	611,827	34.7
Notes Receivable	3,526	0.2
Inventory	416,113	23.6
Other Current	98,738	5.6
Total Current	**1,331,208**	**75.5**
Fixed Assets	340,295	19.3
Other Non-current	91,686	5.2
Total Assets	**1,763,189**	**100.0**
Accounts Payable	352,638	20.0
Bank Loans	8,816	0.5
Notes Payable	47,606	2.7
Other Current	273,294	15.5
Total Current	**682,354**	**38.7**
Other Long Term	215,109	12.2
Deferred Credits	1,763	0.1
Net Worth	863,963	49.0
Total Liab & Net Worth	**1,763,189**	**100.0**
Net Sales	11,449,279	100.0
Gross Profit	2,049,421	17.9
Net Profit After Tax	160,290	1.4
Working Capital	648,854	—

RATIOS	UQ	MED	LQ
SOLVENCY			
Quick Ratio (times)	2.3	1.2	0.7
Current Ratio (times)	3.7	2.1	1.4
Curr Liab To Nw (%)	26.9	67.0	176.3
Curr Liab To Inv (%)	79.5	153.5	306.0
Total Liab To Nw (%)	37.7	100.8	254.0
Fixed Assets To Nw (%)	12.5	30.4	76.2
EFFICIENCY			
Coll Period (days)	13.0	18.3	26.5
Sales To Inv (times)	54.2	30.7	20.3
Assets To Sales (%)	10.3	15.4	24.5
Sales To Nwc (times)	37.3	19.9	11.6
Acct Pay To Sales (%)	1.5	2.9	4.2
PROFITABILITY			
Return On Sales (%)	2.0	0.8	0.3
Return On Assets (%)	11.3	5.3	1.9
Return On Nw (%)	24.7	13.8	4.7

SIC 5148 FRSH FRTS, VGTBLES
(NO BREAKDOWN)
2002 (314 Establishments)

	$	%
Cash	302,006	13.2
Accounts Receivable	1,004,400	43.9
Notes Receivable	13,728	0.6
Inventory	187,610	8.2
Other Current	215,064	9.4
Total Current	**1,722,808**	**75.3**
Fixed Assets	425,554	18.6
Other Non-current	139,564	6.1
Total Assets	**2,287,926**	**100.0**
Accounts Payable	780,183	34.1
Bank Loans	6,864	0.3
Notes Payable	164,731	7.2
Other Current	590,284	25.8
Total Current	**1,542,062**	**67.4**
Other Long Term	194,474	8.5
Deferred Credits	0	0.0
Net Worth	551,390	24.1
Total Liab & Net Worth	**2,287,926**	**100.0**
Net Sales	14,036,356	100.0
Gross Profit	2,386,181	17.0
Net Profit After Tax	196,509	1.4
Working Capital	180,746	—

RATIOS	UQ	MED	LQ
SOLVENCY			
Quick Ratio (times)	1.9	1.1	0.8
Current Ratio (times)	2.5	1.4	1.1
Curr Liab To Nw (%)	44.2	130.3	282.4
Curr Liab To Inv (%)	256.3	552.3	999.9
Total Liab To Nw (%)	56.2	152.7	346.2
Fixed Assets To Nw (%)	13.8	35.8	72.0
EFFICIENCY			
Coll Period (days)	19.2	27.4	37.8
Sales To Inv (times)	131.3	81.6	44.7
Assets To Sales (%)	11.9	16.3	25.6
Sales To Nwc (times)	47.5	21.9	10.5
Acct Pay To Sales (%)	2.5	4.7	7.5
PROFITABILITY			
Return On Sales (%)	2.1	0.7	0.1
Return On Assets (%)	12.5	4.3	0.6
Return On Nw (%)	35.5	12.8	1.7

SIC 5149 GRCRS,RLTD PRDS,NEC (NO BREAKDOWN) 2002 (251 Establishments)
SIC 5153 GRAIN,FIELD BEANS (NO BREAKDOWN) 2002 (510 Establishments)
SIC 5159 FRM-PRD MTRLS,NEC (NO BREAKDOWN) 2002 (43 Establishments)
SIC 5162 PLSTCS MTRLS,B SHPS (NO BREAKDOWN) 2002 (66 Establishments)

	SIC 5149 $	SIC 5149 %	SIC 5153 $	SIC 5153 %	SIC 5159 $	SIC 5159 %	SIC 5162 $	SIC 5162 %
Cash	180,108	10.6	447,246	6.6	594,349	13.9	100,996	8.6
Accounts Receivable	474,058	27.9	969,032	14.3	718,350	16.8	510,854	43.5
Notes Receivable	6,797	0.4	20,329	0.3	64,138	1.5	14,093	1.2
Inventory	457,067	26.9	1,958,393	28.9	957,799	22.4	271,281	23.1
Other Current	86,655	5.1	582,774	8.6	547,314	12.8	34,056	2.9
Total Current	**1,204,685**	**70.9**	**3,977,774**	**58.7**	**2,881,950**	**67.4**	**931,280**	**79.3**
Fixed Assets	350,021	20.6	1,938,064	28.6	923,592	21.6	157,366	13.4
Other Non-current	144,427	8.5	860,609	12.7	470,348	11.0	85,730	7.3
Total Assets	**1,699,133**	**100.0**	**6,776,447**	**100.0**	**4,275,890**	**100.0**	**1,174,376**	**100.0**
Accounts Payable	414,588	24.4	664,092	9.8	513,107	12.0	324,128	27.6
Bank Loans	8,496	0.5	27,106	0.4	4,276	0.1	1,174	0.1
Notes Payable	71,364	4.2	718,303	10.6	282,209	6.6	36,406	3.1
Other Current	402,694	23.7	1,389,172	20.5	833,798	19.5	176,156	15.0
Total Current	**897,142**	**52.8**	**2,798,673**	**41.3**	**1,633,390**	**38.2**	**537,864**	**45.8**
Other Long Term	251,472	14.8	799,620	11.8	491,727	11.5	160,890	13.7
Deferred Credits	1,699	0.1	13,553	0.2	42,759	1.0	0	0.0
Net Worth	548,820	32.3	3,164,601	46.7	2,108,014	49.3	475,622	40.5
Total Liab & Net Worth	**1,699,133**	**100.0**	**6,776,447**	**100.0**	**4,275,890**	**100.0**	**1,174,376**	**100.0**
Net Sales	5,626,268	100.0	15,907,153	100.0	8,852,774	100.0	3,658,492	100.0
Gross Profit	1,586,608	28.2	1,781,601	11.2	2,328,280	26.3	947,549	25.9
Net Profit After Tax	90,020	1.6	143,164	0.9	433,786	4.9	40,243	1.1
Working Capital	307,543	—	1,179,101	—	1,248,560	—	393,416	—

RATIOS	5149 UQ	5149 MED	5149 LQ	5153 UQ	5153 MED	5153 LQ	5159 UQ	5159 MED	5159 LQ	5162 UQ	5162 MED	5162 LQ
SOLVENCY												
Quick Ratio (times)	1.5	0.8	0.5	0.8	0.4	0.2	1.6	0.8	0.4	2.0	1.1	0.8
Current Ratio (times)	2.5	1.6	1.1	1.7	1.3	1.2	3.0	1.8	1.5	2.7	1.9	1.3
Curr Liab To Nw (%)	37.3	96.4	210.0	51.5	91.5	152.7	30.0	71.5	115.8	41.2	87.2	230.6
Curr Liab To Inv (%)	92.8	156.0	293.4	109.1	138.3	191.7	73.8	119.3	210.6	103.4	155.1	438.5
Total Liab To Nw (%)	55.1	122.8	303.3	70.4	116.9	203.1	34.1	82.5	203.8	62.0	118.7	313.4
Fixed Assets To Nw (%)	11.1	32.7	74.0	42.6	62.0	83.0	12.3	36.3	67.1	6.0	21.7	55.1
EFFICIENCY												
Coll Period (days)	18.1	27.9	43.4	9.9	16.6	28.1	6.6	24.8	47.8	37.6	47.1	58.8
Sales To Inv (times)	24.0	13.7	7.9	13.5	8.5	5.7	21.2	7.5	3.9	44.9	15.0	6.6
Assets To Sales (%)	19.9	30.2	47.0	32.3	42.6	54.9	22.7	48.3	76.0	21.4	32.1	46.0
Sales To Nwc (times)	25.7	11.8	6.4	29.4	19.8	11.0	12.9	5.9	3.6	14.1	9.0	5.6
Acct Pay To Sales (%)	3.2	5.6	10.6	1.5	3.0	5.9	1.3	3.8	6.3	5.6	7.1	10.7
PROFITABILITY												
Return On Sales (%)	3.8	1.3	0.4	1.8	0.9	0.1	4.7	2.5	0.4	2.5	1.2	0.3
Return On Assets (%)	13.2	4.5	0.9	4.2	2.2	0.2	10.4	4.6	2.1	8.2	4.2	0.8
Return On Nw (%)	40.5	13.5	4.8	9.5	5.2	0.4	25.7	7.0	3.4	26.7	11.4	1.7

SIC 5169 — CHEM, ALLD PRDTS, NEC (NO BREAKDOWN) — 2002 (263 Establishments)

	$	%
Cash	257,874	12.5
Accounts Receivable	773,621	37.5
Notes Receivable	8,252	0.4
Inventory	433,227	21.0
Other Current	121,716	5.9
Total Current	**1,594,690**	**77.3**
Fixed Assets	367,212	17.8
Other Non-current	101,086	4.9
Total Assets	**2,062,988**	**100.0**
Accounts Payable	528,125	25.6
Bank Loans	10,315	0.5
Notes Payable	76,331	3.7
Other Current	391,967	19.0
Total Current	**1,006,738**	**48.8**
Other Long Term	202,173	9.8
Deferred Credits	8,252	0.4
Net Worth	845,825	41.0
Total Liab & Net Worth	**2,062,988**	**100.0**
Net Sales	6,367,247	100.0
Gross Profit	2,031,152	31.9
Net Profit After Tax	171,916	2.7
Working Capital	587,952	—

RATIOS	UQ	MED	LQ
SOLVENCY			
Quick Ratio (times)	1.7	1.0	0.7
Current Ratio (times)	2.5	1.7	1.2
Curr Liab To Nw (%)	41.0	93.4	233.4
Curr Liab To Inv (%)	119.9	188.6	314.0
Total Liab To Nw (%)	55.2	122.7	288.4
Fixed Assets To Nw (%)	7.8	24.7	64.5
EFFICIENCY			
Coll Period (days)	32.9	42.7	54.6
Sales To Inv (times)	21.7	14.1	8.9
Assets To Sales (%)	23.8	32.4	45.8
Sales To Nwc (times)	19.0	10.3	5.2
Acct Pay To Sales (%)	4.7	6.9	11.5
PROFITABILITY			
Return On Sales (%)	4.7	1.4	0.5
Return On Assets (%)	12.0	4.5	1.3
Return On Nw (%)	31.9	11.6	3.3

SIC 5171 — PETRO BLK STNS, TMNL (NO BREAKDOWN) — 2002 (391 Establishments)

	$	%
Cash	345,174	10.4
Accounts Receivable	872,891	26.3
Notes Receivable	36,509	1.1
Inventory	484,570	14.6
Other Current	192,500	5.8
Total Current	**1,931,644**	**58.2**
Fixed Assets	1,068,710	32.2
Other Non-current	318,622	9.6
Total Assets	**3,318,976**	**100.0**
Accounts Payable	627,286	18.9
Bank Loans	19,914	0.6
Notes Payable	129,440	3.9
Other Current	501,166	15.1
Total Current	**1,277,806**	**38.5**
Other Long Term	604,053	18.2
Deferred Credits	6,638	0.2
Net Worth	1,430,479	43.1
Total Liab & Net Worth	**3,318,976**	**100.0**
Net Sales	14,883,300	100.0
Gross Profit	1,964,596	13.2
Net Profit After Tax	119,066	0.8
Working Capital	653,838	—

RATIOS	UQ	MED	LQ
SOLVENCY			
Quick Ratio (times)	1.4	0.9	0.6
Current Ratio (times)	2.3	1.5	1.1
Curr Liab To Nw (%)	36.6	80.8	193.1
Curr Liab To Inv (%)	156.7	265.1	495.0
Total Liab To Nw (%)	50.7	128.4	301.8
Fixed Assets To Nw (%)	31.8	71.2	153.1
EFFICIENCY			
Coll Period (days)	13.1	20.4	29.9
Sales To Inv (times)	66.0	35.6	19.3
Assets To Sales (%)	15.8	22.3	32.8
Sales To Nwc (times)	43.0	20.2	10.1
Acct Pay To Sales (%)	3.0	3.9	5.3
PROFITABILITY			
Return On Sales (%)	1.4	0.4	(0.1)
Return On Assets (%)	4.9	1.9	(0.3)
Return On Nw (%)	11.3	5.0	(0.4)

SIC 5172 — PETRO PRDTS, NEC (NO BREAKDOWN) — 2002 (475 Establishments)

	$	%
Cash	308,485	9.9
Accounts Receivable	981,544	31.5
Notes Receivable	24,928	0.8
Inventory	420,662	13.5
Other Current	158,917	5.1
Total Current	**1,894,536**	**60.8**
Fixed Assets	956,616	30.7
Other Non-current	264,861	8.5
Total Assets	**3,116,013**	**100.0**
Accounts Payable	716,683	23.0
Bank Loans	21,812	0.7
Notes Payable	99,712	3.2
Other Current	492,331	15.8
Total Current	**1,330,538**	**42.7**
Other Long Term	573,346	18.4
Deferred Credits	6,232	0.2
Net Worth	1,205,897	38.7
Total Liab & Net Worth	**3,116,013**	**100.0**
Net Sales	14,163,695	100.0
Gross Profit	2,138,718	15.1
Net Profit After Tax	113,310	0.8
Working Capital	563,998	—

RATIOS	UQ	MED	LQ
SOLVENCY			
Quick Ratio (times)	1.4	0.9	0.7
Current Ratio (times)	2.1	1.4	1.1
Curr Liab To Nw (%)	52.3	99.0	214.6
Curr Liab To Inv (%)	169.0	307.5	604.9
Total Liab To Nw (%)	75.4	157.7	316.5
Fixed Assets To Nw (%)	35.3	73.4	135.4
EFFICIENCY			
Coll Period (days)	14.2	24.7	35.4
Sales To Inv (times)	78.5	38.8	19.2
Assets To Sales (%)	14.5	22.0	32.9
Sales To Nwc (times)	47.0	20.7	11.0
Acct Pay To Sales (%)	3.0	4.1	6.2
PROFITABILITY			
Return On Sales (%)	1.3	0.5	0.1
Return On Assets (%)	5.5	2.4	0.4
Return On Nw (%)	15.2	6.9	0.9

SIC 5181 — BEER AND ALE (NO BREAKDOWN) — 2002 (103 Establishments)

	$	%
Cash	489,363	13.7
Accounts Receivable	367,915	10.3
Notes Receivable	7,144	0.2
Inventory	717,970	20.1
Other Current	303,619	8.5
Total Current	**1,886,011**	**52.8**
Fixed Assets	896,570	25.1
Other Non-current	789,410	22.1
Total Assets	**3,571,991**	**100.0**
Accounts Payable	367,915	10.3
Bank Loans	53,580	1.5
Notes Payable	64,296	1.8
Other Current	460,787	12.9
Total Current	**946,578**	**26.5**
Other Long Term	732,258	20.5
Deferred Credits	3,572	0.1
Net Worth	1,889,583	52.9
Total Liab & Net Worth	**3,571,991**	**100.0**
Net Sales	13,530,269	100.0
Gross Profit	3,341,976	24.7
Net Profit After Tax	378,848	2.8
Working Capital	939,433	—

RATIOS	UQ	MED	LQ
SOLVENCY			
Quick Ratio (times)	1.7	0.9	0.4
Current Ratio (times)	3.9	2.2	1.3
Curr Liab To Nw (%)	16.3	43.6	94.1
Curr Liab To Inv (%)	80.2	124.2	181.9
Total Liab To Nw (%)	28.2	77.6	202.7
Fixed Assets To Nw (%)	25.0	42.6	77.2
EFFICIENCY			
Coll Period (days)	1.5	4.6	19.4
Sales To Inv (times)	33.6	21.3	14.1
Assets To Sales (%)	20.0	26.4	34.6
Sales To Nwc (times)	22.6	15.4	8.1
Acct Pay To Sales (%)	1.1	2.5	3.5
PROFITABILITY			
Return On Sales (%)	4.4	2.1	0.7
Return On Assets (%)	13.9	9.0	2.3
Return On Nw (%)	29.3	18.4	6.2

SIC 5182 WINE, DSTLLD BVRGES
(NO BREAKDOWN)
2002 (61 Establishments)

	$	%
Cash	182,982	8.1
Accounts Receivable	544,427	24.1
Notes Receivable	2,259	0.1
Inventory	971,384	43.0
Other Current	185,241	8.2
Total Current	**1,886,293**	**83.5**
Fixed Assets	185,241	8.2
Other Non-current	187,499	8.3
Total Assets	**2,259,033**	**100.0**
Accounts Payable	621,234	27.5
Bank Loans	0	0.0
Notes Payable	45,181	2.0
Other Current	481,174	21.3
Total Current	**1,147,589**	**50.8**
Other Long Term	295,933	13.1
Deferred Credits	2,259	0.1
Net Worth	813,252	36.0
Total Liab & Net Worth	**2,259,033**	**100.0**
Net Sales	6,345,598	100.0
Gross Profit	1,764,076	27.8
Net Profit After Tax	209,405	3.3
Working Capital	738,704	—

RATIOS	UQ	MED	LQ
SOLVENCY			
Quick Ratio (times)	1.0	0.5	0.3
Current Ratio (times)	2.4	1.6	1.3
Curr Liab To Nw (%)	63.7	168.2	289.0
Curr Liab To Inv (%)	71.8	94.3	141.5
Total Liab To Nw (%)	71.7	212.3	359.2
Fixed Assets To Nw (%)	9.1	19.4	53.9
EFFICIENCY			
Coll Period (days)	18.5	40.5	51.8
Sales To Inv (times)	9.9	7.4	3.7
Assets To Sales (%)	25.0	35.6	47.0
Sales To Nwc (times)	17.5	10.5	5.2
Acct Pay To Sales (%)	4.9	8.5	15.7
PROFITABILITY			
Return On Sales (%)	4.7	1.8	0.9
Return On Assets (%)	13.2	5.3	2.1
Return On Nw (%)	54.6	20.2	7.5

SIC 5191 FARM SUPPLIES
(NO BREAKDOWN)
2002 (640 Establishments)

	$	%
Cash	250,352	9.0
Accounts Receivable	598,062	21.5
Notes Receivable	27,817	1.0
Inventory	731,583	26.3
Other Current	166,901	6.0
Total Current	**1,774,715**	**63.8**
Fixed Assets	706,548	25.4
Other Non-current	300,422	10.8
Total Assets	**2,781,685**	**100.0**
Accounts Payable	420,034	15.1
Bank Loans	11,127	0.4
Notes Payable	183,591	6.6
Other Current	481,232	17.3
Total Current	**1,095,984**	**39.4**
Other Long Term	283,731	10.2
Deferred Credits	2,782	0.1
Net Worth	1,399,188	50.3
Total Liab & Net Worth	**2,781,685**	**100.0**
Net Sales	5,831,625	100.0
Gross Profit	1,277,126	21.9
Net Profit After Tax	75,811	1.3
Working Capital	678,731	—

RATIOS	UQ	MED	LQ
SOLVENCY			
Quick Ratio (times)	1.4	0.7	0.4
Current Ratio (times)	2.6	1.6	1.2
Curr Liab To Nw (%)	32.6	67.0	142.5
Curr Liab To Inv (%)	87.9	140.6	214.4
Total Liab To Nw (%)	42.2	92.1	192.8
Fixed Assets To Nw (%)	24.5	45.8	76.1
EFFICIENCY			
Coll Period (days)	20.1	31.0	47.3
Sales To Inv (times)	13.5	8.5	5.8
Assets To Sales (%)	33.0	47.7	61.3
Sales To Nwc (times)	18.8	10.0	5.2
Acct Pay To Sales (%)	3.0	5.3	8.8
PROFITABILITY			
Return On Sales (%)	2.7	1.3	0.2
Return On Assets (%)	6.0	2.8	0.5
Return On Nw (%)	12.1	6.0	1.1

SIC 5192 BKS,PRDCLS,NWSPPRS
(NO BREAKDOWN)
2002 (45 Establishments)

	$	%
Cash	156,082	10.9
Accounts Receivable	476,837	33.3
Notes Receivable	2,864	0.2
Inventory	333,642	23.3
Other Current	133,170	9.3
Total Current	**1,102,595**	**77.0**
Fixed Assets	158,946	11.1
Other Non-current	170,401	11.9
Total Assets	**1,431,942**	**100.0**
Accounts Payable	558,457	39.0
Bank Loans	4,296	0.3
Notes Payable	150,354	10.5
Other Current	721,699	50.4
Total Current	**1,434,806**	**100.2**
Other Long Term	306,435	21.4
Deferred Credits	0	0.0
Net Worth	(309,299)	(21.6)
Total Liab & Net Worth	**1,431,942**	**100.0**
Net Sales	3,788,206	100.0
Gross Profit	1,208,438	31.9
Net Profit After Tax	79,552	2.1
Working Capital	(332,211)	—

RATIOS	UQ	MED	LQ
SOLVENCY			
Quick Ratio (times)	1.6	0.9	0.7
Current Ratio (times)	3.0	1.9	1.2
Curr Liab To Nw (%)	34.7	106.0	219.2
Curr Liab To Inv (%)	76.0	145.6	302.3
Total Liab To Nw (%)	72.5	171.6	323.7
Fixed Assets To Nw (%)	7.9	18.1	45.2
EFFICIENCY			
Coll Period (days)	28.1	44.5	75.2
Sales To Inv (times)	13.8	8.3	5.3
Assets To Sales (%)	26.1	37.8	63.1
Sales To Nwc (times)	15.2	6.9	4.4
Acct Pay To Sales (%)	5.6	6.9	18.1
PROFITABILITY			
Return On Sales (%)	6.2	1.3	0.0
Return On Assets (%)	14.7	2.3	0.0
Return On Nw (%)	33.1	7.9	2.5

SIC 5193 FLWRS,FLRSTS SPPLS
(NO BREAKDOWN)
2002 (111 Establishments)

	$	%
Cash	188,610	10.7
Accounts Receivable	461,829	26.2
Notes Receivable	14,102	0.8
Inventory	398,372	22.6
Other Current	121,627	6.9
Total Current	**1,184,540**	**67.2**
Fixed Assets	445,965	25.3
Other Non-current	132,203	7.5
Total Assets	**1,762,708**	**100.0**
Accounts Payable	294,372	16.7
Bank Loans	1,763	0.1
Notes Payable	59,932	3.4
Other Current	315,525	17.9
Total Current	**671,592**	**38.1**
Other Long Term	336,677	19.1
Deferred Credits	3,525	0.2
Net Worth	750,914	42.6
Total Liab & Net Worth	**1,762,708**	**100.0**
Net Sales	5,246,155	100.0
Gross Profit	1,935,831	36.9
Net Profit After Tax	152,138	2.9
Working Capital	512,948	—

RATIOS	UQ	MED	LQ
SOLVENCY			
Quick Ratio (times)	2.2	1.1	0.6
Current Ratio (times)	4.7	2.0	1.4
Curr Liab To Nw (%)	20.6	56.3	141.5
Curr Liab To Inv (%)	64.5	126.4	279.9
Total Liab To Nw (%)	33.7	87.3	214.1
Fixed Assets To Nw (%)	19.2	44.6	71.4
EFFICIENCY			
Coll Period (days)	19.8	35.6	52.6
Sales To Inv (times)	31.8	10.5	6.8
Assets To Sales (%)	24.4	33.6	61.4
Sales To Nwc (times)	14.0	8.7	4.2
Acct Pay To Sales (%)	3.1	4.9	8.6
PROFITABILITY			
Return On Sales (%)	4.8	1.5	0.5
Return On Assets (%)	11.0	4.4	1.4
Return On Nw (%)	20.1	8.9	2.2

	SIC 5194 TBCCO,TBCCO PRDTS (NO BREAKDOWN) 2002 (135 Establishments)		SIC 5198 PNTS,VRNSHS,SUPPL (NO BREAKDOWN) 2002 (50 Establishments)		SIC 5199 NNDRBL GDS,NEC (NO BREAKDOWN) 2002 (541 Establishments)		SIC 52 BLD MTLS HDW GDN SUP (NO BREAKDOWN) 2002 (2355 Establishments)	
	$	%	$	%	$	%	$	%
Cash	269,699	9.6	117,591	9.3	137,347	15.6	133,512	10.4
Accounts Receivable	800,668	28.5	402,087	31.8	308,151	35.0	245,200	19.1
Notes Receivable	5,619	0.2	0	0.0	4,402	0.5	6,419	0.5
Inventory	1,202,407	42.8	488,068	38.6	205,140	23.3	512,225	39.9
Other Current	174,179	6.2	59,428	4.7	61,630	7.0	69,324	5.4
Total Current	**2,452,572**	**87.3**	**1,067,174**	**84.4**	**716,670**	**81.4**	**966,680**	**75.3**
Fixed Assets	241,605	8.6	141,615	11.2	115,336	13.1	233,647	18.2
Other Non-current	115,184	4.1	55,635	4.4	48,424	5.5	83,445	6.5
Total Assets	**2,809,361**	**100.0**	**1,264,424**	**100.0**	**880,430**	**100.0**	**1,283,772**	**100.0**
Accounts Payable	334,314	11.9	269,322	21.3	194,575	22.1	181,012	14.1
Bank Loans	14,047	0.5	0	0.0	6,163	0.7	3,851	0.3
Notes Payable	143,277	5.1	31,611	2.5	36,098	4.1	53,918	4.2
Other Current	536,588	19.1	221,274	17.5	172,564	19.6	209,255	16.3
Total Current	**1,028,226**	**36.6**	**522,207**	**41.3**	**409,400**	**46.5**	**448,036**	**34.9**
Other Long Term	269,699	9.6	127,707	10.1	84,521	9.6	181,012	14.1
Deferred Credits	0	0.0	6,322	0.5	0	0.0	1,284	0.1
Net Worth	1,511,436	53.8	608,188	48.1	386,509	43.9	653,440	50.9
Total Liab & Net Worth	**2,809,361**	**100.0**	**1,264,424**	**100.0**	**880,430**	**100.0**	**1,283,772**	**100.0**
Net Sales	23,217,860	100.0	3,902,543	100.0	3,155,663	100.0	3,360,660	100.0
Gross Profit	1,950,300	8.4	1,264,424	32.4	981,411	31.1	1,004,837	29.9
Net Profit After Tax	185,743	0.8	54,636	1.4	75,736	2.4	67,213	2.0
Working Capital	1,424,346	—	544,967	—	307,270	—	518,644	—

RATIOS	UQ	MED	LQ	UQ	MED	LQ	UQ	MED	LQ	UQ	MED	LQ
SOLVENCY												
Quick Ratio (times)	2.3	1.1	0.7	2.0	0.9	0.6	2.1	1.1	0.6	1.9	0.9	0.4
Current Ratio (times)	6.1	2.5	1.5	3.6	1.9	1.4	3.5	1.9	1.3	4.6	2.4	1.5
Curr Liab To Nw (%)	18.2	63.4	171.2	32.9	70.5	216.4	31.5	74.8	199.5	22.0	52.6	135.8
Curr Liab To Inv (%)	34.0	76.5	142.1	46.2	115.6	160.5	74.4	153.0	378.6	40.6	75.4	129.2
Total Liab To Nw (%)	24.8	72.5	244.3	37.0	99.4	270.7	40.5	100.8	234.0	29.9	81.9	202.6
Fixed Assets To Nw (%)	5.2	13.9	29.0	4.9	16.9	39.6	7.5	18.4	45.6	12.3	27.4	59.9
EFFICIENCY												
Coll Period (days)	9.9	13.1	18.6	22.5	30.7	43.1	22.3	36.5	51.1	12.1	25.6	39.8
Sales To Inv (times)	29.2	21.0	13.5	11.6	8.5	4.6	40.2	12.9	6.6	10.6	6.5	4.2
Assets To Sales (%)	9.0	12.1	15.8	24.0	32.4	48.6	18.7	27.9	41.5	29.5	38.2	51.4
Sales To Nwc (times)	32.2	19.5	10.2	11.8	7.0	4.7	17.7	9.0	5.2	10.7	6.1	3.9
Acct Pay To Sales (%)	0.7	1.2	2.0	3.8	6.4	10.9	2.5	5.0	8.9	2.7	4.3	6.9
PROFITABILITY												
Return On Sales (%)	0.9	0.5	0.2	2.6	1.3	0.1	4.1	1.3	0.1	3.2	1.3	0.2
Return On Assets (%)	7.4	4.0	2.1	7.5	4.8	0.4	14.7	4.6	0.4	8.4	3.3	0.5
Return On Nw (%)	16.0	8.6	4.6	20.8	7.9	0.3	32.5	12.2	1.3	17.4	6.9	1.3

	SIC 5211 LMBR, BLDNG MTRLS (NO BREAKDOWN) 2002 (1319 Establishments)		SIC 5231 PNT, GLS, WLPR STRS (NO BREAKDOWN) 2002 (92 Establishments)		SIC 5251 HARDWARE STORES (NO BREAKDOWN) 2002 (509 Establishments)		SIC 5261 RET NSRS, GDN STRS (NO BREAKDOWN) 2002 (313 Establishments)	
	$	%	$	%	$	%	$	%
Cash	161,514	10.5	71,739	13.9	79,914	9.2	120,592	10.2
Accounts Receivable	379,942	24.7	121,801	23.6	109,447	12.6	113,498	9.6
Notes Receivable	9,229	0.6	1,032	0.2	2,606	0.3	3,547	0.3
Inventory	535,303	34.8	153,284	29.7	419,547	48.3	547,393	46.3
Other Current	78,451	5.1	34,579	6.7	44,300	5.1	61,479	5.2
Total Current	**1,164,439**	**75.7**	**382,435**	**74.1**	**655,814**	**75.5**	**846,509**	**71.6**
Fixed Assets	283,034	18.4	98,576	19.1	136,375	15.7	266,012	22.5
Other Non-current	90,755	5.9	35,096	6.8	76,439	8.8	69,754	5.9
Total Assets	**1,538,228**	**100.0**	**516,107**	**100.0**	**868,628**	**100.0**	**1,182,275**	**100.0**
Accounts Payable	224,581	14.6	98,576	19.1	102,498	11.8	211,627	17.9
Bank Loans	6,153	0.4	1,032	0.2	2,606	0.3	3,547	0.3
Notes Payable	63,067	4.1	14,967	2.9	23,453	2.7	62,661	5.3
Other Current	230,735	15.0	63,482	12.3	120,739	13.9	216,356	18.3
Total Current	**524,536**	**34.1**	**178,057**	**34.5**	**249,296**	**28.7**	**494,191**	**41.8**
Other Long Term	201,508	13.1	79,996	15.5	133,769	15.4	186,799	15.8
Deferred Credits	1,538	0.1	0	0.0	869	0.1	2,365	0.2
Net Worth	810,646	52.7	258,054	50.0	484,694	55.8	498,920	42.2
Total Liab & Net Worth	**1,538,228**	**100.0**	**516,107**	**100.0**	**868,628**	**100.0**	**1,182,275**	**100.0**
Net Sales	4,249,249	100.0	1,633,250	100.0	2,015,378	100.0	2,912,007	100.0
Gross Profit	1,143,048	26.9	656,567	40.2	707,398	35.1	928,930	31.9
Net Profit After Tax	84,985	2.0	32,665	2.0	44,338	2.2	46,592	1.6
Working Capital	639,903	—	204,378	—	406,518	—	352,318	—

RATIOS	UQ	MED	LQ	UQ	MED	LQ	UQ	MED	LQ	UQ	MED	LQ
SOLVENCY												
Quick Ratio (times)	2.2	1.2	0.6	2.0	1.0	0.7	1.6	0.8	0.4	1.0	0.4	0.1
Current Ratio (times)	4.6	2.6	1.6	3.9	2.3	1.5	5.8	3.1	1.9	3.2	1.7	1.3
Curr Liab To Nw (%)	21.4	49.2	117.6	25.3	51.7	103.0	15.3	38.0	92.8	32.8	92.6	217.7
Curr Liab To Inv (%)	43.4	83.1	145.9	60.7	117.3	224.9	27.4	49.9	83.7	56.8	81.5	121.5
Total Liab To Nw (%)	27.4	73.3	175.1	32.0	70.8	172.2	23.7	60.0	158.5	49.4	131.3	304.6
Fixed Assets To Nw (%)	13.4	26.8	57.7	11.9	26.1	66.0	8.2	21.6	47.5	14.9	38.8	82.7
EFFICIENCY												
Coll Period (days)	23.0	33.6	44.2	17.9	25.2	39.4	7.3	16.1	28.7	3.9	10.2	19.4
Sales To Inv (times)	12.1	7.7	5.3	21.6	11.2	7.9	6.9	4.8	3.5	10.2	5.6	3.5
Assets To Sales (%)	28.0	36.2	48.3	24.4	31.6	40.6	33.3	43.1	56.1	30.1	40.6	53.8
Sales To Nwc (times)	9.9	6.2	4.0	13.4	7.1	4.9	8.2	4.8	3.3	13.8	7.8	4.9
Acct Pay To Sales (%)	2.9	4.4	6.4	3.3	5.0	7.2	2.6	4.4	7.2	2.5	5.4	10.6
PROFITABILITY												
Return On Sales (%)	3.1	1.3	0.3	2.4	1.5	(0.5)	4.0	1.6	0.3	2.8	1.0	0.1
Return On Assets (%)	8.6	3.5	0.7	9.2	3.3	(1.3)	8.8	3.6	0.5	7.1	2.4	0.2
Return On Nw (%)	16.5	7.0	1.6	17.6	7.1	(3.6)	15.9	6.8	1.0	17.8	6.5	1.1

SIC 5271 MOBILE HOME DEALERS (NO BREAKDOWN) 2002 (122 Establishments)

	$	%
Cash	196,424	12.3
Accounts Receivable	119,771	7.5
Notes Receivable	17,566	1.1
Inventory	817,634	51.2
Other Current	132,546	8.3
Total Current	**1,283,941**	**80.4**
Fixed Assets	234,750	14.7
Other Non-current	78,251	4.9
Total Assets	**1,596,942**	**100.0**
Accounts Payable	89,429	5.6
Bank Loans	7,985	0.5
Notes Payable	156,500	9.8
Other Current	595,659	37.3
Total Current	**849,573**	**53.2**
Other Long Term	213,990	13.4
Deferred Credits	1,597	0.1
Net Worth	531,782	33.3
Total Liab & Net Worth	**1,596,942**	**100.0**
Net Sales	3,441,685	100.0
Gross Profit	850,096	24.7
Net Profit After Tax	68,834	2.0
Working Capital	434,368	—

RATIOS	UQ	MED	LQ
SOLVENCY			
Quick Ratio (times)	0.8	0.3	0.1
Current Ratio (times)	2.7	1.4	1.1
Curr Liab To Nw (%)	55.2	223.1	477.3
Curr Liab To Inv (%)	73.9	102.9	140.2
Total Liab To Nw (%)	82.8	302.2	563.2
Fixed Assets To Nw (%)	15.2	38.8	73.3
EFFICIENCY			
Coll Period (days)	1.1	6.6	19.7
Sales To Inv (times)	6.3	4.3	2.8
Assets To Sales (%)	32.6	46.4	67.9
Sales To Nwc (times)	22.6	11.5	3.8
Acct Pay To Sales (%)	0.3	1.2	2.9
PROFITABILITY			
Return On Sales (%)	3.0	1.0	0.1
Return On Assets (%)	6.9	1.9	0.3
Return On Nw (%)	25.1	8.8	1.1

SIC 53 GEN MERCHANDISE (NO BREAKDOWN) 2002 (402 Establishments)

	$	%
Cash	164,469	14.4
Accounts Receivable	60,534	5.3
Notes Receivable	2,284	0.2
Inventory	555,083	48.6
Other Current	78,809	6.9
Total Current	**861,179**	**75.4**
Fixed Assets	204,444	17.9
Other Non-current	76,524	6.7
Total Assets	**1,142,147**	**100.0**
Accounts Payable	158,758	13.9
Bank Loans	2,284	0.2
Notes Payable	28,554	2.5
Other Current	174,749	15.3
Total Current	**364,345**	**31.9**
Other Long Term	143,911	12.6
Deferred Credits	1,142	0.1
Net Worth	632,749	55.4
Total Liab & Net Worth	**1,142,147**	**100.0**
Net Sales	2,806,258	100.0
Gross Profit	973,772	34.7
Net Profit After Tax	47,706	1.7
Working Capital	496,834	—

RATIOS	UQ	MED	LQ
SOLVENCY			
Quick Ratio (times)	1.5	0.6	0.2
Current Ratio (times)	6.2	2.8	1.6
Curr Liab To Nw (%)	16.9	41.8	100.4
Curr Liab To Inv (%)	29.4	53.0	97.6
Total Liab To Nw (%)	21.8	65.5	164.5
Fixed Assets To Nw (%)	7.6	23.7	55.9
EFFICIENCY			
Coll Period (days)	1.5	5.1	17.2
Sales To Inv (times)	9.0	5.2	3.5
Assets To Sales (%)	27.1	40.7	57.0
Sales To Nwc (times)	11.0	5.5	3.2
Acct Pay To Sales (%)	2.3	4.9	7.7
PROFITABILITY			
Return On Sales (%)	3.5	1.2	0.1
Return On Assets (%)	8.7	3.5	0.3
Return On Nw (%)	17.9	6.2	0.7

SIC 5311 DEPARTMENT STORES (NO BREAKDOWN) 2002 (143 Establishments)

	$	%
Cash	372,773	11.8
Accounts Receivable	214,818	6.8
Notes Receivable	6,318	0.2
Inventory	1,535,320	48.6
Other Current	170,592	5.4
Total Current	**2,299,821**	**72.8**
Fixed Assets	647,614	20.5
Other Non-current	211,660	6.7
Total Assets	**3,159,095**	**100.0**
Accounts Payable	426,478	13.5
Bank Loans	6,318	0.2
Notes Payable	47,386	1.5
Other Current	473,865	15.0
Total Current	**954,047**	**30.2**
Other Long Term	533,887	16.9
Deferred Credits	3,159	0.1
Net Worth	1,668,002	52.8
Total Liab & Net Worth	**3,159,095**	**100.0**
Net Sales	7,212,546	100.0
Gross Profit	2,488,328	34.5
Net Profit After Tax	72,125	1.0
Working Capital	1,345,774	—

RATIOS	UQ	MED	LQ
SOLVENCY			
Quick Ratio (times)	1.4	0.6	0.2
Current Ratio (times)	4.9	2.6	1.6
Curr Liab To Nw (%)	19.4	45.6	92.5
Curr Liab To Inv (%)	32.4	52.8	93.6
Total Liab To Nw (%)	25.1	76.6	176.9
Fixed Assets To Nw (%)	8.1	33.0	84.0
EFFICIENCY			
Coll Period (days)	1.8	6.1	21.2
Sales To Inv (times)	6.6	4.6	3.5
Assets To Sales (%)	32.0	43.8	64.9
Sales To Nwc (times)	8.5	5.1	3.1
Acct Pay To Sales (%)	3.0	5.6	7.9
PROFITABILITY			
Return On Sales (%)	2.8	1.0	0.1
Return On Assets (%)	6.8	2.3	0.1
Return On Nw (%)	16.2	4.5	0.2

SIC 5331 VARIETY STORES (NO BREAKDOWN) 2002 (172 Establishments)

	$	%
Cash	117,155	16.7
Accounts Receivable	23,852	3.4
Notes Receivable	702	0.1
Inventory	366,897	52.3
Other Current	52,613	7.5
Total Current	**561,219**	**80.0**
Fixed Assets	98,213	14.0
Other Non-current	42,092	6.0
Total Assets	**701,524**	**100.0**
Accounts Payable	112,244	16.0
Bank Loans	0	0.0
Notes Payable	13,329	1.9
Other Current	113,647	16.2
Total Current	**239,220**	**34.1**
Other Long Term	57,525	8.2
Deferred Credits	0	0.0
Net Worth	404,779	57.7
Total Liab & Net Worth	**701,524**	**100.0**
Net Sales	1,916,732	100.0
Gross Profit	680,440	35.5
Net Profit After Tax	47,918	2.5
Working Capital	321,999	—

RATIOS	UQ	MED	LQ
SOLVENCY			
Quick Ratio (times)	1.4	0.5	0.2
Current Ratio (times)	6.5	2.9	1.6
Curr Liab To Nw (%)	16.4	39.6	127.9
Curr Liab To Inv (%)	27.3	51.7	97.4
Total Liab To Nw (%)	18.4	55.2	157.2
Fixed Assets To Nw (%)	5.7	18.9	40.7
EFFICIENCY			
Coll Period (days)	0.7	2.9	14.2
Sales To Inv (times)	11.9	5.7	3.8
Assets To Sales (%)	21.3	36.6	52.0
Sales To Nwc (times)	14.5	6.1	3.3
Acct Pay To Sales (%)	1.9	4.1	7.7
PROFITABILITY			
Return On Sales (%)	3.9	1.6	0.3
Return On Assets (%)	12.4	4.9	0.8
Return On Nw (%)	26.0	10.1	1.6

	SIC 5399 MISC GNRL MRCH STRS (NO BREAKDOWN) 2002 (87 Establishments) $	%	SIC 54 FOOD STORES (NO BREAKDOWN) 2002 (561 Establishments) $	%	SIC 5411 GROCERY STORES (NO BREAKDOWN) 2002 (455 Establishments) $	%	SIC 5421 MEAT, FISH MARKETS (NO BREAKDOWN) 2002 (11 Establishments) $	%
Cash	155,549	14.2	338,234	13.5	365,850	13.0	63,141	7.3
Accounts Receivable	72,298	6.6	170,370	6.8	166,039	5.9	155,691	18.0
Notes Receivable	6,573	0.6	12,527	0.5	16,885	0.6	0	0.0
Inventory	452,408	41.3	663,940	26.5	776,727	27.6	235,267	27.2
Other Current	84,346	7.7	165,358	6.6	180,110	6.4	58,818	6.8
Total Current	**771,174**	**70.4**	**1,350,429**	**53.9**	**1,505,611**	**53.5**	**512,917**	**59.3**
Fixed Assets	234,419	21.4	899,451	35.9	1,024,379	36.4	283,704	32.8
Other Non-current	89,825	8.2	255,554	10.2	284,237	10.1	68,331	7.9
Total Assets	**1,095,418**	**100.0**	**2,505,434**	**100.0**	**2,814,227**	**100.0**	**864,952**	**100.0**
Accounts Payable	116,114	10.6	428,429	17.1	484,047	17.2	179,910	20.8
Bank Loans	4,382	0.4	5,011	0.2	2,814	0.1	26,814	3.1
Notes Payable	60,248	5.5	50,109	2.0	59,099	2.1	4,325	0.5
Other Current	152,263	13.9	440,956	17.6	379,921	13.5	178,179	20.6
Total Current	**333,007**	**30.4**	**924,505**	**36.9**	**925,881**	**32.9**	**389,228**	**45.0**
Other Long Term	159,932	14.6	551,196	22.0	616,316	21.9	198,939	23.0
Deferred Credits	1,095	0.1	7,516	0.3	5,628	0.2	865	0.1
Net Worth	601,384	54.9	1,022,217	40.8	1,266,402	45.0	275,920	31.9
Total Liab & Net Worth	**1,095,418**	**100.0**	**2,505,434**	**100.0**	**2,814,227**	**100.0**	**864,952**	**100.0**
Net Sales	2,565,382	100.0	11,285,739	100.0	13,212,333	100.0	3,544,885	100.0
Gross Profit	856,838	33.4	3,171,293	28.1	3,184,172	24.1	1,552,660	43.8
Net Profit After Tax	38,481	1.5	203,143	1.8	198,185	1.5	258,777	7.3
Working Capital	438,167	—	425,924	—	579,730	—	123,689	—

RATIOS	UQ	MED	LQ	UQ	MED	LQ	UQ	MED	LQ	UQ	MED	LQ
SOLVENCY												
Quick Ratio (times)	2.2	0.8	0.2	1.0	0.5	0.3	1.0	0.5	0.2	1.4	0.5	0.3
Current Ratio (times)	7.0	3.1	1.9	2.6	1.6	1.0	2.6	1.6	1.1	2.9	1.1	1.0
Curr Liab To Nw (%)	13.3	35.2	86.6	30.3	61.3	135.8	30.6	61.3	136.7	61.9	90.6	153.3
Curr Liab To Inv (%)	28.0	55.9	101.9	72.6	126.0	206.7	71.8	119.0	188.7	92.5	155.4	192.7
Total Liab To Nw (%)	18.1	61.4	124.0	47.0	107.3	277.0	48.5	105.2	277.3	61.9	136.3	289.0
Fixed Assets To Nw (%)	9.2	21.8	50.1	33.1	75.4	155.9	34.3	77.5	161.5	27.0	86.0	89.1
EFFICIENCY												
Coll Period (days)	2.2	7.0	15.3	1.1	3.3	7.9	1.1	2.9	6.9	2.6	6.6	14.6
Sales To Inv (times)	9.4	5.5	3.4	30.5	19.5	13.1	29.6	19.6	13.9	37.3	20.4	12.1
Assets To Sales (%)	29.1	42.7	65.9	15.4	22.2	34.1	15.3	21.3	31.2	13.9	24.4	46.1
Sales To Nwc (times)	10.1	5.7	3.0	41.3	19.6	10.8	41.3	20.8	11.1	97.1	36.0	9.7
Acct Pay To Sales (%)	2.2	4.2	7.2	2.3	3.3	4.8	2.3	3.2	4.6	1.0	3.0	6.2
PROFITABILITY												
Return On Sales (%)	4.1	1.0	(0.3)	2.5	1.0	0.3	2.2	1.0	0.3	2.7	1.8	1.0
Return On Assets (%)	7.1	2.5	(0.8)	10.9	4.4	1.1	9.4	4.4	1.4	12.6	4.5	3.9
Return On Nw (%)	11.8	4.6	(0.2)	26.0	10.3	3.3	24.8	10.0	3.5	48.9	19.7	3.5

SIC 5431 FRT,VGTBLE MARKETS
(NO BREAKDOWN)
2002 (21 Establishments)

	$	%
Cash	280,855	20.0
Accounts Receivable	224,684	16.0
Notes Receivable	1,404	0.1
Inventory	165,704	11.8
Other Current	87,065	6.2
Total Current	**759,712**	**54.1**
Fixed Assets	602,433	42.9
Other Non-current	42,128	3.0
Total Assets	**1,404,273**	**100.0**
Accounts Payable	262,599	18.7
Bank Loans	0	0.0
Notes Payable	29,490	2.1
Other Current	235,918	16.8
Total Current	**528,007**	**37.6**
Other Long Term	231,705	16.5
Deferred Credits	4,213	0.3
Net Worth	640,348	45.6
Total Liab & Net Worth	**1,404,273**	**100.0**
Net Sales	6,383,059	100.0
Gross Profit	2,374,498	37.2
Net Profit After Tax	274,472	4.3
Working Capital	231,705	—

RATIOS	UQ	MED	LQ
SOLVENCY			
Quick Ratio (times)	1.4	1.0	0.3
Current Ratio (times)	4.1	1.3	1.2
Curr Liab To Nw (%)	11.9	66.2	288.8
Curr Liab To Inv (%)	72.7	227.7	359.6
Total Liab To Nw (%)	41.2	129.3	307.6
Fixed Assets To Nw (%)	41.0	73.2	170.8
EFFICIENCY			
Coll Period (days)	1.7	4.8	21.6
Sales To Inv (times)	58.6	36.3	16.6
Assets To Sales (%)	16.2	22.0	40.6
Sales To Nwc (times)	44.1	17.5	4.8
Acct Pay To Sales (%)	1.5	2.5	5.6
PROFITABILITY			
Return On Sales (%)	5.4	1.3	0.3
Return On Assets (%)	12.5	6.4	1.2
Return On Nw (%)	60.5	11.1	2.4

SIC 5461 RETAIL BAKERIES
(NO BREAKDOWN)
2002 (16 Establishments)

	$	%
Cash	106,888	10.2
Accounts Receivable	46,109	4.4
Notes Receivable	0	0.0
Inventory	55,540	5.3
Other Current	107,936	10.3
Total Current	**316,473**	**30.2**
Fixed Assets	418,122	39.9
Other Non-current	313,329	29.9
Total Assets	**1,047,924**	**100.0**
Accounts Payable	102,697	9.8
Bank Loans	0	0.0
Notes Payable	24,102	2.3
Other Current	263,029	25.1
Total Current	**389,828**	**37.2**
Other Long Term	347,911	33.2
Deferred Credits	8,383	0.8
Net Worth	301,802	28.8
Total Liab & Net Worth	**1,047,924**	**100.0**
Net Sales	2,454,155	100.0
Gross Profit	1,288,431	52.5
Net Profit After Tax	(17,179)	(0.7)
Working Capital	(73,355)	—

RATIOS	UQ	MED	LQ
Quick Ratio (times)	0.8	0.5	0.2
Current Ratio (times)	1.9	1.0	0.6
Curr Liab To Nw (%)	24.8	33.4	49.4
Curr Liab To Inv (%)	292.1	498.5	999.9
Total Liab To Nw (%)	34.1	56.9	95.5
Fixed Assets To Nw (%)	45.7	72.4	106.4
Coll Period (days)	4.4	5.0	11.3
Sales To Inv (times)	98.0	58.0	51.9
Assets To Sales (%)	18.6	42.7	61.0
Sales To Nwc (times)	119.4	17.7	14.2
Acct Pay To Sales (%)	2.2	3.4	5.9
Return On Sales (%)	2.8	1.8	(2.3)
Return On Assets (%)	14.6	8.1	(3.4)
Return On Nw (%)	28.8	14.0	11.3

SIC 5499 MISC FOOD STORES
(NO BREAKDOWN)
2002 (49 Establishments)

	$	%
Cash	198,746	15.3
Accounts Receivable	124,703	9.6
Notes Receivable	0	0.0
Inventory	355,924	27.4
Other Current	105,218	8.1
Total Current	**784,591**	**60.4**
Fixed Assets	371,512	28.6
Other Non-current	142,889	11.0
Total Assets	**1,298,992**	**100.0**
Accounts Payable	220,829	17.0
Bank Loans	0	0.0
Notes Payable	19,485	1.5
Other Current	693,661	53.4
Total Current	**933,975**	**71.9**
Other Long Term	281,881	21.7
Deferred Credits	11,691	0.9
Net Worth	71,445	5.5
Total Liab & Net Worth	**1,298,992**	**100.0**
Net Sales	4,059,350	100.0
Gross Profit	1,879,479	46.3
Net Profit After Tax	109,602	2.7
Working Capital	(149,384)	—

RATIOS	UQ	MED	LQ
Quick Ratio (times)	1.1	0.6	0.3
Current Ratio (times)	2.6	1.4	1.0
Curr Liab To Nw (%)	31.8	53.8	119.9
Curr Liab To Inv (%)	73.9	136.2	318.5
Total Liab To Nw (%)	36.4	101.2	308.8
Fixed Assets To Nw (%)	12.9	67.3	135.9
Coll Period (days)	1.5	11.7	33.2
Sales To Inv (times)	24.0	15.8	9.0
Assets To Sales (%)	20.4	32.0	47.7
Sales To Nwc (times)	34.7	14.1	6.2
Acct Pay To Sales (%)	2.4	4.4	6.2
Return On Sales (%)	4.5	2.0	(0.3)
Return On Assets (%)	15.1	4.5	(1.1)
Return On Nw (%)	35.8	8.1	(5.7)

SIC 55 AUTO DEALER SVC STATN
(NO BREAKDOWN)
2002 (2467 Establishments)

	$	%
Cash	429,409	10.1
Accounts Receivable	331,623	7.8
Notes Receivable	21,258	0.5
Inventory	2,321,362	54.6
Other Current	276,353	6.5
Total Current	**3,380,005**	**79.5**
Fixed Assets	671,749	15.8
Other Non-current	199,825	4.7
Total Assets	**4,251,579**	**100.0**
Accounts Payable	420,906	9.9
Bank Loans	8,503	0.2
Notes Payable	582,466	13.7
Other Current	1,381,764	32.5
Total Current	**2,393,639**	**56.3**
Other Long Term	501,686	11.8
Deferred Credits	8,503	0.2
Net Worth	1,347,751	31.7
Total Liab & Net Worth	**4,251,579**	**100.0**
Net Sales	14,660,617	100.0
Gross Profit	2,902,802	19.8
Net Profit After Tax	234,570	1.6
Working Capital	986,366	—

RATIOS	UQ	MED	LQ
Quick Ratio (times)	0.6	0.3	0.1
Current Ratio (times)	1.8	1.3	1.1
Curr Liab To Nw (%)	82.2	206.5	413.5
Curr Liab To Inv (%)	81.9	102.4	126.9
Total Liab To Nw (%)	116.2	255.2	493.9
Fixed Assets To Nw (%)	14.2	31.8	71.2
Coll Period (days)	2.6	6.2	15.3
Sales To Inv (times)	10.1	6.3	4.2
Assets To Sales (%)	21.8	29.0	41.0
Sales To Nwc (times)	31.2	16.6	7.9
Acct Pay To Sales (%)	0.5	1.2	3.8
Return On Sales (%)	2.4	1.1	0.3
Return On Assets (%)	8.0	3.8	1.0
Return On Nw (%)	31.1	13.5	4.5

SIC 5511 NEW,USED CAR DLRS
(NO BREAKDOWN)
2002 (1224 Establishments)

	$	%
Cash	670,648	9.6
Accounts Receivable	405,183	5.8
Notes Receivable	27,944	0.4
Inventory	4,380,169	62.7
Other Current	579,831	8.3
Total Current	**6,063,775**	**86.8**
Fixed Assets	628,732	9.0
Other Non-current	293,409	4.2
Total Assets	**6,985,916**	**100.0**
Accounts Payable	426,141	6.1
Bank Loans	6,986	0.1
Notes Payable	1,439,099	20.6
Other Current	2,871,211	41.1
Total Current	**4,743,437**	**67.9**
Other Long Term	558,873	8.0
Deferred Credits	6,986	0.1
Net Worth	1,676,620	24.0
Total Liab & Net Worth	**6,985,916**	**100.0**
Net Sales	27,832,335	100.0
Gross Profit	3,785,198	13.6
Net Profit After Tax	389,653	1.4
Working Capital	1,320,338	—

RATIOS	UQ	MED	LQ
SOLVENCY			
Quick Ratio (times)	0.4	0.2	0.1
Current Ratio (times)	1.5	1.3	1.1
Curr Liab To Nw (%)	169.4	294.3	498.6
Curr Liab To Inv (%)	91.2	104.9	121.0
Total Liab To Nw (%)	189.2	333.8	572.2
Fixed Assets To Nw (%)	13.0	27.2	56.4
EFFICIENCY			
Coll Period (days)	2.9	5.5	11.7
Sales To Inv (times)	8.1	6.3	4.9
Assets To Sales (%)	20.4	25.1	32.2
Sales To Nwc (times)	35.7	21.8	12.8
Acct Pay To Sales (%)	0.4	0.7	1.2
PROFITABILITY			
Return On Sales (%)	2.0	1.1	0.4
Return On Assets (%)	8.2	4.2	1.5
Return On Nw (%)	36.6	18.6	6.9

SIC 5521 USED CAR DEALERS
(NO BREAKDOWN)
2002 (75 Establishments)

	$	%
Cash	99,667	8.1
Accounts Receivable	175,955	14.3
Notes Receivable	14,765	1.2
Inventory	650,912	52.9
Other Current	79,981	6.5
Total Current	**1,021,280**	**83.0**
Fixed Assets	171,034	13.9
Other Non-current	38,144	3.1
Total Assets	**1,230,458**	**100.0**
Accounts Payable	92,284	7.5
Bank Loans	1,230	0.1
Notes Payable	115,663	9.4
Other Current	361,756	29.4
Total Current	**570,933**	**46.4**
Other Long Term	221,482	18.0
Deferred Credits	0	0.0
Net Worth	438,043	35.6
Total Liab & Net Worth	**1,230,458**	**100.0**
Net Sales	4,732,531	100.0
Gross Profit	993,832	21.0
Net Profit After Tax	94,651	2.0
Working Capital	450,347	—

RATIOS	UQ	MED	LQ
SOLVENCY			
Quick Ratio (times)	1.4	0.4	0.1
Current Ratio (times)	6.4	1.8	1.2
Curr Liab To Nw (%)	21.3	150.4	327.1
Curr Liab To Inv (%)	40.0	85.0	125.3
Total Liab To Nw (%)	66.0	240.7	505.1
Fixed Assets To Nw (%)	9.3	27.9	61.3
EFFICIENCY			
Coll Period (days)	2.9	7.3	25.9
Sales To Inv (times)	13.8	7.0	4.5
Assets To Sales (%)	16.3	26.0	41.6
Sales To Nwc (times)	30.1	11.9	5.0
Acct Pay To Sales (%)	0.4	1.4	3.0
PROFITABILITY			
Return On Sales (%)	2.5	0.8	0.1
Return On Assets (%)	9.0	2.4	0.1
Return On Nw (%)	36.3	11.0	1.1

SIC 5531 AUTO,HOME SPPL STRS
(NO BREAKDOWN)
2002 (359 Establishments)

	$	%
Cash	123,014	12.0
Accounts Receivable	171,195	16.7
Notes Receivable	6,151	0.6
Inventory	409,022	39.9
Other Current	59,457	5.8
Total Current	**768,839**	**75.0**
Fixed Assets	206,049	20.1
Other Non-current	50,230	4.9
Total Assets	**1,025,118**	**100.0**
Accounts Payable	185,546	18.1
Bank Loans	3,075	0.3
Notes Payable	32,804	3.2
Other Current	162,994	15.9
Total Current	**384,419**	**37.5**
Other Long Term	153,768	15.0
Deferred Credits	2,050	0.2
Net Worth	484,881	47.3
Total Liab & Net Worth	**1,025,118**	**100.0**
Net Sales	2,879,545	100.0
Gross Profit	1,065,432	37.0
Net Profit After Tax	66,230	2.3
Working Capital	384,420	—

RATIOS	UQ	MED	LQ
SOLVENCY			
Quick Ratio (times)	1.4	0.7	0.4
Current Ratio (times)	3.8	2.2	1.4
Curr Liab To Nw (%)	28.4	67.6	165.3
Curr Liab To Inv (%)	51.5	86.8	130.4
Total Liab To Nw (%)	37.2	96.2	256.6
Fixed Assets To Nw (%)	14.8	33.9	75.5
EFFICIENCY			
Coll Period (days)	11.7	22.3	34.0
Sales To Inv (times)	11.0	7.3	4.5
Assets To Sales (%)	26.7	35.6	48.8
Sales To Nwc (times)	12.8	6.9	4.1
Acct Pay To Sales (%)	3.7	6.1	9.5
PROFITABILITY			
Return On Sales (%)	3.3	1.4	0.2
Return On Assets (%)	8.9	3.8	0.6
Return On Nw (%)	20.6	8.9	1.1

SIC 5541 GASLNE SVC STATIONS
(NO BREAKDOWN)
2002 (304 Establishments)

	$	%
Cash	528,999	12.3
Accounts Receivable	421,479	9.8
Notes Receivable	30,106	0.7
Inventory	705,333	16.4
Other Current	197,837	4.6
Total Current	**1,883,754**	**43.8**
Fixed Assets	1,900,957	44.2
Other Non-current	516,097	12.0
Total Assets	**4,300,808**	**100.0**
Accounts Payable	658,024	15.3
Bank Loans	4,301	0.1
Notes Payable	94,618	2.2
Other Current	649,421	15.1
Total Current	**1,406,364**	**32.7**
Other Long Term	1,053,698	24.5
Deferred Credits	17,203	0.4
Net Worth	1,823,543	42.4
Total Liab & Net Worth	**4,300,808**	**100.0**
Net Sales	18,699,165	100.0
Gross Profit	3,104,061	16.6
Net Profit After Tax	168,292	0.9
Working Capital	477,390	—

RATIOS	UQ	MED	LQ
SOLVENCY			
Quick Ratio (times)	1.1	0.6	0.4
Current Ratio (times)	2.0	1.3	0.9
Curr Liab To Nw (%)	35.5	66.1	143.1
Curr Liab To Inv (%)	136.6	213.7	320.8
Total Liab To Nw (%)	55.5	126.0	301.2
Fixed Assets To Nw (%)	45.5	97.2	207.5
EFFICIENCY			
Coll Period (days)	3.3	6.2	13.5
Sales To Inv (times)	54.1	35.7	22.2
Assets To Sales (%)	15.1	23.0	35.2
Sales To Nwc (times)	60.7	25.0	13.6
Acct Pay To Sales (%)	2.3	3.1	4.5
PROFITABILITY			
Return On Sales (%)	1.5	0.7	0.0
Return On Assets (%)	6.0	2.7	0.0
Return On Nw (%)	16.9	6.6	0.6

	SIC 5551 BOAT DEALERS (NO BREAKDOWN) 2002 (170 Establishments)		SIC 5561 RCRTNL VHCLE DLRS (NO BREAKDOWN) 2002 (154 Establishments)		SIC 5571 MOTORCYCLE DEALERS (NO BREAKDOWN) 2002 (130 Establishments)		SIC 5599 ATMTVE DLRS,NEC (NO BREAKDOWN) 2002 (51 Establishments)	
	$	%	$	%	$	%	$	%
Cash	161,640	8.3	179,598	7.8	266,610	10.3	111,735	8.9
Accounts Receivable	89,583	4.6	62,168	2.7	90,595	3.5	129,311	10.3
Notes Receivable	11,685	0.6	4,605	0.2	15,531	0.6	10,044	0.8
Inventory	1,334,013	68.5	1,701,572	73.9	1,801,556	69.6	647,813	51.6
Other Current	60,371	3.1	92,101	4.0	72,476	2.8	72,816	5.8
Total Current	**1,657,292**	**85.1**	**2,040,044**	**88.6**	**2,246,768**	**86.8**	**971,719**	**77.4**
Fixed Assets	249,275	12.8	214,136	9.3	297,671	11.5	244,813	19.5
Other Non-current	40,897	2.1	48,353	2.1	44,003	1.7	38,919	3.1
Total Assets	**1,947,464**	**100.0**	**2,302,533**	**100.0**	**2,588,442**	**100.0**	**1,255,451**	**100.0**
Accounts Payable	185,009	9.5	188,808	8.2	300,259	11.6	173,252	13.8
Bank Loans	9,737	0.5	11,513	0.5	15,531	0.6	3,766	0.3
Notes Payable	212,274	10.9	276,304	12.0	349,440	13.5	131,822	10.5
Other Current	671,875	34.5	1,061,467	46.1	786,886	30.4	164,465	13.1
Total Current	**1,078,895**	**55.4**	**1,538,092**	**66.8**	**1,452,116**	**56.1**	**473,305**	**37.7**
Other Long Term	231,748	11.9	193,413	8.4	222,606	8.6	189,573	15.1
Deferred Credits	3,895	0.2	0	0.0	0	0.0	3,766	0.3
Net Worth	632,926	32.5	571,028	24.8	913,720	35.3	588,807	46.9
Total Liab & Net Worth	**1,947,464**	**100.0**	**2,302,533**	**100.0**	**2,588,442**	**100.0**	**1,255,451**	**100.0**
Net Sales	4,007,128	100.0	5,965,111	100.0	7,210,145	100.0	3,099,879	100.0
Gross Profit	1,045,860	26.1	1,151,266	19.3	1,643,913	22.8	706,772	22.8
Net Profit After Tax	76,135	1.9	113,337	1.9	201,884	2.8	3,100	0.1
Working Capital	578,397	—	501,952	—	794,652	—	498,414	—

RATIOS	UQ	MED	LQ	UQ	MED	LQ	UQ	MED	LQ	UQ	MED	LQ
SOLVENCY												
Quick Ratio (times)	0.4	0.2	0.1	0.3	0.1	0.0	0.4	0.2	0.1	1.1	0.3	0.1
Current Ratio (times)	2.2	1.4	1.1	1.6	1.3	1.1	2.1	1.4	1.2	2.9	1.6	1.1
Curr Liab To Nw (%)	71.5	200.9	444.5	131.1	322.9	565.3	77.8	194.3	309.3	51.3	143.3	411.6
Curr Liab To Inv (%)	59.5	87.6	103.5	76.3	90.0	101.1	65.0	86.5	98.1	54.5	93.8	120.9
Total Liab To Nw (%)	109.0	242.2	512.6	171.7	339.5	573.9	101.8	218.7	352.8	53.3	196.1	545.5
Fixed Assets To Nw (%)	10.3	26.6	69.9	11.4	25.5	58.2	12.4	23.1	48.7	13.4	40.2	94.8
EFFICIENCY												
Coll Period (days)	1.1	4.0	9.5	0.4	1.7	4.4	1.1	3.3	6.2	5.0	13.5	23.6
Sales To Inv (times)	4.1	2.9	2.3	4.2	3.4	2.7	5.9	4.0	3.2	9.9	5.9	2.6
Assets To Sales (%)	38.7	48.6	62.9	32.4	38.6	49.4	27.6	35.9	43.4	27.6	40.5	53.8
Sales To Nwc (times)	17.0	9.2	4.6	21.8	13.1	7.3	16.8	11.5	7.5	20.0	9.6	4.8
Acct Pay To Sales (%)	0.7	1.6	3.6	0.3	0.8	2.1	1.0	2.0	4.9	1.4	4.9	7.7
PROFITABILITY												
Return On Sales (%)	3.0	1.3	0.2	2.9	1.4	0.5	5.5	2.1	0.8	2.3	0.9	0.0
Return On Assets (%)	6.2	2.9	0.5	7.3	4.0	1.3	14.7	5.9	2.4	6.7	1.8	0.1
Return On Nw (%)	27.9	10.9	3.4	33.7	16.4	5.1	39.9	18.4	8.5	23.8	9.4	0.7

SIC 56 APPAREL ACCES STORES (NO BREAKDOWN) 2002 (2744 Establishments) · SIC 5611 MNS,BYS CLTHNG STRS (NO BREAKDOWN) 2002 (821 Establishments) · SIC 5621 WOMENS CLTHNG STRS (NO BREAKDOWN) 2002 (776 Establishments) · SIC 5632 WMNS ACCY,SPCTY STR (NO BREAKDOWN) 2002 (62 Establishments)

	SIC 56 $	%	SIC 5611 $	%	SIC 5621 $	%	SIC 5632 $	%
Cash	63,789	14.9	61,207	14.7	61,038	16.3	58,182	12.6
Accounts Receivable	20,978	4.9	22,900	5.5	18,349	4.9	44,791	9.7
Notes Receivable	1,284	0.3	833	0.2	1,498	0.4	0	0.0
Inventory	238,031	55.6	233,168	56.0	195,098	52.1	231,803	50.2
Other Current	22,690	5.3	22,900	5.5	22,468	6.0	22,163	4.8
Total Current	**346,772**	**81.0**	**341,008**	**81.9**	**298,451**	**79.7**	**356,939**	**77.3**
Fixed Assets	59,936	14.0	54,961	13.2	57,294	15.3	70,649	15.3
Other Non-current	21,405	5.0	20,402	4.9	18,723	5.0	34,170	7.4
Total Assets	**428,113**	**100.0**	**416,371**	**100.0**	**374,468**	**100.0**	**461,758**	**100.0**
Accounts Payable	63,361	14.8	62,456	15.0	49,430	13.2	74,343	16.1
Bank Loans	856	0.2	1,249	0.3	749	0.2	1,385	0.3
Notes Payable	10,703	2.5	9,160	2.2	6,740	1.8	8,773	1.9
Other Current	62,076	14.5	59,541	14.3	56,919	15.2	70,188	15.2
Total Current	**136,996**	**32.0**	**132,406**	**31.8**	**113,838**	**30.4**	**154,689**	**33.5**
Other Long Term	41,527	9.7	36,641	8.8	34,077	9.1	58,643	12.7
Deferred Credits	0	0.0	0	0.0	0	0.0	0	0.0
Net Worth	249,590	58.3	247,324	59.4	226,553	60.5	248,426	53.8
Total Liab & Net Worth	**428,113**	**100.0**	**416,371**	**100.0**	**374,468**	**100.0**	**461,758**	**100.0**
Net Sales	1,089,346	100.0	986,661	100.0	1,040,189	100.0	1,126,239	100.0
Gross Profit	445,543	40.9	415,384	42.1	420,236	40.4	552,983	49.1
Net Profit After Tax	31,591	2.9	29,600	3.0	27,045	2.6	46,176	4.1
Working Capital	209,776	—	208,602	—	184,613	—	202,250	—

RATIOS	SIC 56 UQ	MED	LQ	SIC 5611 UQ	MED	LQ	SIC 5621 UQ	MED	LQ	SIC 5632 UQ	MED	LQ
SOLVENCY												
Quick Ratio (times)	1.8	0.6	0.2	1.6	0.6	0.2	2.3	0.7	0.2	1.3	0.6	0.3
Current Ratio (times)	6.4	3.0	1.7	6.2	3.0	1.8	7.2	3.2	1.8	5.4	2.3	1.7
Curr Liab To Nw (%)	14.7	38.3	95.5	17.2	40.7	93.3	12.5	35.8	90.9	20.7	52.6	110.9
Curr Liab To Inv (%)	24.8	48.2	84.3	25.5	47.2	81.6	24.8	49.7	91.5	30.4	63.2	102.3
Total Liab To Nw (%)	18.9	50.3	126.7	19.7	50.0	118.0	16.7	43.2	119.2	28.0	78.1	163.9
Fixed Assets To Nw (%)	6.1	17.8	41.6	5.4	16.7	39.3	6.1	18.2	46.0	8.0	18.7	41.2
EFFICIENCY												
Coll Period (days)	1.5	5.8	18.8	2.2	8.0	22.3	1.1	6.0	20.1	6.2	17.4	36.1
Sales To Inv (times)	7.4	4.7	3.0	6.6	4.3	2.8	9.0	5.8	3.6	8.8	5.7	3.8
Assets To Sales (%)	27.8	39.3	58.1	29.8	42.2	60.1	24.7	36.0	55.5	28.5	41.0	64.1
Sales To Nwc (times)	9.2	4.9	2.9	8.1	4.6	2.9	10.1	5.3	3.1	9.7	4.9	3.2
Acct Pay To Sales (%)	2.7	5.1	8.4	3.1	5.4	8.8	2.2	4.4	7.2	2.9	4.9	8.8
PROFITABILITY												
Return On Sales (%)	5.2	1.7	0.0	4.9	1.5	(0.1)	5.2	1.7	0.0	4.9	2.1	0.4
Return On Assets (%)	13.2	4.0	0.1	12.4	3.3	(0.1)	13.4	4.8	0.0	10.7	3.8	1.1
Return On Nw (%)	24.5	7.3	0.5	23.3	5.7	0.2	24.7	7.9	0.3	25.8	11.1	2.3

SIC 5641 CHDRNS, INFNT WR STR
(NO BREAKDOWN)
2002 (116 Establishments)

	$	%
Cash	65,024	14.8
Accounts Receivable	10,544	2.4
Notes Receivable	0	0.0
Inventory	271,521	61.8
Other Current	18,893	4.3
Total Current	**365,982**	**83.3**
Fixed Assets	55,798	12.7
Other Non-current	17,574	4.0
Total Assets	**439,354**	**100.0**
Accounts Payable	72,933	16.6
Bank Loans	439	0.1
Notes Payable	10,984	2.5
Other Current	61,949	14.1
Total Current	**146,305**	**33.3**
Other Long Term	36,027	8.2
Deferred Credits	0	0.0
Net Worth	257,022	58.5
Total Liab & Net Worth	**439,354**	**100.0**
Net Sales	1,372,981	100.0
Gross Profit	553,311	40.3
Net Profit After Tax	39,816	2.9
Working Capital	219,677	—

RATIOS	UQ	MED	LQ
SOLVENCY			
Quick Ratio (times)	1.5	0.4	0.1
Current Ratio (times)	5.6	3.0	1.6
Curr Liab To Nw (%)	17.8	44.0	101.0
Curr Liab To Inv (%)	23.0	52.5	83.1
Total Liab To Nw (%)	24.0	58.8	121.3
Fixed Assets To Nw (%)	4.7	18.1	37.0
EFFICIENCY			
Coll Period (days)	0.4	1.8	11.2
Sales To Inv (times)	8.0	5.2	3.6
Assets To Sales (%)	23.3	32.0	46.7
Sales To Nwc (times)	10.0	5.4	3.2
Acct Pay To Sales (%)	2.3	4.7	8.5
PROFITABILITY			
Return On Sales (%)	4.8	1.5	0.2
Return On Assets (%)	13.5	4.0	0.4
Return On Nw (%)	21.1	6.4	1.2

SIC 5651 FMLY CLTHNG STRS
(NO BREAKDOWN)
2002 (217 Establishments)

	$	%
Cash	83,216	16.0
Accounts Receivable	23,925	4.6
Notes Receivable	2,600	0.5
Inventory	272,532	52.4
Other Current	26,525	5.1
Total Current	**408,798**	**78.6**
Fixed Assets	79,575	15.3
Other Non-current	31,726	6.1
Total Assets	**520,099**	**100.0**
Accounts Payable	55,651	10.7
Bank Loans	520	0.1
Notes Payable	14,563	2.8
Other Current	57,210	11.0
Total Current	**127,944**	**24.6**
Other Long Term	49,410	9.5
Deferred Credits	520	0.1
Net Worth	342,225	65.8
Total Liab & Net Worth	**520,099**	**100.0**
Net Sales	1,163,532	100.0
Gross Profit	438,652	37.7
Net Profit After Tax	32,579	2.8
Working Capital	280,854	—

RATIOS	UQ	MED	LQ
SOLVENCY			
Quick Ratio (times)	2.6	0.8	0.3
Current Ratio (times)	8.4	4.0	1.8
Curr Liab To Nw (%)	10.9	28.7	72.4
Curr Liab To Inv (%)	18.3	42.3	75.7
Total Liab To Nw (%)	12.1	35.8	117.3
Fixed Assets To Nw (%)	7.0	18.0	37.7
EFFICIENCY			
Coll Period (days)	1.7	4.2	20.7
Sales To Inv (times)	7.3	4.3	2.8
Assets To Sales (%)	33.2	44.7	63.4
Sales To Nwc (times)	8.6	4.1	2.5
Acct Pay To Sales (%)	2.2	4.3	7.3
PROFITABILITY			
Return On Sales (%)	6.8	1.9	0.0
Return On Assets (%)	13.7	3.7	(0.1)
Return On Nw (%)	21.1	6.4	0.1

SIC 5661 SHOE STORES
(NO BREAKDOWN)
2002 (433 Establishments)

	$	%
Cash	55,846	12.8
Accounts Receivable	13,089	3.0
Notes Receivable	873	0.2
Inventory	278,358	63.8
Other Current	22,687	5.2
Total Current	**370,853**	**85.0**
Fixed Assets	48,429	11.1
Other Non-current	17,016	3.9
Total Assets	**436,298**	**100.0**
Accounts Payable	75,480	17.3
Bank Loans	1,309	0.3
Notes Payable	11,344	2.6
Other Current	64,571	14.8
Total Current	**152,704**	**35.0**
Other Long Term	38,831	8.9
Deferred Credits	0	0.0
Net Worth	244,763	56.1
Total Liab & Net Worth	**436,298**	**100.0**
Net Sales	1,115,852	100.0
Gross Profit	445,225	39.9
Net Profit After Tax	26,780	2.4
Working Capital	218,149	—

RATIOS	UQ	MED	LQ
SOLVENCY			
Quick Ratio (times)	1.3	0.4	0.1
Current Ratio (times)	5.7	3.0	1.7
Curr Liab To Nw (%)	18.4	41.5	101.1
Curr Liab To Inv (%)	24.6	44.6	73.7
Total Liab To Nw (%)	21.0	54.0	137.4
Fixed Assets To Nw (%)	5.5	15.1	34.2
EFFICIENCY			
Coll Period (days)	0.7	3.3	9.5
Sales To Inv (times)	6.0	3.9	2.7
Assets To Sales (%)	28.2	39.1	57.6
Sales To Nwc (times)	8.4	4.8	2.9
Acct Pay To Sales (%)	3.6	5.8	9.5
PROFITABILITY			
Return On Sales (%)	4.3	1.5	0.0
Return On Assets (%)	10.8	3.6	0.0
Return On Nw (%)	20.1	6.2	0.3

SIC 5699 MISC APPRL,ACCY STR
(NO BREAKDOWN)
2002 (319 Establishments)

	$	%
Cash	75,896	14.7
Accounts Receivable	30,978	6.0
Notes Receivable	2,581	0.5
Inventory	272,604	52.8
Other Current	21,684	4.2
Total Current	**403,743**	**78.2**
Fixed Assets	84,156	16.3
Other Non-current	28,397	5.5
Total Assets	**516,296**	**100.0**
Accounts Payable	87,254	16.9
Bank Loans	1,549	0.3
Notes Payable	23,233	4.5
Other Current	74,863	14.5
Total Current	**186,899**	**36.2**
Other Long Term	80,542	15.6
Deferred Credits	0	0.0
Net Worth	248,855	48.2
Total Liab & Net Worth	**516,296**	**100.0**
Net Sales	1,330,660	100.0
Gross Profit	546,901	41.1
Net Profit After Tax	45,242	3.4
Working Capital	216,844	—

RATIOS	UQ	MED	LQ
SOLVENCY			
Quick Ratio (times)	1.6	0.5	0.1
Current Ratio (times)	5.3	2.6	1.5
Curr Liab To Nw (%)	15.7	47.6	122.1
Curr Liab To Inv (%)	27.7	55.7	93.0
Total Liab To Nw (%)	25.6	76.2	171.2
Fixed Assets To Nw (%)	10.2	22.5	58.8
EFFICIENCY			
Coll Period (days)	1.5	5.5	21.0
Sales To Inv (times)	8.1	4.8	3.2
Assets To Sales (%)	27.0	38.8	54.8
Sales To Nwc (times)	10.8	5.9	3.3
Acct Pay To Sales (%)	2.8	5.7	9.7
PROFITABILITY			
Return On Sales (%)	6.5	2.3	0.4
Return On Assets (%)	18.2	6.0	0.9
Return On Nw (%)	38.8	14.3	3.6

	SIC 57 FURN, HOME FURNISHGS (NO BREAKDOWN) 2002 (3488 Establishments) $	%	SIC 5712 FURNITURE STORES (NO BREAKDOWN) 2002 (1642 Establishments) $	%	SIC 5713 FLR CVRNG STRS (NO BREAKDOWN) 2002 (616 Establishments) $	%	SIC 5714 DRPRY, UPHLSTRY STR (NO BREAKDOWN) 2002 (23 Establishments) $	%
Cash	114,861	13.9	121,205	12.5	87,031	14.8	83,185	23.9
Accounts Receivable	140,478	17.0	139,628	14.4	144,072	24.5	34,109	9.8
Notes Receivable	4,132	0.5	5,818	0.6	2,352	0.4	696	0.2
Inventory	345,410	41.8	455,731	47.0	179,943	30.6	136,438	39.2
Other Current	55,365	6.7	62,057	6.4	41,752	7.1	18,448	5.3
Total Current	**660,246**	**79.9**	**784,439**	**80.9**	**455,150**	**77.4**	**272,876**	**78.4**
Fixed Assets	126,430	15.3	143,507	14.8	100,556	17.1	43,507	12.5
Other Non-current	39,664	4.8	41,694	4.3	32,343	5.5	31,673	9.1
Total Assets	**826,340**	**100.0**	**969,640**	**100.0**	**588,049**	**100.0**	**348,056**	**100.0**
Accounts Payable	135,520	16.4	129,932	13.4	91,148	15.5	48,728	14.0
Bank Loans	3,305	0.4	1,939	0.2	2,940	0.5	9,049	2.6
Notes Payable	24,790	3.0	29,089	3.0	14,701	2.5	0	0.0
Other Current	172,705	20.9	192,959	19.9	124,078	21.1	102,677	29.5
Total Current	**336,320**	**40.7**	**353,919**	**36.5**	**232,867**	**39.6**	**160,454**	**46.1**
Other Long Term	90,897	11.0	102,781	10.6	64,686	11.0	24,712	7.1
Deferred Credits	1,653	0.2	970	0.1	1,176	0.2	0	0.0
Net Worth	397,470	48.1	511,970	52.8	289,320	49.2	162,890	46.8
Total Liab & Net Worth	**826,340**	**100.0**	**969,640**	**100.0**	**588,049**	**100.0**	**348,056**	**100.0**
Net Sales	2,388,266	100.0	2,418,055	100.0	2,244,462	100.0	1,094,516	100.0
Gross Profit	917,094	38.4	974,476	40.3	805,762	35.9	439,995	40.2
Net Profit After Tax	52,542	2.2	55,615	2.3	51,623	2.3	20,796	1.9
Working Capital	323,926	—	430,520	—	222,283	—	112,422	—

RATIOS	UQ	MED	LQ	UQ	MED	LQ	UQ	MED	LQ	UQ	MED	LQ
SOLVENCY												
Quick Ratio (times)	1.8	0.8	0.3	1.9	0.7	0.2	2.1	1.0	0.5	2.1	0.8	0.3
Current Ratio (times)	4.2	2.2	1.4	4.9	2.4	1.5	4.0	2.2	1.4	5.8	1.8	1.2
Curr Liab To Nw (%)	24.1	64.0	153.5	20.5	57.2	139.7	25.4	58.4	139.9	10.0	59.3	197.7
Curr Liab To Inv (%)	46.3	81.4	143.2	39.2	67.0	109.1	67.9	118.9	225.3	38.7	113.6	180.8
Total Liab To Nw (%)	31.1	83.5	201.1	27.2	78.1	180.1	32.0	75.0	180.0	15.3	87.8	216.0
Fixed Assets To Nw (%)	9.3	22.5	48.6	8.4	21.4	46.0	12.1	26.5	49.8	9.0	21.3	47.1
EFFICIENCY												
Coll Period (days)	5.8	16.8	36.1	4.4	16.3	43.4	11.0	21.4	34.7	3.5	6.8	30.3
Sales To Inv (times)	12.4	6.4	4.0	7.7	5.2	3.5	26.0	13.5	7.5	17.4	6.9	4.5
Assets To Sales (%)	23.6	34.6	52.9	28.0	40.1	62.6	19.6	26.2	37.2	17.7	31.8	57.1
Sales To Nwc (times)	13.9	6.9	3.8	10.5	5.5	2.9	17.2	9.1	5.3	18.2	5.3	3.2
Acct Pay To Sales (%)	2.6	4.6	7.7	2.8	4.7	7.5	2.1	3.5	5.6	1.6	2.8	4.8
PROFITABILITY												
Return On Sales (%)	4.1	1.5	0.1	4.1	1.6	0.2	4.4	1.6	0.2	6.0	0.5	(0.9)
Return On Assets (%)	11.1	3.9	0.3	8.8	3.4	0.5	17.2	5.8	0.6	15.5	1.2	(5.0)
Return On Nw (%)	25.8	8.4	1.3	19.9	6.8	1.2	36.2	11.8	2.0	29.2	4.2	0.3

	SIC 5719 MISC HMFRNSHNGS STR (NO BREAKDOWN) 2002 (204 Establishments)		SIC 5722 HSHLD APPLNCE STRS (NO BREAKDOWN) 2002 (267 Establishments)		SIC 5731 RDO,TV,ELECTRNC STR (NO BREAKDOWN) 2002 (268 Establishments)		SIC 5734 COMPTR,SOFTWRE STRS (NO BREAKDOWN) 2002 (306 Establishments)	
	$	%	$	%	$	%	$	%
Cash	89,293	14.7	137,300	14.2	107,867	15.6	111,221	19.2
Accounts Receivable	46,165	7.6	135,366	14.0	93,346	13.5	191,161	33.0
Notes Receivable	2,430	0.4	1,934	0.2	4,840	0.7	1,159	0.2
Inventory	311,614	51.3	427,371	44.2	269,667	39.0	124,545	21.5
Other Current	30,979	5.1	68,650	7.1	44,945	6.5	52,714	9.1
Total Current	**480,481**	**79.1**	**770,621**	**79.7**	**520,665**	**75.3**	**480,800**	**83.0**
Fixed Assets	91,723	15.1	149,870	15.5	135,525	19.6	70,672	12.2
Other Non-current	35,231	5.8	46,411	4.8	35,264	5.1	27,805	4.8
Total Assets	**607,435**	**100.0**	**966,902**	**100.0**	**691,454**	**100.0**	**579,277**	**100.0**
Accounts Payable	116,020	19.1	176,943	18.3	139,674	20.2	145,399	25.1
Bank Loans	607	0.1	1,934	0.2	6,915	1.0	4,634	0.8
Notes Payable	11,541	1.9	39,643	4.1	23,509	3.4	17,378	3.0
Other Current	116,021	19.1	210,784	21.8	145,205	21.0	129,179	22.3
Total Current	**244,189**	**40.2**	**429,304**	**44.4**	**315,303**	**45.6**	**296,590**	**51.2**
Other Long Term	63,781	10.5	112,161	11.6	98,878	14.3	70,672	12.2
Deferred Credits	3,037	0.5	967	0.1	2,074	0.3	4,055	0.7
Net Worth	296,428	48.8	424,470	43.9	275,199	39.8	207,960	35.9
Total Liab & Net Worth	**607,435**	**100.0**	**966,902**	**100.0**	**691,454**	**100.0**	**579,277**	**100.0**
Net Sales	1,725,668	100.0	2,835,490	100.0	2,033,688	100.0	2,574,564	100.0
Gross Profit	740,312	42.9	921,534	32.5	785,004	38.6	885,650	34.4
Net Profit After Tax	43,142	2.5	34,026	1.2	34,573	1.7	66,939	2.6
Working Capital	236,292	—	341,317	—	205,362	—	184,210	—

RATIOS	UQ	MED	LQ	UQ	MED	LQ	UQ	MED	LQ	UQ	MED	LQ
SOLVENCY												
Quick Ratio (times)	1.1	0.5	0.2	1.4	0.6	0.3	1.4	0.7	0.3	2.1	1.2	0.6
Current Ratio (times)	3.9	2.2	1.4	3.2	2.0	1.3	3.2	1.8	1.2	3.2	1.7	1.2
Curr Liab To Nw (%)	26.7	63.7	148.2	33.8	79.6	187.8	30.3	70.9	160.0	34.3	99.6	239.1
Curr Liab To Inv (%)	38.5	66.2	117.7	57.0	89.9	134.8	54.0	99.4	164.9	94.5	184.3	453.7
Total Liab To Nw (%)	36.9	80.1	190.0	43.0	104.3	247.5	37.6	98.4	233.1	43.5	130.5	301.0
Fixed Assets To Nw (%)	9.2	20.6	44.4	10.8	25.0	55.4	12.4	30.9	72.1	8.7	20.9	51.3
EFFICIENCY												
Coll Period (days)	1.1	5.7	19.2	5.8	11.3	25.2	4.8	14.6	26.9	14.4	27.7	43.6
Sales To Inv (times)	8.4	5.4	3.5	9.2	6.5	4.6	10.8	6.9	4.7	45.0	21.0	11.5
Assets To Sales (%)	24.3	35.2	47.5	25.2	34.1	48.8	24.8	34.0	52.0	15.8	22.5	33.9
Sales To Nwc (times)	14.0	6.4	4.0	15.7	7.6	4.2	16.3	8.7	4.8	21.8	11.8	6.3
Acct Pay To Sales (%)	3.1	5.2	9.6	3.0	5.5	9.4	3.2	5.9	8.8	2.4	4.8	8.0
PROFITABILITY												
Return On Sales (%)	4.4	1.5	0.0	3.1	1.1	0.1	3.9	1.2	(0.2)	4.1	1.6	0.1
Return On Assets (%)	11.6	4.5	0.0	8.5	3.2	0.2	11.8	3.0	(0.7)	17.3	5.9	0.7
Return On Nw (%)	27.3	9.9	0.3	21.7	7.9	1.4	29.8	8.4	(0.1)	54.9	17.6	1.8

SIC 5735 RCD,PRRCRDED TP STR (NO BREAKDOWN) 2002 (49 Establishments)
SIC 5736 MSCL INSTRMNT STRS (NO BREAKDOWN) 2002 (113 Establishments)
SIC 58 EATING, DRINKG PLACES (NO BREAKDOWN) 2002 (530 Establishments)
SIC 5812 EATING PLACES (NO BREAKDOWN) 2002 (513 Establishments)

	SIC 5735 $	SIC 5735 %	SIC 5736 $	SIC 5736 %	SIC 58 $	SIC 58 %	SIC 5812 $	SIC 5812 %
Cash	137,539	14.5	95,104	7.9	264,195	13.5	273,976	13.4
Accounts Receivable	25,611	2.7	126,404	10.5	93,936	4.8	100,185	4.9
Notes Receivable	19,919	2.1	3,612	0.3	15,656	0.8	16,357	0.8
Inventory	539,723	56.9	741,568	61.6	127,205	6.5	134,943	6.6
Other Current	38,891	4.1	50,560	4.2	136,989	7.0	141,077	6.9
Total Current	**761,683**	**80.3**	**1,017,248**	**84.5**	**637,981**	**32.6**	**666,538**	**32.6**
Fixed Assets	139,436	14.7	142,054	11.8	1,015,682	51.9	1,061,145	51.9
Other Non-current	47,428	5.0	44,542	3.7	303,335	15.5	316,913	15.5
Total Assets	**948,547**	**100.0**	**1,203,844**	**100.0**	**1,956,998**	**100.0**	**2,044,596**	**100.0**
Accounts Payable	241,879	25.5	225,119	18.7	207,442	10.6	220,816	10.8
Bank Loans	949	0.1	4,815	0.4	5,871	0.3	6,134	0.3
Notes Payable	13,280	1.4	61,396	5.1	48,925	2.5	51,115	2.5
Other Current	488,501	51.5	189,004	15.7	454,023	23.2	476,391	23.3
Total Current	**744,609**	**78.5**	**480,334**	**39.9**	**716,261**	**36.6**	**754,456**	**36.9**
Other Long Term	50,273	5.3	134,830	11.2	620,369	31.7	656,315	32.1
Deferred Credits	0	0.0	0	0.0	9,785	0.5	12,268	0.6
Net Worth	153,665	16.2	588,680	48.9	610,583	31.2	621,557	30.4
Total Liab & Net Worth	**948,547**	**100.0**	**1,203,844**	**100.0**	**1,956,998**	**100.0**	**2,044,596**	**100.0**
Net Sales	2,781,663	100.0	2,254,390	100.0	4,856,074	100.0	5,073,439	100.0
Gross Profit	1,093,194	39.3	924,300	41.0	2,816,523	58.0	2,927,374	57.7
Net Profit After Tax	55,633	2.0	45,088	2.0	189,387	3.9	197,864	3.9
Working Capital	17,074	—	536,914	—	(78,280)	—	(87,918)	—

RATIOS	UQ	MED	LQ	UQ	MED	LQ	UQ	MED	LQ	UQ	MED	LQ
	SIC 5735			SIC 5736			SIC 58			SIC 5812		
SOLVENCY												
Quick Ratio (times)	0.9	0.2	0.0	0.8	0.4	0.1	1.1	0.5	0.2	1.1	0.5	0.2
Current Ratio (times)	3.3	1.8	1.2	3.7	1.9	1.4	1.9	1.0	0.5	1.8	1.0	0.5
Curr Liab To Nw (%)	23.5	75.0	146.5	24.5	80.2	250.4	23.1	55.0	138.6	23.3	55.7	142.1
Curr Liab To Inv (%)	41.6	71.9	110.3	37.9	67.1	97.9	300.6	708.0	999.9	311.8	722.3	999.9
Total Liab To Nw (%)	28.7	77.6	159.7	37.4	101.1	305.0	38.7	111.2	349.6	41.8	114.0	359.4
Fixed Assets To Nw (%)	6.6	18.8	35.8	7.6	16.5	42.2	59.3	110.7	239.5	59.2	111.1	240.3
EFFICIENCY												
Coll Period (days)	0.4	1.8	4.9	5.2	11.0	24.3	0.7	2.9	9.5	0.7	2.9	9.5
Sales To Inv (times)	7.0	4.6	3.4	4.4	3.2	2.4	134.6	79.3	41.5	134.7	80.1	40.2
Assets To Sales (%)	24.4	34.1	48.0	38.0	53.4	67.5	22.9	40.3	65.4	23.1	40.3	64.6
Sales To Nwc (times)	11.4	7.0	3.8	9.4	4.8	2.9	36.0	15.9	7.9	36.0	16.5	8.1
Acct Pay To Sales (%)	7.1	11.2	14.5	3.4	5.5	13.1	1.9	3.0	4.6	1.9	3.1	4.7
PROFITABILITY												
Return On Sales (%)	4.6	1.2	0.4	3.4	1.4	0.2	6.4	2.5	0.1	6.4	2.6	0.0
Return On Assets (%)	16.5	4.8	1.2	6.6	2.9	0.7	13.3	5.3	0.1	13.7	5.5	0.1
Return On Nw (%)	35.3	12.5	3.8	14.0	7.4	2.1	41.3	13.8	2.6	41.5	14.0	2.9

SIC 5813 DRINKING PLACES
(NO BREAKDOWN)
2002 (17 Establishments)

	$	%
Cash	129,472	15.2
Accounts Receivable	25,554	3.0
Notes Receivable	5,111	0.6
Inventory	40,034	4.7
Other Current	88,585	10.4
Total Current	**288,756**	**33.9**
Fixed Assets	428,449	50.3
Other Non-current	134,583	15.8
Total Assets	**851,788**	**100.0**
Accounts Payable	39,182	4.6
Bank Loans	0	0.0
Notes Payable	24,702	2.9
Other Current	174,617	20.5
Total Current	**238,501**	**28.0**
Other Long Term	135,434	15.9
Deferred Credits	0	0.0
Net Worth	477,853	56.1
Total Liab & Net Worth	**851,788**	**100.0**
Net Sales	2,218,198	100.0
Gross Profit	1,483,974	66.9
Net Profit After Tax	42,146	1.9
Working Capital	50,255	—

RATIOS	UQ	MED	LQ
SOLVENCY			
Quick Ratio (times)	2.6	0.5	0.1
Current Ratio (times)	5.4	1.2	0.5
Curr Liab To Nw (%)	9.4	21.1	120.0
Curr Liab To Inv (%)	118.6	530.2	999.9
Total Liab To Nw (%)	19.9	32.5	165.0
Fixed Assets To Nw (%)	67.7	80.0	132.9
EFFICIENCY			
Coll Period (days)	0.9	2.9	3.7
Sales To Inv (times)	114.1	71.2	47.6
Assets To Sales (%)	20.1	38.4	93.6
Sales To Nwc (times)	15.2	7.6	3.9
Acct Pay To Sales (%)	1.8	2.6	3.1
PROFITABILITY			
Return On Sales (%)	6.6	0.7	0.2
Return On Assets (%)	11.0	2.4	0.5
Return On Nw (%)	21.8	3.5	0.6

SIC 59 MISC RETAIL STORES
(NO BREAKDOWN)
2002 (4221 Establishments)

	$	%
Cash	122,167	13.9
Accounts Receivable	124,803	14.2
Notes Receivable	3,516	0.4
Inventory	360,348	41.0
Other Current	50,975	5.8
Total Current	**661,809**	**75.3**
Fixed Assets	157,323	17.9
Other Non-current	59,765	6.8
Total Assets	**878,897**	**100.0**
Accounts Payable	161,717	18.4
Bank Loans	2,637	0.3
Notes Payable	43,066	4.9
Other Current	173,142	19.7
Total Current	**380,562**	**43.3**
Other Long Term	129,198	14.7
Deferred Credits	1,758	0.2
Net Worth	367,379	41.8
Total Liab & Net Worth	**878,897**	**100.0**
Net Sales	2,468,812	100.0
Gross Profit	930,742	37.7
Net Profit After Tax	59,251	2.4
Working Capital	281,247	—

RATIOS	UQ	MED	LQ
SOLVENCY			
Quick Ratio (times)	1.6	0.7	0.3
Current Ratio (times)	4.1	2.1	1.4
Curr Liab To Nw (%)	23.4	60.0	146.8
Curr Liab To Inv (%)	45.5	82.6	169.6
Total Liab To Nw (%)	33.8	85.1	208.6
Fixed Assets To Nw (%)	10.1	25.4	61.6
EFFICIENCY			
Coll Period (days)	5.5	16.4	31.0
Sales To Inv (times)	16.7	7.8	3.9
Assets To Sales (%)	24.0	35.6	53.0
Sales To Nwc (times)	13.1	7.1	4.0
Acct Pay To Sales (%)	2.6	4.8	8.3
PROFITABILITY			
Return On Sales (%)	4.1	1.4	0.1
Return On Assets (%)	11.1	3.9	0.3
Return On Nw (%)	24.1	8.1	1.1

SIC 5912 DRG STRS,PRPRTRY ST
(NO BREAKDOWN)
2002 (456 Establishments)

	$	%
Cash	129,205	15.3
Accounts Receivable	152,850	18.1
Notes Receivable	5,067	0.6
Inventory	344,546	40.8
Other Current	57,424	6.8
Total Current	**689,092**	**81.6**
Fixed Assets	96,270	11.4
Other Non-current	59,114	7.0
Total Assets	**844,476**	**100.0**
Accounts Payable	168,895	20.0
Bank Loans	1,689	0.2
Notes Payable	9,289	1.1
Other Current	115,694	13.7
Total Current	**295,567**	**35.0**
Other Long Term	103,870	12.3
Deferred Credits	1,689	0.2
Net Worth	443,350	52.5
Total Liab & Net Worth	**844,476**	**100.0**
Net Sales	4,201,373	100.0
Gross Profit	991,524	23.6
Net Profit After Tax	96,632	2.3
Working Capital	393,525	—

RATIOS	UQ	MED	LQ
SOLVENCY			
Quick Ratio (times)	2.0	1.0	0.5
Current Ratio (times)	4.6	2.7	1.6
Curr Liab To Nw (%)	22.8	47.4	118.9
Curr Liab To Inv (%)	43.4	77.4	134.7
Total Liab To Nw (%)	28.8	69.2	174.1
Fixed Assets To Nw (%)	6.8	16.4	35.2
EFFICIENCY			
Coll Period (days)	7.7	14.2	21.7
Sales To Inv (times)	18.0	12.7	9.3
Assets To Sales (%)	15.5	20.1	27.6
Sales To Nwc (times)	15.8	9.7	6.7
Acct Pay To Sales (%)	2.3	3.7	5.6
PROFITABILITY			
Return On Sales (%)	3.8	1.6	0.5
Return On Assets (%)	19.2	7.4	2.2
Return On Nw (%)	34.8	14.3	4.7

SIC 5921 LIQUOR STORES
(NO BREAKDOWN)
2002 (25 Establishments)

	$	%
Cash	145,248	10.8
Accounts Receivable	28,243	2.1
Notes Receivable	14,794	1.1
Inventory	681,857	50.7
Other Current	34,966	2.6
Total Current	**905,108**	**67.3**
Fixed Assets	227,286	16.9
Other Non-current	212,492	15.8
Total Assets	**1,344,886**	**100.0**
Accounts Payable	199,043	14.8
Bank Loans	0	0.0
Notes Payable	99,522	7.4
Other Current	153,317	11.4
Total Current	**451,882**	**33.6**
Other Long Term	224,596	16.7
Deferred Credits	(1,345)	(0.1)
Net Worth	669,753	49.8
Total Liab & Net Worth	**1,344,886**	**100.0**
Net Sales	5,037,026	100.0
Gross Profit	1,274,368	25.3
Net Profit After Tax	110,815	2.2
Working Capital	453,226	—

RATIOS	UQ	MED	LQ
SOLVENCY			
Quick Ratio (times)	1.7	0.5	0.2
Current Ratio (times)	4.6	2.3	1.6
Curr Liab To Nw (%)	20.9	48.9	112.3
Curr Liab To Inv (%)	39.8	55.0	99.6
Total Liab To Nw (%)	47.1	69.6	307.6
Fixed Assets To Nw (%)	5.5	24.5	55.2
EFFICIENCY			
Coll Period (days)	1.1	3.5	6.8
Sales To Inv (times)	14.7	10.7	6.1
Assets To Sales (%)	13.3	26.7	37.1
Sales To Nwc (times)	18.4	8.2	5.7
Acct Pay To Sales (%)	1.8	3.9	6.2
PROFITABILITY			
Return On Sales (%)	4.3	1.6	0.4
Return On Assets (%)	11.4	5.5	2.6
Return On Nw (%)	30.5	10.8	4.9

SIC 5932 USED MERCH STRES
(NO BREAKDOWN)
2002 (91 Establishments)

	$	%
Cash	167,213	12.1
Accounts Receivable	139,575	10.1
Notes Receivable	19,347	1.4
Inventory	490,585	35.5
Other Current	189,324	13.7
Total Current	**1,006,044**	**72.8**
Fixed Assets	295,733	21.4
Other Non-current	80,152	5.8
Total Assets	**1,381,929**	**100.0**
Accounts Payable	135,429	9.8
Bank Loans	1,382	0.1
Notes Payable	37,312	2.7
Other Current	250,129	18.1
Total Current	**424,252**	**30.7**
Other Long Term	240,456	17.4
Deferred Credits	0	0.0
Net Worth	717,221	51.9
Total Liab & Net Worth	**1,381,929**	**100.0**
Net Sales	2,362,272	100.0
Gross Profit	1,181,136	50.0
Net Profit After Tax	144,099	6.1
Working Capital	581,792	—

RATIOS	UQ	MED	LQ
SOLVENCY			
Quick Ratio (times)	1.8	0.8	0.2
Current Ratio (times)	6.6	2.8	1.5
Curr Liab To Nw (%)	12.3	34.1	119.2
Curr Liab To Inv (%)	32.1	72.5	126.3
Total Liab To Nw (%)	29.4	89.2	200.7
Fixed Assets To Nw (%)	9.5	29.3	73.9
EFFICIENCY			
Coll Period (days)	5.1	14.3	43.4
Sales To Inv (times)	10.2	5.0	2.6
Assets To Sales (%)	35.3	58.5	91.2
Sales To Nwc (times)	10.6	5.9	2.2
Acct Pay To Sales (%)	0.9	2.9	6.1
PROFITABILITY			
Return On Sales (%)	7.7	3.4	0.5
Return On Assets (%)	11.9	5.1	1.1
Return On Nw (%)	26.1	13.6	2.6

SIC 5941 SPTG GDS, BCYLE SHPS
(NO BREAKDOWN)
2002 (487 Establishments)

	$	%
Cash	84,128	12.1
Accounts Receivable	42,412	6.1
Notes Receivable	2,086	0.3
Inventory	415,078	59.7
Other Current	24,334	3.5
Total Current	**568,038**	**81.7**
Fixed Assets	90,385	13.0
Other Non-current	36,850	5.3
Total Assets	**695,273**	**100.0**
Accounts Payable	254,470	36.6
Bank Loans	2,781	0.4
Notes Payable	20,163	2.9
Other Current	148,788	21.4
Total Current	**426,202**	**61.3**
Other Long Term	90,386	13.0
Deferred Credits	0	0.0
Net Worth	178,685	25.7
Total Liab & Net Worth	**695,273**	**100.0**
Net Sales	1,815,334	100.0
Gross Profit	666,228	36.7
Net Profit After Tax	36,307	2.0
Working Capital	141,836	—

RATIOS	UQ	MED	LQ
SOLVENCY			
Quick Ratio (times)	1.0	0.4	0.1
Current Ratio (times)	3.8	2.2	1.4
Curr Liab To Nw (%)	31.4	73.9	165.9
Curr Liab To Inv (%)	38.1	63.6	88.7
Total Liab To Nw (%)	44.6	95.5	233.6
Fixed Assets To Nw (%)	8.1	19.6	50.6
EFFICIENCY			
Coll Period (days)	0.7	4.8	15.7
Sales To Inv (times)	6.4	4.2	3.0
Assets To Sales (%)	29.4	38.3	50.0
Sales To Nwc (times)	10.1	6.1	4.1
Acct Pay To Sales (%)	4.4	7.8	12.1
PROFITABILITY			
Return On Sales (%)	3.5	1.5	0.1
Return On Assets (%)	8.9	3.9	0.3
Return On Nw (%)	22.5	8.0	1.1

SIC 5942 BOOK STORES
(NO BREAKDOWN)
2002 (103 Establishments)

	$	%
Cash	462,099	18.4
Accounts Receivable	123,059	4.9
Notes Receivable	2,511	0.1
Inventory	1,122,599	44.7
Other Current	120,548	4.8
Total Current	**1,830,816**	**72.9**
Fixed Assets	424,428	16.9
Other Non-current	256,164	10.2
Total Assets	**2,511,408**	**100.0**
Accounts Payable	424,428	16.9
Bank Loans	0	0.0
Notes Payable	75,342	3.0
Other Current	328,995	13.1
Total Current	**828,765**	**33.0**
Other Long Term	359,131	14.3
Deferred Credits	2,511	0.1
Net Worth	1,321,001	52.6
Total Liab & Net Worth	**2,511,408**	**100.0**
Net Sales	5,320,780	100.0
Gross Profit	2,059,142	38.7
Net Profit After Tax	90,453	1.7
Working Capital	1,002,051	—

RATIOS	UQ	MED	LQ
SOLVENCY			
Quick Ratio (times)	1.7	0.7	0.2
Current Ratio (times)	4.5	2.4	1.7
Curr Liab To Nw (%)	21.7	45.7	108.2
Curr Liab To Inv (%)	32.2	68.4	112.7
Total Liab To Nw (%)	27.3	67.9	163.0
Fixed Assets To Nw (%)	10.3	23.4	59.9
EFFICIENCY			
Coll Period (days)	2.9	5.8	14.2
Sales To Inv (times)	8.3	5.4	3.7
Assets To Sales (%)	30.6	47.2	59.9
Sales To Nwc (times)	9.7	6.3	3.5
Acct Pay To Sales (%)	2.4	5.3	9.6
PROFITABILITY			
Return On Sales (%)	3.8	1.4	0.1
Return On Assets (%)	8.3	3.3	0.3
Return On Nw (%)	15.1	7.2	0.5

SIC 5943 STATIONERY STORES
(NO BREAKDOWN)
2002 (217 Establishments)

	$	%
Cash	88,554	14.5
Accounts Receivable	181,993	29.8
Notes Receivable	611	0.1
Inventory	188,711	30.9
Other Current	24,427	4.0
Total Current	**484,296**	**79.3**
Fixed Assets	97,714	16.0
Other Non-current	28,704	4.7
Total Assets	**610,714**	**100.0**
Accounts Payable	131,914	21.6
Bank Loans	1,221	0.2
Notes Payable	161,228	26.4
Other Current	120,312	19.7
Total Current	**414,675**	**67.9**
Other Long Term	76,339	12.5
Deferred Credits	611	0.1
Net Worth	119,089	19.5
Total Liab & Net Worth	**610,714**	**100.0**
Net Sales	2,158,000	100.0
Gross Profit	738,036	34.2
Net Profit After Tax	30,212	1.4
Working Capital	69,621	—

RATIOS	UQ	MED	LQ
SOLVENCY			
Quick Ratio (times)	2.0	1.2	0.7
Current Ratio (times)	3.6	2.0	1.3
Curr Liab To Nw (%)	28.9	69.0	171.7
Curr Liab To Inv (%)	72.9	133.3	255.6
Total Liab To Nw (%)	35.1	95.0	206.9
Fixed Assets To Nw (%)	12.0	24.6	56.4
EFFICIENCY			
Coll Period (days)	22.3	28.5	35.4
Sales To Inv (times)	22.5	12.4	6.7
Assets To Sales (%)	20.7	28.3	38.0
Sales To Nwc (times)	14.7	8.0	4.7
Acct Pay To Sales (%)	3.6	5.4	7.4
PROFITABILITY			
Return On Sales (%)	2.2	0.7	(0.4)
Return On Assets (%)	7.6	2.4	(1.3)
Return On Nw (%)	13.9	5.0	(2.9)

SIC 5944 JEWELRY STORES (NO BREAKDOWN) 2002 (364 Establishments)

	$	%
Cash	113,485	9.5
Accounts Receivable	81,232	6.8
Notes Receivable	3,584	0.3
Inventory	770,505	64.5
Other Current	57,340	4.8
Total Current	**1,026,146**	**85.9**
Fixed Assets	117,069	9.8
Other Non-current	51,367	4.3
Total Assets	**1,194,582**	**100.0**
Accounts Payable	198,301	16.6
Bank Loans	4,778	0.4
Notes Payable	29,865	2.5
Other Current	191,133	16.0
Total Current	**424,077**	**35.5**
Other Long Term	136,182	11.4
Deferred Credits	1,195	0.1
Net Worth	633,128	53.0
Total Liab & Net Worth	**1,194,582**	**100.0**
Net Sales	1,981,065	100.0
Gross Profit	881,574	44.5
Net Profit After Tax	45,564	2.3
Working Capital	602,069	—

RATIOS	UQ	MED	LQ
SOLVENCY			
Quick Ratio (times)	1.1	0.4	0.1
Current Ratio (times)	4.8	2.8	1.7
Curr Liab To Nw (%)	20.8	49.5	124.2
Curr Liab To Inv (%)	27.4	48.9	75.0
Total Liab To Nw (%)	28.9	69.5	164.1
Fixed Assets To Nw (%)	5.0	12.2	30.3
EFFICIENCY			
Coll Period (days)	3.3	12.3	30.3
Sales To Inv (times)	3.5	2.5	1.7
Assets To Sales (%)	44.1	60.3	90.0
Sales To Nwc (times)	5.1	3.0	1.8
Acct Pay To Sales (%)	4.3	7.9	13.9
PROFITABILITY			
Return On Sales (%)	5.0	1.9	0.1
Return On Assets (%)	7.3	3.1	0.1
Return On Nw (%)	12.9	6.6	0.4

SIC 5945 HOBBY,TOY,GME SHPS (NO BREAKDOWN) 2002 (81 Establishments)

	$	%
Cash	77,521	12.9
Accounts Receivable	19,230	3.2
Notes Receivable	6,009	1.0
Inventory	345,538	57.5
Other Current	29,445	4.9
Total Current	**477,743**	**79.5**
Fixed Assets	73,915	12.3
Other Non-current	49,277	8.2
Total Assets	**600,935**	**100.0**
Accounts Payable	76,319	12.7
Bank Loans	1,202	0.2
Notes Payable	15,023	2.5
Other Current	116,581	19.4
Total Current	**209,125**	**34.8**
Other Long Term	77,521	12.9
Deferred Credits	4,207	0.7
Net Worth	310,082	51.6
Total Liab & Net Worth	**600,935**	**100.0**
Net Sales	1,544,820	100.0
Gross Profit	651,914	42.2
Net Profit After Tax	15,448	1.0
Working Capital	268,618	—

RATIOS	UQ	MED	LQ
Quick Ratio (times)	1.4	0.4	0.1
Current Ratio (times)	4.8	2.8	1.7
Curr Liab To Nw (%)	19.9	41.2	116.7
Curr Liab To Inv (%)	28.3	45.5	83.2
Total Liab To Nw (%)	26.2	61.8	173.5
Fixed Assets To Nw (%)	6.6	14.7	31.7
Coll Period (days)	1.3	2.6	5.0
Sales To Inv (times)	6.9	4.8	3.5
Assets To Sales (%)	31.1	38.9	47.2
Sales To Nwc (times)	10.0	5.7	3.6
Acct Pay To Sales (%)	2.0	6.0	8.0
Return On Sales (%)	3.7	0.6	(2.2)
Return On Assets (%)	11.7	1.6	(4.7)
Return On Nw (%)	19.6	4.1	(4.2)

SIC 5946 CMRA,PHOTO SUPPL ST (NO BREAKDOWN) 2002 (62 Establishments)

	$	%
Cash	154,222	16.7
Accounts Receivable	91,425	9.9
Notes Receivable	0	0.0
Inventory	398,946	43.2
Other Current	60,027	6.5
Total Current	**704,620**	**76.3**
Fixed Assets	171,768	18.6
Other Non-current	47,098	5.1
Total Assets	**923,486**	**100.0**
Accounts Payable	215,172	23.3
Bank Loans	1,847	0.2
Notes Payable	14,776	1.6
Other Current	122,824	13.3
Total Current	**354,619**	**38.4**
Other Long Term	116,359	12.6
Deferred Credits	0	0.0
Net Worth	452,508	49.0
Total Liab & Net Worth	**923,486**	**100.0**
Net Sales	2,708,170	100.0
Gross Profit	1,015,564	37.5
Net Profit After Tax	81,245	3.0
Working Capital	350,001	—

RATIOS	UQ	MED	LQ
Quick Ratio (times)	1.4	0.6	0.3
Current Ratio (times)	3.2	1.9	1.6
Curr Liab To Nw (%)	31.7	71.7	134.3
Curr Liab To Inv (%)	51.2	80.1	111.8
Total Liab To Nw (%)	44.4	90.6	166.5
Fixed Assets To Nw (%)	8.9	26.9	58.4
Coll Period (days)	4.4	8.6	14.2
Sales To Inv (times)	9.5	6.8	4.9
Assets To Sales (%)	23.9	34.1	46.8
Sales To Nwc (times)	14.0	8.0	4.7
Acct Pay To Sales (%)	4.3	7.2	9.3
Return On Sales (%)	3.0	1.6	0.2
Return On Assets (%)	11.5	4.4	0.4
Return On Nw (%)	27.7	8.2	1.3

SIC 5947 GFT,NVLTY,SVENR SHP (NO BREAKDOWN) 2002 (296 Establishments)

	$	%
Cash	87,886	16.9
Accounts Receivable	17,681	3.4
Notes Receivable	3,640	0.7
Inventory	259,499	49.9
Other Current	25,483	4.9
Total Current	**394,189**	**75.8**
Fixed Assets	96,207	18.5
Other Non-current	29,642	5.7
Total Assets	**520,038**	**100.0**
Accounts Payable	65,525	12.6
Bank Loans	2,080	0.4
Notes Payable	13,521	2.6
Other Current	92,567	17.8
Total Current	**173,693**	**33.4**
Other Long Term	81,126	15.6
Deferred Credits	0	0.0
Net Worth	265,219	51.0
Total Liab & Net Worth	**520,038**	**100.0**
Net Sales	1,319,893	100.0
Gross Profit	603,191	45.7
Net Profit After Tax	50,156	3.8
Working Capital	220,496	—

RATIOS	UQ	MED	LQ
Quick Ratio (times)	2.0	0.6	0.1
Current Ratio (times)	6.8	2.8	1.6
Curr Liab To Nw (%)	12.8	39.8	95.2
Curr Liab To Inv (%)	24.9	53.9	93.4
Total Liab To Nw (%)	16.9	62.7	144.7
Fixed Assets To Nw (%)	9.4	25.2	54.3
Coll Period (days)	0.4	4.2	12.1
Sales To Inv (times)	7.6	5.1	3.3
Assets To Sales (%)	28.9	39.4	55.9
Sales To Nwc (times)	8.3	5.0	3.0
Acct Pay To Sales (%)	2.2	4.3	8.5
Return On Sales (%)	7.2	2.0	0.0
Return On Assets (%)	15.2	4.9	(0.1)
Return On Nw (%)	30.6	9.8	0.9

	SIC 5948 LGGAGE,LTHR GDS STR (NO BREAKDOWN) 2002 (28 Establishments) $	%	SIC 5949 SEWING,NDLWK,PC GDS (NO BREAKDOWN) 2002 (72 Establishments) $	%	SIC 5961 CTLG,ML-ORDER HSES (NO BREAKDOWN) 2002 (224 Establishments) $	%	SIC 5962 MERCH MCHNE OPRTRS (NO BREAKDOWN) 2002 (79 Establishments) $	%
Cash	69,318	10.2	55,780	10.5	278,032	18.3	169,883	13.0
Accounts Receivable	42,135	6.2	19,124	3.6	199,028	13.1	70,567	5.4
Notes Receivable	3,398	0.5	531	0.1	3,039	0.2	6,534	0.5
Inventory	328,243	48.3	331,490	62.4	539,351	35.5	197,326	15.1
Other Current	99,221	14.6	17,000	3.2	135,217	8.9	60,112	4.6
Total Current	**542,315**	**79.8**	**423,925**	**79.8**	**1,154,667**	**76.0**	**504,422**	**38.6**
Fixed Assets	111,453	16.4	70,123	13.2	223,337	14.7	683,453	52.3
Other Non-current	25,825	3.8	37,186	7.0	141,295	9.3	118,918	9.1
Total Assets	**679,593**	**100.0**	**531,234**	**100.0**	**1,519,299**	**100.0**	**1,306,793**	**100.0**
Accounts Payable	117,570	17.3	73,842	13.9	296,263	19.5	141,134	10.8
Bank Loans	0	0.0	3,719	0.7	3,039	0.2	3,920	0.3
Notes Payable	4,078	0.6	7,437	1.4	48,618	3.2	69,260	5.3
Other Current	157,665	23.2	58,435	11.0	255,242	16.8	203,860	15.6
Total Current	**279,313**	**41.1**	**143,433**	**27.0**	**603,162**	**39.7**	**418,174**	**32.0**
Other Long Term	59,804	8.8	33,999	6.4	232,452	15.3	325,392	24.9
Deferred Credits	1,359	0.2	0	0.0	9,116	0.6	3,920	0.3
Net Worth	339,117	49.9	353,802	66.6	674,569	44.4	559,307	42.8
Total Liab & Net Worth	**679,593**	**100.0**	**531,234**	**100.0**	**1,519,299**	**100.0**	**1,306,793**	**100.0**
Net Sales	1,637,573	100.0	1,252,910	100.0	5,203,079	100.0	4,341,505	100.0
Gross Profit	740,183	45.2	561,304	44.8	2,128,059	40.9	2,010,117	46.3
Net Profit After Tax	(37,664)	(2.3)	28,817	2.3	104,062	2.0	39,074	0.9
Working Capital	263,002	—	280,492	—	551,505	—	86,248	—

RATIOS	UQ	MED	LQ	UQ	MED	LQ	UQ	MED	LQ	UQ	MED	LQ
SOLVENCY												
Quick Ratio (times)	0.9	0.2	0.1	1.2	0.3	0.1	1.7	0.7	0.3	1.2	0.5	0.3
Current Ratio (times)	4.5	2.0	1.4	5.8	3.8	2.2	3.4	1.9	1.3	2.7	1.1	0.8
Curr Liab To Nw (%)	27.9	102.3	151.6	14.6	29.9	63.7	26.5	62.6	147.7	19.3	77.5	150.0
Curr Liab To Inv (%)	38.9	74.8	157.3	20.4	35.6	59.6	60.8	101.3	207.3	87.4	227.8	308.2
Total Liab To Nw (%)	31.7	129.7	186.6	18.0	34.6	93.2	33.9	92.4	214.8	49.8	123.9	348.8
Fixed Assets To Nw (%)	8.7	23.6	52.9	4.5	12.0	40.4	7.2	16.8	45.5	74.8	126.6	229.8
EFFICIENCY												
Coll Period (days)	0.0	7.7	26.3	0.2	2.6	12.4	5.3	10.6	29.2	1.5	4.2	10.4
Sales To Inv (times)	7.6	4.4	3.4	5.2	4.1	2.5	16.6	9.4	6.3	28.6	22.9	15.0
Assets To Sales (%)	23.6	41.5	71.3	27.8	42.4	67.9	20.3	29.2	50.4	22.9	30.1	46.7
Sales To Nwc (times)	13.6	6.5	3.2	7.6	4.4	2.7	16.1	7.9	4.3	54.8	22.0	7.4
Acct Pay To Sales (%)	4.0	6.2	9.6	2.4	5.4	8.6	2.7	5.3	8.6	1.5	3.3	4.9
PROFITABILITY												
Return On Sales (%)	1.6	(0.6)	(6.8)	3.5	1.5	0.4	5.2	1.8	0.0	2.9	0.7	(0.7)
Return On Assets (%)	2.2	(1.8)	(14.9)	7.0	3.9	0.9	16.7	5.8	(0.1)	5.8	2.2	(2.5)
Return On Nw (%)	6.1	(0.5)	(23.4)	10.7	5.7	1.4	33.0	12.1	0.8	13.8	4.1	(7.4)

	SIC 5963 DRCT SLLNG ESTBMNTS (NO BREAKDOWN) 2002 (48 Establishments) $	%	SIC 5983 FUEL OIL DEALERS (NO BREAKDOWN) 2002 (224 Establishments) $	%	SIC 5984 LQFD PETRO GAS DLRS (NO BREAKDOWN) 2002 (145 Establishments) $	%	SIC 5992 FLORISTS (NO BREAKDOWN) 2002 (67 Establishments) $	%
Cash	133,434	14.1	248,631	19.6	214,330	15.4	88,124	18.2
Accounts Receivable	156,146	16.5	306,983	24.2	205,979	14.8	67,788	14.0
Notes Receivable	946	0.1	2,537	0.2	9,742	0.7	1,937	0.4
Inventory	213,873	22.6	115,436	9.1	161,443	11.6	106,523	22.0
Other Current	110,723	11.7	93,871	7.4	89,073	6.4	29,536	6.1
Total Current	**615,122**	**65.0**	**767,458**	**60.5**	**680,567**	**48.9**	**293,908**	**60.7**
Fixed Assets	261,190	27.6	343,771	27.1	555,309	39.9	146,227	30.2
Other Non-current	70,029	7.4	157,297	12.4	155,877	11.2	44,062	9.1
Total Assets	**946,341**	**100.0**	**1,268,526**	**100.0**	**1,391,753**	**100.0**	**484,197**	**100.0**
Accounts Payable	141,951	15.0	147,149	11.6	114,124	8.2	69,240	14.3
Bank Loans	0	0.0	1,269	0.1	1,392	0.1	2,421	0.5
Notes Payable	49,210	5.2	45,667	3.6	64,021	4.6	5,810	1.2
Other Current	291,473	30.8	318,400	25.1	251,906	18.1	95,387	19.7
Total Current	**482,634**	**51.0**	**512,485**	**40.4**	**431,443**	**31.0**	**172,858**	**35.7**
Other Long Term	46,371	4.9	166,176	13.1	297,836	21.4	126,376	26.1
Deferred Credits	2,839	0.3	2,537	0.2	0	0.0	0	0.0
Net Worth	414,497	43.8	587,328	46.3	662,474	47.6	184,963	38.2
Total Liab & Net Worth	**946,341**	**100.0**	**1,268,526**	**100.0**	**1,391,753**	**100.0**	**484,197**	**100.0**
Net Sales	3,042,897	100.0	4,145,510	100.0	2,863,689	100.0	1,508,402	100.0
Gross Profit	1,314,532	43.2	1,115,142	26.9	1,242,841	43.4	808,503	53.6
Net Profit After Tax	176,488	5.8	41,455	1.0	77,320	2.7	28,660	1.9
Working Capital	132,488	—	254,973	—	249,124	—	121,050	—

RATIOS	5963 UQ	MED	LQ	5983 UQ	MED	LQ	5984 UQ	MED	LQ	5992 UQ	MED	LQ
SOLVENCY												
Quick Ratio (times)	1.2	0.7	0.3	2.0	1.1	0.7	2.6	1.1	0.5	2.5	1.1	0.6
Current Ratio (times)	2.9	1.6	1.0	2.8	1.6	1.1	3.8	2.0	1.0	3.7	2.2	1.4
Curr Liab To Nw (%)	38.9	81.4	156.7	25.9	75.0	150.7	17.5	38.9	88.4	22.8	43.4	90.2
Curr Liab To Inv (%)	90.9	200.5	445.1	247.2	483.1	917.2	128.1	216.4	444.4	77.0	127.7	253.3
Total Liab To Nw (%)	51.4	118.6	210.5	38.1	99.9	221.4	34.3	74.8	191.3	33.3	60.9	153.8
Fixed Assets To Nw (%)	18.6	57.7	106.1	26.2	49.0	100.7	37.1	70.6	134.7	34.4	50.6	83.3
EFFICIENCY												
Coll Period (days)	4.0	22.3	32.7	16.4	23.7	35.4	15.9	24.8	35.3	9.1	14.2	24.5
Sales To Inv (times)	30.5	19.0	6.2	98.4	44.6	25.5	33.2	21.3	13.4	31.8	15.4	8.4
Assets To Sales (%)	19.9	31.1	44.6	23.3	30.6	41.7	36.2	48.6	71.7	22.4	32.1	43.8
Sales To Nwc (times)	20.3	11.4	6.4	28.7	10.5	6.4	17.7	7.9	4.7	18.5	10.1	5.2
Acct Pay To Sales (%)	2.1	4.1	7.9	1.6	2.9	4.6	2.0	3.2	5.6	2.1	3.5	6.0
PROFITABILITY												
Return On Sales (%)	7.9	3.0	0.3	2.3	0.5	(0.5)	4.9	2.4	0.1	3.5	1.0	(0.3)
Return On Assets (%)	22.3	10.5	0.6	7.1	1.7	(1.8)	9.0	3.9	0.3	10.2	2.7	(0.7)
Return On Nw (%)	50.5	23.3	3.0	17.5	3.6	(2.0)	21.2	6.9	2.2	16.8	4.2	(1.0)

SIC 5995 OPTICAL GDS STORES (NO BREAKDOWN) 2002 (17 Establishments)

	$	%
Cash	201,525	12.1
Accounts Receivable	176,543	10.6
Notes Receivable	11,658	0.7
Inventory	381,399	22.9
Other Current	46,635	2.8
Total Current	**817,760**	**49.1**
Fixed Assets	446,354	26.8
Other Non-current	401,385	24.1
Total Assets	**1,665,499**	**100.0**
Accounts Payable	366,410	22.0
Bank Loans	16,655	1.0
Notes Payable	8,327	0.5
Other Current	984,310	59.1
Total Current	**1,375,702**	**82.6**
Other Long Term	557,943	33.5
Deferred Credits	8,327	0.5
Net Worth	(276,473)	(16.6)
Total Liab & Net Worth	**1,665,499**	**100.0**
Net Sales	3,668,500	100.0
Gross Profit	2,267,133	61.8
Net Profit After Tax	88,044	2.4
Working Capital	(557,942)	—

RATIOS	UQ	MED	LQ
SOLVENCY			
Quick Ratio (times)	0.9	0.5	0.3
Current Ratio (times)	2.2	1.5	1.1
Curr Liab To Nw (%)	40.5	68.8	136.4
Curr Liab To Inv (%)	93.1	160.7	188.9
Total Liab To Nw (%)	82.3	190.1	434.6
Fixed Assets To Nw (%)	45.5	77.1	205.0
EFFICIENCY			
Coll Period (days)	9.7	14.2	26.1
Sales To Inv (times)	14.8	9.9	7.5
Assets To Sales (%)	34.1	45.4	58.6
Sales To Nwc (times)	49.3	13.8	7.9
Acct Pay To Sales (%)	4.6	5.9	9.5
PROFITABILITY			
Return On Sales (%)	5.5	1.1	0.1
Return On Assets (%)	15.6	3.7	0.3
Return On Nw (%)	58.3	13.0	3.7

SIC 5999 MISC RTL STRS, NEC (NO BREAKDOWN) 2002 (1121 Establishments)

	$	%
Cash	115,833	12.2
Accounts Receivable	195,587	20.6
Notes Receivable	3,798	0.4
Inventory	353,196	37.2
Other Current	54,119	5.7
Total Current	**722,533**	**76.1**
Fixed Assets	173,750	18.3
Other Non-current	53,169	5.6
Total Assets	**949,452**	**100.0**
Accounts Payable	151,912	16.0
Bank Loans	3,798	0.4
Notes Payable	60,765	6.4
Other Current	226,919	23.9
Total Current	**443,394**	**46.7**
Other Long Term	153,812	16.2
Deferred Credits	4,747	0.5
Net Worth	347,499	36.6
Total Liab & Net Worth	**949,452**	**100.0**
Net Sales	2,608,385	100.0
Gross Profit	993,795	38.1
Net Profit After Tax	73,035	2.8
Working Capital	279,139	—

RATIOS	UQ	MED	LQ
SOLVENCY			
Quick Ratio (times)	1.6	0.8	0.3
Current Ratio (times)	3.5	1.9	1.3
Curr Liab To Nw (%)	28.9	74.9	188.4
Curr Liab To Inv (%)	60.8	97.5	200.6
Total Liab To Nw (%)	41.9	104.9	258.9
Fixed Assets To Nw (%)	12.6	30.8	67.1
EFFICIENCY			
Coll Period (days)	11.3	25.6	42.0
Sales To Inv (times)	17.0	8.3	4.2
Assets To Sales (%)	25.9	36.4	52.5
Sales To Nwc (times)	14.6	7.6	4.5
Acct Pay To Sales (%)	2.3	4.5	7.9
PROFITABILITY			
Return On Sales (%)	4.1	1.3	0.2
Return On Assets (%)	11.5	3.6	0.6
Return On Nw (%)	27.2	8.2	1.8

SIC 61 CREDIT AGENC EX BANK (NO BREAKDOWN) 2002 (335 Establishments)

	$	%
Cash	339,243	23.3
Accounts Receivable	222,765	15.3
Notes Receivable	39,311	2.7
Inventory	42,223	2.9
Other Current	396,027	27.2
Total Current	**1,039,569**	**71.4**
Fixed Assets	250,428	17.2
Other Non-current	165,982	11.4
Total Assets	**1,455,979**	**100.0**
Accounts Payable	163,070	11.2
Bank Loans	18,928	1.3
Notes Payable	266,444	18.3
Other Current	701,781	48.2
Total Current	**1,150,223**	**79.0**
Other Long Term	147,054	10.1
Deferred Credits	7,280	0.5
Net Worth	151,422	10.4
Total Liab & Net Worth	**1,455,979**	**100.0**
Net Sales	2,104,016	100.0
Gross Profit	1,159,313	55.1
Net Profit After Tax	220,922	10.5
Working Capital	(110,654)	—

RATIOS	UQ	MED	LQ
SOLVENCY			
Quick Ratio (times)	2.4	1.0	0.1
Current Ratio (times)	3.5	1.5	1.1
Curr Liab To Nw (%)	21.4	94.8	546.2
Curr Liab To Inv (%)	98.5	108.5	512.6
Total Liab To Nw (%)	32.6	143.4	674.3
Fixed Assets To Nw (%)	7.2	20.9	53.7
EFFICIENCY			
Coll Period (days)	5.7	16.1	54.6
Sales To Inv (times)	56.2	3.4	0.6
Assets To Sales (%)	18.0	69.2	263.7
Sales To Nwc (times)	18.7	7.6	3.1
Acct Pay To Sales (%)	0.7	1.7	3.6
PROFITABILITY			
Return On Sales (%)	15.9	8.1	2.4
Return On Assets (%)	33.4	7.5	2.2
Return On Nw (%)	78.0	36.0	10.9

SIC 6141 PRSNL CRDT INSTUTNS (NO BREAKDOWN) 2002 (17 Establishments)

	$	%
Cash	317,639	10.4
Accounts Receivable	1,252,231	41.0
Notes Receivable	161,874	5.3
Inventory	24,434	0.8
Other Current	589,464	19.3
Total Current	**2,345,642**	**76.8**
Fixed Assets	284,043	9.3
Other Non-current	424,536	13.9
Total Assets	**3,054,221**	**100.0**
Accounts Payable	106,898	3.5
Bank Loans	0	0.0
Notes Payable	152,711	5.0
Other Current	772,718	25.3
Total Current	**1,032,327**	**33.8**
Other Long Term	699,417	22.9
Deferred Credits	18,325	0.6
Net Worth	1,304,152	42.7
Total Liab & Net Worth	**3,054,221**	**100.0**
Net Sales	2,221,252	100.0
Gross Profit	1,274,999	57.4
Net Profit After Tax	297,648	13.4
Working Capital	1,313,315	—

RATIOS	UQ	MED	LQ
SOLVENCY			
Quick Ratio (times)	3.0	1.7	1.0
Current Ratio (times)	5.0	3.1	1.7
Curr Liab To Nw (%)	22.0	88.7	212.9
Curr Liab To Inv (%)	41.8	520.9	999.9
Total Liab To Nw (%)	46.5	210.3	657.9
Fixed Assets To Nw (%)	1.5	10.1	28.7
EFFICIENCY			
Coll Period (days)	29.2	245.1	999.9
Sales To Inv (times)	65.8	35.6	5.4
Assets To Sales (%)	82.2	137.5	209.0
Sales To Nwc (times)	5.3	2.2	0.9
Acct Pay To Sales (%)	0.8	2.0	8.0
PROFITABILITY			
Return On Sales (%)	19.4	11.5	7.0
Return On Assets (%)	13.0	6.2	3.1
Return On Nw (%)	76.0	27.3	9.4

	SIC 6153 SHORT-TERM BUS CRDT (NO BREAKDOWN) 2002 (16 Establishments)		SIC 6159 MISC BUS CRDT INSTN (NO BREAKDOWN) 2002 (26 Establishments)		SIC 6162 MTG BKRS, CORRSPNDNT (NO BREAKDOWN) 2002 (135 Establishments)		SIC 6163 LOAN BROKERS (NO BREAKDOWN) 2002 (141 Establishments)	
	$	%	$	%	$	%	$	%
Cash	996,034	10.0	1,274,972	12.9	547,646	21.3	150,140	30.2
Accounts Receivable	3,466,200	34.8	2,589,477	26.2	313,675	12.2	54,190	10.9
Notes Receivable	49,802	0.5	138,369	1.4	82,276	3.2	11,932	2.4
Inventory	617,541	6.2	454,641	4.6	123,413	4.8	3,480	0.7
Other Current	3,157,429	31.7	1,759,263	17.8	907,602	35.3	106,887	21.5
Total Current	**8,287,006**	**83.2**	**6,216,722**	**62.9**	**1,974,612**	**76.8**	**326,629**	**65.7**
Fixed Assets	288,850	2.9	1,106,952	11.2	367,669	14.3	116,831	23.5
Other Non-current	1,384,488	13.9	2,559,826	25.9	228,829	8.9	53,692	10.8
Total Assets	**9,960,344**	**100.0**	**9,883,500**	**100.0**	**2,571,110**	**100.0**	**497,152**	**100.0**
Accounts Payable	258,969	2.6	513,942	5.2	79,704	3.1	108,876	21.9
Bank Loans	0	0.0	59,301	0.6	59,136	2.3	3,977	0.8
Notes Payable	448,215	4.5	978,467	9.9	532,220	20.7	103,905	20.9
Other Current	9,053,953	90.9	2,806,914	28.4	1,257,273	48.9	243,108	48.9
Total Current	**9,761,137**	**98.0**	**4,358,624**	**44.1**	**1,928,333**	**75.0**	**459,866**	**92.5**
Other Long Term	1,195,241	12.0	2,549,942	25.8	190,262	7.4	41,263	8.3
Deferred Credits	0	0.0	19,767	0.2	0	0.0	4,972	1.0
Net Worth	(996,034)	(10.0)	2,955,167	29.9	452,515	17.6	(8,949)	(1.8)
Total Liab & Net Worth	**9,960,344**	**100.0**	**9,883,500**	**100.0**	**2,571,110**	**100.0**	**497,152**	**100.0**
Net Sales	2,455,706	100.0	5,265,583	100.0	2,191,910	100.0	2,029,192	100.0
Gross Profit	1,213,119	49.4	2,074,640	39.4	1,218,702	55.6	1,189,107	58.6
Net Profit After Tax	36,836	1.5	405,450	7.7	249,878	11.4	213,065	10.5
Working Capital	(1,474,131)	—	1,858,098	—	46,279	—	(133,237)	—

RATIOS	UQ	MED	LQ	UQ	MED	LQ	UQ	MED	LQ	UQ	MED	LQ
SOLVENCY												
Quick Ratio (times)	1.7	1.2	0.1	1.4	1.0	0.4	2.1	0.5	0.1	3.0	1.2	0.3
Current Ratio (times)	2.5	1.5	1.2	2.5	1.4	1.1	2.9	1.3	1.1	4.1	1.7	1.1
Curr Liab To Nw (%)	86.6	223.8	430.8	18.5	101.7	545.1	32.5	176.7	821.0	17.2	50.4	254.4
Curr Liab To Inv (%)	39.4	153.6	999.9	103.3	435.4	999.9	98.5	106.0	114.6	64.7	302.9	750.4
Total Liab To Nw (%)	128.2	293.7	554.7	71.8	390.8	690.6	56.5	261.8	898.8	22.2	62.6	347.0
Fixed Assets To Nw (%)	1.2	4.0	8.2	5.1	10.1	36.0	6.5	16.8	49.7	14.3	32.9	65.1
EFFICIENCY												
Coll Period (days)	46.0	68.1	365.0	7.3	34.0	999.9	5.5	16.1	48.4	4.0	12.3	27.0
Sales To Inv (times)	60.6	38.4	1.0	56.2	36.5	16.8	1.3	0.6	0.4	55.5	28.1	0.7
Assets To Sales (%)	119.0	405.6	677.2	39.7	187.7	735.9	26.8	117.3	302.6	14.6	24.5	115.3
Sales To Nwc (times)	2.3	1.4	1.0	15.6	6.2	0.7	14.1	5.9	3.4	23.5	12.5	6.2
Acct Pay To Sales (%)	0.3	6.9	13.8	0.8	1.7	6.5	0.7	1.8	3.2	0.6	1.4	3.0
PROFITABILITY												
Return On Sales (%)	16.0	6.1	(19.8)	14.6	4.6	(1.3)	18.1	5.8	1.4	14.5	8.7	3.3
Return On Assets (%)	6.8	4.6	(2.8)	4.1	1.5	(1.5)	18.7	5.1	1.1	67.6	19.2	4.4
Return On Nw (%)	32.8	9.8	(2.5)	25.4	8.7	(1.2)	67.0	28.3	5.9	98.9	52.6	24.1

SIC 62 SEC,COM BROKERS,SVS
(NO BREAKDOWN)
2002 (137 Establishments)

	$	%
Cash	1,985,378	25.0
Accounts Receivable	1,357,998	17.1
Notes Receivable	103,240	1.3
Inventory	182,655	2.3
Other Current	2,263,330	28.5
Total Current	**5,892,601**	**74.2**
Fixed Assets	682,970	8.6
Other Non-current	1,365,940	17.2
Total Assets	**7,941,511**	**100.0**
Accounts Payable	865,625	10.9
Bank Loans	55,591	0.7
Notes Payable	222,362	2.8
Other Current	2,104,500	26.5
Total Current	**3,248,078**	**40.9**
Other Long Term	635,320	8.0
Deferred Credits	55,591	0.7
Net Worth	4,002,522	50.4
Total Liab & Net Worth	**7,941,511**	**100.0**
Net Sales	10,999,323	100.0
Gross Profit	4,531,721	41.2
Net Profit After Tax	912,944	8.3
Working Capital	2,644,523	—

RATIOS	UQ	MED	LQ
SOLVENCY			
Quick Ratio (times)	2.5	1.2	0.3
Current Ratio (times)	4.4	2.0	1.2
Curr Liab To Nw (%)	18.5	52.4	204.1
Curr Liab To Inv (%)	144.2	210.0	680.0
Total Liab To Nw (%)	26.7	71.9	230.8
Fixed Assets To Nw (%)	3.2	10.3	23.9
EFFICIENCY			
Coll Period (days)	5.5	21.5	47.5
Sales To Inv (times)	39.4	5.1	2.6
Assets To Sales (%)	26.3	72.2	138.1
Sales To Nwc (times)	16.5	4.3	1.4
Acct Pay To Sales (%)	1.0	3.9	11.7
PROFITABILITY			
Return On Sales (%)	15.4	3.8	(0.8)
Return On Assets (%)	19.7	4.4	(1.2)
Return On Nw (%)	39.6	15.4	0.8

SIC 6211 SECURITY BRKRS,DLRS
(NO BREAKDOWN)
2002 (78 Establishments)

	$	%
Cash	3,085,439	25.6
Accounts Receivable	1,916,347	15.9
Notes Receivable	228,997	1.9
Inventory	289,260	2.4
Other Current	4,146,060	34.4
Total Current	**9,666,103**	**80.2**
Fixed Assets	940,095	7.8
Other Non-current	1,446,299	12.0
Total Assets	**12,052,497**	**100.0**
Accounts Payable	1,373,985	11.4
Bank Loans	12,052	0.1
Notes Payable	337,470	2.8
Other Current	3,688,064	30.6
Total Current	**5,411,571**	**44.9**
Other Long Term	711,097	5.9
Deferred Credits	48,210	0.4
Net Worth	5,881,619	48.8
Total Liab & Net Worth	**12,052,497**	**100.0**
Net Sales	13,015,656	100.0
Gross Profit	8,017,644	61.6
Net Profit After Tax	819,986	6.3
Working Capital	4,254,532	—

RATIOS	UQ	MED	LQ
Quick Ratio	2.2	1.2	0.2
Current Ratio	4.2	2.0	1.2
Curr Liab To Nw	23.6	75.8	213.8
Curr Liab To Inv	155.3	593.1	883.4
Total Liab To Nw	34.2	96.2	266.0
Fixed Assets To Nw	3.4	10.1	22.8
Coll Period	5.3	21.0	77.2
Sales To Inv	39.4	4.1	2.6
Assets To Sales	18.7	92.6	159.8
Sales To Nwc	15.9	2.8	1.3
Acct Pay To Sales	0.9	3.8	11.4
Return On Sales	9.9	2.7	(7.1)
Return On Assets	11.4	3.1	(6.7)
Return On Nw	37.1	8.3	(9.0)

SIC 6221 COMMDTY BRKR,DLR
(NO BREAKDOWN)
2002 (11 Establishments)

	$	%
Cash	230,845	14.2
Accounts Receivable	790,076	48.6
Notes Receivable	0	0.0
Inventory	169,070	10.4
Other Current	295,872	18.2
Total Current	**1,485,863**	**91.4**
Fixed Assets	95,915	5.9
Other Non-current	43,893	2.7
Total Assets	**1,625,671**	**100.0**
Accounts Payable	305,626	18.8
Bank Loans	0	0.0
Notes Payable	139,808	8.6
Other Current	326,760	20.1
Total Current	**772,194**	**47.5**
Other Long Term	159,315	9.8
Deferred Credits	0	0.0
Net Worth	694,162	42.7
Total Liab & Net Worth	**1,625,671**	**100.0**
Net Sales	12,505,162	100.0
Gross Profit	1,200,496	9.6
Net Profit After Tax	250,103	2.0
Working Capital	713,669	—

RATIOS	UQ	MED	LQ
Quick Ratio	1.7	1.0	0.4
Current Ratio	2.2	1.4	1.1
Curr Liab To Nw	24.7	259.0	939.7
Curr Liab To Inv	144.2	170.2	381.8
Total Liab To Nw	46.1	259.0	971.2
Fixed Assets To Nw	2.6	9.7	13.6
Coll Period	16.4	32.3	53.9
Sales To Inv	137.6	5.1	2.2
Assets To Sales	7.0	13.0	40.3
Sales To Nwc	51.4	19.6	15.6
Acct Pay To Sales	3.3	4.9	12.5
Return On Sales	2.0	1.0	0.2
Return On Assets	24.1	2.2	2.0
Return On Nw	40.0	32.9	19.7

SIC 6282 INVESTMENT ADVICE
(NO BREAKDOWN)
2002 (38 Establishments)

	$	%
Cash	1,014,821	26.3
Accounts Receivable	478,471	12.4
Notes Receivable	23,152	0.6
Inventory	11,576	0.3
Other Current	841,181	21.8
Total Current	**2,369,201**	**61.4**
Fixed Assets	273,963	7.1
Other Non-current	1,215,470	31.5
Total Assets	**3,858,634**	**100.0**
Accounts Payable	212,225	5.5
Bank Loans	92,607	2.4
Notes Payable	69,455	1.8
Other Current	690,696	17.9
Total Current	**1,064,983**	**27.6**
Other Long Term	297,114	7.7
Deferred Credits	57,880	1.5
Net Worth	2,438,657	63.2
Total Liab & Net Worth	**3,858,634**	**100.0**
Net Sales	4,853,628	100.0
Gross Profit	1,456,088	30.0
Net Profit After Tax	664,947	13.7
Working Capital	1,304,218	—

RATIOS	UQ	MED	LQ
Quick Ratio	3.9	1.5	0.4
Current Ratio	5.7	3.0	1.5
Curr Liab To Nw	12.8	25.8	37.1
Curr Liab To Inv	212.1	212.1	212.1
Total Liab To Nw	17.9	35.0	63.6
Fixed Assets To Nw	2.4	9.2	14.2
Coll Period	3.7	18.1	44.9
Sales To Inv	5.0	5.0	5.0
Assets To Sales	37.5	79.5	153.3
Sales To Nwc	5.8	4.2	1.4
Acct Pay To Sales	0.8	2.5	9.6
Return On Sales	27.9	14.0	(0.8)
Return On Assets	21.6	7.9	(6.6)
Return On Nw	45.1	13.1	5.3

SIC 65 — REAL ESTATE
(NO BREAKDOWN)
2002 (776 Establishments)

	$	%
Cash	556,054	12.9
Accounts Receivable	353,461	8.2
Notes Receivable	90,520	2.1
Inventory	202,593	4.7
Other Current	568,985	13.2
Total Current	**1,771,613**	**41.1**
Fixed Assets	1,823,339	42.3
Other Non-current	715,543	16.6
Total Assets	**4,310,495**	**100.0**
Accounts Payable	250,009	5.8
Bank Loans	12,931	0.3
Notes Payable	271,561	6.3
Other Current	1,099,177	25.5
Total Current	**1,633,678**	**37.9**
Other Long Term	1,112,108	25.8
Deferred Credits	38,794	0.9
Net Worth	1,525,915	35.4
Total Liab & Net Worth	**4,310,495**	**100.0**
Net Sales	2,843,334	100.0
Gross Profit	1,259,597	44.3
Net Profit After Tax	187,660	6.6
Working Capital	137,935	—

RATIOS	UQ	MED	LQ
SOLVENCY			
Quick Ratio (times)	1.9	0.7	0.2
Current Ratio (times)	3.5	1.5	0.7
Curr Liab To Nw (%)	10.4	38.9	120.8
Curr Liab To Inv (%)	96.3	438.3	999.9
Total Liab To Nw (%)	31.0	108.1	315.0
Fixed Assets To Nw (%)	20.9	76.0	191.7
EFFICIENCY			
Coll Period (days)	5.5	17.0	41.3
Sales To Inv (times)	96.6	23.2	4.1
Assets To Sales (%)	48.3	151.6	414.9
Sales To Nwc (times)	12.3	5.2	1.9
Acct Pay To Sales (%)	1.4	3.0	7.6
PROFITABILITY			
Return On Sales (%)	13.6	4.7	(0.2)
Return On Assets (%)	11.2	3.3	(0.3)
Return On Nw (%)	33.9	10.7	0.6

SIC 6512 — NRSDNTL BLDG OPTRS
(NO BREAKDOWN)
2002 (171 Establishments)

	$	%
Cash	648,404	8.3
Accounts Receivable	546,847	7.0
Notes Receivable	101,557	1.3
Inventory	242,175	3.1
Other Current	742,150	9.5
Total Current	**2,281,133**	**29.2**
Fixed Assets	4,320,091	55.3
Other Non-current	1,210,876	15.5
Total Assets	**7,812,100**	**100.0**
Accounts Payable	296,860	3.8
Bank Loans	7,812	0.1
Notes Payable	437,478	5.6
Other Current	1,703,037	21.8
Total Current	**2,445,187**	**31.3**
Other Long Term	2,663,927	34.1
Deferred Credits	15,624	0.2
Net Worth	2,687,362	34.4
Total Liab & Net Worth	**7,812,100**	**100.0**
Net Sales	2,878,445	100.0
Gross Profit	1,257,880	43.7
Net Profit After Tax	290,723	10.1
Working Capital	(164,054)	—

RATIOS	UQ	MED	LQ
SOLVENCY			
Quick Ratio (times)	1.5	0.6	0.1
Current Ratio (times)	3.0	1.4	0.5
Curr Liab To Nw (%)	8.3	29.4	117.4
Curr Liab To Inv (%)	102.9	623.1	999.9
Total Liab To Nw (%)	40.3	108.4	312.7
Fixed Assets To Nw (%)	41.7	113.7	289.5
EFFICIENCY			
Coll Period (days)	8.0	19.8	40.2
Sales To Inv (times)	98.4	36.1	13.2
Assets To Sales (%)	80.7	271.4	593.7
Sales To Nwc (times)	13.6	5.3	1.8
Acct Pay To Sales (%)	1.6	4.2	8.3
PROFITABILITY			
Return On Sales (%)	18.8	6.9	0.0
Return On Assets (%)	7.3	3.0	0.1
Return On Nw (%)	21.1	9.7	2.5

SIC 6513 — APMNT BLDG OPRTRS
(NO BREAKDOWN)
2002 (96 Establishments)

	$	%
Cash	721,833	8.8
Accounts Receivable	631,604	7.7
Notes Receivable	164,053	2.0
Inventory	114,837	1.4
Other Current	721,833	8.8
Total Current	**2,354,160**	**28.7**
Fixed Assets	4,527,862	55.2
Other Non-current	1,320,627	16.1
Total Assets	**8,202,649**	**100.0**
Accounts Payable	352,714	4.3
Bank Loans	0	0.0
Notes Payable	656,212	8.0
Other Current	1,345,234	16.4
Total Current	**2,354,160**	**28.7**
Other Long Term	3,297,465	40.2
Deferred Credits	336,309	4.1
Net Worth	2,214,715	27.0
Total Liab & Net Worth	**8,202,649**	**100.0**
Net Sales	2,743,361	100.0
Gross Profit	899,822	32.8
Net Profit After Tax	106,991	3.9
Working Capital	0	—

RATIOS	UQ	MED	LQ
SOLVENCY			
Quick Ratio (times)	1.9	0.8	0.2
Current Ratio (times)	4.8	1.6	0.7
Curr Liab To Nw (%)	8.2	36.7	106.1
Curr Liab To Inv (%)	237.0	996.6	999.9
Total Liab To Nw (%)	52.1	162.3	611.6
Fixed Assets To Nw (%)	62.9	181.2	488.1
EFFICIENCY			
Coll Period (days)	4.8	13.1	32.0
Sales To Inv (times)	339.3	103.8	9.8
Assets To Sales (%)	119.8	299.0	433.3
Sales To Nwc (times)	8.9	3.5	1.7
Acct Pay To Sales (%)	1.7	3.0	6.4
PROFITABILITY			
Return On Sales (%)	10.3	2.3	(6.3)
Return On Assets (%)	5.2	0.8	(1.9)
Return On Nw (%)	28.2	5.9	(4.5)

SIC 6514 — DWLG OPTRS,EXC APTS
(NO BREAKDOWN)
2002 (11 Establishments)

	$	%
Cash	225,837	5.6
Accounts Receivable	108,886	2.7
Notes Receivable	217,771	5.4
Inventory	254,067	6.3
Other Current	116,951	2.9
Total Current	**923,512**	**22.9**
Fixed Assets	2,242,238	55.6
Other Non-current	867,053	21.5
Total Assets	**4,032,803**	**100.0**
Accounts Payable	116,951	2.9
Bank Loans	0	0.0
Notes Payable	0	0.0
Other Current	282,296	7.0
Total Current	**399,247**	**9.9**
Other Long Term	1,411,482	35.0
Deferred Credits	0	0.0
Net Worth	2,222,074	55.1
Total Liab & Net Worth	**4,032,803**	**100.0**
Net Sales	1,443,897	100.0
Gross Profit	548,681	38.0
Net Profit After Tax	174,712	12.1
Working Capital	524,265	—

RATIOS	UQ	MED	LQ
SOLVENCY			
Quick Ratio (times)	2.6	0.5	0.3
Current Ratio (times)	7.6	1.7	0.9
Curr Liab To Nw (%)	5.7	17.6	25.8
Curr Liab To Inv (%)	46.4	270.8	999.9
Total Liab To Nw (%)	36.9	86.3	200.8
Fixed Assets To Nw (%)	53.6	86.9	143.7
EFFICIENCY			
Coll Period (days)	10.2	20.7	39.8
Sales To Inv (times)	159.9	32.3	1.3
Assets To Sales (%)	128.6	279.3	505.2
Sales To Nwc (times)	27.6	2.5	1.6
Acct Pay To Sales (%)	1.1	1.8	4.6
PROFITABILITY			
Return On Sales (%)	19.5	4.8	0.6
Return On Assets (%)	11.0	4.3	0.2
Return On Nw (%)	16.6	7.7	0.4

	SIC 6515 MBLE HME SITE OPTRS (NO BREAKDOWN) 2002 (10 Establishments) $	%	SIC 6519 RL PRPTY LSSRS,NEC (NO BREAKDOWN) 2002 (32 Establishments) $	%	SIC 6531 RL ESTE AGNTS,MGRS (NO BREAKDOWN) 2002 (260 Establishments) $	%	SIC 6541 TTLE ABSTRCT OFFCS (NO BREAKDOWN) 2002 (12 Establishments) $	%
Cash	229,712	9.3	425,743	11.6	401,748	20.2	1,249,335	39.6
Accounts Receivable	61,751	2.5	165,159	4.5	238,662	12.0	271,320	8.6
Notes Receivable	24,700	1.0	11,011	0.3	61,654	3.1	0	0.0
Inventory	340,863	13.8	150,478	4.1	39,777	2.0	0	0.0
Other Current	34,580	1.4	216,542	5.9	278,441	14.0	536,331	17.0
Total Current	**691,606**	**28.0**	**968,933**	**26.4**	**1,020,282**	**51.3**	**2,056,986**	**65.2**
Fixed Assets	1,674,676	67.8	2,326,907	63.4	658,310	33.1	697,230	22.1
Other Non-current	103,741	4.2	374,360	10.2	310,261	15.6	400,670	12.7
Total Assets	**2,470,023**	**100.0**	**3,670,200**	**100.0**	**1,988,853**	**100.0**	**3,154,886**	**100.0**
Accounts Payable	49,400	2.0	143,138	3.9	145,186	7.3	220,842	7.0
Bank Loans	29,640	1.2	0	0.0	9,944	0.5	0	0.0
Notes Payable	128,441	5.2	113,776	3.1	149,164	7.5	6,310	0.2
Other Current	269,233	10.9	363,350	9.9	501,191	25.2	1,208,321	38.3
Total Current	**476,714**	**19.3**	**620,264**	**16.9**	**805,485**	**40.5**	**1,435,473**	**45.5**
Other Long Term	817,578	33.1	1,115,741	30.4	306,284	15.4	110,421	3.5
Deferred Credits	0	0.0	18,351	0.5	9,944	0.5	0	0.0
Net Worth	1,175,731	47.6	1,915,844	52.2	867,140	43.6	1,608,992	51.0
Total Liab & Net Worth	**2,470,023**	**100.0**	**3,670,200**	**100.0**	**1,988,853**	**100.0**	**3,154,886**	**100.0**
Net Sales	1,409,830	100.0	883,109	100.0	2,977,325	100.0	3,139,190	100.0
Gross Profit	580,850	41.2	484,827	54.9	1,318,955	44.3	2,131,510	67.9
Net Profit After Tax	35,246	2.5	107,739	12.2	211,390	7.1	232,300	7.4
Working Capital	214,892	—	348,669	—	214,797	—	621,513	—

RATIOS	6515 UQ	MED	LQ	6519 UQ	MED	LQ	6531 UQ	MED	LQ	6541 UQ	MED	LQ
SOLVENCY												
Quick Ratio (times)	1.3	0.6	0.2	2.1	1.1	0.1	2.8	0.9	0.3	2.0	1.1	0.6
Current Ratio (times)	2.9	1.5	0.6	2.8	2.0	1.0	3.8	1.5	0.7	3.5	1.1	1.0
Curr Liab To Nw (%)	12.7	23.5	67.9	4.7	15.0	47.4	12.3	47.6	154.6	20.8	79.0	481.6
Curr Liab To Inv (%)	80.5	191.7	745.2	211.6	663.3	999.9	172.2	684.5	999.9	—	—	—
Total Liab To Nw (%)	17.3	58.6	152.5	15.5	64.0	174.3	22.2	91.0	265.4	27.8	90.4	489.6
Fixed Assets To Nw (%)	88.5	102.4	158.6	55.7	85.2	182.4	15.1	50.7	144.0	23.0	38.3	65.3
EFFICIENCY												
Coll Period (days)	0.0	0.7	1.8	4.0	13.9	28.5	6.4	21.2	52.2	7.9	11.0	27.4
Sales To Inv (times)	31.9	4.7	1.0	148.6	49.9	11.8	160.9	44.8	5.1	—	—	—
Assets To Sales (%)	69.4	175.2	329.3	105.0	415.6	770.5	21.3	66.8	203.6	41.7	100.5	127.0
Sales To Nwc (times)	13.1	2.6	2.0	8.7	3.3	1.0	21.2	7.0	3.4	25.4	7.1	2.4
Acct Pay To Sales (%)	0.1	1.5	4.0	1.2	4.3	7.5	1.1	2.5	7.2	0.6	2.3	3.5
PROFITABILITY												
Return On Sales (%)	4.8	1.7	0.8	22.0	2.6	(1.2)	12.7	5.4	0.4	10.3	8.7	2.5
Return On Assets (%)	5.5	1.9	0.2	8.2	4.3	(0.6)	23.6	5.9	0.6	23.3	16.5	3.2
Return On Nw (%)	11.8	6.8	3.1	15.2	6.2	(1.7)	53.4	18.8	3.0	91.2	35.7	18.3

	SIC 6552 SBDVDRS,DVLPRS,NEC (NO BREAKDOWN) 2002 (173 Establishments) $	%	SIC 6553 CMTRY SBDVDRS,DVPR (NO BREAKDOWN) 2002 (11 Establishments) $	%	SIC 67 HOLDG,RE INVESTM COS (NO BREAKDOWN) 2002 (240 Establishments) $	%	SIC 6719 HOLDING COS,NEC (NO BREAKDOWN) 2002 (74 Establishments) $	%
Cash	622,669	8.2	1,111,540	4.6	929,417	17.9	1,522,502	12.9
Accounts Receivable	402,457	5.3	1,522,327	6.3	690,572	13.3	1,498,897	12.7
Notes Receivable	136,684	1.8	48,328	0.2	77,884	1.5	23,605	0.2
Inventory	903,630	11.9	2,537,211	10.5	301,152	5.8	849,768	7.2
Other Current	1,549,080	20.4	4,107,866	17.0	695,764	13.4	1,510,699	12.8
Total Current	**3,614,520**	**47.6**	**9,327,272**	**38.6**	**2,694,789**	**51.9**	**5,405,471**	**45.8**
Fixed Assets	2,505,865	33.0	4,470,324	18.5	1,183,838	22.8	4,083,609	34.6
Other Non-current	1,473,144	19.4	10,366,320	42.9	1,313,644	25.3	2,313,258	19.6
Total Assets	**7,593,529**	**100.0**	**24,163,916**	**100.0**	**5,192,271**	**100.0**	**11,802,338**	**100.0**
Accounts Payable	539,141	7.1	845,737	3.5	1,775,757	34.2	4,956,982	42.0
Bank Loans	30,374	0.4	0	0.0	5,192	0.1	35,407	0.3
Notes Payable	478,392	6.3	24,164	0.1	197,306	3.8	684,536	5.8
Other Current	2,984,257	39.3	3,286,293	13.6	6,765,529	130.3	20,229,207	171.4
Total Current	**4,032,164**	**53.1**	**4,156,194**	**17.2**	**8,743,784**	**168.4**	**25,906,132**	**219.5**
Other Long Term	1,966,724	25.9	3,576,259	14.8	3,821,511	73.6	7,541,694	63.9
Deferred Credits	37,968	0.5	483,278	2.0	31,154	0.6	106,221	0.9
Net Worth	1,556,673	20.5	15,948,185	66.0	(7,404,178)	(142.6)	(21,751,709)	(184.3)
Total Liab & Net Worth	**7,593,529**	**100.0**	**24,163,916**	**100.0**	**5,192,271**	**100.0**	**11,802,338**	**100.0**
Net Sales	4,880,160	100.0	7,008,096	100.0	6,886,301	100.0	14,067,149	100.0
Gross Profit	2,117,989	43.4	4,190,841	59.8	3,332,970	48.4	5,837,867	41.5
Net Profit After Tax	229,368	4.7	(1,415,635)	(20.2)	385,633	5.6	112,537	0.8
Working Capital	(417,644)	—	5,171,078	—	(6,048,995)	—	(20,500,661)	—

RATIOS	UQ	MED	LQ	UQ	MED	LQ	UQ	MED	LQ	UQ	MED	LQ
SOLVENCY												
Quick Ratio (times)	1.1	0.4	0.1	1.8	0.7	0.4	2.0	0.9	0.3	1.8	0.7	0.2
Current Ratio (times)	3.2	1.5	0.9	7.5	2.8	1.2	3.4	1.5	0.7	3.2	1.4	0.7
Curr Liab To Nw (%)	16.0	55.7	170.6	8.5	24.9	52.6	11.7	37.2	149.0	15.3	55.3	200.3
Curr Liab To Inv (%)	70.7	113.0	545.2	105.1	144.3	586.1	191.2	533.0	999.9	128.7	390.4	999.9
Total Liab To Nw (%)	41.9	132.6	448.9	9.9	38.3	137.4	22.4	87.2	227.9	35.1	119.2	325.9
Fixed Assets To Nw (%)	8.1	61.1	148.2	13.3	29.3	51.8	8.4	29.9	102.5	22.2	80.2	217.6
EFFICIENCY												
Coll Period (days)	2.6	12.8	40.4	41.3	46.7	81.0	13.1	34.0	53.7	21.4	38.9	56.1
Sales To Inv (times)	38.8	5.3	1.5	57.6	5.0	3.0	94.2	33.4	12.0	74.3	17.1	6.8
Assets To Sales (%)	71.7	155.6	411.2	150.4	344.8	659.8	36.8	75.4	200.8	41.4	83.9	199.3
Sales To Nwc (times)	7.6	3.4	1.3	3.6	1.2	0.9	19.9	6.2	2.9	17.1	6.4	3.9
Acct Pay To Sales (%)	1.8	3.9	9.3	1.7	2.4	2.7	2.3	4.5	9.4	2.7	5.2	10.2
PROFITABILITY												
Return On Sales (%)	14.0	4.1	0.2	3.6	(1.7)	(36.9)	9.6	2.6	(4.2)	5.3	0.6	(13.8)
Return On Assets (%)	10.4	2.9	0.1	1.0	(2.8)	(4.2)	11.9	2.6	(5.3)	4.6	1.0	(8.2)
Return On Nw (%)	23.1	11.2	1.3	3.5	(3.2)	(6.4)	35.4	7.3	(1.9)	12.0	5.1	(13.2)

SIC 6732 EDCTNL,RLGS,ETC,TRS
(NO BREAKDOWN)
2002 (11 Establishments)

	$	%
Cash	4,015,302	10.6
Accounts Receivable	1,060,646	2.8
Notes Receivable	0	0.0
Inventory	0	0.0
Other Current	11,629,225	30.7
Total Current	**16,705,173**	**44.1**
Fixed Assets	3,447,099	9.1
Other Non-current	17,727,940	46.8
Total Assets	**37,880,212**	**100.0**
Accounts Payable	2,121,292	5.6
Bank Loans	0	0.0
Notes Payable	0	0.0
Other Current	2,575,854	6.8
Total Current	**4,697,146**	**12.4**
Other Long Term	1,856,131	4.9
Deferred Credits	227,281	0.6
Net Worth	31,099,654	82.1
Total Liab & Net Worth	**37,880,212**	**100.0**
Net Sales	4,558,389	100.0
Gross Profit	(984,612)	(21.6)
Net Profit After Tax	(765,809)	(16.8)
Working Capital	12,008,027	—

RATIOS	UQ	MED	LQ
SOLVENCY			
Quick Ratio (times)	2.7	1.5	0.1
Current Ratio (times)	24.5	2.7	0.9
Curr Liab To Nw (%)	2.2	4.4	16.8
Curr Liab To Inv (%)	999.9	999.9	999.9
Total Liab To Nw (%)	3.2	4.9	46.6
Fixed Assets To Nw (%)	0.4	1.5	36.7
EFFICIENCY			
Coll Period (days)	1.0	1.7	52.8
Sales To Inv (times)	999.9	999.9	999.9
Assets To Sales (%)	172.0	831.0	999.9
Sales To Nwc (times)	3.0	0.3	0.1
Acct Pay To Sales (%)	0.6	1.9	2.9
PROFITABILITY			
Return On Sales (%)	0.1	(37.0)	(403.3)
Return On Assets (%)	3.6	(3.1)	(4.3)
Return On Nw (%)	4.8	(3.2)	(8.5)

SIC 6794 PATENT OWNERS,LESSO
(NO BREAKDOWN)
2002 (81 Establishments)

	$	%
Cash	445,880	18.5
Accounts Receivable	409,728	17.0
Notes Receivable	81,946	3.4
Inventory	161,481	6.7
Other Current	286,808	11.9
Total Current	**1,385,843**	**57.5**
Fixed Assets	385,626	16.0
Other Non-current	638,693	26.5
Total Assets	**2,410,162**	**100.0**
Accounts Payable	233,786	9.7
Bank Loans	0	0.0
Notes Payable	33,742	1.4
Other Current	737,510	30.6
Total Current	**1,005,038**	**41.7**
Other Long Term	371,164	15.4
Deferred Credits	14,461	0.6
Net Worth	1,019,499	42.3
Total Liab & Net Worth	**2,410,162**	**100.0**
Net Sales	3,837,838	100.0
Gross Profit	2,168,378	56.5
Net Profit After Tax	280,162	7.3
Working Capital	380,805	—

RATIOS	UQ	MED	LQ
Quick Ratio	1.7	1.0	0.6
Current Ratio	3.5	1.6	1.1
Curr Liab To Nw	19.4	37.1	153.0
Curr Liab To Inv	266.0	568.9	999.9
Total Liab To Nw	25.2	60.3	171.3
Fixed Assets To Nw	7.7	21.0	50.2
Coll Period	13.5	30.5	50.4
Sales To Inv	131.8	46.5	19.1
Assets To Sales	36.8	62.8	99.5
Sales To Nwc	23.1	8.5	4.4
Acct Pay To Sales	2.0	3.8	6.8
Return On Sales	10.1	5.1	0.9
Return On Assets	18.7	7.2	1.5
Return On Nw	47.9	18.7	3.1

SIC 6799 INVESTORS, NEC
(NO BREAKDOWN)
2002 (41 Establishments)

	$	%
Cash	1,169,195	26.5
Accounts Receivable	489,738	11.1
Notes Receivable	44,121	1.0
Inventory	145,598	3.3
Other Current	657,395	14.9
Total Current	**2,506,047**	**56.8**
Fixed Assets	772,110	17.5
Other Non-current	1,133,898	25.7
Total Assets	**4,412,055**	**100.0**
Accounts Payable	3,966,437	89.9
Bank Loans	0	0.0
Notes Payable	291,196	6.6
Other Current	14,992,163	339.8
Total Current	**19,249,796**	**436.3**
Other Long Term	11,678,710	264.7
Deferred Credits	17,648	0.4
Net Worth	(26,534,099)	(601.4)
Total Liab & Net Worth	**4,412,055**	**100.0**
Net Sales	1,601,472	100.0
Gross Profit	744,684	46.5
Net Profit After Tax	70,465	4.4
Working Capital	(16,743,749)	—

RATIOS	UQ	MED	LQ
Quick Ratio	2.0	0.5	0.1
Current Ratio	3.7	1.2	0.3
Curr Liab To Nw	10.6	35.4	220.3
Curr Liab To Inv	548.6	999.9	999.9
Total Liab To Nw	14.5	93.2	343.0
Fixed Assets To Nw	6.6	17.5	118.4
Coll Period	14.2	35.1	56.2
Sales To Inv	129.4	93.5	20.2
Assets To Sales	37.3	275.5	780.2
Sales To Nwc	8.3	3.6	0.4
Acct Pay To Sales	2.5	4.9	20.3
Return On Sales	5.6	(0.7)	(128.7)
Return On Assets	2.8	(5.6)	(42.6)
Return On Nw	18.5	3.0	(24.0)

SIC 70 HOTELS,RE LODGG PLA
(NO BREAKDOWN)
2002 (283 Establishments)

	$	%
Cash	651,942	10.3
Accounts Receivable	253,181	4.0
Notes Receivable	37,977	0.6
Inventory	151,909	2.4
Other Current	329,136	5.2
Total Current	**1,424,145**	**22.5**
Fixed Assets	4,354,720	68.8
Other Non-current	550,670	8.7
Total Assets	**6,329,535**	**100.0**
Accounts Payable	329,136	5.2
Bank Loans	12,659	0.2
Notes Payable	202,545	3.2
Other Current	1,208,941	19.1
Total Current	**1,753,281**	**27.7**
Other Long Term	2,645,745	41.8
Deferred Credits	31,648	0.5
Net Worth	1,898,861	30.0
Total Liab & Net Worth	**6,329,535**	**100.0**
Net Sales	4,712,982	100.0
Gross Profit	3,242,532	68.8
Net Profit After Tax	160,241	3.4
Working Capital	(329,136)	—

RATIOS	UQ	MED	LQ
Quick Ratio	1.8	0.5	0.2
Current Ratio	2.6	1.0	0.4
Curr Liab To Nw	10.2	39.6	90.6
Curr Liab To Inv	428.8	999.9	999.9
Total Liab To Nw	30.0	134.5	369.8
Fixed Assets To Nw	85.4	161.2	346.1
Coll Period	4.8	8.4	18.6
Sales To Inv	144.0	75.3	36.2
Assets To Sales	75.7	134.3	206.2
Sales To Nwc	18.5	8.5	2.8
Acct Pay To Sales	1.4	2.7	5.2
Return On Sales	8.5	1.8	(3.0)
Return On Assets	7.7	1.6	(2.8)
Return On Nw	20.3	5.6	(4.6)

SIC 7011 HOTELS AND MOTELS
(NO BREAKDOWN)
2002 (251 Establishments)

	$	%
Cash	637,596	9.6
Accounts Receivable	285,590	4.3
Notes Receivable	39,850	0.6
Inventory	152,757	2.3
Other Current	318,799	4.8
Total Current	**1,434,592**	**21.6**
Fixed Assets	4,629,215	69.7
Other Non-current	577,821	8.7
Total Assets	**6,641,628**	**100.0**
Accounts Payable	338,723	5.1
Bank Loans	6,642	0.1
Notes Payable	212,532	3.2
Other Current	1,268,551	19.1
Total Current	**1,826,448**	**27.5**
Other Long Term	3,480,213	52.4
Deferred Credits	33,208	0.5
Net Worth	1,301,759	19.6
Total Liab & Net Worth	**6,641,628**	**100.0**
Net Sales	4,805,809	100.0
Gross Profit	3,306,397	68.8
Net Profit After Tax	158,592	3.3
Working Capital	(391,856)	—

RATIOS	UQ	MED	LQ
SOLVENCY			
Quick Ratio (times)	1.7	0.5	0.2
Current Ratio (times)	2.3	0.9	0.4
Curr Liab To Nw (%)	12.8	43.2	92.5
Curr Liab To Inv (%)	473.0	999.9	999.9
Total Liab To Nw (%)	45.6	189.6	413.1
Fixed Assets To Nw (%)	98.4	198.3	388.1
EFFICIENCY			
Coll Period (days)	4.8	8.6	18.6
Sales To Inv (times)	151.2	88.4	38.8
Assets To Sales (%)	75.2	138.2	208.0
Sales To Nwc (times)	19.7	9.2	2.9
Acct Pay To Sales (%)	1.5	2.8	5.5
PROFITABILITY			
Return On Sales (%)	8.5	1.3	(3.2)
Return On Assets (%)	7.7	1.2	(3.0)
Return On Nw (%)	26.0	5.9	(5.7)

SIC 7032 SPORTING, RCRTNL CAM
(NO BREAKDOWN)
2002 (14 Establishments)

	$	%
Cash	233,680	10.9
Accounts Receivable	34,302	1.6
Notes Receivable	19,295	0.9
Inventory	32,158	1.5
Other Current	90,041	4.2
Total Current	**409,476**	**19.1**
Fixed Assets	1,541,430	71.9
Other Non-current	192,946	9.0
Total Assets	**2,143,852**	**100.0**
Accounts Payable	137,207	6.4
Bank Loans	0	0.0
Notes Payable	64,316	3.0
Other Current	199,377	9.3
Total Current	**400,900**	**18.7**
Other Long Term	145,782	6.8
Deferred Credits	0	0.0
Net Worth	1,597,170	74.5
Total Liab & Net Worth	**2,143,852**	**100.0**
Net Sales	1,256,654	100.0
Gross Profit	853,268	67.9
Net Profit After Tax	36,443	2.9
Working Capital	8,576	—

RATIOS	UQ	MED	LQ
SOLVENCY			
Quick Ratio (times)	5.2	0.9	0.5
Current Ratio (times)	11.7	2.0	0.8
Curr Liab To Nw (%)	1.8	3.5	33.7
Curr Liab To Inv (%)	219.3	343.4	999.9
Total Liab To Nw (%)	2.5	16.0	33.7
Fixed Assets To Nw (%)	63.5	82.4	102.5
EFFICIENCY			
Coll Period (days)	2.6	17.0	19.4
Sales To Inv (times)	68.5	50.2	22.0
Assets To Sales (%)	94.6	170.6	262.2
Sales To Nwc (times)	10.9	5.8	1.6
Acct Pay To Sales (%)	0.7	2.0	4.3
PROFITABILITY			
Return On Sales (%)	11.0	(0.4)	(3.1)
Return On Assets (%)	4.8	(0.2)	(3.3)
Return On Nw (%)	8.1	2.5	(2.6)

SIC 7033 TRAILER PRKS, CMPSTS
(NO BREAKDOWN)
2002 (13 Establishments)

	$	%
Cash	240,004	18.4
Accounts Receivable	9,131	0.7
Notes Receivable	6,522	0.5
Inventory	70,436	5.4
Other Current	53,478	4.1
Total Current	**379,571**	**29.1**
Fixed Assets	787,838	60.4
Other Non-current	136,958	10.5
Total Assets	**1,304,367**	**100.0**
Accounts Payable	33,914	2.6
Bank Loans	30,000	2.3
Notes Payable	53,479	4.1
Other Current	155,220	11.9
Total Current	**272,613**	**20.9**
Other Long Term	151,306	11.6
Deferred Credits	32,609	2.5
Net Worth	847,839	65.0
Total Liab & Net Worth	**1,304,367**	**100.0**
Net Sales	1,292,732	100.0
Gross Profit	917,840	71.0
Net Profit After Tax	94,369	7.3
Working Capital	106,958	—

RATIOS	UQ	MED	LQ
SOLVENCY			
Quick Ratio (times)	7.2	0.6	0.3
Current Ratio (times)	9.1	1.6	0.5
Curr Liab To Nw (%)	5.4	12.3	90.4
Curr Liab To Inv (%)	87.7	199.0	691.3
Total Liab To Nw (%)	5.4	15.2	140.0
Fixed Assets To Nw (%)	48.4	88.7	115.6
EFFICIENCY			
Coll Period (days)	0.6	1.1	10.1
Sales To Inv (times)	47.1	20.7	12.6
Assets To Sales (%)	47.7	100.9	135.6
Sales To Nwc (times)	10.0	4.0	2.6
Acct Pay To Sales (%)	0.4	2.2	6.2
PROFITABILITY			
Return On Sales (%)	8.2	5.7	2.5
Return On Assets (%)	9.3	6.0	3.0
Return On Nw (%)	13.3	9.9	4.3

SIC 72 PERSONAL SERVICES
(NO BREAKDOWN)
2002 (304 Establishments)

	$	%
Cash	126,990	15.9
Accounts Receivable	125,393	15.7
Notes Receivable	5,591	0.7
Inventory	62,297	7.8
Other Current	75,077	9.4
Total Current	**395,348**	**49.5**
Fixed Assets	290,720	36.4
Other Non-current	112,614	14.1
Total Assets	**798,682**	**100.0**
Accounts Payable	127,789	16.0
Bank Loans	1,597	0.2
Notes Payable	27,954	3.5
Other Current	271,552	34.0
Total Current	**428,892**	**53.7**
Other Long Term	206,858	25.9
Deferred Credits	8,786	1.1
Net Worth	154,146	19.3
Total Liab & Net Worth	**798,682**	**100.0**
Net Sales	1,943,265	100.0
Gross Profit	1,039,647	53.5
Net Profit After Tax	83,560	4.3
Working Capital	(33,544)	—

RATIOS	UQ	MED	LQ
SOLVENCY			
Quick Ratio (times)	2.5	1.1	0.4
Current Ratio (times)	3.8	1.8	0.9
Curr Liab To Nw (%)	17.0	39.3	95.8
Curr Liab To Inv (%)	112.5	286.9	659.9
Total Liab To Nw (%)	31.2	83.3	207.3
Fixed Assets To Nw (%)	27.2	61.3	140.0
EFFICIENCY			
Coll Period (days)	11.3	29.6	45.3
Sales To Inv (times)	72.9	28.4	12.0
Assets To Sales (%)	25.7	41.1	78.7
Sales To Nwc (times)	15.7	7.6	4.7
Acct Pay To Sales (%)	1.5	2.8	5.5
PROFITABILITY			
Return On Sales (%)	6.7	2.4	0.3
Return On Assets (%)	16.0	4.7	0.6
Return On Nw (%)	36.8	9.5	2.1

SIC 7213 LINEN SUPPLY (NO BREAKDOWN) 2002 (21 Establishments)

	$	%
Cash	215,934	12.6
Accounts Receivable	382,168	22.3
Notes Receivable	15,424	0.9
Inventory	217,648	12.7
Other Current	123,390	7.2
Total Current	**954,564**	**55.7**
Fixed Assets	551,831	32.2
Other Non-current	207,365	12.1
Total Assets	**1,713,760**	**100.0**
Accounts Payable	142,242	8.3
Bank Loans	0	0.0
Notes Payable	15,424	0.9
Other Current	301,622	17.6
Total Current	**459,288**	**26.8**
Other Long Term	308,477	18.0
Deferred Credits	(1,714)	(0.1)
Net Worth	947,709	55.3
Total Liab & Net Worth	**1,713,760**	**100.0**
Net Sales	3,669,722	100.0
Gross Profit	1,383,485	37.7
Net Profit After Tax	84,404	2.3
Working Capital	495,276	—

RATIOS	UQ	MED	LQ
SOLVENCY			
Quick Ratio (times)	2.6	1.4	0.8
Current Ratio (times)	4.2	2.1	1.4
Curr Liab To Nw (%)	15.7	39.5	82.4
Curr Liab To Inv (%)	118.0	242.9	542.7
Total Liab To Nw (%)	19.3	61.4	190.1
Fixed Assets To Nw (%)	30.1	54.1	101.1
EFFICIENCY			
Coll Period (days)	31.8	35.8	44.6
Sales To Inv (times)	26.2	11.8	9.5
Assets To Sales (%)	35.1	46.7	83.1
Sales To Nwc (times)	15.4	7.5	4.6
Acct Pay To Sales (%)	0.9	2.7	4.0
PROFITABILITY			
Return On Sales (%)	5.4	2.3	0.0
Return On Assets (%)	13.2	4.8	0.1
Return On Nw (%)	20.3	6.8	2.1

SIC 7216 DRYCLNG PLT,EXC RGS (NO BREAKDOWN) 2002 (19 Establishments)

	$	%
Cash	150,109	14.2
Accounts Receivable	54,970	5.2
Notes Receivable	10,571	1.0
Inventory	59,198	5.6
Other Current	94,082	8.9
Total Current	**368,930**	**34.9**
Fixed Assets	525,382	49.7
Other Non-current	162,795	15.4
Total Assets	**1,057,107**	**100.0**
Accounts Payable	39,113	3.7
Bank Loans	11,628	1.1
Notes Payable	32,770	3.1
Other Current	205,079	19.4
Total Current	**288,590**	**27.3**
Other Long Term	316,075	29.9
Deferred Credits	0	0.0
Net Worth	452,442	42.8
Total Liab & Net Worth	**1,057,107**	**100.0**
Net Sales	3,547,339	100.0
Gross Profit	1,784,312	50.3
Net Profit After Tax	60,305	1.7
Working Capital	80,340	—

RATIOS	UQ	MED	LQ
SOLVENCY			
Quick Ratio (times)	1.5	0.9	0.3
Current Ratio (times)	2.3	1.2	0.6
Curr Liab To Nw (%)	23.9	38.9	107.4
Curr Liab To Inv (%)	134.0	356.4	999.9
Total Liab To Nw (%)	39.3	131.7	287.9
Fixed Assets To Nw (%)	38.2	134.8	214.6
EFFICIENCY			
Coll Period (days)	10.2	16.1	17.2
Sales To Inv (times)	130.2	54.0	27.2
Assets To Sales (%)	22.0	29.8	88.8
Sales To Nwc (times)	14.0	9.9	7.6
Acct Pay To Sales (%)	1.1	1.7	3.6
PROFITABILITY			
Return On Sales (%)	3.8	2.0	0.4
Return On Assets (%)	6.0	3.6	1.5
Return On Nw (%)	14.2	8.3	5.3

SIC 7217 CRPT,UPHLSTRY CLNG (NO BREAKDOWN) 2002 (35 Establishments)

	$	%
Cash	44,919	8.8
Accounts Receivable	138,840	27.2
Notes Receivable	1,021	0.2
Inventory	26,033	5.1
Other Current	47,981	9.4
Total Current	**258,794**	**50.7**
Fixed Assets	200,604	39.3
Other Non-current	51,044	10.0
Total Assets	**510,442**	**100.0**
Accounts Payable	55,128	10.8
Bank Loans	0	0.0
Notes Payable	70,441	13.8
Other Current	121,995	23.9
Total Current	**247,564**	**48.5**
Other Long Term	144,966	28.4
Deferred Credits	1,021	0.2
Net Worth	116,891	22.9
Total Liab & Net Worth	**510,442**	**100.0**
Net Sales	1,791,025	100.0
Gross Profit	836,409	46.7
Net Profit After Tax	78,805	4.4
Working Capital	11,230	—

RATIOS	UQ	MED	LQ
SOLVENCY			
Quick Ratio (times)	2.0	1.1	0.3
Current Ratio (times)	2.4	1.4	0.5
Curr Liab To Nw (%)	45.4	60.9	91.9
Curr Liab To Inv (%)	371.3	568.3	999.9
Total Liab To Nw (%)	62.7	94.6	240.6
Fixed Assets To Nw (%)	35.9	61.3	178.8
EFFICIENCY			
Coll Period (days)	7.7	36.9	57.3
Sales To Inv (times)	270.4	103.8	47.5
Assets To Sales (%)	18.2	28.5	38.6
Sales To Nwc (times)	17.5	11.6	6.2
Acct Pay To Sales (%)	1.1	2.4	5.1
PROFITABILITY			
Return On Sales (%)	7.4	2.0	(0.3)
Return On Assets (%)	33.3	9.6	(0.8)
Return On Nw (%)	68.4	37.6	4.4

SIC 7218 INDUSTRIAL LNDRERS (NO BREAKDOWN) 2002 (25 Establishments)

	$	%
Cash	262,270	10.8
Accounts Receivable	512,399	21.1
Notes Receivable	7,285	0.3
Inventory	220,987	9.1
Other Current	140,849	5.8
Total Current	**1,143,790**	**47.1**
Fixed Assets	981,085	40.4
Other Non-current	303,554	12.5
Total Assets	**2,428,429**	**100.0**
Accounts Payable	313,267	12.9
Bank Loans	9,714	0.4
Notes Payable	36,426	1.5
Other Current	517,256	21.3
Total Current	**876,663**	**36.1**
Other Long Term	296,268	12.2
Deferred Credits	7,285	0.3
Net Worth	1,248,213	51.4
Total Liab & Net Worth	**2,428,429**	**100.0**
Net Sales	4,407,312	100.0
Gross Profit	2,291,802	52.0
Net Profit After Tax	92,554	2.1
Working Capital	267,127	—

RATIOS	UQ	MED	LQ
SOLVENCY			
Quick Ratio (times)	2.2	1.0	0.6
Current Ratio (times)	3.0	1.7	0.9
Curr Liab To Nw (%)	24.0	47.1	87.8
Curr Liab To Inv (%)	111.8	399.2	575.8
Total Liab To Nw (%)	61.3	112.4	181.1
Fixed Assets To Nw (%)	39.9	67.8	146.0
EFFICIENCY			
Coll Period (days)	28.5	34.2	40.9
Sales To Inv (times)	44.6	12.0	6.8
Assets To Sales (%)	31.2	55.1	76.9
Sales To Nwc (times)	11.6	7.8	4.0
Acct Pay To Sales (%)	2.2	3.3	5.1
PROFITABILITY			
Return On Sales (%)	5.5	1.6	0.1
Return On Assets (%)	9.4	4.7	0.2
Return On Nw (%)	14.5	7.7	0.4

SIC 7221 PHOTO STDIOS,PRTRT
(NO BREAKDOWN)
2002 (12 Establishments)

	$	%
Cash	34,384	21.6
Accounts Receivable	9,073	5.7
Notes Receivable	0	0.0
Inventory	17,988	11.3
Other Current	4,457	2.8
Total Current	**65,902**	**41.4**
Fixed Assets	85,959	54.0
Other Non-current	7,322	4.6
Total Assets	**159,183**	**100.0**
Accounts Payable	12,894	8.1
Bank Loans	0	0.0
Notes Payable	4,298	2.7
Other Current	25,151	15.8
Total Current	**42,343**	**26.6**
Other Long Term	13,053	8.2
Deferred Credits	0	0.0
Net Worth	103,787	65.2
Total Liab & Net Worth	**159,183**	**100.0**
Net Sales	686,134	100.0
Gross Profit	404,133	58.9
Net Profit After Tax	34,993	5.1
Working Capital	23,559	—

RATIOS	UQ	MED	LQ
SOLVENCY			
Quick Ratio (times)	1.2	0.7	0.4
Current Ratio (times)	1.7	1.3	1.0
Curr Liab To Nw (%)	28.6	65.1	96.7
Curr Liab To Inv (%)	94.7	235.4	507.5
Total Liab To Nw (%)	37.8	116.0	152.4
Fixed Assets To Nw (%)	69.1	99.1	116.8
EFFICIENCY			
Coll Period (days)	4.0	10.4	16.8
Sales To Inv (times)	51.1	33.1	17.9
Assets To Sales (%)	21.5	23.2	34.0
Sales To Nwc (times)	26.7	16.7	11.6
Acct Pay To Sales (%)	3.1	3.8	5.6
PROFITABILITY			
Return On Sales (%)	3.3	0.8	0.4
Return On Assets (%)	14.3	3.5	1.3
Return On Nw (%)	15.2	7.6	1.8

SIC 7231 BEAUTY SHOPS
(NO BREAKDOWN)
2002 (38 Establishments)

	$	%
Cash	62,010	17.8
Accounts Receivable	27,173	7.8
Notes Receivable	348	0.1
Inventory	24,386	7.0
Other Current	34,490	9.9
Total Current	**148,407**	**42.6**
Fixed Assets	135,169	38.8
Other Non-current	64,797	18.6
Total Assets	**348,373**	**100.0**
Accounts Payable	27,521	7.9
Bank Loans	348	0.1
Notes Payable	11,845	3.4
Other Current	110,435	31.7
Total Current	**150,149**	**43.1**
Other Long Term	104,163	29.9
Deferred Credits	7,316	2.1
Net Worth	86,745	24.9
Total Liab & Net Worth	**348,373**	**100.0**
Net Sales	1,445,531	100.0
Gross Profit	796,488	55.1
Net Profit After Tax	54,930	3.8
Working Capital	(1,742)	—

RATIOS	UQ	MED	LQ
SOLVENCY			
Quick Ratio (times)	1.7	0.6	0.2
Current Ratio (times)	2.2	1.2	0.6
Curr Liab To Nw (%)	24.9	51.7	446.2
Curr Liab To Inv (%)	193.3	440.7	871.5
Total Liab To Nw (%)	35.3	157.3	522.4
Fixed Assets To Nw (%)	34.8	83.0	227.4
EFFICIENCY			
Coll Period (days)	1.1	7.0	25.2
Sales To Inv (times)	161.9	52.9	39.9
Assets To Sales (%)	19.6	24.1	46.2
Sales To Nwc (times)	35.4	19.3	13.6
Acct Pay To Sales (%)	0.5	2.0	3.1
PROFITABILITY			
Return On Sales (%)	4.5	2.7	0.8
Return On Assets (%)	18.2	7.0	2.5
Return On Nw (%)	59.3	17.1	7.2

SIC 7261 FNRL SVC,CRMTRIES
(NO BREAKDOWN)
2002 (50 Establishments)

	$	%
Cash	122,687	11.5
Accounts Receivable	189,899	17.8
Notes Receivable	16,003	1.5
Inventory	77,880	7.3
Other Current	98,150	9.2
Total Current	**504,619**	**47.3**
Fixed Assets	364,862	34.2
Other Non-current	197,366	18.5
Total Assets	**1,066,847**	**100.0**
Accounts Payable	38,406	3.6
Bank Loans	0	0.0
Notes Payable	37,340	3.5
Other Current	85,348	8.0
Total Current	**161,094**	**15.1**
Other Long Term	357,393	33.5
Deferred Credits	16,003	1.5
Net Worth	532,357	49.9
Total Liab & Net Worth	**1,066,847**	**100.0**
Net Sales	1,405,596	100.0
Gross Profit	910,826	64.8
Net Profit After Tax	44,979	3.2
Working Capital	343,525	—

RATIOS	UQ	MED	LQ
SOLVENCY			
Quick Ratio (times)	4.3	1.8	0.9
Current Ratio (times)	6.4	3.2	1.9
Curr Liab To Nw (%)	11.8	23.2	46.4
Curr Liab To Inv (%)	114.6	214.0	514.3
Total Liab To Nw (%)	26.5	71.0	219.0
Fixed Assets To Nw (%)	23.1	57.9	109.4
EFFICIENCY			
Coll Period (days)	30.7	42.0	53.9
Sales To Inv (times)	44.3	21.0	14.5
Assets To Sales (%)	52.5	75.9	110.8
Sales To Nwc (times)	7.5	5.1	2.4
Acct Pay To Sales (%)	1.8	2.5	4.6
PROFITABILITY			
Return On Sales (%)	6.3	2.6	0.7
Return On Assets (%)	6.9	3.2	1.1
Return On Nw (%)	14.2	5.1	1.1

SIC 7299 MISC PRSNL SVCS, NEC
(NO BREAKDOWN)
2002 (76 Establishments)

	$	%
Cash	144,426	20.7
Accounts Receivable	113,029	16.2
Notes Receivable	7,675	1.1
Inventory	46,049	6.6
Other Current	80,935	11.6
Total Current	**392,114**	**56.2**
Fixed Assets	215,593	30.9
Other Non-current	90,005	12.9
Total Assets	**697,712**	**100.0**
Accounts Payable	290,248	41.6
Bank Loans	3,489	0.5
Notes Payable	11,861	1.7
Other Current	500,957	71.8
Total Current	**806,555**	**115.6**
Other Long Term	195,359	28.0
Deferred Credits	14,652	2.1
Net Worth	(318,854)	(45.7)
Total Liab & Net Worth	**697,712**	**100.0**
Net Sales	1,816,958	100.0
Gross Profit	962,988	53.0
Net Profit After Tax	72,678	4.0
Working Capital	(414,441)	—

RATIOS	UQ	MED	LQ
SOLVENCY			
Quick Ratio (times)	3.3	1.3	0.4
Current Ratio (times)	5.5	1.8	1.0
Curr Liab To Nw (%)	14.6	37.0	95.9
Curr Liab To Inv (%)	46.4	195.9	426.2
Total Liab To Nw (%)	24.1	77.4	178.0
Fixed Assets To Nw (%)	19.8	49.2	97.6
EFFICIENCY			
Coll Period (days)	2.9	19.5	40.2
Sales To Inv (times)	72.7	21.1	9.3
Assets To Sales (%)	22.8	38.4	91.7
Sales To Nwc (times)	13.8	6.4	3.9
Acct Pay To Sales (%)	2.0	3.9	8.4
PROFITABILITY			
Return On Sales (%)	9.1	1.4	(0.1)
Return On Assets (%)	23.9	3.6	(0.2)
Return On Nw (%)	51.9	14.1	1.6

	SIC 73 MISC BUSINESS SVS (NO BREAKDOWN) 2002 (5726 Establishments) $	%	SIC 7311 ADVRTSNG AGENCIES (NO BREAKDOWN) 2002 (302 Establishments) $	%	SIC 7312 OUTDR ADVRTSNG SVCS (NO BREAKDOWN) 2002 (11 Establishments) $	%	SIC 7319 ADVERTISING, NEC (NO BREAKDOWN) 2002 (27 Establishments) $	%
Cash	214,357	18.9	225,052	19.4	307,832	6.7	341,226	22.8
Accounts Receivable	367,469	32.4	532,468	45.9	748,906	16.3	526,805	35.2
Notes Receivable	7,939	0.7	11,601	1.0	13,784	0.3	4,490	0.3
Inventory	68,050	6.0	27,841	2.4	0	0.0	19,456	1.3
Other Current	117,954	10.4	120,646	10.4	257,293	5.6	224,490	15.0
Total Current	**775,769**	**68.4**	**917,608**	**79.1**	**1,327,815**	**28.9**	**1,116,467**	**74.6**
Fixed Assets	241,577	21.3	172,849	14.9	2,572,928	56.0	170,613	11.4
Other Non-current	116,819	10.3	69,604	6.0	693,771	15.1	209,524	14.0
Total Assets	**1,134,165**	**100.0**	**1,160,061**	**100.0**	**4,594,514**	**100.0**	**1,496,604**	**100.0**
Accounts Payable	259,724	22.9	341,058	29.4	606,476	13.2	285,851	19.1
Bank Loans	13,610	1.2	8,120	0.7	0	0.0	0	0.0
Notes Payable	95,270	8.4	25,521	2.2	9,189	0.2	17,959	1.2
Other Current	417,372	36.8	379,341	32.7	546,747	11.9	553,744	37.0
Total Current	**785,976**	**69.3**	**754,040**	**65.0**	**1,162,412**	**25.3**	**857,554**	**57.3**
Other Long Term	191,674	16.9	78,884	6.8	583,503	12.7	341,225	22.8
Deferred Credits	7,939	0.7	5,800	0.5	0	0.0	1,497	0.1
Net Worth	148,576	13.1	321,337	27.7	2,848,599	62.0	296,328	19.8
Total Liab & Net Worth	**1,134,165**	**100.0**	**1,160,061**	**100.0**	**4,594,514**	**100.0**	**1,496,604**	**100.0**
Net Sales	3,259,095	100.0	4,658,880	100.0	2,400,478	100.0	4,507,843	100.0
Gross Profit	1,495,925	45.9	1,719,127	36.9	1,423,483	59.3	1,690,441	37.5
Net Profit After Tax	48,886	1.5	102,495	2.2	146,429	6.1	(94,665)	(2.1)
Working Capital	(10,207)	—	163,568	—	165,403	—	258,913	—

RATIOS	UQ	MED	LQ	UQ	MED	LQ	UQ	MED	LQ	UQ	MED	LQ
SOLVENCY												
Quick Ratio (times)	2.4	1.3	0.7	1.8	1.2	0.8	1.8	1.1	0.8	1.7	1.2	0.7
Current Ratio (times)	3.2	1.7	1.1	2.2	1.3	1.0	3.4	1.3	0.8	2.5	1.3	1.0
Curr Liab To Nw (%)	25.0	66.2	173.1	51.6	144.6	360.0	5.8	15.2	454.8	29.4	94.7	377.3
Curr Liab To Inv (%)	171.2	490.1	999.9	489.8	999.9	999.9	999.9	999.9	999.9	999.9	999.9	999.9
Total Liab To Nw (%)	36.4	93.6	238.5	75.2	169.4	427.4	5.8	15.2	563.7	54.4	130.1	426.9
Fixed Assets To Nw (%)	10.5	29.0	73.0	12.6	31.4	71.5	46.4	77.7	309.1	9.2	24.3	53.2
EFFICIENCY												
Coll Period (days)	27.0	44.5	67.5	31.8	48.9	69.7	38.5	67.2	81.1	43.5	59.3	71.9
Sales To Inv (times)	116.1	34.9	12.9	285.4	80.1	25.0	142.2	71.2	0.2	999.9	685.4	218.4
Assets To Sales (%)	21.4	34.8	66.6	17.9	24.9	36.7	37.4	191.4	567.1	15.4	33.2	67.1
Sales To Nwc (times)	17.7	8.4	4.3	42.1	13.4	7.2	5.2	2.2	1.0	21.8	12.3	4.9
Acct Pay To Sales (%)	1.6	3.8	7.6	3.4	7.2	12.4	1.3	4.5	13.6	2.1	3.4	5.4
PROFITABILITY												
Return On Sales (%)	6.6	1.9	(1.4)	4.6	1.3	0.0	9.2	3.7	(1.0)	6.4	0.4	(4.8)
Return On Assets (%)	19.1	5.4	(3.6)	19.1	5.7	0.0	24.3	7.1	(0.5)	17.7	3.6	(8.6)
Return On Nw (%)	47.9	14.4	(2.0)	60.8	22.5	2.7	336.7	36.3	3.0	64.6	25.7	(11.7)

	SIC 7322 ADJSTMNT,CLCTN SVCS (NO BREAKDOWN) 2002 (32 Establishments)		SIC 7331 DRCT ML ADVRTSG SVC (NO BREAKDOWN) 2002 (90 Establishments)		SIC 7334 PHTCPYNG,DPLCTNG SV (NO BREAKDOWN) 2002 (81 Establishments)		SIC 7335 COMMRCL PHOTOGRAPHY (NO BREAKDOWN) 2002 (26 Establishments)	
	$	%	$	%	$	%	$	%
Cash	216,317	24.7	332,765	18.1	77,952	12.5	110,023	16.8
Accounts Receivable	249,596	28.5	534,998	29.1	172,117	27.6	138,838	21.2
Notes Receivable	31,528	3.6	9,192	0.5	17,461	2.8	0	0.0
Inventory	0	0.0	56,993	3.1	48,642	7.8	24,886	3.8
Other Current	107,721	12.3	158,109	8.6	23,697	3.8	63,525	9.7
Total Current	**605,162**	**69.1**	**1,092,057**	**59.4**	**339,869**	**54.5**	**337,272**	**51.5**
Fixed Assets	180,410	20.6	518,451	28.2	217,017	34.8	291,430	44.5
Other Non-current	90,205	10.3	227,972	12.4	66,726	10.7	26,196	4.0
Total Assets	**875,777**	**100.0**	**1,838,480**	**100.0**	**623,612**	**100.0**	**654,898**	**100.0**
Accounts Payable	177,783	20.3	235,325	12.8	99,778	16.0	98,890	15.1
Bank Loans	4,379	0.5	5,515	0.3	1,247	0.2	0	0.0
Notes Payable	55,174	6.3	49,639	2.7	49,889	8.0	2,620	0.4
Other Current	349,435	39.9	454,105	24.7	106,014	17.0	347,095	53.0
Total Current	**586,771**	**67.0**	**744,584**	**40.5**	**256,928**	**41.2**	**448,605**	**68.5**
Other Long Term	387,093	44.2	378,727	20.6	144,055	23.1	326,794	49.9
Deferred Credits	3,503	0.4	25,739	1.4	0	0.0	2,620	0.4
Net Worth	(101,590)	(11.6)	689,430	37.5	222,629	35.7	(123,121)	(18.8)
Total Liab & Net Worth	**875,777**	**100.0**	**1,838,480**	**100.0**	**623,612**	**100.0**	**654,898**	**100.0**
Net Sales	3,604,021	100.0	5,267,851	100.0	1,918,806	100.0	1,799,170	100.0
Gross Profit	1,293,844	35.9	2,191,426	41.6	1,047,668	54.6	980,548	54.5
Net Profit After Tax	158,577	4.4	147,500	2.8	76,752	4.0	59,373	3.3
Working Capital	18,391	—	347,473	—	82,941	—	(111,333)	—

RATIOS	UQ	MED	LQ	UQ	MED	LQ	UQ	MED	LQ	UQ	MED	LQ
SOLVENCY												
Quick Ratio (times)	2.3	1.1	0.7	2.2	1.3	0.8	2.1	1.2	0.6	2.8	1.2	0.4
Current Ratio (times)	2.6	1.4	1.0	2.9	1.5	1.1	3.0	1.5	0.9	3.3	1.7	1.1
Curr Liab To Nw (%)	26.5	105.0	331.3	25.4	84.6	185.9	25.0	48.7	133.9	7.4	47.5	101.4
Curr Liab To Inv (%)	—	—	—	376.7	928.5	999.9	161.2	334.4	999.9	187.3	655.0	999.9
Total Liab To Nw (%)	56.0	129.2	374.1	53.3	114.7	253.5	44.1	88.8	226.5	24.6	63.0	148.9
Fixed Assets To Nw (%)	14.3	46.2	91.3	27.9	58.7	113.7	28.0	64.8	132.2	39.7	74.1	122.1
EFFICIENCY												
Coll Period (days)	10.3	27.7	47.5	21.2	37.4	55.3	27.9	36.3	50.2	9.7	58.4	74.7
Sales To Inv (times)	—	—	—	290.6	66.3	25.8	105.0	43.2	20.3	154.0	67.2	34.4
Assets To Sales (%)	13.2	24.3	33.4	24.5	34.9	59.1	27.6	32.5	47.2	25.2	36.4	56.6
Sales To Nwc (times)	59.1	16.1	12.0	30.1	10.4	5.7	22.0	9.3	6.1	19.4	9.6	4.5
Acct Pay To Sales (%)	0.9	2.7	4.7	1.5	3.3	6.4	2.6	5.0	8.1	2.3	3.7	9.4
PROFITABILITY												
Return On Sales (%)	7.5	3.6	(0.1)	7.6	1.8	(0.5)	10.8	2.9	(0.5)	5.3	1.1	(0.8)
Return On Assets (%)	31.6	8.6	(0.2)	20.3	5.6	(2.0)	23.9	5.9	(1.1)	10.0	2.6	(3.0)
Return On Nw (%)	98.5	18.2	3.6	56.0	17.3	(1.5)	66.2	20.6	3.9	43.9	6.6	0.7

SIC 7336 COMMRCL ART, GR DSGN (NO BREAKDOWN) — 2002 (125 Establishments)
SIC 7338 SCRTRL, CRT RRPTNG (NO BREAKDOWN) — 2002 (11 Establishments)
SIC 7342 DSNFCTNG, PST CNTRL (NO BREAKDOWN) — 2002 (42 Establishments)
SIC 7349 BLDNG MAINT SVC, NEC (NO BREAKDOWN) — 2002 (224 Establishments)

	SIC 7336 $	SIC 7336 %	SIC 7338 $	SIC 7338 %	SIC 7342 $	SIC 7342 %	SIC 7349 $	SIC 7349 %
Cash	104,618	18.6	49,573	10.5	103,535	14.9	152,825	17.4
Accounts Receivable	194,050	34.5	217,175	46.0	184,834	26.6	334,633	38.1
Notes Receivable	6,750	1.2	1,888	0.4	15,287	2.2	7,905	0.9
Inventory	33,748	6.0	0	0.0	23,625	3.4	26,349	3.0
Other Current	26,998	4.8	12,275	2.6	56,979	8.2	72,021	8.2
Total Current	**366,164**	**65.1**	**280,911**	**59.5**	**384,260**	**55.3**	**593,733**	**67.6**
Fixed Assets	164,239	29.2	98,673	20.9	192,478	27.7	211,671	24.1
Other Non-current	32,061	5.7	92,536	19.6	118,127	17.0	72,899	8.3
Total Assets	**562,464**	**100.0**	**472,120**	**100.0**	**694,865**	**100.0**	**878,303**	**100.0**
Accounts Payable	74,808	13.3	75,067	15.9	54,894	7.9	86,952	9.9
Bank Loans	2,812	0.5	0	0.0	695	0.1	12,296	1.4
Notes Payable	33,185	5.9	30,688	6.5	31,269	4.5	34,254	3.9
Other Current	200,800	35.7	99,617	21.1	130,635	18.8	226,602	25.8
Total Current	**311,605**	**55.4**	**205,372**	**43.5**	**217,493**	**31.3**	**360,104**	**41.0**
Other Long Term	129,367	23.0	91,119	19.3	101,450	14.6	145,798	16.6
Deferred Credits	3,375	0.6	0	0.0	7,644	1.1	1,757	0.2
Net Worth	118,117	21.0	175,629	37.2	368,278	53.0	370,644	42.2
Total Liab & Net Worth	**562,464**	**100.0**	**472,120**	**100.0**	**694,865**	**100.0**	**878,303**	**100.0**
Net Sales	1,980,507	100.0	2,248,190	100.0	2,099,290	100.0	3,527,321	100.0
Gross Profit	960,546	48.5	658,720	29.3	1,303,659	62.1	1,245,144	35.3
Net Profit After Tax	33,669	1.7	(22,482)	(1.0)	111,262	5.3	165,784	4.7
Working Capital	54,559	—	75,539	—	166,767	—	233,629	—

RATIOS	7336 UQ	7336 MED	7336 LQ	7338 UQ	7338 MED	7338 LQ	7342 UQ	7342 MED	7342 LQ	7349 UQ	7349 MED	7349 LQ
SOLVENCY												
Quick Ratio (times)	2.3	1.1	0.6	2.1	1.3	0.9	2.7	1.7	0.7	3.0	1.3	0.9
Current Ratio (times)	2.9	1.5	0.8	2.2	1.3	1.0	4.1	2.3	1.0	3.4	1.8	1.2
Curr Liab To Nw (%)	21.0	76.9	255.9	55.1	66.5	84.5	21.9	38.7	85.1	27.7	60.1	165.3
Curr Liab To Inv (%)	187.0	425.9	999.9	—	—	—	266.9	515.4	999.9	309.9	999.9	999.9
Total Liab To Nw (%)	34.5	111.4	314.2	61.6	84.5	202.1	32.1	65.8	142.5	44.1	90.2	226.0
Fixed Assets To Nw (%)	20.4	39.7	103.2	19.2	29.2	56.9	26.8	36.5	74.1	18.2	36.1	79.7
EFFICIENCY												
Coll Period (days)	26.9	47.1	62.6	41.5	63.7	68.7	21.5	25.9	35.8	27.4	36.7	53.7
Sales To Inv (times)	84.0	32.4	17.0	—	—	—	270.7	60.4	39.7	431.5	138.3	36.5
Assets To Sales (%)	19.9	28.4	45.2	10.2	21.0	38.5	22.5	33.1	47.7	16.5	24.9	39.5
Sales To Nwc (times)	22.2	8.8	5.1	22.8	16.3	10.8	13.6	9.1	5.9	25.2	12.3	7.1
Acct Pay To Sales (%)	1.7	3.6	6.7	2.0	2.2	6.0	1.8	2.2	3.8	1.1	2.1	4.4
PROFITABILITY												
Return On Sales (%)	5.9	1.2	(1.3)	3.7	1.1	0.5	7.4	4.1	1.2	7.1	3.1	0.6
Return On Assets (%)	18.8	5.1	(2.7)	8.9	7.3	4.4	23.7	9.6	3.3	27.3	10.8	2.6
Return On Nw (%)	49.9	15.6	(3.2)	22.3	8.8	(14.2)	41.1	24.0	6.1	55.2	28.3	8.0

SIC 7352 MEDCL EQPT RNTL
(NO BREAKDOWN)
2002 (59 Establishments)

	$	%
Cash	72,608	9.1
Accounts Receivable	227,399	28.5
Notes Receivable	11,170	1.4
Inventory	98,141	12.3
Other Current	55,852	7.0
Total Current	**465,170**	**58.3**
Fixed Assets	267,293	33.5
Other Non-current	65,428	8.2
Total Assets	**797,891**	**100.0**
Accounts Payable	78,991	9.9
Bank Loans	5,585	0.7
Notes Payable	30,320	3.8
Other Current	126,865	15.9
Total Current	**241,761**	**30.3**
Other Long Term	189,898	23.8
Deferred Credits	798	0.1
Net Worth	365,434	45.8
Total Liab & Net Worth	**797,891**	**100.0**
Net Sales	1,561,431	100.0
Gross Profit	977,456	62.6
Net Profit After Tax	65,580	4.2
Working Capital	223,409	—

RATIOS	UQ	MED	LQ
SOLVENCY			
Quick Ratio (times)	3.3	1.5	0.7
Current Ratio (times)	5.5	2.1	1.2
Curr Liab To Nw (%)	13.4	42.0	104.3
Curr Liab To Inv (%)	93.3	219.6	647.1
Total Liab To Nw (%)	18.9	89.8	208.6
Fixed Assets To Nw (%)	30.7	66.4	140.0
EFFICIENCY			
Coll Period (days)	44.7	70.1	93.1
Sales To Inv (times)	33.7	19.3	8.3
Assets To Sales (%)	39.1	51.1	85.1
Sales To Nwc (times)	10.8	4.8	3.0
Acct Pay To Sales (%)	2.9	4.8	6.2
PROFITABILITY			
Return On Sales (%)	8.8	3.6	0.5
Return On Assets (%)	12.7	6.5	1.3
Return On Nw (%)	27.2	14.0	4.7

SIC 7353 HVY CONST EQPT RNTL
(NO BREAKDOWN)
2002 (109 Establishments)

	$	%
Cash	256,034	7.6
Accounts Receivable	673,773	20.0
Notes Receivable	30,320	0.9
Inventory	346,993	10.3
Other Current	178,549	5.3
Total Current	**1,485,669**	**44.1**
Fixed Assets	1,644,006	48.8
Other Non-current	239,189	7.1
Total Assets	**3,368,864**	**100.0**
Accounts Payable	262,771	7.8
Bank Loans	0	0.0
Notes Payable	154,968	4.6
Other Current	720,937	21.4
Total Current	**1,138,676**	**33.8**
Other Long Term	825,372	24.5
Deferred Credits	16,844	0.5
Net Worth	1,387,972	41.2
Total Liab & Net Worth	**3,368,864**	**100.0**
Net Sales	3,785,240	100.0
Gross Profit	1,586,016	41.9
Net Profit After Tax	143,839	3.8
Working Capital	346,993	—

RATIOS	UQ	MED	LQ
SOLVENCY			
Quick Ratio (times)	2.0	1.0	0.5
Current Ratio (times)	3.0	1.6	1.0
Curr Liab To Nw (%)	20.5	52.0	179.2
Curr Liab To Inv (%)	120.0	247.7	999.9
Total Liab To Nw (%)	38.4	132.2	274.5
Fixed Assets To Nw (%)	54.1	96.9	169.2
EFFICIENCY			
Coll Period (days)	38.9	53.7	78.2
Sales To Inv (times)	36.0	9.3	6.6
Assets To Sales (%)	54.7	89.0	141.6
Sales To Nwc (times)	17.2	7.1	3.5
Acct Pay To Sales (%)	2.7	4.5	8.8
PROFITABILITY			
Return On Sales (%)	7.6	2.7	0.2
Return On Assets (%)	8.5	3.3	0.3
Return On Nw (%)	28.1	10.4	2.1

SIC 7359 EQPT RNTL,LSING,NEC
(NO BREAKDOWN)
2002 (349 Establishments)

	$	%
Cash	103,779	10.0
Accounts Receivable	135,951	13.1
Notes Receivable	8,302	0.8
Inventory	146,329	14.1
Other Current	94,439	9.1
Total Current	**488,800**	**47.1**
Fixed Assets	464,931	44.8
Other Non-current	84,061	8.1
Total Assets	**1,037,792**	**100.0**
Accounts Payable	71,608	6.9
Bank Loans	5,189	0.5
Notes Payable	55,003	5.3
Other Current	211,709	20.4
Total Current	**343,509**	**33.1**
Other Long Term	260,486	25.1
Deferred Credits	5,189	0.5
Net Worth	428,608	41.3
Total Liab & Net Worth	**1,037,792**	**100.0**
Net Sales	1,684,727	100.0
Gross Profit	990,619	58.8
Net Profit After Tax	67,389	4.0
Working Capital	145,291	—

RATIOS	UQ	MED	LQ
SOLVENCY			
Quick Ratio (times)	1.6	0.8	0.2
Current Ratio (times)	3.2	1.5	0.8
Curr Liab To Nw (%)	21.5	55.3	140.6
Curr Liab To Inv (%)	82.7	193.0	531.4
Total Liab To Nw (%)	37.6	103.4	245.0
Fixed Assets To Nw (%)	37.2	82.6	169.7
EFFICIENCY			
Coll Period (days)	12.4	33.2	55.5
Sales To Inv (times)	34.4	15.5	5.7
Assets To Sales (%)	41.7	61.6	96.5
Sales To Nwc (times)	13.6	6.4	3.1
Acct Pay To Sales (%)	1.3	2.9	6.7
PROFITABILITY			
Return On Sales (%)	7.1	2.1	(0.7)
Return On Assets (%)	9.8	3.1	(1.3)
Return On Nw (%)	23.8	8.1	(1.0)

SIC 7361 EMPLOYMENT AGENCIES
(NO BREAKDOWN)
2002 (115 Establishments)

	$	%
Cash	167,504	16.5
Accounts Receivable	479,163	47.2
Notes Receivable	15,228	1.5
Inventory	4,061	0.4
Other Current	118,775	11.7
Total Current	**784,731**	**77.3**
Fixed Assets	119,791	11.8
Other Non-current	110,654	10.9
Total Assets	**1,015,176**	**100.0**
Accounts Payable	72,077	7.1
Bank Loans	7,106	0.7
Notes Payable	37,562	3.7
Other Current	264,961	26.1
Total Current	**381,706**	**37.6**
Other Long Term	90,351	8.9
Deferred Credits	5,076	0.5
Net Worth	538,043	53.0
Total Liab & Net Worth	**1,015,176**	**100.0**
Net Sales	5,287,375	100.0
Gross Profit	1,533,339	29.0
Net Profit After Tax	148,047	2.8
Working Capital	403,025	—

RATIOS	UQ	MED	LQ
SOLVENCY			
Quick Ratio (times)	4.6	1.9	1.1
Current Ratio (times)	5.8	2.3	1.5
Curr Liab To Nw (%)	17.0	50.5	119.3
Curr Liab To Inv (%)	486.8	775.6	999.9
Total Liab To Nw (%)	20.6	55.9	159.4
Fixed Assets To Nw (%)	7.1	17.1	28.9
EFFICIENCY			
Coll Period (days)	31.8	44.4	56.9
Sales To Inv (times)	493.8	88.0	13.9
Assets To Sales (%)	13.0	19.2	33.3
Sales To Nwc (times)	16.8	9.5	6.0
Acct Pay To Sales (%)	0.4	1.3	3.1
PROFITABILITY			
Return On Sales (%)	5.4	2.1	(1.0)
Return On Assets (%)	29.7	9.8	(5.0)
Return On Nw (%)	59.3	21.4	0.3

	SIC 7363 HELP SUPPLY SVCS (NO BREAKDOWN) 2002 (183 Establishments)		SIC 7371 CSTM CMPTR PRGMG SV (NO BREAKDOWN) 2002 (808 Establishments)		SIC 7372 PREPACKAGED SFTWARE (NO BREAKDOWN) 2002 (299 Establishments)		SIC 7373 CPTR INTGTD SYS DGN (NO BREAKDOWN) 2002 (679 Establishments)	
	$	%	$	%	$	%	$	%
Cash	291,235	16.0	377,757	27.2	3,827,309	27.7	239,942	18.8
Accounts Receivable	808,177	44.4	436,087	31.4	3,136,459	22.7	505,410	39.6
Notes Receivable	9,101	0.5	6,944	0.5	27,634	0.2	7,658	0.6
Inventory	27,303	1.5	31,943	2.3	221,072	1.6	77,854	6.1
Other Current	216,607	11.9	158,324	11.4	2,169,269	15.7	146,773	11.5
Total Current	**1,352,423**	**74.3**	**1,011,055**	**72.8**	**9,381,743**	**67.9**	**977,637**	**76.6**
Fixed Assets	249,370	13.7	201,378	14.5	1,796,210	13.0	174,852	13.7
Other Non-current	218,426	12.0	176,379	12.7	2,639,047	19.1	123,800	9.7
Total Assets	**1,820,219**	**100.0**	**1,388,812**	**100.0**	**13,817,000**	**100.0**	**1,276,289**	**100.0**
Accounts Payable	109,213	6.0	668,019	48.1	3,924,028	28.4	338,217	26.5
Bank Loans	27,303	1.5	12,499	0.9	13,817	0.1	11,487	0.9
Notes Payable	41,865	2.3	224,988	16.2	7,682,252	55.6	39,565	3.1
Other Current	627,976	34.5	573,579	41.3	3,288,446	23.8	373,952	29.3
Total Current	**806,357**	**44.3**	**1,479,085**	**106.5**	**14,908,543**	**107.9**	**763,221**	**59.8**
Other Long Term	404,089	22.2	286,095	20.6	1,699,491	12.3	178,680	14.0
Deferred Credits	9,101	0.5	22,221	1.6	276,340	2.0	14,039	1.1
Net Worth	600,672	33.0	(398,589)	(28.7)	(3,067,374)	(22.2)	320,349	25.1
Total Liab & Net Worth	**1,820,219**	**100.0**	**1,388,812**	**100.0**	**13,817,000**	**100.0**	**1,276,289**	**100.0**
Net Sales	8,966,596	100.0	3,229,795	100.0	16,103,730	100.0	4,064,615	100.0
Gross Profit	2,044,384	22.8	1,757,008	54.4	10,660,669	66.2	1,662,428	40.9
Net Profit After Tax	98,633	1.1	(29,068)	(0.9)	(1,320,506)	(8.2)	40,646	1.0
Working Capital	546,066	—	(468,030)	—	(5,526,800)	—	214,416	—

RATIOS	UQ	MED	LQ	UQ	MED	LQ	UQ	MED	LQ	UQ	MED	LQ
SOLVENCY												
Quick Ratio (times)	3.4	1.6	0.9	3.0	1.5	0.8	2.2	1.3	0.7	2.1	1.2	0.7
Current Ratio (times)	4.1	2.0	1.3	3.7	1.9	1.1	3.5	1.9	1.0	2.9	1.5	1.1
Curr Liab To Nw (%)	25.9	67.6	168.6	21.1	50.7	129.8	25.3	47.7	96.1	37.3	101.6	247.8
Curr Liab To Inv (%)	264.1	819.6	999.9	329.5	873.1	999.9	655.6	999.9	999.9	273.0	665.5	999.9
Total Liab To Nw (%)	31.7	94.6	231.4	27.7	67.3	162.5	31.3	68.9	132.3	47.3	123.1	312.6
Fixed Assets To Nw (%)	7.3	19.1	39.0	7.4	16.6	41.9	5.9	13.8	33.6	7.6	19.9	49.6
EFFICIENCY												
Coll Period (days)	23.0	38.3	51.1	33.4	52.9	75.8	35.0	55.0	75.6	29.2	48.8	72.8
Sales To Inv (times)	470.9	168.6	44.9	170.9	55.9	17.9	214.4	76.0	31.8	125.4	45.3	17.0
Assets To Sales (%)	12.5	20.3	33.8	24.1	43.0	94.6	42.5	85.8	152.4	21.7	31.4	56.2
Sales To Nwc (times)	25.5	11.5	6.9	11.3	6.0	2.6	6.3	3.1	1.6	20.4	9.6	4.7
Acct Pay To Sales (%)	0.2	0.6	2.0	1.5	3.5	7.4	2.1	4.3	6.6	2.2	4.9	9.5
PROFITABILITY												
Return On Sales (%)	4.1	1.0	0.0	6.2	1.1	(13.3)	5.8	(2.2)	(31.6)	5.9	2.0	(0.8)
Return On Assets (%)	20.6	6.0	(0.4)	16.8	3.1	(23.1)	9.9	(2.1)	(33.3)	19.6	6.0	(2.2)
Return On Nw (%)	39.6	18.0	1.0	40.1	9.5	(21.1)	17.0	(1.7)	(64.3)	54.7	17.4	0.2

SIC 7374 DATA PROC, PRPRTN
(NO BREAKDOWN)
2002 (165 Establishments)

	$	%
Cash	233,146	17.7
Accounts Receivable	356,964	27.1
Notes Receivable	3,952	0.3
Inventory	31,613	2.4
Other Current	152,796	11.6
Total Current	**778,471**	**59.1**
Fixed Assets	317,447	24.1
Other Non-current	221,291	16.8
Total Assets	**1,317,209**	**100.0**
Accounts Payable	484,733	36.8
Bank Loans	7,903	0.6
Notes Payable	40,833	3.1
Other Current	1,008,983	76.6
Total Current	**1,542,452**	**117.1**
Other Long Term	443,900	33.7
Deferred Credits	2,634	0.2
Net Worth	(671,777)	(51.0)
Total Liab & Net Worth	**1,317,209**	**100.0**
Net Sales	3,128,762	100.0
Gross Profit	1,548,737	49.5
Net Profit After Tax	(21,901)	(0.7)
Working Capital	(763,981)	—

RATIOS	UQ	MED	LQ
SOLVENCY			
Quick Ratio (times)	2.2	1.2	0.6
Current Ratio (times)	2.9	1.7	0.9
Curr Liab To Nw (%)	24.2	52.9	120.0
Curr Liab To Inv (%)	383.3	999.9	999.9
Total Liab To Nw (%)	36.9	86.7	189.8
Fixed Assets To Nw (%)	13.8	36.9	82.2
EFFICIENCY			
Coll Period (days)	29.9	48.9	78.5
Sales To Inv (times)	269.5	49.6	17.4
Assets To Sales (%)	25.3	42.1	90.0
Sales To Nwc (times)	18.0	7.5	4.2
Acct Pay To Sales (%)	1.9	3.4	7.8
PROFITABILITY			
Return On Sales (%)	7.0	1.0	(6.7)
Return On Assets (%)	13.9	2.3	(20.3)
Return On Nw (%)	37.0	11.4	(8.9)

SIC 7375 INFRMTN RTRVL SVCS
(NO BREAKDOWN)
2002 (76 Establishments)

	$	%
Cash	942,881	23.8
Accounts Receivable	812,145	20.5
Notes Receivable	39,617	1.0
Inventory	91,119	2.3
Other Current	542,750	13.7
Total Current	**2,428,512**	**61.3**
Fixed Assets	835,915	21.1
Other Non-current	697,256	17.6
Total Assets	**3,961,683**	**100.0**
Accounts Payable	1,434,129	36.2
Bank Loans	0	0.0
Notes Payable	206,008	5.2
Other Current	5,791,980	146.2
Total Current	**7,432,117**	**187.6**
Other Long Term	677,448	17.1
Deferred Credits	23,770	0.6
Net Worth	(4,171,652)	(105.3)
Total Liab & Net Worth	**3,961,683**	**100.0**
Net Sales	4,671,796	100.0
Gross Profit	2,153,698	46.1
Net Profit After Tax	(523,241)	(11.2)
Working Capital	(5,003,605)	—

RATIOS	UQ	MED	LQ
SOLVENCY			
Quick Ratio (times)	1.8	1.1	0.4
Current Ratio (times)	2.6	1.5	0.7
Curr Liab To Nw (%)	26.5	56.2	125.7
Curr Liab To Inv (%)	489.0	911.4	999.9
Total Liab To Nw (%)	38.0	71.4	166.1
Fixed Assets To Nw (%)	7.8	20.3	71.5
EFFICIENCY			
Coll Period (days)	20.8	45.6	71.2
Sales To Inv (times)	230.7	40.8	16.9
Assets To Sales (%)	27.6	84.8	172.4
Sales To Nwc (times)	12.5	7.3	2.1
Acct Pay To Sales (%)	3.8	7.7	15.2
PROFITABILITY			
Return On Sales (%)	5.5	(0.6)	(71.1)
Return On Assets (%)	8.7	(3.1)	(62.6)
Return On Nw (%)	17.6	(4.6)	(84.0)

SIC 7376 COMP FACLTS MNGMNT
(NO BREAKDOWN)
2002 (17 Establishments)

	$	%
Cash	314,680	10.5
Accounts Receivable	1,075,904	35.9
Notes Receivable	155,841	5.2
Inventory	32,966	1.1
Other Current	761,225	25.4
Total Current	**2,340,616**	**78.1**
Fixed Assets	482,509	16.1
Other Non-current	173,823	5.8
Total Assets	**2,996,948**	**100.0**
Accounts Payable	347,646	11.6
Bank Loans	0	0.0
Notes Payable	0	0.0
Other Current	854,130	28.5
Total Current	**1,201,776**	**40.1**
Other Long Term	215,780	7.2
Deferred Credits	17,982	0.6
Net Worth	1,561,410	52.1
Total Liab & Net Worth	**2,996,948**	**100.0**
Net Sales	10,334,303	100.0
Gross Profit	2,707,587	26.2
Net Profit After Tax	361,701	3.5
Working Capital	1,138,840	—

RATIOS	UQ	MED	LQ
SOLVENCY			
Quick Ratio (times)	1.6	0.9	0.6
Current Ratio (times)	2.5	1.5	1.2
Curr Liab To Nw (%)	28.7	143.4	246.4
Curr Liab To Inv (%)	412.4	481.4	999.9
Total Liab To Nw (%)	55.4	180.8	250.7
Fixed Assets To Nw (%)	8.8	16.4	57.2
EFFICIENCY			
Coll Period (days)	34.3	44.2	67.9
Sales To Inv (times)	388.3	50.3	29.3
Assets To Sales (%)	20.8	29.0	38.0
Sales To Nwc (times)	17.4	11.0	5.6
Acct Pay To Sales (%)	1.8	3.1	4.7
PROFITABILITY			
Return On Sales (%)	5.9	3.3	0.8
Return On Assets (%)	29.8	10.5	2.4
Return On Nw (%)	83.6	27.1	4.5

SIC 7377 COMP RNTL, LEASING
(NO BREAKDOWN)
2002 (17 Establishments)

	$	%
Cash	357,249	13.8
Accounts Receivable	396,080	15.3
Notes Receivable	0	0.0
Inventory	137,204	5.3
Other Current	326,184	12.6
Total Current	**1,216,717**	**47.0**
Fixed Assets	968,196	37.4
Other Non-current	403,847	15.6
Total Assets	**2,588,760**	**100.0**
Accounts Payable	284,764	11.0
Bank Loans	0	0.0
Notes Payable	157,914	6.1
Other Current	458,210	17.7
Total Current	**900,888**	**34.8**
Other Long Term	657,545	25.4
Deferred Credits	119,083	4.6
Net Worth	911,244	35.2
Total Liab & Net Worth	**2,588,760**	**100.0**
Net Sales	4,243,869	100.0
Gross Profit	2,189,836	51.6
Net Profit After Tax	288,583	6.8
Working Capital	315,829	—

RATIOS	UQ	MED	LQ
SOLVENCY			
Quick Ratio (times)	1.5	1.1	0.4
Current Ratio (times)	3.4	1.4	0.9
Curr Liab To Nw (%)	38.2	65.2	255.6
Curr Liab To Inv (%)	270.8	540.1	770.0
Total Liab To Nw (%)	49.8	224.2	407.0
Fixed Assets To Nw (%)	35.1	93.8	295.2
EFFICIENCY			
Coll Period (days)	24.8	35.8	79.9
Sales To Inv (times)	367.8	102.5	20.2
Assets To Sales (%)	42.4	61.0	136.1
Sales To Nwc (times)	22.4	7.8	2.1
Acct Pay To Sales (%)	5.6	7.1	7.7
PROFITABILITY			
Return On Sales (%)	9.0	7.9	2.6
Return On Assets (%)	14.4	4.4	3.3
Return On Nw (%)	46.1	32.1	6.8

	SIC 7378 COMP MAINT,REPAIR (NO BREAKDOWN) 2002 (102 Establishments)		SIC 7379 COMP RLTD SVCS, NEC (NO BREAKDOWN) 2002 (452 Establishments)		SIC 7381 DTCTV,ARMRD CAR SVC (NO BREAKDOWN) 2002 (68 Establishments)		SIC 7382 SECURITY SYS SVCS (NO BREAKDOWN) 2002 (82 Establishments)	
	$	%	$	%	$	%	$	%
Cash	121,691	19.8	157,235	18.3	203,575	14.5	82,168	11.9
Accounts Receivable	222,485	36.2	372,037	43.3	721,638	51.4	260,315	37.7
Notes Receivable	615	0.1	1,718	0.2	11,232	0.8	2,071	0.3
Inventory	103,867	16.9	33,509	3.9	16,848	1.2	57,311	8.3
Other Current	44,866	7.3	80,765	9.4	189,535	13.5	51,097	7.4
Total Current	**493,524**	**80.3**	**645,264**	**75.1**	**1,142,828**	**81.4**	**452,962**	**65.6**
Fixed Assets	90,346	14.7	138,332	16.1	155,840	11.1	135,336	19.6
Other Non-current	30,730	5.0	75,611	8.8	105,297	7.5	102,193	14.8
Total Assets	**614,600**	**100.0**	**859,207**	**100.0**	**1,403,965**	**100.0**	**690,491**	**100.0**
Accounts Payable	105,097	17.1	203,632	23.7	123,549	8.8	98,050	14.2
Bank Loans	7,990	1.3	12,029	1.4	4,212	0.3	0	0.0
Notes Payable	18,438	3.0	39,524	4.6	49,139	3.5	14,500	2.1
Other Current	177,619	28.9	397,812	46.3	547,546	39.0	420,509	60.9
Total Current	**309,144**	**50.3**	**652,997**	**76.0**	**724,446**	**51.6**	**533,059**	**77.2**
Other Long Term	73,138	11.9	9,451	1.1	358,011	25.5	164,337	23.8
Deferred Credits	2,458	0.4	2,578	0.3	0	0.0	690	0.1
Net Worth	229,860	37.4	194,181	22.6	321,508	22.9	(7,595)	(1.1)
Total Liab & Net Worth	**614,600**	**100.0**	**859,207**	**100.0**	**1,403,965**	**100.0**	**690,491**	**100.0**
Net Sales	2,069,360	100.0	3,291,981	100.0	5,462,899	100.0	1,972,831	100.0
Gross Profit	993,293	48.0	1,389,216	42.2	1,535,075	28.1	980,497	49.7
Net Profit After Tax	45,526	2.2	88,883	2.7	120,184	2.2	72,995	3.7
Working Capital	184,380	—	(7,733)	—	418,382	—	(80,097)	—

RATIOS	UQ	MED	LQ	UQ	MED	LQ	UQ	MED	LQ	UQ	MED	LQ
SOLVENCY												
Quick Ratio (times)	2.4	1.2	0.7	2.8	1.5	0.9	2.3	1.3	0.9	2.2	1.2	0.6
Current Ratio (times)	3.5	1.7	1.2	3.2	1.8	1.2	2.6	1.6	1.2	2.9	1.5	0.9
Curr Liab To Nw (%)	26.7	71.3	209.2	29.2	72.0	166.3	50.3	106.8	223.5	38.3	82.0	228.7
Curr Liab To Inv (%)	103.5	240.4	842.5	242.1	650.7	999.9	509.3	999.9	999.9	178.2	569.1	999.9
Total Liab To Nw (%)	35.6	86.8	227.3	38.2	93.6	220.8	75.8	126.7	292.5	63.7	141.3	392.1
Fixed Assets To Nw (%)	10.5	22.6	41.5	6.6	18.4	44.9	8.6	18.0	34.7	22.5	42.1	80.3
EFFICIENCY												
Coll Period (days)	22.3	35.4	49.6	30.5	48.2	67.2	35.0	55.9	71.2	32.9	51.5	68.6
Sales To Inv (times)	57.3	22.1	8.8	159.1	54.2	18.1	168.8	122.6	76.8	44.9	21.5	11.4
Assets To Sales (%)	18.7	29.7	44.7	17.1	26.1	38.9	16.6	25.7	37.6	25.1	35.0	56.3
Sales To Nwc (times)	17.9	9.2	5.6	19.2	10.4	5.6	18.1	11.0	5.7	12.8	7.9	5.6
Acct Pay To Sales (%)	1.8	3.5	7.4	1.5	3.5	7.8	0.6	1.9	6.2	2.1	4.6	8.2
PROFITABILITY												
Return On Sales (%)	7.6	1.8	0.1	7.0	2.7	0.2	4.5	2.6	1.0	6.1	2.2	0.4
Return On Assets (%)	23.2	7.9	0.3	30.9	9.1	0.2	19.8	9.0	2.9	19.3	5.5	1.3
Return On Nw (%)	54.2	18.8	0.9	68.6	27.8	4.0	54.8	23.6	9.1	69.0	20.2	6.8

	SIC 7384 PHOTOFNSHNG LBRTRS (NO BREAKDOWN) 2002 (51 Establishments) $	%	SIC 7389 BUS SERVICES, NEC (NO BREAKDOWN) 2002 (1108 Establishments) $	%	SIC 75 AUTO REPAIR,SVS,GAR (NO BREAKDOWN) 2002 (596 Establishments) $	%	SIC 7513 TRCK RNTL,NO DRVRS (NO BREAKDOWN) 2002 (43 Establishments) $	%
Cash	126,436	13.9	143,186	17.6	86,398	13.3	441,592	6.2
Accounts Receivable	161,910	17.8	224,542	27.6	105,886	16.3	740,735	10.4
Notes Receivable	2,729	0.3	5,695	0.7	3,248	0.5	21,367	0.3
Inventory	98,238	10.8	90,305	11.1	129,272	19.9	277,776	3.9
Other Current	54,576	6.0	81,357	10.0	47,421	7.3	733,613	10.3
Total Current	**443,889**	**48.8**	**545,085**	**67.0**	**372,225**	**57.3**	**2,215,083**	**31.1**
Fixed Assets	409,324	45.0	200,949	24.7	228,012	35.1	4,373,187	61.4
Other Non-current	56,396	6.2	67,525	8.3	49,370	7.6	534,184	7.5
Total Assets	**909,609**	**100.0**	**813,559**	**100.0**	**649,607**	**100.0**	**7,122,454**	**100.0**
Accounts Payable	82,774	9.1	133,424	16.4	81,201	12.5	334,755	4.7
Bank Loans	3,638	0.4	24,407	3.0	1,299	0.2	0	0.0
Notes Payable	68,221	7.5	31,729	3.9	28,583	4.4	548,429	7.7
Other Current	136,442	15.0	330,304	40.6	139,665	21.5	1,880,328	26.4
Total Current	**291,075**	**32.0**	**519,864**	**63.9**	**250,748**	**38.6**	**2,763,512**	**38.8**
Other Long Term	236,498	26.0	132,610	16.3	157,206	24.2	2,378,899	33.4
Deferred Credits	0	0.0	2,441	0.3	2,598	0.4	149,572	2.1
Net Worth	382,036	42.0	158,644	19.5	239,055	36.8	1,830,471	25.7
Total Liab & Net Worth	**909,609**	**100.0**	**813,559**	**100.0**	**649,607**	**100.0**	**7,122,454**	**100.0**
Net Sales	2,072,002	100.0	2,385,804	100.0	1,962,559	100.0	5,707,095	100.0
Gross Profit	1,006,993	48.6	1,009,195	42.3	822,312	41.9	1,797,735	31.5
Net Profit After Tax	37,296	1.8	81,117	3.4	54,952	2.8	45,657	0.8
Working Capital	152,814	—	25,221	—	121,477	—	(548,429)	—

RATIOS	UQ	MED	LQ	UQ	MED	LQ	UQ	MED	LQ	UQ	MED	LQ
SOLVENCY												
Quick Ratio (times)	2.4	1.4	0.4	2.4	1.2	0.6	1.9	0.8	0.4	0.9	0.4	0.2
Current Ratio (times)	3.2	2.1	1.1	3.6	1.8	1.1	3.5	1.8	1.0	1.8	0.9	0.5
Curr Liab To Nw (%)	22.0	36.1	83.4	20.7	64.7	171.9	21.6	61.2	156.6	29.7	90.5	232.2
Curr Liab To Inv (%)	205.7	332.4	585.5	116.0	267.5	814.9	77.4	153.4	431.5	512.8	999.9	999.9
Total Liab To Nw (%)	32.6	56.1	145.6	35.7	94.8	241.1	37.9	104.6	270.9	79.9	267.7	492.0
Fixed Assets To Nw (%)	46.1	69.5	110.7	14.3	38.4	85.0	24.1	53.4	138.5	72.0	183.1	427.0
EFFICIENCY												
Coll Period (days)	16.4	28.9	40.2	21.9	36.9	58.0	8.2	21.2	35.2	22.6	36.5	52.2
Sales To Inv (times)	48.0	31.0	16.8	62.3	20.9	9.1	43.0	18.7	7.6	62.8	30.5	12.7
Assets To Sales (%)	33.2	43.9	55.5	21.0	34.1	60.9	21.2	33.1	57.9	63.9	124.8	211.9
Sales To Nwc (times)	12.3	7.4	5.0	17.9	8.9	4.6	19.0	9.5	5.5	25.5	5.4	4.2
Acct Pay To Sales (%)	1.8	3.5	5.8	1.7	4.1	7.7	2.1	3.5	5.8	1.6	3.4	6.0
PROFITABILITY												
Return On Sales (%)	5.5	0.5	(2.3)	7.8	2.3	(0.3)	5.0	1.7	(0.1)	2.2	0.7	(2.0)
Return On Assets (%)	10.3	0.8	(5.0)	21.2	6.8	(0.9)	15.1	4.2	(0.3)	1.8	0.5	(1.0)
Return On Nw (%)	25.9	1.7	(11.9)	51.2	17.6	1.4	39.0	12.1	1.4	7.1	3.3	(2.9)

SIC 7514 PASSENGER CAR RNTL
(NO BREAKDOWN)
2002 (16 Establishments)

	$	%
Cash	158,404	6.5
Accounts Receivable	70,673	2.9
Notes Receivable	17,059	0.7
Inventory	314,371	12.9
Other Current	399,665	16.4
Total Current	**960,172**	**39.4**
Fixed Assets	1,169,753	48.0
Other Non-current	307,061	12.6
Total Assets	**2,436,986**	**100.0**
Accounts Payable	70,673	2.9
Bank Loans	0	0.0
Notes Payable	253,447	10.4
Other Current	718,910	29.5
Total Current	**1,043,030**	**42.8**
Other Long Term	723,785	29.7
Deferred Credits	0	0.0
Net Worth	670,171	27.5
Total Liab & Net Worth	**2,436,986**	**100.0**
Net Sales	1,999,168	100.0
Gross Profit	1,091,546	54.6
Net Profit After Tax	131,945	6.6
Working Capital	(82,858)	—

RATIOS	UQ	MED	LQ
SOLVENCY			
Quick Ratio (times)	0.3	0.2	0.2
Current Ratio (times)	1.6	0.8	0.3
Curr Liab To Nw (%)	64.0	149.7	631.2
Curr Liab To Inv (%)	132.5	999.9	999.9
Total Liab To Nw (%)	143.0	361.2	878.4
Fixed Assets To Nw (%)	48.6	221.2	607.6
EFFICIENCY			
Coll Period (days)	5.3	9.2	26.5
Sales To Inv (times)	99.3	43.2	5.1
Assets To Sales (%)	81.1	121.9	215.9
Sales To Nwc (times)	13.1	6.1	2.9
Acct Pay To Sales (%)	0.3	1.3	3.4
PROFITABILITY			
Return On Sales (%)	5.0	0.3	(0.8)
Return On Assets (%)	5.4	0.3	(0.8)
Return On Nw (%)	36.3	6.5	(7.8)

SIC 7515 PASSENGER CAR LSNG
(NO BREAKDOWN)
2002 (12 Establishments)

	$	%
Cash	327,152	3.0
Accounts Receivable	752,450	6.9
Notes Receivable	21,810	0.2
Inventory	119,956	1.1
Other Current	3,598,672	33.0
Total Current	**4,820,040**	**44.2**
Fixed Assets	3,805,868	34.9
Other Non-current	2,279,159	20.9
Total Assets	**10,905,067**	**100.0**
Accounts Payable	65,430	0.6
Bank Loans	43,620	0.4
Notes Payable	1,886,577	17.3
Other Current	4,045,780	37.1
Total Current	**6,041,407**	**55.4**
Other Long Term	2,835,318	26.0
Deferred Credits	10,905	0.1
Net Worth	2,017,437	18.5
Total Liab & Net Worth	**10,905,067**	**100.0**
Net Sales	5,706,471	100.0
Gross Profit	1,729,061	30.3
Net Profit After Tax	119,836	2.1
Working Capital	(1,221,367)	—

RATIOS	UQ	MED	LQ
SOLVENCY			
Quick Ratio (times)	2.3	0.1	0.0
Current Ratio (times)	3.0	1.2	0.4
Curr Liab To Nw (%)	130.7	215.5	979.3
Curr Liab To Inv (%)	128.2	999.9	999.9
Total Liab To Nw (%)	210.5	705.3	990.3
Fixed Assets To Nw (%)	4.0	121.9	295.4
EFFICIENCY			
Coll Period (days)	6.4	17.0	61.4
Sales To Inv (times)	72.4	59.6	24.0
Assets To Sales (%)	95.4	191.1	220.1
Sales To Nwc (times)	7.4	3.5	3.3
Acct Pay To Sales (%)	0.2	0.3	0.9
PROFITABILITY			
Return On Sales (%)	5.0	(0.2)	(0.5)
Return On Assets (%)	2.3	(0.1)	(0.3)
Return On Nw (%)	7.1	(1.5)	(4.2)

SIC 7532 TP,BDY RPR,PNT SHPS
(NO BREAKDOWN)
2002 (105 Establishments)

	$	%
Cash	76,031	16.1
Accounts Receivable	92,088	19.5
Notes Receivable	4,722	1.0
Inventory	81,698	17.3
Other Current	28,807	6.1
Total Current	**283,346**	**60.0**
Fixed Assets	156,313	33.1
Other Non-current	32,585	6.9
Total Assets	**472,244**	**100.0**
Accounts Payable	78,865	16.7
Bank Loans	0	0.0
Notes Payable	17,001	3.6
Other Current	98,699	20.9
Total Current	**194,565**	**41.2**
Other Long Term	108,616	23.0
Deferred Credits	2,361	0.5
Net Worth	166,702	35.3
Total Liab & Net Worth	**472,244**	**100.0**
Net Sales	2,117,686	100.0
Gross Profit	823,780	38.9
Net Profit After Tax	50,824	2.4
Working Capital	88,781	—

RATIOS	UQ	MED	LQ
SOLVENCY			
Quick Ratio (times)	1.7	0.9	0.6
Current Ratio (times)	2.7	1.6	1.0
Curr Liab To Nw (%)	33.7	57.4	133.7
Curr Liab To Inv (%)	112.3	200.3	543.5
Total Liab To Nw (%)	41.7	104.6	205.5
Fixed Assets To Nw (%)	22.6	47.5	123.7
EFFICIENCY			
Coll Period (days)	9.0	15.7	26.2
Sales To Inv (times)	66.0	29.2	15.5
Assets To Sales (%)	17.1	22.3	33.1
Sales To Nwc (times)	26.8	13.6	8.0
Acct Pay To Sales (%)	2.1	3.6	5.1
PROFITABILITY			
Return On Sales (%)	4.3	0.9	(0.9)
Return On Assets (%)	16.0	3.7	(2.2)
Return On Nw (%)	39.8	15.0	(0.2)

SIC 7534 TIRE RTRDNG,RPR SHP
(NO BREAKDOWN)
2002 (15 Establishments)

	$	%
Cash	232,276	16.1
Accounts Receivable	411,171	28.5
Notes Receivable	1,443	0.1
Inventory	538,130	37.3
Other Current	23,083	1.6
Total Current	**1,206,103**	**83.6**
Fixed Assets	304,411	21.1
Other Non-current	(67,807)	(4.7)
Total Assets	**1,442,707**	**100.0**
Accounts Payable	428,484	29.7
Bank Loans	0	0.0
Notes Payable	34,625	2.4
Other Current	145,713	10.1
Total Current	**608,822**	**42.2**
Other Long Term	152,927	10.6
Deferred Credits	0	0.0
Net Worth	680,958	47.2
Total Liab & Net Worth	**1,442,707**	**100.0**
Net Sales	3,571,057	100.0
Gross Profit	1,028,464	28.8
Net Profit After Tax	74,992	2.1
Working Capital	597,281	—

RATIOS	UQ	MED	LQ
SOLVENCY			
Quick Ratio (times)	1.6	1.1	0.7
Current Ratio (times)	3.5	2.2	1.4
Curr Liab To Nw (%)	51.7	100.5	195.8
Curr Liab To Inv (%)	65.6	98.3	165.7
Total Liab To Nw (%)	62.8	142.4	298.4
Fixed Assets To Nw (%)	20.5	28.9	81.9
EFFICIENCY			
Coll Period (days)	34.7	39.1	48.9
Sales To Inv (times)	10.4	7.9	6.6
Assets To Sales (%)	30.5	40.4	60.4
Sales To Nwc (times)	19.0	6.9	5.5
Acct Pay To Sales (%)	8.3	13.8	16.6
PROFITABILITY			
Return On Sales (%)	3.2	1.0	0.2
Return On Assets (%)	5.5	2.9	1.0
Return On Nw (%)	19.1	6.8	1.2

SIC 7536 ATMTV GLS RPLCMT SH
(NO BREAKDOWN)
2002 (27 Establishments)

	$	%
Cash	91,187	10.7
Accounts Receivable	213,905	25.1
Notes Receivable	852	0.1
Inventory	133,797	15.7
Other Current	68,177	8.0
Total Current	**507,918**	**59.6**
Fixed Assets	250,550	29.4
Other Non-current	93,743	11.0
Total Assets	**852,211**	**100.0**
Accounts Payable	124,423	14.6
Bank Loans	0	0.0
Notes Payable	14,488	1.7
Other Current	136,353	16.0
Total Current	**275,264**	**32.3**
Other Long Term	190,895	22.4
Deferred Credits	6,818	0.8
Net Worth	379,234	44.5
Total Liab & Net Worth	**852,211**	**100.0**
Net Sales	3,838,788	100.0
Gross Profit	1,758,165	45.8
Net Profit After Tax	72,937	1.9
Working Capital	232,654	—

RATIOS	UQ	MED	LQ
SOLVENCY			
Quick Ratio (times)	2.3	1.4	0.7
Current Ratio (times)	3.4	2.3	1.8
Curr Liab To Nw (%)	21.4	38.7	81.1
Curr Liab To Inv (%)	82.9	119.0	221.9
Total Liab To Nw (%)	29.9	48.6	105.3
Fixed Assets To Nw (%)	20.6	41.0	68.9
EFFICIENCY			
Coll Period (days)	19.6	25.2	33.3
Sales To Inv (times)	31.4	18.9	12.4
Assets To Sales (%)	18.7	22.2	41.6
Sales To Nwc (times)	13.3	8.4	5.7
Acct Pay To Sales (%)	2.8	4.0	6.2
PROFITABILITY			
Return On Sales (%)	2.5	1.3	0.1
Return On Assets (%)	13.2	5.5	0.2
Return On Nw (%)	20.8	8.9	3.0

SIC 7537 ATMTV TRANS RPR SHP
(NO BREAKDOWN)
2002 (11 Establishments)

	$	%
Cash	13,013	3.2
Accounts Receivable	42,291	10.4
Notes Receivable	5,286	1.3
Inventory	137,852	33.9
Other Current	4,880	1.2
Total Current	**203,322**	**50.0**
Fixed Assets	124,839	30.7
Other Non-current	78,482	19.3
Total Assets	**406,643**	**100.0**
Accounts Payable	29,685	7.3
Bank Loans	0	0.0
Notes Payable	23,179	5.7
Other Current	70,755	17.4
Total Current	**123,619**	**30.4**
Other Long Term	113,047	27.8
Deferred Credits	0	0.0
Net Worth	169,977	41.8
Total Liab & Net Worth	**406,643**	**100.0**
Net Sales	1,145,473	100.0
Gross Profit	521,190	45.5
Net Profit After Tax	56,128	4.9
Working Capital	79,703	—

RATIOS	UQ	MED	LQ
SOLVENCY			
Quick Ratio (times)	1.3	0.4	0.1
Current Ratio (times)	3.2	1.3	0.6
Curr Liab To Nw (%)	20.7	38.8	71.9
Curr Liab To Inv (%)	51.5	100.7	242.6
Total Liab To Nw (%)	26.0	40.8	463.8
Fixed Assets To Nw (%)	29.2	36.0	115.4
EFFICIENCY			
Coll Period (days)	4.0	10.6	15.0
Sales To Inv (times)	16.8	13.0	6.5
Assets To Sales (%)	22.3	35.5	56.7
Sales To Nwc (times)	10.7	8.9	3.8
Acct Pay To Sales (%)	1.2	2.3	5.1
PROFITABILITY			
Return On Sales (%)	9.1	4.3	0.3
Return On Assets (%)	35.1	5.6	0.8
Return On Nw (%)	50.3	38.2	1.7

SIC 7538 GNRL ATMTVE RPR SHP
(NO BREAKDOWN)
2002 (189 Establishments)

	$	%
Cash	72,775	13.6
Accounts Receivable	87,223	16.3
Notes Receivable	2,676	0.5
Inventory	147,691	27.6
Other Current	33,178	6.2
Total Current	**343,543**	**64.2**
Fixed Assets	161,604	30.2
Other Non-current	29,966	5.6
Total Assets	**535,113**	**100.0**
Accounts Payable	69,030	12.9
Bank Loans	1,605	0.3
Notes Payable	20,869	3.9
Other Current	124,147	23.2
Total Current	**215,651**	**40.3**
Other Long Term	108,092	20.2
Deferred Credits	0	0.0
Net Worth	211,370	39.5
Total Liab & Net Worth	**535,113**	**100.0**
Net Sales	1,760,240	100.0
Gross Profit	711,137	40.4
Net Profit After Tax	58,088	3.3
Working Capital	127,892	—

RATIOS	UQ	MED	LQ
SOLVENCY			
Quick Ratio (times)	1.9	0.8	0.4
Current Ratio (times)	3.8	2.0	1.1
Curr Liab To Nw (%)	23.1	54.3	145.0
Curr Liab To Inv (%)	58.6	118.0	294.1
Total Liab To Nw (%)	36.0	92.9	210.5
Fixed Assets To Nw (%)	22.7	43.6	85.7
EFFICIENCY			
Coll Period (days)	7.7	19.7	30.9
Sales To Inv (times)	30.2	13.0	6.4
Assets To Sales (%)	20.0	30.4	44.9
Sales To Nwc (times)	17.0	9.3	6.1
Acct Pay To Sales (%)	2.5	3.7	5.5
PROFITABILITY			
Return On Sales (%)	4.8	1.8	0.0
Return On Assets (%)	14.8	5.3	0.2
Return On Nw (%)	45.4	13.4	2.9

SIC 7539 ATMTVE RPR SHPS, NEC
(NO BREAKDOWN)
2002 (84 Establishments)

	$	%
Cash	83,225	16.6
Accounts Receivable	100,271	20.0
Notes Receivable	1,003	0.2
Inventory	119,323	23.8
Other Current	28,578	5.7
Total Current	**332,400**	**66.3**
Fixed Assets	138,876	27.7
Other Non-current	30,081	6.0
Total Assets	**501,357**	**100.0**
Accounts Payable	61,166	12.2
Bank Loans	1,504	0.3
Notes Payable	16,043	3.2
Other Current	81,721	16.3
Total Current	**160,434**	**32.0**
Other Long Term	93,754	18.7
Deferred Credits	0	0.0
Net Worth	247,169	49.3
Total Liab & Net Worth	**501,357**	**100.0**
Net Sales	1,474,579	100.0
Gross Profit	613,425	41.6
Net Profit After Tax	44,237	3.0
Working Capital	171,966	—

RATIOS	UQ	MED	LQ
SOLVENCY			
Quick Ratio (times)	3.6	1.2	0.6
Current Ratio (times)	5.5	2.4	1.3
Curr Liab To Nw (%)	13.4	45.7	153.6
Curr Liab To Inv (%)	65.6	110.8	222.4
Total Liab To Nw (%)	18.0	70.4	197.5
Fixed Assets To Nw (%)	18.0	38.2	85.5
EFFICIENCY			
Coll Period (days)	13.5	29.9	40.2
Sales To Inv (times)	29.2	12.6	6.7
Assets To Sales (%)	25.0	34.0	47.7
Sales To Nwc (times)	17.9	7.7	4.0
Acct Pay To Sales (%)	2.1	3.3	5.3
PROFITABILITY			
Return On Sales (%)	5.9	2.3	0.1
Return On Assets (%)	17.5	6.0	0.4
Return On Nw (%)	36.9	16.6	1.3

	SIC 7542 CARWASHES (NO BREAKDOWN) 2002 (14 Establishments)		SIC 7549 ATMTVE SVCS,NEC (NO BREAKDOWN) 2002 (60 Establishments)		SIC 76 MISC REPAIR SERVICE (NO BREAKDOWN) 2002 (1065 Establishments)		SIC 7622 RADIO,TV REPAIR (NO BREAKDOWN) 2002 (64 Establishments)	
	$	%	$	%	$	%	$	%
Cash	231,210	15.5	79,233	13.6	100,252	15.4	144,849	21.6
Accounts Receivable	89,501	6.0	78,650	13.5	173,163	26.6	152,896	22.8
Notes Receivable	19,392	1.3	1,165	0.2	2,604	0.4	671	0.1
Inventory	47,734	3.2	76,320	13.1	132,151	20.3	130,095	19.4
Other Current	71,599	4.8	40,199	6.9	50,777	7.8	39,564	5.9
Total Current	**459,436**	**30.8**	**275,567**	**47.3**	**458,947**	**70.5**	**468,075**	**69.8**
Fixed Assets	893,514	59.9	256,924	44.1	156,237	24.0	135,460	20.2
Other Non-current	138,726	9.3	50,104	8.6	35,804	5.5	67,060	10.0
Total Assets	**1,491,676**	**100.0**	**582,595**	**100.0**	**650,988**	**100.0**	**670,595**	**100.0**
Accounts Payable	88,009	5.9	66,998	11.5	88,534	13.6	67,060	10.0
Bank Loans	0	0.0	1,165	0.2	2,604	0.4	2,682	0.4
Notes Payable	0	0.0	32,043	5.5	22,785	3.5	12,741	1.9
Other Current	732,413	49.1	92,633	15.9	132,150	20.3	119,366	17.8
Total Current	**820,422**	**55.0**	**192,839**	**33.1**	**246,073**	**37.8**	**201,849**	**30.1**
Other Long Term	537,003	36.0	254,594	43.7	104,809	16.1	102,601	15.3
Deferred Credits	4,475	0.3	3,496	0.6	1,953	0.3	0	0.0
Net Worth	129,776	8.7	131,666	22.6	298,153	45.8	366,145	54.6
Total Liab & Net Worth	**1,491,676**	**100.0**	**582,595**	**100.0**	**650,988**	**100.0**	**670,595**	**100.0**
Net Sales	3,766,859	100.0	1,417,506	100.0	1,788,429	100.0	1,827,234	100.0
Gross Profit	1,951,233	51.8	756,948	53.4	765,448	42.8	765,611	41.9
Net Profit After Tax	214,711	5.7	12,758	0.9	50,076	2.8	73,089	4.0
Working Capital	(360,986)	—	82,728	—	212,874	—	266,226	—

RATIOS	UQ	MED	LQ	UQ	MED	LQ	UQ	MED	LQ	UQ	MED	LQ
SOLVENCY												
Quick Ratio (times)	2.0	1.0	0.4	2.4	0.9	0.4	2.9	1.2	0.6	4.3	1.7	0.7
Current Ratio (times)	3.1	1.8	0.6	3.3	1.6	0.9	4.5	2.2	1.3	5.9	2.5	1.4
Curr Liab To Nw (%)	12.0	21.7	126.0	11.9	57.5	124.3	19.8	55.1	140.0	11.1	43.7	112.8
Curr Liab To Inv (%)	171.8	580.7	911.5	85.9	188.9	795.2	76.9	148.2	373.0	62.0	141.7	316.0
Total Liab To Nw (%)	26.5	77.1	168.4	51.1	142.4	596.4	31.4	81.2	208.2	16.1	58.2	189.7
Fixed Assets To Nw (%)	48.0	98.2	190.5	50.9	147.5	337.2	15.1	37.1	83.8	13.1	25.7	72.2
EFFICIENCY												
Coll Period (days)	1.8	2.6	15.6	4.2	19.7	34.9	24.1	37.8	54.2	20.8	40.9	51.1
Sales To Inv (times)	89.0	51.4	34.3	97.9	35.2	16.1	33.9	13.7	7.0	29.0	16.0	8.5
Assets To Sales (%)	22.8	39.6	68.3	23.3	41.1	64.9	25.6	36.4	51.2	28.5	36.7	50.8
Sales To Nwc (times)	13.6	8.6	5.7	29.6	10.3	5.9	12.3	6.9	4.3	12.0	6.5	3.8
Acct Pay To Sales (%)	1.6	2.6	3.4	1.7	3.0	7.4	2.1	4.1	7.2	1.3	3.3	7.2
PROFITABILITY												
Return On Sales (%)	8.6	6.9	1.6	6.0	2.3	(0.1)	4.8	1.8	(0.1)	6.1	2.7	0.4
Return On Assets (%)	25.1	12.6	1.6	16.5	6.7	0.1	13.1	4.9	(0.1)	19.8	6.1	1.0
Return On Nw (%)	67.9	39.1	17.0	54.3	17.2	7.9	34.8	11.4	0.7	37.4	10.9	1.2

SIC 7623 RFRGRTN SVC,RPR
(NO BREAKDOWN)
2002 (91 Establishments)

	$	%
Cash	142,424	22.1
Accounts Receivable	199,135	30.9
Notes Receivable	1,933	0.3
Inventory	72,823	11.3
Other Current	72,179	11.2
Total Current	**488,494**	**75.8**
Fixed Assets	117,935	18.3
Other Non-current	38,022	5.9
Total Assets	**644,451**	**100.0**
Accounts Payable	86,356	13.4
Bank Loans	1,289	0.2
Notes Payable	23,845	3.7
Other Current	127,601	19.8
Total Current	**239,091**	**37.1**
Other Long Term	94,090	14.6
Deferred Credits	4,511	0.7
Net Worth	306,759	47.6
Total Liab & Net Worth	**644,451**	**100.0**
Net Sales	1,964,790	100.0
Gross Profit	725,008	36.9
Net Profit After Tax	64,838	3.3
Working Capital	249,403	—

RATIOS	UQ	MED	LQ
SOLVENCY			
Quick Ratio (times)	3.3	1.5	0.8
Current Ratio (times)	4.0	2.2	1.6
Curr Liab To Nw (%)	31.0	68.0	126.8
Curr Liab To Inv (%)	117.2	243.0	585.3
Total Liab To Nw (%)	38.6	83.7	215.3
Fixed Assets To Nw (%)	12.2	26.9	78.1
EFFICIENCY			
Coll Period (days)	29.6	39.8	59.1
Sales To Inv (times)	66.9	26.3	12.6
Assets To Sales (%)	24.3	32.8	40.2
Sales To Nwc (times)	11.1	7.4	4.6
Acct Pay To Sales (%)	2.3	4.1	8.0
PROFITABILITY			
Return On Sales (%)	5.0	1.6	0.2
Return On Assets (%)	15.1	5.1	0.5
Return On Nw (%)	25.0	10.4	0.7

SIC 7629 ELECTL RPR SHPS,NEC
(NO BREAKDOWN)
2002 (166 Establishments)

	$	%
Cash	118,284	14.6
Accounts Receivable	230,896	28.5
Notes Receivable	2,430	0.3
Inventory	161,222	19.9
Other Current	70,485	8.7
Total Current	**583,317**	**72.0**
Fixed Assets	175,805	21.7
Other Non-current	51,041	6.3
Total Assets	**810,163**	**100.0**
Accounts Payable	106,131	13.1
Bank Loans	3,241	0.4
Notes Payable	25,115	3.1
Other Current	155,551	19.2
Total Current	**290,038**	**35.8**
Other Long Term	112,613	13.9
Deferred Credits	4,051	0.5
Net Worth	403,461	49.8
Total Liab & Net Worth	**810,163**	**100.0**
Net Sales	2,282,149	100.0
Gross Profit	1,049,789	46.0
Net Profit After Tax	79,875	3.5
Working Capital	293,279	—

RATIOS	UQ	MED	LQ
SOLVENCY			
Quick Ratio (times)	2.7	1.2	0.7
Current Ratio (times)	4.4	2.3	1.4
Curr Liab To Nw (%)	24.7	56.0	146.1
Curr Liab To Inv (%)	83.8	140.4	356.4
Total Liab To Nw (%)	36.9	95.7	229.0
Fixed Assets To Nw (%)	14.9	33.0	84.3
EFFICIENCY			
Coll Period (days)	26.3	35.8	51.8
Sales To Inv (times)	34.0	11.8	6.9
Assets To Sales (%)	25.5	35.5	44.3
Sales To Nwc (times)	11.3	6.9	4.6
Acct Pay To Sales (%)	2.3	4.6	7.1
PROFITABILITY			
Return On Sales (%)	5.2	2.3	0.4
Return On Assets (%)	15.1	6.2	1.0
Return On Nw (%)	42.5	13.9	2.1

SIC 7641 REUPHLSTRY,FURN RPR
(NO BREAKDOWN)
2002 (18 Establishments)

	$	%
Cash	38,127	20.5
Accounts Receivable	34,593	18.6
Notes Receivable	0	0.0
Inventory	21,760	11.7
Other Current	10,414	5.6
Total Current	**104,894**	**56.4**
Fixed Assets	68,628	36.9
Other Non-current	12,461	6.7
Total Assets	**185,983**	**100.0**
Accounts Payable	29,571	15.9
Bank Loans	0	0.0
Notes Payable	2,604	1.4
Other Current	50,215	27.0
Total Current	**82,390**	**44.3**
Other Long Term	53,564	28.8
Deferred Credits	0	0.0
Net Worth	50,029	26.9
Total Liab & Net Worth	**185,983**	**100.0**
Net Sales	718,081	100.0
Gross Profit	337,498	47.0
Net Profit After Tax	40,213	5.6
Working Capital	22,504	—

RATIOS	UQ	MED	LQ
SOLVENCY			
Quick Ratio (times)	1.9	1.0	0.5
Current Ratio (times)	2.9	1.5	1.0
Curr Liab To Nw (%)	25.7	32.8	64.3
Curr Liab To Inv (%)	60.0	220.3	999.9
Total Liab To Nw (%)	32.4	38.4	162.3
Fixed Assets To Nw (%)	13.3	51.2	101.5
EFFICIENCY			
Coll Period (days)	10.4	20.8	43.5
Sales To Inv (times)	105.9	47.5	13.7
Assets To Sales (%)	13.0	25.9	50.5
Sales To Nwc (times)	61.5	8.6	5.1
Acct Pay To Sales (%)	1.4	3.1	8.1
PROFITABILITY			
Return On Sales (%)	8.3	2.2	(1.6)
Return On Assets (%)	42.5	7.5	(4.9)
Return On Nw (%)	44.2	18.1	0.1

SIC 7692 WELDING REPAIR
(NO BREAKDOWN)
2002 (48 Establishments)

	$	%
Cash	78,281	18.3
Accounts Receivable	75,715	17.7
Notes Receivable	4,278	1.0
Inventory	63,309	14.8
Other Current	32,938	7.7
Total Current	**254,521**	**59.5**
Fixed Assets	156,562	36.6
Other Non-current	16,683	3.9
Total Assets	**427,766**	**100.0**
Accounts Payable	50,904	11.9
Bank Loans	2,139	0.5
Notes Payable	10,266	2.4
Other Current	65,021	15.2
Total Current	**128,330**	**30.0**
Other Long Term	61,170	14.3
Deferred Credits	428	0.1
Net Worth	237,838	55.6
Total Liab & Net Worth	**427,766**	**100.0**
Net Sales	1,016,071	100.0
Gross Profit	451,136	44.4
Net Profit After Tax	40,643	4.0
Working Capital	126,191	—

RATIOS	UQ	MED	LQ
SOLVENCY			
Quick Ratio (times)	6.5	1.5	0.5
Current Ratio (times)	10.5	2.3	1.3
Curr Liab To Nw (%)	7.8	30.4	89.1
Curr Liab To Inv (%)	58.4	119.9	774.2
Total Liab To Nw (%)	17.2	44.9	118.9
Fixed Assets To Nw (%)	22.0	57.3	104.7
EFFICIENCY			
Coll Period (days)	16.4	27.7	46.4
Sales To Inv (times)	53.4	25.0	8.6
Assets To Sales (%)	29.4	42.1	60.4
Sales To Nwc (times)	12.2	6.1	4.0
Acct Pay To Sales (%)	1.4	3.2	6.6
PROFITABILITY			
Return On Sales (%)	5.3	2.4	0.8
Return On Assets (%)	24.0	5.5	1.5
Return On Nw (%)	33.4	10.3	3.0

	SIC 7694 ARMTRE REWNDNG SHPS (NO BREAKDOWN) 2002 (77 Establishments)		SIC 7699 REPAIR SVCS,NEC (NO BREAKDOWN) 2002 (593 Establishments)		SIC 78 MOTION PICTURES (NO BREAKDOWN) 2002 (191 Establishments)		SIC 7812 MTN PCTRE,VDEO PROD (NO BREAKDOWN) 2002 (108 Establishments)	
	$	%	$	%	$	%	$	%
Cash	89,504	12.4	88,179	13.9	183,061	15.6	98,583	18.9
Accounts Receivable	194,887	27.0	170,648	26.9	254,642	21.7	125,185	24.0
Notes Receivable	722	0.1	3,172	0.5	1,173	0.1	1,043	0.2
Inventory	187,669	26.0	137,026	21.6	70,408	6.0	21,907	4.2
Other Current	44,029	6.1	47,578	7.5	91,530	7.8	46,423	8.9
Total Current	**516,811**	**71.6**	**446,603**	**70.4**	**600,814**	**51.2**	**293,141**	**56.2**
Fixed Assets	161,684	22.4	157,326	24.8	429,488	36.6	166,392	31.9
Other Non-current	43,308	6.0	30,450	4.8	143,163	12.2	62,071	11.9
Total Assets	**721,803**	**100.0**	**634,379**	**100.0**	**1,173,465**	**100.0**	**521,604**	**100.0**
Accounts Payable	76,511	10.6	92,619	14.6	566,784	48.3	396,419	76.0
Bank Loans	2,887	0.4	2,538	0.4	19,949	1.7	13,562	2.6
Notes Payable	10,827	1.5	27,278	4.3	281,632	24.0	183,083	35.1
Other Current	101,775	14.1	138,929	21.9	692,343	59.0	433,974	83.2
Total Current	**192,000**	**26.6**	**261,364**	**41.2**	**1,560,708**	**133.0**	**1,027,038**	**196.9**
Other Long Term	98,165	13.6	107,845	17.0	281,632	24.0	118,404	22.7
Deferred Credits	722	0.1	1,903	0.3	8,214	0.7	5,738	1.1
Net Worth	430,916	59.7	263,267	41.5	(677,089)	(57.7)	(629,576)	(120.7)
Total Liab & Net Worth	**721,803**	**100.0**	**634,379**	**100.0**	**1,173,465**	**100.0**	**521,604**	**100.0**
Net Sales	1,831,987	100.0	1,786,983	100.0	2,429,534	100.0	1,557,027	100.0
Gross Profit	668,675	36.5	773,764	43.3	1,241,492	51.1	803,426	51.6
Net Profit After Tax	16,488	0.9	42,888	2.4	41,302	1.7	42,040	2.7
Working Capital	324,811	—	185,239	—	(959,894)	—	(733,897)	—

RATIOS	UQ	MED	LQ	UQ	MED	LQ	UQ	MED	LQ	UQ	MED	LQ
SOLVENCY												
Quick Ratio (times)	3.8	1.7	0.9	2.6	1.1	0.6	1.6	1.0	0.4	1.9	1.0	0.3
Current Ratio (times)	5.9	2.8	1.7	4.2	2.0	1.3	2.4	1.3	0.7	2.7	1.3	0.6
Curr Liab To Nw (%)	13.5	41.1	67.8	21.4	58.6	166.0	28.3	58.7	162.1	21.3	53.9	140.5
Curr Liab To Inv (%)	52.5	97.1	180.3	76.8	148.9	415.5	181.3	422.8	999.9	241.4	672.8	999.9
Total Liab To Nw (%)	18.4	53.3	114.2	32.1	92.1	241.7	44.7	107.3	289.1	38.1	88.6	213.9
Fixed Assets To Nw (%)	9.9	29.8	60.0	17.9	42.1	84.6	27.3	77.4	173.4	23.5	67.0	115.0
EFFICIENCY												
Coll Period (days)	32.5	41.3	51.5	23.4	38.0	55.3	18.8	38.9	61.4	20.4	40.2	58.4
Sales To Inv (times)	14.9	10.2	6.4	33.1	13.1	6.4	155.8	32.9	12.1	191.0	99.7	18.5
Assets To Sales (%)	29.2	39.4	53.4	25.4	35.5	52.9	27.3	48.3	87.2	22.6	33.5	63.0
Sales To Nwc (times)	9.9	6.8	3.5	13.0	7.1	4.3	23.5	11.1	5.0	22.5	11.1	5.1
Acct Pay To Sales (%)	2.4	4.0	5.5	1.9	4.1	7.4	1.9	4.7	10.1	1.3	4.0	8.3
PROFITABILITY												
Return On Sales (%)	2.8	0.7	(0.6)	4.8	1.7	(0.1)	6.6	1.7	(2.6)	7.6	1.8	(4.1)
Return On Assets (%)	7.9	1.2	(1.5)	13.1	4.7	(0.4)	14.0	3.6	(6.0)	18.1	6.2	(12.7)
Return On Nw (%)	12.4	2.6	(2.8)	37.5	12.2	1.2	45.1	14.0	(2.4)	64.2	21.7	0.3

	SIC 7819 SVCS ALLD MTN PICT (NO BREAKDOWN) 2002 (40 Establishments) $	%	SIC 7822 MTN PICT,TAPE DIST (NO BREAKDOWN) 2002 (13 Establishments) $	%	SIC 7841 VIDEO TAPE RENTAL (NO BREAKDOWN) 2002 (14 Establishments) $	%	SIC 79 AMUSE RECREATION SVCS (NO BREAKDOWN) 2002 (617 Establishments) $	%
Cash	148,368	10.6	482,248	17.0	526,138	9.7	397,797	13.2
Accounts Receivable	352,724	25.2	856,699	30.2	357,991	6.6	238,076	7.9
Notes Receivable	1,400	0.1	2,837	0.1	5,424	0.1	15,068	0.5
Inventory	110,576	7.9	357,431	12.6	737,679	13.6	129,586	4.3
Other Current	60,186	4.3	164,531	5.8	705,134	13.0	226,021	7.5
Total Current	**673,254**	**48.1**	**1,863,746**	**65.7**	**2,332,366**	**43.0**	**1,006,548**	**33.4**
Fixed Assets	634,063	45.3	371,615	13.1	1,524,174	28.1	1,648,448	54.7
Other Non-current	92,380	6.6	601,391	21.2	1,567,567	28.9	358,621	11.9
Total Assets	**1,399,697**	**100.0**	**2,836,752**	**100.0**	**5,424,107**	**100.0**	**3,013,617**	**100.0**
Accounts Payable	165,164	11.8	417,003	14.7	900,402	16.6	256,157	8.5
Bank Loans	4,199	0.3	79,429	2.8	0	0.0	6,027	0.2
Notes Payable	32,193	2.3	25,531	0.9	2,326,942	42.9	66,300	2.2
Other Current	309,333	22.1	1,906,297	67.2	1,339,754	24.7	1,042,712	34.6
Total Current	**510,889**	**36.5**	**2,428,260**	**85.6**	**4,567,098**	**84.2**	**1,371,196**	**45.5**
Other Long Term	356,923	25.5	238,287	8.4	705,134	13.0	922,167	30.6
Deferred Credits	1,400	0.1	22,694	0.8	16,272	0.3	21,095	0.7
Net Worth	530,485	37.9	147,511	5.2	135,603	2.5	699,159	23.2
Total Liab & Net Worth	**1,399,697**	**100.0**	**2,836,752**	**100.0**	**5,424,107**	**100.0**	**3,013,617**	**100.0**
Net Sales	2,755,309	100.0	5,102,072	100.0	7,053,455	100.0	3,016,634	100.0
Gross Profit	1,333,570	48.4	2,474,505	48.5	3,900,561	55.3	1,954,779	64.8
Net Profit After Tax	16,532	0.6	(117,348)	(2.3)	(7,053)	(0.1)	45,250	1.5
Working Capital	162,365	—	(564,514)	—	(2,234,732)	—	(364,648)	—

RATIOS	UQ	MED	LQ	UQ	MED	LQ	UQ	MED	LQ	UQ	MED	LQ
SOLVENCY												
Quick Ratio (times)	1.7	1.2	0.8	1.7	0.9	0.6	0.6	0.4	0.1	1.7	0.8	0.3
Current Ratio (times)	2.3	1.4	1.0	2.5	1.1	0.9	2.6	1.1	0.6	2.8	1.3	0.7
Curr Liab To Nw (%)	33.2	76.9	183.6	43.2	56.2	289.4	21.1	47.5	134.1	9.6	27.1	77.5
Curr Liab To Inv (%)	159.6	340.8	999.9	184.1	198.3	238.7	118.1	284.7	451.5	296.4	733.7	999.9
Total Liab To Nw (%)	70.0	125.7	361.6	45.4	59.7	323.1	24.3	58.2	161.1	21.1	66.6	181.6
Fixed Assets To Nw (%)	61.9	104.2	276.5	3.9	17.2	26.3	18.3	65.4	95.8	53.5	102.0	179.6
EFFICIENCY												
Coll Period (days)	29.2	50.4	65.0	37.8	49.7	89.3	8.4	18.5	999.9	4.8	18.5	40.5
Sales To Inv (times)	122.5	30.0	13.7	13.7	10.6	8.5	18.9	12.1	5.2	98.2	43.3	22.2
Assets To Sales (%)	30.4	50.8	89.2	49.8	55.6	161.2	45.4	76.9	141.3	42.3	99.9	200.0
Sales To Nwc (times)	43.3	12.8	6.3	17.8	5.5	3.9	21.0	8.0	3.4	18.6	8.5	3.5
Acct Pay To Sales (%)	2.6	4.1	8.2	4.0	10.8	20.3	10.2	13.3	24.8	1.8	3.5	6.5
PROFITABILITY												
Return On Sales (%)	4.3	1.3	(1.5)	4.3	2.0	(16.0)	6.4	1.2	(8.9)	6.9	1.7	(3.0)
Return On Assets (%)	12.4	2.0	(2.9)	10.3	3.7	(6.7)	12.2	0.9	(12.2)	8.6	1.9	(2.7)
Return On Nw (%)	32.4	6.3	(7.1)	50.9	14.0	(6.8)	33.0	1.1	(8.5)	18.7	4.5	(2.7)

	SIC 7922 THTRCL PRDCRS,SVCS (NO BREAKDOWN) 2002 (84 Establishments)		SIC 7929 ENTRS, ENTRTNMNT GRP (NO BREAKDOWN) 2002 (29 Establishments)		SIC 7933 BOWLING CENTERS (NO BREAKDOWN) 2002 (17 Establishments)		SIC 7941 SPTS CLBS,MGRS,PMTR (NO BREAKDOWN) 2002 (14 Establishments)	
	$	%	$	%	$	%	$	%
Cash	277,932	15.4	494,230	23.5	54,256	17.5	540,475	19.8
Accounts Receivable	308,613	17.1	437,446	20.8	3,720	1.2	141,943	5.2
Notes Receivable	9,024	0.5	27,340	1.3	2,170	0.7	0	0.0
Inventory	84,823	4.7	35,753	1.7	11,161	3.6	103,728	3.8
Other Current	214,766	11.9	403,798	19.2	10,853	3.5	403,991	14.8
Total Current	**895,158**	**49.6**	**1,398,567**	**66.5**	**82,160**	**26.5**	**1,190,137**	**43.6**
Fixed Assets	573,912	31.8	260,785	12.4	203,384	65.6	472,233	17.3
Other Non-current	335,685	18.6	443,756	21.1	24,492	7.9	1,067,302	39.1
Total Assets	**1,804,755**	**100.0**	**2,103,108**	**100.0**	**310,036**	**100.0**	**2,729,672**	**100.0**
Accounts Payable	167,842	9.3	1,179,844	56.1	12,711	4.1	548,664	20.1
Bank Loans	0	0.0	0	0.0	0	0.0	0	0.0
Notes Payable	63,166	3.5	33,650	1.6	2,790	0.9	90,079	3.3
Other Current	1,949,136	108.0	1,341,782	63.8	58,908	19.0	1,389,403	50.9
Total Current	**2,180,144**	**120.8**	**2,555,276**	**121.5**	**74,409**	**24.0**	**2,028,146**	**74.3**
Other Long Term	227,399	12.6	157,734	7.5	222,916	71.9	524,097	19.2
Deferred Credits	9,024	0.5	4,206	0.2	0	0.0	43,675	1.6
Net Worth	(611,812)	(33.9)	(614,108)	(29.2)	12,711	4.1	133,754	4.9
Total Liab & Net Worth	**1,804,755**	**100.0**	**2,103,108**	**100.0**	**310,036**	**100.0**	**2,729,672**	**100.0**
Net Sales	4,236,514	100.0	2,815,406	100.0	636,624	100.0	2,928,833	100.0
Gross Profit	2,058,946	48.6	1,421,780	50.5	448,820	70.5	1,423,413	48.6
Net Profit After Tax	148,278	3.5	(171,740)	(6.1)	19,735	3.1	114,224	3.9
Working Capital	(1,284,986)	—	(1,156,709)	—	7,751	—	(838,009)	—

RATIOS	UQ	MED	LQ	UQ	MED	LQ	UQ	MED	LQ	UQ	MED	LQ
SOLVENCY												
Quick Ratio (times)	1.6	0.9	0.4	1.7	1.2	0.6	2.9	0.8	0.3	5.0	0.7	0.3
Current Ratio (times)	2.9	1.6	0.9	4.0	1.8	1.2	3.2	1.4	0.5	9.5	1.3	0.7
Curr Liab To Nw (%)	10.0	34.3	110.3	8.1	32.7	82.2	9.1	22.8	63.0	7.5	34.3	131.5
Curr Liab To Inv (%)	225.6	706.4	999.9	626.1	999.9	999.9	434.8	733.7	999.9	217.6	439.0	733.5
Total Liab To Nw (%)	12.1	43.0	142.1	17.0	32.7	83.9	14.9	40.1	205.4	7.5	78.0	599.8
Fixed Assets To Nw (%)	22.0	46.5	96.6	5.0	11.6	24.4	67.7	105.5	230.0	8.5	13.3	42.8
EFFICIENCY												
Coll Period (days)	6.6	23.7	41.5	16.1	46.4	82.9	0.0	0.4	2.9	7.7	11.4	28.8
Sales To Inv (times)	241.1	55.1	26.8	207.3	111.5	51.0	135.8	89.7	67.3	149.1	48.7	8.8
Assets To Sales (%)	22.2	42.6	122.8	18.6	74.7	250.3	28.8	48.7	80.7	53.9	93.2	198.2
Sales To Nwc (times)	19.7	9.6	5.5	9.6	6.9	2.0	29.1	20.6	6.5	17.2	9.0	0.8
Acct Pay To Sales (%)	1.7	3.8	6.8	3.5	6.4	11.7	1.3	2.3	3.9	1.1	2.4	19.0
PROFITABILITY												
Return On Sales (%)	8.8	2.2	(2.0)	6.9	(0.4)	(12.5)	6.1	2.2	0.1	2.3	0.6	(16.0)
Return On Assets (%)	25.8	3.7	(3.1)	8.7	(0.8)	(17.2)	10.8	4.1	0.2	2.8	0.6	(4.9)
Return On Nw (%)	48.7	8.9	(4.3)	27.4	(0.5)	(15.5)	57.3	8.9	0.9	4.6	0.7	(42.2)

Balance sheet data:

	SIC 7948 RCNG,INCL TRCK OPER $	%	SIC 7991 PHYSCL FTNSS FACLTS $	%	SIC 7992 PUBLIC GOLF COURSES $	%	SIC 7993 CN-OPRTD AMSMNT DVC $	%
	(NO BREAKDOWN) 2002 (14 Establishments)		(NO BREAKDOWN) 2002 (27 Establishments)		(NO BREAKDOWN) 2002 (46 Establishments)		(NO BREAKDOWN) 2002 (26 Establishments)	
Cash	1,834,910	8.7	148,895	13.2	182,720	9.5	389,037	14.6
Accounts Receivable	780,364	3.7	58,656	5.2	53,854	2.8	181,196	6.8
Notes Receivable	21,091	0.1	4,512	0.4	5,770	0.3	45,299	1.7
Inventory	63,273	0.3	39,480	3.5	94,245	4.9	162,543	6.1
Other Current	1,940,363	9.2	87,983	7.8	50,009	2.6	119,909	4.5
Total Current	**4,640,001**	**22.0**	**339,526**	**30.1**	**386,598**	**20.1**	**897,984**	**33.7**
Fixed Assets	12,106,185	57.4	630,549	55.9	1,394,445	72.5	1,396,271	52.4
Other Non-current	4,344,728	20.6	157,919	14.0	142,329	7.4	370,385	13.9
Total Assets	**21,090,914**	**100.0**	**1,127,994**	**100.0**	**1,923,372**	**100.0**	**2,664,640**	**100.0**
Accounts Payable	1,117,818	5.3	41,736	3.7	61,548	3.2	194,519	7.3
Bank Loans	0	0.0	1,128	0.1	23,080	1.2	0	0.0
Notes Payable	21,091	0.1	7,896	0.7	32,697	1.7	61,287	2.3
Other Current	2,488,728	11.8	354,190	31.4	575,089	29.9	559,574	21.0
Total Current	**3,627,637**	**17.2**	**404,950**	**35.9**	**692,414**	**36.0**	**815,380**	**30.6**
Other Long Term	5,926,547	28.1	436,533	38.7	690,491	35.9	866,008	32.5
Deferred Credits	210,909	1.0	4,512	0.4	11,540	0.6	5,329	0.2
Net Worth	11,325,821	53.7	281,999	25.0	528,927	27.5	977,923	36.7
Total Liab & Net Worth	**21,090,914**	**100.0**	**1,127,994**	**100.0**	**1,923,372**	**100.0**	**2,664,640**	**100.0**
Net Sales	17,316,021	100.0	990,337	100.0	1,658,079	100.0	4,118,454	100.0
Gross Profit	8,138,530	47.0	804,154	81.2	1,273,405	76.8	2,112,767	51.3
Net Profit After Tax	(917,749)	(5.3)	48,527	4.9	(8,290)	(0.5)	185,330	4.5
Working Capital	1,012,364	—	(65,424)	—	(305,816)	—	82,604	—

RATIOS:

RATIOS	7948 UQ	MED	LQ	7991 UQ	MED	LQ	7992 UQ	MED	LQ	7993 UQ	MED	LQ
SOLVENCY												
Quick Ratio (times)	2.3	0.7	0.2	1.6	0.2	0.1	1.5	0.3	0.1	2.1	1.0	0.4
Current Ratio (times)	2.3	1.1	0.7	2.0	0.8	0.4	2.3	0.9	0.2	2.7	1.5	0.5
Curr Liab To Nw (%)	12.6	29.1	36.8	15.7	67.8	297.6	7.1	15.5	77.3	20.9	52.9	156.1
Curr Liab To Inv (%)	999.9	999.9	999.9	277.7	999.9	999.9	298.7	649.1	965.4	182.6	423.2	999.9
Total Liab To Nw (%)	40.2	79.1	123.1	35.6	179.5	749.6	22.6	76.5	204.3	21.4	135.2	268.5
Fixed Assets To Nw (%)	92.3	127.2	149.1	60.9	150.2	491.2	85.1	149.5	273.0	76.5	102.1	270.5
EFFICIENCY												
Coll Period (days)	2.4	16.8	28.5	4.8	11.0	23.7	0.7	1.8	6.6	1.9	8.4	36.1
Sales To Inv (times)	316.7	245.4	114.7	198.8	64.6	23.5	62.3	43.9	20.5	69.4	38.2	14.9
Assets To Sales (%)	63.4	121.8	210.0	33.1	113.9	183.0	72.1	116.0	171.2	36.7	64.7	97.8
Sales To Nwc (times)	62.6	9.3	2.1	24.6	8.8	5.8	16.4	12.1	6.7	31.2	16.0	5.0
Acct Pay To Sales (%)	1.5	3.0	3.7	0.8	1.9	3.0	1.0	3.2	4.4	1.1	2.5	4.2
PROFITABILITY												
Return On Sales (%)	7.6	4.8	(0.7)	10.5	3.2	(0.2)	5.4	2.1	(0.7)	5.9	2.8	0.8
Return On Assets (%)	5.2	4.1	(0.6)	9.2	3.0	(0.2)	6.2	1.9	(0.2)	12.5	4.7	1.6
Return On Nw (%)	12.5	9.8	(0.6)	30.9	10.3	0.7	12.3	6.4	(0.1)	40.3	13.0	5.1

	SIC 7996 AMUSEMENT PARKS (NO BREAKDOWN) 2002 (10 Establishments)		SIC 7997 MBRSHP SPT,RCTN CLB (NO BREAKDOWN) 2002 (219 Establishments)		SIC 7999 AMUSEMENT,RCRTN,NEC (NO BREAKDOWN) 2002 (127 Establishments)		SIC 80 HEALTH SERVICES (NO BREAKDOWN) 2002 (1296 Establishments)	
	$	%	$	%	$	%	$	%
Cash	1,389,738	12.5	405,185	8.1	230,979	17.8	1,489,958	12.8
Accounts Receivable	300,183	2.7	345,158	6.9	67,477	5.2	2,165,095	18.6
Notes Receivable	0	0.0	5,002	0.1	11,679	0.9	34,921	0.3
Inventory	433,598	3.9	140,064	2.8	98,620	7.6	232,806	2.0
Other Current	333,538	3.0	215,098	4.3	119,382	9.2	1,082,546	9.3
Total Current	**2,457,057**	**22.1**	**1,110,507**	**22.2**	**528,137**	**40.7**	**5,005,326**	**43.0**
Fixed Assets	6,748,568	60.7	3,641,664	72.8	583,936	45.0	4,586,276	39.4
Other Non-current	1,912,279	17.2	250,115	5.0	185,562	14.3	2,048,692	17.6
Total Assets	**11,117,904**	**100.0**	**5,002,286**	**100.0**	**1,297,635**	**100.0**	**11,640,294**	**100.0**
Accounts Payable	433,598	3.9	225,103	4.5	99,918	7.7	954,504	8.2
Bank Loans	0	0.0	5,002	0.1	3,893	0.3	23,281	0.2
Notes Payable	0	0.0	105,048	2.1	36,334	2.8	256,086	2.2
Other Current	2,757,240	24.8	735,336	14.7	290,670	22.4	2,712,189	23.3
Total Current	**3,190,838**	**28.7**	**1,070,489**	**21.4**	**430,815**	**33.2**	**3,946,060**	**33.9**
Other Long Term	11,873,922	106.8	1,805,825	36.1	325,706	25.1	3,340,764	28.7
Deferred Credits	77,825	0.7	70,032	1.4	0	0.0	46,561	0.4
Net Worth	(4,024,681)	(36.2)	2,055,940	41.1	541,114	41.7	4,306,909	37.0
Total Liab & Net Worth	**11,117,904**	**100.0**	**5,002,286**	**100.0**	**1,297,635**	**100.0**	**11,640,294**	**100.0**
Net Sales	15,167,673	100.0	2,715,682	100.0	2,233,451	100.0	15,336,356	100.0
Gross Profit	10,086,503	66.5	1,911,840	70.4	1,386,973	62.1	7,300,105	47.6
Net Profit After Tax	348,856	2.3	8,147	0.3	42,436	1.9	368,073	2.4
Working Capital	(733,781)	—	40,018	—	97,322	—	1,059,266	—

RATIOS	UQ	MED	LQ	UQ	MED	LQ	UQ	MED	LQ	UQ	MED	LQ
SOLVENCY												
Quick Ratio (times)	0.9	0.5	0.1	1.7	0.9	0.5	1.7	0.7	0.2	2.3	1.4	0.8
Current Ratio (times)	1.2	1.0	0.3	2.3	1.3	0.8	3.7	1.3	0.7	3.2	1.9	1.2
Curr Liab To Nw (%)	9.4	49.3	72.1	10.0	21.5	42.6	10.0	36.1	110.2	15.3	29.7	78.4
Curr Liab To Inv (%)	593.1	722.5	859.8	356.5	811.2	999.9	92.2	430.5	999.9	489.8	914.5	999.9
Total Liab To Nw (%)	48.0	190.8	312.5	24.0	56.9	137.0	32.3	87.2	193.9	36.1	80.8	183.8
Fixed Assets To Nw (%)	164.0	256.0	340.9	92.1	123.8	184.9	25.3	80.9	182.4	39.6	69.8	118.6
EFFICIENCY												
Coll Period (days)	4.8	5.5	13.9	21.0	35.0	68.7	1.1	6.8	15.9	30.7	47.1	63.2
Sales To Inv (times)	50.6	42.5	33.1	82.4	38.4	22.6	112.8	33.8	13.4	124.7	62.3	38.4
Assets To Sales (%)	41.7	73.3	129.2	105.0	184.2	284.4	24.5	58.1	122.8	38.3	75.9	128.0
Sales To Nwc (times)	37.7	24.1	3.9	12.0	6.5	3.4	25.4	8.0	3.2	14.3	6.9	4.0
Acct Pay To Sales (%)	2.0	3.9	5.5	2.5	4.3	7.4	1.6	3.0	6.3	2.0	3.5	6.2
PROFITABILITY												
Return On Sales (%)	10.6	0.2	(5.7)	5.2	0.1	(4.3)	7.1	3.3	(1.6)	6.2	2.2	(0.9)
Return On Assets (%)	9.4	2.4	(5.0)	2.9	0.1	(2.7)	16.1	4.9	(3.1)	9.4	2.7	(1.1)
Return On Nw (%)	59.8	23.4	(6.3)	5.1	0.2	(3.9)	38.5	13.5	2.7	18.9	6.3	(0.8)

SIC 8011 OFCS,CLNS OF MDL DR (NO BREAKDOWN) 2002 (193 Establishments)

	$	%
Cash	550,252	20.8
Accounts Receivable	486,761	18.4
Notes Receivable	5,291	0.2
Inventory	50,263	1.9
Other Current	280,417	10.6
Total Current	**1,372,984**	**51.9**
Fixed Assets	965,586	36.5
Other Non-current	306,872	11.6
Total Assets	**2,645,442**	**100.0**
Accounts Payable	343,907	13.0
Bank Loans	0	0.0
Notes Payable	140,208	5.3
Other Current	1,095,214	41.4
Total Current	**1,579,329**	**59.7**
Other Long Term	706,333	26.7
Deferred Credits	5,291	0.2
Net Worth	354,489	13.4
Total Liab & Net Worth	**2,645,442**	**100.0**
Net Sales	6,835,767	100.0
Gross Profit	3,445,227	50.4
Net Profit After Tax	232,416	3.4
Working Capital	(206,345)	—

RATIOS	UQ	MED	LQ
SOLVENCY			
Quick Ratio (times)	2.5	1.2	0.5
Current Ratio (times)	3.3	1.5	0.8
Curr Liab To Nw (%)	18.4	45.0	173.9
Curr Liab To Inv (%)	311.7	809.9	999.9
Total Liab To Nw (%)	32.1	95.6	270.3
Fixed Assets To Nw (%)	27.6	71.8	151.8
EFFICIENCY			
Coll Period (days)	20.8	39.4	60.2
Sales To Inv (times)	134.1	58.6	21.6
Assets To Sales (%)	20.8	38.7	75.8
Sales To Nwc (times)	26.1	7.9	3.7
Acct Pay To Sales (%)	0.8	2.7	6.2
PROFITABILITY			
Return On Sales (%)	7.9	1.0	(1.7)
Return On Assets (%)	17.8	2.7	(3.8)
Return On Nw (%)	50.2	11.9	(5.9)

SIC 8021 OFCS,CLNS OF DNTSTS (NO BREAKDOWN) 2002 (14 Establishments)

	$	%
Cash	107,359	12.5
Accounts Receivable	144,290	16.8
Notes Receivable	0	0.0
Inventory	15,460	1.8
Other Current	46,379	5.4
Total Current	**313,488**	**36.5**
Fixed Assets	382,198	44.5
Other Non-current	163,186	19.0
Total Assets	**858,872**	**100.0**
Accounts Payable	54,968	6.4
Bank Loans	0	0.0
Notes Payable	0	0.0
Other Current	257,661	30.0
Total Current	**312,629**	**36.4**
Other Long Term	311,771	36.3
Deferred Credits	0	0.0
Net Worth	234,472	27.3
Total Liab & Net Worth	**858,872**	**100.0**
Net Sales	1,745,675	100.0
Gross Profit	860,618	49.3
Net Profit After Tax	115,215	6.6
Working Capital	859	—

RATIOS	UQ	MED	LQ
SOLVENCY			
Quick Ratio (times)	3.6	1.3	0.1
Current Ratio (times)	4.9	2.7	0.2
Curr Liab To Nw (%)	0.7	12.2	32.1
Curr Liab To Inv (%)	264.1	714.9	999.9
Total Liab To Nw (%)	30.2	60.7	71.6
Fixed Assets To Nw (%)	20.4	34.5	164.7
EFFICIENCY			
Coll Period (days)	30.3	39.1	49.9
Sales To Inv (times)	56.3	35.1	18.1
Assets To Sales (%)	43.3	49.2	113.3
Sales To Nwc (times)	4.9	4.6	4.3
Acct Pay To Sales (%)	0.5	1.8	2.0
PROFITABILITY			
Return On Sales (%)	24.5	8.2	(13.8)
Return On Assets (%)	45.5	9.6	(35.6)
Return On Nw (%)	63.1	48.5	13.1

SIC 8042 OFCS,CLNS OPTMTRSTS (NO BREAKDOWN) 2002 (13 Establishments)

	$	%
Cash	84,900	12.5
Accounts Receivable	100,521	14.8
Notes Receivable	8,830	1.3
Inventory	85,579	12.6
Other Current	28,525	4.2
Total Current	**308,355**	**45.4**
Fixed Assets	226,173	33.3
Other Non-current	144,669	21.3
Total Assets	**679,197**	**100.0**
Accounts Payable	72,674	10.7
Bank Loans	0	0.0
Notes Payable	67,920	10.0
Other Current	105,275	15.5
Total Current	**245,869**	**36.2**
Other Long Term	249,266	36.7
Deferred Credits	0	0.0
Net Worth	184,062	27.1
Total Liab & Net Worth	**679,197**	**100.0**
Net Sales	1,924,071	100.0
Gross Profit	1,241,026	64.5
Net Profit After Tax	28,861	1.5
Working Capital	62,486	—

RATIOS	UQ	MED	LQ
SOLVENCY			
Quick Ratio (times)	1.8	1.0	0.4
Current Ratio (times)	3.1	1.8	1.2
Curr Liab To Nw (%)	46.2	89.4	161.5
Curr Liab To Inv (%)	86.0	160.3	181.9
Total Liab To Nw (%)	155.3	241.5	381.3
Fixed Assets To Nw (%)	36.0	144.5	213.4
EFFICIENCY			
Coll Period (days)	20.8	26.1	55.9
Sales To Inv (times)	39.0	25.8	9.7
Assets To Sales (%)	29.6	35.3	46.2
Sales To Nwc (times)	27.9	7.8	6.6
Acct Pay To Sales (%)	3.2	3.7	11.5
PROFITABILITY			
Return On Sales (%)	4.4	1.7	(1.0)
Return On Assets (%)	10.3	4.6	(4.4)
Return On Nw (%)	32.5	7.0	(22.2)

SIC 8049 OFCS HLTH PRNRS,NEC (NO BREAKDOWN) 2002 (14 Establishments)

	$	%
Cash	546,252	20.7
Accounts Receivable	1,000,142	37.9
Notes Receivable	7,917	0.3
Inventory	5,278	0.2
Other Current	79,166	3.0
Total Current	**1,638,755**	**62.1**
Fixed Assets	519,863	19.7
Other Non-current	480,279	18.2
Total Assets	**2,638,897**	**100.0**
Accounts Payable	142,500	5.4
Bank Loans	0	0.0
Notes Payable	73,889	2.8
Other Current	1,129,448	42.8
Total Current	**1,345,837**	**51.0**
Other Long Term	443,335	16.8
Deferred Credits	7,917	0.3
Net Worth	841,808	31.9
Total Liab & Net Worth	**2,638,897**	**100.0**
Net Sales	11,423,797	100.0
Gross Profit	6,168,850	54.0
Net Profit After Tax	411,257	3.6
Working Capital	292,918	—

RATIOS	UQ	MED	LQ
SOLVENCY			
Quick Ratio (times)	5.9	1.4	1.0
Current Ratio (times)	5.9	1.4	1.1
Curr Liab To Nw (%)	13.1	107.6	206.4
Curr Liab To Inv (%)	999.9	999.9	999.9
Total Liab To Nw (%)	26.1	133.6	469.4
Fixed Assets To Nw (%)	29.4	41.0	78.3
EFFICIENCY			
Coll Period (days)	33.0	52.6	80.7
Sales To Inv (times)	550.3	550.3	550.3
Assets To Sales (%)	9.1	23.1	43.3
Sales To Nwc (times)	27.2	14.4	4.1
Acct Pay To Sales (%)	0.7	1.4	2.6
PROFITABILITY			
Return On Sales (%)	8.6	3.0	1.0
Return On Assets (%)	22.7	16.2	5.7
Return On Nw (%)	391.4	36.3	17.7

SIC 8051 SKLLD NRSNG CR FCLT (NO BREAKDOWN) 2002 (111 Establishments)

	$	%
Cash	889,714	10.3
Accounts Receivable	1,546,202	17.9
Notes Receivable	60,466	0.7
Inventory	51,828	0.6
Other Current	561,470	6.5
Total Current	**3,109,680**	**36.0**
Fixed Assets	4,258,534	49.3
Other Non-current	1,269,786	14.7
Total Assets	**8,638,000**	**100.0**
Accounts Payable	578,746	6.7
Bank Loans	0	0.0
Notes Payable	172,760	2.0
Other Current	1,710,324	19.8
Total Current	**2,461,830**	**28.5**
Other Long Term	3,766,168	43.6
Deferred Credits	155,484	1.8
Net Worth	2,254,518	26.1
Total Liab & Net Worth	**8,638,000**	**100.0**
Net Sales	8,698,892	100.0
Gross Profit	3,009,817	34.6
Net Profit After Tax	(26,097)	(0.3)
Working Capital	647,850	—

RATIOS	UQ	MED	LQ
SOLVENCY			
Quick Ratio (times)	2.0	1.2	0.6
Current Ratio (times)	2.7	1.6	0.9
Curr Liab To Nw (%)	20.1	39.6	116.0
Curr Liab To Inv (%)	999.9	999.9	999.9
Total Liab To Nw (%)	82.3	148.6	418.0
Fixed Assets To Nw (%)	68.8	134.3	258.1
EFFICIENCY			
Coll Period (days)	24.1	31.4	43.8
Sales To Inv (times)	442.3	267.5	184.0
Assets To Sales (%)	60.8	99.3	184.5
Sales To Nwc (times)	16.8	8.0	4.9
Acct Pay To Sales (%)	1.9	2.7	5.8
PROFITABILITY			
Return On Sales (%)	4.4	0.5	(3.6)
Return On Assets (%)	3.8	0.4	(2.8)
Return On Nw (%)	11.5	2.4	(8.5)

SIC 8052 INTRMDT CRE FCLTS (NO BREAKDOWN) 2002 (35 Establishments)

	$	%
Cash	446,387	12.5
Accounts Receivable	553,520	15.5
Notes Receivable	3,571	0.1
Inventory	17,855	0.5
Other Current	174,984	4.9
Total Current	**1,196,317**	**33.5**
Fixed Assets	1,778,405	49.8
Other Non-current	596,373	16.7
Total Assets	**3,571,095**	**100.0**
Accounts Payable	182,126	5.1
Bank Loans	7,142	0.2
Notes Payable	160,699	4.5
Other Current	435,674	12.2
Total Current	**785,641**	**22.0**
Other Long Term	1,357,016	38.0
Deferred Credits	7,142	0.2
Net Worth	1,421,296	39.8
Total Liab & Net Worth	**3,571,095**	**100.0**
Net Sales	4,613,818	100.0
Gross Profit	2,191,564	47.5
Net Profit After Tax	78,435	1.7
Working Capital	410,676	—

RATIOS	UQ	MED	LQ
SOLVENCY			
Quick Ratio (times)	2.0	1.3	0.8
Current Ratio (times)	2.9	1.8	1.0
Curr Liab To Nw (%)	10.5	43.0	110.4
Curr Liab To Inv (%)	999.9	999.9	999.9
Total Liab To Nw (%)	27.0	102.7	301.2
Fixed Assets To Nw (%)	38.2	80.1	309.4
EFFICIENCY			
Coll Period (days)	25.4	44.9	60.1
Sales To Inv (times)	544.8	391.5	142.5
Assets To Sales (%)	59.4	77.4	132.9
Sales To Nwc (times)	15.4	7.4	6.3
Acct Pay To Sales (%)	2.7	3.8	4.9
PROFITABILITY			
Return On Sales (%)	2.2	0.4	(2.2)
Return On Assets (%)	6.4	0.4	(1.6)
Return On Nw (%)	21.1	1.5	(2.2)

SIC 8059 NRSNG,PRSNL CRE,NEC (NO BREAKDOWN) 2002 (44 Establishments)

	$	%
Cash	837,811	6.9
Accounts Receivable	886,380	7.3
Notes Receivable	0	0.0
Inventory	48,569	0.4
Other Current	1,202,077	9.9
Total Current	**2,974,837**	**24.5**
Fixed Assets	7,176,036	59.1
Other Non-current	1,991,320	16.4
Total Assets	**12,142,193**	**100.0**
Accounts Payable	631,394	5.2
Bank Loans	0	0.0
Notes Payable	157,849	1.3
Other Current	1,784,902	14.7
Total Current	**2,574,145**	**21.2**
Other Long Term	5,633,977	46.4
Deferred Credits	352,124	2.9
Net Worth	3,581,947	29.5
Total Liab & Net Worth	**12,142,193**	**100.0**
Net Sales	6,188,681	100.0
Gross Profit	1,992,755	32.2
Net Profit After Tax	(74,264)	(1.2)
Working Capital	400,692	—

RATIOS	UQ	MED	LQ
SOLVENCY			
Quick Ratio (times)	1.4	0.9	0.5
Current Ratio (times)	2.8	1.5	1.0
Curr Liab To Nw (%)	8.6	45.5	193.5
Curr Liab To Inv (%)	999.9	999.9	999.9
Total Liab To Nw (%)	66.8	264.2	784.5
Fixed Assets To Nw (%)	68.7	183.2	565.9
EFFICIENCY			
Coll Period (days)	13.5	26.1	47.8
Sales To Inv (times)	369.2	199.2	114.1
Assets To Sales (%)	53.2	196.2	372.0
Sales To Nwc (times)	18.0	8.1	3.1
Acct Pay To Sales (%)	2.2	3.2	5.4
PROFITABILITY			
Return On Sales (%)	6.6	1.3	(4.2)
Return On Assets (%)	3.7	0.4	(3.4)
Return On Nw (%)	35.3	4.5	(10.2)

SIC 8062 GNL MDL,SRGL HSPTLS (NO BREAKDOWN) 2002 (442 Establishments)

	$	%
Cash	5,465,022	7.1
Accounts Receivable	10,006,379	13.0
Notes Receivable	153,944	0.2
Inventory	1,462,471	1.9
Other Current	6,696,577	8.7
Total Current	**23,784,393**	**30.9**
Fixed Assets	35,099,298	45.6
Other Non-current	18,088,454	23.5
Total Assets	**76,972,145**	**100.0**
Accounts Payable	4,618,329	6.0
Bank Loans	0	0.0
Notes Payable	307,889	0.4
Other Current	9,159,685	11.9
Total Current	**14,085,903**	**18.3**
Other Long Term	23,322,560	30.3
Deferred Credits	153,944	0.2
Net Worth	39,409,738	51.2
Total Liab & Net Worth	**76,972,145**	**100.0**
Net Sales	70,294,196	100.0
Gross Profit	30,718,564	43.7
Net Profit After Tax	1,476,178	2.1
Working Capital	9,698,490	—

RATIOS	UQ	MED	LQ
SOLVENCY			
Quick Ratio (times)	2.0	1.4	1.0
Current Ratio (times)	3.0	2.0	1.5
Curr Liab To Nw (%)	14.5	22.2	37.7
Curr Liab To Inv (%)	548.1	859.5	999.9
Total Liab To Nw (%)	43.8	74.9	128.8
Fixed Assets To Nw (%)	57.0	75.2	106.7
EFFICIENCY			
Coll Period (days)	42.2	52.2	63.2
Sales To Inv (times)	85.0	58.9	42.5
Assets To Sales (%)	77.9	109.5	137.8
Sales To Nwc (times)	11.5	6.9	4.2
Acct Pay To Sales (%)	2.7	3.9	6.4
PROFITABILITY			
Return On Sales (%)	5.1	2.3	(0.5)
Return On Assets (%)	4.5	2.0	(0.4)
Return On Nw (%)	8.4	3.7	(0.1)

	SIC 8063 PSYCHIATRIC HSPTLS (NO BREAKDOWN) 2002 (15 Establishments)		SIC 8069 SPTY HSPL EX PSYTRC (NO BREAKDOWN) 2002 (34 Establishments)		SIC 8071 MDCL LBRTRS (NO BREAKDOWN) 2002 (62 Establishments)		SIC 8072 DENTAL LABORATORIES (NO BREAKDOWN) 2002 (16 Establishments)	
	$	%	$	%	$	%	$	%
Cash	1,571,513	13.8	10,477,160	13.0	599,410	16.8	34,722	8.7
Accounts Receivable	2,106,738	18.5	11,686,063	14.5	966,905	27.1	161,239	40.4
Notes Receivable	0	0.0	80,594	0.1	17,840	0.5	2,794	0.7
Inventory	34,163	0.3	805,935	1.0	103,470	2.9	5,587	1.4
Other Current	717,430	6.3	9,107,068	11.3	299,704	8.4	20,754	5.2
Total Current	**4,429,844**	**38.9**	**32,156,820**	**39.9**	**1,987,329**	**55.7**	**225,096**	**56.4**
Fixed Assets	4,703,151	41.3	27,724,176	34.4	1,013,288	28.4	139,687	35.0
Other Non-current	2,254,779	19.8	20,712,539	25.7	567,298	15.9	34,324	8.6
Total Assets	**11,387,774**	**100.0**	**80,593,535**	**100.0**	**3,567,915**	**100.0**	**399,107**	**100.0**
Accounts Payable	854,083	7.5	4,432,644	5.5	346,088	9.7	48,691	12.2
Bank Loans	0	0.0	0	0.0	0	0.0	37,516	9.4
Notes Payable	318,858	2.8	564,155	0.7	82,062	2.3	16,363	4.1
Other Current	2,858,331	25.1	12,089,030	15.0	1,177,412	33.0	68,248	17.1
Total Current	**4,031,272**	**35.4**	**17,085,829**	**21.2**	**1,605,562**	**45.0**	**170,818**	**42.8**
Other Long Term	3,154,413	27.7	20,712,539	25.7	656,496	18.4	75,032	18.8
Deferred Credits	0	0.0	0	0.0	3,568	0.1	0	0.0
Net Worth	4,202,089	36.9	42,795,167	53.1	1,302,289	36.5	153,257	38.4
Total Liab & Net Worth	**11,387,774**	**100.0**	**80,593,535**	**100.0**	**3,567,915**	**100.0**	**399,107**	**100.0**
Net Sales	18,699,136	100.0	74,692,804	100.0	6,955,000	100.0	1,683,996	100.0
Gross Profit	10,845,499	58.0	30,250,586	40.5	3,783,520	54.4	626,447	37.2
Net Profit After Tax	(317,885)	(1.7)	(5,975,424)	(8.0)	236,470	3.4	43,784	2.6
Working Capital	398,572	—	15,070,991	—	381,767	—	54,278	—

RATIOS	8063 UQ	8063 MED	8063 LQ	8069 UQ	8069 MED	8069 LQ	8071 UQ	8071 MED	8071 LQ	8072 UQ	8072 MED	8072 LQ
SOLVENCY												
Quick Ratio (times)	2.0	1.2	0.9	2.3	1.6	0.9	2.6	1.8	0.8	5.2	1.7	0.6
Current Ratio (times)	2.4	1.8	1.1	2.8	2.2	1.4	3.5	2.1	1.1	5.3	2.2	0.9
Curr Liab To Nw (%)	27.1	43.3	84.9	13.9	24.7	36.5	18.7	39.9	103.4	14.6	35.5	206.7
Curr Liab To Inv (%)	999.9	999.9	999.9	999.9	999.9	999.9	260.9	611.5	963.6	477.8	730.9	999.9
Total Liab To Nw (%)	41.7	102.6	134.0	26.9	56.2	121.6	31.6	84.8	187.7	32.3	82.2	261.9
Fixed Assets To Nw (%)	56.6	94.3	137.1	27.0	49.6	97.4	25.1	48.0	102.6	29.5	54.7	119.2
EFFICIENCY												
Coll Period (days)	23.4	35.5	55.3	49.3	58.0	75.0	27.7	56.8	81.8	35.6	40.2	48.8
Sales To Inv (times)	999.9	438.8	278.5	211.8	133.1	46.9	78.2	51.0	29.1	96.8	53.3	32.3
Assets To Sales (%)	35.7	60.9	94.3	63.1	107.9	155.1	28.7	51.3	80.9	20.8	23.7	30.6
Sales To Nwc (times)	47.1	11.6	3.4	8.1	4.7	3.4	16.4	7.0	4.6	23.5	8.4	6.1
Acct Pay To Sales (%)	1.3	2.4	4.5	1.6	3.8	6.2	2.8	4.5	7.8	2.1	3.0	4.3
PROFITABILITY												
Return On Sales (%)	6.7	2.0	(1.8)	3.9	0.0	(12.8)	7.8	4.0	0.0	3.7	0.9	0.0
Return On Assets (%)	9.9	6.9	(4.9)	3.4	0.8	(7.0)	17.0	6.4	0.1	11.8	1.6	0.2
Return On Nw (%)	20.3	14.5	1.6	9.8	1.7	(3.0)	33.6	15.6	5.8	10.9	3.8	2.1

	SIC 8082 HME HLTH CRE SVCS (NO BREAKDOWN) 2002 (113 Establishments) $	%	SIC 8093 SPTY OTPNT CLNS,NEC (NO BREAKDOWN) 2002 (105 Establishments) $	%	SIC 8099 HLTH,ALLD SVCS,NEC (NO BREAKDOWN) 2002 (68 Establishments) $	%	SIC 81 LEGAL SERVICES (NO BREAKDOWN) 2002 (78 Establishments) $	%
Cash	516,119	16.6	932,081	16.0	834,669	16.6	472,364	33.0
Accounts Receivable	1,141,059	36.7	1,036,940	17.8	1,201,722	23.9	229,025	16.0
Notes Receivable	6,218	0.2	11,651	0.2	30,169	0.6	20,040	1.4
Inventory	102,602	3.3	58,255	1.0	266,491	5.3	17,177	1.2
Other Current	323,352	10.4	803,919	13.8	719,022	14.3	233,319	16.3
Total Current	**2,089,350**	**67.2**	**2,842,846**	**48.8**	**3,052,073**	**60.7**	**971,925**	**67.9**
Fixed Assets	628,049	20.2	2,178,738	37.4	1,282,172	25.5	390,774	27.3
Other Non-current	391,753	12.6	803,920	13.8	693,882	13.8	68,708	4.8
Total Assets	**3,109,152**	**100.0**	**5,825,504**	**100.0**	**5,028,127**	**100.0**	**1,431,407**	**100.0**
Accounts Payable	397,971	12.8	378,658	6.5	502,813	10.0	94,473	6.6
Bank Loans	21,764	0.7	5,826	0.1	0	0.0	5,726	0.4
Notes Payable	102,602	3.3	168,940	2.9	65,366	1.3	98,767	6.9
Other Current	820,817	26.4	937,905	16.1	2,730,272	54.3	596,896	41.7
Total Current	**1,343,154**	**43.2**	**1,491,329**	**25.6**	**3,298,451**	**65.6**	**795,862**	**55.6**
Other Long Term	705,777	22.7	1,106,846	19.0	543,038	10.8	362,146	25.3
Deferred Credits	6,218	0.2	11,651	0.2	25,141	0.5	22,903	1.6
Net Worth	1,054,003	33.9	3,215,678	55.2	1,161,497	23.1	250,496	17.5
Total Liab & Net Worth	**3,109,152**	**100.0**	**5,825,504**	**100.0**	**5,028,127**	**100.0**	**1,431,407**	**100.0**
Net Sales	7,583,298	100.0	11,202,892	100.0	9,559,177	100.0	6,091,094	100.0
Gross Profit	3,586,900	47.3	4,828,446	43.1	4,531,050	47.4	3,203,915	52.6
Net Profit After Tax	401,915	5.3	291,275	2.6	353,690	3.7	822,298	13.5
Working Capital	746,196	—	1,351,517	—	(246,378)	—	176,063	—

RATIOS	UQ	MED	LQ	UQ	MED	LQ	UQ	MED	LQ	UQ	MED	LQ
SOLVENCY												
Quick Ratio (times)	2.3	1.5	1.0	2.7	1.6	1.0	2.9	2.0	0.8	2.4	1.0	0.4
Current Ratio (times)	3.1	1.8	1.2	4.0	2.2	1.4	4.2	2.9	1.4	3.3	1.3	0.9
Curr Liab To Nw (%)	26.5	66.0	148.0	12.9	33.2	75.9	15.1	26.9	53.8	25.7	80.6	248.9
Curr Liab To Inv (%)	521.5	942.4	999.9	280.9	612.1	999.9	150.2	248.9	481.7	138.0	269.5	283.6
Total Liab To Nw (%)	38.8	86.8	220.8	24.7	53.5	133.2	21.5	37.5	123.4	41.0	138.6	478.3
Fixed Assets To Nw (%)	9.1	27.6	58.4	27.1	53.2	99.2	12.1	39.8	75.7	24.0	49.8	140.2
EFFICIENCY												
Coll Period (days)	34.3	53.7	78.7	19.0	32.3	51.8	33.6	44.5	66.5	8.4	35.4	75.2
Sales To Inv (times)	168.6	72.6	32.3	192.6	51.3	22.8	49.2	29.9	14.4	9.6	8.1	7.3
Assets To Sales (%)	27.7	41.0	65.7	35.1	52.0	79.1	34.2	52.6	90.7	12.2	23.5	40.4
Sales To Nwc (times)	15.8	7.5	4.5	12.5	7.0	3.9	7.7	5.9	3.0	19.6	10.0	5.2
Acct Pay To Sales (%)	1.3	3.3	7.8	1.5	2.6	3.8	2.2	4.3	6.8	0.9	3.4	8.5
PROFITABILITY												
Return On Sales (%)	8.5	4.6	0.6	6.1	2.4	0.5	8.1	3.4	0.6	35.2	4.8	0.0
Return On Assets (%)	15.9	10.0	2.1	11.8	4.7	1.2	14.2	6.9	0.5	178.7	10.9	0.1
Return On Nw (%)	44.9	17.7	7.6	23.0	6.9	2.1	24.2	11.2	0.8	563.2	91.0	4.5

Balance Sheet

	SIC 8111 LEGAL SERVICES (NO BREAKDOWN) 2002 (78 Establishments)		SIC 82 EDUCATIONAL SERVICE (NO BREAKDOWN) 2002 (753 Establishments)		SIC 8211 ELMNTRY,SCNDRY SCLS (NO BREAKDOWN) 2002 (356 Establishments)		SIC 8221 COLLEGES,UNVRSTES (NO BREAKDOWN) 2002 (141 Establishments)	
	$	%	$	%	$	%	$	%
Cash	472,364	33.0	4,310,816	20.1	6,335,690	24.6	12,611,053	10.7
Accounts Receivable	229,025	16.0	1,887,322	8.8	1,751,329	6.8	6,718,037	5.7
Notes Receivable	20,040	1.4	85,787	0.4	51,510	0.2	589,302	0.5
Inventory	17,177	1.2	300,256	1.4	128,774	0.5	589,302	0.5
Other Current	233,319	16.3	2,916,772	13.6	3,992,000	15.5	13,907,515	11.8
Total Current	**971,925**	**67.9**	**9,500,953**	**44.3**	**12,259,303**	**47.6**	**34,415,209**	**29.2**
Fixed Assets	390,774	27.3	8,149,801	38.0	9,838,348	38.2	48,912,027	41.5
Other Non-current	68,708	4.8	3,796,092	17.7	3,657,188	14.2	34,533,069	29.3
Total Assets	**1,431,407**	**100.0**	**21,446,846**	**100.0**	**25,754,839**	**100.0**	**117,860,305**	**100.0**
Accounts Payable	94,473	6.6	1,394,045	6.5	1,210,477	4.7	3,417,949	2.9
Bank Loans	5,726	0.4	0	0.0	0	0.0	0	0.0
Notes Payable	98,767	6.9	514,724	2.4	489,342	1.9	2,121,485	1.8
Other Current	596,896	41.7	4,589,625	21.4	4,764,646	18.5	13,436,075	11.4
Total Current	**795,862**	**55.6**	**6,498,394**	**30.3**	**6,464,465**	**25.1**	**18,975,509**	**16.1**
Other Long Term	362,146	25.3	3,388,602	15.8	4,429,832	17.2	21,332,715	18.1
Deferred Credits	22,903	1.6	257,362	1.2	360,568	1.4	1,178,603	1.0
Net Worth	250,496	17.5	11,302,488	52.7	14,499,974	56.3	76,373,478	64.8
Total Liab & Net Worth	**1,431,407**	**100.0**	**21,446,846**	**100.0**	**25,754,839**	**100.0**	**117,860,305**	**100.0**
Net Sales	6,091,094	100.0	14,100,490	100.0	18,449,025	100.0	49,604,505	100.0
Gross Profit	3,203,915	52.6	7,952,676	56.4	10,792,680	58.5	20,734,683	41.8
Net Profit After Tax	822,298	13.5	479,417	3.4	387,430	2.1	99,209	0.2
Working Capital	176,063	—	3,002,559	—	5,794,838	—	15,439,700	—

RATIOS

	UQ	MED	LQ	UQ	MED	LQ	UQ	MED	LQ	UQ	MED	LQ
SOLVENCY												
Quick Ratio (times)	2.4	1.0	0.4	2.5	1.2	0.5	3.0	1.3	0.5	2.2	1.1	0.5
Current Ratio (times)	3.3	1.3	0.9	4.1	2.1	1.2	4.7	2.3	1.2	3.2	2.1	1.3
Curr Liab To Nw (%)	25.7	80.6	248.9	8.9	21.9	61.0	9.4	24.4	65.5	7.4	15.5	35.8
Curr Liab To Inv (%)	138.0	269.5	283.6	976.0	999.9	999.9	999.9	999.9	999.9	976.0	999.9	999.9
Total Liab To Nw (%)	41.0	138.6	478.3	21.4	51.0	124.5	26.9	60.3	134.0	24.7	43.9	85.4
Fixed Assets To Nw (%)	24.0	49.8	140.2	44.1	80.3	113.3	70.0	91.1	140.9	38.8	75.5	110.5
EFFICIENCY												
Coll Period (days)	8.4	35.4	75.2	5.8	22.3	49.8	0.4	4.8	24.8	14.6	31.4	55.5
Sales To Inv (times)	9.6	8.1	7.3	311.4	108.4	52.6	696.3	281.1	141.3	119.3	71.5	44.2
Assets To Sales (%)	12.2	23.5	40.4	56.6	152.1	260.4	58.6	139.6	221.6	170.4	237.6	354.4
Sales To Nwc (times)	19.6	10.0	5.2	10.4	4.6	2.3	10.5	4.7	2.5	6.5	3.3	2.2
Acct Pay To Sales (%)	0.9	3.4	8.5	1.4	3.3	6.5	0.8	2.2	4.5	3.0	5.4	8.5
PROFITABILITY												
Return On Sales (%)	35.2	4.8	0.0	7.9	2.3	(4.6)	5.9	0.9	(4.6)	7.1	1.8	(6.5)
Return On Assets (%)	178.7	10.9	0.1	8.5	1.6	(2.6)	5.8	0.7	(2.6)	4.1	1.1	(2.7)
Return On Nw (%)	563.2	91.0	4.5	17.1	3.0	(3.2)	13.8	1.0	(4.1)	7.5	1.4	(4.5)

	SIC 8222 JUNIOR COLLEGES (NO BREAKDOWN) 2002 (74 Establishments)		SIC 8231 LIBRARIES (NO BREAKDOWN) 2002 (14 Establishments)		SIC 8243 DATA PROC SCHOOLS (NO BREAKDOWN) 2002 (13 Establishments)		SIC 8249 VOCTNL SCHLS, NEC (NO BREAKDOWN) 2002 (47 Establishments)	
	$	%	$	%	$	%	$	%
Cash	4,370,088	14.4	1,836,885	19.3	62,409	20.4	604,026	22.6
Accounts Receivable	2,185,044	7.2	780,438	8.2	39,159	12.8	628,080	23.5
Notes Receivable	242,783	0.8	0	0.0	0	0.0	8,018	0.3
Inventory	182,087	0.6	9,518	0.1	2,447	0.8	58,799	2.2
Other Current	3,702,434	12.2	828,026	8.7	13,155	4.3	221,833	8.3
Total Current	**10,682,436**	**35.2**	**3,454,867**	**36.3**	**117,170**	**38.3**	**1,520,756**	**56.9**
Fixed Assets	14,202,784	46.8	4,330,481	45.5	115,334	37.7	820,513	30.7
Other Non-current	5,462,610	18.0	1,732,193	18.2	73,423	24.0	331,413	12.4
Total Assets	**30,347,830**	**100.0**	**9,517,541**	**100.0**	**305,927**	**100.0**	**2,672,682**	**100.0**
Accounts Payable	910,435	3.0	142,763	1.5	22,333	7.3	227,178	8.5
Bank Loans	0	0.0	0	0.0	0	0.0	0	0.0
Notes Payable	212,435	0.7	161,798	1.7	3,671	1.2	85,526	3.2
Other Current	4,977,044	16.4	1,503,772	15.8	55,984	18.3	775,078	29.0
Total Current	**6,099,914**	**20.1**	**1,808,333**	**19.0**	**81,988**	**26.8**	**1,087,782**	**40.7**
Other Long Term	6,008,871	19.8	1,513,289	15.9	80,459	26.3	138,979	5.2
Deferred Credits	91,043	0.3	180,833	1.9	5,813	1.9	16,036	0.6
Net Worth	18,148,002	59.8	6,015,086	63.2	137,667	45.0	1,429,885	53.5
Total Liab & Net Worth	**30,347,830**	**100.0**	**9,517,541**	**100.0**	**305,927**	**100.0**	**2,672,682**	**100.0**
Net Sales	14,174,605	100.0	1,184,658	100.0	1,876,853	100.0	4,584,360	100.0
Gross Profit	9,667,081	68.2	745,150	62.9	1,212,447	64.6	3,021,093	65.9
Net Profit After Tax	1,119,794	7.9	74,633	6.3	230,853	12.3	499,695	10.9
Working Capital	4,582,522	—	1,646,534	—	35,182	—	432,974	—

RATIOS	UQ	MED	LQ	UQ	MED	LQ	UQ	MED	LQ	UQ	MED	LQ
SOLVENCY												
Quick Ratio (times)	1.8	1.1	0.7	3.9	1.4	1.2	2.0	1.2	0.4	2.5	1.3	0.9
Current Ratio (times)	3.5	2.1	1.4	12.5	2.6	1.2	2.2	1.3	1.0	3.5	1.5	1.1
Curr Liab To Nw (%)	9.5	17.1	33.2	1.7	24.1	61.0	17.0	23.5	71.9	9.8	31.6	217.4
Curr Liab To Inv (%)	886.8	999.9	999.9	165.4	582.7	999.9	127.4	999.9	999.9	342.3	999.9	999.9
Total Liab To Nw (%)	16.2	39.8	98.9	12.9	37.6	213.9	17.0	23.5	99.4	11.4	45.0	217.4
Fixed Assets To Nw (%)	68.0	86.2	106.3	52.3	73.9	98.3	22.2	33.8	111.7	20.1	44.1	92.5
EFFICIENCY												
Coll Period (days)	7.3	21.7	44.2	41.6	109.2	585.0	8.4	14.1	38.3	21.2	49.1	106.6
Sales To Inv (times)	113.1	68.0	33.5	493.3	493.3	493.3	230.9	136.6	42.2	351.8	178.8	66.8
Assets To Sales (%)	146.4	214.1	296.9	196.5	803.4	999.9	15.8	16.3	53.9	34.8	58.3	158.5
Sales To Nwc (times)	9.4	4.6	1.7	3.2	1.8	0.7	16.0	12.2	8.2	20.4	7.0	3.5
Acct Pay To Sales (%)	1.7	3.9	7.5	0.2	1.5	17.8	2.2	4.4	6.8	1.3	3.2	4.3
PROFITABILITY												
Return On Sales (%)	15.4	4.1	(0.1)	4.3	(2.7)	(162.8)	11.4	1.7	(11.5)	13.8	6.9	0.7
Return On Assets (%)	9.5	3.1	(0.1)	0.0	(0.1)	(9.6)	132.5	3.2	(20.4)	27.2	8.2	1.1
Return On Nw (%)	14.7	5.5	(0.5)	0.0	(2.7)	(9.7)	321.2	83.6	(28.7)	61.5	18.5	0.7

	SIC 8299 SCLS,EDCTL SVCS,NEC (NO BREAKDOWN) 2002 (102 Establishments)		SIC 83 SOC SEV (NO BREAKDOWN) 2002 (827 Establishments)		SIC 8322 INDVDL,FMLY SVCS (NO BREAKDOWN) 2002 (343 Establishments)		SIC 8331 JOB TRNNG,RLTD SVCS (NO BREAKDOWN) 2002 (119 Establishments)	
	$	%	$	%	$	%	$	%
Cash	284,381	21.2	622,549	18.7	491,171	20.1	585,797	21.8
Accounts Receivable	160,971	12.0	482,725	14.5	354,327	14.5	529,367	19.7
Notes Receivable	4,024	0.3	16,646	0.5	9,775	0.4	8,061	0.3
Inventory	81,827	6.1	69,912	2.1	39,098	1.6	120,921	4.5
Other Current	207,921	15.5	466,078	14.0	359,215	14.7	255,279	9.5
Total Current	**739,124**	**55.1**	**1,657,910**	**49.8**	**1,253,586**	**51.3**	**1,499,425**	**55.8**
Fixed Assets	409,134	30.5	1,228,452	36.9	928,582	38.0	964,684	35.9
Other Non-current	193,164	14.4	442,775	13.3	261,469	10.7	223,033	8.3
Total Assets	**1,341,422**	**100.0**	**3,329,137**	**100.0**	**2,443,637**	**100.0**	**2,687,142**	**100.0**
Accounts Payable	272,309	20.3	286,306	8.6	215,040	8.8	249,904	9.3
Bank Loans	0	0.0	9,987	0.3	9,775	0.4	0	0.0
Notes Payable	81,827	6.1	76,570	2.3	43,985	1.8	53,743	2.0
Other Current	604,981	45.1	629,207	18.9	469,178	19.2	405,758	15.1
Total Current	**959,117**	**71.5**	**1,002,070**	**30.1**	**737,978**	**30.2**	**709,405**	**26.4**
Other Long Term	107,313	8.0	545,978	16.4	354,328	14.5	255,279	9.5
Deferred Credits	24,146	1.8	36,621	1.1	19,549	0.8	8,061	0.3
Net Worth	250,846	18.7	1,744,468	52.4	1,331,782	54.5	1,714,397	63.8
Total Liab & Net Worth	**1,341,422**	**100.0**	**3,329,137**	**100.0**	**2,443,637**	**100.0**	**2,687,142**	**100.0**
Net Sales	2,308,816	100.0	5,259,300	100.0	4,363,638	100.0	4,894,612	100.0
Gross Profit	1,182,114	51.2	2,250,980	42.8	1,854,546	42.5	2,192,786	44.8
Net Profit After Tax	64,647	2.8	136,742	2.6	231,273	5.3	151,733	3.1
Working Capital	(219,993)	—	655,840	—	515,608	—	790,020	—

RATIOS	UQ	MED	LQ	UQ	MED	LQ	UQ	MED	LQ	UQ	MED	LQ
SOLVENCY												
Quick Ratio (times)	2.2	1.0	0.4	3.2	1.3	0.7	3.2	1.5	0.7	4.8	2.2	1.0
Current Ratio (times)	3.9	1.9	1.0	5.0	2.0	1.1	5.0	2.3	1.2	6.6	2.9	1.3
Curr Liab To Nw (%)	10.3	34.6	91.8	8.7	27.3	77.9	8.1	26.2	68.4	8.0	21.1	60.1
Curr Liab To Inv (%)	112.0	573.4	999.9	187.9	914.8	999.9	211.0	963.4	999.9	102.7	339.4	964.8
Total Liab To Nw (%)	12.1	47.6	155.9	13.9	53.9	144.1	14.9	52.0	131.3	10.3	41.0	102.5
Fixed Assets To Nw (%)	15.9	43.0	87.8	22.9	60.8	113.6	25.8	61.4	110.4	31.4	57.3	91.2
EFFICIENCY												
Coll Period (days)	10.6	32.7	48.2	13.1	30.7	51.3	11.3	31.0	53.1	26.3	36.5	51.5
Sales To Inv (times)	113.3	49.4	12.0	226.2	64.4	20.2	285.8	58.9	17.1	107.8	27.4	14.9
Assets To Sales (%)	26.7	58.1	117.9	33.7	63.3	134.1	27.5	56.0	111.7	36.9	54.9	90.0
Sales To Nwc (times)	15.7	7.6	3.2	14.9	5.8	2.5	14.1	5.9	2.7	13.2	5.8	2.6
Acct Pay To Sales (%)	1.3	2.9	7.8	1.5	2.9	5.7	1.2	2.6	5.1	1.2	2.7	5.3
PROFITABILITY												
Return On Sales (%)	7.1	1.1	(4.5)	7.2	1.9	(2.0)	9.5	2.6	(1.0)	6.2	2.6	(1.3)
Return On Assets (%)	12.3	3.0	(6.1)	12.2	2.9	(2.7)	19.4	4.1	(1.6)	11.2	4.9	(1.7)
Return On Nw (%)	33.4	10.0	(0.4)	27.2	5.6	(5.0)	41.6	7.8	(2.5)	21.7	6.5	(2.4)

	SIC 8351 CHILD DAY CARE SVCS (NO BREAKDOWN) 2002 (47 Establishments) $	%	SIC 8361 RESIDENTIAL CARE (NO BREAKDOWN) 2002 (158 Establishments) $	%	SIC 8399 SOCIAL SVCS, NEC (NO BREAKDOWN) 2002 (160 Establishments) $	%	SIC 84 MUSEUM, BOT, ZOO GARD (NO BREAKDOWN) 2002 (88 Establishments) $	%
Cash	423,390	15.0	831,480	12.0	1,036,113	21.3	1,557,222	10.9
Accounts Receivable	273,792	9.7	976,989	14.1	608,048	12.5	314,302	2.2
Notes Receivable	2,823	0.1	34,645	0.5	43,779	0.9	42,859	0.3
Inventory	5,645	0.2	90,077	1.3	131,338	2.7	300,015	2.1
Other Current	355,646	12.6	727,545	10.5	948,555	19.5	1,900,098	13.3
Total Current	**1,061,296**	**37.6**	**2,660,736**	**38.4**	**2,767,833**	**56.9**	**4,114,496**	**28.8**
Fixed Assets	1,445,170	51.2	3,090,334	44.6	1,143,130	23.5	6,186,030	43.3
Other Non-current	316,131	11.2	1,177,930	17.0	953,419	19.6	3,985,918	27.9
Total Assets	**2,822,597**	**100.0**	**6,929,000**	**100.0**	**4,864,382**	**100.0**	**14,286,444**	**100.0**
Accounts Payable	361,292	12.8	471,172	6.8	389,151	8.0	271,442	1.9
Bank Loans	42,339	1.5	27,716	0.4	0	0.0	0	0.0
Notes Payable	64,920	2.3	124,722	1.8	189,711	3.9	357,161	2.5
Other Current	601,213	21.3	1,365,013	19.7	958,283	19.7	1,014,338	7.1
Total Current	**1,069,764**	**37.9**	**1,988,623**	**28.7**	**1,537,145**	**31.6**	**1,642,941**	**11.5**
Other Long Term	1,007,668	35.7	1,753,037	25.3	544,811	11.2	1,100,057	7.7
Deferred Credits	11,290	0.4	200,941	2.9	38,915	0.8	14,286	0.1
Net Worth	733,875	26.0	2,986,399	43.1	2,743,511	56.4	11,529,160	80.7
Total Liab & Net Worth	**2,822,597**	**100.0**	**6,929,000**	**100.0**	**4,864,382**	**100.0**	**14,286,444**	**100.0**
Net Sales	5,567,252	100.0	6,773,216	100.0	5,709,369	100.0	3,652,888	100.0
Gross Profit	2,315,977	41.6	2,478,997	36.6	2,592,054	45.4	2,681,220	73.4
Net Profit After Tax	334,035	6.0	(121,918)	(1.8)	39,966	0.7	178,992	4.9
Working Capital	(8,468)	—	672,113	—	1,230,688	—	2,471,555	—

RATIOS	UQ	MED	LQ	UQ	MED	LQ	UQ	MED	LQ	UQ	MED	LQ
SOLVENCY												
Quick Ratio (times)	1.4	0.7	0.3	2.0	1.1	0.6	3.4	1.4	0.5	6.7	1.5	0.4
Current Ratio (times)	1.6	1.0	0.5	3.1	1.7	1.0	8.6	2.1	1.1	14.5	3.8	1.5
Curr Liab To Nw (%)	21.4	62.1	109.0	11.6	29.5	85.1	4.8	27.4	92.8	1.7	3.6	10.7
Curr Liab To Inv (%)	999.9	999.9	999.9	751.6	999.9	999.9	198.2	999.9	999.9	127.8	492.4	999.9
Total Liab To Nw (%)	50.6	90.1	161.2	20.9	74.5	204.9	9.9	54.0	137.7	2.3	10.4	24.4
Fixed Assets To Nw (%)	75.5	114.6	172.2	36.7	75.5	143.5	5.1	27.2	93.5	24.8	54.5	85.2
EFFICIENCY												
Coll Period (days)	3.3	16.1	59.1	14.5	32.5	49.1	8.4	23.2	44.2	1.5	5.8	13.9
Sales To Inv (times)	317.8	132.4	39.7	413.7	144.2	54.6	260.7	110.8	43.8	69.6	34.0	15.9
Assets To Sales (%)	21.9	50.7	118.1	41.1	102.3	274.2	35.3	85.2	165.5	191.3	391.1	687.9
Sales To Nwc (times)	22.5	9.0	4.0	16.6	6.4	2.8	13.3	4.8	1.5	5.6	2.3	0.9
Acct Pay To Sales (%)	1.1	2.5	8.6	2.1	3.1	5.9	1.6	3.8	6.5	1.2	4.0	6.0
PROFITABILITY												
Return On Sales (%)	8.9	1.1	(2.7)	4.7	0.5	(6.5)	6.5	2.1	(2.5)	20.7	2.3	(25.7)
Return On Assets (%)	20.7	1.2	(3.3)	5.9	0.7	(3.4)	10.2	2.0	(5.1)	11.2	0.6	(4.7)
Return On Nw (%)	49.7	9.0	(5.7)	18.1	3.4	(4.8)	21.7	5.2	(8.0)	12.3	1.1	(4.9)

	SIC 8412 MUSEUMS, ART GALLRS (NO BREAKDOWN) 2002 (75 Establishments)		SIC 86 MEMBERSHIP ORGANIZATI (NO BREAKDOWN) 2002 (695 Establishments)		SIC 8611 BUSINESS ASSNS (NO BREAKDOWN) 2002 (141 Establishments)		SIC 8621 PRFSSNL ORGNZTNS (NO BREAKDOWN) 2002 (110 Establishments)	
	$	%	$	%	$	%	$	%
Cash	1,563,968	10.6	1,012,512	21.6	990,704	28.8	1,455,100	25.2
Accounts Receivable	324,597	2.2	318,754	6.8	436,873	12.7	537,001	9.3
Notes Receivable	59,018	0.4	18,750	0.4	3,440	0.1	63,516	1.1
Inventory	324,597	2.2	131,252	2.8	123,838	3.6	127,033	2.2
Other Current	2,050,864	13.9	890,634	19.0	822,146	23.9	1,189,486	20.6
Total Current	**4,323,044**	**29.3**	**2,371,902**	**50.6**	**2,377,001**	**69.1**	**3,372,136**	**58.4**
Fixed Assets	6,226,364	42.2	1,490,642	31.8	550,391	16.0	952,744	16.5
Other Non-current	4,205,010	28.5	825,010	17.6	512,551	14.9	1,449,326	25.1
Total Assets	**14,754,418**	**100.0**	**4,687,554**	**100.0**	**3,439,943**	**100.0**	**5,774,206**	**100.0**
Accounts Payable	295,088	2.0	276,566	5.9	364,634	10.6	456,162	7.9
Bank Loans	0	0.0	4,688	0.1	3,440	0.1	0	0.0
Notes Payable	413,124	2.8	65,626	1.4	41,279	1.2	80,839	1.4
Other Current	826,247	5.6	890,634	19.0	970,064	28.2	1,304,971	22.6
Total Current	**1,534,459**	**10.4**	**1,237,514**	**26.4**	**1,379,417**	**40.1**	**1,841,972**	**31.9**
Other Long Term	988,547	6.7	454,693	9.7	316,475	9.2	542,775	9.4
Deferred Credits	14,754	0.1	173,439	3.7	175,437	5.1	340,678	5.9
Net Worth	12,216,658	82.8	2,821,908	60.2	1,568,614	45.6	3,048,781	52.8
Total Liab & Net Worth	**14,754,418**	**100.0**	**4,687,554**	**100.0**	**3,439,943**	**100.0**	**5,774,206**	**100.0**
Net Sales	4,079,187	100.0	4,238,295	100.0	4,479,092	100.0	6,149,314	100.0
Gross Profit	2,855,431	70.0	2,144,577	50.6	1,504,975	33.6	3,265,286	53.1
Net Profit After Tax	224,355	5.5	55,098	1.3	76,145	1.7	86,090	1.4
Working Capital	2,788,585	—	1,134,388	—	997,584	—	1,530,164	—

RATIOS	UQ	MED	LQ	UQ	MED	LQ	UQ	MED	LQ	UQ	MED	LQ
SOLVENCY												
Quick Ratio (times)	6.7	1.5	0.4	3.5	1.3	0.6	2.1	1.1	0.6	2.1	1.2	0.6
Current Ratio (times)	14.9	5.1	1.7	7.1	2.4	1.2	4.3	1.8	1.1	3.9	2.1	1.2
Curr Liab To Nw (%)	1.2	3.3	7.0	4.6	18.9	58.3	22.2	48.7	136.4	13.8	39.5	108.1
Curr Liab To Inv (%)	107.1	455.6	999.9	219.6	740.1	999.9	217.1	942.9	999.9	587.8	999.9	999.9
Total Liab To Nw (%)	2.1	6.3	20.1	9.8	38.1	108.2	38.1	70.5	192.2	28.7	56.4	139.7
Fixed Assets To Nw (%)	20.1	51.8	82.3	11.4	38.8	88.6	6.4	17.4	58.9	9.5	20.8	49.5
EFFICIENCY												
Coll Period (days)	0.7	5.7	13.9	4.0	17.2	33.8	9.5	21.9	40.9	13.1	19.9	31.0
Sales To Inv (times)	67.8	34.0	17.7	107.3	35.7	16.1	125.6	44.6	10.8	129.5	61.6	28.2
Assets To Sales (%)	191.3	361.7	714.2	51.2	110.6	203.6	40.1	76.8	126.4	50.2	93.9	139.7
Sales To Nwc (times)	5.2	2.3	0.9	8.4	3.8	1.7	7.2	3.1	1.9	10.8	5.0	1.9
Acct Pay To Sales (%)	1.1	3.8	6.4	1.8	4.1	8.2	2.2	4.6	10.3	3.0	5.3	7.7
PROFITABILITY												
Return On Sales (%)	20.7	1.0	(25.7)	7.3	1.2	(5.4)	6.1	2.1	(3.8)	4.2	0.7	(4.4)
Return On Assets (%)	11.6	0.3	(4.8)	7.5	1.4	(4.2)	8.4	2.3	(4.5)	9.1	1.1	(3.5)
Return On Nw (%)	12.3	0.9	(5.1)	11.9	3.0	(6.1)	22.5	5.3	(5.0)	13.4	3.7	(6.9)

SIC 8631 LABOR ORGANIZATIONS
(NO BREAKDOWN)
2002 (16 Establishments)

SIC 8641 CIVIC, SOCL ASSNS
(NO BREAKDOWN)
2002 (156 Establishments)

SIC 8661 RELIGIOUS ORGNZTNS
(NO BREAKDOWN)
2002 (168 Establishments)

SIC 8699 MBRSHP ORGNZTNS, NEC
(NO BREAKDOWN)
2002 (103 Establishments)

	SIC 8631 $	SIC 8631 %	SIC 8641 $	SIC 8641 %	SIC 8661 $	SIC 8661 %	SIC 8699 $	SIC 8699 %
Cash	1,430,937	31.5	784,300	16.9	906,206	14.1	1,050,821	26.0
Accounts Receivable	45,427	1.0	301,654	6.5	186,383	2.9	169,748	4.2
Notes Receivable	4,543	0.1	18,563	0.4	19,281	0.3	28,291	0.7
Inventory	0	0.0	120,662	2.6	83,551	1.3	218,248	5.4
Other Current	794,964	17.5	761,097	16.4	970,475	15.1	840,658	20.8
Total Current	**2,275,871**	**50.1**	**1,986,276**	**42.8**	**2,165,896**	**33.7**	**2,307,766**	**57.1**
Fixed Assets	1,417,309	31.2	1,851,692	39.9	3,489,856	54.3	824,491	20.4
Other Non-current	849,477	18.7	802,863	17.3	771,238	12.0	909,364	22.5
Total Assets	**4,542,657**	**100.0**	**4,640,831**	**100.0**	**6,426,990**	**100.0**	**4,041,621**	**100.0**
Accounts Payable	127,194	2.8	222,760	4.8	179,956	2.8	181,873	4.5
Bank Loans	0	0.0	0	0.0	0	0.0	4,042	0.1
Notes Payable	0	0.0	18,563	0.4	199,237	3.1	36,375	0.9
Other Current	717,740	15.8	839,991	18.1	706,968	11.0	735,574	18.2
Total Current	**844,934**	**18.6**	**1,081,314**	**23.3**	**1,086,161**	**16.9**	**957,864**	**23.7**
Other Long Term	449,723	9.9	329,499	7.1	1,034,746	16.1	169,748	4.2
Deferred Credits	0	0.0	264,527	5.7	32,135	0.5	64,666	1.6
Net Worth	3,248,000	71.5	2,965,491	63.9	4,273,948	66.5	2,849,343	70.5
Total Liab & Net Worth	**4,542,657**	**100.0**	**4,640,831**	**100.0**	**6,426,990**	**100.0**	**4,041,621**	**100.0**
Net Sales	4,171,402	100.0	2,687,221	100.0	3,602,573	100.0	5,142,011	100.0
Gross Profit	988,622	23.7	1,663,390	61.9	2,334,467	64.8	2,164,787	42.1
Net Profit After Tax	(796,738)	(19.1)	10,749	0.4	219,757	6.1	(51,420)	(1.0)
Working Capital	1,430,937	—	904,962	—	1,079,735	—	1,349,902	—

RATIOS	SIC 8631 UQ	SIC 8631 MED	SIC 8631 LQ	SIC 8641 UQ	SIC 8641 MED	SIC 8641 LQ	SIC 8661 UQ	SIC 8661 MED	SIC 8661 LQ	SIC 8699 UQ	SIC 8699 MED	SIC 8699 LQ
SOLVENCY												
Quick Ratio (times)	23.7	1.8	0.7	3.8	1.4	0.6	4.2	1.5	0.4	5.9	1.4	0.6
Current Ratio (times)	30.4	4.7	0.8	7.5	2.8	1.2	10.3	2.7	1.0	13.8	3.6	1.5
Curr Liab To Nw (%)	1.4	14.9	39.0	3.7	11.4	26.6	2.3	7.9	31.5	2.5	9.3	39.2
Curr Liab To Inv (%)	999.9	999.9	999.9	194.8	579.0	999.9	309.7	803.7	999.9	120.8	357.6	882.0
Total Liab To Nw (%)	1.4	22.1	48.8	5.7	19.3	52.5	6.2	27.5	89.2	4.1	16.8	68.9
Fixed Assets To Nw (%)	10.0	21.7	77.3	24.3	58.5	92.5	39.3	91.2	142.4	4.3	17.2	50.5
EFFICIENCY												
Coll Period (days)	7.7	8.4	9.1	6.9	20.8	49.3	0.7	5.1	19.0	2.4	9.5	22.3
Sales To Inv (times)	999.9	999.9	999.9	81.0	32.0	18.0	76.2	32.9	14.4	88.6	25.4	9.3
Assets To Sales (%)	76.9	108.9	168.9	102.9	172.7	282.4	84.8	178.4	370.9	44.7	78.6	211.5
Sales To Nwc (times)	4.9	2.8	1.5	8.0	4.1	1.4	10.2	3.5	1.2	8.0	3.6	1.5
Acct Pay To Sales (%)	2.3	4.0	10.1	1.6	3.9	8.2	1.7	2.9	7.1	1.5	3.7	7.2
PROFITABILITY												
Return On Sales (%)	5.4	(4.3)	(43.5)	7.9	0.3	(11.2)	8.9	1.8	(1.5)	6.8	1.0	(6.4)
Return On Assets (%)	2.3	(4.6)	(136.9)	5.4	0.2	(5.5)	6.0	1.3	(1.1)	9.9	2.9	(7.0)
Return On Nw (%)	3.7	(5.9)	(427.2)	6.9	0.2	(6.5)	8.3	1.8	(2.9)	13.1	3.9	(8.2)

	SIC 87 ENGINEERING MGMT SVC (NO BREAKDOWN) 2002 (4065 Establishments)		SIC 8711 ENGINEERING SVCS (NO BREAKDOWN) 2002 (1146 Establishments)		SIC 8712 ARCHITECTURAL SVCS (NO BREAKDOWN) 2002 (218 Establishments)		SIC 8713 SURVEYING SERVICES (NO BREAKDOWN) 2002 (57 Establishments)	
	$	%	$	%	$	%	$	%
Cash	258,267	18.0	220,612	13.9	174,853	10.5	135,746	14.4
Accounts Receivable	538,056	37.5	734,846	46.3	845,957	50.8	307,313	32.6
Notes Receivable	8,609	0.6	6,349	0.4	3,331	0.2	13,197	1.4
Inventory	47,349	3.3	55,550	3.5	21,649	1.3	16,026	1.7
Other Current	175,047	12.2	201,567	12.7	196,501	11.8	99,924	10.6
Total Current	**1,027,328**	**71.6**	**1,218,924**	**76.8**	**1,242,291**	**74.6**	**572,206**	**60.7**
Fixed Assets	265,441	18.5	260,291	16.4	319,732	19.2	312,026	33.1
Other Non-current	142,046	9.9	107,925	6.8	103,247	6.2	58,446	6.2
Total Assets	**1,434,815**	**100.0**	**1,587,140**	**100.0**	**1,665,270**	**100.0**	**942,678**	**100.0**
Accounts Payable	264,006	18.4	187,283	11.8	228,142	13.7	53,733	5.7
Bank Loans	7,174	0.5	11,110	0.7	11,657	0.7	943	0.1
Notes Payable	87,524	6.1	68,247	4.3	46,628	2.8	71,644	7.6
Other Current	559,578	39.0	499,949	31.5	634,467	38.1	296,942	31.5
Total Current	**918,282**	**64.0**	**766,589**	**48.3**	**920,894**	**55.3**	**423,262**	**44.9**
Other Long Term	235,309	16.4	233,309	14.7	161,531	9.7	252,638	26.8
Deferred Credits	11,479	0.8	9,523	0.6	28,310	1.7	0	0.0
Net Worth	269,745	18.8	577,719	36.4	554,535	33.3	266,778	28.3
Total Liab & Net Worth	**1,434,815**	**100.0**	**1,587,140**	**100.0**	**1,665,270**	**100.0**	**942,678**	**100.0**
Net Sales	3,857,030	100.0	4,278,005	100.0	4,638,635	100.0	2,132,756	100.0
Gross Profit	1,693,236	43.9	1,848,098	43.2	2,203,352	47.5	1,151,688	54.0
Net Profit After Tax	146,567	3.8	162,564	3.8	143,798	3.1	119,434	5.6
Working Capital	109,046	—	452,335	—	321,397	—	148,944	—

RATIOS	SIC 87 UQ	MED	LQ	SIC 8711 UQ	MED	LQ	SIC 8712 UQ	MED	LQ	SIC 8713 UQ	MED	LQ
SOLVENCY												
Quick Ratio (times)	2.7	1.4	0.8	2.7	1.5	0.9	2.7	1.5	0.9	4.3	2.0	1.1
Current Ratio (times)	3.5	1.8	1.2	3.4	1.9	1.3	3.1	1.7	1.2	5.5	2.6	1.4
Curr Liab To Nw (%)	24.5	66.8	162.9	30.7	76.6	163.7	39.9	87.4	220.1	15.6	38.2	81.6
Curr Liab To Inv (%)	174.7	552.7	999.9	156.9	369.4	999.9	195.5	825.6	999.9	173.5	257.6	376.7
Total Liab To Nw (%)	35.8	95.6	220.1	42.3	104.2	213.9	46.1	120.0	265.8	28.6	54.4	138.5
Fixed Assets To Nw (%)	10.1	25.4	62.3	10.1	23.1	52.5	11.8	28.9	53.2	21.8	38.9	83.4
EFFICIENCY												
Coll Period (days)	38.3	61.3	89.1	48.2	70.1	97.8	58.4	86.7	117.9	50.0	75.1	87.8
Sales To Inv (times)	129.4	36.1	11.1	129.4	27.7	11.0	276.3	61.4	15.5	32.4	28.8	12.1
Assets To Sales (%)	25.1	37.2	58.8	26.8	37.1	50.3	26.1	35.9	47.5	33.5	44.2	56.6
Sales To Nwc (times)	14.4	7.3	4.1	13.1	7.1	4.4	16.0	7.2	4.4	10.1	5.5	3.8
Acct Pay To Sales (%)	1.5	3.9	8.1	1.3	3.2	6.8	2.1	5.0	8.7	0.6	2.3	3.5
PROFITABILITY												
Return On Sales (%)	7.4	2.6	0.0	6.9	3.0	0.5	5.3	1.0	(1.0)	7.2	3.4	1.0
Return On Assets (%)	21.0	6.6	(0.1)	20.2	8.0	1.4	16.5	2.5	(2.3)	16.3	7.6	1.6
Return On Nw (%)	46.8	17.2	1.6	41.6	18.5	4.8	28.9	9.1	(3.7)	29.2	18.4	7.0

Balance Sheet Data

	SIC 8721 ACCTNG, AUDTNG, BKPNG (NO BREAKDOWN) 2002 (147 Establishments) $	%	SIC 8731 COMMRCL PHYS RSRCH (NO BREAKDOWN) 2002 (322 Establishments) $	%	SIC 8732 COMMRCL NPHYS RSRCH (NO BREAKDOWN) 2002 (118 Establishments) $	%	SIC 8733 NCMMRCL RSCH ORGNZTN (NO BREAKDOWN) 2002 (127 Establishments) $	%
Cash	85,166	18.7	1,092,301	26.1	407,416	21.2	1,086,159	30.6
Accounts Receivable	142,550	31.3	786,792	18.8	687,995	35.8	567,926	16.0
Notes Receivable	3,643	0.8	20,925	0.5	24,983	1.3	0	0.0
Inventory	15,485	3.4	192,513	4.6	69,184	3.6	88,738	2.5
Other Current	42,810	9.4	673,796	16.1	203,707	10.6	603,422	17.0
Total Current	**289,654**	**63.6**	**2,766,327**	**66.1**	**1,393,285**	**72.5**	**2,346,245**	**66.1**
Fixed Assets	106,115	23.3	803,532	19.2	269,048	14.0	646,016	18.2
Other Non-current	59,662	13.1	615,204	14.7	259,440	13.5	557,278	15.7
Total Assets	**455,431**	**100.0**	**4,185,063**	**100.0**	**1,921,773**	**100.0**	**3,549,539**	**100.0**
Accounts Payable	31,880	7.0	2,025,570	48.4	570,767	29.7	756,052	21.3
Bank Loans	911	0.2	0	0.0	7,687	0.4	24,847	0.7
Notes Payable	12,297	2.7	255,289	6.1	76,871	4.0	237,819	6.7
Other Current	140,272	30.8	1,757,727	42.0	916,685	47.7	3,833,502	108.0
Total Current	**185,360**	**40.7**	**4,038,586**	**96.5**	**1,572,010**	**81.8**	**4,852,220**	**136.7**
Other Long Term	86,077	18.9	1,075,561	25.7	361,294	18.8	525,331	14.8
Deferred Credits	1,822	0.4	46,036	1.1	23,061	1.2	31,946	0.9
Net Worth	182,172	40.0	(975,120)	(23.3)	(34,592)	(1.8)	(1,859,958)	(52.4)
Total Liab & Net Worth	**455,431**	**100.0**	**4,185,063**	**100.0**	**1,921,773**	**100.0**	**3,549,539**	**100.0**
Net Sales	1,459,715	100.0	5,024,085	100.0	4,792,451	100.0	3,549,539	100.0
Gross Profit	815,981	55.9	2,235,718	44.5	1,859,471	38.8	1,380,771	38.9
Net Profit After Tax	176,626	12.1	(60,289)	(1.2)	67,094	1.4	(170,378)	(4.8)
Working Capital	104,294	—	(1,272,259)	—	(178,725)	—	(2,505,975)	—

RATIOS

	8721 UQ	MED	LQ	8731 UQ	MED	LQ	8732 UQ	MED	LQ	8733 UQ	MED	LQ
SOLVENCY												
Quick Ratio (times)	3.1	1.4	0.8	2.8	1.3	0.6	2.5	1.3	0.9	4.9	1.6	0.6
Current Ratio (times)	4.0	1.9	1.1	4.3	2.2	1.1	3.1	1.8	1.2	7.3	2.8	1.1
Curr Liab To Nw (%)	17.7	52.3	137.9	15.9	42.1	98.7	32.4	70.1	170.7	6.9	22.4	65.0
Curr Liab To Inv (%)	90.7	162.6	897.3	172.0	398.5	999.9	127.3	299.4	999.9	316.0	830.3	999.9
Total Liab To Nw (%)	28.1	87.4	201.0	23.1	62.8	154.7	42.3	82.4	191.5	11.1	40.6	95.6
Fixed Assets To Nw (%)	12.7	29.5	84.3	8.9	24.5	59.0	7.6	23.1	51.8	5.0	14.8	49.2
EFFICIENCY												
Coll Period (days)	30.3	51.5	72.3	31.8	55.5	79.2	32.5	58.4	82.7	25.6	57.7	92.0
Sales To Inv (times)	374.7	20.2	14.2	49.0	12.0	4.1	125.8	18.9	5.5	183.8	45.7	9.5
Assets To Sales (%)	18.0	31.2	55.0	36.1	83.3	286.5	26.3	40.1	65.4	35.1	100.0	621.4
Sales To Nwc (times)	15.4	7.5	4.7	9.2	3.8	0.7	14.4	8.7	4.9	7.3	2.3	0.9
Acct Pay To Sales (%)	0.7	2.2	4.7	2.6	6.5	18.2	2.2	3.5	6.3	2.6	6.8	25.3
PROFITABILITY												
Return On Sales (%)	21.9	5.9	0.8	5.9	(0.5)	(161.2)	7.6	2.5	(1.6)	3.7	(2.6)	(140.8)
Return On Assets (%)	63.5	12.5	2.2	12.5	(2.9)	(49.0)	17.9	5.9	(3.1)	8.5	(3.9)	(36.9)
Return On Nw (%)	117.5	37.3	5.4	24.3	(0.1)	(57.2)	44.0	15.8	0.6	19.5	(1.6)	(31.8)

	SIC 8734 TESTING LABRTRS (NO BREAKDOWN) 2002 (132 Establishments)		SIC 8741 MANAGEMENT SERVICES (NO BREAKDOWN) 2002 (370 Establishments)		SIC 8742 MNGMNT CNSLTNG SVCS (NO BREAKDOWN) 2002 (658 Establishments)		SIC 8743 PUBLIC RLTNS SVCS (NO BREAKDOWN) 2002 (69 Establishments)	
	$	%	$	%	$	%	$	%
Cash	123,792	12.9	786,828	16.9	221,421	21.2	193,215	18.7
Accounts Receivable	336,830	35.1	1,108,078	23.8	391,665	37.5	411,228	39.8
Notes Receivable	6,717	0.7	74,493	1.6	5,222	0.5	5,166	0.5
Inventory	29,749	3.1	88,460	1.9	43,866	4.2	29,964	2.9
Other Current	77,731	8.1	698,368	15.0	118,023	11.3	133,288	12.9
Total Current	**574,819**	**59.9**	**2,756,227**	**59.2**	**780,197**	**74.7**	**772,861**	**74.8**
Fixed Assets	302,284	31.5	1,066,176	22.9	162,933	15.6	189,082	18.3
Other Non-current	82,528	8.6	833,386	17.9	101,310	9.7	71,294	6.9
Total Assets	**959,631**	**100.0**	**4,655,789**	**100.0**	**1,044,440**	**100.0**	**1,033,237**	**100.0**
Accounts Payable	63,336	6.6	842,698	18.1	237,088	22.7	174,617	16.9
Bank Loans	6,717	0.7	4,656	0.1	7,311	0.7	12,399	1.2
Notes Payable	42,224	4.4	153,641	3.3	84,600	8.1	50,629	4.9
Other Current	223,594	23.3	1,177,914	25.3	407,331	39.0	408,128	39.5
Total Current	**335,871**	**35.0**	**2,178,909**	**46.8**	**736,330**	**70.5**	**645,773**	**62.5**
Other Long Term	176,572	18.4	987,028	21.2	125,333	12.0	119,855	11.6
Deferred Credits	2,879	0.3	41,902	0.9	6,267	0.6	12,399	1.2
Net Worth	444,309	46.3	1,447,950	31.1	176,510	16.9	255,210	24.7
Total Liab & Net Worth	**959,631**	**100.0**	**4,655,789**	**100.0**	**1,044,440**	**100.0**	**1,033,237**	**100.0**
Net Sales	2,317,949	100.0	8,953,440	100.0	3,203,804	100.0	3,677,000	100.0
Gross Profit	1,168,246	50.4	2,739,753	30.6	1,387,247	43.3	1,687,743	45.9
Net Profit After Tax	120,533	5.2	349,184	3.9	140,967	4.4	117,664	3.2
Working Capital	238,948	—	577,318	—	43,867	—	127,088	—

RATIOS	UQ	MED	LQ	UQ	MED	LQ	UQ	MED	LQ	UQ	MED	LQ
SOLVENCY												
Quick Ratio (times)	4.1	1.7	1.0	1.9	1.2	0.6	2.5	1.3	0.7	2.4	1.4	0.6
Current Ratio (times)	4.3	2.2	1.2	2.7	1.6	1.1	3.1	1.6	1.1	2.7	1.8	1.0
Curr Liab To Nw (%)	17.6	42.8	100.5	22.5	60.3	225.5	25.3	79.4	223.5	27.2	75.3	144.0
Curr Liab To Inv (%)	230.9	771.8	999.9	607.1	999.9	999.9	139.5	478.4	999.9	321.6	901.7	999.9
Total Liab To Nw (%)	32.0	74.7	188.7	55.0	130.0	340.8	36.7	105.0	294.1	35.6	99.5	165.1
Fixed Assets To Nw (%)	27.8	57.1	105.9	11.4	40.8	98.5	8.4	22.9	54.4	9.5	24.4	48.4
EFFICIENCY												
Coll Period (days)	41.3	55.7	83.4	27.7	48.8	67.2	32.1	51.8	75.6	42.0	54.6	70.5
Sales To Inv (times)	283.8	89.4	27.5	102.0	63.5	36.5	171.8	29.7	10.2	281.6	78.0	13.2
Assets To Sales (%)	28.4	41.4	54.3	25.7	52.0	115.3	22.0	32.6	48.6	21.9	28.1	57.6
Sales To Nwc (times)	12.7	6.9	4.4	19.4	9.3	5.0	18.4	8.3	4.6	14.0	8.1	4.9
Acct Pay To Sales (%)	1.1	2.3	4.7	2.3	4.6	9.8	1.4	3.9	8.1	1.7	3.6	9.4
PROFITABILITY												
Return On Sales (%)	7.5	2.8	0.4	6.1	2.2	0.0	8.1	2.6	0.1	8.9	2.5	0.0
Return On Assets (%)	17.0	6.7	0.4	14.7	4.0	0.1	25.6	8.3	0.4	23.1	5.0	(1.3)
Return On Nw (%)	38.1	12.9	4.1	45.5	12.6	1.0	55.2	22.5	4.6	63.2	18.0	5.7

	SIC 8744 FCLTS SPPRT SVCS (NO BREAKDOWN) 2002 (56 Establishments)		SIC 8748 BUS CNSLTNG,NEC (NO BREAKDOWN) 2002 (645 Establishments)		SIC 89 MISC SERVICES (NO BREAKDOWN) 2002 (44 Establishments)		SIC 8999 SERVICES, NEC (NO BREAKDOWN) 2002 (44 Establishments)	
	$	%	$	%	$	%	$	%
Cash	454,825	13.4	156,017	19.7	109,877	24.8	109,877	24.8
Accounts Receivable	1,564,733	46.1	318,370	40.2	129,815	29.3	129,815	29.3
Notes Receivable	16,971	0.5	6,336	0.8	3,987	0.9	3,987	0.9
Inventory	37,336	1.1	25,343	3.2	19,937	4.5	19,937	4.5
Other Current	427,671	12.6	78,403	9.9	61,586	13.9	61,586	13.9
Total Current	**2,501,536**	**73.7**	**584,469**	**73.8**	**325,202**	**73.4**	**325,202**	**73.4**
Fixed Assets	634,718	18.7	141,762	17.9	85,066	19.2	85,066	19.2
Other Non-current	257,961	7.6	65,733	8.3	32,786	7.4	32,786	7.4
Total Assets	**3,394,215**	**100.0**	**791,964**	**100.0**	**443,054**	**100.0**	**443,054**	**100.0**
Accounts Payable	675,449	19.9	125,922	15.9	109,434	24.7	109,434	24.7
Bank Loans	0	0.0	3,168	0.4	9,747	2.2	9,747	2.2
Notes Payable	217,230	6.4	91,868	11.6	11,519	2.6	11,519	2.6
Other Current	885,890	26.1	402,318	50.8	559,135	126.2	559,135	126.2
Total Current	**1,778,569**	**52.4**	**623,276**	**78.7**	**689,835**	**155.7**	**689,835**	**155.7**
Other Long Term	424,277	12.5	137,009	17.3	110,764	25.0	110,764	25.0
Deferred Credits	0	0.0	6,336	0.8	3,101	0.7	3,101	0.7
Net Worth	1,191,369	35.1	25,343	3.2	(360,646)	(81.4)	(360,646)	(81.4)
Total Liab & Net Worth	**3,394,215**	**100.0**	**791,964**	**100.0**	**443,054**	**100.0**	**443,054**	**100.0**
Net Sales	12,478,732	100.0	2,364,072	100.0	1,554,575	100.0	1,554,575	100.0
Gross Profit	3,356,779	26.9	1,118,206	47.3	861,235	55.4	861,235	55.4
Net Profit After Tax	461,713	3.7	99,291	4.2	121,257	7.8	121,257	7.8
Working Capital	722,967	—	(38,807)	—	(364,633)	—	(364,633)	—

RATIOS	UQ	MED	LQ	UQ	MED	LQ	UQ	MED	LQ	UQ	MED	LQ
SOLVENCY												
Quick Ratio (times)	1.5	1.1	1.0	3.2	1.5	0.8	2.7	1.3	0.4	2.7	1.3	0.4
Current Ratio (times)	2.0	1.4	1.2	4.3	1.9	1.2	4.1	2.1	0.8	4.1	2.1	0.8
Curr Liab To Nw (%)	72.7	110.1	297.3	21.2	62.6	156.9	26.6	58.5	130.9	26.6	58.5	130.9
Curr Liab To Inv (%)	999.9	999.9	999.9	168.8	539.4	999.9	174.2	370.2	775.1	174.2	370.2	775.1
Total Liab To Nw (%)	84.6	156.2	366.4	28.2	85.9	202.0	34.6	69.0	195.6	34.6	69.0	195.6
Fixed Assets To Nw (%)	15.0	32.9	78.0	10.8	22.8	56.2	5.7	25.7	70.3	5.7	25.7	70.3
EFFICIENCY												
Coll Period (days)	38.9	56.6	74.5	34.0	62.1	87.2	24.5	42.3	68.9	24.5	42.3	68.9
Sales To Inv (times)	703.1	162.3	66.8	144.0	40.6	13.8	40.0	16.2	9.6	40.0	16.2	9.6
Assets To Sales (%)	21.0	27.2	43.3	22.7	33.5	51.7	12.1	28.5	54.0	12.1	28.5	54.0
Sales To Nwc (times)	35.0	13.8	9.0	14.4	8.1	4.1	14.7	8.0	4.5	14.7	8.0	4.5
Acct Pay To Sales (%)	2.3	4.9	8.9	1.5	4.2	8.1	1.3	5.1	6.2	1.3	5.1	6.2
PROFITABILITY												
Return On Sales (%)	4.9	2.3	1.1	9.0	3.5	0.2	9.1	3.1	0.3	9.1	3.1	0.3
Return On Assets (%)	17.9	7.5	3.3	27.5	10.5	0.6	40.5	11.7	2.4	40.5	11.7	2.4
Return On Nw (%)	58.2	23.7	11.0	62.9	23.6	4.0	67.3	23.6	11.1	67.3	23.6	11.1

APPENDIX - SIC NUMBERS APPEARING IN THIS DIRECTORY